The
Complete Diary
of a Cotswold Lady

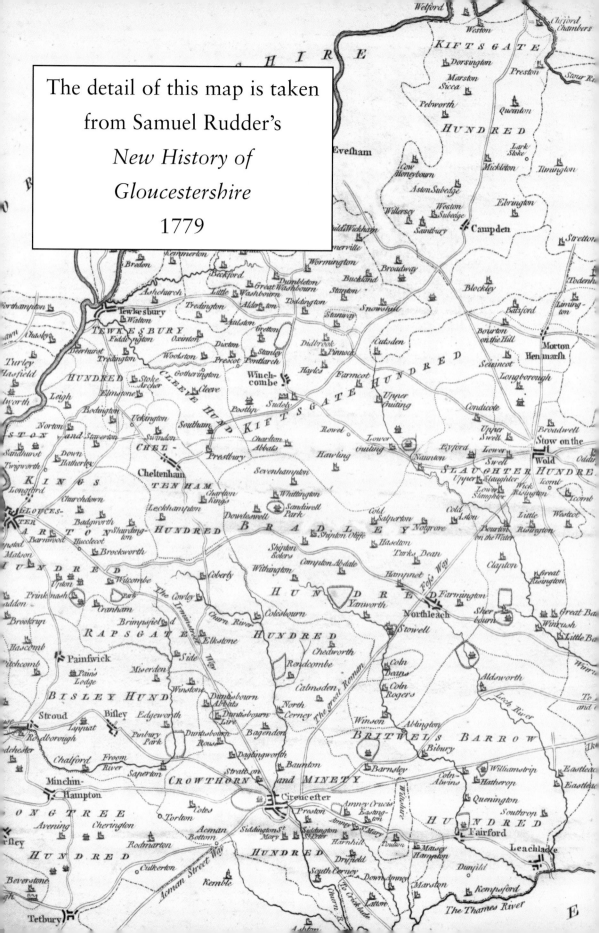

The detail of this map is taken from Samuel Rudder's *New History of Gloucestershire* 1779

The
Complete Diary
of a Cotswold Lady

The Diaries of Agnes Witts

1747-1825

in 5 volumes

Edited by Alan Sutton

Volume 1

The Lady of Rodborough

Introduction

&

Diaries covering the Period

1788-1793

AMBERLEY

The Complete Diary of a Cotswold Lady

Volume 1

The Lady of Rodborough

First published 2008 by
Amberley Publishing
Cirencester Road
Chalford
Stroud
Gloucestershire
GL6 8PE

ISBN 978-1-84868-010-4

Typesetting and origination by Amberley Publishing
Printed in England by Asterim Limited
Bound in Scotland by Hunter & Foulis

Preface

The Complete Diary of a Cotswold Lady has almost come about by accident. Although the diaries have always been known about, little attention has been paid to them. Nicholas Kingsley in his 1984 catalogue of the Witts Family Papers said 'These diaries are of much less interest than her son's, being primarily concerned with family and social news . . .'. It is difficult to argue with this sentiment if one is looking for diary entries of importance and relevance to the history of Gloucestershire, but from a social perspective they are fascinating and with soap opera addiction they hook the reader and provide a glimpse into the life of the gentry in the late eighteenth century and Regency period.

Work started on the diaries of her son, Francis Edward Witts, back in 1982 and after more than a quarter of a century, they have been published in 2008 as *The Complete Diary of a Cotswold Parson*. Towards the latter stages of work on the Cotswold Parson it was necessary to read through his mother's diaries, previously left to one side. When I started on the Agnes diaries in 2005 I immediately said to the the current Francis Witts, (Agnes Witts's great-great-great-grandson), these must be published, and without second bidding Francis immediately put a programme of typing in place.

Agnes Witts was an amazing woman, a power house of energy and extremely self-centred. The French Revolution and the Napoleonic Wars hardly get a mention, for what matters to Agnes was her own social life and the advancement of her favourite son, Francis.

This first volume is of especial interest to those living in the Stroud Valleys. The diaries commence in 1788 with looming financial problems and end in the spring of 1793 with the pending disaster of her husband's bankruptcy, and yet through all of this crisis Agnes goes about life as if in a form of denial as she forges her social circle and plans her card evenings.

The later volumes show life taking a different twist, but as with all good soap operas, the reader has to wait and see.

Alan Sutton
March 2008

The detail of this map is
taken from Joseph Skelton's
*Antiquities of
Oxfordshire*

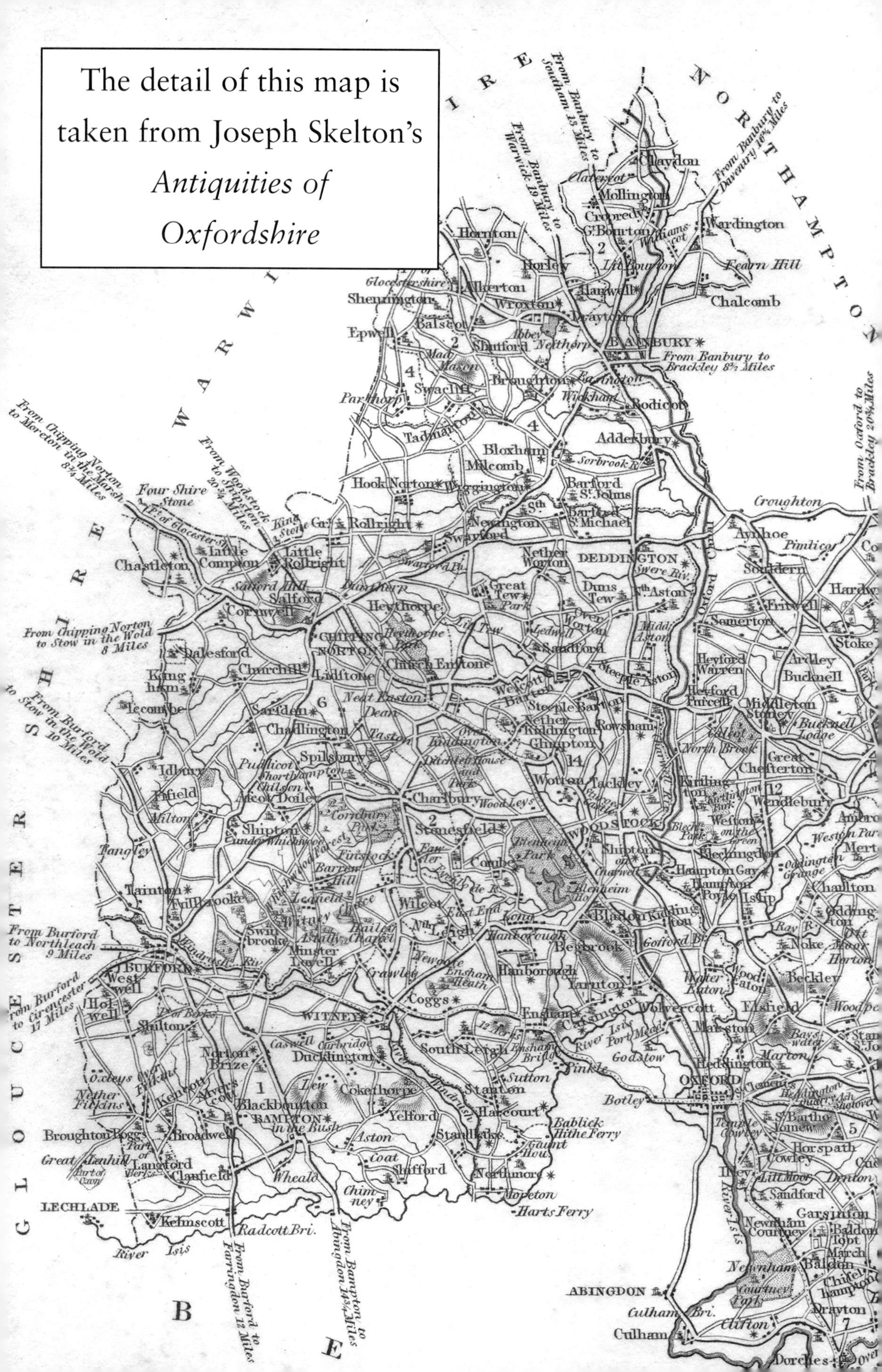

Foreword

I am not in *Who's Who* (though I slipped in as 1s when my father was alive); but, if I was, I could well have included under hobbies "writing forewords". This is the fourth I have written for family papers, the first three for my great-great-grandfather, the Reverend F. E. Witts, and now this one for his mother, Agnes née Travell.

I had been brought up to understand that Agnes' diaries were not as interesting as her son's, and had even been encouraged to deposit them at the Climatic Research Unit at U.E.A. in Norwich (because there were so many and such regular references to the weather). I am deeply indebted to Alan Sutton for proving me wrong, and for showing me what fascinating reading her diaries actually are (and not only for meteorological historians).

She had a hard time with her husband's bankruptcy, but she soldiered on bravely and entertainingly, and Alan has done an amazing job piecing together the various bits of the family history jigsaw drawing both on her diaries and her son's. I write this foreword sitting under the splendid Joseph Wright portrait of Agnes, and alongside her husband Edward's High Sheriff staff. How these two family heirlooms escaped the bailiffs I do not know, and I trust that the Commissioners, on reading this, will not be moved to reopen their files.

When the *Complete Diary of a Cotswold Parson* and the *Complete Diary of a Cotswold Lady* are fully published, Alan and I will have placed before you 15 volumes of old family papers. "Not enough!" I hear you cry. Do not worry, dear reader, we have all Lady Lyttelton's papers up our sleeves, so there are many more volumes to come one day; please be patient.

Francis E. B. Witts

Upper Slaughter
Easter 2008

Contents

List of Illustrations   11
A Note on the Editorial Process   19
Introduction   21
F173   20 April — 3 September 1788   47
F174   4 September 1788 — 6 March 1789   78
F175   7 March — 18 August 1789   107
F176   19 August 1789 — 27 January 1790   136
F177   28 January — 27 June 1790   166
F178   28 June — 7 December 1790   192
F179   8 December 1790 — 20 May 1791   225
F180   21 May — 11 September 1791   255
F181   12 September 1791 — 29 February 1792   288
F182   1 March — 6 August 1792   318
F183   7 August — 13 December 1792   346
F184   14 December 1792 — 25 May 1793   383

List of Illustrations

Anderson. *Shropshire: Its Early History and Antiquities*, John Corbett Anderson, 1864.
Bigland. *Historical, Monumental and Genealogical Collections, relative to the County of Gloucester; printed from the original papers of the late Ralph Bigland*. 1791.
BOTT. *The Book of the Thames*
CMAG. Cheltenham Museum and Art Gallery.
Corry. *The History of Bristol*, John Corry, 1816.
Crapelet. *Souvenirs de Londres en 1814 et 1816*, G. A. Crapelet, Paris, 1817.
DG. *Delineations of Gloucestershire*, J. & H. S. Storer and J. N. Brewer, 1826.
Evans. *The History of Bristol*, John Evans, 1816.
Glover. *The History of the County of Derby*, Stephen Glover, 1829.
HCA. *The History of Calwich Abbey*, Mary Teresa Fortescue, 1915.
Knight. *Old England a Pictorial Museum of Regal, Ecclesiastical, Baronial, Municipal and Popular Antiquities*, Charles Knight, 1845.
Lee. *History of the Town and Parish of Tetbury*, Alfred T. Lee, 1857.
Papworth. Papworth's *Select Views of London*,1816.
PE. *Picturesque Excursions*, Arthur Freeling, *c*.1840.
Rudder. *A New History of Gloucestershire*, Samuel Rudder, 1779.
Rutter. *Delineations of the North Western Division of the County of Somerset*, John Rutter, 1829.
WFP. Witts Family Papers.

The codes in italics at the end of each illustration relate to the catalogue of the Alan Sutton Image Archive.

Illustrations in Colour Section.

1. Agnes Witts, née Travell (1747-1825), by Joseph Wright of Derby, painted at Bath *c*.1776. Collection: Francis E. B. Witts.
2. Edward Witts (1746-1816), by George Romney. Collection: Francis E. B. Witts.
3. Francis Edward Witts (1783-1854), by F. Liston, 1787. Collection: Francis E. B. Witts.
4. Francis Travell (1728-1801).
5. Witts family group by John Hamilton Mortimer, *c*.1769. From left to right: John Witts (1750-1816), Richard Witts (1747-1815), Edward Witts (1746-1816) and Apphia Witts, later Lady Lyttelton (1743-1840). Family tradition has it that the second left is Richard, but there remains a strong suspicion that it is his eldest brother, Broome (1744-1827). Collection: Francis E. B. Witts.
6. Ferdinando Tracy Travell. (1740-1808). Collection: Francis E. B. Witts.
7. Anthony Tracy-Keck, M.P., of Great Tew (1712-1767), by an unknown enameller, *c*.1736.

Reproduced by kind permission of the Earl of Wemyss and March, KT.

8. Anthony Tracy-Keck, M.P., of Great Tew, Oxfordshire (1712-1767), his wife Lady Susan Douglas-Hamilton (d.1755), their daughters Henrietta Charlotte, Viscountess Hereford (1742-1817) and Susan, Lady Elcho (1745-1835), by Edward Alcock of Birmingham, c. 1748. Reproduced by kind permission of the Earl of Wemyss and March, KT.

9. Francis, 7th Earl of Wemyss (1723-1808). Reproduced by kind permission of the Earl of Wemyss and March, KT.

10. Francis, Lord Elcho (1749-1808), pastel by Archibald Skirving, Rome 1790. Lord Elcho was the son of the 7th Earl of Wemyss; and father of the 8th Earl of Wemyss and 4th Earl of March. Reproduced by kind permission of the Earl of Wemyss and March, KT.

11. The Charteris Children by George Romney, 1781. Francis Charteris (1772-1853) succeeded his grandfather as the 8th Earl of Wemyss in 1808, obtaining a reversal of his great-uncle's Jacobite 1746 attainder in 1826, thereby securing formal recognition of the title. His sisters in the picture are Susan (died 1816), who married General Sir Henry Clinton and Henrietta Charlotte (1773-1838) who married the 6th Earl of Stamford. Henrietta suffered a mental affliction and was removed from her husband and children, and later, by coincidence, lived at Swerford Park in Oxfordshire, formerly the home of Agnes and Edward Witts who had been forced to sell the house in 1793 at the time of Edward's financial difficulties. Agnes visited Henrietta on more than one occasion at Swerford. Reproduced by kind permission of the Earl of Wemyss and March, KT.

12. Francis, 8th Earl of Wemyss and 4th Earl of March (1772-1853), pastel by Archibald Skirving, Rome 1790. Francis was known to his family as 'Pear-face'. He was the son of Lord Elcho (1749-1808), and grandson of Francis, 7th Earl of Wemyss (1723-1808. He inherited Stanway from his aunt, Henrietta in 1817. Reproduced by kind permission of the Earl of Wemyss and March, KT.

13. The Witts family group, c.1769-1770 by Richard Cosway (1742-1821). Exhibited at the Royal Academy in 1770 as 'The portraits of a gentleman, his wife and sister, in the character of Fortitude introducing Hope as the companion to Distress'. Broome Witts (1738-1769) of Witney, a linen draper in Bread Street in the City of London, was first cousin to the Witts siblings of Chipping Norton (Alice, Apphia, Broome, Sarah, Edward, Richard and John). The families were tied ever closer by the fact that the two Broomes married two sisters, respectively Elizabeth London (1738-1837) and Amelia London (1742-1832). Witney Broome and Elizabeth had three children, Broome Philips Witts (1767-1845), see plate 14; Edward London Witts (1768-1841) and Maria Amelia Witts (1769-1830). Witney Broome died in 1769 and this unusual memorial painting by Cosway, still in its original frame, is an allegory showing Broome as Fortitude introducing his sister Sarah Witts (1745-1797), represented as Hope standing with her anchor, to Broome's widow Elizabeth shown seated as Distress. Tate, London, 2008.

14. Broome Philips Witts (1767-1845). Collection: Stephen Lloyd.

15. Edward Witts (1746-1816). Collection: Francis E. B. Witts.

16. King George III and the fair quaker. The exact allusion to the Fair Quaker is unclear. As a young man George had a fling with one Hannah Lightfoot who was referred to as 'the fair quaker'. There was also a contemporary play in circulation, *The Fair Quaker of Deal*. Also Mrs. Dorothy Jordan was in town during the royal visit. Anyway, this cartoon was published in October 1788, celebrating the King's five-week visit to the town. Cheltenham Museum and Art Gallery.

17. Their Majesties with the three eldest princesses at Cheltenham. A contemporary engraving showing the King taking the Cheltenham Waters. Cheltenham Museum and Art Gallery.
18. Thomas Hughes of Cheltenham, solicitor and lessee of the well who built the first assembly rooms in the town in 1783. The Hughes family were well acquainted with Edward and Agnes Witts.
19. Cirencester. A contemporary aquatint with hand colouring by J. C. Stadler after Joseph Farington R.A. (1747-1821), published in 1793.
20. The Bath Races from *The Comforts of Bath*, by Thomas Rowlandson, 1798.
21. A view of Wallbridge, Stroud *c*.1790 with Rodborough as the backdrop. The coloured items on the hillside are dyed woollen cloths hung out on tenters. Stroud Museum, The Museum in the Park, Stratford Park, Stroud.
22. South-east view of Woodchester by Samuel Lysons, 1792. This fine view was drawn by Lysons at exactly the time when Edward and Agnes Witts were living with their three sons at Bownham House, Rodborough. The gateway to Bownham House was less than 100 metres from the point at which Lysons executed his view, and this would have been the view facing the family when they left the front gate between 1791 and 1793.

Illustrations in the Text

1. Note by Susan Keck *c*.1752. *WFP Z6. B1017-13*
2. James Leigh (1724-1774) with his wife Caroline née Brydges and their son James Henry Leigh (1765-1823). *C0204-54*
3. The Dutton Family at Sherborne, 1765, by Johan Zoffany. The family group is probably James Dutton (1744-1820), second from the right. He became 1st Baron Sherborne in 1784. On the left are presumably his parents, James Lenox Dutton (formerly Naper) and Jane, née Bond. The old lady on the right is probably a grandmother. William Naper and the other siblings are not shown. *C0204-57*
4. Johan de Witt (1625-1672); by Schouleer and Houbraken after Caspar Netscher, line engraving, 1670. Collection: Stephen Lloyd. *A0922-01*
5. Oxford; engraved by William and John Walker from an original drawing by Dayas, published 1 February 1792 by Harrison & Company, 18 Paternoster Row. *B0809-15*
6. Cheltenham Church; drawn and engraved by Thomas Bonnor, *Bigland. A0917-40*
7. Bath from the Avon; by J. C. Nattes. *B0403-04*
8. Weymouth. *B1119-25*
9. Wyke and Portland 1821; aquatint published July 1821 by J.W. Upham, Weymouth. *B1119-07*
10. Upway House, Dorset; the seat of Sir George Gould. *B1119-08*
11. Lulworth Castle. *B1120-02*
12. Weymouth. *B1120-01*
13. Portsmouth. *B1120-03*
14. Carisbrooke Castle, Isle of Wight; Nelson's *Handbook to the Isle of Wight* W.H. Davenport Adams. *A0930-22*
15. Southampton from the water. *B1120-06*
16. The Water Gate at Southampton; 1786. *B1120-10*
17. Oxford. *A0708-59*

18. King George III; the Long Room, Cheltenham, 1786. C0204-06
19. Their Majesties at the Wells. *B1120-11*
20. Thomas Hughes. *C0204-05a*
21. Cheltenham Wells; CMAG. *B0712-07*
22. Shipton Court; the seat of Sir John Reade. *B1119-02*
23. Blenheim Palace; from *The Beauties of England and Wales. B1119-05*
24. Taking tea; from the frontispiece of volume 3 of *Clarissa Harlowe* by Samuel Richardson. *B1120-14*
25. Temple Bar; 1799. *A0929-05a*
26. Stow-on-the-wold. *B1029-15*
27. The High Street, Cheltenham; from a drawing by John Claude Nattes, 1804. *B0722-09*
28. Piccadilly with White Horse Street to the right, *c.*1790. *C0204-52*
29. Ranelagh Rotunda. *B1121-22a*
30. A view of the front of the old opera house in the Haymarket; built by John Vanbrugh, 1705, from a watercolour by W. Capon, 1783. *A0910-02*
31. The Tower of London from the area of Wapping; aquatint by William Daniell, 1804. *071121-25a*
32. Kensington Palace. *B1121-40a*
33. Epsom. *C0127-02*
34. Chelsea Hospital with Ranelagh Rotunda. *B1120-31a*
35. Old Drury Lane Theatre; 1811. *B1227-11*
36. Haymaking; William, after James Ward, 1793. *B1121-54a*
37. Caroline, Duchess of Marlborough; after Romney, 1791. *B1121-46*
38. The effects of Cheltenham waters; S. W. Fores. *C0204-02*
39. Sandywell; *Rudder. B0324-11*
40. Old Well Walk. CMAG. *B0712-22*
41. North-west view of Blenheim; John Boydell, 1752. *B1120-37a*
42. Card players; John Opie, engraved by John Dean. *B1121-47*
43. The final parting; from the frontispiece of volume 7 of *Clarissa Harlowe* by Samuel Richardson. *B1120-17*
44. School days; William Redmore Bigg, engraved by John Jones. *B1121-52a*
45. The birth of a daughter. *B1121-55a*
46. Woodchester and Rodborough Common in 1797; Samuel Lysons. *B1027-40*
47. Great concern felt & expresss'd; from the frontispiece of volume 6 of *Clarissa Harlowe* by Samuel Richardson. *B1120-16*
48. Minchinhampton; by Kip *c.*1707, from Atkyns' *Ancient and Present State of Glostershire. B1025-06*
49. Berkeley; *Rudder. B0324-05*
50. Westminster Bridge, Hall & Abbey; 1804. *A0909-89*
51. East front Kensington Palace. *B1121-41a*
52. Rodborough; *Bigland. B1029-07*
53. Revd. William Cockin, 1766-1841; from A. T. Playne, *Minchinhampton and Avening.* 1915. *B1029-22*
54. Adlestrop. *C0204-56*
55. Oddington House; CMAG. *B0804-05*
56. Williamstrip; *Rudder. B0324-16*

57. Shooting on Minchinhampton Common; *c.*1790. *C0204-58*

58. Rodborough Manor (earlier called Hill House); T. Way, Lithographer. *B0809-01*

59. Prinknash Park; *DG. A0924-32*

60. Tetbury Church from the Bath bridge. *B1029-18*

61. The Abbey House, Cirencester; *DG. A0924-13*

62. Stonehouse; *Bigland. B1029-14*

63. Quedgeley; *Bigland. B1029-06*

64. Brimscombe Port; *DG. A0924-47*

65. A view of Stroud from Lodgmore, drawn by Samuel Lysons. *C1318-8 & C0318-9*

66. Thames and Severn Canal above Chalford Chapel Lock, 1838. *C0204-10*

67. Stroud; *Bigland. B1029-16*

68. Painswick; *Bigland. B1029-05*

69. Avening; drawn and engraved by Thomas Bonnor, *Bigland. A0917-24*

70. Minchinhampton; drawn and engraved by Thomas Bonnor, *Bigland. A0917-53*

71. View of Bath showing the South Parade, bridge etc.; from *The Beauties of England & Wales.* *B0325-14*

72. Old Rooms, Abbey Walks, Bath, 1785; William Blackamore. *C0204-37*

73. The Pump Room and Colonnade; from an engraving by J. C. Nattes, 1806. *B0403-03*

74. The Interior of the Pump Room; from an engraving by J. C. Nattes, 1806. *B0403-01*

75. Old Theatre, Orchard Street, Bath, 1804; T. Woodfall. *C0204-38*

76. Cartoon by James Gillray; Bath, 13 January 1796. *B0403-11a*

77. Field Place, Paganhill, Stroud; from *Notes and Recollection of Stroud*, P. H. Fisher, 1891. *B1102-01*

78. St. Michaels the Abbey and South Parade, Bath, 1788; Samuel Grimm. *C0204-35*

79. Bisley; drawn and engraved by Thomas Bonnor, *Bigland. A0917-32*

80. The Leasowes; *Gregory. B0325-76*

81. The winding valley, Malvern. *B0930-24*

82. Kings Stanley; *Bigland. B1029-11*

83. Berkeley Castle; drawn and engraved by Thomas Bonnor, *Bigland. A0917-28*

84. Newnham Ferry. *B1103-20*

85. Chepstow castle and bridge. *C0204-23*

86. Chepstow Castle. *A0708-31A*

87. Piercefield, Monmouthshire. *B1103-01a*

88. Tintern Abbey; 1807. *C0123-12*

89. Raglan Castle; 1793. *C0123-08*

90. Brecon Priory. *C0204-25*

91. Briton Ferry. *C0123-25*

92. Cardiff Castle. *C0204-26*

93. Cardiff Castle, 1812. *C0123-10*

94. Newport Castle; William Orme, 1806. *B1120-51a*

95. Newport Castle and Bridge. *C0204-24*

96. Monmouth Bridge. *C0123-23*

97. Monnow Bridge, Monmouth. *C0123-28*

98. Highnam Court. *DG. A0924-31*

99. Nailsworth from Watledge Hill. *C0125-02*
100. The Old Well Walk, Cheltenham, from the Sherborne entrance; from a lithograph by Hullmandel. *B0722-08*
101. Leonard Stanley. *B1029-13*
102. The Thames and Severn Canal at the Tunnel House (eastern portal). *B0809-12*
103. Cirencester; Farington and Stadler, 1 June 1793. *C0106-01a*
104. Calwich Abbey; from *The History of Calwich Abbey* by Mary Teresa Fortescue, 1914. *B0325-83*
105. John Granville 1800; Master John Granville of Calwich Abbey, Staffordshire (1779-1801), painting by John Hoppner (1758-1810). Detroit Institute of Arts. *B0324-01a*
106. View of Worcester in 1785; water-colour by Samuel Lysons. *B1005-02a*
107. North Nibley; *Rudder*. *B0324-14*
108. Warren Hastings; by Sir William Beechey R.A. *B1112-01*
109. Kings Weston; *DG*. *A0924-15*
110. Spring Park, Woodchester; *DG*. *A0924-07*
111. Brimscombe Port, men towing trow. *C0204-11*
112. Priory, Leonard Stanley. *B1103-10a*
113. Fairford Church; *DG*. *A0924-26*
114. Staines Church, 1811. *B1120-47a*
115. Maidstone Church. *C0306-01*
116. Canterbury Cathedral. *C0116-05*
117. Kingsgate, near Broadstairs; *PE*. *A0909-74*
118. Dandelion, Garlinge, near Margate; *PE*. *A0909-80*
119. The Theatre, Hawley Square, Margate, Kent, built 1787; *PE*. *A0909-71*
120. Margate; *PE*. *A0909-68*
121. Old Church, Margate; *PE*. *A0909-72*
122. Ramsgate, 1808. *B1120-50a*
123. Gateway at Kingsgate, near Broadstairs; *PE*. *A0909-73*
124. Sandwich. *C0115-04*
125. Dover Castle, 1786. *C0116-04*
126. Dover, 1805. *C0116-0*
127. Dover, 1803; Serres after John Thomas. *B1121-15a*
128. Fort Rock, Margate; *PE*. *A0909-78*
129. Ramsgate Harbour. *C0115-04*
130. Margate, 1802. *C0116-08*
131. Tunbridge Wells, from the Frant Road. *A0704-10*
132. Richard Cumberland, dramatist. *B0331-12*
133. Tunbridge Wells, the Walk. *A0704-11A*
134. Bayham Abbey ruins. *B1114-06*
135. Boxhill and Burford Bridge, Surrey; 1811. *C0127-07*
136. Norbury Park, Surrey; William Lock. *B1114-09*
137. Leatherhead Church. *C0127-04*
138. St. Paul's and Blackfriars Bridge; 1805. *A0909-88*
139. Covent Garden Theatre, prior to the fire in September 1808. *B1020-01*

140. Oxford from the meadows; drawn by W. Westall. *B0809-24*

141. Witney from the Market Cross; published 1 June 1823, by J. Skelton, Magdalen Bridge, Oxford. *B0930-11*

142. Detail from Sandywell; *Rudder. B0324-11*

143. Charlton Kings; the seat of Dodington Hunt Esq., *Bigland. A0917-39*

144. Tom Paine. *B1114-10a*

145. Bath from the Avon; by J. C. Nattes. This view is taken just a little bit further north from North Parade where Agnes and Edward were staying. It was painted from the east bank of the Avon looking towards Pulteney Bridge. *B0403-05*

146. The Comforts of Bath — Supper; by Thomas Rowlandson. *B0713-16*

147. The Comforts of Bath — Dancing; by Thomas Rowlandson. *B0713-14*

148. The Comforts of Bath — The Concert; by Thomas Rowlandson. *B0713-13*

149. Royal and Lansdown Crescents in 1819; engraving by W. Watts. *B0403-06*

150. Hysterics and fainting; from the frontispiece of volume 6 of *Clarissa Harlowe* by Samuel Richardson. *B1120-19*

151. Gatcombe; *DG. A0924-08*

A Note on the Editorial Process

Punctuation and Spelling

The diaries of Agnes Witts have been reproduced as accurately as is reasonably possible. Her punctuation was erratic and most of the time omitted all together. The spelling of people's names is often inconsistent: in many cases she started using one version, and then, later, when she found out the correct spelling, she put it in as it should have been. In this transcription I have reproduced what she wrote, even if the word or name is incorrect. There are few words which cannot be read, but even so I cannot guarantee total accuracy. There have been three transcription checks, but it is nonetheless possible that mis-readings may have slipped through.

Footnotes

Footnotes have been introduced in an attempt to help the reader to understand some of the diarist's references and comments, especially in relation to people. They are not intended as any form of academic apparatus, nor are they referenced. In many instances the information comes from works included in the Bibliography. In others they have come from correspondence, conversations or personal visits to places or websites. More information on sources is given in the Bibliography, Biographical Index, Subject Index and Appendices in Volume Five. In order to make the notes as easy to use as possible they have been placed at the base of each page as true footnotes, instead of as endnotes. Generally speaking, an individual is introduced to the reader once in the footnotes and then not referred to again unless there is something specific to point out. As a result, the footnotes are particularly heavy in Volume One and then lessen considerably as time goes by. As for the method of choosing who, or who not, to footnote, the simple answer is that if they can be identified with relative ease, then they are noted. When there is an entry for 'Mr Campbell' it is difficult to know exactly to whom the diarist was referring, but when the entry is for 'Mr Campbell of Shirvan' there is something firmer to go on. In this way some minor people are noted, while more illustrious individuals may not be. Fuller details on individuals are provided in the Biographical Index in Volume Five.

Method of Illustrating the Volumes

The collection of illustrations for *The Complete Diary of a Cotswold Parson* started back in 1985. Since then I have built up a large and valuable collection of eighteenth- and early nineteenth-century engravings and of nineteenth-century lithographs. In addition, there are mezzotints and aquatints and the collection has almost taken on a life of its own, separate to the diaries. In addition to this I have used illustrations from several libraries from Weimar to Cheltenham. Illustrations from the families associated with the diarist have added yet more to the collection. When the decision was made to publish *The Complete Diary of a Cotswold Lady* alongside that of her son, it was a simple matter to dip into this collection to provide embellishment.

As a general rule, I have tried to maintain the closest possible link between the date of the illustration and the date of the diary entry. In extreme cases—such as the Pantile Walk in Tunbridge, for which the image is dated 1748—I have had to stray outside the chronological limits, but these are the exception.

Introduction

Agnes Witts was a remarkable woman with great zest for life. She required constant amusement and bored easily. Her favourite pastimes were cards and stimulating conversation, her social circle was wide and well-connected, her attachment to her faith consistent and strong.

In a remarkable series of sixty-two diaries covering the years 1788–1824 Agnes Witts recorded her life in a structured and unvarying manner. She noted the weather, the doings of the day and letters received and written. A day without a letter was a dark day in her life. She loved to maintain a wide correspondence among a large circle of family, friends and acquaintance.

Commencing on 20 April 1788 the diaries hardly miss a day and the final entry is for Christmas Day 1824, just two weeks before her death at the age of seventy-six. Gaps in the diary are very few and usually occur only during times of serious illness. The only noteworthy gap is from 1 January to 20 March 1801, when the family was living in Copenhagen. The diary entries <u>exist</u> for this period, but cannot be read because the ink has faded away completely.

How Agnes acquired the habit of recording her life is unknown, although she may have taken the idea from her elder sister, Anne, who kept an appointment diary to which she added other information as an *aide memoire*. One thing we do know from the diaries is that Agnes was meticulous and structured in her approach to her daily entries, and this studied attention says much about her personality. All the diaries are exactly the same size and the form and style of entry remained consistent throughout the thirty-seven years. This is very different from the diaries of her son, Francis, who took on her habit of maintaining a diary, but his entries varied considerably in style and content and the physical diaries themselves vary in shape, size and style.

The diary entries are matter-of-fact, betraying little emotion, which appears to have been reserved for her letters. Unfortunately, few letters survive, but from those that do it is possible to build a better picture of how she approached the recording of her life and her communications with others. A few letters to her son Francis surivive in the Witts Family Papers (WFP) and some to other members of the family are in the Gloucestershire Records Office. One specific letter to her sister-in-law during a moment of extreme crisis provides a good example of this pattern. The business of her husband, Edward Witts, had failed and the family had left their Gloucestershire home to stay with their close friends John and Harriet Granville in Staffordshire, before heading north to live more economically in Edinburgh. From Calwich Abbey, near Dovedale, Agnes wrote to Apphia, Lady Lyttelton:

… Mr. Witts had left me here with our good & kind friends, while he went into Oxfordshire, in the vain hope of concluding his unfortunate affairs in some measure to his satisfaction, but the very harsh & cruel treatment we continue to meet with leaves us little hope of a speedy, or happy conclusion, & has so much depress'd my spirits that I have had no power to attend to any thing … all our property which we had packe'd up before we left Bownham House, under the eye & permission

of an official Man, empowerd by the Comissioners to superintend our removal & sent them up to London in readiness to be put on board a vessel for Scotland have been for the last week unpacke'd & ransacke'd by one of the Assigne's by orders from the commissioners under the false idea we had removed more than we were allow'd, how it will all end I know not, but I have little doubt we shall unfairly be the sufferers … the various difficulties I have to struggle with one who has not suffer'd in a similar manner can form any idea, to which the very small assistance have met with except from my own Brothers & Sisters & Neices & the very hospitable friends are now & have been so long with, has not a little contributed) to encrease, till cruel experience has taught me the contrary, I thought that to be unfortunate was a certain claim to compassion from those who term themselves friends but we have found it otherwise, our sole trust is in the Almighty who I doubt not will give us equal power to our inclination, "to strive for, & protect our beloved Boys …

The tragedy in this letter was not reflected in the matter-of-fact way in which Agnes recorded events of that day in her diary:

Friday June 14ᵗʰ. An intire bright fine Day, with rather a cold wind but I had small enjoyment of anything our boy from being extremely low & unwell, the morning much broke by archery & a visit from Mr. Wright & Miss Frances Berresford, and some packing of mine, all but Miss Cardin and the 4 children went to dine at Mrs. Milles at Snelson, a sociable friendly visit, a table at whist & casino not at home till near eleven o'clock. Wrote to Lady Lyttelton.

The reference in the extract to 'our boy' is interesting. Agnes had suffered several miscarriages before giving birth to Francis Edward in 1783. After this successful birth she safely bore two more sons: George in 1785 and Edward in 1786. Notwithstanding the fact that the children numbered three, Agnes often behaved as if there was only one—her beloved Francis. On 26 February of each year she underlined the date and usually commented about it being his birthday, a fact she normally ignored for George and Edward. Hardly a week went by without mother writing to son, and son to mother—sometimes twice and on occasion even more. There was a bond between mother and son that is quite remarkable, and the importance of their relationship and her influence on Francis cannot be overstated. When she died, Francis mourned her very much. She demanded her son's attention and, if more than a week went by without a communication, a questioning letter would be sent off. Agnes was undoubtedly the power within the family. She loved her husband very deeply, but his lack of attention to his business matters, and his blundering attempts to put them right, angered the organised Agnes and much of the paperwork she took upon herself. An example of her disappointment is a diary entry when they were in Edinburgh: *20 June 1795: … but my spirits were so oppress'd by the discovery of very ill conduct of one most dearly beloved by me, I could enjoy nothing. …*

The bond between Edward and Agnes was deep and they made a good couple. If Edward was away on business Agnes would record her gloom, and when he returned she would note the return of 'my best friend'.

Edward Witts was born in 1746. He inherited the family wool-stapling business in Chipping Norton, but seemingly paid inadequate attention to it. His main love in life appears to have been travel. As a youth of sixteen he had been in North Wales and, later, wars permitting, he travelled in France, the Channel Islands and Ireland, as well as making extensive tours throughout England and Wales. A surviving passport and letters of introduction are dated 1770, and letters survive to his sister, Apphia, Lady Lyttelton, between 1768 and 1773, from his continental tours. After his marriage to Agnes Travell the wanderlust continued. However, he accepted his responsibilities as a country gentleman and was a justice of the peace, a deputy lieutenant for Oxfordshire and, in 1779, high sheriff of the county, but it remains a fact that his financial affairs were in less than good order. Edward married Agnes in 1775 and at about that time bought Swerford Park.

The diaries of Agnes are mainly a social record, but a few facts do stand out, and the first record of the coming troubles occurred in the summer of 1790, when Swerford was put up for sale and the family moved to Bownham House, Rodborough, near Stroud. Edward and Agnes quickly formed a strong social set and continued to act as gentry, notwithstanding their looming problems. The family's financial circumstances meant that plans for Charterhouse or Merchant Taylors School for Francis were put aside and he went to school at Elmore Court near Gloucester, while the two younger boys, George and Edward, remained in the nursery at Bownham and later at a day school in Cheltenham. Edward and Agnes used their chaise and horses in a whirlwind of social visits, local and away, until, to the absolute horror of Agnes, the full extent of their financial position was revealed to her in March 1793. The next few months were a period of misery as the reality of their predicament sank in. The family removed to Edinburgh to reduce costs, arriving in July 1793.

The diaries in this volume cover the period from 20 April 1788 (the first surviving diary) to 25 May 1793, when the family was at Calwich Abbey en route for their exile in economical Edinburgh.

Little is known of the life of Edward and Agnes before 1788. Following their marriage in 1775 they moved into Swerford Park. Many years later, Francis, as an undergraduate at Oxford, walked to Swerford to spend a day with his Uncle Ferdinando and his cousins at Swerford House. He recorded his thoughts on Swerford Park then, a place he had not seen since he was a seven-year-old boy:

Saturday March 23d. (1805) Swerford.

Walked with Mrs. Travell & Martha Buxton to my Father's very pretty old place of his own creation Swerford Park, the most romantic Dell, I have seen in Oxfordshire; now occupied by a Mr. & Mrs. Chinner, people unworthy of so nice a place.

We also know of Agnes's miscarriage problems from Francis's diary. The Witts Family Papers are effectively a huge jig-saw puzzle and by diligent work it is possible to build a good picture. This particular jig-saw piece comes from 4 February 1826, when Francis was reflecting on the death of his aunt Anne:

... she was the eldest of four daughters of John Travell Esqr of Swerford, and on his demise, they removed to Cheltenham as an eligible residence for single gentlewomen, near their relatives at Stanway & Sandywell Park; a little country town, not then a public place; my Mother was the youngest. The two intermediate sisters died; one Miss Frances Travell, a great while ago: my Aunt

Catherine in 1804. For many years, the unmarried sisters inhabited a house in the George Inn Yard, now an appendage, I think, to that inn, but in former days one of the best houses in the place. It was there, that I was born; my mother, after several miscarriages, having come to Cheltenham to lie in, to avail herself of the skill of a celebrated accoucheur of the place, the late Mr Clark.

Two journals exists (WFP F154 & F172) of a tour the couple made to Scarborough in 1777, but apart from these there is very little to go on, so the presumption must be made that the style of life Agnes recorded in 1788 had been the case for the years before, except that now there was the much-longed-for family.

One striking fact that comes across in the diaries is the bond of family and the importance of friends. There is evidence in the Witts Family Papers to show that there was a strong connection between the Travell, Tracy-Keck and Witts families. One small note survives, catalogued and included in a bundle as WFP Z6, from Susan Keck, later to become Lady Elcho. This appears to be *c.*1752.

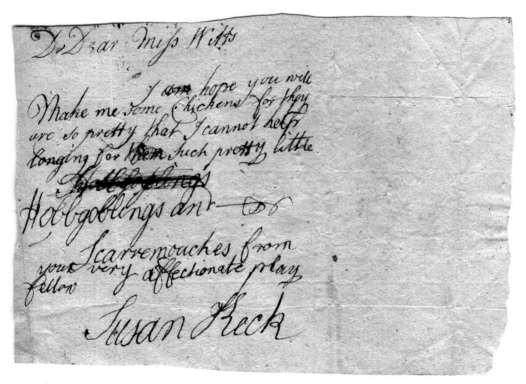

1. *Note by Susan Keck c.1752.*

Other families were allied by the bond of being fellow gentry and some were tied closer by alliance in marriage, the most obvious case being the Rollinson family of Chadlington. Lock Rollinson was a friend of Edward's in his youth and in 1774 they had travelled together in Wales and Ireland. By 1788 Lock Rollinson was dead, and so was his sister, Martha, who had married Agnes's brother Ferdinando, leaving him a disconsolate widower with two daughters. The Rollinson family connection remained close, and, by coincidence, another Rollinson girl, also a Martha, daughter of Lock, married John Dolphin, curate at Lower Slaughter, bringing the family connection closer to Ferdinando's living at Upper Slaughter.

Other local gentry in Oxfordshire included the Tyrwhitt, Penyston and Western families and, to a lesser extent, the Hastings, Drake, Wiltshire and Leigh families. Charles and Mary Western in particular were good friends of Edward and Agnes Witts, and although much younger than the Wittses, Agnes in particular took on an almost maternal approach to the couple and some of the most moving entries from the diaries surround the death of young Tom Western on 4 May 1789.

Other deep and long-standing friendships are difficult to unravel and it is not known how or where they began, but one common denominator appears to be Cheltenham. In particular there is the Snow / Paul / Delabere / Granville connection, followed later by the Lee connection. One of Agnes's closest friends was Miss Anne Snow. She lived in London and appears to have been the sister of Robert Snow, banker of the firm of Denne Cornelius, Robert Snow & William Sanby, Senior & Junior, 217 Strand. She was probably also sister to George Snow of Langton in Dorset, who married Elizabeth Paul, sister of the philanthropist Sir George Onesiphorus Paul of Hill House, Rodborough, near Stroud. Anne Snow was also a friend of the Revd John Granville of Calwich Abbey, Staffordshire, and the Revd John Delabere of Cheltenham. John Delebere's sisters, Harriet and Anne, married, respectively, John Granville (born Dewes) and his brother, Bernard Dewes. The Delabere family of Southam were one

2. James Leigh (1724-1774) with his wife Caroline née Brydges and their son James Henry Leigh (1765-1823).

of the leading gentry families in the area and would have known the Travells, and therefore Agnes. The friendship and connection probably went back a long way.

With these friends, plus family, and with less close friends and acquaintance, it seems that a detailed social diary was planned by Agnes. There were frequent trips, usually centred on fashionable watering places, where at various times during the excursion friends and family come and go. The most common centres were Cheltenham and Bath, but London, Margate and Tunbridge Wells were also included in the itinerary. Taking the waters for medicinal purposes, drinking sea water and bathing for health rather than for pleasure were all part of the general excuses for a social gathering of the Agnes Witts clan.

One other person of note should be mentioned: Elizabeth, Lady Cavendish-Bentinck, *née* Cumberland. Elizabeth was the daughter of Richard Cumberland, the dramatist, and and Elizabeth, *née* Ridge. Richard and Elizabeth Cumberland had four sons and three daughters, and Elizabeth was the eldest of the daughters. For reasons which are unclear, Richard Cumberland came to an arrangement whereby Elizabeth was entrusted to Agnes and Edward Witts, who brought her up. Elizabeth was probably born between 1760 and 1762; on 23 December 1782 she married Edward Charles Cavendish-Bentinck, second son of William, 2nd Duke of Portland, and only brother to the Whig leader and Prime Minister (1783 and 1807–1809) William, 3rd Duke of Portland (1738–1809), who more than once rescued his younger brother Edward from his financial scrapes. Of his marriage to Elizabeth Cumberland, the gossip Mrs Mary Delaney said the alliance was 'likely to produce serious consequences to the health of the Duke of Portland'.

Agnes and Elizbath remained close during this period, as the visits and correspondence show. Elizabeth had two sons, William, born 1784, and Charles, born 1785, plus two daughters, Harriet and Charlotte, dates of birth unknown, although we do know from the diary that one was born in January 1789. There was therefore an additional bond between the two women, for Agnes had borne Francis in 1783, George in 1785 and Edward in 1786.

The Travell Family

The first references to the Travell family are to John Travell as linen draper in the united parishes of St Mary Woolnoth and St Mary Woolchurch, London. The family was mentioned in several City of London records: they appear to have been successful in business and at least one seems to have been an alderman. One reference for 'London Inhabitants within the walls, 1695' lists 'John, £600, linen draper, widr, St. Mary, Woolchurch.' This same John Travell purchased Swerford in Oxfordshire from Sir Thomas Rowe when he was thirty-four years old. He died in 1745 at the age of eighty-seven. John had been unfortunate in losing wives. His first, Elizabeth Thornton, died in 1689 at the age of twenty-three, probably in child-birth. His second, Frances Blagrave, he married at the same time as he bought Swerford. She died just two years later—thus the reason for the 1695 survey listing him as a widower. His third wife, Frances Conant, was to provide him with several children and to secure the succession.

John and Frances had six children: John, Jane, Elizabeth, William, Alexander and Thomas. Jane was baptised at St Mary Woolnoth in 1702 and buried at Bath Abbey in 1767; no record of her life has yet been found. Elizabeth was born in 1703 and died an infant in 1705. William was born in 1704 and buried at Swerford in 1775. Alexander was born in 1705 and probably died an infant. Thomas was born in 1708 and no record has been found beyond his being buried at Swerford. John senior died in 1745; his third wife, Frances, outlived him, and died and was buried at Swerford in 1757 at the ripe age of ninety.

John Travell of Swerford House was born in 1699 and baptised at St Mary Woolnoth. This appears to demonstrate that a residence and business in London was maintained, and presumably the linen-draping business continued to provide the income for the family. It is also fair to surmise that the introduction to the Witts family may have come through the London textile trade. John married well, for his bride was Anne, daughter of John Tracy, Esq., of Stanway, Gloucestershire, by Anne, his wife, the daughter of Sir Robert Atkyns of Sapperton, Gloucestershire, author of the first major county history, *The Ancient and Present State of Glostershire*.

If we adopt the policy of going no further back than the seventeenth century, the Tracy line commences with John Tracy, 3rd Viscount Tracy of Rathcoole (1617–1687), who married, *c.* 1655, Elizabeth Leigh (16??–1688), daughter of Thomas Leigh, 1st Baron Stoneleigh.

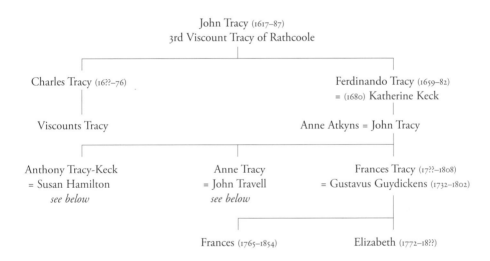

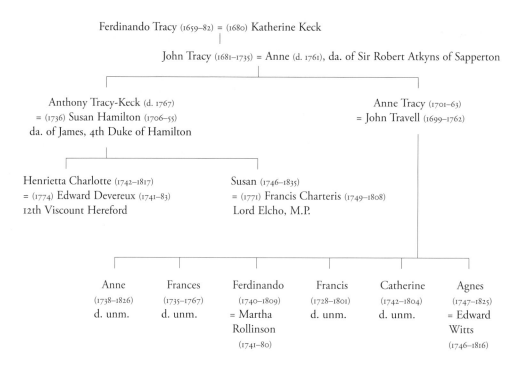

Ferdinando Tracy (1659–82) = (1680) Katherine Keck

John Tracy (1681–1735) = Anne (d. 1761), da. of Sir Robert Atkyns of Sapperton

Anthony Tracy-Keck (d. 1767)
= (1736) Susan Hamilton (1706–55)
da. of James, 4th Duke of Hamilton

Anne Tracy (1701–63)
= John Travell (1699–1762)

Henrietta Charlotte (1742–1817)
= (1774) Edward Devereux (1741–83)
12th Viscount Hereford

Susan (1746–1835)
= (1771) Francis Charteris (1749–1808)
Lord Elcho, M.P.

Anne	Frances	Ferdinando	Francis	Catherine	Agnes
(1738–1826)	(1735–1767)	(1740–1809)	(1728–1801)	(1742–1804)	(1747–1825)
d. unm.	d. unm.	= Martha Rollinson (1741–80)	d. unm.	d. unm.	= Edward Witts (1746–1816)

In 1788 Agnes Witts had four living siblings, Francis Travell, Ferdinando Travell, Anne Travell and Catherine Travell, all of them older than her, for she was the youngest but one out of a brood of thirteen.

Little is known of Francis, although he appears to have gained the epithet of 'Beau' Travell. He never married and lived between the family home in Swerford and Cheltenham. It was the habit in the family for the senior male and female siblings to be referred to as 'Mr' and 'Mrs,' so Anne, although unmarried, was referred to as Mrs Travell, whereas her sister Catherine was called 'Aunt Catherine'. The same applied to Francis, and whilst alive he was referred to as 'Mr Travell;' after he died, in 1801, Ferdinando, the next brother down, received the title.

Although unmarried, Francis fathered two illegitimate sons by Elizabeth Hitchman, Francis Hitchman (1763–1790) and George Hitchman (1767–1808). Although this was shocking by the mores of the day, it seems to have been accepted by the family and Agnes frequently referred to her nephew 'Frank'. It appears that Francis was not helpful to Agnes and Edward during their financial crisis, and when he died Agnes hinted at the past problems:

23 June 1801: a letter from my Bror. Ferdinand, informing me of the melancholy news of the death of my Brother Travell on the 21st at Cheltenham after a short illness, which at his advanced time of life nature could not combat. Natural affection made me feel the shock however separation & untoward circumstances lessened the afflictn.

The next surviving male in the family was Ferdinando Tracy Travell; he was named after his great-grandfather, a Tracy. His family, especially his sister Agnes, referred to him in their diaries as Ferdinand. He was born in 1740 and completed his education at Wadham College, Oxford, matriculating in 1757, obtaining his B.A. in 1761 and his M.A. in 1764.

He acquired the living of Upper Slaughter in 1764, through the patronage of his Tracy aunts. In 1832 his nephew, Francis Witts, the son of our diarist, bought the advowson from Mr Lawrence of Sandywell Park, but much of the surrounding estate appears to have been owned by Lord Sherborne. There was a connection with the Dutton / Naper family (the family of Lord Sherborne), as Ferdinando's second daughter, Jane, married William Naper, younger brother of Lord Sherborne. The aunts at Sandywell Park were also a major influence on the family, and a diary entry by Francis Witts of 1826 provides the information: *Thursday 2 February 1826: ...*

3. The Dutton Family at Sherborne, 1765. The family group is probably James Dutton (1744-1820), second from the right. He became 1st Baron Sherborne in 1784. On the left are presumably his parents, James Lenox Dutton (formerly Naper) and Jane, née Bond. The old lady on the right is probably a grandmother. William Naper and the other siblings are not shown.

Had my Aunt lived till May she would have been 88 years of age ... she was the eldest of four daughters of John Travell Esqr of Swerford, and on his demise, they removed to Cheltenham as an eligible residence for single gentlewomen, near their relatives at Stanway & Sandywell Park ... The relative at Stanway was Viscountess Hereford, the Travell sisters' first cousin; the relatives at Sandywell were aunts on the Tracy side. Agnes Witts in her diary for January 1789 recorded visiting three aged aunts at Sandywell, and these aunts led to Ferdinando acquiring the rectory of Upper Slaughter. The living was quite valuable and a welcome additional income for a young clergyman of twenty-four.

Little is known of Ferdinando's wife, Martha Rollinson. She was referred to fleetingly in the diaries, and there is a portrait in oils of her by Allan Ramsay in the Hunterian Art Gallery, University of Glasgow. All that we know is that she was the daughter of Thomas Rollinson of Chadlington, Oxfordshire, and died in 1780, aged thirty-nine. The two daughters of the marriage fared better. The elder, Martha, married firstly John Buxton, and had two daughters by him who survived to adulthood, Martha and Jane; Harriet and George died in infancy. John Buxton died in 1790 at the relatively early age of thirty-four. Martha then married William Whalley, a young man of little fortune who had recently become incumbent of Waltham Abbey, but his family had apparently been known to Ferdinando Travell for many years. The younger daughter, Jane, was also widowed early. Her husband, William Naper, the brother of Lord Sherborne, died in 1791 at the age of forty-two. Jane then married Henry Rycroft, Knight Harbinger to the King. Agnes was close to both of her nieces.

Ferdinando acquired a second living in 1766, becoming rector of Blunsdon in Wiltshire on the death of Henry Gabel—a living he held until his death. He was now a wealthy man. He had inherited the family lands and Swerford House, he had two livings, and may be said to have been comfortable. In his later years Ferdinando appointed his son-in-law William Whalley as curate at Upper Slaughter.

Apart from immediate family, Agnes had aunts and cousins. Anne Tracy's younger sister, Frances, married Colonel Gustavus Guydickens (1732–1802). Through his father, Melchior, there was a family link to George Canning, the future prime minister. Gustavus had a distinguished military career and was also privileged to be part of Queen Charlotte's household. He appears to have fallen into financial disgrace and died in the King's Bench prison.

Frances and Gustavus had two daughters: Frances, born March 1765, died 25 March 1854; and Elizabeth, born 3 September 1772 and still living in 1854. One curious incident is a reference to Gustavus which seems to differ from an honourable army career and a position in the Queen's household: *he was a Swede by birth, a Soldier of fortune, a man of expence and disreputable character; dying, I believe, in the Kings Bench at a very advanced age ...* This extract from a later diary entry by Francis Witts does not accord with the facts otherwise known, although it may have been that his father Melchior was Swedish by birth. What brought about the downfall of Gustavus is not known.

Mrs Guydickens and the Misses Guydickens feature throughout the diaries of Agnes and Francis Witts.

There were at least two, possibly three, other Miss / Mrs Tracys at Stanway. Agnes was particularly close to Mrs Eliza Tracy. Presumably two of these ladies were sisters to Frances Guydickens; the third was presumably their sister-in-law, Mary, née Dodwell, the widow of Thomas Tracy of Sandywell, who had been M.P. for Gloucestershire and had died in 1770.

The Tracy Family Connection

The family was proud of the Tracy connection. An ancient family, followers of William the Conqueror, the branches split as Tracy of Coscomb, Tracy of Rathcoole, Tracy of Stanway and Tracy of Toddington. The line that ended in the Travell (and subsequently Witts) family was from John Tracy, 3rd Viscount Tracy of Rathcoole (c.1593–1662). He married, c.1655, Elizabeth Leigh (d.1688), daughter of Thomas Leigh, 1st Baron Stoneleigh, thereby introducing a distant link to the Leigh family, to which Francis Witts referred in his diaries. Agnes was also well acquainted with the two branches of the Leigh family in Oxfordshire.

The Stanway line commenced in 1533 with Richard Tracy, the younger son of Sir William Tracy of Toddington. He had acquired Stanway at the Reformation, but his line failed with his grandsons and passed to a distant cousin as mentioned above, Ferdinando, youngest son of the head of the family, John, 3rd Viscount Tracy of Toddington.

Ferdinando (named after Ferdinando II, Medici Grand Duke of Tuscany from 1620 to 1670) married Katherine, the daughter of successful barrister Sir Anthony Keck, M.P., who had bought the estate of Great Tew in Oxfordshire. Their son John married Anne, the daughter of Sir Robert Atkyns, famed for writing the first history of the county, *The Ancient and Present State of Glostershire* (1712).

John and Anne Tracy lived at her father's house, Swell Bowl, near Stow-on-the-Wold, until 1709, before moving to Stanway, where they brought up their fifteen children. Their eldest son, Robert, Whig M.P. for Tewkesbury (1734–1741) and for Worcester (1748–

1754), was to his great disappointment beaten for Worcester in 1761, and damaged his fortune by expensive electioneering. He had, in 1735, married Anna-Maria, daughter of Sir Roger Hudson, from Kent, a director of the South Sea Company, but died childless in 1767, when Stanway passed to his twin brother John, a Cursitor Baron of the Exchequer, who had inherited the fortune of his maternal grandfather, Sir Robert Atkyns. Mr Baron Tracy visited Stanway only once a year, and conducted all the business of the estate by letter. Another brother, Thomas, an ensign in the 9th Regiment of Foot, had married Mary, daughter of Sir William Dodwell, and heiress of Sevenhampton and Sandywell near Andoversford. Their son, Dodwell Tracy, died at Paris on the Grand Tour, aged twenty, in 1768. Another brother, Anthony, who had changed his name to Keck to inherit the Great Tew estate through his paternal grandmother Catherine (Katherine) Keck in 1729, was later described by *Jackson's Oxford Journal* as 'A Gentleman universally admired for the ingenuous openness of his Disposition, engaging Affability, and peculiar Integrity towards his Friends.'

Anthony Keck married Susan, daughter of the 4th Duke of Hamilton, in 1736. Susan died in 1754 and Anthony himself died of happiness ('apoplexy') in 1767 at Epsom races, when his horse won its heat, leaving two daughters, Henrietta Charlotte and Susan, aged twenty-five and twenty-two.

Under the terms of Robert Tracy's will, Henrietta Charlotte Keck inherited Stanway on the death of her uncle John in 1773, being obliged to procure an Act of Parliament to change her name to Tracy. She was Maid of Honour to George III's Queen Charlotte and in 1774, aged thirty-two, married Edward Devereux, 12th Viscount Hereford.

The Tracy family of Stanway died out in 1817 with the death of Viscountess Hereford, first cousin to Agnes, and Stanway House was inherited by Francis Charteris, the 8th Earl of Wemyss and 4th Earl of March, son of Francis Charteris (Lord Elcho) and his wife Susan (*née* Tracy-Keck). Agnes was close to Lady Hereford and to Lady Elcho. She also remained close to the older members of the family and it appears that at least two sisters out of the fifteen siblings, plus Thomas's widow, Mary, were living at Sandywell after the death of Thomas and Dodwell, but all appear to have died by the close of the eighteenth century.

The Witts Family

The Witts family originated in the Netherlands, probably under the name de Witt. Family tradition is that they were connected with John (1625-72) and his brother, Cornelius de Witt (1623–72). John was appointed Grand Pensionary of Holland in 1653 at the age of 28, and held office until his death in 1672. In 1650 Cornelius became burgomaster of Dordrecht and a member of the States of Holland and West Friesland. He was afterwards appointed to the post of *ruwaard* or governor of the land of Putten and bailiff of Beierland.

In 1667 Cornelius was the deputy chosen by the States of Holland to accompany Lieutenant-Admiral Michiel de Ruyter in his famous raid on the English at Medway. Cornelius de Witt on this occasion distinguished himself greatly by his coolness and intrepidity. Compelled by illness to leave the fleet, he found on his return to Dort that the Orange party were in the ascendant, and he and his brother John were the objects of popular suspicion and hatred. They were arrested on false accusations of treason, but did not confess, despite heavy torture, and were ultimately unlawfully condemned to be banished. They were assassinated by a carefully organised lynch mob on the day they were to be released, victims of a conspiracy by the Orangists Johan Kievit and Lieutenant-Admiral Cornelis Tromp. The bodies of both were horribly mutilated and their hearts were carved out to be exhibited as trophies.

4. *Johan de Witt (1625-1672).*

When the English Witts family were granted their Coat of Arms at the end of the eighteenth century, they aimed to copy the De Witt Coat of Arms, but in fact miscopied it, ending up with three hares rather than two hounds and a hare.

Two brothers, Edward and Thomas Witts, settled in England at Aldbourne in Wiltshire, possibly as Protestant exiles from the Spanish enforcement of Roman Catholicism. The date is unknown, but the main period of migration for most immigrants to England from the southern Netherlands was after the commencement of the Eighty Years War in 1568. They may have been weavers or had other skills within the textile industry and joined many others of their countrymen escaping oppression and settling in the woollen cloth industry areas of the west of England. Migration was primarily caused by the war, but some, especially with viable trades, moved for sound economic reasons.

Edward flourished, but Thomas became poor. The parish register of Aldbourne for the Civil War period is missing, having been removed to St Omer in France for 'safe-keeping' and never having been returned, and so early references to Edward and Thomas are unavailable. The first documentary evidence is for the marriage of Edward Witts of Aldbourne to Joane Hinton (Jane Fenton?) in 1649. Their son, Edward (1650–1715), also of Aldbourne, married (secondly) Miriam Adams. Their son, Edward (1676–1736), married Sarah Broome of Witney in 1701 and they presumably made their main home at Witney, but also maintained strong links with Aldbourne. The Broome family was one of distinction in the Witney area and the marriage alliance would have been deemed a good one. Sarah's father, Richard, was the last of the male line of that branch and so presumably some of the Broome family wealth devolved on Edward and Sarah.

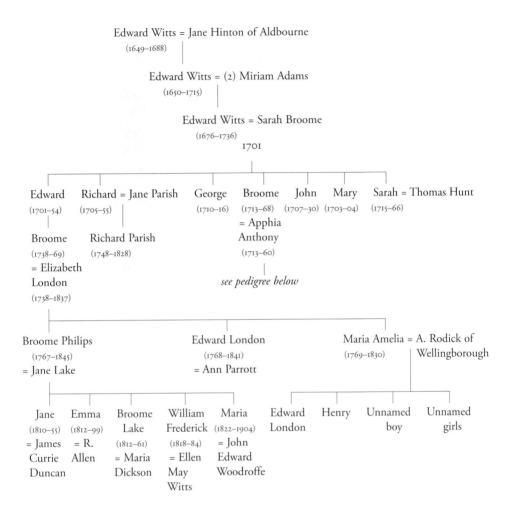

Of the seven children, our interest is in the sixth born, Broome Witts (1713–1768). Broome married Apphia Anthony in 1741 and they settled in Chipping Norton, Oxfordshire, where Broome became a prominent member of society. He was a successful woolstapler and carried on his business in Chipping Norton and at Friday Street in London, sharing his time between the two establishments and residing at both. He was also the Receiver-General of Taxes for Oxfordshire. Apphia died in 1760 and he followed her in 1768 after an attack of smallpox. Broome may not have been the originator of the business, for it appears that a firm of linen drapers operating under the name of Witts & Porter had been active in Friday Street as early as 1740. Broome could have started the business in his twenties, but it is more likely that it commenced under Edward, following his move from Aldbourne to Witney.

The business continued at Friday Street following Broome's death and the tenancy was held by widow Witts. This was probably the widow of Edward, who had died in 1754. She seems to have been assisted by her son, Broome (another Broome, nephew to Broome of Chipping Norton) and eventually also by her grandson, Broome P. Witts—the line of the Witney Wittses.

The Witney Wittses

It seems from the above that Edward and Broome were quite close and were in partnership together, continuing to develop their father's business. The eldest brother, Edward, made his base at Witney and almost certainly maintained strong contacts with the 'Aldbourne Wittses.' Like his brother, Broome, Edward became prominent in his town. He was twice bailiff and had a shop and warehouse adjoining the town hall, rented Farm Mills and was a general dealer, chapman and wool dealer.

Edward died in 1754, presumably leaving the business to his wife and son. This son, Broome (1738–1769), together with his first cousin, also named Broome (*see* pedigree— Broome Witts, 1744–1827) then married two sisters bearing the surname London, of Kingston-upon-Thames. 'Chipping Norton' Broome married the youngest, Amelia; 'Witney' Broome married the eldest, Elizabeth. 'Witney' Broome and his bride then moved to new suburbs near Camberwell, setting up the branch of the 'Witney Wittses' that we might refer to as the 'Champion Hill Wittses'.

At a period between the 1770s and 1790s the business changed, with the emphasis being placed on silk instead of wool. The major centre of silk manufacture was at Spitalfields, little more than a fifteen-minute walk from Friday Street. By the 1790s the driving force of the business was the grandson, Broome Philips Witts, and he was wealthy enough at the turn of the century to buy a spacious house in Brunswick Square. In 1794 he was in partnership as Witts & Rowley at 21 Friday Street, silk weavers & muslin warehousemen.

Broome's brother was Edward London Witts. A year younger than Broome, he appears to have taken no interest in the family company and ran his own businesses. He also operated from Friday Street, at number 44, advertising himself as a stationer and paper hanger (1792–1794). From 1794 he was at 34 St Paul's Churchyard in partnership with William Jennings, but this was dissolved in 1797. Other partnerships followed: from 1800 to 1803 it was Witts & Baldwin, then from 1804 to 1805 Witts & Palmer, and thereafter he seems to have traded alone. He remained a bachelor until late in life, living with his mother at Champion Hill.

The Chipping Norton Wittses

As mentioned above, Broome Witts married Apphia Anthony in 1741.

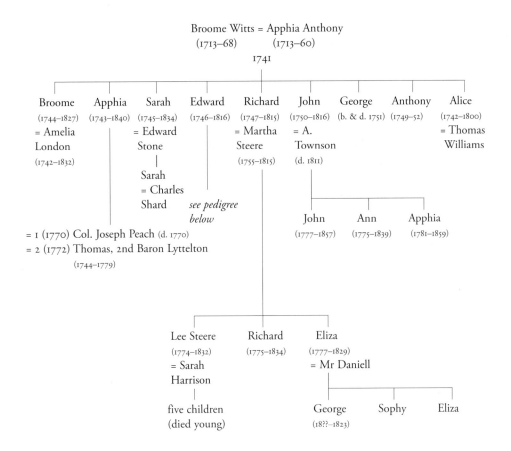

Of their nine children, it is known that George and Anthony died young. All the others, Broome, Apphia, Sarah, Edward, Richard, John and Alice, lived full lives, although Alice is not mentioned in family documents.

The eldest surviving member of Edward's family was Alicia Williams, *née* Witts. The diaries and the Witts Family Papers are silent about her apart from one fleeting reference which could easily have been missed: 13 May 1789 ... *Very hot & windy, went soon after Breakfast taking Lady Lyttelton with us to see M*ʳˢ· *Williams in her retreat at Rotherhithe, a small hut shell in a Garden, her appearance & the visit alltogether very singular.*

The eldest son, Broome, took no interest in the family business. He married Amelia London and by January 1792 had settled at Nibley House, North Nibley, Gloucestershire, as a gentleman farmer; in fact, Edward and Agnes accompanied him on viewings of the property when he was considering it. He was a churchman, but Amelia retained her

Nonconformist views and attended Rowland Hill's tabernacle at Wotton-under-Edge. Broome regretted the move and soon after 1802 the house and estate were sold by the Smythe family and Broome managed to get out of his tenancy. He then moved to Cookham, near Maidenhead, where he managed to buy an attractive estate adjoining the banks of the Thames named 'The Retreat.' He and Amelia lived here on the Berkshire side of the river for a number of years, and then bought a villa on the opposite, named Cookham Grove, living together until his death in 1827. The marriage produced no children. They were well respected in the area and considered rather more than gentry.

Following Edward Witts's business failure there was some friction in the family when the support expected from his elder brother was not forthcoming. Letters from Edward to his sister, Lady Lyttelton, describe the bad feeling:

My Brother Broome, came yesterday to me, by my desire: but his Visit turned out the very reverse, of what I expected. & whatever feeling you discoverd in his mind on the occasions, that arose when you was at Nibley—it was all evaporated before he came under my Roof: as instead of Sympathy or compassion—, he seemed to regret that our settled income was so secured, as to prevent him the effect of Bankruptcy. in truth that is all we have left; & tho' I asked him to be a Trustee to my Affairs, he said very calmly, he was so little of a Man of bussiness that he hardly ever choze to put pen to paper.—His contempt of the World, from having restored a once broken fortune, ought not to have appeard in a House of distress—& is totally the reverse of Richard, who tho he has lately raised Money to assist me has sent a Letter worthy of a Brother & a friend in Affiction.

This letter, written in March 1793 from Rodborough, seems to indicate that bankruptcy might be avoided—but it was not to be, and eventually all was sold, expect for certain items allowed by the commissioner. What benefit Broome might have gained from Edward's eventual bankruptcy is not clear. A further eight years on and friendly terms were restored. The family stayed at Nibley House between November 1800 and January 1801. What the broken fortune was that Broome reversed is unknown.

The next eldest of the Chipping Norton Wittses was the most famous of the family. Apphia had been engaged to her cousin, Richard Witts, and after three years of exchanging letters she sailed to India in 1769 to marry him, only to find on her arrival that he had died. They had not seen each other since he departed for India in 1763, when she was just a seventeen-year-old girl.

Within a matter of months she found a husband—someone a little older and with a distinguished career behind him, for Colonel Joseph Peach had been in the army since 1746 and had fought in the Canada campaign of 1754–1755. He was present at the successful attack at the Heights of Abraham in Quebec in 1759 where he was wounded and General Wolfe was killed. In the late 1760s he found himself in India as Governor of Calcutta and was on hand to comfort the young lady who had expected to meet her fiancé. They married in 1770, but the union was short-lived, for within six months Joseph was also dead. Apphia returned to England, a rich young widow.

With her new-found wealth and a decided taste for rural life in splendid surroundings she bought Leasowes near Hagley, once the residence of the poet William Shenstone. The grounds at Leasowes had been the glory and the downfall of Shenstone. He was the first to use the

French term '*Ferme Ornée*'—it exactly expressed the character of his grounds. Humphrey Repton said that he never strolled over the scenery of Leasowes without lamenting the constant disappointment to which Shenstone exposed himself by a vain attempt to unite the incompatible objects of ornament and profit. 'Thus,' continued Repton, 'the poet lived under the continual mortification of disappointed hope, and with a mind exquisitely sensible, he felt equally the sneer of the great man at the magnificence of his attempt and the ridicule of the farmer at the misapplication of his paternal acres.' The 'sneer of the great man' is perhaps an allusion to what Dr Johnson said of George, 1st Baron Lyttelton:—that he 'looked with disdain' on 'the petty State' of his neighbour. 'For a while,' says Dr Johnson, 'the inhabitants of Hagley affected to tell their acquaintance of the little fellow that was trying to make himself admired; but when by degrees the Leasowes forced themselves into notice, they took care to defeat the curiosity which they could not suppress, by conducting their visitants perversely to inconvenient points of view, and introducing them at the wrong end of a walk to detect a deception; injuries of which Shenstone would heavily complain.'

Shenstone died in 1763, and Apphia Peach bought the estate in 1771, when it was still at its peak.

To buy an estate of such repute is an interesting insight into the mind of such a young woman. What was it that induced her to buy a property which must have demanded great expenditure and great knowledge to maintain? Was it a well-planned decision, or was it a whim? It was not long before word of Apphia Peach's fortune of £28,000 reached the ears of Thomas Lyttelton. Although he could be charming, he already had a formidable reputation as a profligate, a gambler and a rake. Quite how Apphia was taken in by him is a mystery, but, in a whirlwind romance, seemingly cynical on his part and sincere on hers, the couple gained the blessing of George, 1st Baron Lyttelton (the 'Good Lord Lyttelton,' Thomas's father) and married on 26 June 1772.

That Thomas was a man of great capabilities was clear enough. They were attested by Chatham, Burke and Shelburne, and yet these gifts were lent towards misdoings. The elder Lord Lyttelton said there was a streak of madness in his son's character which might exempt his misdoings from punishment in the next world. Charles James Fox called him 'a very bad man—downright wicked.' Horace Walpole, in his *Last Journals*, August 1773, writes that his 'natural parts' were better than his father's, but that his 'detestable character was devoid of every principle and sentiment that became a man; [that his] ingratitude, profligacy, extravagance, and want of honour and decency seemed to aim at nothing but afflicting his father, shocking mankind, and disgracing himself.'

The marriage lasted only eight months. In February 1773 a separation was agreed upon and Thomas went off to live with a mistress and their illegitimate child.

Lord Lyttelton championed his daughter-in-law's cause and seems to have been very close to her. The Queen told him that 'she had made a new acquaintance with a relative of his which gave her pleasure, as Mrs. Lyttelton had a universal good character.' The pair seem to have got on remarkably well and the London season suited them both, with the elderly lord at his brightest for years and Apphia also enjoying herself. Unfortunately, his protection did not last long, for he died on 22 August 1773. This good lord, to whom Henry Fielding had dedicated his novel *Tom Jones*, had a rather bitter last laugh at his son, for on his death the profligate son discovered his father to be indebted to the sum of £26,000!

At this same time, Apphia appears to have been looking after Henry Peach, the nephew of her late husband. A letter of the period by Mrs Hood recorded:

The poor woman has carved very ill for herself. She meets, however, with great regard from all others. The being presented is still deferred from the child who lives with her being taken dangerously ill, and she giving her attendance to him night and day ...

A 'flashback' in the diaries of Francis Witts from 1840, the day of her funeral, provides information on the subject of Henry:

Monday 13 April: Of the last hours of my aged Aunt, who would have completed her 97th. year, if she had survived till May the 8th., I learnt that towards the last her sufferings appeared very great in struggling for breath; that her form had been wasted to a shadow, and the symptoms those of a person dying of a deep decline. ... The Memorandum accompanying the will provides that she shall be interned in a vault which she caused to be made very many years ago in Jesus Chapel, in Great Malvern Church, and whither she caused to be removed the remains of her adopted son, Henry Peach, Nephew of her first husband, Col Peach, a youth to whom she had greatly attached herself, and who, dying young, had been buried at Cardington in Shropshire, the parish of which my Uncle John was the incumbent.

Little is known of Henry Peach. Was he in India with his uncle, or did Apphia only seek him out when she was back in England? Whichever, she seems to have doted on him and by the fact that he was originally buried at Cardington it may have been that in the late stages of his illness she took him to the country retreat of her brother, John, where he died. From the family papers it appears that he was still at Pembroke College, Oxford, in 1787.

A novel which appeared in 1775 under the title *The Correspondents, An Original Novel* was rumoured to have been genuine letters between Apphia and her father-in-law. Horace Walpole believed them to be true, but they were almost certainly forgeries, although they did give Apphia celebrity status for a while. Fanny Burney, the author of the novel *Evelina*, writing in 1782, tells of a party at which she met Mrs Boscawen, Mrs Chapone, Hannah More, Mrs Carter, Mrs Baker, Mr Wraxall, General Paoli, Mrs Garrick, Sir Joshua Reynolds and 'all the belles esprits.' She wrote:

I was also gratified by meeting with the lady of the late young Lord Lyttelton, who was made very celebrated by the book called the Correspondents, which was asserted to be written by her and the old Lord Lyttelton, but proves to be an impertinent forgery. She is still pretty, though a little passée, and very elegant and pleasing in her manners.

This extract shows that Apphia was at the heart of society and, interestingly, many of those people became long-standing friends, as young Francis witnessed eighteen years later:

13 May 1800: We all met & dined at Lady Lytteltons ... Lady Lytteltons universal kindness was extreme I assisted as Landlord, & she behaved to me with the greatest affection: in a kind aunt some little eccentricities may be forgiven. We returned home after dinner & prepared to attend a party there at 8 o'clock. I cannot say, it was any thing very charming, but I was highly delighted by the kind &

*friendly manner, in which Principal Gordon met us. General Paoli was also there. We were introduced
to Mr Boldero the Banker. We supped there, & returned after midnight.*

Apphia, Lady Lyttelton, does not feature much in the following few years. Her estranged
husband developed a parliamentary career on the side of the Tories (partially explaining
Fox's bitter statements) and much is written about him—but nowhere near as much as was
later written on his dramatic end. Dr Johnson put it this way:

*Sir, it is the most extraordinary thing that has happened in my day—I heard it with my own
ears from his uncle, Lord Westcote. I am so glad to have every evidence of the spiritual world
that I am willing to believe it.*

Johnson's friend, Dr William Adams, replied, 'You have evidence enough—good evidence, which
needs no support.' Dr Johnson growled out, 'I like to have more!' Thus the Doctor was willing to
believe what it suited him to believe, even though he had the tale at third or fourth hand; for Lord
Westcote was not with the 'Wicked Lord Lyttelton' at the time of his death, on 27 November
1779. Dr Johnson's observations were made on 12 June 1784. Lord Westcote was Thomas
Lyttelton's uncle and his report—presumably as he gave it to Johnson—was as follows:

*On Thursday the 25th of November, 1779, Thomas Lord Lyttelton, when he came to breakfast,
declared to Mrs. Flood, wife of Frederick Flood Esq. of the Kingdom of Ireland, and to the three Miss
Amphletts (who were lodged in his house in Hill Street, London, where he then also was) that he had
had an extraordinary dream the Night before. He said he thought he was in a room which a Bird flew
into, which appearance was suddenly changed into that of a Woman dressed in white, who bade him
prepare to die, to which he answered 'I hope not soon, not in two months.' She replied: 'Yes, in three
days.' He said he did not much regard it because he could in some measure account for it, for that a
few days before he had been with Mrs. Dawson when a Robin Redbreast flew into her room.*

*When he had dressed himself that day to go to the House of Lords, he said he thought he did not
look as if he was likely to die. In the Evening of the following Day, being Friday, he told the eldest
Miss Amphlett, that she look'd melancholy; but, said he 'You are foolish and fearfull, I have lived
two Days and God willing I will live out the third: On the morning of Saturday he told the same
ladies that he was very well, and believ'd he shou'd bilk the Ghost. Some hours afterwards he went
with them, Mr. Fortescue and Captain Wolseley, to Pitt Place at Epsom; withdrew to his bedchamber
soon after eleven o'clock at night, talked cheerfully to his servant, and particularly inquir'd of him
what care had been taken to provide good Rolls for his breakfast the Next Morning; step'd into bed
with his waistcoat on, and as his servant was pulling it off, put his hand to his side, sank back, and
immediately expired without a groan.*

*He ate a good Dinner after his arrival at Pitt Place that Day, took an egg for supper and did not
seem to be at all out of order, except that while he was eating his Soup at Dinner he had a Rising in
his Throat, a Thing which had often happened to him before and which obliged him to spit some of
it out. His Physician, Dr. Fothergill, told me Lord Lyttelton had, in the summer preceding, a bad pain
in his side, and he judged that some great Vessel in the part where he had felt the pain, had given way,
and to that he conjectured his death was owing. His Declaration of his Dream and his Expressions
above mentioned, consequential thereunto, were upon a close inquiry asserted to me to have been so,*

by Mrs. Flood, the eldest Miss Amphlett, Captain Wolseley and his valet-de-chambre, Faulkner, who dressed him on the Thursday, and the manner of his Death was related to me by William Stuckey, in the presence of Mr. Fortescue and Captain Wolseley, Stuckey being the Servant who attended him in his bed chamber, and in whose arms he died.

What precisely Apphia did following the death of her estranged husband is not known. Nor do we know what happened to her £28,000, but we may surmise that her husband squandered it. A 'flashback' in the diaries of Francis Witts provides the answer:

Tuesday 31 July 1827: ... Death soon removed the worthy colonel, and his young widow, a sincere mourner, returned to her native land with twenty thousand pounds, which he had left her, and many romantic ideas. She in an evil hour accepted the addresses of the profligate, selfish, unprincipled Mr Lyttelton; he deserted her, she took refuge in the protection of his excellent Father, who then lived. The solid good of her Indian thousands was commuted for a settlement of £1000 per ann. on the Hagley Property.

At some point Lady Lyttelton moved to Southall Park and in this first volume of Agnes Witts' diaries she is visited there. But by 1801 she was again resident in London. Apphia, Lady Lyttelton, features throughout the diaries of Agnes Witts, and due to her great age, also in much of the diary of Francis Witts.

The next daughter of Broome Witts was not to have such an illustrious life. In 1769 Sarah Witts married Edward Stone (1743–1811). Her father-in-law, also an Edward Stone, had received his B.A. from Wadham College, Oxford, in 1724 and was rector of Horsenden in Buckinghamshire from 1737 until his death in 1768. He moved to Chipping Norton in 1758. He achieved some fame for his discovery of aspirin, for while in Chipping Norton he discovered that willow bark cured pain. He wrote to the Royal Society in 1763 to inform them of this. Later the active ingredient in the bark was identified as aspirin.

Edward and Sarah had one known daughter, Sarah, born about 1775, and perhaps a son, Edward, who, if he existed, died without issue. This Sarah went on to marry widower Charles Shard in London on 16 June 1807.

Edward, like his father, went to Wadham and received his B.A. in 1762. He followed his father into the Church and succeeded him as rector of Horsenden, holding the living from 1769 until his death in 1811. Edward was also perpetual curate of Princes Risborough. He died on 15 February 1811 and was buried at Winkfield in Berkshire. Edward Stone was for forty-two years rector of the adjoining parish of Horsenden St Michael and vicar of Stagsden, Bedfordshire. He was apparently an amiable character, beloved by all who knew him. He was also a Justice of the Peace for Oxfordshire and Buckinghamshire, and, from 1783 to 1793, rector of Hartwell with Little Hampden. In Princes Risborough he 'retired' from duties in 1800. Edward also held Owlsweek Manor in 1769. He was listed in the 1784 Buckinghamshire Poll Book as living in Princes Risborough. Agnes and Edward visited the Stones on 25 October 1792.

After Sarah came Edward (1746-1816) the husband of Agnes, as mentioned above in this introduction.

Richard Witts was the next in line. After Edward's financial embarrassment, Richard had acted kindly and, unlike elder brother Broome, provided assistance, but this was not to last and other issues came to the fore. Later in 1793 Edward wrote to his favourite and influential sister Apphia seeking her help:

Edinburgh 28th Octb. 1793

My Dear Lady Lyttelton
You may render me a very essential Service, if you will allow me to trouble Mr. Du Val to go to my Brother Richards in Harley St., & to Mr. W. in Friday Street, & if he fails of success there to Mr. Daniel his Solicitor, to Enquire where he is at present, or has been for the last two Months; as I have had no answer to three Letters I have wrote to him of great importance to my Comfort at present, & am indeed very much distressed by his Silence—the fact is he has in his hands about £50—of my Son's Money, given to them at Sundry times by their Several Relations, which we find it necessary now to employ in their Service as well the £100—you have so generously adopted. ... Mr. Witts of Friday Street can inform Mr Du Val where Mr. Daniel lives, who hears from him frequently, & I should be obliged to him to say to Mr. Witts in Friday Street, that a Letter from him would be very acceptable, especialy if he has seen lately my Brother Richards Son which he often does ...

It appears that the money raised for Francis and George was still in the hands of Richard, who acted as a trustee. Richard was also a trustee for his eldest son, Lee Steere Witts, who had inherited a fortune from his grandfather, Lee Steere, Esq. Richard had done well in his marriage and the connection would have been approved of within the family, for the Steere pedigree went back to the Norman Conquest, and they had lands and wealth to match. Martha Steere (1755–1815) married Richard in 1774 and later in the same year Lee Steere Witts was born. There were two other children, Richard and an unnamed daughter who became Mrs Daniells. The following 'flashback' from Francis Witts fleshes out the scanty information:

17 November 1827: ... Mr Lee Steere, the eldest Son, took with the fortune, which was very ample, the name of his maternal grandfather, & has been from the period of his coming of age alienated from his father's family: having been at variance with his Father, who was an incautious man, and having, more through carelessness than any improper motive, failed to keep regular accounts of expenditure on his Son's account during his minority subsequently to his grandfather's decease, was unable to render such a statement as was satisfactory to the interested advisers of the young man, who had yielded himself to their guidance, & who succeeded in detaching him from both his parents & indeed his whole family ...

The solicitor, Mr Daniell, was also to become involved with the family. He seems to have been the son of an East India Company merchant living in Harley Street, close to Richard Witts, and at about this time he married Richard's daughter.

How badly Richard mismanaged his son's affairs is not known, but, on coming of age in 1796, Lee Steere acted with viciousness towards his father and they were estranged from that point onwards. It appears that Richard may have been bankrupted in 1813 and he died two years later.

Edward Witts was desperate to get his hands on the £50 that Richard held and Lady Lyttelton was the go-between. Any kind feelings such as those expressed in early 1793 now evaporated. The story will be continued in the Introduction to Volume Two.

The youngest surviving child of the family of Broome Witts and Apphia Anthony was John Witts (1750–1816). Little information is given in either letters or diaries, but some basics have been pieced together. He obtained his degree at Oxford (Pembroke College) and then married Miss A. Townson in 1775. He was ordained in 1777 and, through a family connection (the Hunt family), obtained the living of Cardington in Shropshire, which he held until his death in 1816.

John's brother-in-law, Robert Townson (1762–1827), was a noted mineralogist, geologist and traveller and lived at Lydley Hayes intermittently from 1788 with his sister and his brother-in-law. In 1797 he published *Travels in Hungary*, a journey he made in 1793. He later travelled to Australia, where he made his fortune.

In January 1790 John stayed with Edward and Agnes at Swerford Park and officiated at Swerford church for a few weeks, a period enjoyed by all apart from John's wife, who was difficult. They saw John at Bownham House in May 1791, but after this Agnes and Edward Witts did not see John for many years: *28 September 1810: ... the day was ushered in most agreeably by the early arrival of our good brother John out of Shropshire who we had not seen for 19 years* ... John's wife died the following year and after that very little is heard until John's own death in 1816.

As usual it is Francis Witts who throws more light on the family. In a 'flashback' when Francis was on a visit to Shropshire many years later we are provided with more basic information:

Friday 16 September 1825: ... Mʳ Hunt of Boreatton ... was a relation of mine; his father having married my grandfather Broome Witts's sister. ... There has been of late years little intercourse between the Witts family and the Boreatton Hunts; the chief intimacy subsisting was with Lady Lyttelton and my Uncle John's family; Cardington, my Uncle's Shropshire living, being in the gift of the Hunts, and at no great distance from Church Stretton.

Another 'flashback' occurred many years later, while Francis was on a visit to the vicinity:

9 July 1845: On the summit of Caer Caradoc, many years since, and long discontinued, was held an annual meeting of a club formed in the neighbourhood among the gentry and clergy, where the fame and praise of Caractacus, and his distant, dim renown, were extolled in speeches and verses. In the heart of these hills to the East of Stretton, three or four miles distant, is the parish and village of Cardington, of which my Uncle John Witts was for many years the Incumbent, having been presented to the living by his cousin, Hunt of Boreatton. He did not live in the village, the Parsonage being then not a suitable residence, but rented a house at some little distance, Lydleys Hayes – where he brought up his family, of which my cousins John and Apphia are the survivors ...

The above information summarises the family of Edward and Agnes Witts. Most of this short introduction has been distilled from the detailed introduction to 'The Nomad,' Volume One of *The Complete Diary of a Cotswold Parson*, the diary of Francis Edward Witts, 1783–1854.

The Diaries in this Volume

The diaries in this volume are catalogued in the Witts Family Papers as F173 to F184 inclusive.

The handwriting is not too difficult to read and Agnes Witts' style is remarkably consistent from 1788 through to 1824. Her format is simple and unvarying. She always commenced the daily entry with the weather, followed by the notable events of the day and ended with a record of letters received and sent. The diaries were clearly intended as an *aide memoire* and not for posterity. This forms a major difference between her diaries and those of her son, Francis, for he seems to have had half an eye on future generations reading what he had written.

The diaries begin on 20 April 1788, when the family was living at Swerford, near Chipping Norton in Oxfordshire. Over the following two years it becomes evident that trade in Edward's business was bad and that the family needed to economise. For some reason, possibly through the consciousness that their financial embarrassment required them to move away from the neighbourhood, they selected Stroud in Gloucestershire. Edward had already put Swerford Park on the market while they were still there, and one person viewing it was Warren Hastings, lately Governor-General of India, on behalf of an acquaintance.

The house they settled on was Bownham House in Rodborough, near Stroud. It was rented from John Cooper of Woodchester and remained the family home for two years. The choice of Rodborough is interesting, but the reason why the location was chosen is not known for sure. It was adjacent to an acquaintance, Sir George Onesiphorous Paul, a relation of Anne Snow, a close friend of Agnes Witts, and it seems likely that the availability of the property was made known through this channel. It is also likely that Edward had many business contacts among the local clothiers and some of these contacts may have been good friends. Their landlord, John Cooper, was a wealthy clothier himself and he and Edward may have been on reasonably good terms. It was also close to Cheltenham, where Agnes could gain some comfort from her sisters, and Sandywell, where her aunts lived.

Francis was sent to a small private school at Elmore Court near Gloucester, and the younger boys remained in the nursery until August 1792, when they were settled as day scholars at Cheltenham.

Once settled in Rodborough social life began, and within a matter of weeks they were into a routine with frequent dinner parties and no lack of invitations. In fact, it seems as if Agnes felt somewhat superior to some of the clothiers' families and from a social point of view they would have been seen as occupying a position among the local gentry.

Life at Bownham went on much as usual. There are frequent references in Agnes's diaries to Edward making business trips, but he always came back depressed, his efforts unrewarded. By the beginning of 1793 financial matters took a decided turn for the worse and Agnes began to understand the seriousness of their position. On one trip away Edward wrote home and in a letter received on 26 February 1793 (Francis's birthday) Agnes recorded how she felt: *received a letter from Mr. Witts which did not mend my spirits* ... The following day her eldest brother Francis visited her at Bath, where she was at the time: *My Brother Travell breakfasted with us, after which accompanied by Dr. Baker as a Chaperon & introductory I went to make a very anxious visit to my Bror. Ferdinand & both his daughters, which passed off well, tho with strong feelings on each side* ... Exactly why she needed to be accompanied by a chaperon is not known, but presumably there had been stormy words prior to this and she needed some moral support before facing him. Ferdinando was a trustee of their marriage settlement and this almost certainly had some bearing on the matter.

By 8 March 1793 Edward Witts was back in Bath: ... *the day past very mournfully by the recapitulation of many dismal events from Mr. Witts, detail of his London businesses which terminated far worse than I expected & gave very little power of supporting myself, walk'd miserably about with him in the morning & was very ill all the evening* with hysterics. Eleven days later they were back at Rodborough and received a visit from Edward's elder brother, Broome: B. Witts arrives from Nibley ... interesting and distressing conversation. ... never more low in my life. Two days after this visit, Edward wrote a sorrowful letter to his sister:

Bownham House 21. March 1793

Dear Lady Lyttelton

I am much obliged to you—for all the kind expressions in your Letter of the 17th: & take an early opportunity to answer it: as the Crisis of our Journey, I hope is not far distant: for when a Plan is once formed, the sooner it is accomplishd in all respects the better. but you seem not to understand that the Education of our Boys—under our own Eyes, as well under our Roof, is absolutely necessary to our reduced income, & for which Motive, we move to Scotland where oeconomy & Education, go hand in hand.—The Charter House & Merchants Taylors, must therefore give way to the necessity, the deprivation of Trade, makes necessary, tho it will allow us the society we should have lost; & the opportunity of watching their morals & principles; which our new Situation will afford; I hope, & repay us, for the Exile, we pursue on such well founded motives. We have not yet fixed what Servant attends my wife, one English one is absolutely necessary; & Lord & Lady Elcho last week dedicated part of 3 days to a full Consideration & plan for our removal, Situation & Reception in Scotland whenever we go ... & nobody can be better informed in all Respects than they are. My Brother Broome, came yesterday to me, by my desire: but his Visit turned out the very reverse, of what I expected. & whatever feeling you discoverd in his mind on the occasions, that arose when you was at Nibley—it was all evaporated before he came under my Roof: as instead of Sympathy or compassion, he seemed to regret that our settled income was so secured, as to prevent him the effect of Bankruptcy. in truth that is all we have left; & tho' I asked him to be a Trustee to my Affairs, he said very calmly, he was so little of a Man of bussiness that he hardly ever choze to put pen to paper.—His contempt of the World, from having restored a once broken fortune, ought not to have appeard in a House of distress—& is totally the reverse of Richard, who tho he has lately raised Money to assist me has sent a Letter worthy of a Brother & a friend in Affiction. Molly the Boys Servt is the person we wish to take with us & Kitty has had several offers thro' my Wife: but at present is not informed of them: when she is you shall hear. My two Sisters from Cheltenham come to us tomorrow & probably stay till we go—We therefore shall not have an opportunity of seeing the party of Nibley again, & indeed parting Scenes without congenial feelings, are better avoided—the Settlement my Brother, had the hardness to tell my Wife to her face, was too much for her—perhaps you are a stranger to. it is £2500 of my personalty & my Estate at Chip Norton which now produces—about £110.—in all perhaps £210. besides the Annuity for my Life of ye D. of Malbro', which if my Brother had had the happiness of being a Father; he would not think too much for their maintainance & Education, so far different am I in that respect, that any bounty will be thankfully received by me; to extend that Education, beyond the narrow limits I am now engaging in—I confess I am much hurt, wounded minds as ours are, XXX ill bear oppressive Treatment. My Wife presses her kind Regards to those of your affectionate

Friend & Brother
Edwd: Witts.

This letter explains what was left to the distraught family. They had sufficient remaining to generate an annual income of about £210, but even this was subject to the trustees of the marriage settlement, one of whom was Ferdinando. As for Broome, why he desired the bankruptcy is not clear. On 19 April 1793 Agnes recorded a visit to her brother, seemingly less difficult than the previous visit, but with morbid tinges: *I went in the chaise to Upper Slaughter, rather a doleful visit being the last time I was to see my Bror. Ferdinand perhaps for ever. ...*

On 30 April they finally left Bownham for good and proceeded to Calwich, in south Staffordshire, near to the border with Derbyshire, to stay with their good and faithful friends John and Harriet Granville. From there Edward disappeared into Oxfordshire on business for a few days, and Agnes wrote a very pained letter to Lady Lyttelton.

On 17 June they left Calwich, stayed overnight at Manchester and arrived at Blackpool on 19 June, where they remained until 5 July, and which they left, according to Agnes 'with little regret'. The family, despite their distress, took the opportunity of looking around the Lake District and eventually arrived at Dumfries on 14 July. Two days later they were nearing their destination, when Agnes recorded with horror the poverty of their new country:

... we only went a stage of 19 miles to a very poor Inn call'd Noble House before we arrived there the country rather mended upon us being not quite so hilly & rather better planted and cultivated, & roads smoother. Here our accomodations were very moderate & our attendants worse, neither shoes or stockings, short petticoats & jackets, & dirt and filth of every kind very intolerable to my feelings however we got a good nights sleep all 5 in one room, for security.

When they arrived in Edinburgh they took lodgings in 2 George's Square. Agnes suffered from depression and recorded her low feelings frequently in her diary entries. They took a new under-maid, Kitty, but on 26 July she ran away. By September they were settling in, and on the third of the month the vessel containing all their packing cases landed—thirteen cases were carried to their lodgings in two carts. Things were looking up and on the last day of the month Agnes was sounding almost optimistic: *... taking another look & our favorit House in North Hanover Street, which grew more in favour on another survey.* Edward wrote to Lady Lyttelton on 23 October with the happier news that they were getting settled!

These last few paragraphs give a flavour of the opening of Volume Two, 'Exile.' Volume One therefore finishes on 25 May 1793 when Agnes was still at Calwich. Volume Two commences on 26 May 1793 and ends on 19 December 1800, when the family were in Copenhagen. It covers the majority of their exile period when, for financial reasons, they lived in Edinburgh until the summer of 1798, and then moved to Weimar in Germany for the education of Francis and George. They left Weimar in the summer of 1800, spent a few weeks in Leipzig and Dresden, moved north to the coast and took ship to Copenhagen, remaining there until they were evacuated along with other British subjects prior to Nelson's attack on the city.

Witts Family Papers F173

1788

Sunday April 20th.

Quite a hot summer Day, Dr. Williams did the Duty at Swerford Church, attempted to walk afterwards but found it quite to hot walk'd in the evening rec'd a Letter from Mrs. Eliza: Tracy.

Monday April 21st.

Fine again, but too windy to be pleasant My Sisr. Catherine Mr. Witts & I dined at Mr. Tyrwhitts happy to see them again, & the children so well recover'd the S. Pox. attempted to visit Mrs. Rollinson but she was gone out. not at home till near 9 at night but good driving light.

Tuesday April 22d.

Again very windy, & towards afternoon quite wet, I was very ill all Day, play'd at Cribage at night & Mr. Witts read in the Pharos, rather disappointed in it.

Wensday April 23d.

Mild & pleasant but cloudy, & at noon it turn'd again to rain, children & all caught by it in the farm yard & staid half an hour in the Barn. evening spent as the former one had been.

Thursday April 24th..

Soon after Breakfast My Sister Travell, Francis & myself, set out to spend the Day with Mrs. Rollinson, did some little businesses at Chip by the way, a fine Day but windy Mr. Witts join'd us at Dinner found Mr. & Mrs. Tyrwhitt & Mr. Western with Mrs. Rollinson. wrote to Dr. Wall.

Friday April 25th.

Most prodigious high wind, but dry quite unpleasant moving out but still I walk'd out twice, tho scarce able to stand. Francis quite ill all Day with a feverish complaint wrote to Lord Edward Bentinck on Mr. Caseys account.

Saturday April 26th.

Very similar weather quite unpleasant. my dear Francis much better but I dare not venture to let him go out, rec'd a Letter from Doctor Wall.

Sunday April 27th.

Much pleasanter weather, mild & fine Mr Witts went to Church at Kingham chiefly with a Design to enquire after Mrs. Western me was ill.[1] Dr Bandinell did the Duty at Swerford Church very well walket out in the evening again wrote to Miss Snow.

Monday April 28th.

Very fine Day, dined at the Childrens hour & set out for Oxford at ½ past three, leaving my Sisters & the Boys to take care of each other, had a very pleasant drive, Dr Wall drank Tea with us at the Star & sat till 9 o'clock in a very friendly way giving one medical advice.

Tuesday April 29th.

A most uncommon cloudless Day quite hot Dr Wall breakfasted with us, shop'd & made visits, had an early Dinner at the Inn & returnd home to a late Tea an extreme pleasant drive & found my little loves' all well.

5. *Oxford.*

---

1. Charles and Mary Western were good friends of Edward and Agnes Witts, and, although much younger, Agnes in particular took on an almost maternal approach to the couple. The basic biographical details are as follows: Charles Western (1760–1835), Mary Western, *née* Goostrey (1762–1849). The couple married at St James' Palace, London, on 7 July 1782. They had five children—four boys and one girl. The girl, Hannah Maria Western, was born in 1787 and died in 1851. Of the boys, Thomas was born in 1785 and died on 5 May 1790 at Kingham, with Agnes Witts by his bedside. The second boy was Charles William Western, born on 8 May 1786 and died five months later, on 20 October 1786. The third son fared less well: Maximilian Western was born on 20 January 1789 and died on 30 April 1789. The fourth and final boy did much better: Charles Maximilian Thomas Western was born on 4 June 1790 at Tiverton in Devon and, after gaining a commission in the army as a lieutenant-colonel, joined the Portuguese service. He married Harriet Clarke and had five children, four of whom were born in Portugal. He died in 1824. Therefore, out of their five children, Charles and Mary had the distress of seeing four predecease them.

Wensday April 30th.

Day exactly the same as fine & warm as possible Mr Witts at Banbury at a Court Meeting. My Bror Travell & Frank here for an hour.[2] My Sisr Catherine & the Boys Drank Tea with him at Swerford, My Sisr Anne & I went to Chip: late in the evening rec'd Letters from Mrs. Drake & Miss Anne Snow, from the former on the subject of visiting them at Amersham.

Thursday May 1st.

Such a Hot fine Day seldom known so early, too hot to be comfortable sitting with all the Doors & windows open, Mr Witts all morning at Mr Penystons, Mrs. Rollinson & her daughter Mary came early to Dine, truly sorry to see her so low & indifferent. My Br Travell Drank Tea here; wrote to Mrs. Drake.

Friday May 2d.

Again very hot till towards evening when it changed wonderfully to extreme cold & looket like rain My Brother & Francis dined here, walket with them in the evening & play'd at Cribage wrote to Mrs. Buxton.[3]

Saturday May 3d.

Cold & stormy a surprizing change to ones feeling, I walket out in spite of high wind, & walket to Swerford in the afternoon great delight to the children rec'd a Letter from Lord Edward Bentinck, & wrote to Miss Anne Snow.

Sunday May 4th.

Still rather windy but fine from much sunshine Dr Williams did the Duty at Church, I visited both the Sunday schools & carried them some new Books, walket home from Church with my Brother Travell took a little airing in the afternoon with my Sisr Catherine & 2 eldest Boys & wrote to Mrs. Granville.

Monday May 5th.

Very similar Day but warmer, Mr Witts went quite early to Chipping Norton & return'd in time to go with me to dine at Mrs. Westerns to see Miss Wiltshire who were first come to Kingham a lively pleasant visit & charming bright evening to return home in. My Sisters & Francis went down to Swerford to dine with my Brother Travell rec'd a Letter from Mrs. Tyrwhitt.

Tuesday May 6th.

Fine warm cloudy Day shewing great signs of rain, which came in mixed Showers in the evening, walket after Breakfast, & again in the evening to Swerford, kept in a Cottage an hour till the chaise could be fetch'd great delight to the children, play'd at Cribage at night.

---

2. Brother Travell was Agnes' eldest brother, Francis (1728–1801). The other brother was Ferdinando. Francis did not marry, but had two illegitimate sons: Francis (Frank, 1763–1790) and George (1767–1808). Their mother was Elizabeth Hitchman.

3. Mrs Buxton was Martha Buxton, *née* Travell, the daughter of Agnes' brother Ferdinando, and therefore her niece.

Wednesday May 7th·

Very fine warm morning frequent small showers, and at Dinner time a very powerfull one which made it too wet to walk much any part of the Day spent much time in looking over Maps & Books of roads, to plan our intended Journey by, wrote to Lady E Bentinck & rec'd Letters from Mrs· Buxton & Miss Snow.

Thursday May 8th·

A charming Day after the rain, took Mrs· Biggerstaff, who had arrived the night before to walk over all the premises, My Brother Travell & Frank dined here so walket with them in the evening.

Friday May 9th·

Violent high wind & storms, & in the afternoon, settled rain for three or four hours. My Sister Catherine & I took Mrs· Biggerstaff to Chip: & then over to Cornwell to pay a visit to Mrs· Penyston, her Mother Mrs· Asheton there a formal business then went to Chadlington to dine with Mrs· Rollinson where Mr Witts join'd us, Miss Jane Western with her. My Sisr Travell dined at Swerford.

Saturday May 10th·

A mild pleasant Day without much Sun till the afternoon walket a good deal in the morning Mr & Mrs· Tyrwhitt came to Dinner in a most friendly way, walket after Dinner to Cold Bath &c, vastly pleasant as they always are, wrote to Mrs· Buxton.

Sunday May 11th·

Very similar day to yesterday most pleasant being out of Doors, Mr Earle return'd & did his own Duty at church went again in the afternoon & took my little George for the first time great delight & he behav'd most well; my Sisr Travell & I went afterwards to Wigginton to call on Mrs· Jones to enquire after Mrs· Payn home to Tea & walket again to hear the Nightingales.

Monday May 12th·

Fine hot Day, much alarm'd early in the Morning by Mr Witts's Dressing room chimney being on fire, but by great care & exertion it was soon got under without any other damage than causing much fright walket a good deal both Morning & evening surveying the Men catching fish &c wrote to Miss Snow.

Tuesday May 13th·

Another extreme fine Day, quite summer walket much, to Swerford in the evening visiting the sick play'd at Cribbage afterwards as usual.

Wensday May 14th·

No change in the weather excepting being rather colder, My Brother Travell & Frank call'd here in the Morning, & drank Tea likewise, by way of a take leave visit, we walket part of the way home with them. rec'd Letters from Mrs· Granville & Mrs· Naper.

Thursday May 15th.

Fine but disagreeably windy, & towards evening very cold & unpleasant, My Sister went away to Mrs. Rollinsons for a few Days, I was full of employs all Day. at night wrote to Mrs. Savage.

Friday May 16th.

Fine in the Morning, but rain'd fast from 9 to 11 & then clear'd up & was very fine again, the Boys caught in it When taking their morning walk. M^r & Mrs. Penyston dined here, not being able to get anybody to meet them, I dreaded the formality of the Day but it turn'd out better than could be expected.

Saturday May 17th.

Very fine Day but still windy I rose early to see the two little Boys bath'd for the second time this season, Mr Witts all the Morn: at Chip: I engaged in many employs. rec'd a Letter from Mrs. Tyrwhitt & answer'd it, & wrote to M^{rs.} E: Tracy & Dr Wall.

Sunday May 18th.

Still fine weather, but rather flighting. Dr Williams did duty at Swerford church after which attended both schools, walket various times in the Day, but very far from well all Day. rec'd a Letter from my Sister Travell.

Monday May 19th.

Perfectly fine till Dinner time when there was some distant Thunder & some trifling showers but not enough to prevent walking — transacted many different kinds of business, & wrote to My Sister Travell.

Tuesday May 20th.

Most delightfull weather still, rather too hot to move much in a morning. Mr Witts at Chip, walket to the Village in the evening. rec'd a long Letter from Miss Anne Snow, with an account of her great escape by taking a wrong medicine. Much shocket at it.

Wensday May 21st.

Still hotter & more burning, but walket to see the workmen in the water, M^{rs.} & Miss Rollinson & Miss Western dined here, walket with them in the evening to cold Bath &c. rec'd Letter from Dr Wall & wrote to Miss Anne Snow.

Thursday May 22^{d.}

Very fine & hot but still cloudy at times. Mr Witts all morning at Chip: & I very busy with preparations for our approaching Journey, Mr Francis dined here & I went to Chip: in the afternoon to see Mr Bulley & other business. rec'd Letters from L^{dy.} Shrewsbury & Mrs. Savage, & wrote to Mrs. Naper & my Bro^r Ferdinand.

Friday May 23^{d.}

Just the same weather looking like rain but none coming, still more busy from Morn: to night heartily fatigued by it. rec'd Letters from M^{rs.} E: Tracy & Mrs. Buxton.

6. Cheltenham Church.

Saturday May 24th

A very hot burning Day, tho high wind set out soon after 9 from home, leaving my two sweet little loves with unspeakable regret, dined at Stow, & Drank Tea with Mrs. Tracy at Sandywell, the comfort of the Days Journey impeded by one of our Horses that was put to Ldy. Shrewsburys chaise to convey our servants running rusty, but no accident happend got to Cheltenham as it was dark.

Sunday May 25th

If possible a still hotter Day, or the heat of the place & being much fatigued made me think so went to Church in the Morning, & made some visits Miss Delabere & two Gentlemen Drank Tea at my Sisters walket & sat on the well walk.

Monday May 26th

No kind of change in the weather but for the hotter, we left Cheltenham at 9 sending the Servants some hours before, going ourselves with Posthorses much pleased with the views for the first 18 miles were unlucky in bad horses, dined at the X hands[4] & got to Bath at seven, much pleased with our comfortable Lodgings in Bennet Street, Lady Shrewsbury sat ½ an hour with us.[5]

---

4.   The Cross Hands at Old Sodbury.
5.   Elizabeth Talbot, *née* Bishop, (1724-1809). Her Husband George Talbot, 17th Earl of Shrewsbury had died the previous year.

Tuesday May 27th.

If possible still hotter than ever, my Bror Travell breakfasted with us, I made some visits & did some business, had a comfortable Dinner at home drank Tea with Mrs. Western, & when near Dark walket with her & her Daughters in the Crescent Fields much fatigued, by the heat.

Wensday May 28th.

Not so much sun but close & equaly hot, a few drops of rain at various times but came to nothing, went soon after Breakfast to Newton to call on Mrs. Langton spent two hours with her very pleasantly got much intelligence about Weymouth. Dined at Mr Wiltshires, & drank Tea with them in Spring Gardens & home early wrote to Mrs. Tracy.

Thursday May 29th.

Considerably cooler, & some rain fell in the afternoon, early in the Day full of many businesses & at noon went with Ellen Wiltshire to Bath Ford to see Mr J: Wiltshires children, to carry him an account of them to Weymouth, return'd to Mr Wiltshires again to Dinner excellent entertainment, return'd home to our Lodgings after Tea, to prepare for our departure the next Morning.

Friday May 30th.

Quite a cold heavy looking Day & small rain the greater part of it; but by laying the dust made our Journey more pleasant; My Br Travell breakfasted with us, delay'd setting out by

7. Bath from the Avon.

getting no places in the Coach for the Servants, but set off by ½ past nine, a most charming road all the way to Salisbury, & Country unequal & very uncultivated all the way to Warminster, & from thence in general dull, dined very comfortably at Deptford Inn, & saw Wilton in the afternoon, too dull a sky to shew the Pictures off to advantage but much pleased with many of them & the Sculpture to Judge ——— very fine.[6] Went to the Antelope Inn at Salisbury clean & good but slow.

Saturday May 31st.

Rather cloudy but little rain fell, only flying showers & in the afternoon was very fine, Dᴱ & Mʳˢ· Paul sat with us while we eat our Breakfast, after which Mᴱ Witts, Francis & I, set out for Wardour Castle a drive of 16 miles chiefly over & most naked country, but amply repaid when we got there by the grandeur of the general scenery, the House most superb far beyond description very well shewn, some excellent Pictures, & the plantations & variety of ground about the house most striking, dined very comfortably at the Arundel Arms & then went on to Mᴱ Beckfords at Font Hill,[7] a fine approach & place the water in a good stile, & the House & furniture very excellent, the Turkish apartment particularly pleasing good road to Salisbury by Wilton, drop'd Francis at the Inn & went to Sup at Dᴱ Pauls, meeting Dᴱ & Miss Baker very conversible & pleasant. Much pleased by Mʳˢ· Pauls obliging easy manner quite a Snow.[8]

Sunday June 1st.

A most charming Day throughout scarce a cloud in the sky, breakfasted at the Inn, & went to Dᴱ Pauls to attend them to service at the Cathedral well perform'd, walket about the Town till nearly time to go to evening service, dined with the Pauls in the afternoon took the Carriage & survey'd the scite of old Sarum well worthy of observation & the clearness of the evening made each object delightfull, all adjourn'd to here & supper at Dᴱ Bakers quite a setting forth but rather a dull business altogether, walket home to the Inn with the Pauls much pleased by their uncommon attention.

Monday June 2d.

Just such another delightfull Day as the former only still warmer left Salisbury before 9: a pleasant open drive of 22 miles to Blandford, where we went without stopping, the Crown a

---

6.   This word is not legible.
7.   William Beckford (1760–1844) was a novelist, art critic, travel writer and politician. He was M.P. for Wells (1784–1790) and Hindon (1790–1795 and 1806–1820). At the age of ten, Beckford inherited a large fortune from his father, a former Lord Mayor of London, also William Beckford, consisting of £1 million in cash, land at Fonthill with a mansion and several sugar plantations in Jamaica. This allowed him to indulge his interest in art and architecture, as well as writing. Beckford's life was colourful, but a scandal surrounding his relationship with the young William Courtenay, later Viscount Courtenay and 9th Earl of Devon, resulted in his exclusion from society. Having studied under Sir William Chambers and Alexander Cozens, Beckford journeyed in Italy in 1782 and promptly wrote a book on his travels, *Dreams, Waking Thoughts & Incidents* (1783). Shortly afterwards came his best-known work, the Gothic novel *Vathek* (1786). His other principal writings were *Memoirs of Extraordinary Painters* (1780), a satirical work, and *Letters from Italy with Sketches of Spain & Portugal* (1835), full of brilliant descriptions of scenes and manners. Beckford's fame, however, rests as much upon his extravagances as a builder and collector as upon his literary efforts. In undertaking his building works he managed to dissipate his fortune. In 1788 he was about to begin work on Fonthill Abbey and he later had the Fonthill Splendens mansion demolished and the contents sold.
8.   The Paul and Snow families were related by marriage.

good Inn & the Town chearfull while Dinner was getting, walket up to Mr Snows at Langton more than a mile to see his three Boys, fine children in a melancholly situation poor things; the place tolerable, on our road to Dorchester we went three miles to the left to see Abbey Milton Lord Miltons, drove thro' his new Village in a pretty vale the new House built in the Castle stile is well connected with the old Church close to it, by a colonnade, which is used as a Green House, the shape of the ground & the plantations fine & pleasing, the House is only made to accomodate a large family, not finely furnished & very few Pictures worthy observation, and there is a large suite of appartments not fitted up. In the old Church is a fine Monument to the Lady of the presant Lord Milton the figure of his presant Lordship hanging over her in an attitude of contemplative Grief. a pleasant drive from thence to Dorchester wch. is a large Town with three small churches, we were sent out of what is esteemed the best Inn by want of Room, but were very well accomodated at the second best.

Tuesday June 3^d.

Most pleasant weather no kind of change, left Dorchester at 11 after walking about the Town & soon got to Weymouth, 8 miles of a Hilly & very open Country, a fine first view of the Sea at five miles distance, landed at the Kings Head a quiet good Inn, Mr J. Wiltshire soon join'd us & assisted us in seeking for Lodgings wch. were soon procured, a whole small House in the Market Street very comfortable well furnish'd & very neat & clean, got into it in the afternoon after a good Dinner at the Inn, very busy all the evening in unpacking & settling. rec'd a Letter from Nurse with a charming account of my little loves at home,[9] two Letters from Miss Snow & one from M^rs. Naper & wrote to Miss Snow.

8. *Weymouth.*

---

9.   Francis had joined his parents on the trip, George and Edward having been left in the nursery at Swerford Park.

Wensday June 4th.

Equally fine weather, began drinking a draught of the Sea Water, very nauseous, finish'd settling our House in order, walket out a little on the Esplanade, went to some Shops, began buying bargains Mr Wiltshire call'd on me in the afternoon, after Tea went out in the chaise to a village call'd Preston two miles off, a heavy Hilly-Dragg post on the sands at night wrote to Nurse.

Thursday June 5th.

Much the same weather Mr & Mrs. Wiltshire call'd here in the Morning, Mr Witts went an airing with him in his open Carriage & she went with me to see an exhibition of work at the school wch. Miss Savage is at, & then drove together on the sands in the afternoon. Mr W. Francis & I drove to the Village of Upway 4 miles distant, drank Tea there at a Gardiners House very pleasant, after we came home walket about in pursuit of Lodgings for Ldy. Hereford rec'd a Letter from her & answer'd it.

Friday June 6th.

Quite as fine a day as the former went again Lodging hunting for the Viscountess, then call'd in the Chaise at the school for Miss Savage, & took her an airing on the Portland Sands much pleased by the Sea views. Mr Witts & the children walket on the Sands & picked shells while I drove about, brought Charlotte home to Dinner walket in the evening & took her home, Mr & Mrs. England call'd in the Morning. wrote to Mrs. Granville.

9. Wyke and Portland.

Saturday June 7th.

Fine Morning, but stormy towards evening, attended my Francis in his first dip into the Sea on here he behaved as well as possible, drank my Sea Water on the Beach & walket afterwards but found I was as sick as if I had staid in Bed, Mr Witts rode out I never went out of the House all Morning, Mrs. Bunton call'd here but I was dressing to dine at Mr J: Wiltshires, after Tea we air'd towards Upway she in the Chaise with me & Mr Witts in their open Carriage, the Sea very rough & beautifull to look on wrote to Mrs. Bunton.

Sunday June 8th.

High Wind which made it a very unpleasant Day tho bright sunshine & the dust intolerably troublesome, went to Church a singular low, & long Church, tolerable preaching & reading, but a strange clerk & still stranger singing after church went to Mrs. Buntons at Billfield two miles from Weymouth, a beautifull spot commanding a fine view of the Western ocean & Portland Isle, an excellent House very elegantly fitted up, found here a very pleasing old Lady, & happy in renewing her old acquaintance with Mr Witts, nothing could be more polite, her Son, his Wife & children with her walket all over the shrubbery & premises, in the evening air'd to Upway in search of Strawberries, wrote to Mrs. Savage, & at 10 o'clock Bath'd in the Tepid Bath not a pleasant operation being ill contrived but slept very well after it.

Monday June 9th.

Most violent high North east wind, quite unpleasant moving, & dust dreadfull, walket a little in the Morning merely for exercise, Dined at Mr J: Wiltshires to meet his Father, & his friend Mr Jeffries & Charlotte Savage, after Tea air'd with them to Wick & so on those Sands, very rough Sea. Bath'd again in warm Bath.

10. Upway House.

Tuesday June 10th.

Very windy still, walket a little on the sands after seeing Francis dip'd & again at noon to some shops, M^r & M^{rs.} J: Wiltshire dined here, & all air'd to Upway after Tea pleasant evening, wrote to Mrs. Naper & rec'd a Letter from Lady Hereford.

Wensday June 11th.

A very fine Day not near so high a wind M^r & Mrs. Wiltshire here an hour in the Morning to look over smuggled goods, I air'd afterwards on the sands. Mr Witts & Francis walket. busy at accounts in the afternoon, after Tea air'd again to Upway, & Bathd in the warm Bath.

Thursday June 12th.

An extreme fine Day little or no wind & warm sun, visited Mrs. Langton & went a shopping with her in the Morning, call'd on M^r & Mrs. Dytts who were just arrived at the Hottel, after Tea took Mrs. Wiltshire in the Chaise an airing to Wick & on those sands, Mr Witts & the Boy out a walking, on my return walket on the sands with M^r & Mrs. Langton. rec'd Letters from Miss Snow, & my Bro^r Ferdinand, & wrote to L^{dy.} Hereford. went into the warm Bath at night.

Friday June 13th.

A close warm cloudy day looking like rain but none came, Mr Witts & Francis Bath'd we all three went in the Morning to call on Mrs. Bunton, I afterwards drove on the sands, after Tea walket about Weymouth & among the shiping & late join'd the Langtons on the sands. wrote to Mrs. E. Tracy & rec'd a Letter from Nurse with a charming account of my little darlings.

Saturday June 14th.

Quite a hot Day & but little wind, went out at one o'clock to see how the world went sat a little w^{h.} Mrs. Langton meeting Buntons there, Mrs. Wiltshire dined here in her Husbands absence & was more pleasant than usual, she & I aird after Tea to Upway, after wch. I joind Mr Witts & a party & walket on the sands came home & read in Lady Hawks new novel not much struck with it.

Sunday June 15th.

Most prodigious fine Day, but towards night grew stormy & looket very much like rain but none fell, went to Church at Wick sat in Mrs. Buntons seat, service strangely perform'd, much disagreeable singing, air'd on the Sands afterwards a full Mall. dined very agreably with M^r & Mrs. Dytts, walk'd with her late in the evening on the sands, rec'd Letters from Mrs. Naper & Mrs. Bunton & wrote to Miss A: Snow.

Monday June 16th.

A cloudy Morning, but it turnd out a very fine Day & towards evening, wonderfully hot; set out at 10 o'clock accompanied by Mrs. Bunton, her Son & Daughter in their Chaise, on an excursion of three Days, a fine drive of 20 miles to Bridport, stopp'd at Winterbourne for Hay & water excellent roads chiefly over a very Hilly barren Country till within a Mile or two of the Town, which is handsome, wide open streets, dined very well at the Bull & had a most delightfull drive of 9 or 10 Miles to Lyme, the greater part of the way commanding a most rich & extensive views, & very frequently noble peeps of the Sea, from whence we were never distant more than 3 or 4 miles, the approach to the Town of Lyme is beautifull, a sad Town wth. narrow streets the beach charming to look upon but very moderate bathing, the Sun hot dusty & unpleasant, after Tea walket on the walk, sat in the shed or rooms had a merry supper & to bed in very poor apartments.

Tuesday June 17th.

A very close broiling Day rather unfortunate for moving, & it made the elder M^rs. Bunton very ill, two miles from Lyme turnd out of the road to see a fine Sea & Rocks view but it by no means answerd the extreme heat & fatigue of climbing the Hills one of the most enchanting rides of 16 miles I ever saw, rich tho hilly, two miles from Sidmouth left the great Exeter road & winded thro a sweet Valley crowded with fruit trees & sweet spizes running thro it,[10] Sidmouth is a miserable Town, but a lovely beach to the eye but wretched bathing a very neat walk & shed, Inn very good but slow in time got a mighty good Dinner, returnd 10 miles on the same road & then turn'd off to Axminster but mistaking the road did not get there till ten o'clock at night full Moon favor'd us much & if possible shew'd off the beauties of the country to greater advantage, good Inn & poor M^rs. Bunton much better.

Wensday June 18th.

Very hot again in the Morning but grew much cooler & proved a most delightfull Day for travelling, after a very comfortable breakfast went to see the Carpet Manufactory, much entertain'd by it sat a quarter of an hour watching a Woman form a large Bird in the corner of a carpet very curious afterwards went to survey a Manufactory of Tapes on some of the Looms 18 different peices are made in width, Axminster is 12 miles from Bridport the first six miles thro a new & beautifull Country, & at the Village of Charmouth came again into the Lyme road to Bridport, where we got again a very good Dinner and return'd to Weymouth between 8 & 9 well pleased with our excursion, as well as our companions, the younger M^rs. Bunton being a very sensible pleasant young Woman. rec'd a Letter from L^dy. Hereford.

Thursday June 19th.

Very early in the Morning most sharp rain attended with Thunder, but ceased by 9 o'clock, tho continuing cloudy & close all Day, I sat very quiet till time to go to Dine at Mr Englands at Stafford two miles beyond Dorchester, a large Parsonage in a dull low situation, where we met M^r & M^rs. Bunton, Mr Yeo & Mr Englands Bro^r & Sister, not an unpleasant visit I came home with M^rs. Bunton in her Chaise a very chatty tétètété,[11] when I came home had the joy of a excellent account of my little loves in a Letter f^m. Nurse.

Friday June 20th.

Cold & stormy throughout the whole Day, Northeast wind & flying showers, made some visits & dawdled about with M^rs. Langton, went in the afternoon to Drink Tea at Bellfield with the Buntons very sociable & pleasant Mr Hanbury & a Mr Payn a Clergyman, there play'd three rubbers at Whist with success, not at home till quite dark wrote to M^rs. Naper.

---

10.   The word appears like 'spizes' but is at the bottom of the page and written in a cramped hand.
11.   *Tête-à-tête.* Agnes Witts was aware that there should be accents, but was unclear as to what they should be.

Saturday June 21ˢᵗ·

Quite a Sultry Day tho much wind went a shopping with Mʳˢ· Langton, afterwards walket on the Sands with Miss Smith & Mʳ Sackville Lloyd, much entertain'd by his being become so much the Count. dined at Col: Langtons very free & pleasant only as four, walked late in the evening on the beach the tide too much in to walk on the Sands. rec'd a Letter from my Sister Travell.

Sunday June 22ᵈ·

A very fine Day went to Church in our own street, Mʳ & Mʳˢ· Dytts sat ½ an hour with us afterwards & then I air'd on the Sands & my two companions walket. Mʳ & Mʳˢ· Wiltshire dined with us I took her to Upway after Tea & on my return walket for ½ an hour on the Beach rec'd Letters from Mʳˢ· Tyrwhitt, Mʳˢ· Naper, & Mʳˢ· E: Tracy & wrote to My Sister Travell:

Monday June 23ᵈ·

An almost entire wet Day, beginning just as I went to Bathe for the first time but it did not spoil the pleasure of my plunge, tho it prevented our spending an agreable Day with Mʳ & Mʳˢ· Dytts, in a Yacht they had engaged to go a Days sailing, were at home all Day, working, reading, & writing, wrote to Lᵈʸ Edward Bentinck & Mʳˢ· Tyrwhitt.

Tuesday June 24ᵗʰ·

Very fine Morning but grew stormy towards Noon, & brightened up again, went out directly after Breakfast to see the Dytts's go abroad their Yacht went with them for an hour or two, & return'd in a boat, Mʳˢ· Wiltshire being of our party, the change from one Vessel to another made me very sick for a short time & the Sea was rough, but well pleased altogether & Francis delighted came home & dress't in haste to Dine at Bellfield, meeting Col: & & Mʳˢ· Langton Admiral & Governor Arbuthnot[12] & Mʳ Payn sat down unto a very handsome Dinner play'd at whist & home late rec'd Letters from Lᵈʸ Hereford & Miss Anne Snow.

11. Lulworth Castle.

---

12. Admiral Mariot Arbuthnot (1711–1794), who commanded the Royal Navy's North American station during the Revolutionary War. A native of Weymouth, Arbuthnot entered the navy in the late 1720s, became a lieutenant in 1739, commander in 1746 and post captain in 1747. In 1759, during the Seven Years' War, he commanded H.M.S. *Portland*, one of the ships employed under Commodore Robert Duff in the blockade of Quiberon Bay, and was present at the defeat of the French on 20 November. From 1775 to 1778 he was naval commissioner resident at Halifax, Nova Scotia. He was Lieutenant-Governor of Nova Scotia from 1776 to 1778. In 1779 he was made vice-admiral and commander-in-chief of the American station. Soon after arriving at his destination, he was blockaded in New York City harbour by the French fleet under Count d'Estaing. In December 1779 Arbuthnot conveyed the troops of Sir Henry Clinton to Charleston, South Carolina, and co-operated with him in laying siege to that city. In 1781 he fought the French Newport squadron in the Battle of Cape Henry, before returning to England. Arbuthnot appears in contemporary accounts (*Morning Chronicle*, 18 May 1781) as a coarse, blustering, foul-mouthed bully.

Wensday June 25th.

A very unpromising Morning for our jaunt to Lulworth Castle as it rain'd when I bath'd early, & at times continued so till Dinner time but we were not daunted I went in M$^{rs.}$ Buntons Coach, & Mr Bunton with Mr Witts, a varied drive of 14 miles part very indifferent road, over a Hilly country ill cultivated, & now & then peeps at the Sea, it is a good Castle like House but not much worth seeing, the Chapel a little distance from the House newly built in the Garden is well worth seeing neat large & handsome but unlike a Cornish Chapel, had a comfortable merry Dinner at the Alehouse in the Village, walked to see the Cove & return'd home to Weymouth as it was dark. rec'd a Letter from Nurse, the Dear Loves quite well.

Thursday June 26th.

A very fine Day throughout, busy all Morning in contriving our little intended Voyage w$^h.$ M^r & M$^{rs.}$ Dytts, they & Miss Baldwyn & the Bunton Family drank Tea with us & play'd at Cards, rec'd a Letter from L$^{dy.}$ Edward Bentinck & wrote to M$^{rs.}$ Bunton.

Friday June 27th.

An equal fine Day very promising for our intended Jaunt, w$^{ch.}$ was quite agreed upon for the next Day & Vessel engaged, visited M$^{rs.}$ Langton &c, in the Morning, in the afternoon took a quiet airing to Upway to procure some strawberries to take on board. to bed early.

Saturday June 28th.

Such a total change in the weather there was no possibility of going our voyage tho all was in readiness & we got up at 5 o'clock in the Morning to be ready, much rain & high wind, made us feel glad to be safe on dry land tho a good deal disappointed at noon air'd on the Sands for a little air & exercise drank Tea with the Langtons, but too bad an evening to walk out. rec'd a Letter from M$^{rs.}$ Guydickens.

Sunday June 29th.

Disagreable cold northeast wind with a few flying showers till mid:day a fine evening not pleasant bathing, went to Church visited the Dytts air'd on the Sands, dined at Mr Wiltshires 2 girls from the school there, air'd with her after Tea afterwards walket on the Beach with Langtons &c.

Monday June 30th.

Windy but dry & warm & looking like Thunder, stroled about with M$^{rs.}$ Langton & went to survey Mr Welds Yacht a very compleat Vessel in point of accomodation, dined at M$^{rs.}$ Buntons, meeting Englands, Wiltshires, Thodbers & a set of them, which made up the company 16, a handsome Dinner, but too large a circle to make the Day so agreable as it would have been, play'd at Whist. wrote to M$^{rs.}$ Tuckett & Miss Snow.

July 1st.

Very similar Day not pleasant bathing walket a little in the Morning, & air'd after Tea on the Abbotsbury road, a very fine view of the Western Ocean, went to see a beautiful calf at a Farm on the road, afterwards walket on the beach with Langtons &c. wrote to M$^{rs.}$ Rollinson.

Wensday July 2ᵈ·

Fine Day but wind always high at Weymouth, had several visitors in the Morning, then stroled with Mʳˢ· Langton, Drank Tea at Bellfield very agreably & walket all over the premises, sorry to take leave of Mʳ & Mʳˢ· Fowel Bunton rec'd Letters from Mʳˢ· Granville, Miss Snow & Nurse with a nice account of my little loves.

12. Weymouth.

Thursday July 3ᵈ·

A close cloudy Day looking very like Thunder & consequently very oppressive, went over the Duke of Gloucesters House & walket round his Shrubbery everything much out of repair but a very good House, after Dinner took an hour or two Sail within the Harbour taking with us Francˢ Friend Mastʳ Bastard return'd to Tea & then walk'd on the Beach as usual rec'd Letters from My Sisʳ Travell & Mʳˢ· Masson answer'd the letter & wrote to Dʳ Wall.

Friday July 4ᵗʰ·

Hard rain early in the morning but held up for me to go to Bathe, after breakfast went to some Shops & air'd with Francis on the Portland Sands fine Day but very windy, Col: & Mʳˢ· Langton & Mʳ Sackville Lloyd dined here & were very agreable all walked on the beach late but it was cold & unpleasant.

Saturday July 5ᵗʰ·

Wet & stormy all Day, and at Noon taking Mʳˢ· Wiltshire with me on the Abbotsbury road & afterwards on the Sands Drank Tea with Mʳˢ· Bunton at Bellfield, who had got 2 Miss Payns with her a chatty visit, came home thro' hard rain. wrote to Mʳˢ· Naper.

Sunday July 6ᵗʰ·

A Brilliant fine Day till Dinner time when it grew wet & stormy & was a very wet night, I bath'd, went to Church, air'd on the Sands with Mʳˢ· Wiltshire, Drank Tea at Mʳ Smyths meeting Col & Mʳˢ· Langton. rec'd a Letter from Miss Snow & wrote to Miss Jones

Monday July 7ᵗʰ·

A fine Day but windy to a disagreable degree in the Morning better in the evening, dawdled about the greatest part of the Morning with Mʳˢ· Langton & Miss Smyths going into empty Lodging Houses &c., went to Dorchester & drank Tea, to enquire after stage Coaches & Waggons, walket on the beach on our return; wrote to Miss Snow & my Sister Travell.

Tuesday July 8ᵗʰ·

Very fine Day till 12 o'clock when it became very wet & continued raining 3 or 4 hours, Mʳ & Mʳˢ· Wiltshire dined here, we all went out after Tea in Chaise & Buggy, on the Upway road, where we met all the world airing. cold night but dry.

Wednesday July 9th.

Very lowering Morning & turn'd out too wet to stir out all the Morning. Busy at home with various employs, Drank Tea with Mrs. Bunton, meeting there M^r J: England & Miss England, & two Miss Payns play'd two Pools at Comerce. rec'd a Letter from Nurse with a nice account of the darlings.

Thursday July 10th.

Cloudy & damp early, & very wet towards noon, made some visits & air'd with Mrs. Langton in her Chaise to Upway, Drank Tea with the Langtons meeting Miss Smyth. wrote to Mrs. Guydickens & Nurse & rec'd Letters from both the Miss Snows & Dr Wall.

Friday July 11th.

A damp disagreable Day, tho but little rain fell, walket & drove about with Mrs. Langton for an hour or two, in the evening drove to Upway & by the way went a quar^t of a mile to the left of the road to the mineral spring at Nottington, shocking smelling water & near as bad tasted a strong Chalybeate by turning silver to the colour of copper in two or 3 minutes, on our return walke'd on the Beach with the Langtons, rec'd Letters from Mrs. Tyrwhitt & Mrs. Rollinson & wrote to Miss Snow.

Saturday July 12th.

Tolerably fine again till noon when it again rain'd, which it did at times all Day, & in the evening was a miserable disagreable thick Fog, & very hot & low, Mr Witts rode out in the Morn: I staid at home & rec'd many visitors, in the afternoon went to Bellfield, meeting Higgensons & Payns, several more people expected but all disappointed rather a dull evening, a whist & commerce Table wrote to Mrs. Granville.

Sunday July 13th.

Wonderfull high wind, & flying Showers all Day heard a most excellent Sermon from a Dr Butler, call'd after church on Mrs. Langton & air'd with her; drank Tea with the Wiltshires & air'd to Upway as usual with them. rec'd Letters from Mrs. Bunton & Mrs. Naper.

Monday July 14th.

Cloudy but dry till 12 o'clock when it began pouring with rain & so continued all Day & night Mrs. Langton sat an hour with me in the Morning, too wet to go to them as intended to take our leave of them, full of business all Day beginning to prepare for our removal wrote to Mrs. Elizabeth Tracy.

Tuesday July 15th.

Most violent rain till noon when it clear'd & permited us to attempt making a visit at Bellfield and some others & then air'd a little while on the sands, walket a little on the beach in the evening rec'd a Letter from Miss Snow. Full of business & accomp^{ts} all Day.

Wensday July 16th.

Had been a most violent wet night but fortunately for our approaching Journey clear'd up & we left Weymouth without much regret, between 9 & 10 went 8 miles the same road as to Lullworth, & then to Wareham, a good road but not thro' a very pleasant Country, a tolerable Town, from whence we went 4 miles to Corff, where we dined at a very miserable Inn or Alehouse, where there was literally no Meat or Wine to be got. Corff Castle is a noble old Ruin, well worthy of observation, upon a very high knoll, supposed to be part natural part artificial, at the bottom nearly a mile in circumference, built by King Edgar & finally demolish'd in the Civil Wars. were obliged to go back again to Wareham to get into the road to Pool, wch. is 10 miles very excellent road but over a horrid morrass the greater part of the way Pool is a dirty ill built Town of much shipping Trade, the Quay is well lined with Vessels; The old Antelope Inn a most dreadfull one destitute almost of common necessaries. in the evening wrote to L^{dy.} Hereford.

Thursday July 17th.

An extreme wet Morning but clearing up about 10 we set forth to Christchurch 14 miles the first 4 upon the Ringwod Turnpike road, & then upon a very tolerable cross country road rather sandy, & thro' several villages, a fine rich Corn country & the crops apparently good, Christchurch is small irregular built Town, we found the George Inn very neat & comfortable & had an excellent Dinner. the Church is large & very ancient much in the Cathedral stile, a new Organ putting up; there is a very curious Sculpture Altar piece, the figure of Jesus large as life at the bottom in a recumbent posture, with the root of a Vine arising from his Body & the branches directing the generations to the promised birth of Christ finishing by the wise Mens offerings, & the Angel pointing out the Star in the east; close to the back of the Church is a large House & place belonging to a Mr Brandon a Man of large fortune, the House commands a fine view of the Isle of Wight the Needles &c. with the Rivers Avon & Stour uniting in a fine stile not a hundred yards from the house & running into the Sea; on each side this front of the house is a conservatory & fruit houses with many curious plants wch. the civility of the Gardiner made us benefit by, & at a little distance in the kitchin Garden a Hot House for Vines, a compleat place but out of repair during a Minority; from here 13 miles of very good road & pleasing rich Country to Lymington, the Sea views fine, a neat pretty Town but without any command of Sea, the baths are more than ½ a mile off, well contrived for what they are but much inferior to open sea bathing, we found the Angel where we took up our abode a very comfortable Inn, made more to us by being kept by Mr Baughn an old acquaintance. rec'd Letters from Miss Snow, Miss Adams & Nurse with a charming account of our little Dears, a delightfull fine evening. weather appearing quite clear'd up.

Friday July 18th.

A most glorious fine Morning quite bright & hot, had had but little sleep in the night from a drunken riot in the house, busy in writting & preparing for our voyage to Portsmouth, for wch. purpose had a very early Dinner & was aboard with our Boy & three servants by ½ past one, a neat comfortable Vessel, very civil Captain, & a Man & a Boy on board such fine weather sat on deck all the time not one of us sick, mere 4 hours & a q^t performing the voyage & very beautifull the views both of the Isle of Wight & the opposite shore were on wch. was a fine

13. Portsmouth.

looking place of Mr Robbins's, a small one of Mr Drummonds[13] & another in Castle form call'd Lutterels Folly the first view of Portsmouth Harbour both beautifull & noble, Haslar Hospital a fine object & so are all the surrounding fortifications, we got into a small boat to bring us close to shore & went to the Fountain Inn, one of the most comfortable & the civilest people I ever saw, drank Tea & walket almost round the Fortifications, & afterwards about the fair w$^{ch.}$ was amusing, being merely booths erected for the sale of Toys, Haberdashery, Calves[14] &c. &c. & last for 14 Day's wrote to Miss Snow & rec'd a Letter from my Sister Travell with an entertaining account of the Royal doings at Chelten:[15]

Saturday July 19$^{th.}$

A Fine shewey Morning, grew stormy at Noon, & wet late in the evening; set out about 9 o'clock to walk round the Dockyard &c, much entertain'd & gratified by the sight, which far more than answered even my raised expectation, extremely well shewn, by an intelligent conductor; after taking more than two hours in this survey, we took a Boat to go to the

13.   Robert Drummond of Cadland (1728–1804). Drummond was the seventh son of William Drummond of Machany, 4th Viscount Strathallan, who died at Culloden in 1745. This branch of the family founded Drummonds of Charing Cross, bankers to the royal family, nobility and the rich and famous of the nineteenth century. The Drummond country home was Cadland, near Fawley in Hampshire, an estate overlooking the Solent and with grounds designed by Capability Brown; the main house was designed by Henry Holland.
14.   This does not make any particular sense; the word looks like 'Calves' or 'Calnes'.
15.   During the summer of 1788 George III and Queen Charlotte spent much time at Cheltenham.

Barfleur, a 90 Gun Ship, Captain Knight lately under the command of Admiral Lord Hood, who is now removed & no other yet appointed it is esteem'd a very fine Vessel, & to me a very glorious sight, who had never seen a Man of War before the Officers were very obliging & shew'd us every part even to the Stewards room & stores of Provision, the Admirals Cabin is realy elegant & very roomy & comodious, the staircase up to the Ship as easy as possible, from hence we return'd in the Boat to the Gun Yard & walket home & finding it late determined not to leave Portsmouth this Day, had a good Dinner, & sail'd to the Brewery & Haslar Hospital afterwards by the way, saw 400 Convicts chain'd returning from their daily labour to the Vessel where they are station'd in the Harbour many of them for life, we did not think it worth while to go into the Brewery, but row'd on to the Hospital a very noble & extensive building & well accomodated as may be supposed, as during the last War it had sometimes 2300 patients in it, it has 43 windows in Front & is built in a square Quadrangular form at present there is only 140 in it: the badness of the evening prevented our going out of the Inn after Tea.

Sunday July 20th.

Had been a very Stormy night, the wind was high but dry, at a little after 8 in the Morn: when we went on board our Lymington Vessel to take us to Cowes, both wind & Tide being against us, we did not get there till past twelve, the Sea was very rough & disagreable, Francis & Pressich were both sick I kept on Deck all the time & did not mind it at all. Cowes is a pretty little harbour, a comfortable Inn the Fountain kept by a very civil Widow Woman, when we had dined we walk'd to the Bathing Beach where is three Machines let down by a Rope the Castle is small but in repair & some pieces of Cannon; the Town is neat & it seems as if it would not be a disagreable place for the purpose of bathing from thence to Newport 5 miles we took a Coach & pair taking James in the Carriage wth. us, the other servants being gone on to Lymington, we pass'd by a very large building the general work House for the whole Island wch. we understood was rather abused or would bear an excellent

14. Carisbrooke Castle.

plan, Newport is a large good Town tho without any particular Trade, but is the principal Mart for the whole Island, the Sun is a good Inn where we engaged Beds &c & went to Carisbrooke Castle about a mile, both that & the Village stand beautifully, I have not often past 3 hours more pleasantly than in & about the Castle, which is a noble old ruin Charles the first made it a retreat till forced from it to Hurst Castle just opposite to the Needles. It is now made use of in War time for Sick Soldiers on their first landing from foreign stations; & there is some very comfortable apartments for the Matron of the Castle who with her Sisters & two Nieces are the only inhabitants at present, most civil intelligent people, we drank Tea there most comfortably in a room commanding a very rich view of the Town of Newport & surrounding Country, & a Sea view towards Portsmouth, we walk'd all over the Ruins & saw a well of excellent water which is 300 feet deep, into w$^{ch.}$ they throw pieces of lighted paper to shew the depth, drop a Pin to hear the sound at bottom & all those little wonders. in our way to Newport we walket thro the village of Carisbrooke where there is a fine ring of 8 Bells & some very beautifull Meadows, walket about the Town, had a good Supper & went tired to Bed.

Monday July 21$^{st.}$
A very fine Day, with fine light & shade to shew off the charming views to advantage set off between 9 & 10 in a hired Chaise drove by a Coachman sitting on a Chair, a miserable Carriage & good Horses w$^{ch.}$ are necessary in this Country the Hills being frequent & sharp, the roads in summer are very tolerably good but in Winter I should guess horrid, the views are delightfull & very much varied w$^{h.}$ hill & dale rich & large Corn fields, & peeps of the Sea 4 miles from Newport at a place call'd Swanston we walket over an old Place of Sr Fitzwill$^{m.}$ Barringtons[16] a good Garden Hot House &c. a very civil Gardener w$^{ch.}$ supplied us both with fruit & flowers, we quitted the road to Yarmouth to go to Fresh Water Gate w$^{ch.}$ is about 12 miles from Newport, on a Down leading to it call'd Brook Down is the finest Sea View I ever saw, full of Vessels, & the inland views of the Island charming, here we staid half an hour to walk on the Cliffs & then went on three miles to Yarmouth, the approach to which is extremely pretty it is a small Market Town with several good Houses & Gardens, we took a hurrying Dinner at the George & then hired a Vessel to take us first to the Needles & then home to Lymington, it was the finest Sail to the Needles possible & the sight of them wonderfull but both wind & tide being against us, it was a very tiresome business getting to Lymington where we did not arrive till 9 o'clock damp & cold on the water the approach to the Town at low water is very disagreable, the stream being narrow & the Banks a nasty Green Mud.

Tuesday July 22$^{d.}$
An uninterrupted fine Day, but at times gloomy hot, attempted to Bathe but from the lowness of the tide found it impossible, walket a little about the Town wrote & prepared for our departure after an early Dinner, the whole 17 miles to Southampton most excellent road & thro' a most beautifull Country, the greater part of the way thro the new Forrest;

---

16.   Fitzwilliam Barrington (1708–1792), 8th Baronet, of Barrington Hall, Essex, succeeded to the title in 1776.

Lyndhurst a very pretty Village, at one
end of it a fine place late Sr Phillips
Jen: Clerkes[17] much superior to the
Kings House inhabited by the Duke
of Gloucester which stands in a street
nearly opposite the Inn;[18] the approach
to Southampton must be very fine at high
water, as it was very pleasing at low, the
Town large & the principal street wide
& spacious, we went to the Dolphin a
large & apparently good Inn, drank Tea

15. *Southampton from the water.*

walket to survey the Rooms Baths &c. wrote to M$^{rs.}$ Naper.

Wensday July 23$^{d.}$

Very pleasant sweet Day with a great deal of light & shade, I bath'd early not agreable
Bathing & the Guide a bold disgusting Creature: at 11 o'clock we went in the Chaise to see
Netley Abbey, by land 8 or 9 miles tho across the water not half so much, the first 4 or 5
miles on the Gosport road this a beautiful county & by many handsome places, the rest a
bad cross road & difficult to find; the Ruin is very noble; & much to be lamented it is not
made the most of, as it is greatly too much overgrown, & not possible to see the outside as
could be wish'd, it is very large in particular the church end. we quitted the Carriage at Itchin
Ferry & had a very pleasant sail up by the Quay to Southampton had an excellent Dinner,
walket a great deal about the Town & wrote to Miss Anne Snow & Nurse.

Thursday July 24$^{th.}$

Weather quite as fine, I bath'd again & at 11 left Southampton sending Pressich off to
Oxford & having James to follow after as he could, for the sake seeing Lord Palmerstons at
Broadlands,[19] we went the Ramsey Road to Winchester w$^{ch.}$ is 5 or 6 miles about it is a very
pretty place in a sweet Country & very nicely kept. The House was undergoing a thorough
repair so we could not see it, the kitchen Gardens Hot Houses &c are very good, & the pleasure
ground very pleasing; at Winchester we found great hurry & confusion it being the election
time at the College the White Hart a miserable old House, & very dear or else comfortable
enough, for 5 or 6 miles of either side the Town the country barren & dreary & the land light
& bad, & I think a very dull old Town we were much pleased with the Cathedral which is
admirably well kept, & better worth seeing than any I ever saw, the altar piece is a beautifull

---

17.   Sir Philip Jennings Clerke (1722–1788), of Duddleston Hall, Shropshire, and Lyndhurst, Hampshire, M.P. for
      Totnes (1768–1788). He was created a baronet in October 1774.
18.   H.R.H. Prince William Henry, third son of Frederick, Prince of Wales (1743–1805). William Henry was created
      Duke of Gloucester in 1764. He was a major-general in the army and eventually became a field marshal in 1793. He
      was Warden of the New Forest (1771–1805).
19.   Henry Temple, Viscount Palmerston (1739–1802), succeeded to the title in 1757. The building of the Palladian
      mansion was begun in 1767. Temple commissioned Lancelot 'Capability' Brown to supervise work commenced
      under William Kent and further landscaping, planting, clearing and riverside work created one of his greatest
      masterpieces. During 1788, at the time when Agnes visited, further work was in hand, whereby Brown's *protégé* and
      son-in-law, Henry Holland the younger, added the east front portico and Domed Hall.

16. The Water Gate at Southampton.

piece of old gothic stone work, & there is a fine modern Picture by West of the resurrection of Lazarus, the tomb of William of Wickham, & all his wonders are entertaining; the Close & the environs of the Church are large — but dull, we call'd on Mʳ Woodford but he was not at home but we walk'd in his Prebendal Garden where were many fine flowers. after Tea went to the College in which we were rather disappointed, the Rooms for the poor Collegers are like dirty old Barns & not near so <u>sweet</u>, the school is now rather at a low ebb, as there is not above 40 Commoners, & 70 is the constant number on the foundation.

Friday July 25ᵗʰ·

Most pleasant weather for travelling being Dry & fine, without being hot, left Winchester at 8 o'clock the first 4 or 5 miles dreary & dull but afterwards mended greatly, & changed to rich wooded country & we past several fine places, we went to Aldermaston 26 miles without stopping, there we found the Hinds Head a very moderate Inn in appearance but in time we got an excellent Dinner, & had a most pleasant drive of 18 miles to Wallingford which we reach'd at 7 o'clock much pleased with the country passing Lᵈʸ· Clives at Englefield, Sʳ Frans· Sykes's at Bassldon[20] &c we found the Bear at Wallingford not splendid but comfortable, & had a pleasant walk over the bridge & about the scite of the old Castle well planted & very pretty.

Saturday July 26ᵗʰ·

Much the same weather got to Oxford at 12 o'clock where we found our Servants were landed before us ordered our Dinner at the Star & went to call on Dʳ Wall, Mʳˢ· Cox, & Mʳˢ·

---

20.   Francis William Sykes, 1st Baronet (1732–1804). Sykes entered the service of the East India Company in 1749 and made his fortune there. He bought the estate at Basildon in Berkshire about 1770 and built the mansion house.

17. Oxford.

Wickeham the latter the only one we found at home, as usual quite pleasant & happy to see us, impatient to set forth again to reach home before my little darlings went to Bed which we did, & found them all we could wish; a fine evening walket about till it was dark rec'd Letters from Lady Hereford, Miss Chaplin, Maria Jones & one from Nurse at Oxford.

Sunday July 27th·

Just the same weather very pleasant & heartily glad to find myself once more at home with all my sweet Boys, Mr· Evans did the Duty at Swerford Mr· Earle not being at home, very well pleased with his manner & thought him a well looking Man, went to church again in the evening & visited both the schools. rec'd a Letter from Miss Snow & wrote to Mrs· Tyrwhitt & Mrs· Hyett.

Monday July 28th·

No change of weather being a very fine Day, too busy with unpacking &c to be out till after noon, when I sat out on the Green watching the Green house plants being arranged in the evening wrote to My Sister Travell.

Tuesday July 29th·

Similar weather quite close & hot but not much sun, Mrs· Rollinson & Miss Western & Mr· Earle & Mr· Evans here in the Morning, Mr· Witts at Chip: after Tea He & I walk't to Swerford to call on Miss Earles, very chatty & pleasant. walket about the Parsonage Garden & premises & home quite late & dark. rec'd a Letter from Mrs· Tyrwhitt & wrote to Miss Snow.

Wensday July 30th·

Again close hot weather, Mr· Witts went to see Mr· Penyston & Ldy Fane, Miss Earles sat an hour with me, Francis walket with us in the evening about the Park & Gardens at night wrote to Lady Edward Bentinck.

Thursday July 31st.

Still very fine weather, Mr & Mrs. Western, Miss Maria, & Miss Elizabeth Wiltshire dined here all very pleasant & agreable walket a great deal about both before & after Tea, & after they were gone very busy at accounts.

Friday Augst. 1st.

Very close & hot like Thunder quite oppressive, Mr Witts rode to Chipping Norton, drank Tea at Mr Earles, rather a dull silent visit, play'd at Whist & won both Rubbers, Francis the most lively of the whole party.

Saturday Augst. 2d.

A most prodigeous fine day clear air & bright Sun Mr Witts went early to Mr Penystons, & we dined at Mr Westerns to meet Mr & Mrs. Tyrwhitt which made the visit most agreable to me as their society I always think charming, a beautiful evening to come home in; rec'd a Letter from My Sisr Travell & answer'd it.

Sunday Augst. 3d.

As fine or still finer a Day, wonderfully hot, Mr Evans did the Duty at Swerford, Mr Earle at Hook: Norton sat with his Sisters half an hour after Church in the Morn: & after evening went to Drink Tea at Wiginnton, the visit much in the old stile, wrote to my Brother Ferdinand.

Monday Augst. 4th.

If possible still hotter than ever, ill suited to the variety of business I had to go thro & still less to the Book Club Meeting at C: House at which there were only 19 assembled, & 9 of them Clergyman. Mr Earle steward & both he & his two Sisters did the Honors as well as possible, but it would have been sadly dull to me but for the pleasantness of Mr & Mrs. Tyrwhitt.

Tuesday Augst . 5th.

Not near so hot quite pleasant Mr Evans breakfasted here, to attend Mr Witts to Hook Norton, busy preparing & Dressing to go to Blenm Public Day, sat down 30 to Dinner which would likewise have been dull but for the Tywhitts not at home till ½ past ten. The Dutchess particularly gracious & pleasant.[21] rec'd a Letter from Miss Snow.

Wensday Augst. 6th.

Realy rather a cold wind, cloudy & looking like rain, Mr W. at Chipping Norton & I hard at work, packing & setting things in order to leave at home & go to Cheltenham, scarce allow'd myself time to walk ½ an hour in the evening wrote to Mrs. Rollinson.

Thursday Augst. 7th.

A fine Day much like the former ones left home at Noon to go to Upper Slaughter sorry to leave my little loves again so soon, were long on the road, having many stops & hinderances,

---

21. Caroline Spencer, *née* Russell (1743–1811), daughter of John Russell, 4th Duke of Bedford. She married George Spencer, 4th Duke of Marlborough (1739–1817) in 1762. He had succeeded to the title in 1758.

sorry to find my poor Brother still worse than he had been, much struck with his alter'd looks & alarming complaints tho he was tolerably chearfull. M^r & M^rs. Naper sat two hours with us in the evening glad to see her better.

Friday Aug^st. 8th.

Very similar weather extremely pleasant. M^r & M^rs. Naper came to breakfast we left Slaughter at 12 & dined at Sandywell met with a most pleasing reception from all the Ladies, got to Cheltenham before it was dark; & went to the Rooms & play'd at Whist successfully with Mr Dewes. Mr Napleton &c.

Saturday Aug^st. 9th.

A most pleasant Day bright Sun but not too hot, much visiting all the Morn^g. happy in seeing M^r & M^rs. Granville &c; M^rs. C: Thornton Miss Andrew & Mr Napleton dined here, M^rs. Evans also drank Tea here & went wth. us to the Play orderd by the King where all the Royals were, a most Crowded House, & M^rs. Jordan perform'd charmingly, both in the Maid of the Oaks & the Poor Soilder.[22]

Sunday Aug^st. 10th.

Still very fine weather, a crowded Church with all the Royals, & all that wanted to see them, the Bishop of Glocester Preach'd, the Granvilles sat an hour with us after, Miss Nettleship

18. King George III; the Long Room, Cheltenham.

22. *The Maid of the Oaks* by General John Burgoyne (1722–1792). Burgoyne was a British army officer, a politician and a dramatist. *The Maid of the Oaks* was first performed in 1774. *The Poor Soldier* by John O'Keefe (1747–1833) was first performed at Covent Garden in 1783.

19. Their Majesties at the Wells.

drank Tea here, & we went early to court on the Walks a most new scene & for once amusing, the crowds prodigious, Mr Napleton supp'd here.

*Monday Aug^st.^ 11th.*

No change in the weather Mrs. Tracys here from Sandywell in the Morning shop'd & dawdled about with them, Drank Tea at Mr Delaberes, Mrs. Snell added to their large party, went late with them to the Ball wch. was a small one but good for this season, play'd 3 rubbers at whist wrote to Miss Snow.

*Tuesday Aug^st.^ 12th.*

A very hot wind consequently an unpleasant Day & in the evening hard rain, much visiting in the Morning, My Bro^r^ Travell, Mr Witts & I dined at Mr Delaberes, not very pleasant, intended going to the Play but as neither the King nor Mrs. Wells were to exhibit there exchanged it for the walks & rooms, unsuccessfull at Whist. rec'd a long pleasing Letter from L^dy.^ Ed^d.^ Bentinck & one from my Bro^r^ Ferdinand wth. rather a better account of himself.

*Wensday Aug^st.^ 13th.*

Had been a very wet night, & was very Showery all Day, made some visits & went to hear Careys & Keans[23] Theatric imitations entertaining enough, most of the Delabere party &

23. This was Edmund Kean, an architect's clerk, and Anne Carey, daughter of the eighteenth-century composer and playwright Henry Carey. Their son, Edmund Kean (1787–1833), was to become one of the most famous early nineteenth-century actors, making his first appearance on the stage, aged four, as Cupid in Jean-Georges Noverre's ballet *Cymon*.

Mr Napleton drank Tea here, & all went to the Rooms 7 Card Tables w$^{ch.}$ was better than usual, play'd at Cribbage, w$^{th.}$ M$^{rs.}$ Cox, M$^{rs.}$ Freeman, & Miss Hanbury came home very indifferent with the fashionable cold.

Thursday Aug$^{st.}$ 14$^{th.}$

Very wet early in the Morning but only occasional showers through the Day sat at home all Morning to nurse myself for the evening, Mr Witts went to the Clothing country to see the Mob assembled to do Honor to the Royals & did not come home till Tea time,[24] Mr Egerton & Mr Napleton dined here, & Mr Seward drank Tea here, & all went to the Ball together w$^{ch.}$ was a very poor one, play'd at Cribage with nearly the same party.

Friday Aug$^{st.}$ 15$^{th.}$

A fine Day upon the whole tho with some showers, walk'd to see M$^{rs.}$ Cox at the Cottage & made other visits, My Bro^r dined out; went to the Play to see the Royals & M$^{rs.}$ Wells, Miss Hanbury with us, Francis much delighted, a very poor performance concluded by an address to their Majesties, as a concluding compliment on their leaving Cheltenham. rec'd a Letter from Nurse.

Saturday Aug$^{st.}$ 16$^{th.}$

Warm with short showers but not enough to prevent strolling about, Mr Delaberes whole party to the number of seven dined here very highly agreable, Mr Napleton also drank Tea here all went to the Rooms, which were thin M$^{rs.}$ Wells playing her Imitations.

Sunday Aug$^{st.}$ 17$^{th.}$

A prodigious wet Morning early but clear'd up to permit us to walk to Church but there was much rain fell in the course of the Day, Mr Witts went into Oxfordshire, Mr Napleton preach'd a most excellent Sermon, drank Tea at Mr Delaberes a party of 16, much concern'd to bid adieu to all the agreable Granville party.

Monday Aug$^{st.}$ 18$^{th.}$

Very similar weather, being frequent hard showers, began drinking the waters, walks crowded, after breakfast walket with M$^{rs.}$ C: Thornton & Miss Andrew, My Bro^r & Sister Cath: went to Slaughter Mr Napleton dined here, & M$^{rs.}$ Dunster Mr Seward , Miss Wyndham & Miss Norwood Drank Tea here, & went to the Ball not a good one. play'd at Whist.

---

24. The clothing country was Stroud and its environs. Sir George Onesiphorus Paul lived at Hill House, later renamed Rodborough Manor. It was at Hill House that Sir George entertained King George III and Queen Caroline to breakfast on 14 August 1788. The King made his progress on horseback, the Queen and princesses being in open carriages, escorted by the influential persons of the neighbourhood. His Majesty wore a blue coat with a scarlet collar and a cocked hat. They were taken via Wallbridge to witness a barge going through a lock. After breakfast they were shown around Sir George's woollen cloth manufactory, Southfield Mill in Woodchester. After this they were entertained by Francis, Lord Ducie, at Spring Park, now known as Woodchester Park. The road from Stroud to Nailsworth was new made and turnpiked just after 1780, and at the same time the road leading up the hill as a spur from this road, Bear Hill, was also made, or at least much improved. It was this road leading to the Bear Inn on Rodborough Common that also led to Sir George's estate. At the top of this road past the Bear Inn was Bownham House, which was to become the new home of Edward and Agnes Witts in 1791.

Tuesday Aug^{st.} 19th.

Wet & disagreable again but not sufficient to confine one to the house Mr Witts returnd to Dinner, Miss Delabere & Mr Napleton both dined & supt here, we all Drank Tea with Miss Nettleships, & Miss Anne went with Mr Witts & me to see Mrs. Wells in Isabela & The Irish Widow[25] very well entertain'd rec'd Letters from L^{dy.} Lyttelton, Mrs. Sabine & Miss Anne Snow & wrote to Mrs. Buxton.

Wensday Aug^{st.} 20th.

Showery early in the Morning, fine & hot at Noon & wet in the afternoon, visited & walket as common in the Morning, & drank Tea in the afternoon with M^{rs.} C: Thornton & Miss Andrew, meeting Mrs. Mary Joted & her Niece Miss Jones, & carrying Miss Delabere who with Mr Hugh Hughes had dined here, went to the Rooms for a short time, & then a large party of us went to the Play for the purpose of seeing Mrs. Wells in her Imitations tolerably well entertain'd with them but sick of Peeping Tom of Coventry.[26]

Thursday Aug^{st.} 21st.

Very close hot Morning looking like rain but none fell till Dinner time & continued wet all the evening, the usual sport of visiting wth. great vigour, Mr Hughes[27], his Daughter, & two Sons dined here, Mrs. M. Joted, Miss Jones, M^{rs.} C: Thornton & Miss Andrew drank Tea, a very lively party till we went to the Ball which was stupid enough only 8 couple of Dancers tho a full room play'd at Cribbage with Cox's, Hanbury, &c. rec'd a Letter from Miss Anne Snow.

Friday Aug^{st.} 22^d

Had been a very wet night & was uncomfortable moving all Morning, tho no weather or anything keeps people at home in this place, walket about with L^{dy.} Dacre hunting after Lodgings visiting &c. drank Tea with her agreably meeting Mrs. Egerton, all went to the rooms together, play'd at Cribbage, M^{rs.} C: Thornton, Miss Andrew, & Miss Hughes supt here the latter come to stay a few Days wrote to Miss Anne Snow.

Saturday Aug^{st.} 23^d

A finer Day than for several past only a few trifling showers, brought home from the mall as the Morning before by Miss Hanbury soon after Breakfast walket with the Thorntons to Alston to see Mrs. Thos Leigh a droll visit, the Markham family dined here & Mr Pope & Miss Andrew drank Tea, as usual went to the rooms & again play'd at Cribage.

20. *Thomas Hughes.*

---

25.   *Isabella; or the Fatal Marriage* and *The Irish Widow* were both plays by David Garrick (1717–1779).

26.   *Peeping Tom of Coventry; or The Lady Godiva and the Witch of Warwick* was recorded as being performed at Drury Lane. The author is unknown.

27.   Portraits of Thomas Hughes of Cheltenham (1732–1794) and Elizabeth his wife (1728–1786). Thomas Hughes was responsible for the construction of the Assembly Rooms in the High Street, Cheltenham.

Sunday Aug$^{st.}$ 24$^{th.}$

a most beautifull Morn: but several hard showers in the afternoon, after Church walket with a large party to survey Lord Fauconbergs & the Wooden House, Lady Dacre & Miss Lennard, M$^{rs.}$ Egerton Miss Delabere, L$^{d.}$ Mountnorris[28] & M$^{rs.}$ Seward Drank Tea here a very conversible meeting the Gentlemen staid till past ten much talk on Men, Manners, & books.

Monday Aug$^{st.}$ 25$^{th.}$

A very cloudy dull day but with very little rain, went to the Publick breakfast to oblige Miss Hanburys, a sad stupid business only 25 there & tired to death with waiting for it went afterwards with Miss Hanbury to see M$^{rs.}$ Cox home early to dress to receive M$^{rs.}$ Tracys from Sandywell at Dinner, Mr Welsh also dined here, Mr Bowlby & Lady Mary & Miss Hanburys drank Tea here, a very full & agreable Ball, play'd at Whist in a very pleasant set.

Tuesday Aug$^{st.}$ 26$^{th.}$

An intire fine Day without rain, most pleasant moving about, after Breakfast took a walk in the fields with M$^{rs.}$ C: Thornton &c. & made many visits, met her & Miss Andrew, Miss Wyndham, Dr Webster, Mr Ramsey & Mr Seward at Miss Hanburys to Drink Tea a lively visit all adjourned to the rooms, play'd at Cribage.

Wensday Aug$^{st.}$ 27$^{th.}$

A cloudy warm Day without rain, M^{r} B: Hughes came to Breakfast & to take away his Sister, went to Mr Delaberes to hear Mr Seward read the Play of Macbeth much disappointed by the performance, made some visits, Mr Holford dined here, I drank Tea at M$^{rs.}$ Thorntons & went to the Play with Miss Hanburys, a full house but sad performance adjourn'd to good rooms & play'd at Cribage.

Thursday Aug$^{st.}$ 28$^{th.}$

Much the same weather little flying showers & very close, M$^{rs.}$ Naper came at Noon, walket about with her, went to see the wooden house on its progress; Mr Napleton dined, & Mr Boddingtons family & Miss Hollingsworth drank Tea all went to the Ball w$^{ch.}$ was very full, many Grandees I play'd at Whist.

21. Cheltenham Wells.

28. Arthur Annesley, Baron Mountnorris and Viscount Valentia (1744–1816). He married Lucy Fortesecue, sister and heir of Thomas Lyttelton, 2nd Baron Lyttelton of Frankley (the 'Wicked' Lord Lyttelton), second husband of Edward Witts' elder sister, Apphia, Lady Lyttelton. Lady Lyttelton remained on close terms with the family.

Friday Aug^{st.} 29th.

A cold disagreable Day, with thick mist & flying showers, Mrs. Naper went away after Breakfast, to which M^{rs.} C: Thornton Miss Andrew & Mr Napleton were added, My Sister Francis & I went in Miss Hanburys chaise to Charlton to visit Mrs. Evans & Mrs. Pullen, drank Tea very pleasantly at L^{dy.} Dacres meeting Mrs. Egerton went to the rooms & play'd at Cribage with them.

Saturday Aug^{st.} 30th.

Very beautiful fine Morning changed at Noon and was hard rain at night. walket & visited as usual in the Morning, Miss Wyndham, Mr Boddington, Mr Seward, & Mr Napleton dined here, & M^{r} & Mrs. Tighe & Miss Bligh drank Tea here, a very extraordinary dispute between Mr Tighe & Mr Seward, in wch. the former much exposed himself; very full rooms play'd at Whist.

Sunday Aug^{st.} 31st.

Had been a severe night of rain but held up to go to Church tho rain'd frequently in the course of the Day, after Morning Church went to see the Children of the Sunday School to the number of 140,[29] assembled in the Well Room to receive a 3^{d.} Cake from Mr Boddington a pleasing sight, Miss Delabere dined here & we made a Stupid Tea Drinking visit to Miss Nevilles, tho a party of 13. Miss Delabere & Mr Napleton supp'd here. rec'd a very pleasing Letter from Mrs. Tyrwhitt.

Monday Sept. 1st.

Most charming weather, Mrs. Evans breakfasted here, Mrs. Traceys & many others visited in the Morning, M^{r} J: Delabere dined here, Drank Tea at Mrs. Delaberes meeting a large party of Gentlemen, & afterwards went to a crowded Ball. play'd agreably at Whist.

Tuesday Sept. 2^{d.}

No change of weather, after Breakfast Mr Witts went away, walket & visited as usual, Mr Napleton dined here, & was most pleasant, sat ½ an hour with L^{dy.} Dacre, & drank Tea at Miss Norwoods, meeting an odd large party & went to the Rooms with Mrs. Pennant play'd at Whist. rec'd a Letter from Nurse.

Wensday Sept. 3^{d.}

Similar weather, M^{r} & Mrs. Holford Miss Wyndham & Mr Napleton Breakfasted here, walket & visited with the latter, air'd with Lady Dacre on the Bath road, Miss Nettleships & Miss Hughes dined here very pleasant, all Drank Tea at Mrs. Markeham went w^{h.} her to see Mr Tighes scenery & exhibition of Poppets a pretty thing went to the rooms play'd at Cribage.

---

29. The Sunday School movement was founded by Robert Raikes (1736–1811). It began in July 1780 in the home of a Mrs Meredith. Only boys attended, and she heard the lessons of the older boys, who coached the younger. Later, girls also attended. Within two years, several schools opened in and around Gloucester, including Cheltenham. *See* the note in F182 below.

Witts Family Papers F174

1788

Thursday Sep.ʳ 4ᵗʰ·

A bright fine Morning, but turn'd out an unpleasant close thick Day with trifling showers went to see Mʳˢ· Jordan Rehearse in Twelfth Night dined at Mʳ Boddingtons meeting Mʳ & Miss Hollery were very agreable, went to a Dull Ball & play'd at Whist.

Friday Sep.ʳ 5ᵗʰ·

Just such another fine Day, walket visited, & went to see Mʳˢ· Jordan rehearse, Miss Delabere, Miss Dewes, & Mʳˢ· Napleton dined here the latter went with us to Drink Tea with Lady Dacre, & all went together to the Play, much delighted with seeing Mʳˢ· Jordan in Viola & the Romp,[1] rec'd a delightful Letter from Mʳ Witts.

Saturday Sep.ʳ 6ᵗʰ·

Another beautiful Day, much engaged in packing, visiting & all necessary preparations for my departure, dined at Mʳˢ· Markhams, meeting Miss Nettleship & Miss Norwood, went again to the Play with Lady Dacre more than ever charm'd with Mʳˢ· Jordan in Rosalind & the Virgin unmask'd.[2]

Sunday Sep.ʳ 7ᵗʰ·

A very hot Day with bright sunshine very busy in packing up but did not leave Cheltenham till after Church, parted with regret from many agreable acquaintance, got to Sandywell by Dinner, where Mʳ Witts met me rejoiced to see him & to hear a good account of my little Loves at home. found Mʳˢ· Eliza: Tracy very indifferent rather a long evening of conversation rec'd a Letter from Mʳˢ· Naper.[3]

Monday Sep.ʳ 8ᵗʰ·

Still much the same weather but not very pleasant being a fog in the Morn: & hot & close all Day, Mʳ Witts rode to Cheltenham in the Morn: Lord Fauconberg & Miss Hanburys dined here agreable enough.

---

1. Dorothy Jordan, *née* Bland (1762–1816). Viola is a character in *Twelfth Night*. *The Romp* is a musical entertainment in which Mrs Jordan played the part of Priscilla Tomboy, a role she first performed at Drury Lane in 1786.
2. Rosalind is a character in *As You Like It. The Virgin Unmasked* is a play by Henry Fielding (1707–1754).
3. Eliza Tracy was an aunt of Agnes, sister to her late mother, Anne Travell, *née* Tracy (1704–1763). Mrs Naper was Jane Naper, *née* Travell, the daughter of Agnes' brother Ferdinando, and therefore niece to Agnes. There appear to have been three 'Mrs' Tracys. All were aunts, one or two were maternal aunts and at least one, but possibly two out of the three, were widowed by marriage.

Tuesday Sep.ʳ 9ᵗʰ·

No difference in the weather, staid within all the Morning to converse with the Ladies. Mᵉ W. & Francis took a long walk, Mᵉ Thomas dined, after Tea Mʳˢ· Tracy, Mᵉ Witts & I went down to Cheltenham to see Mʳˢ· Jordan perform in Sir Harry Wildair & Roxalana,⁴ well pleased with the former & quite delighted with the latter, a very full house, but had no opportunity of conversing with any of my friends excepting those I sat with Mʳˢ· Buckner & Miss Hanbury a fine Moon made our drive home quite pleasant rec'd a Letter from Mʳˢ· Granville.⁵

Wensday Sep.ʳ 10ᵗʰ·

A dull day but dry & fine thro' out, after Breakfast bid adieu to our kind Sandywell friends, Mᵉ Witts on horseback, had a Jumbling drive to Stow, while dinner was getting ready survey'd Mᵉ Hippisleys Greenhouse and garden reach'd home by Tea time, much pleased by finding my little Boys quite well & grown fat. wrote to my Sister Travell & Mʳˢ· Naper.

Thursday Sep.ʳ 11ᵗʰ·

Had been a good deal of rain in the Morning but turn'd out a bright fine Day quite pleasant, but was too much engaged in a variety of business to walk much out, My Bro.ᵗ Travell call'd in his way to Cheltenham, Mᵉ Witts dined at the C: House at a Justice Meeting. rec'd a Letter from Miss Snow & answer'd it & wrote to Mʳˢ· Tyrwhitt & Mʳˢ· Rollinson.

Friday Sep.ʳ 12ᵗʰ·

A most truly delightfull Day bright sun & very warm, very busy all the Morn: in the afternoon went to Chip: on some errands & returned to the Chappel House to Tea to meet the Boddington family on their route from Cheltenham spent two hours with them very agreably, & returnd home by the clearest Moon that ever shone, rec'd Letters from Mʳˢ· Rollinson, Mʳˢ· Buxton & Mʳˢ· Naper.⁶

Saturday Sep.ʳ 13ᵗʰ·

Quite a warm close Day with Fog early in the Morning & a smart shower at Dinner time, went to Dine with Mʳˢ· Rollinson calling first at Mᵉ Tyrwhitts for ½ an hour, much agreable converse, found Mʳˢ· Biscoe & her Daughter & Miss Western with Mʳˢ· Rollinson, play'd at Cribbage & returnd home late.

Sunday Sep.ʳ 14ᵗʰ·

A universal fine clear Day, rather a cold North wind, Mᵉ Evans did the Duty at Swerford Church indeed is Mᵉ Earles regular Curate, Mᵉ Francis dined here, I went to Church in the evening & to the Sunday Schools, drank Tea at Wiginngton, the visit much as usual, rec'd a Letter from Mʳˢ· Guydickens, my little George went into Breeches.⁷

---

4. Sir Harry Wildair is a character in *The Constant Couple* by George Farquhar (1677–1707). Roxalana is a character in *The Sultan* by Isaac Bickerstaff (1733?–1808?).
5. Mrs Granville was Harriet Granville, *née* Delabere (1754–1825). Harriet and John Granville (1744–1826) of Calwich Abbey, Staffordshire, were possibly the closest friends of Agnes and Edward Witts.
6. The Chapel House was a public house on the crossroads about a mile from Chipping Norton on the Banbury road.
7. George Anthony Witts (1785–1823), second son of Edward and Agnes Witts.

Monday Sepr. 15$^{th.}$

Had been a little frost in the night was a clear bright Day but rather cold, went to Dine at Little Compton, found poor Lady Fane confined to her dressing room with the gout, & M$^{rs.}$ Harward looking dismaly, & in a miserable state of health, had an excellent Dinner, but the visit was rather triste play'd at Quadrille. wrote to Lady Edward Bentinck.

Tuesday Sepr 16$^{th.}$

Had been a great deal of rain in the night but was dry & cloudy till Noon, when it raind very hard for the remainder of the Day, Mr Evans dined here, nothing very bright or striking in him thought his company made the evening long. Wrote to L$^{dy.}$ Lyttelton.[8]

Wensday Sepr 17$^{th.}$

Had been a frost in the night & was an uncommon strong dew in the Morning, bright & fine all Day walket out both Morning & evening with the Children, rec'd a Letter from Miss Anne Snow & wrote to my Sister Travell.

Thursday Sepr 18$^{th.}$

Very hard rain till 11 in the Morn: when it grew better but was showery all Day quite close & warm with heavy clouds, went to Miss Newtons at Salford, to see & converse with her friend Miss Sherston who was in treaty to be Governess to Miss Dewes, pretty well pleased with her general manner & appearance, spent an hour not disagreably, rec'd a Letter from my Sister Travell & wrote to M$^{rs.}$ Granville.[9]

22. Shipton Court, the seat of Sir John Reade.

8.   Apphia, Lady Lyttelton (1744–1840), sister to Edward Witts.
9.   Miss Dewes was a sister-in-law to Harriet Granville.

Friday Sep.' 19th.

An extreme wet Day quite a deluge till Noon when it rather cleared, as we set out to Dine at Sir John Reades & was not a bad night to return home,[10] which we did not till past eleven, met M.' & M.rs. Reade there, a very pleasant visit. wrote to Miss Anne Snow.

Saturday Sep.' 20th.

Dry but cloudy till Noon, when it began raining hard & so continued all Day. M.' Witts at Chipping: Norton much play & fun with the Dear Children & when they were gone to Bed much engaged with accompts. rec'd a Letter from M.rs. Tyrwhitt.

Sunday Sep.' 21st.

A most unterrupted Day of rain, so much so as to make it impossible to go to Church either Morn: or evening read, wrote & play'd a great deal with Children.

Monday Sep.' 22d.

Still harder rain till Noon when it clear'd up for two or three hours, so as to suffer me to take a walk, M.' Witts at M.' Penystons in the Morning wrote to M.rs. Eliza Tracy & worket hard at Accompts.

Tuesday Sep.' 23d.

A cloudy day but with little rain, tho cold & stormy, dawdled about a good deal surveying the workmen altering the Green house wrote to M.rs. Tyrwhitt.

Wensday Sep.' 24th.

Much the same weather little flying showers but not enough to confine me to the house tho I had a bad cold & pain in my head & face. M.' Witts at Chip: wrote to M.rs. Naper & Miss Chaplin.

Thursday Sep.' 25th.

Bright Morning, but a stormy cold disagreable Day, ventured to walk out a little tho much plagued by a bad pain in my Head & Face in the evening wrote some Letters on Business.

Friday Sep.' 26th.

Very wet early in the Day but towards Noon clear'd off, but tho fine & bright, the wind was very high & cold, notwithstanding my face was very bad I walket a little, & helpt to adjust the Green house plants; M.rs. Naper came quite unexpectedly an hour before Dinner rejoiced to see her so tolerably well M.' Francis dined here, much agreable converse both before & after Supper. Rec'd a Letter from my Sis.' Travell.

---

10. Sir John Reade, 6th Baronet (1762–1789). He received his M.A. from Magdalen College, Oxford. He married Jane, only daughter of Sir Chandos Hoskyns, in 1784 and they had five children—one a year until John died in June 1789. Jane, Lady Reade, lived at Oddington until her death in 1847. Sir John was also the rector of Rollright Parva and Little Rollright.

Saturday Sepr 27th.

A much better Day being only now & then flying showers but still cold & stormy, after Breakfast walket a little with M^rs. Naper, after which sat in great comfort till one o'clock when she took her leave, very sorry to part with her so soon; the complaint in my head better but still far from well. wrote to M^rs. Buxton

Sunday Sepr 28th.

Quite a winter Day, high wind & storms & towards evening intirely wet: could only go to Church in the Morning, read much. rec'd a Letter from Miss Snow.

Monday Sepr. 29th.

Better weather clear with a good deal of Sun walket about a good deal, M^r & M^rs. Thos. Leigh made a long civil Morning visit, M^r & M^rs. Western came to dinner, & Mr Evans also very merry play'd at Whist.

Tuesday Sepr 30th.

Disagreable & stormy again very cold only permitted us Ladies to walk to the Green house. The Gentlemen rode out, we had a long chatty Morning Mr Sandby came to Dinner, were very lively & again play'd at Whist rec'd a Letter from M^rs. Eliza: Tracy.

Wensday Octr 1st.

Still a worse day being equally stormy & still more wet, but still attended our friends to Chip. Norton, where we met Tyrwhitts &c, & I took the two eldest Boys whom I left with M^rs. Betts while I went to call on M^rs. Langton whom I found arrived at Over Norton the night before sat an hour with her much talk. rec'd a Letter from M^rs. Tyrwhitt.

Thursday Octr 2^d.

Violent stormy still, but scarce any rain & much warmer, I went to pay a Lying in Visit to M^rs. Penyston all in grand form Miss Apleton with her, but it proved a very pleasant visit & a very nice little Girl. I brought old M^rs. Trinder home with me from C: Norton to spend a day or two wrote to M^rs. Sabine.[11]

Friday Octr 3^d.

Very high wind but warm, walk'd a great deal before it was time to dress to go to Mr Tyrwhitts where we went to Dinner, met Mr Hoskins there all very chearfull & pleasant, play'd a lively Game at Whist interspersed with much converse.

Saturday Octr 4th.

An uncommon mild pleasant Day, tho without much sun, the Gents went soon after Breakfast to Hunt, & Mr Witts in quest of a Poney for Francis, & join'd me at M^rs. Rollinsons when we

---

11. Sarah Sabine, *née* Hunt (17??–1788). Sarah was the daughter of Sarah Hunt, *née* Witts (1715–1766), and therefore first cousin to Edward Witts. Her husband, Joseph, was a trustee of the marriage settlement between Edward and Agnes and the families appear to have been close.

made a visit of an hour, finding Miss O: Adee & Mr Man: Western with her rec'd a Letter from Miss Snow & answer'd it.[12]

Sunday Octr 5th.

Cold, windy, & very unpleasant again, being Wake Sunday, there was a great many common people at Church, early in the Morning the three Boys attended Mrs. Trinder in the Chaise to C: Norton. after Church Mr Witts call'd on Mr Langton but he was not at home.

Monday Octr 6th.

An intire wet Day, no stirring out of the House for either Mother or Children, who of course were much together & very happy in each other rec'd a Letter from Mrs. Naper, with an amended account of her poor Father on his return from Nottingham.

Tuesday Octr 7th.

Quite a contrast to the former Day being dry, bright, & fine, Mr Witts went early to attend the Sessions at Oxford, the two elder Boys walket with me to Swerford, & all three dined with me a happy Party, wrote to Mr Hunt a letter long owed.

Wensday Octr 8th.

Almost an equal fine Day but rather too windy, Mr Thomas sat an hour here, & then came Mrs. Langton & staid near three hours, very chatty & pleasant, Mrs. Rollinson & Miss O: Adee came to Dinner & Mr Witts return'd likewise from Oxford, play'd a merry Game at Whist in the evening. wrote to Mrs. Naper.

Thursday Octr 9th.

More stormy & cold, not pleasant enough to tempt the Ladies to be much out, had a pleasant Morn: of work & converse, Mr Witts at Chip: Mr Hoskins, Mr Price, & Mr Evans all din'd here, quite a Clerical meeting. play'd at whist again.

Friday Octr 10th.

Much the same weather only more Sun Mrs. Rollinson & her friend went away after Breakfast Mr Witts & I walket to Swerford in the evening wrote & did many accompts.

Saturday Octr 11th.

Very indifferent weather frequent misty Showers & very cold, Mr Witts at Chip. I walket a little with the Children, in the evening worket & Mr Witts read received a Letter from Miss Snow.

Sunday Octr 12th.

The same dull sort of weather till Noon when it clear'd up & was bright Sun, went early to the Girls Sunday School & to Church late. immediately after went to make a visit to Mrs. Langton Mr Langton at home & very conversible; in the evening taught & play'd with the young People.

---

12. The Wittses were quite close to the Rollinson family. Agnes' brother, Ferdinando, had married Martha Rollinson (1741–1780), and in his youth Edward had been a close friend of Lock Rollinson, travelling with him to Wales and Ireland.

Monday Octr 13th.

Cloudy Morning, but turn'd out a very bright fine Day, quite a pleasant drive to Dine at Lady Fanes where we met M.^r & Mrs. Naper & my Brother Ferdinand, Dow: Lady Reade, Mrs. Harward & Mrs. Cotton a very lively pleasant visit & a fine night to return home, but was late.

Tuesday Octr 14th.

A truly fine Autumn Day very busy all the Morning, & went to Dine at Mr Westerns, meeting M.^r & Mrs. Savage a very great pleasure, & liked her more & more, were very chearfull & merry, play'd at Whist. wrote to Mrs. Rollinson.

Wensday Octr 15th.

The finest warm Day ever known at the Season, the Gentlemen rode out, & we walket & convers'd most pleasantly, & the evening spent as the former one had been.

Thursday Octr 16th.

Nearly as fine a Day left our agreable friends after Breakfast transacted some business at Chipping Norton in my way home, Mrs. Naper & her Father came to Dinner, delighted to see him much better, poor Mrs. Naper very ill all the evening with one of her bad headaches.

Friday Octr 17th.

The same kind of weather but cloudy till the afternoon when it was beautifully bright & clear. Mr Witts went early to a Justice Meeting at Adderbury the rest walket about till time to Dress when my Bro.^r went to see Mrs. Rollinson, & Mrs. Naper & I to adorn ourselves for the Play at Blenheim Mrs. Penyston coming in the meantime was unable to receive her. Dined early & reach'd Blenheim by seven, a genteel & crowded House the performance of three acts of the Provok'd Husband & the Musical Lady most amusing Lady Elizabeth a capital performance, came home by two o'clock much pleased with our entertainment.[13] rec'd Letters from Mrs. Rollinson & Mrs. Granville.

Saturday Octr 18th.

Had been a sharp frost in the Night but turn'd out a most brilliant fine Day, Breakfasted not till 11 o'clock & by 12 came our agreable friends from Kingham & spent a most lively Day here. Mrs. Naper went away at Noon, my Bro.^r Ferdinand return'd from Chadlington to Dinner, & M.^r & Mrs. Witts came likewise just as we were going to Dinner which created rather a bustle had one Table at Whist & much talk during the course of the evening. rec'd a Letter from Lady Lyttelton.[14]

---

13. *The Provoked Husband* is a play by John Vanbrugh (1664? –1726); under the title of *Journey to London* it was left unfinished at his death. Colley Cibber (1671–1757) completed the play in five acts and it was first performed in 1728. The performance given at Blenheim was obviously a shortened version. *The Musical Lady* is a farce by George Colman the Elder (1732–1794), which premiered in London in 1762. Lady Elizabeth was presumably Lady Elizabeth Spencer (1771–1812), the second daughter of George Spencer, 4th Duke of Marlborough (1739–1817). The event appears to have been a private performance of amateur theatricals for the local gentry.

14. Mr and Mrs Witts were presumably Edward's elder brother, Broome (1744–1827), and his wife, Amelia (1742–1832).

Sunday Oct.ʳ 19ᵗʰ.

Just such another Day, all but my Broᵗ Travell went to Church, & afterwards walket till near Dinner time enjoying the delightfull weather for the season, a very conversable Day rec'd a long Letter from Miss Anne Snow & answer'd it. Mᵗ Francis Dined here.

Monday Oct.ʳ 20ᵗʰ.

Not quite so fine a Day but very pleasant, the Gentlemen rode & Mʳˢ· Witts & I walket Mʳˢ· Rollinson & Mᵗ Evans dined here, very chearfull & agreable, play'd both at Whist & Cribage.

Tuesday Oct.ʳ 21ˢᵗ.

No change of weather, Mʳˢ· Rollinson went away at Noon, the Gentlemen again rode & we walket, evening spent in very pleasant converse & I play'd in Picquet with Mʳˢ· Witts. rec'd a Letter from Mʳˢ· Buxton.

Wensday Oct.ʳ 22ᵈ.

A beautiful warm bright Morning but grew rather cloudy towards Noon. My Broᵗ Ferdinand took his leave of us, much to our regret as he grew better every Day he was here the rest of us went to Chipping Norton to see the old place & people. rec'd a Letter from Mʳˢ· Drake & wrote to Mʳˢ· Elizabeth Tracy.

Thursday Oct.ʳ 23ᵈ.

If possible a still finer Day, quite suited to the purpose we made of it, which was taking my Broᵗ & Sister Witts to see Blenheim, my Husband being engaged staid at home, & Francis & I escorted them as well as we could, just view'd the Parks then the Gardens made a hasty Dinner at Woodstock & return'd by the House, did not get home till near seven, but found it good driving light.

23. Blenheim Palace.

Friday Oct.r 24th.

Not quite so fine a Day being more windy, Mrs. Langton sat two hours here, very chatty as usual, we afterwards walket out rec'd a Letter from Mrs. Naper, & wrote to my Sister Travell.

Saturday Oct.r 25th.

A most beautifull fine Day, walket after Breakfast & went to Dinner at Mrs. Rollinsons the Gentlemen riding, a very pleasant visit, play'd 5 rubbers at Whist with great success.

Sunday Oct.r 26th.

Still the same delightfull weather, walket almost from Breakfast to Church where the service was perform'd by an itinerant Clergyman, return'd home imediately afterwards & found the little loves all quite well.

Monday Oct.r 27th.

Much the same sort of weather as many former days, after breakfast Mrs. Witts & the two eldest Boys & I went to make a Morning Visit to Lady Fane found Mrs. Penyston there a very lively pleasant visit; evening spent as usual in much conversation. wrote to Mrs. Drake.

Tuesday Oct.r 28th.

Rather a more pleasant Day. Walket about a good deal, Mr. Earle here in the Morning rather formal & queer, wrote to Mrs. Naper, & rec'd Letters from Miss Snow & Miss Sabine with an account of her Mothers being brought to Bed of a Son.

Wensday Oct.r 29th.

A much colder Day than many of the former ones, after Breakfast Mrs. Witts & I went to Chipping Norton on some little Businesses & made a Visit to Mrs. Langton lively enough.

Thursday Oct.r 30th.

Very much the same weather went to make a Morning Visit at Wigginton finding the two younger Miss Hoskins's there & Miss Haynes, Mrs. Witts much entertain'd by the variety of droll characters & many odd &c's, Mr. Earle & Mr. Evans dined here, play'd many rubbers at Whist & wrote to Miss Sabine.

Friday Oct.r 31st.

Similar weather, Mr. Witts at a Meeting at Chipping Norton, the three Misses from Wigginton here in the Morning for several hours almost tired with forcing conversation walket about to help out. Rec'd a Letter from Mrs. Drake & answer'd it & wrote to Ldy. Edward Bentinck & Miss Snow.

Saturday Nov.r 1st.

Had been a frost in the Night & was a wonderfull thick Fog till 9 o'clock, Breakfasted early to accomodate My Bro.r & Sis.r Witts on their Journey to Risbro' to see Lady Lyttelton Mr. Witts at Chip: the Boys & I walket for 2 or 3 hours, the brightest fine Day possible, Mr. Roberts call'd here. very busy all Day.

Sunday Nov.ʳ 2.ᵈ

If possible a still thicker Fog which never intirely went off the whole Day, & made it very damp & uncomfortable, Mʳ Evans did the Duty at Church, sat a little while after with Mʳ Earle, & I walket after I came home, rec'd Letters from Mʳˢ· Rollinson & Miss Snow & answer'd them both & did much other writting in the evening.

Monday Nov.ʳ 3.ᵈ

A most tempestous day, with flying rain, & terribly damp, quite unpleasant after so fine a Season, Mʳ Witts at Chip: much engaged all Day with various business & getting ready for our intended Journey. rec'd a Letter from Mʳ Hunt.

Tuesday Nov.ʳ 4.ᵗʰ·

Had been a great deal of hard rain in the night was dry but stormy till 12, & afterwards turn'd out a beautifull bright day propitious, to our intended Journey, set out at 10, at Woodstock we stopt half an hour at Mʳ Walkers, drawn in then to see Mʳ & Mʳˢ· Tyrwhitt who were there at Oxford walket with Mʳˢ· Wickham in the street & invited by her to Dinner but eat Beef Steaks at the Star, by the help of the Moon got pleasantly to Tetsworth to Tea. rec'd Letters from Mʳˢ· E: Tracy & Lᵈʸ· Edward Bentinck answer'd the letter & wrote to Mʳˢ· Dolphin.

Wensday Nov.ʳ 5.ᵗʰ·

A sharp Frost in the night, but was a bright fine Day well suited to travelling, & found it very pleasant, got to Dʳ Drakes at three met with a most pleasing reception from our agree. friends, & charm'd with their pretty situation & new good house; play'd at Whist but much interspersed with conversation.

Thursday Nov.ʳ 6.ᵗʰ·

A very thick Fog in the Morn: but clear'd up at noon to be a very fine Day, after Breakfast walket all over the premises & House & then went in the Coach taking the Boys with us to see Old Mʳ Drakes at Shardeloes, an excellent House & fine place; three Clergymen dined here Mʳ Pritchard, Mʳ Middleston, & Mʳ Anderson; another lively Game at Whist in the evening. wrote to Miss Snow.[15]

Friday Nov.ʳ 7.ᵗʰ·

Still fine weather, but rather cold & windy, went to Morning Prayers at Amersham & survey'd the Monuments of the Drake family in the church there, on our return home sorry to find Lᵈ· Parker & Mʳ Talbot had call'd in our absence. poor Mʳ Willᵐ· Lockwood came to stay all night, & Mʳ & Mʳˢ· Lloyd & their Son Sackville came to Dinner, play'd at Quadrille. rec'd a Letter from Mʳˢ· Naper.

---

15. The Witts connection with the family is unclear. The Drakes appear to have been related to the Tyrwhitt family, and they inherited the estate of Sir John Tyrwhitt in 1760 and thereafter changed their name to Tyrwhitt-Drake. Both father and son were the sitting M.P.s for the family pocket borough of Amersham. William Drake, senior (1723–1796), sat from 1746 to 1796, William Drake, junior (1747–1795), from 1768 to 1795. Drake was reckoned to be one of the richest commoners in England.

Saturday Novr 8th.

Again a thick Fog in the Morning but turn'd out a beautifull bright Day, left our agreable friends after Breakfast, stopt for an hour at Uxbridge where we changed Horses, & visited Mrs. Richard Walford & got to Saville Row at 4 o'clock where we met with the usual kind reception from our good friends, Mr Swinburne, Mrs. Robert Snow, & Dean Paul dined here & we went to Tea at Temple Bar with Mr Snow who was confined then play'd unsuccessfully at Whist. rec'd a Letter from Mrs. Dolphin.[16]

24. *Taking tea.*

Sunday Novr 9th.

Just as fine a Day as before, went to Conduit Street Chappel a good preacher, drove to Hyde Park, & got out to walk, went to Dine with Mr Snow at Temple Bar, Mrs. Ross drank Tea there rather a Dull stupid evening.

Monday Novr 10th.

A most delightfull fine Day, the weather quite wonderfull for the time of Year, very bad accounts rec'd of the Kings melancholly state his death hourly expected, went with Miss Snows to a Gentlemans house in Norfolk Street strand whose windows commanded a fine view of the river & both Bridges, to see the Lord Mayors Procession in 18 Barges finely ornamented, went in the evening to Covent Garden Theatre to see the Highland Reel & the Miser, Fran^{s.} much entertain'd. rec'd a Letter from Nurse with a charming account of my little loves.[17]

Tuesday Novr 11th.

Nearly as fine a day tho not quite so much sun. Mr Witts, Francis & I walket to see the Guydickens,[17] & Hanburys, & thro Hyde Park to meet Miss Snows when Mr Witts rode with Miss Anne & I walket home with Miss Snow thro' the Green Park spent the evening at Temple Bar, meeting the Rosses & playing at Whist. rec'd a Letter from Mrs. Rollinson much struck by her intelligence of the Majors being married.

---

16. Mrs Robert Snow was of the Paul family of Rodborough, Gloucestershire. Dean Paul was John Dean Paul (1775–1852). He was a member of the distinguished family bank, Snow, Sandby & Paul of 217 Strand, but his main love and achievement in life was as a painter, in which he enjoyed much success. He was created a baronet in 1821.

17. *The Highland Reel* by John O'Keefe (1747–1833). This play had only been premiered four days earlier, the first performance being at Covent Garden on 6 November 1788. *The Miser* is much older, being a play by Jean Baptiste Poquelin, better known as 'Molière' (1622–1673), first performed in 1668.

18. The Guydickens family were relations of Agnes Witts, Mrs Frances Guydickens, *née* Tracy (17??–1808), being a sister of the Sandywell ladies, and another aunt of Agnes. She married an army officer of Swedish origin, Gustavus Guydickens (1732–1802), and they had two daughters, both of whom remained maiden ladies: Frances (1765–1854) and Elizabeth (1772–18??).

Wensday Nov.ᵣ 12.ᵗʰ

Very much the same weather went about shopping with Miss Snows, most dreadfull accounts of the Kings insane state, went again as usual to spend the evening at Temple Bar a chearfull Game at Loo. rec'd a Letter from M.ʳˢ Dolphin & answerd it,[19] wrote to M.ʳˢ Naper & a short Letter to M.ʳˢ Granvilles in one of Miss A Snows.[20]

Thursday Nov.ᵣ 13.ᵗʰ

A very wet Day till Noon, when it held up, & M.ʳ Witts & I went in a Hackney Coach to see Miss Rollinson at a school in Queens Square & did some other business, went as usual to Tea at Temple Bar, & were very merry M.ʳ Snow being much recoverd play'd at Loo. rec'd Letters from my Sis.ᵗ Travell & Lady Edward Bentinck.

25. Temple Bar.

Friday Nov.ᵣ 14.ᵗʰ

A Dry bright fine Day but very cold, My Brother Ferdinand came & sat an hour with us after Breakfast then Miss Snow Francis & I sallied forth to see the Wild Beasts at Exeter change, well entertain'd & went to several shops, went again to Temple Bar, a large party of Gentlemen then play'd at Whist; M.ʳ Witts went to the Play at half price.

Saturday Nov.ᵣ 15.ᵗʰ

A Cold frosty Day, Jumbled by myself to Holbourn & about, rather dull sport went to Tea & Supper at M.ʳˢ Ellis's, meeting M.ʳˢ Dolphin & her two Daughters, M.ʳ Warburton & my Brother play'd at Cribage & was very lively & pleasant. rec'd Letters from Lady Edward Bentinck & Nurse.

Sunday Nov.ᵣ 16.ᵗʰ

Just such another Day, but very cold, went to Conduit street Chappell, a very indifferent Preacher, walket to make some visits & at three o'clock went in the Coach to the Park & from thence to dine at Col: Guydickens's only there own family my Bro.ᵗ Ferdinand came to Tea a very chatty evening wrote to Lady Edward Bentinck & Nurse.

---

19.   Mrs Dolphin was Martha Dolphin, *née* Rollinson. She was the daughter of Lock Rollinson, and niece by marriage to Ferdinando Tracy-Travell, being the niece of his late wife, also named Martha. She married John Dolphin, curate at Lower Slaughter.

20.   The fact that Anne Snow was writing to Harriet Granville indicates that there were a series of parallel friendships, probably emanating from mutual Cheltenham connections.

Monday Novr 17th.

Most wonderfull weather for the time of Year, went in the Coach shopping & about, & afterwards walket in Bond Street with Francis to Toyshops &c. went as common to Temple Bar to Tea, & play'd at Whist.

Tuesday Novr 18th.

Frosty, with sun & very fine, bid adieu to our worthy friends with regret as we always do & set out at twelve for Lord Edward Bentincks, 20 miles of good road soon perform'd Mr Witts on Horseback, thought the House & place at Michelefield Green much improved, rec'd a very agreable welcome from both my Lord & Lady thought the latter looket remarkably well, the Children very backward, & kept too strict, & not so much attended to as I think right. had a very chatty evening & play'd at Cribage with wonderfull success.[21]

Wensday Novr 19th.

No frost & rather thick & foggy but very mild & without wind consequently very pleasant walking were out the greatest part of the morning, surveying Green house &c. most excellent Dinner, good eating appearing to be a first rate pleasure, much pleased by my Lords obliging manner to everyone & singular attention to his Wife, the evening spent as before.

Thursday Novr 20th.

Very much the same weather extremely favorable for moving about, after a late Breakfast Lord Edward went to Town to the meeting of the parliament; Mr Witts rode to Moor House to see the Earles & L.^{dy} Edward & I walket, she & I play'd at two handed Cribage interspersed with much lively chat. wrote to Miss Snow, & rec'd a Letter from Nurse.

Friday Novr 21st.

No change of weather Mr Witts Francis & I walket to Michelefield Hall, Mr Ross's half a mile distant, a sad poor place wondered they could like to live there even in summer, Mr Edwd Earle made a morning visit here, & Ld Edward came back to Dinner full of information & news relative to the melancholly state of the King.[22] play'd again at Cribage. wrote to Mrs Naper.

Saturday Novr 22^{d.}

Quite the same weather only still more mild & pleasant walket about the whole Morning dined late, & spent the evening as usual. wrote to Mrs Buxton.

---

21. Lord Edward Charles Cavendish Bentinck (1744–1819). Cavendish Bentinck was M.P. for Lewes (1766–1768), Carlisle (1768–1774), Nottinghamshire (1775–1796) and Clitheroe (1796–1802). He was the son of William Cavendish, 2nd Duke of Portland. He married, in 1782, Elizabeth, daughter of the dramatist Richard Cumberland. Elizabeth was a close friend of Agnes Witts. He was the only brother of the Whig leader and prime minister (1783 and 1807–1809) William, 3rd Duke of Portland (1738–1809), who more than once rescued him from his financial scrapes. Of his marriage to Elizabeth Cumberland, the gossip Mrs Mary Delaney said the alliance was likely to produce serious consequences to the health of the Duke of Portland.
22. King George III suffered his first serious bout of madness in 1788, leading to constitutional concerns.

Sunday Novr. 23^{d.}

Had been a sharp frost in the night but turn'd out a bright fine Day with much Sun, Mr Witts, Francis & I took a long walk to Mr Manners's, Sarrat Mill &c Mr Ross dined & supp'd here a very merry pleasant evening. wrote to M^{rs.} E Tracy & heard from Nurse a nice account of my sweet little Boys.

Monday Novr. 24th.

Just such another Day in all respects, I walket & the Gentlemen rode to visit Mr Edward Earle at Moor House. the evening passt as usual. had ill luck at Cribage. wrote to my Sis^r Travell.

Tuesday Novr. 25th.

No frost but a cold east wind not pleasant enough to walk much out, had much agreable converse with our aimable friends, play'd successfully at Cribage, rec'd a Letter from Miss Snow, & wrote to Mrs. Swabey.

Wensday Novr. 26th.

Again a sharp frost & tho very cold was bright & fine for travelling & roads excellent, we left our pleasing friends after Breakfast with much regret, having spent a week most happily with them. stopp'd at Amersham to send Pressick home by a Coach,[23] & as we pass'd by Mr Drakes Garden at Shardeloes, looket in at the Hot House & Green House & brought away some choice plants got to Aylesbury thro Wendover not a very pleasant country by 4 o'clock & had a good Dinner &c rec'd Letters from Nurse, Mrs. Swabey, Miss Chaplin & Mrs. Hunt, with the sad news of poor Mrs. Sabines death in Ireland, lament her loss much for myself but how greatly for her poor Children. Mr Stone came over from Hartwell & drank Tea with us.[24] wrote to Mrs. Naper.

Thursday Novr. 27th.

Another sharp frost, but quite unlike the former Day, being dreadfully cold, very thick, & flying snow almost the whole Day, got to Hartwell at 11, Mr Stones Parsonage House the worst I ever saw both in point of situation & all respects. Found my poor Sis^r Stone in even still worse health than we expected, able to see very little of us, we went with M^r & Miss Stone to call on Sir Willm. & L^{dy.} Eliza: Lee very politely recd & entertain'd, a very good House, fine sized rooms, day too bad to judge of the place out of Doors,[25] had an early Dinner at Mr Stones & reach'd Thame soon after dark, the Red Lion a very moderate Inn, almost starved with cold. had half an hours conversation with Mr Stratford the Master of the School there.[26]

---

23. Pressich appears to have been Agnes' lady's maid.
24. Edward Stone (1743–1811) was for forty-two years rector of the nearby parish of Horsenden St Michael and vicar of Stagsden in Bedfordshire. He had married Sarah, *née* Witts (1745–1840), sister of Edward Witts.
25. Sir William Lee of Hartwell, 4th Baronet (1726–1799). Lady Elizabeth was the daughter of Simon Harcourt, 1st Earl Harcourt. Edward and Agnes Witts were friends of the Lee and Fiott families at Totteridge in Hertfordshire, and they appear to have been first cousins once removed to Sir William Lee of Hartwell.
26. The search was on for a school for Francis, who was now five years old. There had been thoughts of Merchant Taylors or Charterhouse, but financial concerns now precluded such choices.

Friday Nov.ʳ 28ᵗʰ.

As cold as ever Misty, & the frost apparently going, before we quitted Thame, went to Mʳ Stratfords at the School to make observations in case we should like to place Fran.ˢ there, well pleased upon the whole, a very cold miserable drive to Oxford, did some little business there & eat a hasty Dinner & got home before six very safely tho dark, rejoiced to see my little Dears so well. rec'd a Letter from Miss Anne Snow.

Saturday Nov.ʳ 29ᵗʰ.

Still frosty, thick & cold, but not much wind very busy all Morning with unpacking surveying Green House Stove &c, Mʳ Earle call'd here for half an hour. in the evening play'd with the Children wrote &c. &c. wrote to Mʳˢ. Hunt & my Sister Travell.

Sunday Nov.ʳ 30ᵗʰ.

Very much the same weather, but extremely cold at Church, Mʳ Earle did the Duty walket afterwards. rec'd a Letter from Mʳˢ. Naper, & wrote to Lady Edward Bentinck & Miss Anne Snow.

Monday Dec.ʳ 1ˢᵗ.

The same weather in the Morning but brighten'd at Noon & was very pleasant walking Dʳ Williams. call'd here. wrote to Mʳˢ. Tyrwhitt & Mʳˢ. Rollinson.

Tuesday Dec.ʳ 2ᵈ.

Continued frost, & very much the same kind of weather foggy in a Morning with bright sunshine afterwards, very cold, Mʳ Witts at Chip: walket with the Boys & at night very busy at accompts.

Wensday Dec.ʳ 3ᵈ.

No change of weather, only appearing like Snow & therefore more unpleasant, only went to the Green House & Stove, Mʳ Francis dined here very conversible, after he went finish'd accompts.

Thursday Dec.ʳ 4ᵗʰ.

If possible still colder, some thing of a Ryhme, I thought it too miserable to walk out; Mʳ Roberts came unexpectedly to Dinner & we took him with us to Drink Tea at Wigginton a large circle there, the Swerford Clergymen being there & Miss Hoskins's 2 Tables at Whist rather dull & stupid, & very dark & unpleasant coming home. rec'd a Letter from Mʳˢ. Tyrwhitt.

Friday Dec.ʳ 5ᵗʰ.

Very much the same weather Mʳ Roberts went to Breakfast at Wigginton, Dʳ Drake joined Mʳ Witts & I in our Morning, walk, had two pleasant hours of his Company, Mʳ Earle & Mʳ Evans Join'd Mʳ Roberts here at Dinner. play'd many rubbers at Whist rec'd a Letter from Mʳˢ. Rollinson & answer'd it.

Saturday Dec.ʳ 6ᵗʰ.

No change of weather yet extremely cold, Mʳ Roberts went away after Breakfast, & we went to Dine at Mr Tyrwhitts, finding there D^r & M^rs. Drake & M^rs. Rollinson, most chearfull pleasant visit, as friendly, as chearfull, return'd home with M^rs. Rollinson after playing some rubbers at Whist, & after Supper had a great deal of interesting converse received a Letter from my Sister Travell.

Sunday Decr. 7th.

Still Frost & very cold tho without much wind, Dr Drake did the Duty at Chadlington Church in the absence of Mr Sandby. Soon after church were much alarm'd by an account that Mr Western of Kingham was dangerously ill, Mr Witts took his Horse instantly to go to see him, & M^rs. Rollinson & I could not be easy without soon following him, much shocket by his appearance, as a Paralytic attack was certainly the cause, His eyes much drawn & the use of his left side nearly gone, sent to Oxford for Dr Wall, & did not return home to Dinner at Chad: till after dark, a gloomy melancholly evening.

Monday Decr. 8th.

A clearer Day with much sun after Breakfast set forth again for Kingham with much anxious impatience, found our poor friend much in the same state, Dr Wall had just left him with tolerable good hopes about him, but his state very precarious left M^rs. Rollinson there, & returnd home to Dinner finding my sweet Trio all well in the evening wrote a Letter to Miss Sabine a very painfull task.

Tuesday Decr. 9th.

A thick Fog had been but little frost in the night & thaw'd all Day, Mr Witts went to Chip: & brought back rather a better account of Mr Western. I walket for an hour with the Boys & at night wrote to M^rs. Tyrwhitt & M^rs. Naper.

Wensday Decr. 10th.

Hard Frost, & thick Fog till near Noon when it went off & was very clear & fine, I took Mr Witts as far as Chip: & then went on to see our poor Friend at Kingham, & found him in rather a better state, glad to see me & able to converse, tho only able to get out of his Bed to have it made. M^rs. Rollinson went away soon after I got there, & M^rs. Western & Daughter Jane arrived from Bath in the evening a trying scene the first meeting with the poor invalid but I own I was rejoiced to see them spent a very anxious Day & not less so a night.[27] rec'd Letters from L^dy. Edward Bentinck & Miss Snow very pleasing ones.

Thursday Decr. 11th.

Very much the same kind of Day, Mr Western very low & indifferent in the Morn: from the power of opium, but considerably better towards evening & able to sit up for an hour, Mr Witts came in the Morn: & staid; Mr Earle & Mr Evans call'd & staid half an hour. Much interested for my poor friend & up & down stairs with him all Day long & happy to be of any use or comfort.

---

27.   This was Jane Western, Nee Calvert, (1735-1819), the mother of Revd. Charles Western and his sister, also Jane Western, (1763-1852). It seems rather surprising that Charles Western should have suffered a paralytic attack at the age of twenty-eight.

Friday Dec.ʳ 12ᵗʰ·

Something of a Rhyme, & the Fog never clearly went off, so there was no Sun & consequently very cold; Mʳˢ· Rollinson came to Kingham about 12 & we left it soon after, with tolerable satisfaction having comfortable hopes of Mʳ Westerns recovery, if no unfavourable change took place, call'd at Swerford before I went home on my Brother, & Sisters who came the Day before & home to Dinner, & to my sweet little loves who were all charming; rec'd Letters fᵐ· Mʳˢ· Naper & Mʳˢ· Eliza: Tracy & wrote to Mʳˢ· Savage.

Saturday Dec.ʳ 13ᵗʰ·

More of a Rhyme & thick Fog & consequently dreadfull cold, Mʳ Witts went early to Chip: & we dined at Mʳ Penystons, meeting Mʳ & Mʳˢ· Martyn of Bourton on the Hill agreable people wᶜʰ· took off the natural form of the visit, play'd at Whist with success, & not at home till late, very cold both going & returning but more miserably so there.

Sunday Dec.ʳ 14ᵗʰ·

Not so much of a Rhyme but hard frost with considerable wind which made it horribly cold at Church, where Mʳ Evans did the Duty, my Sisters return'd home from Church with us for an hour & walket a little way back with them. wrote to Miss Snow & heard much amended accounts of Mʳ Western.

Monday Dec.ʳ 15ᵗʰ·

If possible still harder frost, wind & cold, tho clear & bright sunshine we walket a little My Brother, Sisters & Mʳ Francis dined here, & play'd till ten o'clock at three penny Whist, sad dull sport indeed.

Tuesday Dec.ʳ 16ᵗʰ·

Still hard Frost with bright sunshine but not quite so intensely cold as yesterday, walket out a little, My Broʳ Ferdinand sat an hour here in his way to Swerford thought him very tolerably well in the evening heard from Mʳˢ· Buxton & wrote to Mʳˢ· Granville.

Wensday Dec.ʳ 17ᵗʰ·

Very much the same sort of Day but still colder than yesterday, tho I did not find it very terrible going to Kingham, at Chip I drop'd Mʳ Witts, found Mʳ Western certainly better tho his amendment very slow, his Mother & Sisʳ gone to Chad: to wait upon Major Rollinson & his Lady, sat 2 or 3 hours very pleasantly with Mʳ & Mʳˢ· Western rec'd a Letter from Mʳˢ· Tyrwhitt & wrote to Mʳˢ· Naper.

Thursday Dec.ʳ 18ᵗʰ·

Full as cold a Day, if not colder as the frost was quite hard, & no sunshine, Mʳ Witts & I went after Breakfast to Chadlington to make our visit of form to Major Rollinson & his Wife, rather shocket at her appearance & manner, which are very plain & vulgar, could not but be astonish'd at his choice, her daughter Miss Evans a vulgar Irish Girl, poor Mʳˢ· Rollinson very indifferent & much out of spirits. rec'd a Letter from Miss Anne Snow & wrote to Miss Chaplin.

Friday Decr 19th.

Not near so cold, no wind & warm Sun, but still hard frost. Mr Earle & Mr Evans call'd here in the Morning, as did my Sisters from Swerford, walket part of the way home with them quite pleasant out of Doors.

Saturday Decr 20th.

Much the same weather in the Day but thaw'd a little at night, Mr Witts went to Chip: & I walket with the Boys busy with accompts in the evening Mr Witts went likewise to Kingham to call on Mr Western & found him mending tho very slowly

Sunday Decr 21st.

A violent Storm of hail & Snow early in the Morning, but soon clear'd up again & was bright sunshine & froze hard, Mr Earle did the Duty at Church not very cold there. Much enjoyment & instruction with the Children & a good deal of reading.

Monday Decr 22^{d.}

Hard frost & bright sun again not quite such good walking owing to the little Snow that had fallen, but Mr Witts, Francis & I walket to Swerford, sat ½ an hour with my Sisters, Mr Roberts Mr Evans dined here, & Mr Earle came to Tea, with his usual caprice calling it too cold to dine out, playd at Whist with success Mr Roberts lay here.

Tuesday Decr 23^{d.}

Quite as fine a Day & rather more mixd, most pleasant walking with my Boys Mr Witts at Chip: my Sis^t Catherine call'd here in the even^{g.} busy with accompts.

Wensday Decr 24th.

An expected quick thaw, with a high South West wind, & very small rain or mist but still I was not deter'd from putting into execution my design of going to Kingham, dropp'd Mr Witts at Chip: & took Fran^{s.} all the way, roads not so bad as might be thought for; found Mr Western up & better than since his illness tho still a dreadfull invalid. wrote to Lady Edward Bentinck.

Thursday Decr 25th.

Still a thaw but a bright Day with sun & high wind, very cold at Church, Mr Evans did the Duty with much propriety & devotion, walket after I came home from Church.[28]

Friday Decr 26th.

Had been a frost again in the night & froze all Day, accompanied, with high wind & flying storms of snow, which made it bitterly cold & unpleasant, & the roads very rough & bad even to Adlestrop where I made a Morning visit to Mrs. Leigh who I alone saw, out of all the

---

28. One singular point of interest in the Witts family, both for Edward and Agnes, and then later for their son Francis, is that Christmas was so little celebrated. There is hardly ever as much as a passing reference to the event and only once in her later years does Agnes mention eating a turkey—and even then it is at the home of a friend.

numbers that fill the house at this time. had the good fortune to meet M^rs. Buxton & Miss Buxton there from Upper Slaughter sorry to see the former look thin & poorly rec'd a Letter from M^rs. Naper; in the evening Mr W. read the Tragedy of Vimonda to me. not capital.[29]

Saturday Decr 27th.

Hard frost again & very cold but not afraid to walk out, any more than my Sisters to come here from Swerford, Mr Witts read in the evening in the History of China, wrote to M^rs. Rollinson.

Sunday Decr 28th.

Still harder frost & most extremely cold tho there was a great deal of Sun, Mr Evans did the Duty at Church a most excellent Sermon, I went down afterwards to the Girls School & sat half an hour with my Sisters. Rec'd a Letter from M^rs. Rollinson & wrote to Miss Anne Snow.

Monday Decr 29th.

Much more severe frost, & dreadfully cold, being no sun & frequent flying storms of Snow. I never went out all Day but were very busy at work & much engaged with the Children. Mr Witts went to see Mr Western, & found him much better much concern'd to hear of the death of Mr Penystons little Girl. wrote to M^rs. E: Tracy, & rec'd Letters from M^rs. Savage & Miss Sabine, a most excellent Letter & caused me many tears both of pain & pleasure.

Tuesday Decr 30th.

Just such another Day only still colder, never stirr'd out all day, but was very busy in Millinery, too bad a Day even for the Boys to go out had them with me all Day almost. rec'd a most pleasing Letter from L^dy. Edward Bentinck.

Wensday Decr 31st.

One of the most severe dreadfull Days that ever a Year ended with violent driving Snow & high Wind, in the afternoon it rain'd hard for 2 hours & at night Froze hard again. not even Mr Witts went out the whole Day, I worket hard & he read in the account of the Pelew Islands very much entertain'd with it.[30]

1789

Thursday Jan: 1st.

The Year began as it ended with extreme cold & violent driving Snow, but at Noon cleard up & was bright Sun & froze harder than ever at night. Mr Witts rode to Chip: & in the evening read to me again much pleased with our Studies. Received a very kind & agreable Letter from M^rs. Tyrwhitt

29. Andrew Macdonald (*c.* 1755–1788), *The Tragedy of Vimonda* (1788).
30. Now known as the Republic of Palau, the islands are to the north-east of the Philipines. Henry Wilson, the captain of the East India Company packet *Antelope*, was shipwrecked here in 1783, and it was his account, written by George Keate, *An Account of the Pelew Islands*, that Edward Witts would have been reading.

Friday Jan: 2^d.

Clear bright Day with universal Sunshine Mr Witts went on business to Banbury & the Children walket on the Gravel walke wch. had been swept for them. rec'd a Letter from M^rs. Granville & wrote to M^rs. Tyrwhitt.

Saturday Jan: 3^d.

Very disagreable Day thick Fog with a strong Rhyme & intensely cold & dark, busy all Morning preparing for our intended Jaunt into Glocestershire & at night with writting & accompts.

Sunday Jan: 4th.

Dark cold Day but without Snow or Rhyme, but severe black Frost, bitterly cold at Church where Mr Evans did the Duty, Mr Earle being gone. came home again for an hour or two, & then went to Dine at my Bro^r Travells at Swerford, Fran^s with us dull miserable work & very cold, came home at 9 o'clock.

Monday Jan: 5th.

Extreme hard frost & wonderfully cold but from constant sun, not disagreable going in the Chaise to Lower Slaughter roads good & went quick, Mr Witts rode, met with a most kind reception as usual from our good friends, & passt the remainder of the Day in chearfull converse, interspersed with several rubbers at Cribbage. rec'd a Letter from Miss Anne Snow.

Tuesday Jan: 6th.

No change of weather but to being much colder, being high wind & no sun. M^rs. Naper & I went in the Chaise soon after Breakfast to Upper Slaughter principaly to see little Patty Buxton, Mr Witts & Francis walket, thought her a very nice Child,[31] & was much much entertain'd by surveying My Bro^rs. Flower House Mr Hippesley & his Sons visiting there. We came home early & the Upper Slaughter family dine'd here much enjoyment of M^rs. Buxtons company play'd at Cribage

Wensday Jan: 7th.

Quite as severe a Day but more bearable from Sunshine tho the wind was higher M^rs. Naper, M^rs. Buxton, Miss Buxton & I went in the Coach first to make a visit of an hour to M^rs. Hippesley wch. as usual was very lively & pleasant & then to make one of equal length to Lady Reade very chatty in the Coach, Mr Hippesley & Sons & Mr Snell dined here; lively & agreable; M^rs. Naper & I took every opportunity of reading in Mr Cumberlands new Novel of Arundel.[32] play'd at Cribage with very bad success

---

31. There are no other references to Patty Buxton and it seems that she died young. She would have been a great-niece of Agnes Witts.

32. Richard Cumberland (1732–1811). Cumberland was at the height of his fame as a dramatist, competing for popularity with Richard Brinsley Sheridan. Edward and Agnes knew Cumberland quite well, and appear to have acted as guardians, or at least mentors, to his daughter Elizabeth in her youth. Elizabeth was now Lady Elizabeth Bentinck, a regular correspondent with Agnes.

Thursday Jan: 8ᵗʰ·

A continuation of the same weather with constant sunshine, but extremely cold, Mᵣ Naper out a Shooting & Mᵣ Witts went to call on Mᵣ Jones & Mʳˢ· Naper & I went early to Upper Slaughter to work before Dinner, had a very chearfull Day there & play'd at Cribage

Friday Jan: 9ᵗʰ·

Still no change of weather, went early to Dress, dining early to go to the Play at Adlestrop, with which we were far more entertain'd than expected Matilda the Play, the performers Mᵣ Leigh, Mᵣ & Mʳˢ· Twisleton, Miss Twisleton, Mᵣ Oliphant, Mᵣ Thickets & Mᵣ Heynes, Bon Ton the Farce in which none but Mᵣ Oliphant were near so capital as in the Play the Drawing Room made a tolerable good Theatre tho the stage was too small: 24 Spectators out of the Neighbourhood, & the refreshments good & plenty not at home till ½ past one rather fatigued.

Saturday Jan: 10ᵗʰ·

A very dismal Morning, of Wind & Snow tho none fell of any consequence, but yet Mᵣ Witts fullfill'd his intention of going to see Mᵣ Western which he did. Mʳˢ· Naper very indifferent till evening with the head ache when she grew better, & we had a very comfortable evening interspersed with chat & reading Arundel. wrote to My Sister Travell

Sunday Jan: 11ᵗʰ·

A bright fine Day but quite as sharp & cold as ever, went to Church at Upper Slaughter where Mᵣ Williams did the Duty; sat an hour there afterwards: Mᵣ Witts came home to Dinner, as did Mᵣ Buxton to Upper Slaughter, rather a long evening with a little reading. wrote to Lady Edward Bentinck & rec'd a Letter from Nurse with a good account of my little Dears.

26. *Stow-on-the-wold.*

Monday Jan: 12ᵗʰ·

Rather the coldest Day there had been & a most severe frost, Mʳˢ· Naper & I went up to Stow & sat an hour with Mʳˢ· Hippesley who we found very indifferent, came home early to Dress for Stow Ball. the Upper Slaughter family dined here & all but my Brother went with us, who took Francis home wʰ· him, I never saw so bad a meeting only 32, & chiefly Dancers 12 couple, it was a dull evening to me having never anybody to converse with. play'd two rubbers at Whist, did not get home till near three. well tired.

Tuesday Jan: 13ᵗʰ·

A very fearfull Day of Hail, sleet & rain, towards night it came very severe, & shew'd every sign of a lasting thaw, My little Francis came home from U: Slaughter to Dinner on Horseback – much to his delight. working, reading & cribbage fill'd up the Day, Mʳˢ· Naper very indifferent with fatigue.

Wensday Jan: 14ᵗʰ·

A bright Morning, having been again a sharp frost in the Night, which made the earth almost a sheet of Ice; & made it judged improper to attempt going to the Play at Adlestrop, great disappointment to me who was of opinion it might have been done very safely; My Broʳ & Mʳ Buxton here in the Morning. play'd at Cribbage with very ill success wrote to Lady Lyttelton.

Thursday Jan: 15ᵗʰ·

Very much the same weather as the day before; being a small frost in the night & a stormy disagreable Day, went with Mʳˢ· Naper in the chaise at Noon to Upper Slaughter, Mʳ Buxton being ill wᶜʰ· prevented their dining here, found him very indifferent staid there till Dinner time. had ill luck again at Cribbage rec'd Letters from Miss Snow & Nurse & wrote to Mʳˢ· Tyrwhitt & Mʳˢ· Granville.

Friday Jan: 16ᵗʰ·

No material change in the weather, but the earth was more slippery, & the moving deem'd too dangerous to attempt going in the Carriage even to Upper Slaughter, but Mʳ Witts walket there & brought a better account of Mʳ Buxton; began reading Fieldings Amelia aloud,[33] worket a good deal, & play'd at Cribbage with success. rec'd a Letter from Miss Cumberland with the joyfull news that Lᵈʸ· Edwᵈ· Bentinck was safely brought to Bed of a Daughter, wrote to Lord Edward.

Saturday Jan: 17ᵗʰ·

A very compleat thaw, began raining hard about 12 o'clock & so continued for the greater part of the Day, & extremely hard in the evening. Mʳˢ· Naper & I went to make a Morning visit to Mʳˢ· Leigh chearfull & pleasant, invited to another Play, sat ½ an hour very agreably with the Hippesleys call'd at L: Slaughter to take our three Gents with us to Dine at U: Slaughter; very comfortable a Table at Whist & Cribbage I play'd at the former, returning home, we found it

---

33. Henry Fielding (1707–1754). *Amelia* had been published in 1751, so it was by no means a new novel.

impossible to pass thro the brook in the Coach, from the imense quantity of Ice collected got out & were each supported by two Men & walked home in safety; a wonderfull event.

Sunday Jan: 18th.

A most stormy wet Day, & the floods prodigeous tho they went off fast in the course of the Day, not one of us ventured to go to Church much reading, writting, & talking. rec'd a Letter from Lord Edwd. Bentinck & Mrs. C: Western answerd the latter & wrote a very long Letter to Miss Snow, & a Letter of condolence to Mrs. Hyett on the Death of her Father poor Dr. Adams rec'd likewise a Letter from Mrs. Tyrwhitt.

Monday Jan: 19th.

Had been a small Frost in the night was a bright clear Morning, rain'd at Noon & snow'd very hard for some hours at night. after Breakfast, Mr. Naper went to Mr. Westerns & Mr. Witts to Swerford Park Mrs. & Miss Buxton came at 12 o'clock to spend the whole Day very comfortable working & talking party My Brother & Mr. Buxton came to Dinner Cribbage in the evening

Tuesday Jan: 20th.

A bright clear Day & the snow melted fast from the great power of the Sun, My Bror & the two Ladies sat an hour here in the Morning, Mr. Witts return'd home to Dinner, bringing a nice account of my sweet little Boys. went to Drink Tea & play at Cribbage at Upper Slaughter remarkably chearfull & lively. rec'd Letters from Mrs. Catherine Thornton & my Sister Travell

Wensday Jan: 21st.

Damp & close in the Morning, & at Noon began raining violently, & so continued the whole Day & night. Mr. Naper came home to Dinner from Cirencester & we early went to the Play at Adlestrop Venice Preserved & who is the Dupe, with a Prologue between by Mr. Oliphant in the character of Mother Shipton riding on a Broomstick, Mr. Twisleton was very great in Pierre & Mr. Leigh little less so in Jaffier. Mrs. Twisleton was not equal to Belvederes difficult part, the Theatre was very full & we did not get home till past two, thro' some perils from floods in Stow Lane the Upper Slaughter family were obliged to sleep here, the floods being too strong to make it safe for them to go home. rec'd a Letter from Ld. Edward Bentinck & wrote to Mr. Hunt.[34]

Thursday Jan: 22d.

Much the same Morning as the former & turn'd out, another wet Day, Breakfasted late the Gentlemen rode out to enjoy the rain, the Ladies sat working till they were tired & then play'd at Cribbage till Dinner, to which Major Rollinson was added a very chearfull Day. a Table at Whist & another at Cribbage. the Upper Slaughter family went home to Supper. rec'd a Letter from Miss Chaplin.

---

34. *Venice Preserv'd* is an English Restoration play written by Thomas Otway (1652–1685), first performed in 1682. The play contains the characters Pierre, Jaffier and Belividera. *Who's the Dupe* is a farce written by Hannah Cowley (1743–1809), first performed at Drury Lane in 1779.

Friday Jan 23ᵈ·

High wind but no rain thro'out the Day Mʳ Naper & Mʳ Witts went out a Hunting early, My Broʳ came to Breakfast after which Major Rollinson went away & my Broʳ & I set forth to make a Morning visit at Sandywell in Mʳ Napers Chaise, obliged to go the round about way wᶜʰ· made as near 6 hours on the road & only an hour & a ½ there, found my three Aunts all as well as could be expected, had a satisfactory meeting with Mʳ Clarke on the subject of my Boys inoculation, my Broʳ went home to Dinner, we had a comfortable evening & play'd at Cribbage. had the pleasure of receiving a Letter from Lᵈʸ· Edwᵈ· Bentincks own hand, wrote 5 Days after she was brought to Bed were well both herself & little Girl.

Saturday Jan: 24ᵗʰ·

An intire wet Day till quite evening much engaged all the Morning in writting went to Drink Tea at Upper Slaughter, a Table at Whist & Cribbage staid Supper. rec'd a Letter from Mʳˢ· Hyett, & wrote one to Lᵈʸ· Edward Bentinck, & Miss Western on the subject of the Adlestrop Plays.

Sunday Jan: 25ᵗʰ·

Clear weather with high wind & bright Sunshine, Mʳ Naper & Mʳ Witts went to Church at Sherborne, Mʳˢ· Naper, Francis, & I to U: Slaughter & staid an hour after, & walk'd about in the Garden &c after we came home, glad to find the use of our Legs once again. Mʳ Markham & Mʳ Fretwell dined here, the former staid all night.

Monday Jan: 26ᵗʰ·

Quite a disagreable Day violent wind with flying Showers, & immoderately damp, Mʳ Naper early hunting, we left L. Slaughter with much regret, having been highly pleased with our three weeks visit; sorry to leave Jane in such indifferent health, came home quick tho the roads very wet & bad . found my sweet little Boys all that was nice.

Tuesday Jan: 27ᵗʰ·

A very damp disagreable Morning & at Noon turn'd out hard rain & so continued all Day, Mʳ Witts went on business to Banbury, Major Rollinson & his Lady made a long visit here, thought her less unpleasant than when I saw her before, My Sisters came here before they were gone, & walket down to Swerford in extreme hard rain, in spite of all I could say. In the evening I worket, & Mʳ Witts read.

Wensday Jan: 28ᵗʰ·

High wind & dry, I took Mʳ Witts in the Chaise to Chip: Norton, calling at Over Norton by the way but found Mʳˢ· Langton was not come there, then went on to Kingham & sat with poor Mʳˢ· Western for 2 hours, who I found quite well, having lain in 10 Days & the little Boy tolerable,[35] happy in making her chearfull, & hearing good accoᵗ· of Mʳ Western

---

35.   This was Maximilian Western, born on 20 January 1789 and died on 30 April 1789.

Thursday Jan: 29^(th.)

A very thick Fog, which never clearing off made it impossible to go out all Day, even for the Boys, much engaged with them working reading & writting. rec'd a Letter from Miss Snow & wrote to M^(rs.) Naper.

Friday Jan: 30^(th.)

Another very thick Fog, with an inclination to rain which prevented my design of going to make visits at Chadlington, but at Noon it clear'd off, & I went out a walking; My Bro^(r) Travell & M^(r) Francis rode up here & my Sister Travell walket. rec'd a Letter from Miss Western from Bath containing as good an account of her poor Bro^(r) as could be expected.

Saturday Jan: 31^(st.)

An intire bright fine Day from sun rise to sun set, quite warm & like spring & drying fast. I took M^(r) Witts with me as far as Chip: & then went on to visit M^(rs.) Rollinson, meeting M^(rs.) Tyrwhitt on the road coming to see me, sat an hour & ½ at the Upper House & near as long, afterwards with M^(rs.) Tyrwhitt both very pleasant visits. Wrote to Miss Sabine.

Sunday Feb: 1^(st.)

Foggy in the Morning but clear'd off at Noon & was a very fine Day, M^(r) Evans did the Duty at Swerford Church, walket home from Church my Sisters with us & did not come in till near Dinner time when my Bro^(r) Travell & M^(r) Francis Join'd us, they went home early in the evening, wrote to Miss Anne Snow.

Monday Feb: 2^(d.)

A very fine Day, but grew windy & more cold towards evening, walket out a great deal M^(r) Roberts call'd here in the Morning, in the evening engaged with accompts.

Tuesday Feb: 3^(d.)

Very high wind & storms but no rain of any consequence I walket out for an hour & half with M^(r) Witts. M^(r) & M^(rs.) Buxton & Miss Buxton, & my Bro^(r) Ferdinand came to Dinner, very chearfull & pleasant tho poor M^(r) Buxton was attack'd with a violent pain in his stomach in the evening. play'd at Cribbage. rec'd a Letter from M^(rs.) Tyrwhitt.

Wensday Feb: 4^(th.)

Very thick dark Morn: w^(ch.) was succeed'd by hard rain for several hours, M^(r) Witts all Morning at a Turnpike meeting. My Brother & we three Ladies went down to make a visit to my Bro^(r) & Sisters at Swerford. M^(r) Buxton very indifferent all Day, excepting which the Day passt in a most comfortable manner cribage again rec'd a very delightfull long Letter from M^(rs.) Naper

Thursday Feb: 5^(th.)

A most violent high wind but no rain, of any consequence, but on the contrary a great deal of sunshine, we all walk'd out in a party for an hour or two tho' almost blown away. M^(r) & M^(rs.) Tyrwhitt, M^(rs.) Rollinson, & Col: Langton dined here a very chearfull pleasant visit, a Table at Whist & Cribbage & much chearfull conversation, in the evening

Friday Feb: 6ᵗʰ·

Weather very similar in all points Mᵣ Buxton & Mᵣ Witts rode out, tho the former was very indifferent as well as his poor Wife who had a very bad headache. Miss Buxton & I walket together cribbage & conversation as usual in the evening.

Saturday Feb: 7ᵗʰ·

Frequent violent hard showers till after 12, when it became dry tho continued very stormy. our agreable friends left us, & I went to Kingham to see poor Mʳˢ· Western, who I had heard was very ill I dropp'd Mᵣ Witts at Chip: found my poor Friend very indifferent tho not so bad as I expected came home to a late Dinner. began reading the new Novel of Agnes De Courci not very interesting and wrote to Miss Western.³⁶

Sunday Feb: 8ᵗʰ·

If possible rather a more unfavourable Morning but grew better about the same time, Mᵣ W. went to Church but I was fearfull spent the Day in playing with the Boys, much reading & writting wrote to Lady Edward Bentinck.

Monday Feb: 9ᵗʰ·

Most violent high wind, & at noon storms of Hail & cold rain, wᶜʰ· made the air bitterly cold. walket out after Breakfast with Mᵣ Witts for an hour or two, went to dine & sleep at Mʳˢ· Tyrwhitts meeting there Mʳˢ· Rollinson, Col: Langton & Mᵣ Roberts, very chearfull & pleasant, play'd at Whist with success, Mʳˢ· R. staid Supper. rec'd a Letter from Mᵣ Hunt & wrote to Mʳˢ· Naper.

Tuesday Feb: 10ᵗʰ·

Had been a white frost in the night was cold, but clear & fine with constant sunshine all Day; had a most conversible breakfast & hour afterwards with our agreable friends, dropp'd Mᵣ Witts at Chip: & went to Adlestrop to make a visit to Mʳˢ· Thoˢ· Leigh, more agreable than usual by the adition of Mʳˢ· Elizabeth Leigh, a very chearfull pleasant old Maid; & fine drive home rec'd a Letter from Mʳˢ· Buxton, & wrote to Mʳˢ· Catherine Thornton.

Wensday Feb: 11ᵗʰ·

Had been a frost in the night, was a bright shewy Morning, but grew very stormy with frequent hard showers of Snow & rain & so continued all Day, I contrived to walk out for ½ an hour, worket & read in the evening.

Thursday Feb: 12ᵗʰ·

A cold stormy Day but without snow or rain so I walk'd for an hour, Mᵣ Evans & Mᵣ Francis dined, two poor solitary creatures staid till 9 o'clock. rec'd a Letter from Miss Frances Hanbury relating to their having gain'd their cause & answer'd it.

---

36.   Anna Maria Bennett (1760–1808). *Agnes de Courci—A Domestic Tale* was published in 1789.

Friday Feb: 13th

Rather a more mild Day being less wind I went early to Chipping Norton & transacted much business & then went on to make another visit to Mrs Western at Kingham where Mr Witts join'd me from making a visit to Mr Thos Leigh & Mr Penyston, rec'd Letters from Mrs Granville & Miss Western.

Saturday Feb: 14th

A dark disagreable Day, with high wind & frequent small showers, too bad for me to walk out, indeed Mrs Tyrwhitt & Mrs Drake spent the Morning here by appointment, much pleasure as ever in their society.

Sunday Feb: 15th

A violent stormy Day with frequent showers, after Church walket a little in the Garden &c. very low in the evening from some little discomposures not rendered less by the idea of going the next Day to Cheltenham to fix & settle about the 2 little Boys inoculation

Monday Feb: 16th

A very bright Morning, & sunshine the greater part of the Day, but high wind & slight showers, set out soon after Breakfast Mr Witts & I only in the Chaise, stopt an hour at Stow & eat cold Meat, & got to Cheltenham between 4 & 5, dined very comfortably as well as slept at the George Inn, Mrs Markham & Mr Clarke spent part of the evening with us. rec'd Letters from Mrs Naper & Mrs Travell.

Tuesday Feb: 17th

Mild Day with high wind & but little sun breakfasted early & met Mr Clarke at Sandford House to assist us in the survey of the Lodgings but a very miserable place, but agreed for it as very suitable to the design, visited Miss Hughes, Mrs Markham, & Lady Williams, & got to Sandywell to Dinner, & found our three Aunts well & happy to see us, a long evening of mere conversation.

Wensday Feb: 18th

A very fine mild Day with constant sunshine, Mr Witts & Mrs Tracy walket, I staid within with my Aunts, Mr Thomas dined with us, the same expectation of a long talkative evening

Thursday Feb: 19th

Quite a fine Day till after 12 o'clock when it overclouded & were a continued series of hard showers, left our good friends after breakfast & finding the roads wonderfully good reach'd home in less than 5 hours, only stopping at Stow for Hay & water for the Horses, found our little loves all quite well & happy.

Friday Feb: 20th

A Dry Day, but with high winds & stormy & quite without Sunshine, I walket for an hour & ½ attended by Francis, Mr Witts gone to Chip: Mr Hoskins & Mr Evans sat an hour here in the Morning. rec'd a Letter from Miss Anne Snow & wrote to Mrs Naper & my Sister Travell. –

Saturday Feb: 21ˢᵗ·

Had been a great deal of hard rain in the night, & the Morning looket very lousiey but clear'd up & proved a fine stormy Day with some sun. I left Mʳ Witts at Chip: & went to Chadlington made a long visit to Mʳˢ· Tyrwhitt & Mʳˢ· Drake & a short one to Mʳˢ· Rollinson both pleasant in their way; did some business at Chip: on my return.

Sunday Feb: 22ᵈ·

A fine showery Morning tho had been again a prodigeous wet night, but grew violently windy & tempestuous towards Noon, after Church I went to see Mʳˢ· Langton who was arrived at Over Norton a few days, the ease of the visit somewhat interrupted by Lᵈ· Charles Spencer being there, & in the room the whole time.[37] I was far from well all the evening; so did little of any use.

Monday Feb: 23ᵈ·

Dry till 11 o'clock when it became a most dreadfull tempestuous day, raining harder every hour & so continued all the evening I could never stir out very busy all the Morning in the evening wrote to Miss Anne Snow

Tuesday Feb: 24ᵗʰ·

Extremely stormy again & with frequent hard showers but not continuous rain, I went early in the Day to visit Mʳˢ· Penyston who I found at home, staid an hour, rather formal as usual I then went on to Kingham, found poor Mʳˢ· Western pretty well & happy to see me, staid another hour with her & waded home thro' the worst roads I ever saw. At night wrote to Mʳˢ· Granville.

Wensday Feb: 25ᵗʰ·

A most dreadfull day, wind & rain incessant & that very violent till Mid.Day Mʳ Witts prevented going to Chadlington as he intended near Dinner time I just went as far as the Green House almost blown away in the attempt wrote to Miss Chaplin.

Thursday Feb: 26ᵗʰ·

Still very disagreable weather wet & stormy all Morning & after Mid.Day continued rain & very cold, Mʳ Witts went to Chip: Mʳˢ· Rollinson, the Major & his Wife & Miss Evans came here to Dinner & were chearfull & merry enough; play'd at the noble Game of the Goose till I was heartily tired, but it was a great delight to my Little Francis, who was allowed to sit up & play being his Birth Day compleating 6 years. Rec'd a Letter from Lᵈʸ· Edward Bentinck & nice long one from Mʳˢ· Naper.

Friday Feb: 27ᵗʰ·

Quite a fine Day, mild & pleasant without wind & some Sun; well suited to walking about the place which our friends liked to do & were upon our Legs two hours or more, but Mʳˢ· Rollinson was far from well all the remainder of the Day; Mʳ Earle drank Tea here & play'd at Whist.

---

37.   Lord Charles Spencer (1740–1820), son of Lieutenant-General Sir Charles Spencer, 3rd Duke of Marlborough. Mrs Langton was presumably of the Gore-Langton family of Upper Norton.

Saturday Feb: 28th.

More stormy Day & very cold with some sharp showers of Hail, our Friends left us soon after Breakfast, & they were soon succeeded by Mrs. Langton who sat 2 or 3 hours with me in a very comfortable manner bringing her work, after she went I attempted to walk a little but was soon driven in by apparent storms. My two little Loves began their prepartive Physic for Inoculation.

Sunday Mar: 1st.

A very cold North east wind but no rain tho damp, Mr Earle perform'd the service at Church, & I sat a quarter of an hour with him afterwards Mr Witts going to call on Col: Langton, walket a little with Francis on my return the little ones being confined to the House with their Physic.

Monday March 2d.

Much the same kind of weather, Mr Earle call'd here after Breakfast, Mr Witts, Francis & I walket to Swerford, in the evening Mr Witts read to me Mr Cumberlands new Comedy of the Impostors & I wrote to Ldy. Edward Bentinck.

Tuesday Mar: 3d.

Rather a mild pleasant Day without wind but no sun to last, Mr Witts at Chip: I fully taken up with preparation of going to Cheltenham next Day on the Inoculation plan; but found time to walk out with the Boys in the Morning, & with Mr Witts after Dinner for the first time.

Wensday Mar: 4th.

Had been a slight frost in the night, & a very small sprinkling of snow, & was bitterly cold, set out bag & baggage for Cheltenham, Mr Witts on Horseback Myself, three Boys, & three Maids in two Chaises, staid 2 hours at Stow, had a very comfortable Dinner there made more so by Mrs. Napers & her Fathers spending the greater part of the time with us, tho we thought her very indifferent got to Sandywell by six, which we found warm & comfortable & everything in very good order. rec'd a Letter from My Sister Travell.

Thursday Mar: 5th.

A cold day but dry & pleasant walking, had rested very comfortably, & found all things much to our mind, Papa & Mama, Nurses & Children spent most of the Morning in the Town visiting & shopping; dined early all together, Mr John Delabere sat with us all the time & was full of anecdote; Mr Witts & I walke't into the Town again in the afternoon, drank Tea with Miss Nettleships return'd home early before the Boys went to Bed. rec'd a Letter from Miss Snow.

Friday March 6th.

Had been a sharp Frost in the night was bitterly cold, & upon the Hills a flight of Snow, the Children took their Physic. Mrs. Tracy & my Aunt Eliza spent great part of the Morning here; Miss Delabere & Miss Hughes call'd here in the afternoon Mr Witts Frans. & I walket out almost starved with cold. rec'd a Letter from Mrs. Buxton & answer'd it.

Witts Family Papers F175

1789

Saturday March 7th.

Quite a dismal Winter Day, constant small driving Snow, very damp & cold, no possibility of stirring out of the house for any of us, but Mr Witts. Mr Clarke came early in the Day & inoculated the Boys & Molly a trying scene to me tho I tried to summon up all the fortitude possible. Read & worket a great deal.[1]

Sunday March 8th.

Weather very similar, not quite so bad but unfit to go out of the House, particularly as almost every one of us had got colds. Mr John Delabere sat an hour here before Dinner, & Mr Clarke dined here very conversible & agreable. I wrote to Mrs Naper & Mrs Eliza: Tracy. children very lively but tired of being so much confined to the House.

Monday March 9th.

A showey Morn: but still a severe frost & very early grew stormy & some violent showers of snow fell which kept me a prisoner to the House & the Children also, excepting early in the Morn: Mr Witts walket to Sandywell, & my Sisters call'd here in the evening for a qt of an hour on their way home.

Tuesday March 10th.

Had been a considerable fall of Snow in the night but melted fast, & sufferd me to have a relay of visitors all the Morning, Miss Nettleships, Miss Hughes, & my Sisters, who staid & dined here leaving us before it was dark. rec'd a Letter from Miss Sabine & wrote to Miss Eliza: Tracy & Miss Snow. Children perfectly well & their arms not shewing so much infection as I could wish.[2]

Wensday March 11th.

The most intire Day of Snow I almost ever saw at any season of the Year, small but constant & no wind, it quite prevented the power of stirring out of the House or else we were to have spent the Day with my Sisters at Chelt. Children & all. much working reading & playing with the Boys.

---

1. Molly appears to have been a servant girl.
2. Inoculation against smallpox had been conducted in England since 1717 and was not unusual. The experiments by Edward Jenner two years later were to make vaccination with cowpox a viable alternative and by 1801 the Witts family had got to know him well in Cheltenham social circles; Francis Witts personally assisted Dr Jenner on a few occasions.

Thursday March 12th.

Having been a sharp frost in the night the Snow lay, all but what the power of the Sun melted, My Sis⁺ Travell ventured here, & sat 2 or 3 hours in the Morning, & so did M⁺ Clarke & M⁺ˢ Rooke & her Daughter drank Tea here. rec'd a Letter from M⁺ˢ E Tracy & M⁺ˢ Naper.

Friday March 13th.

There had been in the night a more severe fall of Snow than before, nay indeed I believe than the whole Winter, but it melted fast when the sun came out, but it again prevented our spending the Day with my Sisters M⁺ Witts walket but I was obliged still to submit to walking in the House with the Boys, who still kept free from all complaint, but Molly began to grow indifferent. received a Letter from Lady Lyttelton & wrote to M⁺ˢ Tyrwhitt.

Saturday March 14th.

Snow nearly all gone in the Vale & the air milder with a good deal of Sun, tho it again grew stormy at Noon. M⁺ Witts, Francis & I went to the Town early in the day, found the walking most dreadfull, & worse coming back thro' the fields, made several visits & did much business; Molly had some spots come out on her face the Dear Boys still quite well wrote to M⁺ˢ Naper

Sunday March 15th.

A dry Morning till 11 with rather a mild air, after which continued hard rain for the rest of the Day, walket out with the Boys till it rain'd, in the meadows & orchard; poor little George was very hot & heavy the greater part of the Day, but as good as possible: My Sisters came here in a Chaise to Dinner & went away after Tea

Monday March 16th.

Had been a sharp frost in the Night & being a very cold high wind was more severe than ever went out an airing with the two little Boys & Nurse thro' the Town to the Glocester

27. *The High Street, Cheltenham.*

road, George again much the same in the middle of the Day, Edward yet perfectly well. My Sisters here in the afternoon rec'd a Letter from M^rs. Tyrwhitt.

Tuesday March 17th.

Again a sharp Nights frost, but not quite so cold as the former Day having some warm Sun & the earth much dried; at mid:day walket to Cheltenham visited & shop'd as usual. George much better & some fine spots appearing Edward not yet ill. rec'd a long entertaining Letter from Miss Snow & wrote to M^rs. Tyrwhitt in the evening Mr Witts read to me in Lady Cravens Letters.[3]

Wensday March 18th.

A very perilous Morning with rain & Snow alternately, & had been much snow in the night but it did not lie, at Noon it held up; M^rs. Travell call'd in the Morning, Mr Witts walket out in the afternoon & Mr Clarke sat an hour or two in the evening & was very chatty, little George perfectly well & about 20 fine spots about him, Edward still pretty well but a spot or two visible. Rec'd a Letter from L^dy. Edward Bentinck & wrote to M^rs. Elizabeth Tracy.

Thursday March 19th.

Cold & raw, but dry had been a frost again in the night, Mr Witts & I & the 2 eldest Boys air'd on the Bath road, well Jumbled; Mr Clarke dined here & my Sisters drank Tea here, & as it proved made their last visit, to prevent the foolish fears of some foolish people in the Town, Edward pure well & 2 or 3 spots fully out upon him, wrote to L^dy. Lyttelton & M^rs. Naper.[4]

Friday March 20th.

Small rain in the Morning but clear'd off at Noon, & was a bright fine afternoon walket a little in the meadows before Dinner with the Boys & after Dinner went with Nurse & 2 little Boys in the Chaise to Lord Fauconbergs & the Well where Mr Witts & Francis met us on foot, afterwards air'd on the Dowdeswell road. wrote to Miss Snow, M^rs. Buxton, & L^dy. Edward Bentinck.

Saturday March 21st.

A very bright fine Morning & was a dry pleasant Day tho the Sun did not keep out constantly, directly after Breakfast Mr Witts Francis, & I went in the Chaise to Glocester, roads very bad, walket out about the Town, went to some shops & Mr Witts to see the new Gaol, eat some sandwiches at the Kings Head & home to a late Dinner,[5] little Edward not very well, more eruption appearing Georges filling finely. Mr Clarke drank Tea here rec'd a Letter from M^rs. Naper with a good account of herself.

---

3. Elizabeth Craven, *née* Lady Elizabeth Berkeley (1750–1828). Elizabeth was the third child of the 4th Earl of Berkeley. She married William Craven, 6th Baron Craven, in 1769, but they separated in 1783 after numerous scandals on both sides. Elizabeth travelled widely in Europe and Turkey. Her major work was *A Journey through the Crimea to Constantinople* (1789).

4. Presumably the foolish fears were in relation to catching smallpox from the inoculated children.

5. This is the first reference in the diaries to a 'Sandwich,' named after John Montague, 4th Earl of Sandwich (1718–1792). The use of the word is believed to date from 1762.

Sunday March 22ᵈ

Almost an intire wet Day, excepting an hour or two at Noon, when I sent the Boys & their Maids an airing in the Chaise, poor Edward being very indifferent, being feverish & apparently more disorder wanting to shew itself. My Sisters dined & drank Tea here. wrote to Mʳˢ· Granville

Monday March 23ᵈ

A very cold raw Day, but nearly without either rain or Snow, but I was not tempted to stir out of the House, Edward rather better & all his spots advancing, Georges evidently on the turn. My Sisters & Mʳ Hughes call'd here in the afternoon. wrote to Mʳˢ· Rollinson.

Tuesday March 24ᵗʰ·

Had been a sharp frost in the Night & was a particular cold Day with severe N: East wind Mʳ Witts, Francis & I spent the Morning in driving to Tewkesbury, the roads for the first half dreadfull thought the Town much improved by paving, walket about made some little purchases, drank some Egg:wine at the Inn, & drove on our return home to survey the Chalybeate Spring at Walton a Mile distant where a smart House for the reception of company is nearly finish'd. rec'd Letters from Mʳˢ· E: Tracy, & Mʳˢ· Drake & answer'd the latter.

Wensday March 25ᵗʰ·

Constant small interrupted Snow the whole Day, but melted as it fell, tho most bitterly cold & windy, confined to the House the whole Day the two eldest Boys took a dose. My Sisters dined & drank Tea here. rec'd a Letter from Miss Anne Snow & wrote to Mʳˢ· Eliza Tracy. Edwards spots begining to turn

Thursday March 26ᵗʰ·

Extremely cold but dry suited to all the demonstrations of Joy testified at Cheltenham on the Kings recovery, an Ox roasted whole in the street & given away to the poor with Bread & Beer, Bells ringing & Guns firing, & a large Dinner to 40 Gentlemen at the Swan of which Mʳ Witts was one. I dined with my Sisʳˢ· & Franˢ· hoping to meet Mʳˢ· Naper but disappointed, went with them to drink Tea at Mʳˢ· Markhams meeting Miss Nettleships, brought Mʳ Witts home at 10 o'clock, the Boys got quite well, Molly miserably bad & very full with the disorder.

Friday March 27ᵗʰ·

Had been a very sharp frost in the night but was a very bright fine Day, Mʳˢ· Evans Mʳ Thomas, & Miss Nettleships here in the Morning went in the Chaise to Cheltenham being very far from well. Mʳ John Delabere dined & drank Tea here very chatty – rec'd a Letter from Mʳˢ· Tyrwhitt. poor Molly still in a state much to be lamented, wᶜʰ· made it certain it would be impossible to go home on Monday.

Saturday March 28ᵗʰ·

Miserable cold Day with flying storms of snow & turn'd out very hard rain in the afternoon. Mʳ Witts & I went to dine at my Sisters meeting Mʳ Hugh Hughes who was very conversible;

Mr Bridges Hughes, his Brother & Sister, Miss Norwood & Mr John Delabere drank Tea a Table at whist & cribage at w^ch· I play'd, we staid supper came home a little after 11 rec'd a Letter from M^rs· Naper. Molly a good deal better

Sunday March 29th·
Still very cold tho much sunshine soon after Breakfast Mr Witts & I went to Sandywell to see poor Mr Dunn & walk in the Garden, on our return found Miss Hughes & her Brother Bridges & my Sisters, Miss Nettleships & their Brother drank Tea here, & were very conversible & agreable rec'd a Letter from M^rs· Elizabeth Tracy.

Monday March 30th·
Much the same kind of weather quite as cold, went to Cheltenham at Noon, made some visits & did some business, dined at my Sisters meeting Miss Hughes, & Nanny Dewes, Lord Fauconberg & his Daughter Lady Anne, very chearfull & lively at Tea, came home at 9 o'clock wrote to Miss Anne Snow.

Tuesday March 31st·
Rather a milder air, & in the afternoon turn'd to a mild rain, busy early in the Day packing, Miss Delabere her Bro^r & Niece call'd here walked back with them to the Town, My Sisters dined here, & play'd a rubber or two at Cribage, I was quite fatigued with the labours of the Day; rec'd a Letter from M^rs· Granville

Wensday April 1st·
Somewhat a milder, tho a dryer Air & not quite so cold, but showery, Mr Clarke sat with us while at Breakfast, to make a last visit as we left Sandford House, without any regret but much thankfullness that the Dear Boys had so well got over the inoculation M^rs· Naper met us at Stow, & sat with us while we dined, I thought her rather better but not so much as I could wish. got home by six o'clock, never thought my home so much like a Palace before, & all so neat & comfortable. rec'd a Letter from Miss Sabine.

Thursday April 2^d·
Violent Wet Morning, & continued very stormy the whole Day, I was only able to go to the Green House between the showers, Mr Witts all Day at a Justice Meeting at Banbury, the Boys all Day with me, wrote to M^rs· E: Tracy & M^rs· Savage

Friday April 3^d·
A very sour disagreable Day, with many flying showers, but I ventured to walk out for an hour tho but very indifferent. received Letters from M^rs· Rollinson, M^rs· Buxton, & My Sister Travell & wrote to M^rs· Tyrwhitt.

Saturday April 4th·
A smart fall of Snow early in the Morning, & continued snowing at times the greater part of the Day Mr Witts at Chip: M^rs· Rollinson & M^rs· Naper with her sat two hours with me in the morn: in the evening wrote to M^rs· C: Western & Miss Sabine.

Sunday April 5th.

Sharp frost in the night, but was a very fine Day, with bright sun & no wind, walket both Morning & evening, would not go church for fear of giving alarm of the small Pox, wrote to Lady Lyttelton & a short Letter to Mrs. Naper.

Monday April 6th.

A very pleasant Day, more like Spring than any former one I walket with Mr Witts & Francis to the high wood ground was out more than two hours; in the evening Mr Witts read in the Life of the late King of Prussia, by Powell, a very entertaining Book.

Tuesday April 7th.

The weather changed again to cold & stormy with an east wind, & in the afternoon to a settled rain, Mr Witts & I went to Mrs. Rollinsons for two nights, no company there, had so much conversation no want of Cards in the evening, much pleased to find her rather better, rec'd a Letter from Mrs. Tyrwhitt.

Wensday April 8th.

Cloudy Morn: but a very fine mild Day, walket about the Villige & premises for a great while, Mr Witts much engaged in his Judiciary office, trying to investigate the horrid Murder commited at Chadlington but without affect in the evening play'd at 3 handed Cribbage, rec'd a Letter from Miss Anne Snow.

Thursday April 9th.

A very beautifull Day quite bright & warm, walket about with Mrs. Rollinson after Breakfast & then left her to return home, doing some little business on the way at Chip: found my little Dears all well & lively. Mr Witts read in the King of Prussia wrote to Mrs. Granville.

Friday April 10th.

Much such another Day, went to Church walket afterwards, & in the afternoon, till quite tired & far from well & much out of spirits rec'd a Letter from Miss Snow & wrote to my Sisr Travell

Saturday April 11th.

Neither so warm nor so much sunshine, I walket out several times but feel too much fatigued by it to enjoy it so much as I should busy at accompts rec'd a Letter from Mrs. Naper & answer'd it imediately

Sunday April 12th.

A very cold North east wind, some sun, but very stormy, not very seasonable for Easter, visited the Sunday schools before Church went to Church in the afternoon for the first time glad to sit by the fire the remainder of the evening wrote to Mr Hunt & Miss Snow.

Monday April 13th.

Not quite so cold being bright sunshine the whole Day, Mr Sheldon from Weston came here to an early Breakfast, & was very agreable & pleasant; Mr Witts all the Morn: at a Parish Meeting at Hook: norton I walket with the Boys in the evening worket & heard life of the King of Prussia.

Tuesday April 14th.

An equal bright Day & a much more warm air, Mr & Mrs. Naper came to Dinner, He very pleasant & easy, she as usual affectionate & delightfull to me, walket a little in the afternoon & talk'd more at night play'd at Cribage.

Wensday April 15th.

Much such another Day, Mrs. Naper & I in the chaise & the Gentlemen on Horseback went soon after Breakfast to survey the alteration at Heythrop much pleased with the new manner wch. the Gallery is fitted up; & quite delighted with ye. splendid new Fruit House & Conservatory, left the Gent to pursue their ride went on to Chadlington & sat an hour with Mrs. Rollinson, dined very late & spent the evening as the former one rec'd Letters from Mrs. Charles Western & my Sister Travell

Thursday April 16th.

Not such fine weather colder & more stormy, our agreable friends left us at mid.day taking my sweet Francis with them, who was much delighted at the permission, I felt much at parting with him but could not refuse, worket & read in the evening & wrote a short Letter to Ldy. Edd. Bentinck

Friday April 17th.

Had been a night of rain & was a very mild pleasant day, & vegetation advancing very fast; Mr Witts went to Chip: Mr Evans dined & drank Tea here; misst my Frans. very much.

Saturday April 18th.

Much such another Day having been again rain in the night, & very growing much engaged all Morning; but walket a good deal.

Sunday April 19th.

Very mild & fine but sometimes cloudy, went to church twice, George with me in the afternoon & to the Girls school rec'd Letters from My Brot Ferdinand & Miss Sabine, & answer'd it & wrote to my Sister Travell and Mrs. Buxton. –

Monday April 20th.

A very brilliant Morning quite warm Mr Witts went early to a Justice Meeting at Adderbury I walket, dresst early, and dined at 1 o'clock with the Children & set off at three for Shirborne, Prissick with me, from Burford took a pair of Post Horses, found Mrs. Naper & Mrs. George Talbot an agreable tetetete, worket & conversed the whole evening; infinite joy to see again my sweet Francis quite well & happy & much commended. rec'd a Letter from Mrs. Savage.

Tuesday April y^e^ *21*^st^

Not quite so fine a day being colder & more stormy, an agreable Breakfast the Gentlemen full of the apprehended sport on the Downs, for wch we set out at 12 o'clock, good but short sport, & the pleasure terminating in pain to Jane & myself, by seeing Mrs Talbot in such anxious agitation for Mr Talbot who was one of the Jockies Mr Witts join'd us on the course, & with Mr Isaacs & Mr Twining return'd with us to Shirborne to Dinner rather a long dull evening Mrs Naper being far from well, & all the rest of us rather overset by the events of the Day rec'd a Letter from L^dy^ Ed^d^ Bentinck.

Wensday April 22^d^

A very fine Day, Mrs Naper, Fran^s^ & I in the Coach went to the Downs, where we were detain'd till 5 o'clock, but amply repaid by many races, & most admirable sport, Mr Talbot very successfull; a great deal of company collected rather anxious to return home to Mrs Talbot, the evening spent much like the former. rec'd a Letter from Mr Hunt

Thursday April 23^d^

Dry but stormy, left Shirborne soon after Breakfast, came home very quick happy to salute my little loves quite well, Mrs Rollinson & her two Girls came to us to Dinner, she very indifferent, the 5 Children most happy & joyous together; had much conversation & an hour of 3 handed Cribbage.

Friday April 24th

a bright windy Morning, & in the course of the Day, frequent warm mild Showers very growing, Mrs Rollinson & I walk'd & talk'd much she went away in the evening. Mr Roberts call'd here in the Morning.

Saturday April 25th

Fine in the Morning, but grew cold & stormy at noon, & met in the afternoon Mr Witts the Boys & I walket to Swerford & made some visits. Read & worket in the evening rec'd Letters from Mrs Eliza Tracy & my Sister Travell, & wrote to Mrs Tyrwhitt.

Sunday April 26th

Very cold & stormy with frequent hard showers of rain & hail, went to Church twice, & walk'd a little before Tea not pleasant enough to stay out long rec'd a Letter from Miss Snow & answer'd it & wrote to my Brother Ferdinand.

Monday April 27th

Quite as disagreable weather if anything colder than the Day before, Mr Witts at Chipping Norton I walket a little & was very busy.

Tuesday April 28th

Not much change for the better in the weather, I walked with Mr Witts & the Boys, Mr Evans dined here but went away early I wrote to Mrs Naper.

Wensday April 29ᵗʰ·

Rather milder weather more Sun & less wind & storms, Mᵣ Witts all Day at Chip: at a Justice Meeting, the Boys nice lively companions they dined with me & I walket with them afterwards to Swerford. rec'd a Letter from Miss Anne Snow & answer'd it, & wrote to Mʳˢ· Tyrwhitt.

Thursday April 30ᵗʰ·

Very indifferent weather still I was so much engaged I gave myself very little time to walk, prevented Dining at Mᵣ Tyrwhitts by the Coachmans having bad eyes rec'd a Letter fᵐ· Mʳˢ· Tyrwhitt. Francis had been for three or 4 Days 2 or 3 hours in a Morning with Mᵣ Evans to learn his Latin Grammar & to write.

Friday May 1ˢᵗ·

Cold, stormy & very unlike May Day but yet Mᵣ & Mʳˢ· Tyrwhitt made one a visit of two hours in their Phaeton a pleasing proof of their good will Mᵣ Witts at Chip: Mᵣ Francis Dined here. rec'd a Letter from my Broᵣ Ferdinand & answerd it.

Saturday May 2ᵈ·

A wet moist Morning, & had been a great deal of Rain in the night, continued a dark gloomy Day tho without rain, very busy all the Morn: Mᵣ Witts at Chip: walket with him in the afternoon rec'd a very pleasing affectionate Letter from Mʳˢ· Naper.

Sunday May 3ᵈ·

A most intire wet miserable Day, very small thick rain towards evening more like a Fog too bad to attempt going to Church, but full of business not quite happy or easy about my sweet Francis who had got a very bad cold & was rather feverish.

Monday May 4ᵗʰ·

A thick close Morning very growing & in the afternoon clear & beautifully Fine, we left home at 11 o'clock, feeling much to part from my sweet Boys, Francis's cold better, dined at Oxford going so far with our own Horses, & then Post to Henly, could not gain admittance at the Red Lyon but very well satisfied with our reception at the Bell. Wrote to my Sister Travell.

Tuesday May 5ᵗʰ·

A wonderfull clear fine Day which made the country thro' which we pass'd appear very beautifull, left Henley between 8 & 9, & got to Town at one, landed at the Hottel in Pall Mall; where Mᵣ & Mʳˢ· Naper were; set out walking in search of Lodging which we soon found in Duke Street St. James's neat & comfortable, & were settled in them that night Dine'd at Mᵣ Snows Sir Frank Standish Mᵣ George Snow & his Daughter there very merry & comfortable sat an hour in the evening with Lᵈʸ· Lyttelton who was far from well & home to bed early.[6]

---

6.   Sir Frank Standish, 3rd Baronet, of Duxbury (1746–1812). Sir Frank was a politician and a noted horse breeder.

28. Piccadilly at the junction with White Horse Street.

Wensday May 6th.

A Thick close hot Morning but turned out a bright very fine Day, went a shopping with Mrs. Naper, visited <u>Aunts</u> & many others. Dined at Mrs. Ecles's meeting a very pleasant party,[7] & a still larger in the evening, from thence went to a very large party at Miss Snows which concluded with a lively Dance & jolly Supper not at home till past two.

Thursday May 7th.

A most intire bright fine Day in this Town quite hot, Miss Anne Snow & Mr Richard Witts sat with us while we Breakfasted,[8] I visited about for two hours Dined with Mr & Mrs. Naper at there Hottel, were to have gone to the Opera together but she was so very indifferent we gave it up, Maria Jones came early in the afternoon, all went to see the Shakespeare Gallery in Pall Mall, drank Tea very comfortably when we went to sit ½ an hour with My Aunts in Green Street & from there to Ldy. Fanes. rec'd Letters from Miss Chaplin, Miss Sabine, Mrs. Granville & from Nurse, & wrote to my sweet Francis.

Friday May 8th.

The same delightfull weather continued quite hot, out 4 hours in the Morning visiting &c. dined early at home, to go to the Play with Lady Dacre, but not being likely to turn out a

---

7.   Mrs Ecles features frequently in the diaries, generally in connection with Ferdinando Travell. She may have been born a Rollinson, and thereby be a sister-in-law to Ferdinando. He often stayed with Mrs Ecles in London, Bath and elsewhere. The Rollinsons were also connected to the Dolphin family, so the entry for 14 May below seems to support this hypothesis.

8.   Richard Witts (1747–1815) was a slightly younger brother to Edward Witts. He lived in Harley Street, London.

29. Ranelagh Rotunda.

good performance did not go but drank Tea with Lady Lyttelton & sat an hour with M^rs. Tracy in Norfolk Street, & then went to Ranelagh.[9] Mr Witts & I tete tete, very bad company at first, but some good, & very full towards the last.

Saturday May 9th.

No change in the weather quite as warm, sat an hour with M^rs. Naper early in the Morning meeting Miss Boddington afterwards visited & shopp'd as usual. Dined at Mr Snows in a quiet comfortable way, Miss Snow & I went to a very crowded Opera very hot indeed much good company, Mr Witts went to the Play & took Dean Paul with him rec'd a very good account of my Dear Boys.

Sunday May 10th.

Just such weather, went to S^t. James's Church heard a very dull sermon from Dr Parker made a visit or two, went with the Snows to Kensington Gardens, great mixture of company, dined with the Snows a party of 10 very merry staid with them all the evening & supt there.

Monday May 11th.

Very much the same fine weather M^rs. Naper & Mr Stone met at our Lodgings before I went out when I made some visits, 17 in number & did some business, dined at home very comfortable went early to M^rs. Siddone's benifit with the whole family of the Snows, sat very agreably therefore not much incomoded with heat, the Play Romeo & Juliet, home very late from the crowd. Mr Witts at two Routs.

---

9.   Ranelagh Gardens were pleasure grounds in Chelsea, with the main feature being a rococo rotunda with a diameter of 37m. The gardens and rotunda were closed in 1803 and the rotunda demolished two years later.

30. A view of the front of the old opera house in the Haymarket.

Tuesday May 12ᵗʰ·

Rather a disagreable Day from a strong east wind, which made the dust dreadfull went at 11 o'clock to Hastinge's Trial, sat two hours before any thing began, & then not much gratified either by the trial or appearance,[10] dined with Lady Hereford, meeting my Brother Ferdinand took him with us to an agreable Party at Mʳˢ· Fords some good Musick afterwards went to a smart party at Mʳˢ· Westerns full & hot. rec'd Letters from Lᵈʸ· Edward Bentinck, Mʳˢ· Rollinson & my Sister Travell.

Wensday May 13ᵗʰ·

Very hot & windy, went soon after Breakfast taking Lady Lyttelton with us to see Mʳˢ· Williams in her retreat at Rotherhithe,[11] a small hut shell in a Garden, her appearance & the visit alltogether very singular, when we return'd found Mʳ Sabine & his Son & Daughter just arrived felt much at the first sight of them, glad of the quiet of Dining at home drank Tea at Col: Guydickens's meeting all the Aunt Tracys, sat an hour with the Sabines at Lady Lytteltons, & then went to Ranelagh taking Miss Guydickens's very full & hot. home late

Thursday May 14ᵗʰ·

Again hot & windy, Jo: Sabine breakfasted with us & went with Mʳ Witts to Westminster Hall, Mʳˢ· Naper & Maria Jones called upon me & I went shopping with them & Col:

---

10. Warren Hastings (1732–1818). Hastings had been Governor-General of India, but on his return to England in 1784 had been impeached for misdemeanours by Edmund Burke, abetted by Sir Philip Francis, who had been wounded by Hastings in a duel in India. The impeachment came in 1787 and the trial commenced in 1788, dragging on for seven years, until Hastings was finally acquitted.

11. This must have been Alicia Williams, *née* Witts (1742–1800). Alicia was the eldest of Edward's immediate family. She is very elusive in the diaries and in the Witts Family Papers. Who Mr Williams was and what he was doing in Rotherhithe are unknown.

31. The Tower of London from the area of Wapping.

Sabine for her, & made some visits. Dined very agreably at Lady Dacres a party of 8, a very handsome entertainment, play'd at Cribbage both there & at M$^{rs.}$ Ecles's when we went at 9 o'clock & supt very pleasantly, all the Dolphin family there, & my Bro^r Ferdinand rec'd a charming account of my Dear Boys.

Friday May 15$^{th.}$

A very fine mild Rain till near 10 oclock when it became a clear bright fine Day, took the Miss Snows into the City, to Houndsditch & many other businesses, dined with them meeting M^r & M$^{rs.}$ Colme, Mr Trusson & their own large party very jolly play'd at Whist, M^r & M$^{rs.}$ Ross being added to the party, then went to a crowded Route at the Dow. L$^{dy.}$ Reades, return'd to Saville Row to Supper a very wet night.

Saturday May 16$^{th.}$

A very stormy Day frequent slight Showers, went early with M^r & M$^{rs.}$ Naper to Plernirs the painters, then took M$^{rs.}$ Naper with us to make a Visit at Mr Boddingtons at Clapton very agreable left M$^{rs.}$ N. there, & on our return survey'd Gainsboroughs delightfull exhibition of Pictures much pleased with them dined at home & spent the greater part of the evening very pleasantly at M$^{rs.}$ Buxtons, about 40 people there & supt with Miss Snows.

Sunday May 17$^{th.}$

A very disagreable Day from Morn: to night, thick air, & constant small rain & the dirt intolerable, went to St Georges Church, visited all the Tracys & several others finding everyone at home, dined with the Snows meeting only poor M$^{rs.}$ Watson except their own family, refus'd staying Supper.

Monday May 18th.

Cold & stormy but dry, out several hours in the Morning visiting & shopping, dined at home, went early to a very fine Concert in Hanover Square, Miss Sabine & Miss Stone with me much entertain'd, the Prince of Wales & a good deal of fine company there, at 11 o'clock took Miss Snows & Mr. Witts to Ranelagh, which was thin but very genteel & agreable, meeting many I knew.

Tuesday May 19th.

A much finer Day than many past, call'd first on the Napers, where we met the Hunts, very happy to see them, made visits inumerable Dined at a very late hour at Mr. Arthur Stanhopes a very handsome entertainment 4 Ladies & 7 Gentlemen easy, & very agreable, went at 10 o'clock to sup at Mrs. Ecles's meeeting Mrs. Naper very pleasant. rec'd a charming account of my Dear Boys & wrote to L^{dy.} Edward Bentinck.

Wensday May 20th.

A very fine bright Day excepting a disagreable east wind, made some visits & did some business before two o'clock, when I went w^{h.} Miss Snow & Mrs. Ross & her Children into Kensington Gardens, many genteel people there, dined late at home Mr. Witts being detained at Hastings's Trial drank Tea with Mrs. Naper meeting Maria Jones then went to Lady Fanes, & from thence to Ranelagh with Sabines & Stones not a very elegant pleasant party, & from the extreme crowds quite disagreable, near 4 thousand people supposed to be there, the Snows join'd us wch. made it far better, not at home till ½ past three.

32. Kensington Palace.

Thursday May 21ˢᵗ·

Quite disagreable weather, small thick rain till quite the evening, out in the morning for two hours with Mʳ W. doing little businesses & to the exhibition in Spring Garden of the Sortie of Gibraltar, dined at Mʳ Jones's in Hatton Street meeting the Napers & my Broʳ & other company & in the evening to a talking Party at Mʳˢ· Ords not very brilliant or lively. Wrote to my sweet Francis.

Friday May 22ᵈ·

Very much the same weather dirty & disagreable & in the evening violent hard rain made 11 visits in the course of the Morning meeting many at home, dined at home, went to Drink Tea with Aunt Traceys in Green Street, & then to a very smart pleasant route at Lady Betty Chaplins,[12] many fine people & many of my acquaintance, play'd at Commerce rec'd a Letter from Lady Edward Bentinck.

Saturday May 23ᵈ·

A universal bright fine Day Mʳ & Mʳˢ· R. Witts breakfasted with us, several others friends call'd on us, & we went with my Broʳ & Sisʳ & Mʳˢ· Steer to three exhibitions,[13] dined at Mʳ Trotters meeting several strangers a very handsome entertainment but not much amusement, went afterwards to a Music & Card Party at Ldy. Lytteltons very agreable.

Sunday May 24ᵗʰ·

A thick close unpleasant Day went to church at Sᵗ· Georges, afterwards with the Snows to Kensington Gardens which were genteel & very pleasant, dined in Saville Row, Mʳ Shebeare & Mʳ Warren besides their own family & Mʳˢ· Ross in the evening, supt there & came home late rec'd a Letter from Lady Edward Bentinck.

Monday May 25ᵗʰ·

The same sort of weather, very disagreable & hot, shopp'd visited, & went to see Lear's beautifull paintings & varnishing on Tables &c, dined at Mʳ Ross's meeting Sʳ G: O: Paul Mʳ Shebbeare &c. &c. to the number of 10, all of whom went together to a benifit concert in Hanover Sqʳᵉ· not so well entertain'd as at the last Concert very hot, & bad company. rec'd Letters from Mʳˢ· Swabey & Nurse with a charming account of the Dear Boys.

Tuesday May 26ᵗʰ·

A very thick close Day quite oppressive, Mʳ Witts & I went over Westminster & London Bridge to Sᵗ· Georges in the East to see Dʳ & Mʳˢ· Mayo, met with a most friendly reception on our return visited the Tower much entertain'd by the Armoury, dined at home, & went in the evenᵍ· to an agreable party at Ldy· Clives play'd at Cribbage wrote to Mʳˢ· Swabey & Lady Edward Bentinck.[14]

---

12. Lady Elizabeth Chaplin was the sister of Brownlow Cecil, 9th Earl of Exeter (1725–1793).
13. Richard Witts' wife, Martha (1755–1815), had been born Martha Steere, so presumably Mrs Steere was her mother, sister or sister-in-law.
14. Margaret Clive, *née* Maskelyne, Lady Clive of Plassey (1735–1817). Lady Clive was a society figure and it would be interesting to find out the connection by which Agnes entered this elite circle.

Wensday May 27th

Most charming Day went early shopping, & visiting late, dined with Mrs. Tracy in Green Street meeting Guydickens's, & the Napers Drank Tea, went to Ranelagh with Col. Guydickens & his youngest Daughter, Miss Hanburys, & Miss Fanny Dolphin, the party pleasant, but it was too full & bad company.

Thursday May 28th

Quite as fine a Day, well suited to going to Epsom Races, wch. Mr Witts & I did with Miss Anne & Jane Snow much pleased with the Country which was quite new to me & tho the sport was but moderate, yet well entertain'd by the beauty of the scenery, from the crowds of Carriages & Horseman dispersed upon the varied ground; got a scrambling Dinner at the Town of Epsom, went to the evening race, & returned to Town at ½ past nine thro crowds of Carriages & clouds of dust supt in Saville row heartily fatigued.

Friday May 29th

Near as fine a Day, Miss Anne Snow & I drove about for 4 hours shopping dined very chearfully in Saville Row meeting S^r G: O: Paul,[15] all went together to a Route at Mrs. Ross's very agreable, Mr Witts staid supper but I went to Ranelagh with Mrs. Naper & the two Miss Dolphins the party most pleasant but it was disagreable, bad company very dark, & the floor wretched to walk on.

33. *Epsom.*

15.   Sir George Onesiphorus Paul (1746–1820). Sir George was to become famous for his prison reforms and a large memorial to him is in Gloucester Cathedral. He lived at Hill House, Rodborough, Gloucestershire, and was well known to Edward and Agnes Witts. His sister married into the Snow family; Sir George died without issue. On his death, Hill House went to his nephew, Robert Snow, who changed his name to Robert Snow Paul.

34. Chelsea Hospital with Ranelagh Rotunda.

Saturday May 30[th.]

A stormy disagreable Morning & turn'd to excessive hard rain in the evening; made some visits after Breakfast, & then Miss Snow M[r.] Witts & I went to survey Lees & Kennedys Nursery a delightfull shew of Plants, which sent us home in a poorer state than we went. dined at home & were to have gone in a large pleasant party to Vauxhall, but weather prevented. ourselves & several of the party met in Saville Row, play'd at Loo, had a little Dance & supt.

Sunday May 31[st.]

Dry & fine till mid-day, when there was most frequent & tremendous Showers for the remainder of the Day, took Miss Chaplin after having been at St. Georges Church, into the Park by way of enjoying her company instead of Kensington Gardens, made some visits, & dined late in Saville Row meeting M[r.] & M[rs.] Tho[s.] Chaplin & others staid supper & were very merry.

Monday June 1[st.]

Very showery in the Morning but fine after mid-day Breakfasted very agreably with Miss Pyke & Miss Anne Warburton, made many visits & finish'd much business; dined comfortably enough with M[r.] Sabine & his family in their Lodgings & went with them to Drury Lane Theatre to see M[rs.] Jordan in the Country Girl, a very crowded House & dreadfully hot, but never better entertain'd. rec'd a Letter from Nurse.[16]

---

16. William Wycherley (1641–1715). The Restoration play *The Country Girl* was made famous by David Garrick, who altered it by taking out the licentious passages. Dorothy Jordan, in the character of Peggy, made it very successful.

35. Old Drury Lane Theatre.

Tuesday June 2^d.

A universal warm fine Day M^rs. Naper Breakfasted here but the comfort much interrupted by variety of tradespeople & other business, visited about till time to Dress, dined at Lady Betty Chaplins meeting to the number of 12, a very agreable party, at 9 o'clock went to M^rs. Steers's meeting Boddingtons &c. play'd at Whist, at home early to write &c.

Wensday June 3^d.

A stormy disagreable Morning, & after 6 o'clock the most violent hard rain, quite a deluge, plagued & worried to death by the unpunctuality of tradespeople & the hurry of packing, at 12 o'clock went with Miss Snows to Ranelagh to see the remaining ornaments of the Spanish Ambassadors Ball for the Queen, a very pretty scene & must have been beautifull by Candlelight. could not leave Town till three o'clock, dined comfortably at Stanmore & got to Michelefield Green as it was dark, met with the usual kind reception from our agreable friends, found M^r & Mrs. Cumberland with them wch. prevented our sleeping there, & went after supper to sleep at Mr Ross's. rec'd a good account of my Dear Boys.

Thursday June 4th.

Perpetual hard showers and alternate bright sunshine, wch. prevented all moving except to the Greenhouse & Garden, not much delighted with our Lodging at Michelefield Hall & determined not to make use of it again, day spent very pleasantly, Mr Cumberlands conversation very brilliant, play'd at Cribbage & wrote to Miss Anne Snow & Francis & went to the Bell at Rickmansworth to sleep, very tolerable accomodation distance near 4 miles.

Friday June 5th.

Most wretched Day, perpetual rain till afternoon, much conversation; after Dinner Lady Edward & I in our Chaise took a pleasant airing & return'd to Tea play'd at Whist much enlivened by Mr Cumberlands brilliant wit.

Saturday June 6th.

A tolerable fine Morning, but soon after our arrival from Rickmansworth it became perpetual rain & ceased not till quite evening sat waiting all Day in expectation of being able to take an airing but in vain. a Mr Kingston dined here. play'd both at Whist & Cribbage in the evening.

Sunday June 7th.

A much better Day than many former ones, scarce any rain but very high wind we Breakfasted at our Inn for the sake of going to Church heard an excellent sermon from a London Preacher, sat in Mr Earles seat, Mr Vic: Earle read Prayers, & afterwards we went with him, to see his Brother at Moor House a mile & half distant, an odd old Place, but good Garden & many comforts. did not reach Michelefield Green till Dinner time. in the afternoon took Ldy. Edwd. & Mrs. Cumberland to Langley Bury, Sir Beaumont Hothams to Drink Tea,[17] rather a laughable visit Mr Manners Drank Tea & supt here. rec'd a Letter from Miss Anne Snow & wrote to my Sister Travell.

Monday June 8th.

Quite a universal fine Day like summer come at last, Mr & Mrs. Cumberland & their daughter went away, & Lord Edward to Town to attend the House of Commons but return'd at night. Mr Witts went Trout fishing with Mr Manners, & Ldy. Edward & I went to the Grove to see Ldy. Clarendon,[18] a very pretty place & an obliging reception from thence to Ld. Essexs at Cassiobury to survey the Hot Houses &c rather disappointed;[19] Mr Manners Dined & supt here & play'd many rubbers at Cribbage in the evening

Tuesday June 9th.

As fine a Day but with less sun in the Morning Ldy. Edward & I in the Chaise & Mr Witts on Horseback went to survey the beauties of Moor Park with which we were well pleased in the afternoon were much in the Garden, & play'd at Cribbage in the evening. rec'd a Letter from Mrs. Naper & another from Nurse & wrote to Mrs. Granville a Letter long owed.

Wensday June 10th.

Much the same kind of weather dark heavy cloud: like rain but none fell & in the evening bright & fair. Left Michelefield Green at 9 o'clock always parting with our aimable friends with strong regret, went thro' Amersham to High Wycombe, where we took a very early

---

17. Admiral William Hotham, 1st Baron Hotham (1736–1813). Hotham was the son of Sir Beaumont Hotham (d. 1771) and had a distinguished career in the Royal Navy. He was present at the relief of Gibraltar and in 1790 was Rear Admiral of the Red. It is possible that this was the admiral's brother and not the admiral himself.
18. Charlotte Villiers, *née* Capell, Countess Clarendon (1721–1790).
19. William Capell, 4th Earl of Essex (1732–1799).

Dinner, drank Tea at Tetsworth, where we had Miss Lucy Napleton added to our party, who we stumbled upon out of a stage Coach, sent my Maid in her Place & took her with us to Oxford in the Chaise slept at the Star well tired.

Thursday June 11th.

No change in the weather close & hot, executed some little businesses after Breakfast & made a chearfull visit to Mrs. Wickham, thought our drive home very tedious being so anxious to see my sweet Boys, who met us with mutual Joy, never saw them look better & the place in high beauty & luxuriance, walket about a good deal & rec'd a Letter from my Sister Travell.

Friday June 12th.

A very thick Fog in the Morning but clear'd off, to be a very fine Day, warm & growing, but rather flighting, & our fruit trees shew'd there had been many of such Days, much engaged all Day long with unpacking & setting things in order, hardly allow'd myself time to enjoy the Dear Boys.

Saturday June 13th.

Quite a fine Day, actual summer come at last, so much engaged in setting a variety of things I scarce allow'd myself time to walk out, wrote to Mrs. Tyrwhitt, Mrs. Rollinson & to my Sister Travell.

Sunday June 14th.

Not so fine a Day east wind & realy cold, we walke'd to & from Church, our Horses being gone to Banbury to bring Mr. Sabine & his Son & Daughter here, who arrived to Dinner who were conversible, & the father more agreable than usual walket out in the evening. wrote to L^{dy.} Edwd. Bentinck.

Monday June 15th.

A very fine Day warm sun & clear air, walket out after Breakfast, the Gents' rode to Heythrop & Caroline & I conversed on many subjects relative to her own family & concerns, & shed many tears on the relation of her poor Mothers Death in the evening walket to Swerford. wrote to Mrs. Naper

Tuesday June 16th.

Another very warm fine Day at 12 o'clock. went with Miss Sabine & her Brother in our Chaise to Heythrop, walket over the Conservatory & then took Joseph to take his place in a Coach for London where he was going to keep them at Lincolns Inn, very sorry to part with him, drove by C: Norton home, Mr. Evans dined with us & all took a walk in the evening. all my Boys ill with colds.

Wensday June 17th.

Frequent hard Showers in the course of the Day unable to walk out till quite evening, Gentlemen fishing in the Morning, rec'd Letters from Mrs. Rollinson & Mrs. Drake with the pleasing news of Mrs. Tyrwhitts being brought to Bed of a Son & answer'd it, & wrote to Mrs. Eliza Tracy & Miss Snow.

Thursday June 18th.

The most intire Day of violent hard rain I ever saw, got up early to see the Sabines set off on their Journey at seven o'clock, but they waited in vain till eleven, for a dry hour when they departed almost in a deluge, felt much at parting with poor Caroline, little knowing when I might see her again & seeing the difficulty of her situation. Far from well all Day myself.

Friday June 19th.

Fine Day excepting 2 or 3 slight Showers & some heavy clouds & a little Thunder walket a little in the Morning, M^{r.} & Mrs. Western (glad to see him more recover'd than I expected)[20] Dined here & staid late in the evening, rec'd a most pleasing & affectionate Letter from L^{dy.} Edwd. Bentinck & wrote to Mrs. Rollinson.

Saturday June 20th.

Had been a most violent night of hard rain, the wind extremely high, with some slight showers during the Day, Mr. Witts went to call on Mr. Tyrwhitt, & brought back a very good account of both her & the Baby, I walket a little both Morn: & evening. rec'd a Letter from Miss Snow Mr. Hoskins here in the Morn:

Sunday June 21st.

A stormy Morning, with very heavy threatening clouds, but very little rain till the afternoon, when it came on most violently & continued the whole evening, with some distant Thunder went to Church in the Morning, but prevented by the weather from going in the afternoon, read & play'd with the Boys & very busy at accompts.

Monday June 22^{d.}

Constant violent rain till 5 o'clock in the afternoon, when a high wind dispersed the clouds & it was clear & fine, Mr. Witts took the opportunity of going to Chip: which he had been waiting for all Day. rec'd a Letter from my Sister Travell.

Tuesday June 23^{d.}

Cloudy but dry till mid-day when the showers came so violent & frequent that it might be call'd perpetual hard rain being before engaged went thro it to Drink Tea at Wigginton where I had not been since Decr. last, roads dreadfull & the visit dull & stupid as usual Mr. Harry Davis there rec'd a Letter from Mrs. Naper & wrote to Mrs. Buxton.

Wensday June 24th.

A very nasty Morning with Fogg & flying Mist, which never kindly went off & at Noon turn'd to hard steady rain for the remainder of the Day & dismally cold. Mr. Witts went to Chip: Mr. Tyrwhitt & Mrs. Drake sat an hour with me in the Morn: & Mrs. Rollinson & her Daughter Mary & Mr. Evans Dined here, & the latter staid late. happy to see Mrs. Rollinson in so much better health.

---

20. There is no mention here of the death of the three-month-old Maximilian Western, who died on 30 April 1789.

Thursday June 25[th.]

Constant hard soaking rain excepting for an hour at noon, when my Brother Travell & M[r] Francis took the opportunity of calling here glad to see the latter look better than I expected; pursued a variety of employs in the course of the Day & wrote to Miss Anne Snow.

Friday y[e] 26[th.]

For a great wonder an intire fine Day without rain, strong wind & bright sun which a little served to dry up the extreme damps of the earth, walket several times in the Day, happy to be able to make use of my legs. rec'd a Letter from my Bro[r] Ferdinand & wrote to my Sister Travell.

Saturday June 27[th.]

A very bright shewey Morning but soon clouded, & by 11 o'clock there was a most violent shower, & so continued at frequent intervals the whole of the Day, with a good deal of thunder, not at all suited to our engagement of Dining at M[r] Westerns where we met M[r] & M[rs.] Penyston & M[rs.] Rollinson pleasant visit enough, but the roads more intolerably bad than if in winter & the Kingham water very deep.

Sunday June 28[th.]

Much such another Day only if possible the storms were more heavy, & quite bitterly cold, contrived to get to Church in the Morning, had a most excellent Sermon from M[r] Evans, had much pleasure in the Dear Boys, read, & wrote a great deal of accompts.

Monday June 29[th.]

A cloudy, cold, stormy Day but scarce any rain fell, which made it possible for me to be out a good deal, my Brother Travell & M[r] Francis dined here, too cold in the evening to walk out. wrote to Lady Edward Bentinck.

36. Haymaking.

Tuesday June 30th.

A tolerably fine day with a mixture of clouds & sunshine, but considerably warmer & more like summer, dined at Mrs. Rollinsons meeting M^r & Mrs. Western & Mr Sandby, walket about a great deal, quite a pretty Haymaking scene. rec'd Letters from M^{rs.} E: Tracy & Miss Anne Snow

Wensday July 1st.

Quite the reverse of yesterday in point of weather, being dark, cloudy, & very stormy had been a good deal of rain in the night & begun raining again after Dinner & so continued all the evening, Mr Witts at Chip in the Morning, wrote to Mrs. Naper, & rec'd a Letter from Mrs. Granville

Thursday July 2^{d.}

A close, warm, cloudy Morning but clear'd off at Noon, & was the finest evening possible quite summer. M^r & Mrs. Penyston & her Sister Miss Asheton, Mrs. Rollinson, M^r & Mrs. Western & my Brother Travell & Mr Evans all Dined here, the Day passet off very chearfully, more easy then usual walket out after Tea.

Friday July 3^{d.}

By far the finest Day there had been the whole summer, constant sun & quite a hot air in & out the whole Day enjoying it much, & seeing a whole large field of sandfoid cut down in the Day by 8 Mowers. rec'd a Letter from my Sister Travell & wrote to Mrs. Tywhitt.

Saturday July 4th.

A sad reverse of weather, for there was most violent hard rain in the night accompanied by Thunder, & it proved a most disagreable Day, thick close oppressive air with frequent showers & towards evening it became a settled rain; I was very far from well all Day.

Sunday July 5th.

Constant hard soaking rain till 2 o'clock impossible to go to Church in the Morning, & it was scarce over in the afternoon when it began again but was fine in the evening. went from Church to the Girls Sunday school, & with Mr Witts & the eldest Boys drank Tea with my Bro^r Travell at Swerford much after the old rate. wrote to my Sister Travell.

Monday July 6th.

A bright fine Morning but by 12 became very stormy & showery, & so continued the whole Day, & was close & hot. Mr Witts on horseback & myself, Francis & Prissick in the Chaise went to my Brother Ferdinands at Upper Slaughter, found him tolerably well & agreably surrounded by Mrs. Dolphin & her two charming Daughters no moving out of the House all the evening but much conversation.

Tuesday July 7th.

Cloudy but pleasant all the Morn^g but turn'd out hard rain in the afternoon & all the evening, walket in the Garden in the Morning, the Gents & Miss Fanny Dolphin rode out much pleasant converse & at night play'd at Cribbage.

Wensday July 8th.

Very much the same Day as the last showery in the Morning, & continued rain in the afternoon Mrs. Smith from Ford here the greater part of the Morning, the Gentlemen & & Miss Fanny rode out.

Thursday July 9th.

Heavy clouds & great appearance of rain, but none fell, warm & pleasant, Mr. Witts went into Oxfordshire & did not return till Tea time; Mr. Jones dined here, Mrs. Dolphin, Fanny & I walke'd to see Mrs. Burrows in the evening. rec'd Letters from Ldy. Edwd. Bentinck, Mrs. Tyrwhitt, Mrs. Buxton & Miss Snow.

Friday July 10th.

Quite hard soaking rain the greater part of the Day only clearing up at Tea time, after which my Brother & Mr. Witts rode out, & we Ladies walket a little in the Garden. entertain'd at different times of the Day by reading Mrs. Piozzis Tour into Italy &c. a singular stile.[21]

Saturday July 11th.

Hard showers both Morning & evening but fine between & suffer'd us to walk between; & Mr. Witts & Miss Fanny rode out in the Morning; the Gentlemen went to Dine at Mr. Dixons at Oddington to meet a party; we worket & read & were very comfortable & pleasant together.

Sunday July 12th.

An intire Day of hard soaking rain from Morning till night not an interval of five minutes impossible for any Lady to go to church either time, much reading & walking, & more pleasant conversation wrote to Mrs. Granville.

Monday July 13th.

Thick fog & some rain till 9 o'clock from which time it was dry till near two when a most violent thunder storm came on, & it was hardly dry any more the whole Day; bid adieu to Upper Slaughter with some regret after having spent a very pleasant week with such agreable friends, but always happy to come home to my sweet Boys who we found very well. rec'd a Letter from Mrs. Naper.

Tuesday July 14th.

A tolerably fine Dry, Day, till Dinner time, when it became showery, & towards night became constant flying rain, out a great deal in the Morning, in the Garden &c. wrote to Mrs. Swabey.

Wensday July 15th.

Cloudy but dry till 11 o'clock when it began raining & so continued without ceasing the whole Day, I luckily got a walk before it began. Mr. Witts spent the greater part of the Day at a Turnpike meeting at Chipping. Nor. the Boys all dined with me very happy. rec'd a Letter from my Sist Travell & wrote to Mrs. Naper & Mrs. E: Tracy.

---

21. Hester Lynch Piozzi (1741–1821).

Thursday July 16th.

Very threatening for rain but none fell till three or four in the afternoon when there was 2 or 3 hard showers wch. I just escaped on my return from visiting Mrs. Tyrwhitt, meeting Mrs. Wickham & Mrs. Drake there, my Brother Travell & Frank dined here.

Friday July 17th.

Tolerably fine excepting 2 or three short slight Showers in the afternoon, walket out a great deal, Mr Witts at Chip: some hopes the weather would be fine & Dry. wrote to Miss Chaplin.

Saturday July 18th.

For a wonder no rain the whole Day but warm & very fine & well suited to Haymaking in which were very busy & out many times in the Day amongst it. Mr Tyrwhitt, Dr Drake & his eldest son here in the Morning, rec'd a Letter from Miss A. Snow

Sunday July 19th.

Not so fine a Day, & a smart shower while we were at Church in the afternoon, attended the Sunday schools both before & after, & took a very long walk in the fields in the evening. wrote to Miss Snow & rec'd a Letter from Miss Amelia Sabine.

Monday July 20th.

A most brilliant fine Hot Day throughout, well adapted to carrying a great deal of Hay & making a Rick, we dined at my Brot Travells at Swerford taking Francis with us, rather a better thing than usual, they walket almost home with us wrote to Lady Edward Bentinck.

Tuesday July 21st.

Quite as fine a Morning but before mid-day grew cloudy, with heavy thundery appearance, & at the close of Day it began raining very hard. Mr Hoskins & Mr Evans dined here & walket with us in the evening. rec'd a very friendly Letter from Mrs. Catherine Thornton.

Wensday July 22d.

Fine in the Morning, but was such constant hard Thunder storms from ten to three that it might be almost call'd perpetual violent rain, I was confined in the Green House a considerable time. the earth too wet to venture out in the evening with my Rhumatism, worket & read much & wrote in the Morning to my Sister Travell.

Thursday July 23d.

Very stormy & showery, tho no rain of any great consequence fell, but most threatening clouds which prevented my venturing to accept of my Brother Travells invitation to either dine or drink Tea, in Mr Witts's absence, who went very early in the Morning to Oxford to the Assizes the children dined & were much with me.

Friday July 24th.

Bright & fine till noon when it overcast & there were several slight showers in the course of the Day, Mr Witts return'd from Oxford very early in the Day & we went to Dine at Mrs.

Rollinsons taking Francis with us & meeting my Bro.ʳ Travell, dry in the evening to come home. rec'd a Letter from my Brother Ferdinand, & wrote to Miss A: Sabine

Saturday July 25ᵗʰ·

Cloudy & stormy but no rain fell of any consequence till the evening, when it became very steady & quite put a stop to walking, Mʳ Witts at Chip: in the Morning. wrote to my Brother Ferdinand & Mʳˢ· Naper.

Sunday July 26ᵗʰ·

A very fine pleasant Day, dry air, & a good deal of sun but not very warm went to church twice & walket out in the evening received a Letter from Miss Snow with the dismal account of poor Mʳ & Mʳˢ· Ross's having been thrown out of a Gig & both very much hurt. quite low all Day

Monday July 27ᵗʰ·

A brilliant fine Morning, but changed sadly at Noon to violent Thunderstorms which lasted more or less the whole Day, Mʳ Witts went to Kingham, & Mʳ Roberts sat an hour or two with me & was a very agreable companion wrote to Miss Snow & Mʳˢ· Buxton.

Tuesday July 28ᵗʰ·

As usual very threatening heavy clouds, & hard rain inplaces, but we were fortunate to both go & return from Dining at Lᵈʸ· Fanes without having any, a fine star light night & strong Northern lights. Lady Reade, Mʳˢ· Cotton & Mʳ Sandys at Little Compton, the old Lady much broke & more than ever infirm. play'd at Quadrille a very sad piece of work, to get thro one Pool.

Wensday July 29ᵗʰ·

Gloomy & frequent small showers in the course of the Morning, but fine in the evening, I was nearly wet thro' in one, Dʳ Williams here in the Morning, & in the afternoon we took the eldest Boys to see their Uncles Hay carried in the New close & Drank Tea with my Bro.ʳ rec'd a Letter from my Sister Travell.

Thursday July 30ᵗʰ·

Cloudy but no rain & in the evening a very strong dew, Mʳ Witts at Chip: in the Morning, in the evening walket to the high Wood close to see the new cut Hay. rec'd Letters from Mʳˢ· Naper & Miss Snow, answer'd Miss Snows & wrote to Miss Guydickens.

Friday July 31ˢᵗ·

Cold & stormy till 11 o'clock, when it began raining very hard & continued the whole Day & evening most violently without any cessation, Mʳ Witts return'd from Chip: (where he had been to meet Mʳ Penyston on business) wet thro'. Mʳ & Mʳˢ· Western dined here, & would return home in spite of our intreaties. rec'd a Letter from Mʳˢ· Eliza: Tracy

Saturday Augˢᵗ· 1ˢᵗ·

High wind, but dry & tolerably fine the whole Day, I went soon after Breakfast to see Mʳˢ· Tyrwhitt & after having made her a chatty long visit call'd on Mʳˢ· Rollinson &

returnd home to a four o'clock Dinner; walket out in the evening. rec'd a Letter from Miss Guydickens to refuse going with me to Oxford Races.

Sunday Aug$^{st.}$ *2*$^{d.}$

A very fine warm brilliant Day, till afternoon when it clouded over & was a small shower, at church both times, taking little Edward in the afternoon for the first time & he behaved very well went to the Girls school wrote to my Sister Travell.

Monday Aug$^{st.}$ *3*$^{d.}$

An intire fine Day hot sun, well suited to Haymaking, better than to our meeting of the members of the Book Club at C: House of which Dr Williams was steward, & appointed me his Lady President w$^{ch.}$ I would gladly have waved sat down 20 to Dinner, 9 Clergymen, 4 Laymen & 7 Ladies, upon the whole agreable enough, more so than usual. rec'd a Letter from Miss Chaplin

Tuesday Aug$^{st.}$ *4*$^{th.}$

Still hot & fine, but more oppressive, from heavy clouds some part of the Day & a strong South east wind. My Bro^{r} Travell & Mr Francis breakfasted here, & Mr Earle came in the Morning, & walke'd with us to the High Wood Close where we sat an hour or two surveying the making of the Rick, & carrying the Hay. In the afternoon busy preparing for Oxford Race. rec'd a Letter from Miss Snow & wrote to M$^{rs.}$ C: Thornton.

Wensday Aug$^{st.}$ *5*$^{th.}$

Very heavy & cloudy & in the afternoon strong wind & a little very small flying rain. Set out between 11 & 12 for Oxford Race, stopp'd at Woodstock to bait the Horses & get a hurrying Dinner which from the Inn being so full was obliged to be sent to us to a private house near. went to the course; where was better sport than could have been expected from the Horses & very wet state of the meadow, a good many carriages & smart people, went to the Star to drink Tea & take possession of our apartments, & then to the Musick room, not at all entertain'd both Concert & company very bad supt & went to Bed early to prepare for the fatigues of the next Day

Thursday Aug$^{st.}$ *6*$^{th.}$

A very fine Day excepting high wind which was disagreeable, went to Breakfast with M$^{rs.}$ Wickham meeting D^{r} & M$^{rs.}$ Drake & Mr Tyrwhitt all went together in proper time to the Public Breakfast where was a great mixture of company tho the bad rather prevail'd but the variety of odd figures made it very amusing, visited afterwards & went to the Ladies Ordinary where was about 30, & 6 of them Gentlemen, hot, formal, & rather disagreable went to the Race, where the sport was very moderate indeed went up into the new Stand for the Ladies, w$^{ch.}$ would have been very pleasant but for a cold high wind, home to Dress & then to the Ball with M$^{rs.}$ Drake, which was very full & a great deal of good company, staid late & then a party of fifty adjourn'd to a supper at the Star rather dull & stupid, not in Bed till 5 in the Morn: & got no sleep at all from the great noise in the House.

Friday Aug.^{st.} 7th.

Quite as fine a Day more pleasant from the wind not being so high, breakfasted late made some visits, & left Oxford at one, & home to a late Dinner, found the Dears all well, went to Drink Tea at Mr Earles, meeting Mr Sandby & Mr Evans, rather a dull business, but I was so tired & sleepy I could scarce keep my eyes open & did go to Bed the moment I came home.

Saturday Aug.^{st.} 8th.

A prodigeous fine Day, quite hot, Mr Witts at Chipping Norton, & Mr Hoskins visited me always agreable. Miss Snows came from Town about 8 o'clock most happy to see them a very chatty evening. Mr Sandby Breakfasted here.

Sunday Aug.^{st.} 9th.

Very fine hot weather, tho with too much wind for pleasure, Miss Anne Snow went in the Morning to church & Miss Snow in the evening, where was much violent bad singing & my two Dear eldest Boys gain'd much credit by saying their Catechism in the Church for the first time; took a very pleasant walk in the evening wrote to Mrs. Naper.

Monday Aug.^{st.} 10th.

Just such another fine warm Day too hot to walk much in the Morning, worket & chatted very comfortably, Mr Leigh his Aunt M.^{rs.} E Leigh & Miss Twisleton, (Mrs. Leigh not well enough to come) dined here & also Mr Earle an easy chearfull visit after they were gone walket & play'd a rubber at whist rec'd a Letter from my Sister Travell & wrote to Mrs. Tyrwhitt

Tuesday Aug.^{st.} 11th.

Most charming weather, not quite so hot as the former Days therefore much pleasanter moving walket in the Morning, & after Dinner Miss Anne Snow & I & George went to Heythrope to see the Conservatory & Garden, & coming home by C: Norton & the Chappel House were not at home till supper time wrote to my Sis.^t Travell

Wensday Aug.^{st.} 12th.

A most wonderfull hot Day quite overcoming, we were almost broil'd going in the two Post Chaises to Dine at Mr Leighs at Adlestrop, first making a short visit at the Parsonage, sat down 11 to Dinner, rather formal but Mrs. Leigh is always pleasant & agreable not at home till quite late. rec'd a Letter from Lady Hereford & answer'd it. a small shower at night

Thursday Aug.^{st.} 13th.

Not so hot but much more agreable, out a great deal in the Morning among the Hay in the Valley, drank Tea on the pleasure ground & afterwards walket to visit Mr Earle & brought him & Mr Evans home with us to Cards & Supper. rec'd Letters from Mrs. Tyrwhitt & Mrs. Savage

Friday Aug.^{st.} 14th.

A very pleasant Day fine air & not much sun quite propitious for our friends journey to Sir George Pauls, on wch. they set out at 9 o'clock always sorry to part with them, Mr Witts &

I dined at M.ᵉ Tyrwhitts, no company there, but a most friendly pleasant visit not at home till late. wrote to M.ʳˢ Savage & M.ʳˢ Western & rec'd a Letter from the latter.

Saturday Aug.ˢᵗ 15.ᵗʰ

Much the same kind of weather, till Dinner time when there was a most sudden & violent storm of Hail, w.ᶜʰ did not last long but the remainder of the Day was dull & sober, M.ᵉ Witts at Chip in the Morning, & walket a little in the evening.

Sunday Aug.ˢᵗ 16.ᵗʰ

Very fine clear Day with a good deal of wind, at Church both Morning & evening, after which went to Drink Tea at Wigginton, a visit much in the old stile no one there but the two old Ladies, rec'd Letters from M.ʳˢ Naper & my Sister Travell.

Monday Aug.ˢᵗ 17.ᵗʰ

Weather quite pleasant & similar, went at Mid-day, to call on M.ʳˢ Penyston & spent a very pleasant hour Lady Fane calling there likewise, went to Dine at M.ᵉ Westerns where M.ᵉ Witts met me, & we found our agreable friends M.ᵉ & M.ʳˢ Savage there who I am always happy to meet. rec'd a long Letter from Miss Anne Snow, & answer'd it, & wrote to my Sister Travell.

Tuesday Aug.ˢᵗ 18.ᵗʰ

No change of weather quite as fine, M.ᵉ Evans breakfasted here, & we went to Dine at the Public Day at Blenheim, rather warm going there, the Dutchess not being well did not appear till Ten, but the young Ladies amply supplied her place at Dinner where was 28 in number, only 9 Ladies & those not very resplendent but I fell into a very pleasant party & liked it very well, home between 10 & 11 by the finest light of the stars I ever saw.

37. Caroline, Duchess of Marlborough.

Witts Family Papers F176

1789

Wens.ᵗ August 19ᵗʰ·

Very hot in the Morning & quite broiling in the evening, very busy packing & preparing to leave home dined with the Children at ½ past one, soon after which Mᵉ Witts set off for Enstone to go in a Coach to London on business, & I with Francis for Lower Slaughter, the Sun in our eyes most disagreable, found our friends at Tea with my Brother & Mʳˢ· Ecles's added to them took a little walk afterwards & Mʳˢ· Naper & I had much talk till we went to Bed. rec'd a Letter from Mʳˢ· Dolphin & answer'd it.

Thursday Augˢᵗ· 20ᵗʰ·

Dark & gloomy all the Morning & frequent Showers of small rain, hot & oppressive, Mʳˢ· N. & I went out in the Phaeton but were soon driven back by the rain, drank Tea at Upper Slaughter very chearfully & pleasantly.

Friday Augˢᵗ· 21ˢᵗ·

Much the same Morning as the last but it was a tolerable fine evening, left L. Slaughter at 11, call'd at Sandywell for an hour, thought Mʳˢ· Tracy looket but indifferent, got to Cheltenham at three, met with a pleasing reception from my Sisters my Brother dined out, & Dʳ Napleton dined with us agreable as usual, much concern'd it was the only time we should see him, Mʳˢ· Rollinson, Mʳˢ· Wickham & Mᵉ & Mʳˢ· Western drank Tea, went to the Rooms 5 or 6 Card Tables, I play'd a merry Game at Cribbage with Mᵉ & Mʳˢ· Cox & Mʳˢ· Egerton had the Joy of receiving a Letter from my Dear Husband & one from Mʳˢ· Granville. Mʳˢ· Egerton supt.

Saturday Augˢᵗ· 22ᵈ·

A bright shewey Morning but there was frequent slight showers in the course of the Day, went to the Well in the Morning, not a very brilliant appearance of company, rec'd numerous morning visits & walket a little before Dressing for Dinner to which came Mʳˢ· Rollinson & Mʳˢ· Jones, Mʳˢ· Sprigg & Miss Peggy Hibbert, my Sister Catherine, Francis & I went to the Play Lady Howes ordering sat in her Box very little amused with anything but Tom Thumb rec'd a Letter from Mᵉ Witts & wrote to Mʳˢ· Savage.

Sunday Augˢᵗ· 23ᵈ·

Quite a beautifull Day from Morn: to night, I set out from Cheltenham at little after 9 & got to Sir George Pauls at Hill House near Rodbro' between 12 & one, a most charming drive of 18 miles much struck with the beauty of the place & situation, very agreably rec'd by the Bart. & his & my surrounding friends sat out of Doors & walket till Dinner time soon after which Mr Robert Snow was obliged to set off for London had a syllabub out of Doors, drank Tea late & play'd at Tron Madame. rec'd another Letter from Mr Witts.

Monday Aug.st 24.th
Foggy in the Morning but most delightfully fine all the Day, Mr Snow went away after Breakfast, two Ladies made a visit & at mid-day Miss Snow & I in a Phaeton the rest on Horseback, took a most charming airing, views quite enchanting, & much struck with the many beauties of my Lord Ducies Place at Woodchester Park scarce time to Dress before Dinner, soon after which came two Miss Hawkers pretty Girls who staid the whole evening, we all walke'd & after dark playd at Lottery Tickets. Wrote to Mr Witts & My Sis.^{er} Travell.

Tuesday Aug.st 25.th
Not quite so fine a Day more wind & less warm, & in the afternoon a small shower or two. Miss Snow & I took another very pleasant drive in the Phaeton, & saw many sweet & different views. Mr Snow return'd to Dinner, & M.^r & Mrs Pettat came a little walking in the evening, much lively conversation & a Table at Whist & Cribbage.

Wensday Aug.st 26.th
A gloomy dark morning, & soon after Breakfast began raining & continued several hours, our whole party went in 4 carriages to dine at Mr Hyetts at Painswick where we found M.^r & Mrs Probyn & 4 Daughters & Miss Hunt so sat down 16 to Dinner hot, & dull, but Mrs H. was very civil, & obliging, walket in the Gardens & I came away before Tea was over, yet did not reach Cheltenham till past nine o'clock, where I join'd my Sisters at the rooms for half an hour. found Francis quite well & had the happiness of receiving a long letter from Mr Witts & another from Nurse with a very good account of the Dear Boys at home. wrote to Mrs Naper.

Thursday Aug.st 27.th
A very fine brilliant hot Day several visitors before 12, when I went out & made more & walket a little Miss Hughes dined here, & we went to drink Tea at Mrs Wickhams, meeting Mrs Foley, Mrs Rollinson, & Mrs Jones, & play'd 2 Rubbers at Whist before we went to the Ball, which was a good one in point of numbers but such very bad company that I found it very dull & stupid & glad to come home early. rec'd a Letter from Mr Witts & answer'd it & wrote to Nurse. A letter from Miss Sabine

Friday Aug.st 28.th
Much such another Day, the Morning spent as usual in paying & receiving visits, Mrs Rollinson, & Mrs Jones, & Mrs Wickham dined here M.^r & Mrs Dunster Miss Vernon, Mr Pettyworth & Mr Blackwood drank Tea, & all adjourn'd, to the Rooms which were pretty good ones, play'd at Commerce in a large stupid party, rewarded by dividing a Pool, after which went to see Miss Snows & their Nephew who were arrived at the George Inn & had a merry supper with them

Saturday Aug^{st.} 29th.

Most prodigeously hot, much Hotter than any Day the whole summer, quite oppressive in this warm situation walket to the well with the Snows who breakfasted here, visited & dawdled about as usual, I went to drink Tea at the George with the Snows & Sir G: Paul & all went to the Play well entertain'd by the Brothers & the Commisary in both of which Quick perform'd principal parts.[1] Looket in at dull rooms, supt at the Inn with my friends very gaily. rec'd a Letter from Mr. Witts & Mrs. Buxton.

Sunday Aug^{st.} 30th.

A very thick falling fog in the Morn: & turn'd at Noon to settled hard rain which continued the whole remainder of the Day, got tolerably to church in the Morning, an elegant good sermon by a young divine, confined an hour afterwards at a visit at Mrs. Rollinsons with many others, by driving early & not able to go to church a very long afternoon, drank Tea at the George with the Snows & Sir George Paul, merry & comfortable. wrote a Letter to Mr. Witts.

Monday Aug^{st.} 31st.

Quite a thick damp disagreable Morning, but very little rain fell in the course of the Day tho it appear'd so lowering, went to the Well to begin drinking the waters, visited much after Breakfast, my Brother Ferdinand came to dinner in his way into Shropshire, Miss Snows also dined, & Mrs. Egerton & Miss Upton came to Tea as also Mrs. Rollinson & Mrs. Jones, all went to the Ball wch. was a pretty good one play'd at Cribbage. wrote to Mrs. Tyrwhitt.

38. *The effects of Cheltenham waters.*

1. John Quick (1748–1831). Quick was a London-born actor famed as a comedian. *The Brothers* was a play by Richard Cumberland (1732–1811), who was well known to Agnes and Edward Witts.

39. Sandywell.

Tuesday Sep^{t.} 1st.

Most violent hard rain from Morn: to night quite impossible to go to the well to drink water, my Bro^r went after an early Breakfast Miss Snows here the greater part of the morning my Sis^r Catherine & I went to drink Tea with Mrs. Cox at the Cottage who sent her chaise for us. very good rooms a merry party at Cribbage rec'd a Letter from my Husband with the joyfull news of his speedy arrival & a charming account of my little loves from home.

Wensday Sep^{t.} 2^{d.}

A fine shewey Morning but frequent hard storms in the course of the Day, Mr Witts arrived at Noon by the Coach having travell'd all night, happy to see him return, many visitors in the Morning, Miss Snows dined here, & M^r & Mrs. Wilmot, L^{dy.} Fr. Balmley Miss Vernon, Mr Hardinge & Mr Mackay drank Tea went to the Rooms, & divided another Pool at Commerce

Thursday Sep^{t.} 3^{d.}

Wet disagreable Morning, fine at mid-day but was most violent hard rain in the evening attended with strong thunder & Lightning, carried to the Well in the Morning by Miss Snow, & after breakfast attended both Sisters on a visit to Sandywell,[2] found Mrs. Serle there, drank Tea with Miss Snows & went to the Ball which was more lively & a better than usual. play'd at Cribbage. rec'd a Letter from Mrs. Naper.

---

2.   Sandywell was the home of the Travell sisters' aunts, the Miss Tracys.

Friday Sep.^t 4th.

Much the same kind of weather, went to the Well with M^rs. Cox, frequent showers in the course of the Day but not enough to prevent visiting & parading Miss Snows, Lord Fauconberg, & Mr Dunster dined here very lively & agreable. M^rs. Cox drank Tea play'd at Cribbage at the Rooms which were brilliant 3 Commerce Tables & 4 others

Saturday Sep.^t 5th.

Some few trifling showers in the early part of the Day, & afterwards very fine, M^rs. Tracy & M^rs. Serle here from Sandywell in the Morning, Miss Vernon Mr Hardinge, & Mr Mackay dined here, Miss Snows drank Tea & Mr Witts & I went with them to the Heiress which was miserably perform'd[3] did not stay the farce, but went to the Rooms, where was an unexpected Ball given by Gentlemen, a very lively pleasant one. did not conclude till 12, after which there was a Supper for those that chose to stay. Play'd at whist one rubber.

Sunday Sep.^t 6th.

A very brilliant fine Day quite hot, after Church walke'd with Miss Snows to see M^rs. Cox at her Cottage, Miss Nettleships dined here & sat with me while the rest went to church; drank Tea at Mr Dunsters a party of 15, some conversible others silent & stupid. Miss Snows supt here very lively & gay.

Monday Sep.^t 7th.

Very brilliant shewey Morning but soon grew cloudy & gloomy not carried to the well as usual by M^rs. Cox, Mr J. Delabere breakfasted here, visited & strolled Dined at Lord Fauconbergs meeting Miss Snows & Mr Dunster,[4] a good Dinner & very chearfull, went to the Ball not very full & rather stupid play'd at whist.

Tuesday Sep.^t 8th.

A very pleasant Day not very hot Mr Witts went very early into Oxfordshire, Miss Snow my Sister Catherine, Mr Dunster, Francis & I walk'd to Sandford House, Miss Snows & Mr John Delabere dined here, Miss Lees drank Tea,[5] & we all went to the rooms play'd at Cribbage a good party, supt with Miss Snows, Mr Dunster & M^r J: Delabere of the party

Wensday Sep.^t 9th.

Much the same kind of weather, Miss Snows Breakfasted here, much hurt to learn by a visit from Mr Isaacs how ill Mr Naper was, Miss M. Benfield & Mr J. Delabere dined here Miss Snows drank Tea & we all went to the Beaux Strategen & who is the Dupe bespoke by M^rs. Wilmot tolerably well perform'd.[6] looket in at the Rooms where found Mr Witts return'd. rec'd a Letter from Mr Witts & wrote to M^rs. Naper.

---

3. *The Heiress* by General John Burgoyne (1722–1792). Burgoyne was a British army officer, a politician and a dramatist. *The Heiress* was first performed in 1786.
4. Henry Belasye, Earl Fauconberg (1743–1802). His wife was Charlotte (1743–1790), sister of Peniston, 1st Viscount Melbourne, and daughter of Matthew Lamb.
5. The Miss Lees of Totteridge Park were long-standing friends of Agnes and Edward Witts.
6. *Who's the Dupe* (1779) and *The Belle's Stratagem* (1780) were both plays by Hannah Cowley (1743–1809)

Thursday Sep.^t 10th.

A most uncommon hot oppressive Day with thick air & appearance of thunder enough to make most people unwell, Miss Snows & Mr Baggot dined here, M^rs. Cox drank Tea & we all went to the Ball which was a very good one & much more lively than usual. play'd in a very merry party at Cribbage.

Friday Sep.^t 11th.

From having been hard rain in the night the air was much cool'd & proved a most delightfull fine Day, M^rs. Sprigg & Miss Peggy Hibbert Breakfasted here, walk'd in the fields with Miss Snows & my Sisters, M^r B: Hughes, & his Sister & a Mr Critchett dined here Miss Snows drank Tea & all adjourn'd to lively Rooms.

Saturday Sep.^t 12th.

Quite as fine a Day as the former Mr John Delebere Breakfasted here, Miss Snows sat an hour afterwards, & then bid adieu to Cheltenham to my sincere regret; walket in the fields, M^rs. Tracys from Sandywell, Lord Fauconberg & M^r J: Delabere dined here, all went to the Play bespoke by Lady Frances Balmley,[7] the Play As you like it, Rosalind by M^rs. Wells, who was very great in her imitations the Farce the agreable Surprize.[8] Mr Delabere return'd with us to Supper. rec'd a very agreable Letter fr^m. M^rs. Naper

40. Old Well Walk.

Mrs Wilmot was a popular actress who performed regularly at the Adelphi Theatre in London. Note that Agnes' spelling was awry: this was clearly done from memory.

7. Bespoke in this sense appears to be intended for 'bespeak,' which was a term used to denote a benefit performance. Presumably Lady Frances Balmley underwrote the costs of the performance, or alternatively arranged for it to be put on for the benefit of one or more of the performers.

8. *The Agreeable Surprise* (1781), a comic opera by John O'Keefe (1747–1833), first produced at the Haymarket Theatre, London.

Sunday Sep.^t 13.th

A very fine Morning, but cloudy the latter part of the Day, after Morning church sat with some company on the well walk. Little Willm Coxwell dined here to Francis's great delight, went to Church in the afternoon, sat half an hour with poor Mr Hughes before we went to Drink Tea with Miss Nettleships home early. wrote to Mrs Naper & Mrs Buxton

Monday Sep.^t 14.th

An extreme wet Morning & continued so the greater part of the Day, went down to the well as usual with poor Mrs Cox who was then very ill, & afterwards so bad as her life to be thought in danger from a Paralytic stroke. Mr Marcham & Mr Bignell & his Nephew dined here M.^r & Mrs Fowler & Miss Nettleships drank Tea & Miss Anne went with us to the Ball which was lively & agreable play'd at Whist with 4 Gents.

Tuesday Sep.^t 15.th

Had been a frost in the night was a clear bright Day in general but sometimes cold & cloudy. Mr Witts & I set out at 8 o'clock in the Chaise with Post Horses to go to survey Bownham House two miles from Stroud, a beautifull situation & a shewey House, but inconvenient in some respects an excellent Garden Hot House & Greenhouse.[9] We got a bad Dinner at Stroud & return'd home between 7 & 8, went to the rooms & play'd at whist with success rec'd a Letter from Miss Anne Snow & Nurse

Wensday Sep.^t 16.th

Just such another Morning, but there was frequent hard showers in the course of the Day & was very cold & unpleasant, Mr Witts went very early in the Morning into Oxfordshire, I visited Mrs Cox after breakfast surprized & pleased, to see her so much recover'd, Miss Hughes & her Brother Robert dined here & we join'd a party of 12 to drink Tea with Lady Frances Balmley, crowded & stupid, glad to adjourn to the rooms play'd at whist with bad luck. rec'd a Letter from Mrs Tyrwhitt.

Thursday Sep.^t 17.th

Clear & Frosty, with cold air & warm Sun, walket a little in the Fields, Miss Lee's & Miss Norwood dined here & Mrs Pullen drank Tea. Miss Lees & my Sister Travell & I went to the Ball which was a very good one 16 couple & 5 Card Tables play'd at Whist in an agreable set. wrote to Miss Anne Snow & rec'd a Letter from Mr Witts with a very indifferent account of poor Mr Naper.

Friday Sep.^t 18.th

The same kind of morning but such very frequent showers afterwards it might almost be call'd perpetual rain, made several visits in the Morning & dined at Mr Hughes's meeting

---

9.   Bownham House was shortly to become their new home. Quite how the introduction came about is unknown, but is likely to have been through the Paul or Snow families, who would have been acquainted with the property, just a short distance from Rodborough Manor, the seat of Sir George Onesiphorus Paul. An additional clue is that after talking to the Miss Snows, Agnes wrote to her niece, Jane Naper, and later received an agreeable letter from Jane. The Napers, Snows and Pauls were connected via the Master family of Cirencester. *See* footnote below in F176.

Lady Frances Balmley besides their own family, a very pleasant visit. went to the rooms which were good, play'd at Whist in the same party as the night before. rec'd a Letter from Mᵣ Witts & answer'd it.

Saturday Sepᵗ 19ᵗʰ

Exactly the same kind of Day frequent showers all the Morning, & perpetual rain all the evening, my Sisᵗ Travell, Francis & I went in the Chaise to visit Mʳˢ Lane & Miss Benfield at Charlton & Mʳˢ Ram at Sandford House Mᵣ Clarke dined here & Mᵣ & Mʳˢ Adair, Mᵣ & Mʳˢ Dunster & Miss Bridges drank Tea here & went to the Rooms, where Mᵣ Witts soon follow'd us return'd out of Oxforshire I playd at Cribbage.

Sunday Sepᵗ 20ᵗʰ

Hard rain in the Morning, & tho it did not continue much rain, yet was miserably damp, dirty & uncomfortable the whole Day; went to Church in the Morning where Dᵣ Pargeter preach'd, made some visits afterwards. Drank Tea at Miss Nevilles a party of 12 dull & stupid & bad walking home.

Monday Sepᵗ 21ˢᵗ

A foggy Morning, bright at noon & a hard shower in the afternoon, Mᵣ Witts went to Breakfast at Mᵣ Hyetts at Painswick, & to meet a Person on business,[10] but returnd to Dinner to meet Mᵣ & Mʳˢ Evans, & Mᵣ H: Hughes, Mᵣ & Mʳˢ Ramsay drank Tea & went with us to the Ball which was rather thin but 14 Couple & 4 Card Tables I play'd at Cribbage. rec'd a Letter from Mʳˢ Buxton.

Tuesday Sepᵗ 22ᵈ

Cloudy Morning, & settled rain from 11 to two, I never stirr'd out till evening to nurse a bad cold, Miss Hughes dined here, & Miss Nettleships & Miss Lees drank Tea, the two latter went with Mᵣ Witts & I to the rooms, rather thin, dark & stupid I play'd both at Whist & Cribbage rec'd a Letter from Miss Anne Snow & wrote to Mʳˢ Naper.

Wensday Sepᵗ 23ᵈ

A very fine bright Morning, visited & walke'd as usual, Mᵣ & Miss Vernon dined here both very pleasant & agreable, Mᵣ & Mʳˢ Higginson & Mʳˢ Barnet drank Tea here, all went to very good & pleasant rooms play'd at Whist. rec'd Letters from Mʳˢ Rollinson & Nurse with a good account of the Boys.

Thursday Sepᵗ 24ᵗʰ

As fine a Day as possibly could be at any time of the Year, Mᵣ Witts & I went at 9 o'clock in the Chaise to make another visit to Bownham House, calling upon Mᵣ Cooper by the way

---

10. Edward Witts was suffering badly with his business and was on the point of failure. Already the couple were scaling down by preparing to sell Swerford Park and to rent Bownham House. The business was that of wool stapling, and presumably he bought and sold woollen cloth. Although his home was in Oxfordshire he would have bought widely in the Stroud valleys and would have known many of the merchants and gentry of the area.

& taking him with us, well pleased with his obliging manner & desire of coming into our proposals,[11] made a bad hurrying Dinner at Stroud & did not return home till 9 o'clock, but having both Moon & stars it was very good driving light, found Miss Lee's with my Sister. rec'd Letters from M^rs. Naper & Miss Snow.

Friday Sep^t. 25th.

Nearly as fine a Day, as the former one, I went with M^rs. Higginson & M^rs. Barnet to show them Fauconbridge Lodges & afterwards aird with them on the London road & on my return made some visits drank Tea very agreably at Mr Higginsons & went to full & very pleasant rooms play'd at Whist in the old party. wrote to M^rs. Rollinson & Miss Snow

Saturday Sep^t. 26th.

Much the same kind of weather only not so much sun, very lively at the Well in the Morning, Miss Nettleships breakfasted here, paid so many take leave visits that I was quite tired. Lady Fran^es. Balmley, Sir Willm. Altham, & M^r J: Delabere dined here & we all adjournd to drink Tea at Mr Hughes's where we found a large party & all went to the rooms play'd at Whist.

Sunday Sep^t. 27th.

Quite a fine bright Morning, but changed at Noon, & was wet in the afternoon & evening went to church, & soon after with numerous farewells bid adieu to Cheltenham with much regret having passt 5 very agreable weeks there. got to Sandywell a little while before Dinner, found my Aunt Betty but very indifferent the others tolerable, a large share of talk all the evening, some very interesting, but I was very sleepy & tired.

Monday Sep^t. 28th.

A very disagreable Day, cold & stormy, with some trifling flying storms of rain but none of any consequence, did not leave Sandywell till one o'clock, & reach'd Lower Slaughter but just before Dinner, felt a great deal at finding Mr Naper still confined to his Bed in the same melancholly situation, & of course poor Jane in a very pitiable state, Join'd with Miss Guydickens in doing all possible to keep up her spirits, play'd several rubbers at Cribbage & sat up to a late hour.

Tuesday Sep^t. 29th.

No change for the better in the weather, on the contrary grew worse before Noon & was continued rain for an hour or two; I bid adieu to my poor Niece with an aching heart seeing

---

11. John Cooper was a leading clothier, living in Woodchester and having his Dunkirk Mill works close by. This mill, built in 1748, became too small for his needs and in 1798 a large mill complex was built alongside. By 1800 Cooper was living in Dunkirk Manor on the hillside above the mill. He was in business with Joseph Cooper and in 1814, following a down-turn in trade, he went bankrupt. Bownham House was built *c.* 1740 and altered by the architect Anthony Keck (1766–1770) for James Winchcombe, who by then had acquired it. James died childless in 1781 and the property went to his nephew, Nathaniel Winchcombe (1757–1817), a descendant of the Clifford / Clutterbuck family of Frampton-on-Severn. He also inherited the estate at Frampton and took up residence at Frampton Court, changing his name to Clifford by Royal Sign Warrant in 1801. How Bownham House became the property of John Cooper is unclear, but it may simply have been a matter of Nathaniel selling it to John as it was surplus to his requirements. The house was demolished in the 1960s and now only the stone gate piers survive.

little chance of her dismal scene being soon relieved, & got home to Dinner, found my two sweet little Loves all alive & merry & much grown for the time low & tired; wrote a long Letter to Maria Jones.

Wensday Sep.t 30.th
Cold & very stormy & disagreable but no rain of any consequence fell in the course of the Day, I was far from well, but much engaged with setting things to rights & various bussiness, Miss Lee's came to Dinner on their way from Cheltenham, M.r Earle & M.r Evans Drank Tea & supt here, play'd at Whist back Gammon & chess. rec'd a Letter from M.rs Tyrwhitt & answer'd it.

Thursday Oct.r 1.st
Had been a most tremendous bad night of hail, rain, & wind, & was a very unpromising Morning, but growing rather better I ventured to take Miss Lee's in the Chaise to Heythrope, returning by the C: House & C: Norton after having survey'd the House, & Conservatory, but the rain came on again in the evening when we had a merry game at Cribbage tho I was very far from well all Day.

Friday Oct.r 2.d
Cold stormy & unpleasant tho no rain fell of any consequence, & the night was clear & fine but frosty; Miss Lee's went away before Breakfast, I was much engaged till time to Dress to dine at M.r Tyrwhitts, where we met by appointment Sir John & Lady Reade, very agreable, play'd at Whist with success, not at home till quite late.

Saturday Oct.r 3.d
Weather worse rather than better equally cold & stormy, with frequent hard showers of hail, I never ventured out of the House being very Rhumatic & had sufficient employment of various sorts. M.r Witts went to Chip: rec'd a Letter from Miss Snow & wrote to my Sister Travell.

Sunday Oct.r 4.th
Cold & stormy but no rain & some sun went to Church in the Morning & walket afterwards but not tempting enough to stay out long, wrote & read a great deal in the course of the Day.

Monday Oct.r 5.th
A dismal dark cold Morning, & began raining most violently with tremendous high wind soon after Breakfast, & continued with very small intervals the whole Day, which prevented my going to make two morning visits as I intended, the Boys all caught in the rain out a walking.

Tuesday Octr. 6th.

Stormy cold & very disagreable weather & at Noon, there was most violent rain for two or three hours, in which we had the luck to go to Dine at Lady Fanes,[12] where we met Major & M^rs. Browne, play'd at Quadrille, not at home till past 11, but a fine bright Moon. rec'd a long Letter from Maria Jones.

Wensday Octr. 7th.

Much the same kind of Morning but grew very showery at Noon & so remain'd the whole Day, I went to see M^rs. Penyston, who I found very pleasing & agreable, her little Boy was asleep so could not see him, from there I went to see M^rs. Langton who was lately arrived at Over Norton, free & easy as usual not at home till late rec'd Letters from M^rs. Naper, Miss Forrest & Miss Anne Snow

Thursday Octr. 8th.

Such an intire Day of steady uninterrupted rain there was no possibility of stirring out the whole Day, did a great deal in it. rec'd a Letter from M^rs. Naper & wrote to M^rs. Granville & Miss Dolphin.

Friday Octr. 9th.

A thick, damp foggy Day, with great appearance of rain, but scarce any fell to speak on, I walket a little in the Morning, Mr Witts went in the Chaise to Chip: Norton, expecting to bring home M^rs. Cotton, but she was deter'd from fear of the weather; M^rs. Rollinson came to Dinner, we play'd at three handed Cribbage interspersed with much talk which we kept up till a very late hour.

Saturday Octr. 10th.

Another perfect wet Day almost without ceasing from Morn: to Night, which quite prevented my returning with M^rs. Rollinson as I had intended to Chipping: Norton to transact some business, she left us at Noon. I wrote to M^rs. Buxton.

Sunday Octr. 11th.

Had been a sharp white Frost in the night & was a clear bright Morning, but grew stormy in the afternoon & was very wet again in the evening & all night, I was so extremely ill all Day I could scarce keep off the Sopha, with a most violent Cold & fever with strong Rhumatic pains, sent for Mr Kinglake who order'd me a large dose of James's Powder.

Monday Octr. 12th.

Dark damp Morning with perpetual soft showers, fine at mid-day & very wet again at night I was much recover'd by the dose I had taken, but fearfull almost of stirring down stairs least

---

12. Lady Fane (1706–1792) was the widow Charles Fane, 2nd Viscount Fane (*c.* 1708–1766), M.P. and at various times the British Resident in Florence, Turin and Constantinople. Susanna, Lady Fane, was the youngest daughter of John Marriott, Registrar of the Court of Chancery, of Stuston Hall, near Diss in Norfolk, and of Sonning in Berkshire. In 1726 she had married Sir William Juxon, 2nd Baronet, of Little Compton in Warwickshire. After nine years of widowhood she married Viscount Fane in 1749. After being widowed for a second time she returned to live at Little Compton, the estate of her first husband.

I should inexcuse my complaint. Mr Witts in the Morning at a Justice meeting at Adderbury, rec'd a Letter from M$^{rs.}$ Cotton & answer'd it.

Tuesday Octr 13$^{th.}$

A dismal thick morning & at Noon began being such perpetual heavy showers that it became almost constant rain; I was so well recover'd that I ventured to walk out a little, & we went to dine at Mr Westerns thro worse roads than I even ever knew to Kingham, found 'em pure well spent a chearfull even$^g.$ Play'd at Cribbage.

Wensday Octr 14$^{th.}$

A very thick Fog in the Morning early but clear'd off so well as to be a most delightfull fine Day with warm air & bright sun, the Gentlemen went to a Land Tax meeting at Chip: & I took M$^{rs.}$ Western to visit both the Houses of Leigh at Adlestrop, going by the way to survey Mr Hastings's great works & improvements at Dailsford, a fine situation but a great undertaking to go thro it.[13] Found only Lady Say & Sele & Miss Twisleton at home[14] M$^{rs.}$ Rollinson & her Daughter Patty came to us at Dinner, & we had a chearfull evening again play'd at Cribbage rec'd a Letter from Miss Anne Snow.

Thursday Octr 15$^{th.}$

Nearly as fine a Day without a fog in the Morning, left Kingham soon after breakfast but did not get home till four doing much business at Chip: where I met M$^{rs.}$ Tyrwhitt, & made a visit to M$^{rs.}$ Langton coming home where I found my Boys all well & lively. had the pleasure of receiving a Letter from M$^{rs.}$ Naper with a much amended account of Mr Naper.

Friday Octr 16$^{th.}$

Quite as fine a Day tho a very thick fog in the Morning, I was much engaged, in setting the Plants in order in both Green Houses, sent the Chaise to Shipston to bring Miss Forrest, who came to Dinner, Mr Evans likewise dined here & we play'd at Whist in the evening. rec'd Letters from L$^{dy.}$ Edward Bentinck & Miss Dolphin & wrote to my Sister Travell.

Saturday Octr 17$^{th.}$

Neither Fog nor Sun but a mild pleasant Day, I ventured to walk a little, tho I was lame with a bad Corn, Mr Witts went to Chip: in the Morning, & in the evening read to Miss Forrest & me. rec'd a Letter from Miss Guydickens & wrote to M$^{rs.}$ Naper

---

13. Warren Hastings (1732–1818) was the first Governor-General of British India, from 1773 to 1785. He was impeached in 1787 for corruption, and acquitted in 1795. On returning to England in 1784 as a very rich man, Hastings used his wealth to re-acquire the family estate at Daylesford. The previous owner, Jacob Knight, had set about building a house, but never finished it, leaving it as a rectangular shell. Despite the uncertainty of the pending impeachment, Hastings set about much work on the estate.
14. Elizabeth, Lady Saye & Sele (1741–1816). Elizabeth was the first daughter of William Leigh of Adlestrop. She married Thomas Twisleton in 1767 and became Lady Saye & Sele in 1781 when her husband successfully claimed the title via the Committee of Privileges.

Sunday Oct[r.] 18[th.]

Had been a dismal wet Night & did not clear up till Breakfast time & rain'd hard again in the afternoon went to the Sunday School before church. M[r] Frazier dined here. wrote to M[rs.] Eliza Tracy.

Monday Oct[r.] 19[th.]

A Stormy disagreable Morning, & confirm'd rain by Noon & the whole remainder of the Day & tremendous wind at night. M[r] Witts at Chip: in the Morning & M[r] Roberts made me a visit. reading & work in the evening as usual.

Tuesday Oct[r.] 20[th.]

Had been violent rain in the night clear'd up at Breakfast, but the wind remain'd quite tempestuous but I ventured to walk a little; wrote to Lady Edward Bentinck & rec'd a Letter from my Sister Travell.

Wensday Oct[r.] 21[st.]

Quite a delightfull Day after the many miserable ones we had had, mild air & warm sun walket a good deal, M[r] Witts at Chip: M[r] Evans dined here, & we play'd some spirited rubbers at whist rec'd Letters from M[rs.] Naper & Miss Amelia Sabine.

Thursday Oct[r.] 22[d.]

Nearly but not quite so fine Day having been a frost in the night, M[r] Witts went to Banbury on bussiness, & like many thousand besides staid to see a famous Boxing match between Johnson & Perkins the former successfull & did not return till a very late Dinner hour. I walket a great deal. Wrote to Miss Anne Snow & Miss Sabine.

Friday Oct[r.] 23[d.]

Thick air & very damp the whole Day went to dine with M[rs.] Rollinson, meeting M[r] & M[rs.] Western, a chearfull pleasant Day, & a very merry game at Cribbage in the evening.

Saturday Oct[r.] 24[th.]

Much the same kind of weather only colder & still more disagreable, left M[rs.] Rollinson soon after breakfast & took Miss Forrest to visit M[rs.] Tyrwhitt who we found kind & agreable as usual, did some little businesses at Chip: by the way & return'd home to Dinner finding the loves all well & happy.

Sunday Oct[r.] y[e.] 25[th.]

No change in the weather but to be more cold & disagreable, went to Church but not pleasant enough to walk afterwards connected. wrote & read a great deal rec'd a Letter from M[rs.] Eliza Tracy & wrote to M[rs.] Naper.

Monday Oct[r.] 26[th.]

Rather a more pleasant Day not quite so cold but still without Sun, M[r] Witts set off very early in the Morning to go to Bownham House to meet M[r] Cooper intending to Breakfast with my

Bro.ᵗ At Upper Slaughter by the way, Miss Forrest & I took a good walk but talk'd more.

Tuesday Oct.ᵗ 27.ᵗʰ

A tolerable fine Morning, but soon grew foggy, damp, & too disagreable to think of moving out of the House, but did not find the Day long, from much converse with my agreable Friend, reading working & pleasure in the Dear Boys. wrote to my Sis.ᵗ Travell.

Wensday Oct.ᵗ 28.ᵗʰ

A smart shower in the Morning but soon grew clear & pleasant & allow'd Miss Forrest & I to take a walk to the village & visit the sick & old, M.ᵗ Witts return'd home to a late Dinner having much to tell of his adventures on his Journey rec'd a Letter from M.ʳˢ Granville.

Thursday Oct.ᵗ 29.ᵗʰ

Had been a frost in the night & was a clear bright Morning with all enlivening Sun, but changed at Noon & was wet in the afternoon. I walk'd a great deal with M.ᵗ Witts, & we went to Drink Tea at Wigginton a large party the Hoskin family being there all in the old stile,[15] play'd at whist a clear night to come home by.

Friday Oct.ᵗ 30.ᵗʰ

A very cold Day frost & clear sun in the Morning early, stormy & wet at Noon & all the remainder of the Day, & very severe at night when we return'd home from Dining at M.ᵗ Tyrwhitts, where we met M.ʳˢ Rollinson & Miss Western. Col: Langton & M.ᵗ Roberts; pleasant as ever not at home till very late. M.ᵗ Hoskins here in the Morning

41. *North-west view of Blenheim.*

---

15. It is difficult to know what is meant here as they were drinking tea, not dining. Social customs were changing and the dinner hour moved quite markedly through the eighteenth century. In London, by the 1730s and 1740s, the upper class and gentry were dining at three or four in the afternoon, and by 1770 their dinner hour in London was four or five. By the 1790s the fashionable set were taking dinner between five and six. The usual meaning of 'old style' was in reference to dining at an hour that might have seemed very early and very old-fashioned.

Saturday Octr 31.st.

A very clear Day, sharp frost & severe North east wind which made it bitterly cold, went to Dine at Mr Penystons, meeting M.^r & Mrs. Western & Mr Tahourdin <u>very</u> agreable,[16] again not at home till a very late hour, but a clear bright Moon. rec'd a Letter from Mrs. Naper wrote in very low spirits. feel much for her.

Sunday Novr 1.st.

Continued Frost but not quite so cold a wind & much sun went to Church in the Morning & afterwards walket a little Mr Francis dined here. rec'd a Letter from Mrs. Buxton & wrote to L.^{dy.} Lyttelton Mrs. Tyrwhitt & Mrs. Cotton.

Monday Novr 2.^{d.}

Foggy in the Morning but clear'd off to be bright & pleasant & I walk'd out a little in spite of much bussiness, Mr Evans dined & supt here & we had a Game at Whist.

Tuesday Novr 3.^{d.}

A still thicker fog but never cleared off well, I was much engaged all Day with preparations for our approaching Journey; Mr Witts at Chip: in the Morning. rec'd Letters from Mrs. Tyrwhitt, Miss Anne Snow & my Sister Travell.

Monday Novr 4.th.

A sad wet Morning, till 10 o'clock when it clear'd off & was very fine the remainder of the Day suitable to our proposed Journey, when Miss Forrest, Mr Witts, Francis & I all squeezed very comfortably into the Post Chaise, on our way to Oxford drove about Blenheim Park to shew it Miss Forrest Mrs. Wickham sat with us till our Dinner was ready, & Mr Loveday, Miss F's cousin dined with us, & we did not get to Tetsworth till seven o'clock but the Moon kindly lent her aid, our accomodation bad there as usual. wrote to Mrs. Naper.

Thursday Novr 5.th.

Wet again in the Morning, & clear'd off as the Day before, but the fog remain'd longer & made our drive less pleasant; dined tolerably comfortably at Beauconfield,[17] & reach'd Lady Lytteltons at Southall Park first as it was dark were rec'd by her very kindly in her superb large old Mansion.[18] play'd at Back Gammon & Picquet.

Friday Novr 6.th.

Cold & Foggy in the Morning, but clearer at noon & no rain, survey'd the house & premises after Breakfast Mrs. Glasse the wife of Dr Glasse made a Morning visit here & pleased me well by her chearfull agreable manner, dined very late & play'd again at our Duett Games. wrote to Miss Anne Snow.

---

16.   Charles Tahourdin was rector of Cornwell, between Stow-on-the-Wold and Chipping Norton. He was ordained priest in 1777, became rector in 1785 and died in 1819.

17.   Beaconsfield.

18.   Southall Park was part of the Manor of Hayes in Middlesex. Lady Lyttelton lived here and in Berkeley Street, Mayfair. She later economised and after selling both properties retired to Malvern in Worcestershire.

Saturday Nov.r 7th.

A very dismal Morning, hard rain & very thick fog, but not withstanding we all put our schemes of going to London in practice & it held up at Noon, Lady L. took Miss Forrest & M.r Witts & I follow'd our own invention, leaving our Chaise at Livery Stables & Jumbled about for 4 hours in a Hackney Coach doing much bussiness concluding by making a visit to M.rs. Guydickens & return'd home all in safety to Dinner at Southall.

Sunday Nov.r 8th.

A clear pleasant Frost with continued bright sunshine, went in the two Carriges to Church at Norwood two miles distant, much pleased with the excellent manner in which the service was perform'd by M.r Hinton dined early found the evening long & dull from doing nothing. wrote to M.rs. Catherine Thornton.

Monday Nov.r 9th.

Just the same kind of pleasant seasonable weather, M.r Hinton call'd here in the Morning, M.r Witts & I walk'd in the Park & Wood for an Hour, M.r & M.rs. Hinton came to Dinner & staid all night; play'd at Whist & Chess. rec'd a Letter from Lady Edward Bentinck & one from Nurse.

Tuesday Nov.r 10th.

No change in the weather but being rather colder & the House at Southall Park being very cold & not famous fires we felt it very sensibly M.r Witts went early in the Morning on bussiness to London & return'd to Dinner. M.r & M.rs. Hinton went away after Breakfast, & we three Ladies went first to visit a M.rs. Graham on Hanwell Heath & afterwards not finding her at home went to D.r Glasses at Greenford a very pleasant easy visit, pleased with seeing the young Gentlemen under his care perform their military excercise. play'd a strange Game at Whist at night & wrote to M.rs. Savage & Miss Lee.

Wensday Nov.r 11th.

Quite a beautifull Day for the time of Year, but clouded towards evening & shew'd the frost was going, at Noon we all went an airing in the Coach thro Norwood, Heston, Osterly, Sion, Brentford & over Hanwell Heath home, much pleased with the several scenes evening spent as usual. wrote to my Sister Travell & rec'd a Letter from M.rs. Tyrwhitt.

Thursday Nov.r 12th.

Fog & rain till 10 o'clock when it cleard off & was a very fine Day, M.r Witts & I went to London, for me to appear in the Court of Chancery[19] call'd upon M.rs. Guydickens, who kindly went with me there, the bussiness was soon over, & she went with me shopping till near Dinner time when we dined very comfortably in Bayswater Street, Miss Hanburys came to Drink Tea & staid the evening, & after Supper we went to Sleep at M.r Parrots in Quebec Street very comfortably.[20]

---

19. With financial problems looming it seemed that some affairs needed to be put in order. Quite what this appearance related to is unknown, but may well have related to private property of Agnes secured under their marriage agreement.

20. Mr Parrot was an acting partner in the banking firm of Sir Claude Scott & Company. Lady Lyttelton was friendly with the Parrot family.

Friday Nov.r 13th.

Fog & rain almost the whole Day as unpleasant in London as could be, & as dirty went to Breakfast with the Guydickens, & took Betty with me in Miss Hanburys Chariot to finish my bussinesses left London between 2 & 3 & brought Anne Witts home with us to Southall Park.[21] rec'd Letters from Miss Anne Snow & Mrs. Catherine Thornton & wrote to Mrs. Tyrwhitt.

Saturday Nov.r 14th.

Rain in the Morning, & when it went off, damp wind & very disagreable, Mrs. Graham made a Morning visit here, & afterwards Mr Glasse bringing Mr Dutton with him, play'd at Picquet with Miss Forrest. rec'd a Letter from Nurse & wrote to Miss Guydickens.

Sunday Nov.r 15th.

A most dreadfull wet Day till after 12 o'clock, when it was chiefly dry but very stormy the whole of the Day, we all went to Hanwell Church to hear Mr Glasse who perform'd most charmingly, a most striking sermon, plain pleasing singing, & the whole of the service most devoutly perform'd, the church an elegant new built one, afterwards we went to pay a visit to Mr & Mrs. Glasse, spent an hour very agreably delighted with their 2 little Girls; wrote to Mrs. Catherine Thornton & Nurse.

Monday Nov.r 16th.

A very fine brilliant Morning but changed at mid-day to hard rain, Mr Witts went very early to London taking Anne Witts back again to school & L: Lyttelton, Miss Forrest, Francis & I went in the Coach to visit Mr & Mrs. Hinton at Norwood, Mr Witts returnd to a late Dinner. wrote to Mrs. Buxton & rec'd a Letter from my Sister Travell.

Tuesday Nov.r 17th.

After 10 o'clock it began being very violent hard rain & so continued the whole of the Day. Mr Witts was again obliged to go to Town in the hope of completing his bussiness but in vain, & join'd me at Totteridge Park at Dinner in a Hired Post Chaise, I found the road good thro Harrow on the Hill, Stanmore, & Edgeware about 16 miles, & the country seem'd to abound in many beauties if the weather would have permitted me a sight of them; met with a very polite reception from Mrs. Lee & a real friendly one from her Daughters; a large handsome old House & place, with many comforts in & about it, Mr & Mrs. Fiott (another Daughter) & a Miss Lygett a Lady with them dined & supt at Totteridge, & a Mr Arrowsmith was staying in the House, a lively pleasant middle aged Man, a very handsome Dinner & everything quite in a stile of hospitality; a Table at Whist & Cribbage I play'd at the former.[22]

---

21. Anne Witts was the daughter of Edward's younger brother, John Witts, rector of Lydley Hayes in Shropshire. Anne was at school in London.

22. This appears to have been the first visit to Totteridge and it is not really clear if the friendship with the Miss Lees, who they had met recently in Cheltenham, was recent or had been long-standing. Whichever, it was to last for many years.

Wensday Nov. 18th.

Rather a Fog the whole Day, so as to absence the fine views around which we much regretted, but it was Day with some few gleams of sunshine, set forth on our walk imediately after Breakfast first going all over the premises, & then walking to visit Mrs. Fiott in her new House about a quarter of a mile distant, saw 5 out of her six children, stout & healthy, but not beautifull, she & her companion dined with us again as also Mr Marsham the Curate of the Parish a well behaved Young Man.[23] the same parties at Cards again

Thursday Nov. 19th.

A very fine bright Morning, & the whole Day turn'd out a finer travelling one than could be expected at the time of Year, left our obliging friends at Totteridge in spite of their entreaties at 10 o'clock & fell into the great road at Barnet from whence to St. Albans the road is remarkably pleasant being interspersed with the views of many good seats stopp'd at a very moderate Inn at Market Street where we got a pretty good Dinner, & did not get to Woburn till an hour after dark, but a young Moon & many stars enabled us to go with safety & comfort, found the Bedford Arms a pretty good quiet Inn, supt on Veal Cutlets & went to Bed early wrote to Lady Edwd. Bentinck & Mrs. Naper.

Friday Nov. 20th.

A Cold damp Day with a thick air but scarce any rain fell, left Woburn at 9' o'clock, passing thro' Newport Pagnal, 9 miles of very low dull country indeed the whole of the road to Northampton is miserably dull; we stopp'd at an Ale House in a Village call'd Stoke a little better than half way to bait the Horses dined at Northampton, & took a pair of Post Horses there hopeing to reach Mears Ashby in good time, but having very bad Horses it proved quite otherwise, & we were in much danger, & more alarm'd from the roads & the Horses not taking the Hills, but at last arrived safely, & met with a most kind reception from our good old Friends, to whom were added Captain Thornton & Mr Panting who I was very happy to see after many years absence, play'd at Whist & had some very lively conversation after Supper.

Saturday Nov. 21st.

Much the same kind of weather rather wet towards the afternoon, not tempting enough for any Lady to walk out, & the situation too dirty to think of it with any pleasure, had much pleasant converse, Mr Walker the Clergyman of the Parish here in the evening a very gentlemanlike Man, a Table at Whist & Back Gammon. Wrote to Miss Snow.

Sunday Nov. 22^{d.}

Wet in the Morning but soon clear'd off & was mild & fine with some gleams of sunshine Mr Panting went away early to serve his church at Brockhall, to our general regret; we

23. Thomas Cope Marsham (1761–1817). Marsham was born in Peterborough and educated at Eton; he graduated B.A. in 1784 and M.A. in 1787. He was vicar of Kew and Petersham, Surrey (1801–1817) and curate of Totteridge (1803–1817); he was also chaplain to the Duke of York and to the Prince of Wales. In 1802 he married Penelope Judith, eldest daughter of the Hon. Sir Alexander Maitland, 1st Baronet. Marsham died on 11 December 1817 at Totteridge, Hertfordshire.

had a very dirty walk to Church, the service well perform'd by Mr Walker an excellent usefull Sermon, a chearfull evening of conversation Captain Thornton improving much on acquaintance rec'd a letter from Nurse with a good account of the Dears.

Monday Novr 23^d.

The same dark damp kind of weather, with a mixture of trifling showers & sunshine, Mr Witts rode to Wellinbro: to transact some bussiness with an Attorney,[24] & M^rs. Cath: Thornton, Miss Andrew, & Captain Thornton, went there also to make a wedding visit. M^r & M^rs. Whalley & Miss Kingston her Niece dined here,[25] a lively Game at Whist & another at two handed Cribbage. wrote to Miss Chaplin.

Tuesday Novr 24th.

Rather a better day, tho still cold & damp, the Gentlemen took a long ride, & the Ladies a very dirty walk in the Villiage, very chearfull & merry the whole evening. & played at Whist. wrote to M^rs. Granville

42. Card players.

24.   This attorney was presumably Mr Rodick, the husband of his second cousin, Maria Amelia Rodick, *née* Witts.
25.   Untangling all of the connections is extremely difficult and is an exercise which is unlikely to be completed, even with a lifetime of research. The Whalley family was large and the connections likewise. Agnes and Edward knew members of the Whalley family in London, Oxfordshire and Gloucestershire. William Whalley (177?–1845) was shortly to marry Agnes' niece, Martha Buxton, *née* Travell—much to the disappointment of Agnes, who considered it a poor match. One Whalley, the Revd Peter, was the author of *The History and Antiquities of Northamptonshire*, published in 1791. Peter Whalley was rector of Ecton in 1763 and appears to have been followed by Palmer Whalley, eldest son of Eyre Whalley, instituted as rector in 1763. He held the living, together with that of Wilby from 1782, until his death in 1803. During his ministry of forty years he was confined to his room for long periods due to illness.

Wensday Nov.ʳ 25ᵗʰ·

Very much the same kind of weather clear & bright at Noon the Gentlemen & Miss Anne Andrew rode to Mᵣ Dolbere at Finedon, the rest of us went in the Chaise to Ecton to see the three Mʳˢ· Orlebars, Mᵣ Whalley call'd here in the Morning, play'd at Whist & Cribbage & at Ving'tun after Supper rec'd a Letter from Lord Edward Bentinck.

Thursday Nov.ʳ 26ᵗʰ·

A thick Fog in the Morning but was fine soon, the Gentlemen & Miss Anne rode to Sir Justⁿ· Ishame at Lamport, I never went out having a bad cold, evening spent as before wrote to Miss Forrest.

Friday Nov.ʳ 27ᵗʰ·

Had been a sharp frost in the Night, was a clear bright Day but very cold, & the frost had made the roads so bad that we were more than 2 hours & a half going to Mᵣ Andrews at Harlston, 4 miles beyond Northampton, met with a most friendly reception from my old Friends, who I found surrounded by their seven Daughters many of them grown fine young Women, 2 parties at Whist & Ving t'un after Supper. rec'd Letters from Mʳˢ· Naper, Mʳˢ· Guydickens, & Nurse

Saturday Nov.ʳ 28ᵗʰ·

Very little Frost, & was a dark damp unpleasant Day, left our good friends at mid-day, & went to Northampton, where we dined at Mʳˢ· Wards, a very handsome entertainment meeting Dᵣ Syme the Physician & the two Mʳˢ· Whalleys, play'd both at Whist & Cribbage & return'd home to Mears Ashby late by the Moon, leaving Captain Thornton behind us.

Sunday Nov.ʳ 29ᵗʰ·

A mild Day pleasant Day for the time of Year, went to Church at 2 o'clock the only service in the Day. Mᵣ Walker gave us a most charming Sermon much chearfull converse, with reading & writting fill'd up the Day. wrote to Mʳˢ· Naper & Nurse

Monday Nov.ʳ 30ᵗʰ·

A very cold raw disagreable Day Mᵣ Walker sat an hour here in the Morning, we went in the two Chaises to Drink Tea at Mᵣ Whalleys at Ecton,[26] none but their own family, play'd at Whist & at two handed Cribbage return'd home by a fine bright Moon.

Tuesday Dec.ʳ 1ˢᵗ·

Had been a sharp Frost in the night but soon melted from the heat of the Sun, & was a fine winter Day, were out a walking a great while, play'd both at Whist & Ving'tun in the evening rec'd a Letter from Miss Chaplin with a melancholly detail of her friend Mʳˢ· Howards Death.

---

26. The Revd Palmer Whalley of Ecton, referred to above.

Wensday Dec.ʳ 2.ᵈ

A fine Dry Bright Day without any frost & had been hard
rain in the night, busy in Dressing all Morning to go to Dine
with Dᴿ Syme at Northampton & go to the Concert in the
evening meeting at Dinner Mᴿ & Mʳˢ· Dolben, & the two
Mʳˢ· Whalleys, the Concert was full & agreable, much good
Company, came home by the bright light of the Moon at ½
past twelve, & eat a hearty Supper rec'd a Letter from Nurse

Thursday Dec.ʳ 3.ᵈ

A sharp frost, but such bright warm Sun that it was
quite a delightfull Day, breakfasted late & were
engaged in various bussiness's all the Mornᵍ· Mᴿ & Mʳˢ·
Dolben, & Mᴿ Walker came to Dinner, & the latter
supt. play'd at Whist & Picquet.

43. The final parting.

Friday Dec.ʳ 4.ᵗʰ·

High wind & very stormy, in the Morning, & frequent showers of rain in the course of the
Day, but upon the whole could not be call'd a bad travelling Day for the time of year, as
we left our good old friend at Mears Ashby after Breakfast, Mʳˢ· Cath: Thornton & Miss
Andrew going with me as far as Northampⁿ· parted from them with mutual regret after
having spent a very happy fortnight together; found the road very bad part of the way to
Daventry, where we arrived between 3 & 4 & found our saddles Horses ready to meet us
& bring our Letters, rec'd one from Miss Snow, my Sister Travell & Nurse; got an excellent
Dinner & warm room & spent a comfortable evening.

Saturday Dec.ʳ 5.ᵗʰ·

A very fine Winters Day a dry clear air, with much sunshine, left Daventry a little after nine,
& it was fortunate we got out so early for the roads tho rather better than we had reason to
expect, made us very tedious on the road, & by baiting for an hour & a half at Banbury did
not get home till 5 o'clock, found our little Dears quite well & bonny eat a hearty Dinner &
went early to Bed being well tired & shaken, rec'd a Letter from Mʳˢ· Tyrwhitt & answer'd
it, & wrote to Mʳˢ· Rollinson.

Sunday Dec.ʳ 6.ᵗʰ·

A very stormy damp unpleasant Day with frequent showers, went to Church where Mᴿ
Evans did the Duty, My Sister Travell & Brother Ferdinand who were both at Swerford
came home with us for an hour or two & had much converse on various subjects some very
painfull.[27] rec'd a Letter from Lady Lyttelton & a most pleasing one from Miss Forrest, &
wrote to Mᴿ Glasse & Mʳˢ· Guydickens.

---

27.   One painful topic was the on-going dangerously poor health of William Naper, the son-in-law of Ferdinando, but
      perhaps more pressing at this point was the financial difficulty of Edward and Agnes, which was forcing them to sell
      Swerford Park.

Monday Dec.ʳ 7ᵗʰ·

Had been a very trifling frost in the night, & was one of the most uninterrupted bright fine Days I ever saw at the time of year; Mʳ Witts walke'd to Swerford after breakfast, & brought my Sister Travell back with him, for an hour or two I walk'd a great deal enjoying the fineness of the Day & did much bussiness besides. rec'd Letters from Mʳˢ· Tyrwh & Mʳˢ· Rollinson & wrote to Mʳˢ· Cath: Thornton.

Tuesday Dec.ʳ 8ᵗʰ·

A most disagreable & universal fog the whole Day which prevented my walking down to my Brothers at Swerford as I had intended, I first went to the Green Houses with Mʳ Earle who made a long morning visit here & my Broʳ Travell also late in the Morning. wrote to Miss Chaplin.

Wensday Dec.ʳ 9ᵗʰ·

A still thicker & more disagreable Fog, never stirr'd out, Mʳ Witts went to Chip: & Mʳ & Mʳˢ· Western came to Dinner, a merry Game at Cribb: interlarded with much talk.

Thursday Dec.ʳ 10ᵗʰ·

A happy change in the weather to a clear bright Day the Gentlemen rode to survey Broughton Castle, my Sister Travell here an hour or two in the Morning, Mʳ Earle & Mʳ Evans drank Tea here & augmented our Cribbage party. sat up talking till twelve o'clock.

Friday Dec.ʳ 11ᵗʰ·

Very cold & rather raw, but still without doubt fine winter weather, walkt imediately after Breakfast, my Broʳ Travell here for half an hour Mʳ & Mʳˢ· Western went with us to dine at Mʳˢ· Rollinsons,[28] where we found my Broʳ Ferdinand & Miss Western, play'd many rubbers at Cribbage in the evening. bad fires so almost starved with cold Sam Rollinson came home from Rugby School for his first holidays. Mʳˢ· Langton here in the Mornᵍ· but I could not see her

Saturday Dec.ʳ 12ᵗʰ·

A milder air & much dew indeed quite a fine Day, left Chadlington soon after Breakfast, & went down to Mʳ Tyrwhitts, where I found poor Mʳˢ· T— confined to her Bed with a bad cold & fever, & too ill to see me, but I spent an hour most pleasantly with Mʳˢ· Drake, pick'd up Mʳ Witts on my return thro' Chip: & found the three Dear Boys all well & merry on my return. Wrote to Miss Anne Snow —

Sunday Dec.ʳ 13ᵗʰ·

Much the same kind of weather but grew colder & much more stormy at mid-day, went down in the chaise with the two elder Boys to Swerford soon after Breakfast, my Sister Catherine

---

28. Ferdinando had married Martha Rollinson (1741–1780), presumably the sister of Lock Rollinson. Lock had died in 1788; his widow was Mary, *née* Jones. The eldest son was James Lock Rollinson. A daughter, Anne (1783–1855), was to marry Henry Hippisley (1776–1838). Their third son, Robert William Hippisley (1818–1901), was later to become rector of Stow-on-the-Wold, and a thorn in the side of Agnes' son, Francis Edward Witts. Another daughter, Martha Rollinson, married John Dolphin (1776–1831), curate at Lower Slaughter and later rector of Wakes Colne.

44. School days.

being added to their party, much shock'd to see the declining state of poor M.ʳ Francis's health who looket most dreadfully, after Church went to call on M.ʳˢ· Langton, the Col: & herself very lively & pleasant; came home by C: Norton much engaged by accompts all the evening.

Monday Dec.ʳ 14.ᵗʰ·

Had been a small flight of snow in the night, & was a true miserable winter Day being hard rain & thick fog. M.ʳ Witts went early to Chipping: Norton, myself much engaged both Morning & evening with a variety of bussiness.

Tuesday Dec.ʳ 15.ᵗʰ·

After a most violent night of rain, was a day of very high cold wind & frequent showers, at noon I went down to Swerford to see how poor Frank did & to take leave of the rest of the party, sending the former out in the chaise to see how he bore the motion. engaged in writting & many other bussinesses all the evening.

Wensday Dec.ʳ 16.ᵗʰ·

Rather a finer Day having some sunshine, but very cold & stormy, my Bro.ʳ Travell call'd on us just before we set out for Upper Slaughter M.ʳ Witts on Horseback, Frans· George, Prissick & I in the Chaise roads so bad did not get there till quite Dinner time finding Patty Rollinson with my Brother, rec'd a Letter from M.ʳˢ· C: Thornton & one from M.ʳ Buxton with the good news that his Dear Wife was safely brought to Bed of another Daughter. wrote to Lady Lyttelton.

45. *The birth of a daughter.*

Thursday Decr. 17th.

Much the same kind of weather a little Frost, & very cold & stormy; the Gentlemen went soon after Breakfast to a Meeting at Stow where they dined, & about 2 o'clock I went to Lower Slaughter where I found Mrs. Naper much recover'd her late illness but looking sadly. Mr Naper appear'd much as usual excepting being thinner, & wearing his night Cap; very conversible tho I fear very much out of Spirits at times the Gentlemen return'd from Stow to Tea & we play'd many rubbers at Cribbage with bad success

Friday Decr. 18th.

Very fine & pleasant early in the Day but grew cold & sour at noon & wet at night, the Gent: rode out & the Boys & I walkt. Mr Witts read to me in the evening in the Villiage Curate a good Poem in many parts. wrote to Miss Forrest.

Saturday Decr. 19th.

Extreme hard rain till after mid-day when it clear'd off, Mrs. Naper here for an hour or two in the Morning, Mr Hickman dined here, an uncommon genteel well behaved Gentleman Farmer. reading again in the evening as before

Sunday Decr. 20th.

Quite a mild fine winter Day with bright gleams of sunshine, went to Church both Morn: & evening the service very moderately perform'd by Mr Williams my Brothers Curate who dined here, walk'd a good deal between the Churchs. Wrote to Mr Buxton.

Monday Dec.ʳ 21ˢᵗ.

Quite a fine Day for the shortest Day of the Year, Mʳ Witts & my Brother rode to call on Mʳ Jones at Naunton, while they were gone Mʳ Hippesley & his eldest Son sat an hour with me, & were very agreable. I walket a little & my little Edward & his Nurse came from Swerford Park. We went to dine at Lower Slaughter no change for the better there after playing many rubbers at Cribbage return'd home to Supper. rec'd Letters from Lady Edwᵈ. Bentinck Mʳˢ. Tyrwhitt, Mʳˢ. Granville, Miss Anne Snow, Miss Sabine & my Sister Travell with something a better account of poor Mʳ Francis.

Tuesday Dec.ʳ 22ᵈ.

A most disagreable Day thick mist the whole Day & very frequently hard rain, & most terribly damp & close, but yet my Brother & I ventured to go to make a Morning visit at Sandywell in our Chaise found the roads dreadfull, & our visit sadly short, by the length of time on the road, found them all tolerable, & Miss Guydickens a most happy addition to their party. found Mʳ Jones here on our return, who staid all night & we play'd many rubbers at Cribbage Mʳ Witts & I with uncommon bad luck. wrote to my Sister Travell.

Wensday Dec.ʳ 23ᵈ.

Nearly as disagreable a Day tho not quite so much wet fell, Mʳ Jones went away imediately after Breakfast, & I went to L: Slaughter to spend the Morning with Mʳˢ. Naper, who sent her Chaise for me, much painfull & some pleasurable conversation Mʳ Witts finish'd the Village Curate in the evening to me & rec'd a Letter from Mʳˢ. Guydickens.

Thursday Dec.ʳ 24ᵗʰ.

A universal wet Day from Morn: to night & dreadfully damp & uncomfortable, but my Brother contrived to ride to L: Slaughter, & Mʳ Witts to Stow on business, I read & work'd & enjoy'd the Boys much. Mʳ Witts read to me in the evening in a Novel call'd Athlin & Dunbayne. Wrote to Lady Edward Bentinck.

Friday Dec.ʳ 25ᵗʰ.

Quite the reverse of the former Days being, Dry bright & uncommonly mild for Xmas Day not at all cold even in church walk'd afterwards Mʳˢ. Naper call'd for 5 minutes between the churches Mʳ Williams & the two Mʳ Dolphins dined here, much pleased with both the young Men.

Saturday Dec.ʳ 26ᵗʰ.

Had been a sharp hoar frost in the night, & was a bright fine Morning, but grew stormy & rather wet at mid-day, the Gentlemen rode & I walk'd with the Boys in the Garden, dined at Lower Slaughter, all in the usual stile playing at Cribbage &c. wrote to Mʳˢ. Tyrwhitt.

Sunday Dec.ʳ 27ᵗʰ.

A very miserable Day high winds & storms with constant small rain & Fog, too bad to permit me to go to Church, Farmer Cooke dined here, much reading &c. wrote to Miss Snow.

1. Agnes Witts, née Travell (1747-1825), by Joseph Wright of Derby, painted at Bath *c*.1776.

2. Edward Witts (1746-1816), by George Romney.

3. Francis Edward Witts
(1783-1854),
by F. Liston, 1787.

4. Francis Travell
(1728-1801).

5. Witts family group by John Hamilton Mortimer, *c.*1769. From left to right: John Witts (1750-1816), Richard Witts (1747-1815), Edward Witts (1746-1816) and Apphia Witts, later Lady Lyttelton (1743-1840). Family tradition has it that the second left is Richard, but there remains a strong suspicion that it is his eldest brother, Broome (1744-1827).

6. Ferdinando Tracy Travell

7. Anthony Tracy-Keck, M.P.,
of Great Tew (1712-1767),
by an unknown enameller, c.1736.

8. Anthony Tracy-Keck, M.P., of Great
Tew, Oxfordshire (1712-1767), his wife
Lady Susan Douglas-Hamilton (d.1755),
their daughters Henrietta Charlotte,
Viscountess Hereford (1742-1817), and
Susan, Lady Elcho (1745-1835), by
Edward Alcock of Birmingham, c. 1748.

9. Francis, 7th Earl of Wemyss (1723-1808).

10. Francis, Lord Elcho (1749-1808), pastel by Archibald Skirving, Rome 1790. Lord Elcho was the son of the 7th Earl of Wemyss; and father of the 8th Earl of Wemyss and 4th Earl of March.

11. The Charteris Children by George Romney, 1781. Francis Charteris (1772-1853), succeeded his grandfather as the 8th Earl of Wemyss in 1808, obtaining a reversal of his great-uncle's Jacobite 1746 attainder in 1826, thereby securing formal recognition of the title. His sisters in the picture are Susan (died 1816), who married General Sir Henry Clinton and Henrietta Charlotte (1773-1838), who married the 6th Earl of Stamford. Henrietta suffered a mental affliction and was removed from her husband and children, and later, by coincidence, lived at Swerford Park in Oxfordshire, formerly the home of Agnes and Edward Witts who had been forced to sell the house in 1793 at the time of Edward's financial difficulties. Agnes visited Henrietta on more than one occasion at Swerford.

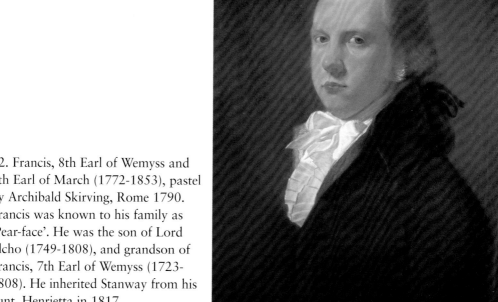

12. Francis, 8th Earl of Wemyss and 4th Earl of March (1772-1853), pastel by Archibald Skirving, Rome 1790. Francis was known to his family as 'Pear-face'. He was the son of Lord Elcho (1749-1808), and grandson of Francis, 7th Earl of Wemyss (1723-1808). He inherited Stanway from his aunt, Henrietta in 1817.

13. The Witts family group, *c*.1769-1770 by Richard Cosway (1742-1821). Exhibited at the Royal Academy in 1770 as 'The portraits of a gentleman, his wife and sister, in the character of Fortitude introducing Hope as the companion to Distress'. Broome Witts (1738-1769), of Witney, a linen draper in Bread Street in the City of London, was first cousin to the Witts siblings of Chipping Norton (Alice, Apphia, Broome, Sarah, Edward, Richard and John). The families were tied ever closer by the fact that the two Broomes married two sisters, respectively Elizabeth London (1738-1837), and Amelia London (1742-1832). Witney Broome and Elizabeth had three children, Broome Philips Witts (1767-1845), *see* plate 14; Edward London Witts (1768-1841), and Maria Amelia Witts (1769-1830). Witney Broome died in 1769 and this unusual memorial painting by Cosway, still in its original frame, is an allegory showing Broome as Fortitude introducing his sister Sarah Witts (1745-1797), represented as Hope standing with her anchor, to Broome's widow Elizabeth shown seated as Distress.

14. Broome Philips Witts (1767-1845).

15. Edward Witts (1746-1816).

16. King George III and the fair quaker.

The exact allusion to the Fair Quaker is unclear. As a young man George had a fling with one Hannah Lightfoot who was referred to as 'the fair quaker'. There was also a contemporary play in circulation, *The Fair Quaker of Deal*. Also Mrs. Dorothy Jordan was in town during the royal visit. Anyway, this cartoon was published in October 1788, celebrating the King's five-week visit to the town.

17. Their Majesties with the three eldest princesses at Cheltenham.

A contemporary engraving showing the King taking the Cheltenham Waters.

18. Thomas Hughes of Cheltenham, solicitor and lessee of the well who built the first assembly rooms in the town in 1783. The Hughes family were well acquainted with Edward and Agnes Witts.

19. Cirencester. A contemporary aquatint with hand colouring by J. C. Stadler after Joseph Farington R.A. (1747-1821), published in 1793.

20. The Bath Races from *The Comforts of Bath*, by Thomas Rowlandson, 1798.

21. A view of Wallbridge, Stroud *c*.1790 with Rodborough as the backdrop to the right. The coloured items on the hillside are dyed woollen cloths hung out on tenters.

22. South-east view of Woodchester by Samuel Lysons, 1792. This fine view was drawn by Lysons at exactly the time when Edward and Agnes Witts were living with their three sons at Bownham House, Rodborough. The gateway to Bownham House was less than 100 metres from the point at which Lysons executed his view, and this would have been the view facing the family when they left the front gate between 1791 and 1793.

Monday Decr 28th.

So fine a Day has seldom been seen on this Day, mild air, very dry, & constant sunshine, Mr Witts went into Oxfordshire before Breakfast, my Brother & I went in the Chaise to Stow for him to do several errands & sat an hour very agreably with Mrs. Hippesley where we found Mr Dixon, in the evening much reading &c. with the Children & wrote to Mrs. Granville.

Tuesday Decr 29th.

An intire change in point of weather stormy & flying hard showers till Noon & then most perpetual rain the remainder of the Day, Mrs. Naper here for an hour in the Morning, & Mr Witts return'd out of Oxfordshire to Dinner most thoroughly wetted & brought a most miserable account of poor Frank, read & workt in the evening & rec'd a long Letter from Mrs. Tyrwhitt.

Wensday Decr 30th.

Tolerably dry & fine till after 12 o'clock, when it began raining most violently, & so continued the Children & I had been wise enough to take our walk & make some visits in the villiage before it began dined again at L. Slaughter, just as usual, some merry rubbers at Cribbage came home thro storms & tempests

Thursday Decr 31st.

A most dreadfull Day such constant violent showers with most strong wind that it might be almost call'd perpetual rain, Mrs. Naper sent her Chaise & I spent two or 3 hours with her very comfortably; Mr Jones came to Dinner, & we play'd at Cribbage with bad success. a darker Day never concluded a Year.

rec'd 201 Letters
wrote 181 Letters.

1790

Friday Jan: 1st.

Had been a Frost in the night & continued freezing all Day in spite of constant Sun I walk'd a good deal, Mr Jones staid here, & we again play'd at Cribbage. rec'd Letters from Miss Anne Snow & my Sister Travell.

Saturday Jan: 2^{d.}

The Frost quite gone, tho very cold, raw, & disagreable, with a very strong wind, but I walk'd a little & the Gentlemen a great deal, dined at Lower Slaughter, much as usual, the poor Mr Napers spirits appear'd worse than ever.

Sunday Jan: 3^{d.}

Had been a night of severe rain but clear'd off in the Morning, & was a bright fine Day, with a damp wind. went to Church at 10 o'clock, the service indifferently perform'd by a Mr Griffiths in the absence of Mr Williams, no church in the evening, walk'd a good deal in the Morning & visited the sick. wrote to Maria Jones & my Sister Travell.

Monday Jan: 4ᵗʰ·

No rain but damp, cold, & disagreable Mʳ Witts went early to Sandywell returning to Dinner. Mʳˢ· Naper here in the Morning for a short time, I walk'd as usual. Mʳ Simon Paget dined here, but a way before it was quite dark. Mʳ Witts read to me in the evening.

Tuesday Jan: 5ᵗʰ·

Very much the same kind of weather which did not tempt me to go out, the Gentlemen rode to L: Slaughter for an hour or two, Mʳˢ· Rollinson, Miss Western Miss & Master Rollinson came to Dinner, much play & delight among all the Children, & we play'd at Cribbage wrote to Miss Amelia Sabine & rec'd a Letter frᵐ· My Sister Travell.

Wensday Jan: 6ᵗʰ·

Nothing more similiar in point of weather than one Day to another, the Ladies never went out of the House, the Gentlemen went in the Chaise to survey Mʳ Hippesleys plantations,[29] Mʳˢ· Naper here for an hour or two in the Morning. the evening passt as the former one.

Thursday Jan: 7ᵗʰ·

Such an uncommon fine Day was hardly ever known at this season, a trifling Frost in the Morning, but perfectly dry, mild & warm & constant Sun from Morn: to night. Mʳˢ· Rollinson & her party went away soon after Breakfast, the Gents rode & the Boys & I walkt in the fields. Dined at Mʳ Napers in the old stile.[30]

Friday Jan: 8ᵗʰ·

Quite a contrast in point of weather very thick fog, consequently cold & raw, went with Mʳˢ· Naper to Mʳ Palmers at Bourton to make a small purchase, & sat an hour or two at L. Slaughter on our return. Mʳ Witts gone to Chip: but return'd to Dinner to meet Mʳ Jones & Mʳ Vernon a merry Game at Cribbage at night,[31] Mʳ Jones as usual taking a Bed.

Saturday Jan: 9ᵗʰ·

As thick a fog as the former Day no stirring out for pleasure, read & worket besides schooling the Boys, & went to Drink Tea at Lower Slaughter playing at Cribbage with success.

Sunday Jan 10ᵗʰ·

Till after mid-day as thick a fog as the former Days when it clear'd a little & permitted me to walk in the Garden; Mʳˢ· Naper came to church in the Morning, not cold there, Mʳ Williams dined here as usual after evening Church.

---

29. John Hippisley (1735–1822), rector of Stow-on-the-Wold. John Hippisley married his relation Margaret Hippisley Cox in 1769, and their second son, Henry, was the Hippisley who married Anne Rollinson, mentioned above.
30. *See* the note above about dining. Presumably they ate in the mid- to late afternoon.
31. The Mr Vernon was presumably Thomas Vernon Dolphin of Eyford Park. He was the father of John Dolphin, the curate of Lower Slaughter.

Monday Jan: 11th.

Rather foggy, with frequent flying showers & at night hard rain with violent gusts of Wind, Mr Jones here in the Morning, & we dined at Lower Slaughter where all things continue just the same.

Tuesday Jan: 12th.

Much such another Day, only with more continued rain & dreadfully damp, going out of the House absolutely impossible, Mr John Dutton dined here great delight to the Boys, much hurt by hearing of the Death of <u>poor Frank</u>, tho it was an event very long to be expected. — sincerely sorry for what my Bro^r Travell must suffer on the melancholly occasion.[32]

Wensday Jan: 13th.

A very dismal Day thick fog & rain, & the greater part steady hard rain, Mr Witts went directly after breakfast to meet Mr Penyston at Chip: & did not return. Richard Hippesley here for an hour in the morn^{g.}[33] My Brother & I went to drink Tea at L. Slaughter where we found Mr Master & his Son.[34] Cribbage as usual rec'd Letters from L^{dy.} Edwd. Bentinck & Miss Snow.

Thursday Jan: 14th.

Fog in the Morning but clear'd off early to be a prodigeous bright fine Day. My Brother & Francis went to Hawling Downs in his Chaise to set out a new road, & Mrs. Naper sending her Chaise for me I spent the whole Morning with her airing with her to the end of Stow Town, Mr Witts return'd home to Dinner I was far from well in the evening.

Friday Jan: 15th.

A white Frost in the Morning which soon went off & was succeeded by a most brilliant warm fine Day, My Brother & <u>all</u> of <u>us</u> <u>5</u> walk'd to see Mrs. Burrows, a great undertaking from the extreme dirt which was greater than I could have had any notion of, dined at L: Slaughter, Mr Markham there & Mr Isaac's return'd, both M^r & Mrs. Naper very far from well, visit renderd doubly melancholly from the idea it was the last this season; & leaving them worse rather than better.

Saturday Jan: 16th.

No frost & a mixture of storms & sunshine without rain so upon the whole a fine Day tho rather colder. bid adieu to Upper Slaughter with gratefull sentiments to my Bro^r for his kindness to me & mine brought our elder Sons with us in our own Chaise & Edwd. Came on a hired one with the Maids; stopt a very little while at Chip: & I went alone to Swerford

---

32. 'Frank' was Francis Hitchman (1763–1790), the illegitimate son of Francis Travell, 'Brother Travell'.
33. Richard Hippisley, son of the Revd John Hippisley, of Stow, took the name and arms of Tuckfield in 1808 and moved to Fulford Park in Devon, the historic seat of the Tuckfield family.
34. The Naper family seemed to mix the use of the Naper and Dutton names. They were the same family with Lord Sherborne at the head. Mr Master was Thomas Master of Cirencester. In 1769 he had married Mary Dutton (d. 1819), the younger sister of William Naper, now lying on his long and lingering deathbed in Lower Slaughter. James Lenox Naper, father of Lord Sherborne, assumed the name Dutton in lieu of Naper in 1748, on inheriting the estate of Sherborne under the will of his maternal uncle, Sir James Dutton, 2nd Baronet.

before I went home to see my Brother & Sisters, found the former much as I expected in his distresst state, came home to a late Dinner. rec'd a Letter from M^rs· Granville

Sunday Jan: 17th·

Something of a Frost but neither bright or fine & very cold & raw, Mr Evans did the Duty at Church & my Sisters return'd home with us & my Brother came soon after & staid here till quite our Dinner time. wrote to M^rs· Rollinson & Miss Anne Snow.

Monday Jan: 18th·

Much the same weather as yesterday only colder, which made me affraid from my Rhumatism to stir out & the Boys had all too bad colds, Mr Witts went to Chip: on the information of some audacious Housebreakers being taken up. My Brother Travell & my Sisters dined here & play'd at Whist the former very low indeed. Mr Earle call'd here in the Morning

Tuesday Jan: 19th·

No change of weather only the wind rather higher part still very trifling, none of us went out but Mr Witts who rode to Chip: much engaged all Day wrote to M^rs· Naper.

Wensday Jan: 20th·

A bright, clear, pleasant Frost with constant sunshine Mr Witts went down to Swerford to take leave of my Brother & Sisters before their departure I walkt for an hour before I went to dress to go to Kingham to which place we found the roads were worse than ever, only us 4, play'd a merry Game at Cribbage.

Thursday Jan: 21st·

Something of a Frost but the most uninterrupted, terrible, thick fog ever seen, but yet the Gentlemen rode out, we Ladies never left the fireside play'd again at Cribbage with much success, rec'd a very pleasing Letter from M^rs· Naper.

Friday Jan: 22^d·

Just such another Day only the fog was rather thicker & towards afternoon became rain, made our dirty drive home still more unpleasant, found our Dear Boys colds rather better. Mr Witts read General Conways Comedy of False appearances to me.[35] wrote to M^rs· Catherine Thornton.

Saturday Jan: 23^d·

Fog early in the Day, but clear'd off & was a mild pleasant Day, engaged in many employments & in the evening very busy at accompts

---

35. Henry Seymour Conway (1721–1795). Conway had a long and distinguished military career, ending up as field marshal. Part of the leisure of his last years was devoted to literary work. He wrote and printed a prologue to the play *The Way to Keep Him*, acted by amateurs at the private theatre at Richmond House, in April 1787, and 'altered from the French,' the original being *Dehors Trompeurs* of Louis de Boissy, a comedy entitled *False Appearances*, which was first performed at Richmond House, and then published in 1789 with a long dedication to Miss Farren, who acted in it at Drury Lane.

Sunday Jan: 24ᵗʰ·

No fog, but a thick mild air & terribly damp, did not venture to take the Boys to church where Mᵣ Earle did the duty, I walkt a little after I came home, rec'd a Letter from Mʳˢ· Naper & answerd it.

Monday Jan: 25ᵗʰ·

Had been a night of severe rain & did not clear off till 10 o'clock when it was very fine but damp, Mᵣ Evans call'd here in the Morning my two Sisters came to Dinner from Slaughter. some reading & Cribbage both in the evening.

Tuesday Jan: 26ᵗʰ·

Had been a small frost in the night but went off & only made it still more dirty walking but I did not mind it; Miss Western came to Dinner from Mʳˢ· Rollinsons to stay a week. Mᵣ Earle & Mᵣ Evans likewise dined here, so we had a very large Party at Cribbage. wrote to Dᵣ Wall on a poor Mans account.

Wensday Jan: 27ᵗʰ·

Very hard rain all night, & was a most violent stormy Day, but dry & with much sunshine, but not pleasant enough for any of us to think of going out but Mᵣ Witts who went to Chip much reading & working & some Cribbage. rec'd a Letter from Lady Lyttelton.

Witts Family Papers F177

1790

Thursday Jan: 28ᵗʰ·

Thick fog in the Morning which terminated in hard rain, thoroughly damp & unpleasant, no stirring out but very favourable to reading working, conversing & playing with the Boys to whom the Magic Lanthorn was exhibited at night & afterwards Cribbage. rec'd a Letter from Dʳ· Wall.

Friday Jan: 29ᵗʰ·

A trifling frost, but a bright fine Day tho cold & windy, we all took a long walk, & all went to Drink Tea at Dʳ Williams's, the Chaise going twice which made some not at home till quite a late hour. a Table at Whist & Cribbage, one of the Miss Heyner's being added to their family party.

Saturday Jan: 30ᵗʰ·

Much such a Day as the former only not quite so bright a Sun, Mʳ Witts went to Chipping: Norton, & we walk'd again & got very dirty play'd at Goose in the evening for the amusement of the Boys, soon sick of it & glad to go to Cribbage as a relief.

Sunday Jan: 31ˢᵗ·

Quite an indifferent Day, cold & stormy with some rain, very dirty going to Church where Mʳ Earle did the Duty, Mʳ Evans being gone into Wales more talking in the course of the Day, than either reading or writting. rec'd a very long & agreable Letter from Miss Forrest.

Monday Feb: 1ˢᵗ·

Dry bright & fine, tho rather a cold wind, walk'd all of us for an hour of more, Mʳˢ· Rollinson came to Dinner, & enlivened our party much by many chearfull anecdotes arising from her Journey to Town to carry Mary to School, rec'd a Letter from Mʳˢ· Naper, & wrote to Mʳˢ· Buxton.

Tuesday Feb: 2ᵈ·

Not a very fine Day, nor much otherwise, flying showers at noon, wᶜʰ made walking not elegible, so we had a long Morning of work & converse, Cribbage as before in the evening. & wrote to Mʳˢ· Naper.

Wensday Feb: 3ᵈ·

An uncommon mild fine Day, for the time of Year tho without sun, Mʳ Wrightsons Fox hounds in & about the Park for an hour or more, much concerned to receive by an early messenger from M^rs. Naper a very bad account of Mr Buxton whose state seemd to be very dangerous, & to request one of my Sisters to go to her, which My Sis^r Cath: did Mr Witts going with her to Chipping Norton. M^rs. Rollinson & Miss Western left us at mid-day; My Sis^r Travell & I walkt & in the even^g. workt & read. wrote to M^rs. Naper.

Thursday Feb: 4th.

Dry, but not so warm or fine a Day as the former one, Mr Hoskins & Mr Price both here for an hour or two in the Morning from Wigginton, walkt out with us, M^r & M^rs. Western came here to Dinner & Mr Earle also, both Cribbage & Picquet in the evening. rec'd Letters from Miss Anne Snow & M^rs. Naper, with something a better account of poor Mr Buxton.

Friday Feb: 5th.

Much the same kind of Day, rather finer, sat all the Morning in the house out of Compliment to M^rs. Western, the Gentlemen rode, evening spent in Cards & much chearfullness. rec'd a Letter from M^rs. Rollinson with an inclosed Letter of my Bro^r Ferdinands giving a better account of Mr Buxton.

Saturday Feb: 6th.

A most uncommon fine Day for the time of Year, mild air & constant sun, & the earth beginning to get dry fast. our Kingham friends left us soon after Breakfast, when we walkt to Swerford to see many sick & poor people.

Sunday Feb: 7th.

A still quiet Day without either sun & wind & yet a very drying air & grown wonderfully under foot, I went to the Sunday School imediately after Breakfast Mr Edward Earle did the Duty at Swerford Church, M^rs. Wosley dined here. I wrote to M^rs. Granville & M^rs. Eliza: Tracy.

Monday Feb: 8th.

No change at all in the weather except being a little colder, My Sister Travell & I went soon after Breakfast to call on M^rs. Penyston a pleasant chatty visit, did several little businesses going & returning, the two Mr Earles drank Tea & play'd at Whist. wrote to M^rs. Tyrwhitt.

Tuesday Feb: 9th.

Dark foggy Morn: but turn'd out a warm fine Day, Mr Witts & my Sister walk'd, but I was too busy with many employs to find time. My Sister & I began reading M^rs. C: Smiths new Novel of Ethebride. rec'd a Letter from M^rs. Tyrwhitt & wrote to M^rs. Naper & Miss Snow.

Wensday Feb: 10th.

Much such another Morning which never well clear'd off, Mr Witts went to Chipping Norton & M^rs. Tyrwhitt made a long visit here pleased to see her look so well & happy as ever in her friendly society rec'd a Letter from my Bro^r Ferdinand with a much amended account of poor Mr Buxton

Thursday Feb: 11ᵗʰ·

Had been a good deal rain of rain in the night, but was a mild pleasant Day, walkt a great deal in & about the Park, the Boys with us entertaind by Ethebride tho not quite satisfied with the Story rec'd a Letter from Mʳˢ· Naper

Friday Feb: 12ᵗʰ·

Cold High wind but constant sunshine the Chaise went early to fetch Mʳ & Mʳˢ· John Witts from Chipping Norton where they had arrived the night before in a Coach out of Shropshire, very happy to see them & they both lookt very well; walkt to Swerford to shew my Brother His temporary Church rec'd a Letter from Mʳˢ· Rollinson

Saturday Feb: 13ᵗʰ·

A bright fine Morning but grew cloudy & stormy at Noon, I perform'd a great feat by walking to Hook: Norton with my Sisᵗ Travell my Broᵗ John Witts, my Husband & 2 eldest Boys, a good deal tired when it was over but liked it much at the time, my Broᵗ Read to us in the evening.

Sunday Feb: 14ᵗʰ·

A cold dry Day without Sun, the two Brothers went early to Hook Norton Church Mʳ J. Witts being to do Mʳ Evans's duty both there & at Swerford while he is here, well pleased with his manner in the church. rec'd a Letter from Miss Snow

Monday Feb: 15ᵗʰ·

Had been a sharp white Frost, much sun & some wind, we all walkt to Swerford read & conversed in the evening as usual. wrote to Lady Edward Bentinck.

Tuesday Feb: 16ᵗʰ·

Thick fog & hard rain till afternoon when it clear'd off & became dry & promising frost day pass'd much as the former one much reading working, talking & laughing

Wensday Feb: 17ᵗʰ·

Had been a considerable hoar frost in the night, but was a most delightfull warm bright Day, Mʳ Witts went to Chipping: Norton & my Sister Travell, George & I went to see Mʳˢ· Tyrwhitt where we found Mʳ Sandby, a delightfull visit George highly pleased with dining with his young friends. Much hurt by hearing a very moderate account of Mʳ Buxton.

Thursday Feb: 18ᵗʰ·

A very thick fog, but went off by 10 or 11 & was a bright fine Day we all walk'd out; in the evening finish'd reading Ethebride, in which we found more to condemn than admire. wrote to my Brother Ferdinand.

Friday Feb: 19ᵗʰ·

Another thick fog but went off in as favourable a manner & was a charming Day the Brothers walk'd to see Dʳ Williams at Wigginton & the three Ladies took a very pleasant walk.

Saturday Feb: 20ᵗʰ·

Quite a mild fine Day with much sun, the Gentlemen rode to Chipping: Norton & we walk'd as usual & for a wonder play'd a rubber or two at Cribbage. rec'd a Letter from Mʳˢ· Swabey

Sunday Feb: 21ˢᵗ·

Early in the Morning a very thick Fog & something of a Rhime, but soon went off & was a most glorious Day, after our return from Swerford Church we only staid to eat sandwichs & attended Mʳ J: Witts to Hooknorton Church, our whole party, servants & all 11 in number, very large congregation & good singing, rec'd a Letter from Miss Chaplin.

Monday Feb: 22ᵈ·

A considerable Frost, but a most delightfull warm fine Day, went to Dinner at Mʳˢ· Rollinsons, the Gentlemen on Horseback, Mʳ Sandby there, two Tables at Cribbage lively & agreable.

Tuesday Feb: 23ᵈ·

Fog in the Morning, but when it clear'd off mild & fine, the Gents took a long ride Ladies all idle. Mʳ Lystee, Mʳˢ· Pigott, & her youngest Daughter call'd in the Morning, & Mʳ & Mʳˢ· Tyrwhitt & Mʳ Andrew Foley dined, a Table at Whist & Cribbage; rec'd a Letter from Mʳˢ· Naper with a sad account of Mʳ Buxton

Wensday Feb: 24ᵗʰ·

Much such another Day only a thicker air, left Chadlington soon after Breakfast but did not get home till near Dinner time having much business & some visits to make at Chipping: Norton found the Dear Boys quite well. rec'd a Letter from Mʳˢ· C: Thornton & wrote to Mʳˢ· Naper.

Thursday Feb: 25ᵗʰ·

Had been much rain in the night & was a stormy Day but Dry, all went to Dine at Mʳ Tyrwhitts the two Brothers going on horseback where we found Mʳ Andrew Foley & Mʳ Lawrance Mʳ Ts uncle a very pleasant visit a Whist & Commerce Table fine Moon to return home by. wrote to Mʳˢ· C: Thornton.

Friday Feb: 26ᵗʰ·

A very disagreable stormy Day much wind & some rain quite a stay at home Day but made memorable to me by being my sweet Francis Birth Day compleating seven years of age, made a Pool at Commerce for him in the evening. rec'd Letters from Mʳˢ· Savage & my Broʳ Ferdinand with a confirm'd bad account of poor Mʳ Buxton.

Saturday Feb: 27ᵗʰ·

A bright pleasant Day, Mʳ Witts went to Chip: directly after Breakfast to meet Mʳ Penyston on the business of apprehending House breakers, & never return'd home till 12 o'clock at night having sent three Men to Oxford Goal. We walk'd talk'd read & work'd.

Sunday Feb: 28th.

A Dry dull Day & colder than it had been, all went to Swerford Church. & Mrs. Witts went with me afterwards to the Sunday School.

Monday Mar: 1st.

Much the same kind of weather only rather warmer, walkt a little with Mr Witts alone, Mrs. Rollinson & Miss Western came to Dine here & return'd home by the Moon a very merry game at Cribbage.

Tuesday Mar: 2d.

A most uncommon warm fine Day tho without sun, the two Brothers went to Breakfast wh. Mr Earle at Swerford, Mrs. J: Witts my Sisr Travell myself & the Boys took a walk there, to see many sick, & poor, & I came back tired to death. Mr Earle drank Tea here & play'd at Whist. rec'd Letters fm. Lady Edwd. Bentinck & Mrs. Naper. Wrote to Anne Snow

Wensday Mar: 3d.

Nearly as fine a Day, tho cold in the Morning, Mr & Mrs. Tyrwhitt came here in their phaeton & staid two hours, after they were gone my Husband went to Chip: He & his Brother having both got colds we indulged then – by playing at Cribbage.

Thursday Mar: 4th.

Much of a frost in the night, but was a delightfull fine Day with constant sunshine, went to Dinner at Mr Westerns, where we met Mr Sandby a whist & Cribbage Table chearfull & lively enough.

Friday Mar: 5th.

Something of a Fog, but mild & fine towards afternoon, the Gentlemen rode out, Mrs. Rollinson & Miss Western came for an hour or two in the Morning, Mrs. J: Witts ill all Day with the Headache & went to Bed after Dinner; much hurt by a bad account of Mr Buxton & wrote to Mrs. Naper.

Saturday Mar: 6th.

Quite a thick fog, & very cold & uncomfortable, left Kingham after Breakfast stopp'd a little while at Chipping: Norton, & on our return home to Dinner found Mr Sandby, who staid all night a talk-ative Game at Cribbage. rec'd a Letter fm. Anne Snow.

Sunday Mar: 7th.

Weather very similar only not quite so cold, Mr Witts went to Hooknorton Church with his Bror, Mrs. Travell & I with the Boys to Swerford afterwards call'd on Mr Earle who was confined by illness. Mr & Mrs. J: Witts went in our Chaise to Enstone imediately after Dinner to proceed on towards London. wrote to Lady Edwd. Bentinck.

Monday Mar: 8th.

Very much the same kind of weather but late in the Day grew very fine; My Sister Travell went away soon after Breakfast to Lower Slaughter where Mr Witts & I soon follow'd her

46. Woodchester and Rodborough Common.

in our way to Bownham House, found M^rs. Naper & my Sis^r Catherine tolerably well, Mr Naper no better at all, much conversation & many rubbers at Cribbage.

Tuesday Mar: 9th.

Fog in the Morning, which cleard off, but no sun the whole Day; M^rs. Naper & I air'd in the Chaise to Bourton my Sisters & Mr Witts walkt to Upper Slaughter, a variety of subjects talkt on thro'out the whole Day; & Cribbage at night

Wensday Mar: 10th.

Had been some rain in the night was a bright Morning, strong wind all Day interspersed with frequent hail storms left Lower Slaughter after Breakfast, dined at the Ram Inn Cirencester very comfortably, took a peep at Bownham House by the way to the Fleece Inn at Rodborough Sir George Paul not being at home; Mr Cooper sat half an hour with us

Thursday Mar: 11th.

A dark foggy Morning, & about Noon, flying thick rain & hard towards evening went up to Bownham House after Breakfast with Mr Cooper, much engaged all the Morning with surveying & giving directions, dined at Mr Coopers at Woodchester, he & Mr Witts spent the evening at a Club held at the Fleece once a fortnight which made my tetetete with M^rs. Cooper long & tedious, play'd at Cribbage & work'd. rec'd a Letter from M^rs. Naper with a sad account of Mr Buxton

Friday Mar: 12th.

Thick in the Morning but clear'd up to be a very
brilliant fine Day, quite warm & delightfull, sat out
after Breakfast, & passing thro' Painswick went
to see Creed Place 4 miles from Glocester, road
excellent & views beautifull, much pleased with the
place & situation, but affraid it would prove too
large for my Broᵉ Witts,[1] dine'd & slept at Mᵉ Hyetts
at Painswick, met with a very friendly reception, no
one there but Mᵉ Chestern the Doctors Son play'd at
Whist & wrote to Mʳˢ· Naper & my Francis.

Saturday Mar 13th.

An unpleasant damp Morning & had been hard rain
in the night, & at Noon began to be very wet again,
left Painswick soon after Breakfast & passing thro'
Stroud, stopp'd to look into Rodborough church

47. *Great concern felt & expresss'd.*

a dismal one indeed, went for a quarter of an hour to Bownham House, from thence to
Minchin Hampton, which Church also we Survey'd & not more gratified, & proceeded on to
Mᵉ Savages at Tetbury where we arrived at Dinner time finding Miss Elizabeth Wiltshire with
them, much conversation, & great concern felt & expresss'd, at Mᵉ John Wiltshires pitiable
situation from the shamefull conduct of his Wife.

Sunday Mar: 14th.

Had been a frost in the night, & was a clear bright Day with a very cold wind, went early
to Church, & again to evening service before Dinner two Sermons, the rest of the Day fully
spent with conversation on various points.

Monday Mar: 15th.

Much such another Day, only with more clouds & stormy appearance, left our agreable
Friends after Breakfast, pass'd thro' Cirencester & stopp'd at Bibury to Bait the Horses &
dine, & got to Burford before it was dark. wrote to Mʳˢ· Hyett.

Tuesday Mar: 16th.

Sharp frost, but a most delightfull bright fine Day left Burford at 10 & got home by one
where we found my Broᵉ John, (who had return'd on Sunday to serve his Churches) & our
Dear Boys rejoiced to see us. Mᵉ Edwᵈ· L. Witts came from Witney to Dinner, a very pleasant
well behaved Young Man play'd at Cribbage in the evening.[2] rec'd Letters from Mʳˢ· Granville,
Miss Amelia Sabine & my Sisᵗ Travell wrote to Mʳˢ· Rollinson & my Sister Travell

---

1. Edward's elder brother, Broome, was seeking premises in central Gloucestershire.
2. Edward London Witts (1768–1841). Edward London was first cousin once removed to Edward Witts, being the younger
son of his first cousin, Broome Witts (not to be confused with Edward's own brother, also named Broome Witts).

Wensday Mar: 17th.

Quite as brilliant a Day if not more so, surprized early in the Morning by notice that Mr &
Mrs. Hastings & a party with them were desirous of seeing this place, about two they came,
a Young Lady of the name of Payn, who I had known when a little Girl & 2 Gentlemen,
staid till four behave'd very politely & appear'd well pleased with the spot evening spent as
the former wrote to my Brother Ferdinand.[3]

Thursday Mar: 18th.

A cold foggy disagreable Morning but after mid-day was fine & very pleasant, Mr Witts & his
Cousin rode to Chipping Norton & I walkt with the Boys evening spent as the former rec'd a
Letter from Mrs. Naper with an amended account of Mr Buxton & wrote to Miss Anne Snow.

Friday Mar: 19th.

Rather cold & stormy, Mr John & Mr Edwd. Witts took a ride together, I never went out not
having been quite well the night before, very busy in cutting out & in many employs. wrote
to Mr Evans & Mrs. Elizabeth Tracy.

Saturday Mar: 20th.

Had been a white Frost but was a brilliant warm fine Day, all the whole party, Boys & all
walkt down to Swerford, from whence the two Mr Edwd. Witts's went to call on Dr Williams.
Rec'd a Letter from my Sisr Travell with a still better accot of Mr Buxton, & one from Ld.
Edwd. Bentinck with the sad news that his Dear Lady had had a dreadfull accident by a fall
from her Horse much alarmd about her. wrote to him imediately & to Mrs. Granville

Sunday Mar: 21st.

Just such another fine Day, went early with the Boys to the Sunday School from Swerford Church,
we all went to evening service at Hook Norton much singing & a crowded Church dined late.
rec'd a Letter from my Bror Ferdinand which did not raise my hopes about Mr Buxton.

Monday Mar: 22d.

Very much the same kind of Day Mr J. Witts went away early in the Morning to Mr Stones
in Bucks, Mr Witts & I in the Chaise & Mr Edward Witts on horseback went to Dine at
Mrs. Rollinsons, the latter went to Witney in the evening where we had a merry Game at
three handed Cribbage

Tuesday Mar. 23d.

Not at all a fine Day, thick misty air, with frequent flying little showers & towards evening
serious rain, left Mrs. Rollinson after Breakfast, Mr Witts going to Chip: while I went to sit an
hour or two with Mrs. Tyrwhitt, did some little errands at Chip:, on my return, delighted to
find my sweet Boys as well as usual rec'd a Letter from Ldy. Edward Bentinck with the joyfull
news of her amendment & one from my Sister Travell & wrote to Mrs. Naper

---

3.   This was presumably Warren Hastings.

Wensday Mar: 24th.

Mild fine rain till Noon when it was bright & fine quite a growing Day, but I was affraid to go out having got a very bad Cold; Mᵣ Hoskins here for ½ an hour. Mᵣ Witts read to me in the evening in the voyage to Botany Bay. rec'd a Letter from Miss Snow & wrote to Mʳˢ· Buxton.

Thursday Mar: 25th.

A charming Day after the rain mild, with fine gleams of sun, my Cold was so very bad I was fearfull of stirring out, Mᵣ Witts took the three Boys a long walk. rec'd a Letter from Mʳˢ· Naper.

Friday Mar: 26th.

A tolerable fine Day, tho with rather a cold wind, yet I ventured out a walking hoping to mend my cold. my Broᵣ John arrived to Tea quite unexpectedly, & much surprized to find his Wife did not propose returning a good deal vex'd at it wrote to my Sister Travell in one of Franˢˢ his first Letter

Saturday Mar: 27th.

Quite a cold disagreable Day with a thick air, did not venture out, much engaged with work, cutting out &c. play'd at 3 handed Cribbage in the evening, not a very <u>lively</u> Day alltogether.

Sunday Mar: 28th.

A fine pleasant Day, with much sun, tho rather a cold wind, after Morning Church Mᵣ Witts & the 2 eldest Boys & I in the Chaise drove to Heythrope, to see the blossom of the Melianthus Tree, in the Conservatory, the drive was pleasant, but disappointed in our errand as it was not fully blown.

Monday Mar: 29th.

Thick fog in the Morning & never clear'd off sufficiently to make it desirable walking besides I was far from well all Day. wrote a Letter to Miss Forrest long owed.

Tuesday Mar: 30th.

Very much the same kind of Day not suitable to the time of year, Mᵣ Hoskins sat here two hours in the Morning, & Mᵣ Edwᵈ· Witts return'd here again to Dinner, play'd at three handed Cribbage in the evening. rec'd a Letter from my Sister Travell with a still worse account of poor Mᵣ Buxton

Wensday Mar: 31st.

A bright Day, but not a pleasant one, from a strong blighting North east wind, Mᵣ Witts myself & 2 eldest Boys spent most of the Morning at Chip: Norton, in paying some little visits & doing much business, Mᵣ Hoskins dined here, & Mᵣ & Mʳˢ· John Witts came to Tea from Risbro' quite a strong party at Cribbage.[4]

---

4. Risboro was Princes Risborough, near which lived Sarah Stone, *née* Witts (1745–1834). She had married Edward
    Stone (1743–1811), rector of the parish of Horsenden.

Thursday Ap: 1ˢᵗ·

A most truly uncomfortable Day being an uncommon high east wind, & more bitterly cold than any part of the winter, but I ventured to walk a little with my Husband & Mᵣ E: Witts, & we all went to Drink Tea at Wigginton much as usual, rather better from Mᵣ Hoskins being there, play'd at Cribbage with success. rec'd Letters from Mʳˢ· Naper & Mᵣ Evans.

Friday Ap: 2ᵈ·

Much such another Day only the wind not quite so turbulent, colder at Church than the whole Day glad to return home & sit by the fireside; play'd at Cribbage in the evening. rec'd Letters from Lᵈʸ· Edward Bentinck & Mʳˢ· Guydickens, answer'd the latter & wrote to Mʳˢ· Naper.

Saturday Ap: 3ᵈ·

Rather a better Day tho, still cold & stormy, Mʳˢ· J: Witts kept her Bed all Day with a bad Nervous head ache,[5] Mᵣ Roberts & Mᵣ Hoskins here in the Morning, & rode with Mᵣ Witts to Chip:, the other Gent's took a long walk with the Boys & I in the evening reading & Cribbage.

Sunday Ap: 4ᵗʰ·

Much the same kind of weather, rather colder than yesterday, Mᵣ Witts & I took my Broᵣ John in the Carriage to Hook Norton Church, where we rec'd the Sacrament, I then attended him to Swerford Church, where we found Mᵣ Edwᵈ· Witts & the Boys, Mʳˢ· J. Witts got a little better, tho unable to go out. rec'd Letters from Mʳˢ· Hyett & my Sister Travell, & wrote to Miss Sabine.

Monday Ap: 5ᵗʰ·

Something warmer & the wind less violent, but still in the same disagreable point, the two Broʳˢ· Went to Morning Prayers at Hook norton & to settle some Parish business, Mᵣ Edᵈ· Witts & I took a very pleasant walk. Cribbage late in the evening. wrote to Miss Snow.

Tuesday Ap: 6ᵗʰ·

Weather still more severe wind higher & little or no sun, I had so much Rhumatic in my head I did not venture out, but workt hard all Day the Gentlemen all rode to Chipping: Norton. evening spent much as usual very chearfully.

Wensday Ap: 7ᵗʰ·

Somewhat a better Day, being much sun, & the wind not so strong tho in the same disagreable corner, Mᵣ Witts spent the whole Day at a Justice Meeting at Chipping. Norton, the rest of us all Dined at Mᵣ Westerns, & return'd home by 8 o'clock quite good driving light. Mʳˢ· J: Witts & I got there by 2 o'clock & chatted & workt before Dinner to which was added Mᵣ Curzon & Mᵣ Sandby. rec'd a Letter from Mʳˢ· Guydickens with an amended account of my Aunt Betty[6]

---

5.   It is hard to avoid the conclusion that Agnes did not like her sister-in-law.
6.   Mrs Guydickens was Frances Guydickens, *née* Tracy. Elizabeth Tracy was her sister, and they were both aunts to Agnes.

Thursday Ap: 8th.

Much such another Day rather warmer , I walk'd down to Swerford Mr Edward Witts with me to see some sick & poor, evening spent as usual. rec'd Letters from M$^{rs.}$ Naper & Miss Anne Snow, & wrote to Mr Stone.

Friday Ap: 9th.

A most dreadfull Day of cold high wind with flying showers of rain & sleet, ill suited to all the movements that took place, M^r & M$^{rs.}$ J: Witts & Mr Edwd Witts all leaving us after Breakfast; & Nurse also, after having lived here 4 Years, the parting was rather dismal on all sides. Mr Witts at a Justice meeting at Adderbury but came home to Dinner. much engaged all Day with a variety of employments.

Saturday Ap: 10th.

Very much the same kind of weather only little or no falling weather wind if possible still more violent; Mr Witts on horseback Francis, Prissick & I in the chaise set out soon after breakfast for Upper Slaughter, where we found my Sis^r Catherine stationary with my Bro^r who was very poorly indeed much talk & some Cribbage fill'd up the evening.

Sunday Ap: 11th.

Something milder, & not quite so strong a wind, my Sis^r Travell & the two Miss Masters came up to Church from L: Slaughter, & Mr Witts Francis & I walkt back with them & sat an hour there very agreably returning home to Dinner very unpleasant walking but dry.

Monday Ap: 12th.

Very much the same kind of weather, Mr Witts set out after Breakfast for Witney where he was to dine with Mr Hoskins in his way to Sessions at Oxford Mr Master call'd here, after which My Bro^r Sister & I went down to L. Slaughter for a couple of hours. play'd at Back Gammon in the evening. wrote to Lady Edward Bentinck.

Tuesday Ap: 13th.

Still bitterly cold & uncomfortable, but after 12 o'clock snow, rain & sleet fell, which gave better hopes & in the evening quite hard; we dined at Mr Napers, rather a triste visit altogether. He never appearing the whole time, she ill with a violent headache & my Brothers complaint worse than ever, play'd a little at Cribbage, & return'd home at the usual hour very dark indeed.

Wensday Ap: 14th.

Rather better weather in the Morning but soon grew stormy with frequent showers of snow & sleet, M$^{rs.}$ Naper & my Sister here for an hour in the Morning the former very indifferent, I attempted to walk but caught in a storm, Mr Witts return'd to Dinner from Oxford full of chearfull anecdote. a very lively game at Cribbage in the evening. wrote to M$^{rs.}$ Rollinson & rec'd a Letter from Miss Snow.

Thursday Ap: 15th.

An interrupted Day of very hard blowing snow, of course miserably cold & uncomfortable quite prevented spending the Morn: at L. Slaughter as I intended. much work & reading & some Cribbage.

Friday Ap: 16th.

The snow much gone, tho the air was not much warmer, but from constant sun, we had intended to have return'd home, but my Bro.ᵗ gladly made a pretence of the bad weather & roads to keep us a Day longer; I spent the greater part of the Morn: with Mʳˢ· Naper, who brought me back after having air'd with her; Mʳ Witts visited Mʳ Hippesley. Lively Cribbage in the evening. rec'd a Letter from Mʳˢ· Tyrwhitt

Saturday Ap: 17th.

A much finer Day, & the Snow going very fast; Mʳ Witts walk'd to L. Slaughter directly after Breakfast, I join'd him in an hour in the Chaise leaving my Bro.ᵗ with particular regret, his dreadfull complaint increasing very rapidly, & his spirits very bad, reach'd home early & found the dear little Boys quite well. work'd & read in the evening. wrote to Mʳˢ· Tyrwhitt.

Sunday Ap: 18th.

A very cold & uncomfortable Day without any Sun, a very good Sermon from Mʳ Evans, glad to have the sound of his voice again; walk'd after I came home from Church. wrote to Mʳˢ· Guydickens.

Monday Ap: 19th.

Rather a milder better Day, tho without sun having less wind, Mʳ Evans call'd here in the Morning, Mʳ Witts & the Boys & I walkt to High wood close, & walk'd again in the afternoon for the first time rec'd a Letter from my Sister Travell with rather a worse account of poor Mʳ Buxton & a Letter from Mʳˢ· Tyrwhitt, & wrote to Miss Anne Snow.

Tuesday Ap: 20th.

Much the same kind of weather being mild & pleasant with a good deal of sun tho the wind keeps in its old disagreable corner, Mʳ W. the three Boys & I walkt to Swerford & in the eveng wrote to Mʳˢ· Hyett, as well as work'd & read.

Wensday Ap: 21st.

Very cold & stormy tho the wind was turn'd to the south, & towards evening, there was a little rain & hail; Walkt in the Morning, Mʳ Evans & Mʳ Hoskins dined here, imediately after Tea both the Gentlemen attended Mʳ Witts to quell a Boxing riot at Hooknorton from whence he did not return till 9 o'clock. Wrote to my Sister Travell

Thursday Ap: 22d.

Somewhat a better Day, milder air tho little sun, Mʳ Hoskins here in the Morning I walked a little Dined at Mʳ Tyrwhitts meeting Mʳ Western, always agreable, not at home till 9 o'clock recd Letters from Mʳˢ· Granville Miss Sabine & Mʳˢ· Naper with a wretched account of Mʳ Buxton.

Friday Ap: 23ᵈ·

Very much the same weather only with a few showers of rain & hail, after an early Breakfast, I went alone in the Chaise to Kingham to see little Thomas Western, by his Papas request who told me the Day before he was alarmingly ill & so indeed I found him, & his poor Parents in a sad state of distress, advised them to send for Dᴿ Wall & promised to give him the meeting there the next Day. came home to Dinner, & went to Drink Tea at Wigginton, being previously engaged, while the rest play'd at Whist I work'd & conversed with Mᴿˢ· Jones.

Saturday Ap: 24ᵗʰ·

Just the same kind of weather flying showers with heavy clouds, but very little moisture fell on the earth, very indifferent all the morning, ill equall to undertake the scene of distress I was going into, Mᴿ Witts went with me to Dinner at Mᴿ Westerns, Dᴿ Wall came before it was dark, & pronounced the Poor Boy in a very alarming state tho a little better than the Day before; he & I sat up with him till near two in the Morning.

Sunday Ap: 25ᵗʰ·

The same weather rather more growing than it had been, the poor Invalid not much better if any, for rather more a composed night, his fever still remaining so strong Dᴿ Wall went away after breakfast I doubt with small hopes, we staid to go to Church with Mᴿ Western, & afterwards left them with sincere concern return'd home to Dinner & took a pleasant walk after the Boys with us. wrote to Mᴿˢ· Naper.

Monday Ap: 26ᵗʰ·

A tolerable fine Day, tho the wind again rather turn'd to the east, & after dark some rain, Mᴿ & Mᴿˢ· Tyrwhitt & Mᴿ Evans dined here the former were as usual most friendly & pleasant rec'd a Letter from my Sister Travell.

Tuesday Ap: 27ᵗʰ·

Rather foggy & unpleasant till noon, when it became clear & fine, Mᴿ Witts rode to Kingham to see how poor Tom: Western was & brought back a miserable account. I was much engaged all Day, with attending the packing up of all the Green house Plants, which with the Gardiner were to go to Bownham House the next Day. rec'd another Letter from my Sisᴿ Travell to tell my Broᴿ Ferdinand was set off for Town.

Wensday Ap: 28ᵗʰ·

Fine & pleasant the early part of the Day but cold & stormy afterwards, walk'd both Morning & evening; just before it was dark arrived most unexpectedly, my Broᴿ John Witts, in his way into Salop whither his Wife was going by a Coach. A very visible eclipse of the Moon just before we went to Bed. waked Francis out of his sleep to survey. rec'd a most melancholly Letter from Mᴿˢ· Western & answer'd it.

Thursday Ap: 29ᵗʰ·

Soft fine rain early in the Morning but soon went off & was again cold & stormy in the afternoon, walk'd but little, spirits very low from the melancholly situation of so many of our friends rec'd a Letter from M$^{rs.}$ Naper which did not mend them. my Bro^r John left us early in the Morning

Friday Ap: 30$^{th.}$
A Stormy Day with frequent showers of slight rain & hail, but too much to make walking pleasant, Mr Penyston here for an hour in the Morning rec'd a most melancholly, but excellent Letter from poor M$^{rs.}$ Western; much concern'd for them.

Saturday May 1$^{st.}$
Rather gloomy weather for the Day very lowering clouds but no rain till afternoon, took a walk in the Morning; when Mr Roberts call'd here; rec'd a Letter from M$^{rs.}$ Tyrwhitt.

Sunday May 2$^{d.}$
A very fine Day; after Morning Church, Mr Witts & I & the two elder Boys went in the Chaise to Chipping Norton to call on Mr Heynes to enquire after poor little Western who we found was all but dead & that they wisht to see us the next Day. walkt out in the evening, & wrote & read much. wrote to my Sister Travell.

Monday May 3$^{d.}$
Quite a summer Day, Mr Witts went early to Chip: on horseback, where I pickt him up & came to Kingham to Dinner, where we found our poor friends in much distress, & the poor Boy apparently in the agonies of Death a terrible scene, we walk'd in the afternoon & tried a little to play at Cribbage. rec'd Letters from my Sister Travell & M$^{rs.}$ Savage.

Tuesday May 4$^{th.}$
A fine Day with a few Clouds, & rather a stormy appearance, Mr Witts went soon after Breakfast for a few hours to L. Slaughter, Mr Western rode part of the way with him, poor M$^{rs.}$ W. & I talk'd & most anxiously wish'd the whole Day for the dissolution of the poor little Boy whose agonies were dreadfull to see. rec'd a Letter from my Bro^r Ferdinand with the long expected tidings of poor Mr Buxtons death, a most happy release. felt strongly for his Dear Widow. wrote to M$^{rs.}$ Savage.

Wensday May 5$^{th.}$
Strong appearance of rain indeed some trifling showers fell in the Morning, but fine in the evening the poor Dear little Boy breath'd his last at 8 o'clock in the Morn: his distressed Parents bore the shock as well as could be expected. the Gentlemen rode out in the Morn: my Sis^r Travell came here to Dinner in her way to Northampton, to meet my Bro^r to go with him to Notts. in the afternoon with much difficulty prevail'd on Mr Western to suffer the poor little Boy to be open'd obliged myself to attend to give others courages, almost too strong an exertion for myself, not able to go home that night as I intended with my Sister. rec'd Letters from M$^{rs.}$ Eliza Tracy & Miss Anne Snow.

Thursday May 6$^{th.}$
Quite a growing Day, had been much hard rain in the night, & was frequent hard showers all Day; My Sis^r & I after an early Breakfast set off for S. Park leaving Mr Witts to comfort

our poor friends, found my sweet Children all well, my Sis^{r} proceeded on in a Chaise for Northampton I had a happy Dinner with the Boys, & return'd to Kingham again before it was dark. play'd at Cribbage

Friday May 7$^{th.}$

Had been a night of Sharp rain & so continued till Breakfast time, but clearing up after mid-day & the sun bright was a most delightfull growing Day, walkt about in the Garden several Days a most sad restless Day to every one from the knowledge the poor Child was to be buried in the evening, for which purpose Mr Evans came to Dinner, & at six o'clock Mr Witts attended the poor Parents in an airing to be out of the way of the melancholly procession; I paid the last respect, by following the poor little Boy to the Grave as the principal Mourner a trying scene wrote to M$^{rs.}$ Naper. Mr Evans staid all night.

Saturday May 8$^{th.}$

A very fine Day tho a North east wind imediately after Breakfast, quitted our poor friends after having spent several dismal Days with them but I hope been of some service to them, by the way home came round by Dailsford to survey Mr Hastings's great works & many curiosties well amused, stopt a little while at Chip: & return'd home with Joy to my trio, in the evening Mr Witts read in the Life of Mr Elwes a well written account of a singular character.[7]

Sunday May 9$^{th.}$

A very fine Day tho a strong wind, went twice to Church, in the afternoon took all the three Boys & went afterwards to the Sunday School. rec'd a Letter from Maria Jones & wrote to M$^{rs.}$ Elizabeth Tracy & Miss Sabine.

Monday May 10$^{th.}$

A thick close disagreable Day, with frequent growing showers, sufficient to keep one in the House all Day, but I was fully employ'd & Mr Witts read a great deal to me in Zeluco, with which I was well entertain'd tho the second reading.[8]

Tuesday May 11$^{th.}$

Thick & foggy but no rain, very busy all Day with Taylors & Mantua Makers,[9] tiresome employ but necessary, & far from well myself made me relish it less. read & workt in the evening.

---

7. John Elwes (formerly Meggott; 1714–1789), landowner and eccentric. In his youth he spent two or three years in Geneva, learning to ride, becoming one of the most daring riders in Europe. He was introduced to Voltaire, whom it was said he resembled. He inherited an estate from his uncle, a notorious miser, who, with a large income and expenditure of only £110 a year, he left at his death a fortune exceeding £250,000. John Elwes seems to have fallen into the character of his uncle, and adopting miserly habits of his own left a sum of £500,000 when he died in 1789.

8. John Moore (1729–1802) was born in Scotland and studied medicine at Glasgow. He served in the army in Flanders and travelled to London and Paris, where he continued his studies. Ultimately, however, it was his studies of human character and morality, rather than his study of medicine, which would lead to his most important work, *Zeluco*. He wrote several other novels, all forgotten today, and an important *Journal During a Residence in France* (1792).

9. Mantua-makers was a term which fell out of use after the eighteenth century. Basically they were dressmakers, following the style and tradition of Mantua in Italy.

Wensday May 12th·

A clear fine Day tho a North east wind
Mr· Witts at Chip: I walkt a little not
quite happy about my Francis who had
got a bad cold & little fever & as I was
to have him the next Morning I sent for
Mr· Kinlake to put him under his case. Mr·
Evans dined here. rec'd a Letter from Mrs·
Naper & wrote to Lady Edward Bentinck.
Rec'd a Letter also frm· Mrs· Western

Thursday May 13th·

Much such another Day, hot sun with cold
high wind, my Dear Boy being rather better
we ventured to leave home at 8 o'clock,
stoppd at Burford for an hour & ½ to bait
the Horses, drank Coffee, & dined very
comfortably at Cirencester, & got easily to
Minchin Hampton by 7 tho 44 miles, drank

48. *Minchinhampton.*

Tea walk'd about the miserable Town, & had much talk with the Gardiner from Bownham.
Wrote to Mrs· Naper from Burford & rec'd Letters from Ldy· Edward Bentinck, Mrs· Tyrwhitt &
my Sisr· Travell, containing a better account of our poor friends from Notts. than I expected.[10]

Friday May 14th·

A very fine warm Day, went directly after Breakfast to Bownham House where we found full
employment in surveying & giving orders, dined at Mr· Coopers at Woodchester, & in the after
noon took a very pleasant airing of 4 or 5 miles to a Romantic villige call'd Horsley, the Minister
of which takes young Gentlemen to educate, but it did seem likely to suit our ideas in any respect.
return'd to our Inn at Hampton as it was dark.[11] wrote to Mrs· Western & my Sisr· Travell

Saturday May 15th·

A still finer Day, almost oppressively hot & the Dust on the great roads intolerable, set
out early staid an hour or two at Bownham, & then took the vale road to Glocester, thro
Stonehouse &c. the greater part of the way a beautifull country & a drive of 12 or 13 miles;
diverged out of the road about 4 miles from Glocester to go to Elmore Court an old seat
belonging to the Guise family, but now inhabited by two young Clergymen, who have form'd
it into a school a most beautifull situation & so well pleased with the terms & appearance
of things in general, that we were nearly determined on placing our sweet Frans· there when
we move into this County, got to Gloucester about 4, got a very moderate Dinner at the
Kings Head which was kept by a new Person, & walkt about all the afternoon to several
Upholsterers in search of furniture. wrote to Mrs· Tyrwhitt.

---

10. This was in relation to Agnes' niece, the recently widowed Martha Buxton.
11. This appears to be a slip of the pen. She presumably intended to write 'did not seem likely to suit our ideas'.

49. Berkeley.

Sunday May 16th.

Quite as fine a Day & a most beautifull evening, went early to visit the Dean & Mrs. Tucker & went with them to service at the Cathedral, after which visited Mrs. Newton, Mrs. Cummerlin, & Mrs. Jennings dined very comfortably at the Deanery, & at 4 o'clock set forth for Newport 18 miles, but diverged from the road to survey Berkeley Castle with the outside of which we were a good deal disappointed, but the inside is envious & worth seeing & very well kept the approach & walks round the Castle pretty & in nice order, & the country in general rich & very beautifully wooded a tolerable good Inn the Red Lyon Newport. rec'd a Letter from my sweet Francis, wch made me very happy in all respects & answer'd it.

Monday May 17th.

A wet Morning & continued very perpetual Showers all the rest of the Day, rather unfavourable for our Journey, but still permitted us to admire the Country thro which we pass'd. took the road thro, Thornbury to give us the opportunity of seeing the old Castle of that name, which is a fine but intire ruin; a very fine view of the river Severn for several miles of the road; the Inns at Bristol dreadfull, all dirt & confusion after a pretty good Dinner went in a Hackney Coach to Upholsters &c. till it was dark.

Tuesday May 18th.

A very fine & pleasant Day after the rain which made the road to Bath quite delightfull when we arrived at 12 took up our abode at the white Lyon, & meaning to stay so short a time did not look after Lodgings, Mrs. Savage made us an early visit after which we visited Mrs. Western & did some bussiness dined very comfortably at our Inn & drank Tea & supt at

Mr Wiltshires a jovial large party of their own family & a M^r & M^rs. Clarke who were with them in the house to stay. Wrote to Miss A Snow & rec'd Letters from Lady Edwd. Bentinck, Miss Snow & Miss Sabine.

Wensday May 19th.

Entirely wet till 4 o'clock when it clear'd off, rather unsuitable to both our bussiness & amusement; went out in the Carriage for two or three hours shopping & visiting, dined with M^rs. Western in the Vineyards, where in the afternoon came a large party from the Wiltshires 2 Tables at Cards I play'd at Cribbage chearfull enough. wrote to L^dy. Edward Bentinck & rec'd Letters from M^rs. Naper & my Dear Francis with a nice account of him & his Brothers. My Brother Travell Breakfasted with us rather low & indifferent.

Thursday May y^e. 20th.

Rather wet early in the Morning but turn'd out a fine Day, my Brother Breakfasted here two of the Miss Westerns sat an hour here, Mr Witts & I went in the Chaise to Bath Ford to see M^r J: Wiltshire & his Children met many of his family there,[12] & went with some of them a drive of a mile or two to a place call'd Warley, a pretty romantic spot belonging to a Mr Skreen,[13] dined at the Inn, & went to Drink Tea with M^rs. Herehill, meeting a Party 2 Tables at Cards play'd at Cribbage when I return'd home wrote to M^rs. Naper.

Friday May 21st.

A very disagreable Day but Dry cold thick east wind, very busy all Morning shopping & walking about, dined at Mr Wiltshires, a party of 11 tho all inmates of their House, a handsome Dinner & chearfull reception, went late to Drink Tea at M^rs. Westerns to meet M^rs. M. Lockwood play'd at Cribbage

Saturday May 22^d.

Dry very early, but wet, & very wet the whole remainder of the Day quite inconvenient to us, who were finishing up our Bath bussinesses. I walk'd a little before Breakfast, went with

---

12. John Wiltshire lived at Shockerwick, Bathford. Quite what it was that his wife did (Tetbury above) is unknown to the editor of these pages, but presumably she had an affair and deserted him.
13. According to historical documents, the Skrine family inhabited the manor of 'Warleigh', near Bath, England, from before 1400 until 1956, when Anna Dorothea Skrine died, aged eighty-one, unmarried and without children. A decade or more after this visit and the new owner, Henry Duncan Skrine (1788–1853), was to demolish the old property, and during 1814–1815 built a new Warleigh House. As a matter of coincidence, Agnes and Edward met up with a collateral descendant in London at a dinner party held by Miss Hughes at her house on 27 October 1801. Edward and Agnes kept in contact and on a visit to Walton-on-Thames met up with them. Their son, Francis Edward Witts, mentioned the visit in his own diary: '*Sunday 4 August: Mrs. Skrine's hospitality made our day pass very pleasantly. Breakfasted with her & accompanied her to Church where Service & a Sermon upon the duty of attending the Sacrament was performed moderately by Mr. D'Ayley. The young Skrines accompanied me over a ferry to Sunbury where I was admitted to poor Mrs. A Snow's bedside & found her tho' in a bad state still rather better than I had expected. Botanized & sketched. Dined very pleasantly en famille with Mrs. Skrine who took us on a walk to Oatlands: the park too narrow: the artificial water very bad, & the place ill kept: it might, I think, be greatly improved: the house is large patched up, & a jumble of styles. Drank tea with Mrs. Skrine on our return ... Tuesday 6 August: Breakfasted with Mrs Skrine to have an opportunity of looking round her pretty little placed & turn over some Engravings of Egyptian Scenery, Architecture & Costume.*'

M^rs. & Miss Western to be introduced to M^rs. M: Hartley, to see her beautifull collection of her own drawings, which far more than answer'd my expectations, & I was much pleased with the visit altogether as nothing could be more polite from there drove thro some of the new buildings in the upper Town & made an agreable visit to Miss Davie's in their summer Lodgings dined at the Inn & staid at home all the evening no temptation to stir it was so terribly wet & dirty. rec'd a Letter from my Sister Travell much disappointed at not receiving one from my sweet Francis. went to Bed quite low.

Sunday May 23^d.

Very hard rain till between 9 & 10 when it gradually clear'd off & was as fine a Day as possible, we left Bath at nine, thinking we had a very melancholly prospect for our Journey, but were luckily mistaken as it grew fine by the time we reach'd Bath Easton, turn'd out of the road to Chippenham, to go to Mr Methuens at Corsham hoping to see the fine collection of Pictures there, but being Sunday were not permitted, dined at Calne 18 miles, a dull miserable old Town, the Wheel a very indifferent Inn tho perhaps the best, drank Tea at the Castle at Marlborough, & finding we had time & the Horses not tired went on to Hungerford 42 miles on the whole, from Marlbro' to the latter rather a dull open exposed country tho' inclosed, between Calne & Marlbro,' on the side of a high barren chalk Hill, is the figure of a Horse cut out admirably, & of a size to be seen at a great distance. the Bear at Hungerford an excellent Inn.

Monday May 24th.

A most tremendous wet Morning, we waited in vain for its holding up till ½ past nine, had about an hour extreme hard rain to go thro' when it fortunately ceased, but was a thick disagreable damp Day, passing thro' Speenhamland we stopp'd for an hour at a villiage call'd Thatcham to bait the Horses, dined at the Crown at Reading, a great but disagreable Inn the Militia being there did not mend it, while Dinner was getting ready walk'd about the Town which was large & handsome, 14 miles to Marlow, completed 40 miles in the Day, the Crown a very comfortable Inn for the place. rec'd a Letter from my sweet Francis wch. made me quite happy, & one from Miss Anne Snow which I answer'd & also wrote to M^rs. Charles Western, M^rs. Buxton & my Sister Travell.

Tuesday May 25th.

Violent rain again till 11 o'clock when it clearly shew'd for a fair Day, & we ventured to leave Marlow, passing thro High Wycombe to Amersham where we only staid a few moments for Hay & water & to send a message to Dr Drakes, & tho the distance to Michelefield Green was only 20 miles, we were more than 4 hours performing it, from the number of Hills & the badness of the roads, met with the same pleasing reception as ever from our agreable friends, & found a Miss Hughes with them a Cousin of Lady Edwards a clever young Woman. play'd at Cribbage in the evening & walk'd in the afternoon. rec'd Letters from M^rs. Charles Western & Miss Anne Snow.

Wensday May 26th.

An uncommon thick oppressive damp Day, certainly thunder in the air, & at Dinner time began raining most violently & continued the whole evening walk'd & saunterd about in the morning, interspersed with much conversation, a very chearfull evening play'd at Cribbage. wrote to my sweet Francis having had the delight of a sweet Letter from him in the Morning.

Thursday May 27th.

A continuation of most violent rain till 12 o'clock when it ceased, & was dry but not fine & rain'd prodigeously all night; when it held up Mr W set off on Horseback for London, after having been waiting for it some hours, paddled a little about in the Garden in the Morning & talk'd without ceasing all the evening a merry Game at Cribbage.

Friday May 28th.

Quite a warm fine pleasant Day, tho lowering towards evening & a trifling storm, dawdled about the greater part of the Morning, Lady Essex made a short visit here;[14] evening spent as usual very chearfully & pleasant rec'd a Letter from Mrs. Naper & my Dear Husband & answer'd it.

Saturday May 29th.

Lowering & cloudy but dry & not unpleasant, Lord & Lady Edward & I all three stuff'd into the Buggy drived round & about Rickmansworth very pleasant; in the evening came a Mr Power from London a good sort of plain Man play'd at Cribbage as usual & equaly merry & conversible rec'd a letter from Miss Forrest & Mr Witts.

Sunday May 30th.

Very much the same kind of weather only now & then a trifling shower, Lady Edward & I took a drive in the Buggy to Watford, going thro Cassiobury Park, & returning thro the Grove Lord Clarendons, Mr Witts return'd to Dinner from London, Sir Beaumont & Lady Hotham & Miss Hotham drank Tea here rec'd a Letter from my beloved Boy.

Monday May 31st.

A very fine Day independant of a violent Thunder storm at mid-day which proved unsuitable to our Jaunt to Bulstrode as it begun just as we enter'd the Park, Lady Edward & I in the Buggy, Miss Hughes & Mrs. Power in the Chaise & the other Gentlemen on Horseback, carrying a cold Dinner the distance about 10 miles, much pleased with the place & situation in general, & quite delighted with the flower Garden & Hot House plants the evening being so fine we had a most pleasant drive home having passt a most lively agreable Day

Tuesday June 1st.

Quite a true hot summer Day throughout, walk'd a good deal about this pretty place in the Morning, & Lady Edward & I in the afternoon, drove to Langley Broom Sr Beaumont Hothams to Drink Tea rather a dull visit, return'd to a very merry Game at Cribbage. rec'd Letters from Mrs. Guydickens & my Sister Travell, answer'd the latter & wrote to Mrs. Naper

14. Harriet, Lady Essex, *née* Harriet Bladen of Glastonbury Abbey, Somerset (1734–1821).

*50. Westminster
Bridge, Hall &
Abbey.*

Wensday June 2ᵈ·

A gloomy hot Day without sun, left Michelefield Green as ever with sincere regret after Breakfast, my Sweet Friend carried me in the Buggy to Watford, where Prissick got into a Coach, & we brought Miss Hughes to Town with us, not much pleased with our Lodgings at the Hotel in Soho Square Dined in Saville Row meeting Mʳ & Mʳˢ· Granville & their Son & Miss Delabere, after Tea drove about visiting & shopping, play'd at Whist & had a chearfull supper.

Thursday June 3ᵈ·

Very much the same kind of weather only not so warm, Miss Hughes attending as we went to hear the Messiah in Westminster Abbey, got excellent places tho we did not go till between 10 & 11, fortunate enough to sit next to Miss Hollingworth wᶜʰ made the hours of waiting more pleasant, much charm'd with the performance wᶜʰ exceeded all imagination, & from being very full the sight was glorious, a terrible crowd returning & we were unfortunate enough to have a pole dashed thro the back pannel of our Chaise in which we went; dined again with the Snows meeting the same party, & all went to Vauxhall; which we found so thin & such bad company that after staying an hour we all return'd to our several habitations I found myself heartily tired with the fatigues of the Day.

Friday June 4ᵗʰ·

A universal fine Day, finding the Hotel so uncomfortable we determined to move & got apartments at Greniers in Albemarle Street a happy change, visited about all Morning, & dined at Mʳ Richard Witts's in Harley Street very pleasantly a small party in the evening,[15] play'd at Whist, went late to Saville Row, where was likewise a small party staid supper & on our return home drove down Sᵗ· James's Street to see the illuminations on the Kings birth Day. rec'd a Letter from my sweet Boy.

---

15.   Richard Witts was the last of Edward's brothers. The others we have met with already in this diary—Broome and John. In age Richard was one year older than Edward. Broome was the eldest, John the youngest.

Saturday June 5ᵗʰ·

Much the same weather, Miss Snow took us in her Coach into the City on various bussiness Upholsterer's &c. &c., & to view the famous Steaming Machine for the use of Kitchens. Miss Hughes had Breakfasted with us, & we Dined at Mʳ Sabines comfortably enough, a Mʳ Hicks a friend of Jo: Sabines dined there also, & we all went to Sadlers Wells where we were much entertain'd by the various performances tho the heat was almost intolerable.

Sunday June 6ᵗʰ·

A fine Day till Dinner time when it became gloomy & in the evening was very wet, went to Sᵗ Georges Church where we heard a very poor Sermon, made some visits & went into Kensington Gardens with Miss Snow & her Niece Jane, poor Anne not being well enough to be of the party, an amazing crowd & a very gay scene, Dined at General Guydickens only their own family, walk'd in Portman Square driven back by the rain; went late to Saville Row where we found a Jolly party & supt there.

Monday June 7ᵗʰ·

A universal fine Day Morning spent in making visits very few found at home. dined at Mʳ Snows in a party of 12 lively & pleasant play'd at Whist with <u>great</u> success, the whole party adjourn'd to Ranelagh except poor Anne we carried Miss Guydickens & Mʳ Shebeare, such imense crowds we never got there till near one in the Morning, there was 4600 people there wᶜʰ made it impossible to move with any comfort or see any one, a merry Tea Drinking in a Box got home with ease, but not till past four, bringing home Miss G<u>ue</u> & 2 Mʳ Lloyds. rec'd Letters from Lᵈʸ· Edwᵈ· Bentinck, Mʳˢ· Naper, & my Sisʳ Travell.

Tuesday June 8ᵗʰ·

Not so fine a Day, & wet in the evening, took Miss Snow with me a shopping, dined early quite in a family way with them, & return'd home to Dress afterwards, to go to Lady Clives where was a party of near 30, Cards & Music, Miss Stowe a most wonderfull performer.[16] rec'd a Letter from Mʳˢ· Charles Western.

Wensday June 9ᵗʰ·

A very fine Day but rather windy walk'd about a good deal in the Morn: with Mʳ Witts chusing Papers &c. Dined in the City with Mʳˢ· Witts of Friday Street, quite pleasant from the obliging reception she gave us & very glad to see her Son Edward,[17] adjourn'd to Saville Row to Cards & Supper; success at Whist, no one there but Mʳ Champney, who was very lively & pleasant. rec'd a Letter from my sweet Francis & answer'd it, & wrote to Lady Edward Bentinck

---

16. Charlotte Wilhelmine Caroline Bachmann, *née* Stöwe (1757–1817). Charlotte Stöwe was born in Berlin, the daughter of a musician. She received training in singing and keyboard playing and at the age of nine sang in the Berliner Liebhaber-Konzerte, whose performances she was later to dominate. In 1785 she married the Berlin violist and instrument maker Carl Ludwig Bachmann.
17. Mrs Witts was the widow of Broome Witts, first cousin to Edward. Edward London Witts we met with a little earlier in the diary.

51. East front Kensington Palace.

Thursday June 10th.

Fine in the Morning but at Noon there was a most violent Storm, & was wet for some hours, visiting & shopping in the Morning Dined with Lady Hereford,[18] only a trio, but very chearfull friendly & pleasant, went in the evening to Mrs. Tracys in Green Street, meeting Mrs. & Miss Guydickens at home early & wrote to Mrs. Naper.

Friday June 11th.

Quite a fine pleasant Day early in the Day concluded my bussiness & sat an hour with Lady Betty Chaplin, at Noon went with Miss Snow into Kensington Gardens remarkably pleasant, a few genteel people, dined in Saville Row, only there own trio, in the evening Mr & Mrs. Elliss, & Mr Shebeare, play'd at Whist & Cribbage a merry Supper to conclude our London Campagn.

Saturday June 12th.

A fine grey Morning & a bright afternoon, plagued & much hurried before we could get away from London, wch we did about eleven & went down to Ldy. Lytteltons at Southall Park, where we were appointed to meet a large set of company wch turn'd out between 30 & 40, who were assembled for a Morning concert, 6 Lady & 4 Gentlemen performers, the most capital player Miss Stowe, much vocal Music, during the Music light refreshments were handed about, & at the conclusion a very elegant cold collation, the company not all dispersed till 5 or 6, & at 7

18.   Lady Hereford (1742–1817), widow of Edward Devereux, 12th Viscount Hereford (1741–1783). Lady Hereford was first cousin to Agnes Witts. She had a house in London and her country home was Stanway House in Gloucestershire.

those that remaind wch were Lady Clive, D^r & M^rs. Jones & M^rs. Penny her Sister & ourselves went to Dinner, Tea & Cards finish'd the evening & much fatigued were we all

Sunday June 13th.

An intire fine hot Day, all went to Norwood Church, where Dr. Jones gave us a very good Sermon, dined early, M^r & M^rs. Hinton being added to our party, Went to Church in the afternoon to Hanwell to hear Mr Glasse,[19] some of the party walkt in the evening, I prefer'd staying to converse with Lady Clive, found the Day very long & quite uninteresting, fatigued by much useless talk.

Monday June 14th.

A still more delightfull Day the air being warmer, left Southall Park before 9 o'clock stopp'd for near three hours at High Wycombe to bait the Horses & got a good early Dinner, the Town full of noise & riot, from the approaching contested election;[20] drank Tea at Oatsworth, & from wrong information ventured to go the new road to Oxford to avoid Shotover Hill, but found it so rough & nearly impassable that we did not arrive there till near dark & almost jumbled to Death, could gain no admittance at the Star from the pretence of being full, went indignantly to the Boar which we found but a very moderate Inn, tho a splendid appearance.

Tuesday June 15th.

Still a warmer Day, tho a thicker air & not so much sun, found myself quite ill from a bad cold & sore throat, left Oxford soon after Breakfast found the drive home long & tedious, made more so probably from my eagerness to see my sweet Boys who we found all well &

---

19. Samuel Glasse (1735–1812). Glasse matriculated at Christ Church, Oxford, in 1752 and graduated B.A. in 1756, M.A. in 1759 and D.D. in 1769. He was rector of Hanwell until 1785, when he resigned the living. He was vicar of Epsom from 1782 and Wansted, Essex, from 1786. He was a prebendary of Wells Cathedral from 1790 and of St Paul's from 1798. His return to Hanwell was clearly on a courtesy visit to see old parishioners and catch up with friends.

20. This was an important election and there was feverish excitement. The Tory (Pittite) party was backed by George Grenville, Marquess of Buckingham (1753–1813), and represented by his brother, William Wyndham Grenville (1759–1834), who Pitt had made Home Secretary. The Whig candidates were championed by Lord George Augustus Henry Cavendish, 3rd Duke of Portland. He had been prime minister in 1783 and was again to take on the role of premier from 1807 to 1809. One particular and popular Whig was selected to run, Ralph Verney, 2nd Earl Verney (1714–1791). Unfortunately, he was living abroad, evading his creditors. In the end a deal was struck and one Tory (Grenville) and one Whig (Verney) were returned unopposed on 22 June 1790. On Verney's return to England the bailiffs arrived at his home of Claydon. Just a little after, Verney's wife died, with tradition stating that Verney escaped the creditors by hiding in the hearse. Verney himself died only four months after the meeting of the new parliament. Of particular interest is that many of the people closely associated with Edward and Agnes Witts were involved in this affair. The Drakes, father and son (of the Drake and Tyrwhitt-Drake family of Shardeloes), were the sitting M.P.s of the adjacent pocket borough of Amersham and they took a close interest in the county contest, although they held a staunchly independent viewpoint. Portland had tried to enlist the support of Sir William Lee, but Lee disclaimed any pretensions on the part of himself or his family and suggested that Portland and Buckingham might divide the representation between them to the general satisfaction of the county—which is precisely what happened. Sir William's cousin, William Lee Antonie of Totteridge Park, Hertfordshire, and of Colworth, Bedfordshire (brother of the Miss Lees and uncle to the Fiott children), was returned for this same parliament for Great Marlow. Of even greater interest is that Edward and Agnes' great friends were Edward Charles Cavendish Bentinck (1744–1819) and Elizabeth Cavendish Bentinck, *née* Cumberland (17?? –1837), who had married in 1782. Edward was the younger brother of the Duke of Portland.

rejoiced to see us, came thro' Blenheim Park wch appear'd in high beauty walk'd out in the afternoon, but was too ill to attend to anything went to Bed early taking James's Powder[21] rec'd a Letter from my Sister Travell.

Wensday June 16th.

Rather a gloomy Day & not very warm, found myself much better for my remedy but not ventured out till after Dinner when I strode a little about, much engaged all Morning in setting all things to rights & overlooking many domestic concerns. rec'd a Letter from Miss Anne Snow & wrote to M^rs. Naper.

Thursday June 17th.

Quite an unpleasant blighting Day hot, with a thick air, & late in the evening some distant thunder & a trifling rain, Mr Witts rode to Banbury, I walk'd a little both Morning & evening Mr Evans drank Tea here. rec'd a Letter from M^rs. Naper with the good news of Mr Napers great amendment & wrote to M^rs. Granville

Friday June 18th.

Had been very severe rain in the night, was gloomy & sultry in the Morning, & in the evening stormy with some small rain, I was far from well & therefore very little tempted to walk out. our Servant James left us, after having behaved in a very unhandsome manner for sometime past rec'd a Letter from M^rs. Rollinson & answerd it & wrote to M^rs. Eliza: Tracy.

Saturday June 19th.

A very peculiar Day for the time of Year, being dark, damp, & very windy, & apparently going to pour every moment, & at Dinner time there was a sharp shower, I went as soon as I had breakfasted dropping Mr Witts at Chipping: Norton by the way, to call on M^rs. Western at Kingham found her but very indifferent & by no means recover'd her lying in, her little baby a nice Boy;[22] the roads so bad almost jumbled to Death, pick'd up Mr Witts & went to dine with M^rs. Rollinson, M^rs. Jones with her, & all her Children at home from school who made a fine noise, & lessen'd the pleasure & comfort of the visit. not at home till late. rec'd an entertaining Letter from Miss Snow.

Sunday June 20th.

A very fine clear Day, with bright sun & strong wind, went twice to church & in the afternoon to the Sunday School, after Tea walk'd about the Park, but far from well all Day. rec'd a Letter from M^rs. Naper & answer'd it & wrote to Miss Anne Snow. in the evening arrived Thomas Johnson our new Man Servant.

---

21. Pulvis Antimonialis (U.S.P.), Antimonial powder, James' powder, Pulvis Jacobi, Pulvis antimonii compositus, James' pulver.—'Antimony oxide, thirty-three grammes (33 Gm.) [1 oz. av., 72 grs.]; precipitated calcium phosphate, sixty-seven grammes (67 Gm.) [2 ozs. av., 159 grs]; to make one hundred grammes (100 Gm.) [3 ozs. av., 231 grs.]. Mix them intimately'. The foregoing is the official substitute for a nostrum first prepared by Dr James, of England, who died in 1776.
22 This child was Charles Maximilian Thomas Western (1790–1824). *See* the footnote in F173.

Monday June 21ˢᵗ

A most strange uncomfortable Morning, gloomy hot but thick, blighting air & little Thunder, mended at Dinner time, & was an uncommon clear bright evening, with strong dew & every appearance of hot weather, quite ill all the Morning but full of bussiness, walkt late in the evening with pleasure. wrote to Mʳˢ· Tyrwhitt

Tuesday June 22ᵈ

The most wonderfull hot Day I ever remember, so dreadfully oppressive, & yet a strong wind there was no being cool, tho keeping ever so quiet it made me quite ill, I yet ventured down to Swerford late in the evening to see my Broʳ & Sisʳ Travell who had arrived to Dinner; there we were follow'd by a most tremendous storm of thunder lightning & rain obliged to send for the Chaise to convey us home wᶜʰ made it so late we were forced to sup there & come home at 11 thro perils & dangers, the flashes of lightning being dreadfull.

Wensday June 23ᵈ

A better Day than could be expected after so severe a Night, tho cloudy & stormy, & towards evening was got almost too cold, what a change of climate, My Broʳ & Sisʳ Travell dined here, Mʳ Evans prevented by the arrival of a friend walkt part of the way home with them after a round. rec'd a Letter from Mʳˢ· Eliza Tracy.

Thursday June 24ᵗʰ

Very wet Morning, but wind rising it became Dry, tho stormy & unpleasant, Mʳ Witts at Chip: & I very busy in preparation for starting again from home; my Sisʳ Travell here in the Morning. I found time to walk a little in the evening. rec'd a Letter from Mʳˢ· Tyrwhitt.

Friday June 25ᵗʰ

Rather stormy & cloudy, but no rain of any consequence only a few trifling showers, left home soon after Breakfast with Francis & Prissick in the Chaise & Mʳ Witts on Horseback, to go to Upper Slaughter, the meeting with Mʳˢ· Buxton very painfull to all parties, & thought she look'd sadly, her little Girls delightfull; My Sisʳ Catherine likewise of the party, who is dreadfully deaf; weather too indifferent to walk much in the evening.

Saturday June 26ᵗʰ

Such perpetual hard showers, that it might be almost call'd an intire wet Day, much work as well as conversation, Mʳ & Mʳˢ· Naper came to Tea, rejoiced to see him once more himself again, & her looking so well.

Sunday June 27ᵗʰ

Very fine Morning, cloudy towards evening with some showers, Mʳ & Mʳˢ· Naper came to church & staid sometime after as well as Miss Dolphins from Eyford where they were with their Brother. Mʳ & Mʳˢ· Naper came again to Tea & we all walk'd a little in the Garden.

Witts Family Papers F178

1790

Monday June 28th.

A most intire clear fine Day, with strong sun & fine air, a great comfort after so much wet, I went in the Morning with my Brother in his Chaise & <u>new Horses</u>, to make a first visit to poor Lady Reade at Oddington,[1] Mr Naper & Mr Witts met us there on Horseback, the latter & my Brother dined at L. Slaughter to meet Ldy. Shirebourne;[2] Mrs. Buxton my Sister Catherine, Francis & I walk'd to Eyford to Drink Tea with Miss Dolphins very chearfull & pleasant.

Tuesday June 29th.

Almost perpetual rain till near Dinner time, a long Morning of work & conversation with Mrs. Buxton, Mr & Mrs. Naper both here in the Morning, Mr Witts spent the Day in Oxfordshire to visit his Boys & his Hay, My Brother & I drank Tea at L. Slaughter, where we found Mr & Mrs. Martin & Daughters & Mrs. Tracy from Sandywell a very agreable visit.

Wensday June 30th.

A very disagreable Day, thick damp air in the Morning, & in the afternoon violent showers Mrs. Buxton my Sisr. Catherine & I spent two or three hours in the Morning at L. Slaughter, after Tea bid adieu to our friends at Upper Slaughter & went to Sandywell Park, much perplex'd as well as vex'd at the alarming sudden illness of one of our Carriage Horses which soon proved fatal; did not get to Mrs. Tracys till quite dark & suppertime, met as usual with a most kind reception from her rec'd a Letter from Miss Snow.

Thursday July 1st.

For a wonder a Day without much rain tho strong appearance, & very cloudy at times walk'd a little both Morning & evening with Mrs. Tracy, much time spent in various conversations, some very interesting.

Friday July 2d.

A very indifferent Day, quite stormy with some thunder, & frequent violent hard showers, left Sandywell Park imediately after Breakfast, went with Post Horses to Painswick, where finding none were obliged to go on to Stroud where from a Bishops Visitation there was such a crowd it was impossible to get either a Dinner or Horses so went on to the Fleece at

---

1. Sir John Reade had died young in 1789.
2. Elizabeth Dutton, Lady Sherborne (1753–1824). Elizabeth was the sister of Thomas William, 1st Earl of Leicester, of Holkham, daughter of Wenman Roberts of Longford, Derbyshire, and the sister-in-law of William Naper.

52. Rodborough.

Rodbro', drank Tea with M^rs. Cooper at Woodchester call'd at Bownham House for an hour or two & got to our old Quarters at Minchin Hampton as it was dark

Saturday July 3^d.

Very cloudy & strong appearance of rain, but scarce any fell, went to Bownham House directly after breakfast surrounded by a variety of tradespeople the whole morning, to give orders to; brought Mr Conyhall the Upholsterer of Glocester back to Hampton to dine with us went in the afternoon to survey Rodbor' & Stroud Churches, call'd at Bownham again for an hour.

Sunday July 4th.

Cloudy but with little rain till the afternoon, when the rain became almost constant, went in the Morning to Stroud Church well pleased with Mr Ellis's <u>matter</u> & <u>manner</u> staid to receive the Sacrament,[3] found our own seat large & comfortable, went to evening service at Hampton, a miserable crowded Church & Mr Cockings manner much inferior to Mr Ellis's.[4] Dined after we came from Church, & never stirrd out of the Inn afterwards it was so wet. wrote to M^rs. Buxton & Miss Anne Snow.

---

3.   William Ellis (1745–1804). The living was held by the Revd James Webster and Ellis was the officiating curate with sole charge of the parish from 1772 until his death in 1804. Ellis was fond of music and drawing, but painting in colour often created bizarre results due to his colour-blindness. He was also something of a humourist and punster.

4.   William Cockin (1766–1841). Between 1786 and 1806 the rector was Henry Charles Jefferies, appointed to the living by Edward Sheppard. At the time of Edward and Agnes Witts arriving, William Cockin was the curate. He was originally curate both of Minchinhampton and Cherington, and after officiating at the former place, it is said, in top boots, he used to gallop off on his horse, which was waiting outside, to do duty at Cherington. There is a story related by Arthur Playne of the manner in which he became rector of Minchinhampton. Joseph Pitt, solicitor, of Cirencester, either owned, or acted for the owner of, the advowson. On the living becoming vacant in 1806, Joseph Pitt expressed a doubt, in Mr Cockin's hearing, as to whom he should appoint, and, as the story goes, Cockin immediately said, 'I bet you £1,000 you don't appoint me.' The bet was taken and Cockin became rector. In 1790 William Cockin would have been a mere twenty-four-year-old.

Monday July 5th

Perpetual violent showers, most ill suited to the
performance of our various bussinesses at Bownham House
where we spent the greater part of the Day returning to
Hampton to Dinner. my little Francis having something of
a rash out upon him left him at home in the afternoon. late
in the evening the 2 Miss Sheppards who live here made us
a visit. could have excused them the favor.[5]

Tuesday July 6th

Showers as frequent, but not quite so violent till the
afternoon, when it was dry & bright but very cold. left
Minchin Hampton at 10 changed Horses at Cirencester &
went on 8 miles to Fairford a place quite new to me, while
Dinner was getting, went in the Carriage ½ a mile to call

53. Revd. William Cockin, 1766-1841.

on M[r] & M[rs] Raymond Barker,[6] & principaly to take a view of the new invented Steaming
Machine they had put up in their Kitchen. after a good Dinner went to Survey the painted glass
windows in the Church, not much entertain'd by it, the clerk who shews it quite a character. in
our way to Faringdon, walk'd over M[r] Barkers Hob Houses & Garden, the distance 11 miles &
the Crown a very comfortable Inn & the Town neat & well seated on rising ground.

Wensday July 7th

A Day without any rain & in general the sun out, quite a comfort, got our breakfast early
& reach'd Witney before 11 o'clock 12 miles of an indifferent road, & miserable flat watery
country as ever I wish to see, thro' Bampton of the Bush & several dirty villages stopp'd two
hours at Witney, M[r] Witts being engaged in bussiness, w[ch] made it too late to reach home by
Dinner so got a very indifferent Dinner at the Litchfield Arms at Enstone & got home to Tea
finding our little Boys particularly well rec'd Letters from M[rs] Catherine Thornton & Miss
Anne Snow & wrote to L[dy] Edw[d] Bentinck.

Thursday July 8th

A very fine Day, strong air & much sun but towards evening grew a little cloudy, walkt
in the Hay fields after Breakfast, dresst & went early to dine at Kingham, & previously

---

5.   The Sheppard family were the local gentry. Edward Sheppard (1725–1803) lived at Gatcombe Park. Edward was
      lord of the manors of Minchinhampton and Avening. The Miss Sheppards were presumably his daughters, but may
      also have been maiden sisters.

6.   John Raymond Barker (17??–1827). Raymond Barker was responsible for developing the landscaped gardens
      at Fairford Park. His son, Thomas, was to play a part in a scandalous divorce in 1805, becoming involved with
      Anne Loveden of Buscot Park. As an M.P, and with his county commitments, Edward Loveden was away on many
      occasions. Anne said she felt neglected, so a young, good-looking visitor 'who had the reputation of flirting with
      every woman he came near', would have been a clear temptation, despite the moral climate of the time. Thomas
      Raymond Barker, the son of a close friend of Edward Loveden, lived a short distance away at Fairford Park, and he
      was a constant visitor to Buscot. Edward supported him at college and even lent him an expensive horse. In 1805
      both friends and servants noticed a growing attachment between Anne and Tom. The divorce case was notorious,
      but this is not the place to narrate it.

to attend the Christening of M^r & M^rs· Western's little Boy Mr Witts standing Proxy for Mr Savage, M^rs· Rollinson, M^rs· Jones, & Master & Miss Rollinson, & Mr Thos· Western & his Sister Caroline there, a good Dinner but rather a dull party. not at home till late. I wrote to M^rs· Tyrwhitt.

Friday July 9th·

Had been severe rain in the night & was very showery till after 12 o'clock. Mr Witts went to Chip: Mr Tyrwhitt & Mr Earle made me long visits at seperate times in the Morning. Took a long walk in the evening it being very pleasant wrote to M^rs· Naper & M^rs· Eliza Tracy.

Saturday July 10th·

A dry but cloudy Morning, & very severe Showers in the afternoon. I fortunately took my walk in the Morning, Mr Earle & Mr Evans dined here – received a Letter from M^rs· Buxton

Sunday July 11th·

Very showery in the Morning but dry & fine in the afternoon, went twice to Church Mr Earle perform'd the service each time, the 2 eldest Boys said their Catechism in the Church visited the Sunday School in the afternoon, & took a very pleasant walk in the evening. rec'd a Letter from L^dy· Edward Bentinck

Monday July 12th·

Perpetual hard showers all Day very hopeless, being a new Moon, Mr Witts at Mr Penyston's in the Morning on bussiness, Dined at Mr Tyrwhitts, meeting Mr Earle & Mr Evans not at home till quite late & rather dark.

Tuesday July 13th·

No change in the weather excepting rather for the worse, Mr Witts set out at mid-day for Oxford to attend both Sessions & Assizes, rode to Enstone, Mr Earle sat ½ an hour with me in the Morning the 3 Boys dined with me, & made the whole Day pass more lively to me by their sweet behaviour rec'd a letter from my Sis^r Travell & a very <u>interesting</u> one from Miss Snow, which I answer'd in the evening, & wrote to several trades people

Wensday July 14th·

Still incessant violent showers with some distant Thunder, no possibility of getting a walk tho ever so short. M^rs· Penyston here in the Morning,[7] thought the Day a very long one without my Dear usual companion, tho the Dear Boys were all that was pleasant.[8] rec'd a Letter from M^rs· Naper & a few lines from Mr Witts & wrote to M^rs· Buxton & my Sister Travell.

---

7. Rebecca Penyston, *née* Assheton. The Assheton family came from Downham near Clitheroe in Lancashire. She married Francis Penyston of Cornwell, between Stow-on-the-Wold and Chipping Norton. Francis was a distant relation of Warren Hastings. Francis and Rebecca had one son and seven daughters, all of whom died unmarried.
8. Working through the Witts Family Papers it becomes clear that Edward and Agnes were very much in love with each other. Agnes was irritated with Edward's lack of attention to his business matters, but nevertheless they were deeply attached to each other and socially they were an amazing double-act.

Thursday July 15th.

Had been a very wet night but for a wonder the Day pass'd without any rain, a strong wind & a good deal of sun suited the poor soak'd Hay, walk'd a little after Breakfast, & drank Tea at Dr Williams's, taking my two eldest Boys with me. Mr Earle & Mr Evans being added to the usual trio. very dull, heartily glad to come home early. rec'd a Letter from my Husband. Edwd. went into breeches.

Friday July 16th.

A universal fine Day quite a rarity & very delightfull walkt a little in the Morning & after the Boys had all dined with me, went to High wood close to enjoy the Haymaking scene wch was most pleasant; most happy to have Mr Witts return home before dark. rec'd another very interesting Letter from Miss Snow & one from Mrs. Granville

Saturday July 17th.

Very unexpectedly thick small rain in the Morning, but soon went off, but continued a thick oppressive hot Day, Mrs. Leigh of Adlestrop bringing her friend Mrs. Gabel with her made a long Morning visit, as did Dr Berkeley on a <u>survey</u> of the <u>Premises</u> for a friend. Mr & Mrs. Tyrwhitt dined here, Mrs. Rollinson prevented coming by illness. enjoy'd the company of our aimable friends very much.

Sunday July 18th.

Rather cloudy, but with sun & wind at intervals which made it very pleasant went to Church twice. little Edward gain'd great applause by saying his Catechism there as well as his Brother. drank Tea with Mr Earle meeting Mr Evans. Not sorry to come home early.

Monday July 19th.

Cloudy but windy, dry with a little sun but not much like the time of year, Mr Witts went to meet Mr Penyston on Justice bussiness in the Morning, we walk'd after Dinner to the High wood ground to see the Hay carried a very great crop.

Tuesday July 20th.

High wind with flying small rain in the Morning & sharp showers in the afternoon wch made it quite a stay at home day to me, but always busy with many employs & amused with my Dear Boys.

Wensday July 21st.

A most violent high wind & quite cold more like March, but being dry our Haymaking was all finish'd, & being finer in the evening I took a long walk to Swerford &c. with Mr Witts & Francis. wrote to Mrs. Tracy of Sandywell.

Thursday July 22d.

A tolerable fine morning tho thick air & no sun, but in the evening more cloudy & thick flying rain, dined early, to go to Chipping: Norton to take the Boys to drink Tea with Mrs.

Betts the weather made it but little pleasure to walk about the Town, brought M^rs. Trinden home to stay a Day or two. wrote a Letter to Miss Forrest.

Friday July 23^d.

An almost intire Day of small rain, damp & cold, Mr Hoskins here in the Morning M^rs. Rollinson & her Son dined here, had expected the Westerns but his illness prevented; rec'd Letters both from Miss Snow & Miss Anne & my Sis^r Travell

Saturday July 24th.

Quite an unpleasant Morning, being a hot thick air, with flying mist, towards evening clear & fine, & a beautifull fine night, Mr Witts & I spent the whole Morning at Kingham not coming home till to a very late Dinner; found poor Mr Western in a most pitiable state of health & spirits & his surrounding family much distresst. Mr Earle & Mr Evans sat an hour or two here in the eveng. after we had taken a walk to the High Wood ground. rec'd a Letter from M^rs. Buxton.

Sunday July 25th.

Much the same kind of Morning but clear'd off at Noon & was a prodigeous fine warm Day, went to church twice, walkt home in the evening, from the Sunday School, having sent M^rs. Trinden home in the Chaise & two of the Maids to attend her. wrote to M^rs. Naper & Miss Snow

Monday July 26th.

Rather a thick Morning again but a very fine Day, very busy all Morning, & after Tea took a walk to the Villige & Francis with us extremely warm & pleasant.

Tuesday July 27th.

Quite a true summer Day, Mr Witts at Chipping: Norton. too full of employment to walk out till after Tea, much anxious interesting conversation & my mind full of hopes & fears.

Wensday July 28th.

No change in the weather, tho the evening was dark & lowering, Mr Witts made an unsuccessfull visit to Dr Berkeley, & we walkt in the evening. & I afterwards wrote a great deal.

Thursday July 29th.

Very fine Morning, cloudy noon & very wet evening, Mr Witts rode to Weston, & Mr Roberts call'd here, very busy all Morning in a blond purification,[9] too wet to walk in the evening rec'd a Letter from M^rs. Ingram & answer'd it.

---

9. Presumably Agnes was attending to her hair. In Venice in the eighteenth century blonde was the desired hair tone and *The Civilization of the Renaissance in Italy* describes the lengths to which ladies of fashion put themselves: 'The Ideal colour sought for both natural and artificial hair was blond. And as the sun was supposed to have the power of making the hair this colour, many ladies would pass their whole time in the open air on sunshiny days. Dyes and other mixtures were also used freely for the same purpose—It is customary, in Venice, to erect square, wooden, open loggias on top of houses, called *altane*. There the greater part of the women of Venice devoted themselves intensely to the art of dyeing their hair blond, employing different kinds of washes and rinses especially devised for this purpose.' What was fashionable in Venice would not have gone unnoticed in England. Hydrogen peroxide was not discovered until 1818, so presumably Agnes was using some of these washes and rinses.

Friday July 30ᵗʰ·

Very much the same kind of weather wet again in evening & very wet in the night. Mʳ Witts went to Chip: in the Morning I very busy preparing for a general packing the whole Day. rec'd a Letter from Mʳˢ· Naper.

Saturday July 31ˢᵗ·

Wet early in the Morning, but was a very fine Day, being clear air & bright sun dined at Lady Fanes, finding as usual Mʳˢ· Cotton & Mʳˢ· Sandys, & Mʳ Reade,[10] the old Lady pretty well & visit much as usual very pleasant drive home wrote to my Sister Travell & rec'd a Letter from Mʳˢ· Charles Western.

Sunday Augˢᵗ· 1ˢᵗ·

Excepting one small shower an intire dry day, but high wind & cloudy, the two Mʳˢ· Ingrams from Wolford came before church to spend the Day with us & went with us Mʳ Evans did the duty Mʳ Earle & he drank Tea here, & we all took a good walk, as much or _more_ conversation than usual in the course of the Day. rec'd a long dismal Letter from Miss Snow.

Monday Augˢᵗ· 2ᵈ·

A most disagreable Day of Storms & much rain in showers, our two Ladies left us imediately after Breakfast, but we met again at the Book Club Meeting, which was worse attended than usual, only 8 Ladies & 7 Gentlemen & went off very flat & dull indeed, Mʳ Witts did the Honours in poor Mʳ Westerns absence; the Books sold very ill, & the Club proved a Bankrupt.

Tuesday Augˢᵗ· 3ᵈ·

Such constant violent showers that it might almost be term'd an absolute wet Day, fully employ'd with a variety of packing preparatory to our final moving, quite fatigued towards night. rec'd another Letter from Miss Snow in the old strain & answer'd it & wrote to Mʳˢ· Charles Western & Mʳˢ· Buxton.

Wensday Augˢᵗ· 4ᵗʰ·

No rain, but high wind, showy clouds & some sunshine & very fine in the evening the whole Morning taken up, with attending upon a Man packing up China & Glass, indulged myself in walking in the evening. Mʳ Witts at Chip in the Morning. rec'd a Letter from my Sisʳ Travell & answerd it.

Thursday Augˢᵗ· 5ᵗʰ·

A tolerable fine Morning but soon became cloudy, & at Noon small rain which continued the whole Day; engaged from Morn: to night in a continued series of packing seldom more fatigued.

---

10.   Mrs Sandys was presumably the wife of the Revd Edwin Bayntun Sandys, later to become Sir Edward Bayntun Sandys, 1st Baronet, of Miserden in Gloucestershire (d. 1838). The family had extensive interests in this area on the Warwickshire / Oxfordshire border and Edward was lord of the manor of Chadlington. Mr Reade is more difficult to identify, but may have been Thomas Reade (1762–1837), the brother of the late Sir John Reade.

54. Adlestrop.

Friday Aug$^{st.}$ 6$^{th.}$

Cloudy Morning, & soon became incessant rain, with violent wind & storms & yet hot & close, as busy or more so in removing things, it being dry when nearly dark I walked for a little while. received a Letter from M$^{rs.}$ Elizabeth Tracy.

Saturday Aug$^{st.}$ 7$^{th.}$

A very disagreable close damp Morning with flying rain, but clearer in the afternooon & fine. in the Morning I made visits at both Houses at Adlestrop leaving Mr Witts at Chip by the way at Mr Leighs I met L$^{dy.}$ Dow. Reade & M$^{rs.}$ Cotton both very pleasant visits. M$^{rs.}$ Wosley & her neice M$^{rs.}$ Smith drank Tea here, & Mr Earle here for an hour or two in the evening. received a Letter from M$^{rs.}$ Buxton.

Sunday Aug$^{st.}$ 8$^{th.}$

Quite dry the whole Day, with a very strong wind, & a mixture of clouds & sunshine. Breakfasted early to go to church at Chadlington taking the two eldest Boys with us to spend the Day all of us with M$^{rs.}$ Rollinson; M^{r} & M$^{rs.}$ Tyrwhitt sat ½ an hour there after church, Mr Lyster dined, & Dr Cobb drank Tea.[11] the Boys quite happy, but I felt very low from many causes received a Letter from Miss Snow & wrote to M$^{rs.}$ Naper. home as it was dark.

---

11.   Mr Lyster may have been Thomas Moses Lyster (*c.* 1752–1821). Dr John Cobb (d. 1827) was the new incumbent of the adjoining parish of Charlbury, where he had been appointed vicar on 27 May 1790.

55. Oddington House.

Monday Aug^st. 9th.

Fine & dry weather again but still a strong wind, incessant & fatiguing bussiness from Morn: to Night with packing up two Loads of goods almost knock'd up by it. Mr Earle & Mr Evans here for ½ an hour in the evening.

Tuesday Aug^st. 10th.

A true summer Day hot sun & clear air, still as busy as ever in quite clearing away by packing up a third Load, & when finish'd glad to take a quiet walk in the cool of the evening.

Wensday Aug^st. 11th.

If possible a still finer Day & very hot I went imediately after Breakfast to call on M^rs. Penyston who I did not find at home, from thence to Lady Reades at Oddington where my visit would have been more pleasant, but for the interruption of poor Lady Harrington who was there also,[12] in the afternoon Mr Witts & I made a farewell visit at Wigginton. rec'd a Letter from M^rs. Naper & my Sister Travell, answer'd the latter & wrote to Miss Snow.

Thursday Aug^st. 12th.

A more disagreable close kind of heat, with heavy clouds, & some trifling showers which obliged me to have the chaise to bring me home before Dinner from Swerford, where I went to see & take leave of some of the Villiagers. Mr Witts at Chip: Drank Tea at Mr Earles where was Mr Evans a very triste kind of bussiness altogether. violent hot close evening.

---

12.   Jane Stanhope, *née* Fleming, Lady Harrington (1755–1824). Jane married General Charles Stanhope, Earl of Harrington (1753–1829), in 1779, bringing with her an independent fortune of £100,000. He served in America in 1776 and in the following year was aide-de-camp to General John Burgoyne at Saratoga. He succeeded to the peerage in 1779 and attained the rank of general in 1802. Their son, Charles Stanhope (1780–1851), married Maria Foote in 1831. She had been the mistress of Colonel Berkeley, afterwards Lord Segrave and Earl Fitzhardinge. Charles Stanhope was an eccentric leader of fashion and was to become one of the most intimate companions of George IV.

Friday Aug^(st.) 13^(th.)

A much pleasanter Day clearer air & bright sun, a constant scene of hurry & bussiness in preparing to remove <u>finally</u> the next Day. took a last walk in the evening & Francis with me wrote to M^(rs.) Tyrwhitt.

Saturday Aug^(st.) 14^(th.)

A very fine hot Day from Morn to night still more bustle & confusion as our departure drew nearer, had an early Dinner of cold Meat that everything might be pack'd up & set off for Burford at 4 o'clock, with many painfull feelings, M^(r) Witts on Horseback, myself the two eldest Boys & Prissick in our Chaise & Edward & the three other Maids in a hired Chaise drank Tea & supt comfortably at the George Inn but much fatigued & agitated by the labours of the Day

Sunday Aug^(st.) 15^(th.)

Not so hot a day, but a brisk wind & much pleasanter for travelling, set off in in the same manner as the Day before, dined at Cirencester & got to Minchin Hampton to Tea, after w^(ch) M^(r) Witts & I went down to Bownham House to make a survey much disappointed to find all the Workmen had been so negligent & the work so backward. rec'd a Letter from Miss Snow.

Monday Aug^(st.) 16^(th.)

Flying rain early in the Morning & a damp air all Day, went to Bownham House early in the Day, much plague'd & perplex'd with a variety of untoward circumstances, came to M. Hampton to Dinner & back again in the afternoon.

Tuesday Aug^(st.) 17^(th.)

Very fine Morning early, but grew cloudy with little flying Mists, after breakfast return'd M^(rs.) Chance's & Miss Sheppards visit directly after which the three Boys, Molly & myself set off for Cheltenham, leaving M^(r) Witts going to Bownham House to hurry on the workmen all he could, rec'd a most warm reception from my Sis^(rs.) with whom was my Brother Travell, & at Dinner we were join'd by M^(r) & M^(rs.) Naper, & M^(r) Hippesley on their way out of Worcestershire, a very chearfull pleasant Day looket in at the rooms w^(ch) were very thin & too hot to to wish to stay. Francis most happy in attending John Granville to the Play. the same party at Supper.

Wensday Aug^(st.) 18^(th.)

Quite a hot fine Day, D^(r) Napleton added to the party at Breakfast,[13] & a great reception of visitors afterwards, the Napers &c. went away afterwards, my Brother dined out, & D^(r) Napleton with us walked with him before Tea, to which came poor M^(rs.) Egerton & her Sister M^(rs.) Rutherford, went to the Rooms which were rather splendid, play'd both at Whist & Cribbage.

Thursday Aug^(st.) 19^(th.)

A close cloudy Day, with strong appearance of rain but none fell to speak of, went to the Well before breakfast to the great delight of the Boys, M^(r) & M^(rs.) Granville & Son & M^(r) J.

---

13.   John Napleton (1738?–1817). Napleton was a contemporary of Ferdinando Travell's at Oxford, and presumably they maintained contact and friendship. He was Chancellor of Hereford Cathedral and bishop's chaplain.

Delabere breakfasted,[14] & soon after I returnd to Bownham (leaving the Boys behind) by the way of Glocester, where I did some bussiness, took a hasty Dinner & returnd to Tea, where I found my Husband well, & having got things in more forwardness than I expected, went to M: Hampton to sleep. rec'd a Letter from Amelia Sabine.

Friday Aug^st. 20th.

An uncommon hot Morning being a very disagreable thick air, but at noon grew clear & was a most beautifull Day & evening imediately after Breakfast Mr Witts & I walk'd down to Bownham, leaving Prissick to follow in the Chaise wth the baggage not proposing to go any more to Hampton, full of employ all Day; dined not uncomfortably tho in a scrambling way.

Saturday Aug^st. 21st.

Much the same kind of weather thro' the Day, but a small shower in the evening, as busy as possible the whole Day, chiefly in unpacking glass & China, walkt a little in the evening tho tired as a Dog, at night wrote to Miss Snow.

Sunday Aug^st. 22^d.

A most charming Day being a clear air & very bright sun, tho a little rain again in the evening. went to Church at Rodborough, thought our rented Pew a very comfortable one, & liked the reading & manner of the Clergyman, dined & set off for Cheltenham at 4 o'clock by the way of Glocester Mr Witts, Prissick & I in the Chaise, got there as it was dark finding my Dear Boys well & happy to see us. rec'd a Letter from M^rs. Naper.

Monday Aug^st. 23^d.

Very pleasant weather, tho appearance of rain in the Morning, went to the Well to drink some water brought home by M^rs. Cox, made visits in the course of the Morning, M^r J: Delabere dined here, took all the Boys in the evening to Mr Tighes representation great delight to them, went afterwards to the Ball which was smart & pleasant, play'd at Whist in a clever party.

Tuesday Aug^st. 24th.

Quite a fine Day tho rather autumnal feeling to the Well as usual, & much visiting in the Morning, Miss Nettleship Dined here, Sr Willm. & Miss Althan,[15] M^rs. F: Tracy & Miss F: Hanbury, Miss Hughes & her Brother drank Tea here, & most of the company adjourn'd to the Rooms play'd at Cribbage in the old set. wrote to M^rs. Naper. Mr Witts left Cheltenham early in the Morning for Bownham.

---

14. John and Harriet Granville have been mentioned above. Their young son was John (1780–1799); *see* the Hoppner portrait in the colour section. John Delabere was the brother of Harriet and he was the last of the ancient family of Delaberes of Southam, living in one of the oldest and most charming buildings in Gloucestershire. He was appointed vicar of Taynton, near Burford in Oxfordshire, in 1784, a living he held until his death in 1810.

15. Sir William Altham of Thetford, Norfolk. Little is known of this family. William Altham, Esq., sat as a county magistrate for several assize sessions. The *Daily Universal Register* for 18 September 1786 recorded, 'St. James', Sept. 16. The King was this day pleased to confer the honour of knighthood on William Altham, of the borough of Thetford, Esq.'

Wensday Aug^(st.) 25^(th.)

Tolerably fine in the Morning but at noon became wet, & rain'd prodigeously all the evening & night, went to the well, & made some visits after breakfast before it begun, Miss Vernon, Miss Hughes, Dr Napleton, & Mr Commeline from Glocester dined, went to the Rooms w^(ch) were miserably dull, not able to make up a Card Party.

Thursday Aug^(st.) 26^(th.)

Continued small rain with very small intermission the whole day, & the air most uncomfortably thick, Francis & I set off at noon for Bownham by the way of Glocester, to join Mr Witts roads tolerable, in spite of the extreme rain, found him most busy & things going on pretty well. rec'd a letter from Lady Edward Bentinck & my Husband & wrote to M^(rs.) Buxton.

Friday Aug^(st.) 27^(th.)

Thick Morning, fine Noon, & wet afternoon, Mr Witts went early to Bibury on bussiness & return'd to Tea, I was full of employ all Day in which Francis's assistance was very usefull.

Saturday Aug^(st.) 28^(th.)

A very fine Day throughout, after Breakfast, Mr Witts, Francis & I set out on our return to Cheltenham, by the Painswick road got time enough to Dress before Dinner to which was added to our home party Dr Napleton, Mr Bernard Dewes & Miss Delabere & her Brother Miss Nettleship drank Tea & we went to full agreable rooms, play'd at Whist in a pleasant party.

Sunday Aug^(st.) 29^(th.)

Not so fine a Day having little sun & strong clouds but no rain, Dr Waters read Prayers & Dr Napleton preach'd both Morning & afternoon & dined with us, we drank Tea at M^(rs.) Markhams meeting other company, from where we went to a Tea drinking meeting at the Rooms lively and agreable enough staid but a short time rec'd a melancholy Letter from Miss Snow from Canterbury

Monday Aug^(st.) 30^(th.)

Some sun, but with strong wind & many clouds, & in the evening small rain, brought back from the well by Miss Hanbury, at 12 went an airing with Mr Champneys in his Curricle beyond Dowdeswell had much interesting converse with him, He dined with us & Dr Napleton drank Tea Miss Nettleship & Miss Markham went with us to a very full agreable Ball, where I play'd again at Whist, not at home till quite late for collation

Tuesday Aug^(st.) 31^(st.)

Quite a disagreable Day, damp falling air, had been much rain in the night, & was very, oppressively hot, got an early breakfast to enable Mr Witts, Francis, & I to reach Bownham early, to receive the first instructions from the Man that had come down from London to put up the Steam Machine in the kitchen who having completed it was to leave his final directions found it answer very well, so much bussiness was quite fatigued at night. rec'd a very friendly Letter f^(m.) M^(rs.) Tyrwhitt.

Wensday Sepr. 1st.

Thick air in the Morning, but fine Day, & remarkable fine bright evening, most fully employ'd all Day, wch prevented me the power of receiving Mrs. Savage & Miss Wiltshire who call'd in the Morning, walkt out of our own premises in the evening, & wrote to Miss Snow.

Thursday Sepr. 2^{d.}

Fine Morning, but wet at Noon & very wet in the afternoon; Francis & I left Bownham early having bussiness of various sorts to transact at Glocester, got to Cheltenham just at my Sisters Dinner time went to a lively Ball & play'd at Whist in a pleasant Party.

Friday Sepr. 3^{d.}

A Cold windy Morning, & after 11 o'clock constant hard showers till the afternoon but yet dabbled about visiting, after having a party of 10 to Breakfast, My B^{r.} Ferdinand & J: Stow came to Dinner, lait from Bownham House where they had lain Dr Napleton of the party also, M^r & Mrs. Adair to Tea with whom I went late to the Rooms for an hour rec'd a Letter from my Dear Husband.

Saturday Sepr. 4th.

A bright tho cold Morning, but soon became very Showery & so continued the whole Day which prevented any moving out of the House from Breakfast, till we went to the rooms in the evening in Cap^{tn.} Fraines Coach.[16] My Bro^{rs.} both went away one to Lady Herefords, the other home. Miss Vernon dined here, & went with us to the rooms which were good & lively play'd at Whist.

Sunday Sepr. 5th.

Quite a wet dismal Day, dry for an hour or two only, just to allow us to go to Morn. Church, & make some visits after. Drank Tea with Mrs. Swinfin, meeting Miss Delabere & two Gentlemen beside their own family party, lively & pleasant enough.

Monday Sepr. 6th.

Cloudy in the Morning, but dry the whole Day, & very fine in the afternoon, did not go to the Well, but walk'd & visited in the Morning, dined at Mr Hughes's where Mr Critchet & his Son were added to their family party, went to the Ball with a train of young Ladies, which prevented my Playing at Cards an odd, but a pretty good Ball.

Tuesday Sepr. 7th.

A fine clear Morning, but very sharp & cold having been much of a Frost, walk'd to & about the Well before Breakfast, & a little shopping afterwards, Mr Champneys took a farewell Breakfast here, Mrs. Eliza: Tracy dined here coming early & Mr Witts arrived to Dinner also, the Markham family, & the Hughes also, & Miss Hanburys drank Tea here, went to the Rooms which were pretty good play'd at Whist.

---

16. Captain Joseph Fraine, R.N., received his commission in 1790.

Wensday Sep.ʳ 8.ᵗʰ

A very bright fine Day tho extremely cold, went to the Well with my Husband & Boys, Mʳ Hutton breakfasted here, walk'd in the fields with Miss Delabere & Miss Nettleship, soon after Dinner Mʳ Witts set off for Upper Slaughter in his way to Oxon. we drank Tea with Mʳˢ. Chapeau, & I took the three Boys to Mʳ Tighes representation, a disagreable crowd; went afterwards to the Rooms play'd at crown Whist with Miss Crew &c. with ill success.[17]

Thursday Sep.ʳ 9.ᵗʰ

Fine early in the Morning, but soon over clouded & was cold & stormy, & in the afternoon small misty rain, walk'd & visited as usual, Miss Nettleship dined here & we all drank Tea at Mʳ Delaberes & play'd a merry game at Cribbage rec'd a Letter from Mʳˢ. Buxton.

Friday Sep.ʳ 10.ᵗʰ

Much the same kind of weather, had rather a working party in the Morning an unusual thing, Miss Benfield Dined, & we drank Tea at Mʳ Sloanes, meeting the Gregg Family & others very lively & pleasant, went to the Rooms & play'd at Whist with success.

Saturday Sep.ʳ 11.ᵗʰ

A fine Morning, & very fine afternoon, walk'd to Sandford House taking all the Boys, Miss Delabere Dined, drank Tea at Mʳ Greggs, after which a very pleasing Concert in wᶜʰ Miss Gregg shone much, & to which 22 people were assembled; Mʳ Witts arrived out of Oxon at the latter part of it. rec'd a Letter from Miss Sabine

Sunday Sep.ʳ 12.ᵗʰ

A dark unpleasant Day throughout tho no rain of any consequence, went to Church in the Morning, & heard an excellent sermon from Mʳ Hatton,[18] made a visit to Mʳˢ. Eliza Tracy at Sandywell, in the afternoon & drank Tea with her found Mʳˢ. Chapeau with my Sisʳˢ. on our return, went to the Rooms late to attend Miss Vernon not unpleasant wrote to Mʳˢ. Naper & Mʳˢ. Buxton.

Monday Sep 13.ᵗʰ

Rather a warmer & finer Day but a small appearance of rain at Night came home early from the well, to go to Breakfast at Mʳˢ. Lanes at Charlton; to welcome the meeting of the 6 Benfield Sisters after a Seperation of more than 25 years, a party of 20 assembled, very chearfull & agreable; Miss Peggy Hibbert returned with us to Dinner to wᶜʰ also came, Mʳ Hutton, Mʳ John Delabere, & Mʳ Llewellyn,[19] the new Clergyman went to the Ball which was thin & lingering, but render'd amusing by many queer figures.

---

17. Crown whist—five-shilling whist. This was a considerable sum of money in 1790. The wages of an agricultural labourer for one week were a mere ten shillings.
18. This was probably the Revd Christopher Hatton (1716–1795), rector of the parishes of Maulden and Marston in Bedfordshire. Hatton died at another fashionable watering place, Bath, on 20 February 1795.
19. The Revd David Llewellyn, curate.

Tuesday Sep.r 14th.

Dark close weather but no rain went to the well, & soon after Breakfast set out to attend our sweet Francis to Elmore Court school, stopping a short time at Glocester on bussiness the trial of the whole Day more than I could well bear & made me quite ill. Dined at Elmore in a large party, which did not mend my painfull strugglles, the Dear Boy far superior in resolution & conduct to his poor Mother, did not get home to Bownham House till an hour after dark but roads so good I was not alarm'd.

Wensday Sep.r 15th.

Rather a shewy morning but soon clouded, & was hard rain & thick mist the whole Day. most busy which with other reasons made us decline Dining with Sir G: Paul to meet much company. wrote to M.rs Savage & Miss Snow.

Thursday Sep.r 16th.

Had been a clear sharp frost in the night, & was a most clear beautifull Day, & Sun quite hot, quite as much engaged, or more so than ever, S.r George call'd on us in the Morning for half an hour quite pleasant, & found time to walk out a little in the evening

Friday Sep.r 17th.

Much the same kind of delightfull weather, quitted home at Noon to return to Cheltenham bring.g Kitty Housemaid on a visit with me, most delightfull Day for travelling, tho the views much obscured came the Painswick road, on our arrival found my B.r Travell just before us, & my Sisters spirits much agitated by the great alarms of fire the Morning before, but my Dear Boys well & merry, took Miss Vernon with us to the Play, well amused, M.r & M.rs Knights first appearance[20] went afterwards to the rooms for a short time rec'd Letters from M.rs Naper & Miss Anne Snow

Saturday Sep.r 18th.

If possible a still finer Day from Morn: to Night, went to the well, walk'd & visited as usual afterwards, M.r Witts & I dined very agreably at M.r Delaberes, intirely a family party excepting M.r Llewellyn, went again to the Play with them, still better amused than the night before not at home till quite late.

Sunday Sep.r 19th.

A very bright fine Morning tho very windy & in the afternoon very lowering, & in the evening quite wet, a dull Sermon from D.r Walters, visiting till near Dinner tine, our little Dears set out to go home at that time; M.r B. Hughes, & Miss Dewes dined here, all drank Tea at M.r Nettleships. rec'd Letters from Lady Hereford & Lady Lyttelton & wrote to M.rs Tyrwhitt.

---

20.   Thomas Knight (17?? –1820). Following an early start at the Richmond Theatre, Knight went on to Bath and increasing fame. In 1787 he married Margaret Farren, sister of the Countess of Derby, Elizabeth Farren. Margaret had also found a taste for the stage and had developed her own career to much acclaim.

Monday Sep.ʳ 20ᵗʰ·

Stormy Morning & indeed the whole Day & at times much rain fell, 6 of the Charlton family breakfasted here after meeting us at the well, Mʳ Evans & Miss Peggy Hibbert dined here, the latter staid all night, & went with us to dull Rooms instead of a Ball which was put off on the Duke of Cumberlands death play'd at Whist.[21] wrote to Lady Edward Bentinck & rec'd a Letter from Mʳˢ· Buxton.

Tuesday Sep.ʳ 21ˢᵗ·

Stormy disagreable Morning but grew fine at Noon & afternoon, went to the Well in the Chaise taking Miss Peggy Hibbert, Miss Hughes also Breakfasted & various people call'd before we set out at one o'clock for Shirbourne where we were to meet Mʳ & Mʳˢ· Naper & Miss Western & the usual &c's a chearfull evening. play'd at Cribbage had the delight of a Letter fᵐ· Francis

Wensday Sep.ʳ 22ᵈ·

A tolerable fine Morning but at noon turn'd to wet & in the evening extreme hard rain, very unpropitious to Burford Races, very good sport & largely attended, brought home the two Mʳˢ· Tracys & Mʳˢ· Craven to Dinner, the latter staid all night Mʳˢ· Craven returning with Mʳ Naper from the Ordinary, Mʳˢ· Naper so much fatigued obliged to go to Bed early.

Thursday Sep.ʳ 23ᵈ·

A dark damp Morning, at Noon fine & very pleasant, but wet again in the evening Mʳˢ· Craven, Miss Western, & myself went in the Coach to the downs, Mʳˢ· Naper being affraid to venture, not so much company, but most wonderfull fine sport not at home till quite late, Mʳ & Mʳˢ· Craven went home from the Course evening spent as the former

56. *Williamstrip.*

---

21.   H.R.H. Henry Frederick, fourth son of Frederick, Prince of Wales (1745–1790), Duke of Cumberland (1766–1790).

Friday Sepr 24th.

Quite a fine bright Day, very warm sun, but cloudy without rain in the afternoon, Mr Witts went early in his own Chaise to survey Mr Hicks Beaches Hot Houses at Williamstrip,[22] & join'd us on the course where was very good sport tho not equal to the former Day, Mr Witts dined at the Ordinary at Burford as well as Mr Naper & did not return till late. took Mr Evans to play with us at Cribbage

Saturday Sepr 25th.

A most beautifull Day throughout left our agreable Friends at Sherborne soon after Breakfast, going thro Upper Slaughter stopp'd there half an hour to see Jane Buxton, bring away some plants &c., lost our road to Stanway where we did not arrive till a late hour, found my Bro.^r Ferdinand & Mrs. Buxton with Lady Hereford, a very cordial reception much good eating, & a great deal of odd conversation play'd at Cribbage

Sunday Sepr 26th.

A mild dull Day but without rain went to Church twice, the Curate rather a miserable performer he dined with us, walk'd a little between the Churches, & talk'd at a great rate the whole Day, almost worn down with it. rec'd a Letter from Molly with a charming account of little Boys.

Monday Sepr 27th.

Very much the same weather my Brother & Mrs. Buxton went home after Breakfast & Lady Hereford & I in our Chaise, & Mr Witts on Horseback went to make a visit at Lord Tracys and a very lively pleasant one it was,[23] my Lady & I afterwards went to make a short visit to Mrs. Holford at Coxcombe a sad dull thing we had of it much crying &c. play'd at 3 handed Cribbage till quite tired rec'd Letters from Miss Snow & my sweet Francis & wrote to Miss Anne Snow & my Sister Travell.

Tuesday Sepr 28th.

As fine a Day as possible constant bright sunshine, wallk'd & prowled about a good deal till time to go to dress to dine at Mrs. Holfords no one there but her niece Miss Gage, yet not so dull a bussiness as I expected, got home between 9 & 10 a very bright fine night.

Wensday Sepr 29th.

Rather a dark gloomy Day but calm & not unpleasant, Lord & Lady Tracy, Dr Tracy[24] & Miss Byam made a Morning visit here chearfull & pleasant we walk'd afterwards, much converse throughout the Day & 3 handed Cribbage in the evening wrote to my sweet Francis.

---

22. Michael Hicks, later Hicks-Beach, of Beverston Castle and Williamstrip Park (1760–1830).
23. Thomas Charles Tracy, 6th Baron and Viscount Tracy of Rathcoole (1719–1792). Thomas married Harriet, *née* Bathurst (17?? –1795), of Clarendon Park in Wiltshire. Thomas was a distant relation of Lady Hereford, representing the other branch of the Tracy family.
24. Dr Tracy was John Tracy (1722–1793); he succeeded his brother Thomas as 7th Baron and Viscount Tracy of Rathcoole. He was Warden of All Souls' College, Oxford, and died unmarried in February 1793, just six months after inheriting the title.

Thursday Sep. 30.th.

A mild pleasant Day tho without much sun & a peculiar bright fine night, left Stanway at nine o'clock, a tedious drive of 4 hours 21 miles to Glocester thro' Tewekesbury, dined & spent 3 or 4 hours in a variety of bussiness, sent as we pass'd near Elmore to enquire after our sweet Boy & rec'd a most pleasing account not at home till late found our little Dears quite well rec'd a Letter from Mrs. Hyett & answer'd it

Friday Octr. 1.st.

Quite a bright fine Day with a sharp cold wind, a variety of bussiness all day not well, & much vex'd by seeing everything around me so backward & unsettled. Walk'd after Dinner on the Common: & at a distance survey'd a curious Race much delight to the Boys who were with us rec'd a Letter from Mrs. Travell & Mrs. Naper & answer'd the latter.

Saturday Octr. 2.^{d.}

A thick close damp Morning but hardly rain enough to speak of & a very fine afternoon. Mr Witts took a ride both to Hampton & Stroud, & we walk'd before it was dark as well as a little in the Morning.

Sunday Octr. 3.^{d.}

Quite a thick Fog in the Morning & never well clear'd off the whole Day, a hot close & very disagreable air. Went to Rodbro' Church in the Morning, & to Stroud in the afternoon taking both the Boys, but found that too great an undertaking getting home so late it was 6 o'clock before we went to Dinner. rec'd a Letter from Miss Anne Snow & wrote to Mrs. Granville.

Monday Octr. 4.th.

As thick a fog in the Morning, but clear'd off rather better, tho was small rain in the afternoon Mr Witts & I went to visit the Savages. after Breakfast, met Mrs. Savage on the road a Horseback

57. *Shooting on Minchinhampton Common.*

who obligingly turn'd back with us & we spent a very chearfull hour with her, he not at home; did some little bussinesses at Hampton as I return'd. rec'd a Letter from my Dear Francis.

Tuesday Oct.ʳ 5.ᵗʰ

An early fog, but became one of the most beautifull bright Days quite hot ever known at the time of year, Mʳ Witts went early to Bibury on bussiness & did not return till a very late Dinner. Mʳˢ· Savage sat an hour with me in the Morning & Mʳ Bridges Hughes[25] came unexpectedly to Dinner & staid all night & was very pleasant & agreable wrote to Francis.

Wensday Oct.ʳ 6.ᵗʰ

A disagreable damp, thick, Day wʰ oppressive heat, & at times trifling showers; walk'd about with Mʳ Hughes before he left us, Mʳ Witts went to return some visits, walk'd a little after Dinner

Thursday Oct.ʳ 7.ᵗʰ

A still more close unpleasant Day & rain at many times in the Day, I was very nervous & far from well, much engaged all Morning in unpacking & settling Books to rights; & in many other matters of that kind.

58. Hill House.

---

25. In his *Magna Britannia*, volume six: 'Devonshire' (1822), Samuel Lysons records the following: 'The manor of Chittleham-holt, which formerly belonged to the Pollards, was afterwards in the family of Bridges, whose heiress brought it to Hughes. The late Bridges Hughes, Esq., barrister at law.' This visit was presumably something to do with financial claims against Edward Witts. One assumption is that Edward had retained the services of Bridges Hughes.

Friday Octr 8th.

Had been a little Frost in the night but was a most bright beautifull Day, tho rain'd a little about the close of evening. M^rs. Master & M^rs. Naper & Miss Master here in the Morning, from Sir George Pauls, bringing with them M^rs. Estcourt & M^rs. Hodges after they left us, we drove to survey the furniture upon Sale at Dunkirk 2 miles off, some of the road very bad, dress'd & went to dine at the Hill House, sat down 13, a very handsome entertainment & all quite in a stile tho very easy & lively a Table at Whist & Cribbage, staid supper, not at home till ½ past 12. rec'd a Letter from M^rs. Hyett. Miss Sheppard here while I was out in Morn^g.

Saturday Octr 9th.

Very much the same kind of weather only rather colder, early in the Day came M^rs. Master & M^rs. Naper accompanied by their Husbands & Miss Master in their way home, spent a pleasant hour in their way to Cirencester & walkd about, M^r & M^rs. Hyett soon succeeded them & made a long visit. wrote to Miss Snow & my Sis^t Travell.

Sunday Octr 10th.

Quite a sharp hoar frost, set out before 9 o'clock Mr Witts, George & I to see our Dear Francis at Elmore Court, the road both good & beautifull, got there time enough for their Chappel service, walk'd afterwards, had an early good Dinner went to Chappel again, a Sermon preach'd by Mr Parsons, well pleased, with the manner of polite attention of all parties, but most with seeing my Dear Child well & all I could wish; a very pleasant drive home before it was quite dark wrote to M^rs. Buxton.

59. Prinknash Park.

Monday Oct.ʳ 11ᵗʰ·

Much such another Morning, but grew cold & stormy towards afternoon, & in the evening small rain. after Breakfast Mͬ Witts & I set forth to visit Col: & Mͬˢ· Durouse at Paradise a mile beyond Painswick a sweet romantic spot, but apparently destitute of comforts, did not find them at home, from thence drove to Mͬ Howells at Prinnage to see after some Pine Plants the Gardiner not being at home no better success there,[26] walk'd over the dismal old Place & house, most miserable altogether & return'd home to a late Dinner, well tired with the unsuccessfull labours of the Morning.

Tuesday Oct.ʳ 12ᵗʰ·

A cold raw disagreable Morning but not till Noon became very wet, with a most violent tempestuous wind, horridly disagreable, & made our Chimneys smoke sadly. very low & uncomfortable all Day. wrote to Miss Sabine

Wensday Oct.ʳ 13ᵗʰ·

A strong contrast to yesterday in point of weather being clear, bright, & fine from Morn: to night well suited to a long expedition, Mͬ Witts & I attended by George took in the Morning, wᶜʰ kept us out till 5 o'clock, first going to see Miss Gorges at Laterton, 8 or 9 miles distant, not finding them at home proceeded on to Mͬ Cresswells at Sherston Pinhincy in Wiltshire, thro' some wretched bad roads, to survey his Hot Houses &c., return'd home thro' Tetbury, having baited ourselves, servants, & Horses, at an ale House on the Bath road. rec'd a Letter from Mͬˢ· Naper & wrote to Mͬˢ· Rollinson. Mͬ Reads family here in Morning

Thursday Oct.ʳ 14ᵗʰ·

A very disagreable Day, high wind, thick mist or small rain, & most dreadfully damp, went for 2 or 3 hours to the sale at Dunkirk House,[27] which neither for the company assembled, nor the commodities to be sold, answerd the trouble of going thro' such very horrid roads as those to that house. smoky Chimneys took from our comfort all Day.

Friday Oct.ʳ 15ᵗʰ·

A Frosty night which produced a clear fine Day tho the wind was still strong, walk'd in the Morning, Mͬ Witts rode to Hampton &c., & we dined at Mͬˢ· Reads at Ebley meeting besides themselves & their three Daughters, a Capⁿ· & Mͬˢ· Bailly a Miss Clutterbuck, & a Mͬˢ· Palmer, a new stile of visiting & entertainment but well enough, play'd at whist & home by the clear light of the Moon rec'd a long Letter from Miss Snow.

---

26. Thomas Bayly Howell (1768–1815). The estate at Prinknash had been bought in 1770 by Howell's father, Thomas Howell of Jamaica. Thomas Bayly Howell was admitted to Lincoln's Inn and called to the Bar in 1790. When William Cobbett projected a new edition of the State Trials he secured Howell as editor. Howell carried out the work from the first volume (1809) to the twenty-first (1814). The remaining twelve volumes were completed by his son, Thomas Jones Howell (1793–1858). In the 1820s this son and Francis Edward Witts, the son of Edward and Agnes, met during their duties as magistrates and a strong friendship developed. In fact it is fair to say that Howell was to become Francis Witts' closest friend,
27. Dunkirk Manor as it came to be called was about to become the home of their landlord, John Cooper.

60. Tetbury Church from the Bath bridge.

Saturday Oct.r 16th.

If possible a still finer Day, I walkt several times tho no great distance, Mr Witts visited Mr Clutterbuck &c., rec'd a Letter from my Sister Travell & wrote to Mrs. Naper.

Sunday Oct.r 17th.

A continuation of the same beautifull weather, went to Stroud Church in the Morning, from a difference in the clocks, there ½ an hour too soon a learn'd but uninteresting Sermon from Mr Ellis after our return home took a very pleasant walk in our own Wood & fields not before explored; wrote a Letter to Lady Lyttelton.

Monday Oct.r 18th.

Constant moderate, but soaking rain the whole Day which prevented my going to Cirencester as I had intended, but fill'd up the Day busily, with setting many things to rights; at night taken up with accounts.

Tuesday Oct.r 19th.

A direct contrast to the former Day, being clear bright, & quite warm, set out by myself & imediately after Breakfast to see Mrs. Master, a very pleasant drive of 11 miles, not tedious being no Hills, a most agreable visit, her manner & reception being so pleasing, found there

61. The Abbey House, Cirencester.

Lady Suffolk,[28] & her Sister, M[rs.] Willes, & Miss Duttons. M[r] & M[rs.] John Pettat & M[r] & M[rs.] Richard Pettat here in my absence. had the pleasure of receiving a Letter from my sweet Boy

Wensday Oct[r] 20[th.]

Quite a disagreable Day, thick Foggy air with very cold wind & at noon a short shower M[r] Witts went to Prinnage after Pine Plants & from thence to Creed Place to call on M[r] Goldbourn to thank him for them, I walk'd a very little at night wrote to Miss Chaplin a Letter long owed, & to my Dear Francis.

Thursday Oct[r] 21[st.]

A still thicker fog, at times sharp rain, a most damp unpleasant Day, but I walkt a little, M[r] & M[rs.] Read & Miss Read, M[r] Wathen, & M[r] Clutterbuck dined here,[29] the two latter pleasant young Men, play'd at Whist & the visit went off very well: rec'd a Letter from M[rs.] Buxton.

Friday Oct[r] 22[d.]

Another thick wetting Fog in the Morn: but clear'd off at Noon to be a clear warm fine Day, but so cloudy an night that the Philosophers must have been disappointed in seeing the eclipse M[r] Witts went with me to make a visit to M[rs.] & Miss Sheppards at Hampton, from thence went to Stroud on several bussinesses w[ch] turn'd out very successfully, being

---

28. Julia, Lady Suffolk (1737–1819), of Charlton House, Malmesbury, wife of John Howard, 15th Earl of Suffolk (1739–1820). She was the daughter of William Kingscote, of Kingscote near Tetbury.

29. James Clutterbuck (1758–1849). James lived at Hyde, Minchinhampton. He was a clothier at St Mary's Mill in the valley below. James later lived at Holcombe and Cheltenham. He became a Justice of the Peace and a Deputy Lieutenant of the county. The other young man was Samuel Wathen of New House, Stroud. He was in business with his brother, Nathaniel Peach Wathen of Stanley House. Nathaniel was shortly to become Captain Nathaniel Peach, commanding the Kings Stanley Riflemen. The brothers were in a partnership as clothiers, presumably working Hope Mill in the Brimscombe Valley.

Market Day the dirt in the streets were beyond belief. rec'd a Letter from Miss Forrest & wrote to M^rs. C: Thornton & my Sister Travell.

Saturday Octr 23^d.

Very foggy again in the Morning but soon turn'd to most violent uninterrupted rain for the whole Day & evening; very propitious to a variety of bussiness & settling within Doors. rec'd a Letter from Lady Lyttelton.

Sunday Octr 24th.

Very thick Fog, but clear'd before Noon to be a most beautifull clear warm Day, went to Rodbro' Church, Mr Witts walk'd home by the Canal side & George attended me to attempt making a visit to M^rs. Pettat & Ryeford who was not at home on our return by Mr Reades call'd in for half an hour; found Miss Hillyar added to their party return'd home thro' Rooksmoor & up Sir G: Pauls hill.[30] wrote to Miss Anne Snow.

Monday Octr 25th.

Much such another foggy Morning but never clear'd off so well as yesterday, tho was mild & pleasant, the Day turn'd out full of events & much bussiness, Mr Lee's the Apothecary from Hampton call'd here. I began riding double, went to Woodchester & boought some trifles at Mr Tyndales large shop which is famous for a variety of different articles.

Tuesday Octr 26th.

Never a clear air, but yet not a fog, but a cold high wind, I went to Painswick, by the way met Col: & M^rs. Durouse, & her Sister Miss Wynne, coming to visit us, very sorry to turn them back, not being so fortunate as to meet M^rs. Hyett at home; on my return made a visit to M^rs. T: Pettat at Ganycocks near Stroud. very far from well & much out of spirits the whole evening.

Wensday Octr 27th.

Much such another Day, only wind higher & more cold, very full of bussiness both in House & Garden the hot Houses being filling with Pine plants. S: Salmon here out of Oxfordshire rec'd a Letter from Miss Snow.

Thursday Octr 28th.

Weather rather more unpleasant being frequent showers & wind still more high & cold, I did not stir out the whole Day, & Mr W. very little having got a bad cold, he assisted me in adjusting my medicines in new Physic Cupboard. Miss Clutterbuck here for an hour in the morning very agreable. rec'd a short Letter from Miss Hyett & answerd it.

Friday Octr 29th.

Something a better Day, tho still cold & stormy, Mr Witts went with me to make a morning visit to M^r & M^rs. John Pettat at Stonehouse where we met Mr R. Pettat, a

---

30. Sir George Onesiphorus Paul lived at Hill House, later renamed Rodborough Manor. It was here at Hill House that Sir George entertained King George III and Queen Caroline to breakfast on 14 August 1788. *See* the note in F173 above.

62. Stonehouse.

chatty, sociable visit,[31] made Stroud on way home to do some little bussinesses. Very far from well all the evening & much vex'd not to receive a letter from my Dear Boy. Miss Wathen call'd here in my absence.

Saturday Oct[r] 30th

Still very cold, but quite Dry & clear tho no sun to signify, but a day well suited to our expedition to Glocester, literaly to market for which purpose we set out at 8 o'clock, hard at Shopping &c. for 4 hours, refresh'd ourselves at the Bell & paid a short visit to M[r] & M[rs] Dimock & on our return home gave ourselves the supreme felicity of picking up our Dear Francis on Quedgley Green where he was in waiting for us from Elmore we had been before concerted, & brought him home, in perfect health & charming spirits.

Sunday Oct[r] 31st

Rather a thick Morning but turn'd out a most beautifull warm bright Day, went to Stroud Church, taking the two eldest Boys, from thence went to call on M[r] & M[rs] Cooper at Woodchester whom finding at Dinner did not get out of the Chaise, but took a drive on Selsley Hill, the view charming, & the air most refreshing & pleasant much delight in the company of my sweet Fran[s]

---

31. The Revd John Pettat (1739–1811), Pettat was vicar of both Leonard Stanley and Stonehouse; the latter church he served for more than forty years. His wife was Martha (1742–1826), eldest daughter of Sir Howe Hicks, Baronet, of Witcombe Park. The other brother was Richard Pettat of Ebley (1741–1809). His wife was Martha Pettat (1739–1809).

63. *Quedgeley.*

Monday Nov.ʳ 1ˢᵗ·

A sad reverse of weather being perpetual rain, wind, & storm the whole Day which ill suited with the smoky state of our Chimnies Mʳ Witts far from well with a bad Cold, & I beginning to sicken with one; much engaged with setting my dressing room Closets in order in which my sweet Boy was happy to assist.

Tuesday Nov.ʳ 2ᵈ·

A better Day, little or no rain but still very windy, therefore little pleasure in walking, my Dear Boy entertain'd himself & me much by reading to me in Gil Blas.³² my cold very bad. rec'd Letters from Miss Snow & Mʳˢ· Buxton, wrote to the latter.

Wensday Nov.ʳ 3ᵈ·

A mild pleasant Morning, but at 2 o'clock turn'd to most steady tho violent rain which continued all the evening. Mʳ Witts Francis & I set out between 12 & one to carry him as far as Quedgley Green on his way to Elmore where he was met by a servant & Horse; parted fᵐ· him with unfeign'd regret, but he always behaves like a Hero, & proceeded on thro' Glocester to dine at Painswick where we were engaged to dine & sleep to meet Sir John & Lady Guise & Miss Guise,³³ a very pleasant visit play'd at Cribbage.

---

32. Alain-René Lesage (1668–1747). Lesage, also spelled Le Sage, was a French novelist and playwright born at Sarzeau, in the peninsula of Rhuys, between the Morbihan and the coast, in Brittany. The first two parts of *Gil Blas de Santillane* were published in 1715.
33. John Guise (1733–1794); Elizabeth, Lady Guise, *née* Wright (17??–1808). The baronetcy was a new creation of 1783, that which had been conferred on his great-great-uncle, Christopher Guise, having become extinct. The family seat was at Highnam Court, but the family owned other properties, including Elmore Court, housing the school where Francis was now studying.

Thursday Nov.ʳ 4ᵗʰ·

Quite a fine mild Day, in the afternoon a trifling shower or two; the Guises went away after Breakfast, but we were prevail'd on to stay another Day; Mᵣ Witts rode to call on Mᵣ Goldbourn, Mʳˢ· Hyett & I walk'd a little but talk'd much more, found Mᵣ Hyett very conversible & well inform'd.[34] Cribbage again in the evening.

Friday Nov.ʳ 5ᵗʰ·

Nearly as fine a Day as the former left our agreable friends after breakfast, & went to call on the Durouses at Paradise, disappointed again in not finding the Col: at home, but sat an hour agreably with her & her Mother & Sisᵗ Mʳˢ· & Miss Wynne, a strange place & miserable uncomfortable House, stopt a few minutes at Stroud in our way home & found the Dear Boys well & bonny rec'd Letters from Mʳˢ· Drake, Miss Anne Snow & my Sister Travell, wrote to Mʳˢ· Drake to thank her for her pleasing intelligence of Mʳˢ· Tyrwhitts safety & the birth of another Son.

Saturday Nov.ʳ 6ᵗʰ·

Quite an uninterrupted Day of violent rain & Wind, & miserably damp, but for a wonder our Chimnies were kind & did not smoke which made the Day pass comfortably, & enabled me to adjust many usefull things wrote to Miss Snow.

Sunday Nov.ʳ 7ᵗʰ·

Rather wet in the Morning, & very damp, dark, & disagreable weather the remainder of the Day, went to Rodbro' Church, Mʳˢ· Tanner our Neighbour dined here, her Son prevented, a very sensible well behaved Woman of her rank, rec'd Letters from Mʳˢ· Rollinson, Mʳˢ· Granville, & my Dear Boy, & wrote to Miss Hughes & my Sisᵗ Travell.

Monday Nov.ʳ 8ᵗʰ·

Something of a Frost which made the air sharp but was a delightfull Day with continued sunshine, I went at Noon to make a visit at Hyde to Mʳˢ· Clutterbuck & Miss Clutterbuck, a pretty odd place a mile from Hampton thro which I went both going & returning to do some errands. I liked my visit much the old Lady quite a wonder from having lost her right arm, & yet being a most excellent needlewoman.[35] very hard at accounts all the evening.

Tuesday Nov.ʳ 9ᵗʰ·

Not so fine a Day being no sunshine quite late in the Day, but calm & very pleasant for riding I mounted my Pillion; & my Husband attended me, first calling on Mᵣ Wathen at his Mill, then to Stroud calling at some Shops from thence to Ganycocks made a short visit to Mᵣ & Mʳˢ· R. Pettat, then to Mᵣ Cooper at Woodchester about a Great Coat, which was a good round but did not fatigue me. rec'd a Letter from Mʳˢ· Charles Western.

---

34. Benjamin Hyett (d. 1810). In 1733 Charles Hyett bought an ancient copyhold estate called the Herrings and on the site built Painswick House, formerly called Buenos Ayres. Charles died in 1738 and the estate passed in turn to his sons Benjamin (d. 1762) and Nicholas (d. 1777) and then to Nicholas' son Benjamin.

35. Ann Clutterbuck, *née* Sheppard (1719–1791), widow of Edmund Clutterback of Hyde (1707–1778). Ann was of the Sheppard family of Minchinhampton. The Miss Clutterbucks were Mary (1747–1841), Elizabeth (1749–1842) and Martha (1753–1810).

Wensday Nov.ʳ 10.ᵗʰ

Much the same kind of weather only rather more wind, Mᵉ Witts took a long ride to various places the Boys & I walk'd very near to Sir Geo: Pauls in the evening wrote to Mʳˢ· Elizabeth Tracy & Mʳˢ· Naper.

Thursday Nov.ʳ 11.ᵗʰ

A disagreable thick foggy Day not pleasant enough to tempt me to walk out at all Mᵉ Witts walk'd to Hampton. Mᵉ Wathen dined here & we found him a very pleasant conversible Young Man. rec'd Letters from Mʳˢ· Naper & Mʳˢ· Buxton answerd the latter imediately.

Friday Nov.ʳ 12.ᵗʰ

As bad if not a more unpleasant Day I attempted to ride out but return'd before I had gone half a mile it wetted so fast; Mᵉ Witts continued his ride to Stroud &c. reading & work in the evening.

Saturday Nov.ʳ 13.ᵗʰ

A most uncommon warm, bright beautiful Day for the time of Year, at Noon I took a delightfull walk, Mᵉ Witts & the Boys with me to the Coal Wharf at Brimscombe & back on the banks of the Canal by Mᵉ Wathens home in the evening wrote to several tradespeople.

Sunday Nov.ʳ 14.ᵗʰ

Very cold & stormy, but quite dry went to Church at Stroud where Mᵉ Dalaway, the Curate of Rodbro' did the Duty for Mᵉ Ellis who changed with him, walk'd from church with Mᵉ R. Pettat to view Mᵉ Cooks Hot House at Lodgmore whose Garden joins to Ganycocks where we stopt to drink Chocolate. rec'd a Letter from my Sister Travell & answerd it & wrote to Miss Anne Snow.

64. *Brimscombe Port.*

65. A view of Stroud from Lodgmore

Monday Nov.ʳ 15ᵗʰ

A very strong cold wind, but bright sunshine for whole Day which made it very pleasant moving out, was scarce in the house the whole morn.ᵍ first walking & sauntering about, & then riding first to Hampton on some errands call'd on Miss Sheppards at their Door, & then went to make a short call on M.ʳˢ Clutterbuck at Hyde returning home by Brimscombe. Rec'd a Letter from Miss Hughes & my Dear Francis wrote to the latter.

Tuesday Nov.ʳ 16ᵗʰ

The day more pleasant, being less wind & not quite so cold, I only walk'd in our own wood & premises, M.ʳ & M.ʳˢ J. Pettat, M.ʳ & M.ʳˢ R. Pettat, Miss Clutterbuck & M.ʳ Thornton, the Apothecary from Stroud dined here, & the three Miss Sheppards drank Tea a Table at Whist & Commerce, quite a Route of three carriages. rec'd a Letter from M.ʳˢ Naper.

Wensday Nov.ʳ 17ᵗʰ

No Sun, but a very pleasant Day being quite without wind, & a fine Sky, at Noon M.ʳ Witts & I ride to Stroud the Hill way, returning by the Canal, on the banks of which I walk'd part of the way to avoid a steep Hill. did many little errands at the Metropolis. work'd in the evening.

Thursday Nov.ʳ 18ᵗʰ

Very much the same kind of weather, but at times more foggy, but we rode to see M.ʳ Sevilles Garden & Hot House at Chalfont[36] with which we were much entertain'd

---

36.   Agnes clearly wrote 'Chalfont', but the village is actually 'Chalford.' William Sevill came from an old clothier family.

66. Thames and Severn Canal above Chalford Chapel Lock.

being both quite unique in their way. Mr Witts dined with a party of Gentlemen at Mr Wathen's, wch made me find the evening long & dull.

Friday Novr 19th

Had been a great deal of rain in the night, & continued Showery till Noon when it became very bright & fine, & I walk'd a great deal. Miss Hughes & my Sis^r Catherine, came from Cheltenham much talk, & Cribbage in the evening.

Saturday Novr 20th

Clear & somewhat frosty early in the Day, but soon became cloudy & frequent showers, & towards evening perpetual. walk'd about the Garden & premises before the weather alter'd much pleasant Morning of walk & conversation & Cards again late in the evening.

Sunday Novr 21st

Had been a severe night of rain & did not clear off till Breakfast time, & was tolerably fine afterwards, went to Church at Stroud, Mr Witts on horseback, the service performed by a Mr Moore admirably reading, writting & much talk; wrote to Mrs Rollinson & Mrs Swabey a Letter long owed.

Monday Novr 22^d.

A most perpetual constant rain the whole Day, scarce a possibility of getting even to the Hot House; more suitable to work & employment of various kinds. rec'd a Letter from M^rs. Drake & a charming one from my Dear Francis.

Tuesday Novr 23^d.

Not much better calculated for stirring, being a very thick fog till Dinner time when it brighten'd & was a frosty evening, when Mr Witts myself & Miss Hughes my Sis^t Cath: not being quite well went to drink Tea with M^r & M^rs. Sheppard not an unpleasant visit play'd at Whist & a fine Moon to light us home.[37]

Wensday Novr 24th.

A most happy change in the weather to a perfect bright fine Day having been a trifling frost, I enjoy'd it much by taking a fine ride to Woodchester, Nailsworth &c. Mr Wathen here in the Morning, & Mr Cooper to Dinner. rec'd Letters from M^rs. E: Tracy, Miss Anne Snow & my Sister Travell.

Thursday Novr 25th.

A most tremendous, & intire Day of violent wind & rain. My Brother Ferdinand & M^rs. Buxton came to Dinner but not till a very late hour from the badness of the weather, both most miserable invalids, & sadly out of spirits, play'd at Cribbage & did as well as we could. wrote to M^rs. Naper.

Friday Novr 26th.

Dark & stormy in the Morning, but clear'd off to be a bright fine Day, tho with a very high cold wind, not pleasant enough to be much out. M^r & M^rs. Pettat made a long Morning visit here Cribbage as usual, but my Brother miserably bad.

Saturday Novr 27th.

Had been a sharp frost in the night but was a delightfull pleasant bright fine Day we all walk'd a good deal & my Bro^t & Sister took an airing & Mrs Witts rode; M^rs. Savage & the two eldest Miss Sheppards here in the Morning & Sir G: O: Paul dined & supt here & was particularly pleasant & agreable

Sunday Novr 28th.

Much the same kind of Day, took M^rs. Buxton & Miss Hughes to Stroud Church, Mr Witts on horseback, heard an excellent sermon from Mr Ellis, after which we air'd to Selsley Hill & back by Nailsworth Hill, the views so beautifull as much to amuse my 2 companions, the rest of the Day rather melancholly, from my Bro^rs. complaint being very bad & M^rs. Buxtons spirits wretched, rec'd a Letter from Miss Sabine.

---

37. Mr and Mrs Sheppard were not married, they were in-laws. Edward Sheppard of Gatcombe Park (1725–1803) had lost his wife, Sarah, the previous year. Presumably this Mrs Sheppard was Jane Sheppard (1725–1799), the widow of his elder brother, Samuel.

67. Stroud.

Monday Nov.ʳ 29.ᵗʰ

A very severe cold wind & strong appearance of snow, too bad for any of us to attempt going out, but yet M.ʳ & M.ʳˢ John Pettat ventured to make a Morning visit on horseback much talking & great difficulty to keep ourselves warm the whole Day. Cribbage as usual in the evening & wrote to my Dear Francis from whom I was much vex'd not to receive a Letter.

Tuesday Nov.ʳ 30.ᵗʰ

Not much change in the weather for the better, only not so high a wind, but at times flying showers of snow, yet I ventured to take a ride & M.ʳ Witts with me as far as Lodgemore & home by Stroud. the 2 M.ʳ Cooks & M.ʳ N: Wathen dined here, Cribbage & Commerce in the evening. much shocked by hearing of an alarming attack M.ʳ Naper had had. Wrote to Miss A: Snow

Wensday Dec.ʳ 1.ˢᵗ

The month usherd in, in a very severe manner, being a most violent driving snow the whole Day, with tremendous east wind, towards night it abated & began to thaw. much work & conversation & cards as usual.

Thursday Dec.ʳ 2.ᵈ

Frost in a manner gone, & the air milder, tho the wind very high which made our Chimnies smoke intolerably & enduced the Ladies to sit in my powdering Room, walkt a little before Dinner rec'd a Letter from my Sister Travell with rather an amended account of Mr Naper & a sweet one from my Dear Francis.

Friday Decr. 3^{d.}

A very disagreable close damp Day poor Mrs. Buxton extremely ill with one of her dreadful Headaches, all the rest of us dined at Sir G: Pauls meeting Mr Hawkes & 2 Sons & Mr Hodson the architect being such a queer party, it was not so pleasant as usual in that House; Whist & Cribbage & home at 10. finding the poor Invalid very ill.

Saturday Decr ye. 4th.

A very pleasant mild Day tho without sun, Mrs. Buxton so very ill it was impossible her Father & she should return as was intended, he & my Sister Catherine took an airing & Mr Witts & I a most pleasant ride; Cribbage in the evening & Mrs. Buxton some what better.

Sunday Decr 5th.

Quite a delightfull fine bright Day M^{rs.} B: sadly ill indeed, Dr Cheston being hourly expected to her, Leaned not to go to Church, the rest went to Rodbro', Dr Cheston here all the Morning in talking to whom I had sufficient employment; Mrs. B. rather better in the evening. wrote to Mrs. Rollinson

Monday Decr 6th.

Quite a sharp hoar frost, but much sun & very fine, my Bro^r left us after breakfast to return home, Mr Witts went with him as far as Cirencester to visit Mr Master & rode back. Mrs. B. somewhat better, Miss Hughes & I walk'd on the common & were completely dirtied. M^r & Mrs. Savage dined & slept here, the 2 eldest Miss Sheppards & Mr Thornbury of Avening dined also.[38] a party at Whist & Commerce. rec'd a Letter from Mrs. Naper & Mrs. Hyett

Tuesday Decr 7th.

No frost, but a damp disagreable air not pleasant enough to stir out but had a nice working Morning, with Mrs. Savage as they did not leave us till noon. wrote to Mrs. Naper & to Dr Cheston with an account of his Patient who was still better than the Day before. rec'd a Letter f^{m.} Miss Snow

---

38.　The Revd N. Thornbury, rector of Avening. Thornbury was something of an amateur antiquary and Agnes' great-grandson, George Backhouse Witts, recorded the following in his archaeological handbook: '... *This lies half a mile to the east of the village of Avening, and two and a half miles from Nailsworth. It is 160 feet long, its greatest width being 60 feet, and greatest height 6 feet. Its direction is east and west, the highest portion of the barrow being at the east end. It was opened in the year 1809 by the Rev. N. Thornbury, Rector of Avening. Three stone chambers were taken out and removed to a grove in the rectory garden, where they are carefully preserved.*'

Witts Family Papers F179

1790

Wensday Dec.ʳ 8ᵗʰ·

Rain & fog the whole Day & quite miserable & uncomfortable, after Breakfast I carried Miss Hughes to Painswick where her Father met her to convey her to Cheltenham very sorry to part with her, went to make a visit to Mʳˢ· Hyett, a lively hour or two. found Mʳˢ· Buxton not quite so well on my return. rec'd a sweet Letter from my Franˢ·

Thursday Dec.ʳ 9ᵗʰ·

A very pleasant mild pleasant Days with beautifull gleams of sun, I walk'd for an hour with Mʳ· Witts. the new Gardiner arrived from London. Mʳˢ· Buxton somewhat better & able to enjoy Cribbage in the evening. rec'd a Letter from Mʳˢ· Naper & wrote to my Sister Travell & Francis.

68. Painswick.

Friday Dec.r 10th.

A fine Morning, a foggy Noon & a bright afternoon, I took Mrs. Buxton an airing late in the Day to Stroud, she was very indifferent all the afternoon tho not in consequence rec'd a Letter fm. Dr. Cheston

Saturday Dec.r 11th.

Rain & thick fog the greater part of the Day, Mrs. Buxton so miserably ill till quite evening that it was quite wretched to see her much taken up by her situation both Mind & Body wrote to Dr. Cheston, My Bror. Ferdinand & Mrs. Naper.

Sunday Dec.r 12th.

Something of a frost, & in general a bright fine Day, Mr. Witts & I went to Stroud Church walkt in the Garden after our return. Mrs. Buxton a good deal better than the former Day; Dr. Cheston came a little before Dinner, & staid till 8 o'clock paying the utmost attention to his Patient rec'd a Letter from Miss Hughes.

Monday Dec.r 13th.

A universal Day of violent hard rain & wind which affected our tiresome chimnies so much we were reduced to sitting all Day in my Bedchamber but it was not uncomfortable; Mrs. Buxton certainly better much reading, work, conversation & Cards wrote to my Bror. Ferdinand & rec'd a Letter from Dear Frans.

Tuesday Dec.r 14th.

A trifling frost, but a strong disagreable Day yet Mrs. Buxton ventured to take an airing went first to Hampton, & then to Chalfont home early evening spent as usual. wrote to Dr. Cheston and Miss Hughes. began reading Mr. Cumberlands Arundell.[1]

Wensday Dec.r 15th.

Quite a stormy unpleasant Day tho but little rain fell, late in the Day took an airing first to Hampton to put Letters in Post & then to Mr. Tyndales at Woodchester to buy bargains.

Thursday Dec.r 16th.

A miserable Day from Morn: to night of rain wind & Fog, fit for nothing but to stay at home; Dr. Cheston call'd here for an hour & found his Dear patient much recover'd. rec'd 2 Letters from my Bror. Ferdinand, one from Mrs. Naper Dr. Cheston & my sweet Francis.

Friday Dec.r 17th.

Had been a little Frost in the night, but was a pleasant Day tho with very little sun, till afternoon when it began being wet & misty, Mrs. Buxton & I went to make a Morning visit to Mrs. Savage at Tetbury, where we met Mrs. Escourt & Mrs. Grimstone a very pleasant visit wrote to my Br. Ferdd.

---

1. *Arundel*, a novel by Richard Cumberland, published in 1789.

Saturday Dec.ʳ 18ᵗʰ·

A very tremendous Morning of wind & snow, but clear'd up in the afternoon, & bitterly cold all Day, M.ʳ Witts & I after an early breakfast went to Elmore to bring home our Dear Francis for the holidays, a mutual delight to all parties, & the Dear fellow as well & happy as possible staid an hour & half to bait the horses & home at 4 o'clock, not finding the roads so bad as we expected. M.ʳˢ· Buxton not near so well as the former Days.

Sunday Dec.ʳ 19ᵗʰ·

Quite a dreadfull Day from Morning to Night continued driving Snow with strong east wind & miserably cold, no possibility of going to Church but most happy in having got Francis at home M.ʳˢ· Buxton very indifferent. received a Letter from Lady Lyttelton & wrote to Miss Snow.

Monday Dec.ʳ 20ᵗʰ·

A Sharp frost with continued Sun consequently very pleasant in spite of the snow on the ground I walkd with M.ʳ Witts & Francis M.ʳˢ· Buxton rather better; Cribbage as usual in the evening playing with great success.

Tuesday Dec.ʳ 21ˢᵗ·

Frost & snow all gone, succeeded by thick fog & hard rain till Dinner time, dreadfully damp & uncomfortable; too bad a Day for M.ʳˢ· Buxton to venture to return home as she intended, but my Sister Catherine set out for L. Slaughter after Breakfast; a very comfortable tetetete Day with my Dear Niece received a Letter from M.ʳˢ· Rollinson & from my Sister Travell.

Wensday Dec.ʳ 22.ᵈ

Something of a frost, which produced a bright fine Day tho with a strong wind. Poor M.ʳˢ· Buxton left us to return home lamented her departure so much I was very low & unwell all Day. M.ʳ Witts & Francis walk'd to Hampton in the Morning & I only in the Garden.

Thursday Dec.ʳ 23.ᵈ

Had been a most tempestuous Night w.ʰ· Thunder lightening &c., was a bright fine Day, tho with strong wind, M.ʳ Witts & Francis walk'd to M.ʳ Wathens we three dined at M.ʳ Pettats at Stonehouse meeting M.ʳ & M.ʳˢ· Hollings from Stroud & Miss Crump. with them M.ʳ & M.ʳˢ· Rich.ᵈ· Pettat, & M.ʳ Tho.ˢ· Pettat a very nice young man just left Rugby School. play'd a merry game at odd three handed Loo, & did not come till past ten by the light of the finest Moon I ever saw.

Friday Dec.ʳ 24ᵗʰ·

Thick fog & small rain till 12 o'clock when it became clear, mild & pleasant, & I set out first to visit M.ʳˢ· & Miss Clutterbuck at Hyde, & from thence to M.ʳˢ· Wathens at Newhouse,[2] most excreble road by Brimscombe, return'd home thro Stroud not much better. wrote to M.ʳˢ· Eliza: Tracy.

---

2.   Newhouse was the home of Samuel Wathen.

Saturday Dec. 25*th.*

Had been considerable rain in the night but was a bright fine Day tho with a strong wind but brilliant for a Xmas Day, went to Church at Stroud which was crowded to a great degree, tho very few communicants, walk'd in the Garden when we came home. wrote to M.rs. Naper & M.rs. Granville

Sunday Dec. 26*th.*

A dreadfull thick wetting fog the whole Day, went to Church at Hampton sitting in M.rs. Sheppards seat, visited them afterwards M.r Schutz there, & Miss Beale of Hyde; M.r Jenkins & M.r N: Wathen call'd here before Dinner; wrote to M.rs. Charles Western.

Monday Dec. 27*th.*

Not near so thick a fog, but still very unpleasant with frequent showers of small rain, walk'd for an hour after breakfast with the Boys drove in by the rain. dined at M.r Wathens at Newhouse, no one there except their own family but Cap.n. Procter from Stroud an agreable young Man; play'd at Ving'tun & staid supper, & the moon rising so late were not at home till between 1 & 2 in the Morning. rec'd a Letter from M.rs. Buxton with an amended account of herself.

Tuesday Dec. 28*th.*

Quite a sharp frost for one night with constant uninterrupted sunshine, took a ride first to Woodchester, & then round by Stroud the bottoms quite gay with many riding parties, liked it much. wrote to M.rs. Buxton.

Wensday Dec. 29*th.*

A very strong Frost but bright & very pleasant, walk'd a good deal with the Boys, Miss Sarah Sheppard, & M.r Schutz here in the Morning, the three M.r Wathens, & their Sister & the two young M.r Coopers dined here, a merry game at Ving'tun, M.r Wathens supt here, & Miss Wathen slept a pleasant young Woman.

Thursday Dec. 30*th.*

A great change in the weather, frost gone, & most violent rain & wind from Morning to Night without ceasing, carried Miss Wathen with us to dine at M.rs. Clutterbucks at Hyde, almost blown over both going & returning, met M.r Wathens there a pleasant visit & very neat & good entertainment play'd many rubbers at Whist.

Friday Dec. 31*st.*

Frost again, with strong sun but cold wind, walk'd soon after Breakfast, before Miss Wathen left us to return home, M.r Witts visited M.r Thornbury at Avening. I had a variety of employs in the course of the Day rec'd a Letter from M.rs. Naper.

rec'd 205 Letters
wrote 161 Letters

69. Avening.

1791

Saturday Jan: 1ˢᵗ·

A Strong thick wetting fog, which never well clear'd off the whole Day, & it was hard rain in the evening, quite a confining Day for Man, Woman, & Child, I work'd a great deal, & Mʳ Witts read to me in Bourgoannes travels into Spain moderately entertaining

Sunday Jan: 2ᵈ·

A sharp frost in the Morning, cold & without sun, & at 12 o'clock turn'd to most violent wind & rain which lasted the whole Day, went to Church at Rodboro', very disagreable coming home a new young Clergyman name unknown but a very tolerable performer. wrote to my Sister Travell Miss Sabine

Monday Jan: 3ᵈ·

Quite a sharp frost, but a wonderfull fine Day, the sun being strong & no wind, Mʳ Witts the Boys & I walk'd on the common & were out a great while; Mʳ Bridges & Mʳ Robert Hughes call'd here for half an hour in the Morning in their way to Avening

Tuesday Jan: 4ᵗʰ·

A sad excuse of weather, being a most dreadfull Day of hail & rain & the wind so violent it was quite alarming, but fortunately our premises escaped much damage, very busy all Morning cutting out & in the evening pleased the Boys by playing with them at Goose rec'd a Letter from Miss Snow.

Wensday Jan: 5th·

Weather not much improved if any wind still very high, & frequent violent storms of snow but not to lye deep, busy with a variety of works, & much entertain'd by having Mr Witts read Mr Burkes famous Pamphlet.[3]

Thursday Jan: 6th·

A strong frost with constant sunshine but such bad moving from the Snow on the ground I was again a Prisoner except to the hot house; M^r & M^rs· Burgh, Cap^tn· Forster & Mr Joshiah Wathen dine'd & supt here, & Captain Forster staid all night play'd at Vingtun & was very chearfull.

Friday Jan: 7th·

Had been a most tremendous night of rain & wind, the latter continued all Day but being dry I walk'd a good deal, accompanied by Mr Forster who did not leave us till noon. Mr Witts read in Mr Burkes Book in the evening. wrote to M^rs· Tyrwhitt & M^rs· Naper.

Saturday Jan: 8th·

The same violent stormy weather but a more drying wind; defied it, & walk'd for an hour or two with Mr Witts & the Boys on the premises. at night play'd at the glorious Game of the Snake to please the Boys.

Sunday Jan: 9th·

Had been a violent night of rain & wind but was dry all Day excepting a hard shower at noon, went to Church at Hampton sat in M^rs· Clutterbucks seat much pleased with the manner of Mr Douglass the new Curate there. rec'd Letters from Lady Edward Bentinck, M^rs· Buxton, & my Sister Travell, & wrote to Lady Lyttelton & M^rs· Buxton.

Monday Jan: 10th·

A wetting fog in the Morning, which soon turn'd to violent rain, & high wind in the evening, prevented intirely stirring out, & much plagued with smoke distresses, which obliged us to dine in my Dressing room. much work & reading.

Tuesday Jan: 11th·

A tolerable mild fine Day with gleams of sunshine, but a hard shower in the afternoon. Mr Witts & I went in the Chaise first to call on M^r & M^rs· Burgh at the Grange near Stroud who not finding at home, we went to Mr Pettats at the Ryeford only her at home, on our return,

---

3.   Edmund Burke (1729–1797). The outbreak of the French Revolution in 1789 was greeted with much enthusiasm by some people in England. Burke was hostile to it and also was alarmed by the favourable English reaction. He wrote *Reflections on the Revolution in France* (1790), which provoked a host of English replies, of which the best known is Thomas Paine's *The Rights of Man* (1791–1792). As a prediction of the course of the Revolution, *Reflections* was strikingly accurate. Burke opposed the French Revolution to the end of his life, demanding war against the new state. His hostility to the Revolution was challenged by Charles James Fox, an ardent supporter of it. Their long friendship came to a dramatic end in a parliamentary debate in May 1791 over the events in France. The two men never spoke to each other again.

made a visit to M^rs· & Miss Reades at Ebley. rec'd Letters from M^rs· Tyrwhitt & M^rs· Naper, answer'd the latter & wrote to Miss Snow. Mr Witts read to me in Mr Edward Sheppards Play of Chaubert. Some good lines.

Wensday Jan: 12th·

Very showery & unpleasant in the Morning but rather clearing towards noon I ventured to mount on my Pilion & Mr Witts with me to call on Miss Wathen, met there Miss Beale & Miss E Lysons, from there went to M^rs· Clutterbucks at Hyde as usual a very pleasant visit, but the wind rising to a most tremendous height had a dreadfull journey home, obliged to dismount on Hampton common & walk home for fear of being blown off, rec'd a long Letter from Miss Anne Snow. Goose with the Boys & Chaubert in the evening served to disipate the horrors of the most dreadfull storms of wind & rain I ever heard.

Thursday Jan: 13th·

Stormy but dry till mid-day, when it became wet in showers, & the wind very high & towards night quite tremendous again: walk'd with the Boys after breakfast for an hour or more, dined at M^rs· Sheppards at Hampton, Mr Schutz still one of the family, & M^rs· Savage only met us, Mr Savage being unwell; play'd at whist & home by 10 o'clock. wrote to Lady Edward Bentinck & rec'd a Letter from Miss Chaplin.

Friday Jan: 14th·

A thick fog in the Morning, which soon turn'd to rain & violent wind as usual, Mr Witts attempted to take a ride but was soon driven back a Day fit for nothing but reading & working, & enjoyment with the Dear Boys. finish'd Chaubert.

Saturday Jan: 15th·

A trifling Frost which made it both bright & dry, tho still stormy, & in the evening much more so. Mr Witts went to Stroud &c. on several calls, & I attempted in the Chaise to make a visit to M^rs· Douglass at Hampton but not finding her at home return'd back within the Hour. in the evening some reading & Goose to please the Boys.

Sunday Jan: 16th·

Incessant fog & small rain the whole day, & towards night wind very high, so miserably damp & uncomfortable would not venture out even to church, much writting of accompts, reading & commerce with the Boys. rec'd a Letter f^m· M^rs· Buxton

Monday Jan: 17th·

The same kind of weather till noon when it clear'd up, & was bright & fine enough to tempt me out a little with the Boys; Miss Clutterbuck, Mr Thornbury, Mr Wathen & his Bro^r Nathen dined here, lively & pleasant enough, play'd at Ving'tun till 10 o'clock.

Tuesday Jan: 18th·

The most cruel day of violent rain & wind of any that has happen'd even in this very bad season, were obliged to go thro it being engaged to dine at M^r R: Pettats, where we met

M^r & M$^{rs.}$ Pettat of Stonehouse & their Son & Daughter,[4] a Miss Scott with them & D^r & M$^{rs.}$ Snowdon, a queer Dinner & rather a laughable visit altogether, a Party at Whist, & another at Ving'tun at which I play'd with success. fortunately it was both dry & light for us to return home

Wensday Jan: 19$^{th.}$

After a most severe night of rain & wind which continued till near noon, it clear'd & was very fine till late at night but so dirty & wet I could not venture to walk, dined at Mr Burghs at the Grange near Stroud; the Party Dr Snowdon, the 2 Mr Wathens, Cap^n Forster, Mr Bryant, & Mr Blackwell M$^{rs.}$ Burghs Brother, a very agreable visit all play'd at Ving'tun staid supper, & returnd home thro' hard rain at one in the Morning wrote to Miss Anne Snow.

Thursday Jan: 20$^{th.}$

Another dreadfull wet & windy Night, but was quite bright & fine till late in the evening when it again rain'd & blew, I just went into the Garden & hot houses, went to Dine & sleep at Mr Savages at Tetbury taking Francis with us met only the two eldest Miss Sheppards who return home in the evening after playing at whist. rec'd a Letter from M$^{rs.}$ Naper & wrote to M$^{rs.}$ Buxton

Friday Jan. 21$^{st.}$

Had been a very trifling frost, & was an intire bright fine Day tho with a strong cold wind. left our agreable friends soon after Breakfast Mr Witts walk'd home from Hampton, when Fran^s attended me to make purchases at Mr Tyndales at Woodchester, & to make a visit to M$^{rs.}$ Cooper, found our little Boys quite well & play'd at Goose with them at night. rec'd a Letter from Miss Gorges.

Saturday Jan: 22$^{d.}$

A sad change for the worse in the weather, being constant small rain the whole Day, & towards night a very high wind, very much engaged all Day, & busy at accompts at night & wrote to Miss Gorges.

Sunday Jan: 23$^{d.}$

Wet early in the Day, but clear'd off so as to permit us both to go & return from Stroud Church in dry, indeed was a clear fine afternoon. Miss Sheppard surprized us by a visit on horseback as soon as we had dined & staid till quite dark. rec'd a Letter from M$^{rs.}$ Granville & wrote to M$^{rs.}$ Naper.

Monday Jan: 24$^{th.}$

Had been a small frost in the night & was a bright fine Morning early, but soon changed to damp & fog & quite unpleasant, walk'd out a little M$^{rs.}$ Read, Miss Elizabeth Read, & her little Brother William here in the Morning, & also Mr Jeffries from Hampton & his

---

4.   The son was Thomas Pettat (1772–1839). Thomas went on to enter the Church and became the rector of Hatherop and Beverstone.

Sister M^rs. Douglass a very pleasant Woman;[5] M^rs. Sheppard & her two youngest daughters drank Tea & play'd at Whist here & staid till 10 o'clock.

Tuesday Jan: 25th.
Very much the same kind of Day, several attempts at rain but none fell to speak on, & towards night the wind was very high, I took Francis with me in the Chaise to make a visit to M^rs. Pettat at Stonehouse, herself & Daughter very pleasant & sociable, on my return call'd on M^rs. Pettat at the Ryeford, He confined with the Gout at night play'd with the Boys at Goose. Mr Witts made an unsuccessfull attempt in the Morning to visit Sr George Paul.

Wensday Jan: 26th.
A foggy thick air, but not unpleasant being quite without wind & the air rather mild, being so calm it was very suitable to taking a walk to the Fort on Rodbro' common which I had never visited before, & was much pleased with, Mr Witts & Fran^s. going with me. rec'd a Letter from M^rs. Eliza Tracy & Miss Anne Snow.

Thursday Jan: 27th.
Small rain & fog in the Morning but clear'd off sufficiently at mid-day to allow me to walk a little before we went to Dine at Mr Coopers where we met Mr Burgh, & Mr Brown & his Son; rather a stupid business, the Gentlemen being long engaged in the evening on our Law business after which, play'd at Whist, supt & came home so late that Francis was quite delighted with being so great a rake for him

Friday Jan: 28th.
Had been a pretty considerable frost in the night, & was a universal bright fine Day I walkt a good deal, Mr Witts rode to make visits at Hampton & we went to Dine at Mr Reades their own family very numerous, & M^r & M^rs. Hill of Stonehouse added to it made the party large & not disagreable; play'd at Whist, & was late home tho we did not stay supper. rec'd a Letter f^m. M^rs. Buxton

Saturday Jan: 29th.
Small rain with some wind early in the Day, but tolerably fine till quite night, when it raind very hard, M^rs. R. Pettat made me such a long Morning visit that it sadly threw me out of all my various employs. rec'd a Letter from M^rs. Naper, & wrote to M^rs. Rollinson & M^rs. Buxton

Sunday Jan: 30th.
A stormy, cold disagreable Day but dry, tho severe black clouds & but little sun; went to Church at Hampton, where Mr Jeffries read prayers & Mr Douglass preach'd a most excellent sermon after Church visited at M^rs. Sheppards, & also at M^rs. Clutterbucks at Hyde to take leave before our Bath Journey. Dull & much out of spirits all the evening , with the approaching departure of my sweet Francis.

---

5.   Jefferies was the rector at Minchinhampton.

70. Minchinhampton.

Monday Jan: 31ˢᵗ·

Quite a mild pleasant Day, with suffcent gleams of sunshine to make the views & country appear beautifull, as I carried my Dear Francis to Elmore Court, George going with us, we all bore the parting better than could be expected & George & I return'd home to Dinner; Mʳ Wathen drank here & staid conversing agreably till between 9 & 10. after which I wrote to Mʳˢ· Eliza Tracy

Tuesday Feb: 1ˢᵗ·

Not cold, but a prodigeous high wind & very stormy, with frequent flying showers Mʳ Witts rode to Hampton, & I walk'd, Captain Forster here for an hour in the Morning, very busy all Day in preparation for our departure; much writting & accompts. dreadfull high wind at night.

Wensday Feb: 2ᵈ·

A continuation of storms early in the Day with some snow, but before noon was very bright with much sun, very fortunate for our drive to Bath went to the Cross hands with our own Horses & from thence past the roads excellent, got to Bath soon after three, & imediately got into a comfortable Parlour appartment on the North Parade next Door to my Broʳ & Mʳˢ· Buxton with whom we dined, & Mʳˢ· Granville Miss Snows, & Mʳ Dalby were added to us to Tea. supp'd also with our friends.

71. *View of Bath showing the South Parade.*

Thursday Feb: 3ᵈ·

Quite a sharp frost & having been a little snow, was hard walking, tho bright sun & otherwise very fine tho cold, went to the Damp room before Breakfast with Mʳˢ· Buxton in the Morning made many visits & saw inumerable people that I knew, dined at Mʳ Granvilles meeting Miss Snows, Mʳˢ· Halford & Miss Gage there in the evening, play'd at whist, call'd in on my Broʳ & Mʳˢ· Buxton late for half an hour.

Friday Feb: 4ᵗʰ·

Continuation of frost, but snow being melted & no wind, it was delightfull pleasant walking visiting with Mʳˢ· Granville almost all Morning, dined at Mʳ Hyetts, meeting Mʳ Sabine & his family, Miss Probyn, & Miss Hunt agreable enough, play'd at Whist, & went late with Mʳˢ· Granville to the Ball at the Lower Rooms very well amused.

Saturday Feb: 5ᵗʰ·

No frost, but tolerably dry & pleasant went to the Pump as usual with Mʳˢ· Buxton, John Sabine breakfasted with us,[6] much visiting as usual dined next Door at my Broʳˢ· my Sister Travell returnd from Lᵈʸ· Shrewsburys, drank Tea & supt with Miss Snow, meeting Mʳ & Mʳˢ· Mason & Daughter play'd at Whist.

---

6. John Sabine was an officer in the Grenadier Guards. His wife was Maria, daughter of Admiral Pasley. John was the son of Joseph and Sarah Sabine. Sarah was first cousin to Edward Witts, and she had died in 1788 (*see* above).

72. Old Rooms, Abbey Walks, Bath.

Sunday Feb: 6th.

Fog in the Morning, & never well clear'd off but still dry good walking, went to St. James's Church, the whole service admirably performd look'd in for a moment into a crowded Pump room made many visits & walk'd in the Crescent with my Sist. Travell, dined at our next Door Friends where was my Brother Travell & Miss Westerns went home early to write. rec'd a Letter from my sweet Francis, answerd it & wrote to Mrs. Naper.

73. The Pump Room and Colonnade.

*74. The Interior
of the
Pump Room.*

Monday Feb: 7ᵗʰ·

Very much the same kind of weather still excellent walking about, but being at home early
to dress, I only kept near home, dined at my Broᵗ Ferdinands meeting my other Broᵗ & Mʳˢ·
C: Western to Tea, went to a stupid party at Mʳˢ· Andres & from thence to the Ball at the
Upper rooms, our Party Mʳˢ· Granville, Miss Snow, Miss Beresford, Miss Sheppards & my
Sisᵗ Travell, not very full but very agreable

Tuesday Feb: 8ᵗʰ·

Quite as fine a Day, Mʳˢ· J. Sabine Breakfasted with us made 11 visits found more than half
at home, dined at Mᵉ Granvilles most comfortably only Mᵉ Dalby there went in the evening
to a Party at Mʳˢ· Westerns well enough play'd many rubbers at half crown Cribbage

Wensday Feb: 9ᵗʰ·

Much the same sort of weather, walkd & visited, & shopp'd with Mʳˢ· Buxton, dined at Mᵉ
Wiltshires besides there own family, Mᵉ & Mʳˢ· Charles Western, Mᵉ Strode & Mʳˢ· Stockton,
a very handsome Dinner, more company in the evening, 2 Tables at Whist. rec'd a Letter
from Molly with a good account of the dear Boys

Thursday Feb: 10ᵗʰ·

Little or no change in the weather not very pleasant but still good moving about, spent two hours
or more, my Broᵗ Ferdinand going with us in surveying Major Velleys collection of dried plants
much entertain'd by them,[7] paid some visits afterwards. dined at Mᵉ Westerns meeting the two
youngest Miss Wiltshires & their brother, more company in the evening 2 Tables at Whist.

7.   Thomas Velley (1748? –1806). Velley graduated from St John's College, Oxford, in 1772. He became lieutenant-
      colonel of the Oxford Militia and was awarded a D.C.L. in 1787. He was a distinguished botanist, especially for the
      study of algae, and after his death his collection was bought by the Liverpool Botanical Gardens.

75. Old Theatre,
Orchard Street,
Bath.

Friday Feb: 11th

Quite a miserable wet Day, with violent high wind & thoroughly disagreable, spent the Morning with the Snows, & at No. 10, dined with M[rs.] Holford; meeting the Granvilles & Snows with all of whom M[r] Witts staid the evening, while I went to M[rs.] M. Hartleys by appointment where I met three Gentlemen, & saw some beautifull drawings, from thence went to M[r] Hyetts where I play'd a rubber at Whist, & staid supper a party of 8 or 9 very pleasant & chearfull.

Saturday Feb: 12th

Had been something of a frost in the night, was a dry bright Day tho very cold, walk'd a good deal with M[rs.] Buxton shopping, dined at No. 10, & went to the Play in the evening with M[r] & M[rs.] Granville much amused both by the Suspicious Husband, & No Song no Supper.[8]

Sunday Feb: 13th

An intire day of hard rain from Morning to night, went to Church at the Abbey in a Chair, heard a most excellent sermon sat an hour or two afterwards with Miss Snows Dined at No. 10, where was also my Bro[r] Travell & to Tea M[r] & M[rs.] Granville & Miss Hoare. eat Bread & cheese there & home early. rec'd a charming Letter from my sweet Francis.

Monday Feb: 14th

Wet early in the Morning, but soon clear'd off, & was a bright windy Day, but very wet again at night, breakfasted very agreably at M[r] Wiltshires, to enjoy M[rs.] Savages Company,

---

8. *The Suspicious Husband* (1747) by Benjamin Hoadly (1706–1757). *No Song, No Supper* (1790) by Stephen Storace (1762–1796). In terms of commercial success, Storace, whose works were produced at the Theatre Royal in Drury Lane, was the success story of his day, meeting popular tastes largely with ballad operas that featured visual spectacle, bold vocal turns and exotic themes.

walkt afterwards with them, dined at M^rs. Birds,
meeting both branches of the Western Family rather a
dull stupid bussiness, play'd at Cribbage till we went to
the Ball, M^rs. Savage & her Sisters added to our party
the society of the former made it so pleasant to me I
have seldom liked a Bath Ball so well, & it was very
full & brilliant

Tuesday Feb: 15th.

Very much the same kind of weather wet early, &
fine, & showery by turns the rest of the Day, busy
all Morning in finishing up all bussiness & pleasure,
dined at No. 10 & drank Tea & supt with Miss
Snows, meeting M^r & M^rs. Granville & Sir G: O: Paul
who was just arrived. play'd at shilling Whist with
wonderfull success. wrote to my Dear Francis.

A Modern Belle going to the Rooms at Bath.

76. Cartoon by James Gillray, Bath, 1796.

Wensday Feb: 16th.

Wet & foggy early, but very fine the remainder of the Day, tho extremely windy & cold call'd
on several people before we quitted Bath at 12 o'clock, wch I did without any very strong
regret, went to the X Hands with Post Horses, my Bro^r Ferd: my Sis^r Travell, & M^rs. Buxton
& Patty join'd us there, & we all Dined together very comfortably seperated about 4, they
to sleep at Tetbury, & we at home, where we arrived at 7 by the clear light of the Moon &
found the Dear Boys quite well.

Thursday Feb: 17th.

A miserable Day, of perpetual thick misty rain, & considerably damp & windy, scarce able to
get to the Hot: House, very full of various employs, rec'd a pleasing Letter from Lady Edward
Bentinck, & wrote to Miss Forrest, a Letter of congratulation on her new appointment.

Friday Feb: 18th.

Quite cold & windy, with frequent flying showers of snow & sleet but none to lie, I walk'd
for an hour or more & did not regard it very busy all Day, wrote to Lady Edwd. Bentinck.

Saturday Feb: 19th.

Weather worse, being colder, & the storms more violent accompanied by hail, too bad
even for me to wish to go out, but had enough to do within, much surprized & agitated by
receiving in a Letter from my Sis^r Travell from Cheltenham that M^rs. Naper were brought to
bed yesterday of a Son, sometime before it was expected, but all going on well; wrote to my
Sis^r Travell by the return of the Messenger.

Sunday Feb: 20th.

Not quite so bad a day being little or no falling weather, but still very cold & uncomfortable,
went to Church at Hampton, where Mr Jeffries did the whole bussiness of the Day, after

Church went to call on M^rs. Sheppard, where was M^rs. Burgh, from thence went to Hyde to call on M^rs. Clutterbuck whom I found very indifferent just as we sat down to Dinner, arrived M^r & M^rs. Hunt, quite unexpectedly from Cheltenham, very glad to see them a large share of easy, but interesting talk.

Monday Feb: 21st.

Something of a fog in the Morning but it went off & was a pleasant mild Day, tho without Sun, breakfasted early for M^r & M^rs. Hunt to set off for Bath, & ourselves for Cheltenham had a pleasant drive tho part of the road very bad found M^rs. Naper quite as well as could be expected & babe tolerable, M^rs. Buxton with her, & my Bro^r Ferdinand at my Sisters. Mr Naper better than I imagined, pretty conversible, play'd at Cribbage recd a Letter from M^rs. Holford & also from Francis.

Tuesday Feb: 22^d.

Fog early in the Day but turn'd out a most beautifull fine warm Day, took a long walk to Bays Hill &c. with a large Party my Bro^r, Sisters, M^rs. Buxton & Miss Hughes. several visitors in the Morning. our Nursery going on extremely well. Cribage again in the evening. rec'd a Letter from Miss Anne Snow & answer'd it.

Wensday Feb: 23^d.

A sad reverse in the weather being perpetual rain & storms, no stirring out but yet some callers came here; the little stranger was named in the Morning by its Grand Papa by the names of James, Lenox William. evening spent much as usual wrote to M^rs. Tracy, M^rs. Tyrwhitt & my dear Francis; Cards as before.

Thursday Feb: 24th.

Something of a Frost but another beautifull fine mild Day with much sunshine Mr Witts set out before Breakfast on a visit into Oxfordshire to M^rs. Rollinson M^rs. Buxton Breakfasted with her Aunts I visited & walk'd much. rec'd a Letter from M^rs. Eliza Tracy.

Friday Feb: 25th.

A thick foggy Morning, which before noon turn'd to violent wind & rain and at night snow, bitterly cold, I breakfasted at my Sisters, & several callers here in the Morning, & my Sister Catherine came in the evening to play at Cribbage with us. wrote to my Husband

Saturday Feb: 26th.

Another dismal day of constant storms of snow & hail with strong & very cold wind, fit for nothing but a variety of home employs, M^rs. Naper not so well to Day I never quitted her Bed my Sis^r Travell left M^r & M^rs. Hunt who were just arrived at their House to come & play at Cribbage with us. rec'd a Letter from my Husband & Lady Lyttelton. My Dear Fran^ss Birth Day

Sunday Feb: 27th.

Miserably cold, damp & uncomfortable & at times flying storms of snow, tho in this vale it did not lye at all, went to Church in the Morning sat with Miss Hughes, visited afterwards with

M^rs. Granville, drank Tea at my Sisters, where were Mr Granville & Mr John Delabere besides their own party. rec'd Letters from Miss Snow & my Dear School Boy. M^rs. N. better

Monday Feb: 28th.
Sharp frost, but tho with little sun, yet being no wind it was pleasant being out; walk'd twice from the top to the very bottom of the Town with M^rs. Buxton, all the party from my Sisters House drank Tea here from various causes rather a dull meeting a little playing at Cribbage rec'd a Letter from my Husband & answerd it & wrote to Lady Lyttelton.

Tuesday Mar: 1st.
Continued frost, but from constant Sun very warm & pleasant. a mixture of visiting & walking, Mr Fretwell added to our party at Dinner, & I went to Drink Tea at my Sisters where was also M^r & M^rs. Talbot & Miss Hughes. rec'd a Letter from Miss Gorges; & wrote to George

Wensday Mar: 2^d.
Nearly the same weather, but not being so much sun was not quite so warm & pleasant; our Friends left us about mid-day to go to Upper Slaughter truly sorry to part with M^rs. Buxton. walk'd with Miss Hughes & my Sister Catherine after they were gone, rec'd Letters from M^rs. Tracy, Mr Witts, & Molly with a good account of the Boys, & wrote to Miss Gorges & Miss Snow.

Thursday Mar: 3^d.
A more bright fine day, tho with more wind, walk'd out with Miss Nettleships & my Sisters, my Dear Husband return'd to Dinner well & chearfull, my Sis^rs. added to our party both at Dinner & in the evening, all our spirits much raised by James Lenox taking to his Mothers Milk; rec'd Letters from M^rs. Tyrwhitt & M^rs. Master & wrote to the latter.

Friday Mar: 4th.
Frost quite gone but still a dry air, tho very mild & pleasant, walk'd a little with my Sisters & Husband, M^rs. Naper able to come into the Drawing room, my Sisters here to Tea & Cards. rec'd Letters from M^rs. Master & Miss Anne Snow, & wrote to M^rs. Buxton.

Saturday Mar: 5th.
Weather much the same as yesterday only still more pleasant, & very fine walking, got quite dry, walkt to Sandford with Miss Delabere & her Brother. my Sis^r Travell & Mr Witts, my Sisters dined here. rec'd a Letter from my beloved Francis.

Sunday Mar: 6th.
Much the same weather only still warmer, went to Church in the Morning & staid the sacrament, afterwards walk'd & visited a little, quite alone all the evening read a little but talk'd more.

Monday Mar: 7th.
A pretty sharp frost, with a cold wind but warm sun, M^rs. Master & her 2 Daughters came here from Cirencester before our breakfast, & staid here for 3 or 4 hours walk'd after they were gone, Mr Talbot dined here & my Sisters drank Tea. wrote to M^rs. Buxton

Tuesday Mar: 8th.

Continued frost, but a much warmer fine Day, Mrs. Naper tolerably well & quite early in the Drawing room, took a fine walk in the fields with my Sis^{rs.} only Mr Witts being gone to Bownham House calling at Elmore School by the way, my Sisters dined here. rec'd a Letter from Molly with a charming account of the Boys.

Wensday Mar: 9th.

Just the same weather but not being very well I staid within the whole Day, busy in many avocations, my Sisters here to Tea & Cards Mrs. Naper pretty well but very weak. rec'd a long Letter from Miss Forrest.

Thursday Mar: 10th.

A very beautifull Day again quite hot in the sun, Mr Witts return'd from Bownham House quite early, bringing a charming account of <u>all</u> my three Dear Boys, I walk'd a little, my Sis^{rs.} dined here. rec'd Letters from Mrs. Buxton & Miss Snow.

Friday Mar: 11th

No frost but mild & pleasant walk'd in the fields with Mr W. & my Sisters began working a Lawn Handkerchief; Mrs. Naper well enough to make one at our Cribbage party. wrote to Lady Edwd. Bentinck & Miss Anne Snow.

Saturday Mar: 12th.

A charming Day with continued sunshine many Morning visitors, walk'd to Bays Hill with the two Miss Gorges, Mrs. Buxton came to Dinner, & my Bro^r & Sis^{rs.} to Tea & Cribbage.

Sunday Mar: 13th.

Not quite so fine a Day being colder & the wind high, went to Church in the Morning, & walk'd a little after, dined so early that Mr Witts & I took a short walk in the fields before Tea. rather a long vacant Day wrote to Mrs. Master.

Monday Mar: 14th.

A dark thick Day with strong appearance of rain but none came to speak of, I was not well so did not go out several callers in the Morning, & a chearfull game at Cribbage with our own home party in the evening. wrote to Mrs. Eliza Tracy.

Tuesday Mar: 15th.

Quite a mild Day, soon after breakfast I went in Mrs. Napers Chaise with my Sister Travell to call on Mrs. Lane & Mrs. Phipps at Charlton, on our return Mrs. Naper went an airing for the first time. My Brother & Sisters dined here.

Wensday Mar: 16th.

Still the same charming weather walk'd in the fields after Breakfast with Mrs. Buxton & Mr Witts quite hot & spring like, Mrs. Naper again went airing, when I made some visits a comfortable evening our own home party.

Thursday Mar: 17ᵗʰ·

No change in the weather, several visitors before Mʳˢ· Naper took her airing, when as usual I walk'd, My Broᵗ & Sisters here to Tea & Cards. rec'd a Letter from Lady Edward Bentinck & one from Molly & wrote to Mʳˢ· Blackwell & my Dear Francis.

Friday Mar: 18ᵗʰ·

Weather more warm & fine than ever thought sufficiently so for Mʳˢ· Naper to venture to go to Church sitting in a Sedan Chair the whole time so she did not suffer Mʳˢ· Buxton & I attended her several visitors afterwards, I walk'd in the fields with Mᵗ Witts, who after taking an early Dinner set out in the Coach for Town, much lamented his departure & very low & uncomfortable I felt.

Saturday Mar: 19ᵗʰ·

Great change in the weather, being stormy & very cold, my Brother & Mʳˢ· Buxton went away & Mᵗ Isaacs came I air'd with Mʳˢ· Naper for an hour, my Sisters here in the evening. rec'd Letters from Mʳˢ· Blackwell Mʳˢ· Master & Miss Anne Snow.

Sunday Mar: 20ᵗʰ·

Hard rain in the Morning, but was dry again before church, but damp & stormy all Day & violent rain & wind at night, I went to Church in the Morning, had many visitors afterwards. My Sisters here in the evening. had the joy of receiving most satisfactory Letters from Mᵗ Witts & Francis & wrote to Miss Anne Snow.

Monday Mar: 21ˢᵗ·

Violent wind & very cold but dry & constant sun, but I had too much of the Rhumatism to venture out. Miss Duttons & their Governess came early in the Day & staid all Day, play'd at Commerce in the evening. I began spinning on my beautifull new Wheel. wrote to my Dear Husband.

Tuesday Mar: 22ᵈ·

A very pleasant quiet mild Day walk'd & visited with Miss Duttons before they went away, air'd with Mʳˢ· Naper towards Dowdeswell. drank Tea at Mᵗ Hughes's meeting Mᵗ & Mʳˢ· Hervy, Mᵗ & Mʳˢ· Amyall, Miss Gorges's, I divided 2 Pools at Commerce. rec'd a Letter from Mᵗ Witts.

Wensday Mar: 23ᵈ·

A still finer Day more sun. many visitors in the Morning, air'd again the same road, reading aloud all the time in Mʳˢ· Inchbaulds new novel of the simple story,⁹ my Sisters & Mᵗ Isaacs dined here I walk'd in the fields afterwards with my Sisᵗ Cath: rec'd an interesting Letter from Mᵗ Witts. rec'd also a Letter from Molly.

---

9. Elizabeth Inchbald (1753–1821) was an English actress, author and playwright, best known today for her first novel, *A Simple Story*.

Thursday Mar: 24th.

No change in the weather still beautifully fine, after receiving visitors air'd and read as before, walk'd in the fields after Dinner with my Sisters, who return'd with me to Tea & cards. rec'd a still more interesting Letter from Mr Witts & one from Miss Anne Snow. Wrote to Mr Witts & Lady Edward Bentinck; & my Dear Francis.

Friday Mar: 25th.

Another beautifull fine Day Mrs. Markham airing with Mrs. Naper I took the opportunity of making many visits, my Sisters dined here & we spent the evening in reading together Mrs. Gunnings wonderfull Pamphlet neither amazed or instructed by it.[10] wrote to Mr Witts & Miss Anne Snow.

Saturday Mar: 26th.

Had been a good deal of rain in the night & was so far wet all Day that we never ventured out or saw anyone, read a great deal the whole Day & talk'd much. rec'd a Letter from Mr Witts.

Sunday Mar: 27th.

Something of a frost in the night but an intire bright fine Day & very warm for the time of year, I went to Church in the Morning & walk'd & visited a little after, Dr Cheston came to Dinner having been sent for on Mr Napers account Mrs. Buxton came to Tea from U: Slaughter & supt also. rec'd letters from my beloved Husband & Son, & wrote to the former.

Monday Mar: 28th.

Rain in the night, & very trifling rain continued till Noon; many callers in the Morn: Mrs. Buxton air'd with Mrs. Naper & I made many take leave visits; walk'd to Sandford in the evening with Mrs. Buxton. read a little & talk'd more in the evening. wrote to Mr Witts.

Tuesday Mar: 29th.

Quite a mild pleasant Day with a strong mixture of light & shade; left Cheltenham between 12 & one, with a variety of contending feelings on bidding adieu to both my Dear Nieces in their different trying situations, thought the drive home long & tedious in spite of the beautifull views. Found my Dear Boys very well & rejoiced to see me. strolled in the Garden till near dark. a dull evening quite alone rec'd a Letter from Mr Witts. wrote to Mrs. Hyett.

Wensday Mar: 30th.

Something of a fog in the Morning & never a very clear air the whole Day tho much finer in the evening, when I walk'd out with the Boys chiefly in the Woods & home premises busy all Day setting things in order, but much out spirits; rec'd a Letter from Mr Witts & answer'd it & wrote to my Dear Francis.

---

10. Susannah Gunning (1739/40–1800). *A Letter from Mrs Gunning, addressed to His Grace the Duke of Argyle.* London: printed for the author and sold by Mr Ridgway [etc.], 1791. A denial of accusations against the character of the author's daughter, Elizabeth Gunning.

Thursday Mar: 31ˢᵗ·

Rather a pleasanter Day but not much, being little or no sun, walk'd after Dinner with the Boys & visited Mʳˢ· Tanner a sad dull Day heartily sick of being alone. rec'd a Letter from my Husband & Mʳˢ· Hyett.

Friday Ap: 1ˢᵗ·

Very much the same weather, in the morning took both the Boys in the Chaise with me first to call on Sᵗ Geo: Paul then shopping to Mʳ Tyndales & home round by Nailsworth Hill too cold to walk in the afternoon.¹¹ rec'd Letters from Mʳ Witts & Miss Anne Snow.

Saturday Ap: 2ᵈ·

After some trifling rain in the night a harsh cold Day with very strong wind tho constant sun, Miss Reade sat an hour with me in the Morning, at Noon arrived my Husband by a Coach to my no small joy, walk'd a little with him in the afternoon but almost starved it was so bitter cold & windy. wrote to Miss Snow

Sunday Ap: 3ᵈ·

A beautifull fine Day from Morn: to night went to Church at Stroud, from whence took a drive to survey Mʳ Cookes sweet situation at Paganhill,¹² but could not get into the new house & home by Rodbro' much entertain'd by surveying a very visible eclipse of the Sun, Mʳ Wathen calld here in the Morn: Mʳ Witts & the Boys walk'd in the afternoon rec'd a Letter from Mʳˢ· Granville & wrote to Mʳˢ· Hyett & Mʳˢ· Tyrwhitt.

77. *Field Place, Paganhill.*

11. Nailsworth Hill is the 'W', an alpine-like zig-zag road running up the steep hill from Nailsworth to the hamlet of Box. It was built as a turnpike road in 1781 by the engineer Dennis Edson for the sum of £220 to replace the old and steep pack-horse road, 'the Ladder.'

12. The estate at Paganhill was bought by Richard Cooke of Lodgemore in 1784, where he built a new house at Farm Hill, above the village, commanding a fine view taking in Stroud, the entrance to Woodchester Valley and the opposite side of the vale of Stonehouse.

Monday Ap: 4th.

Another bright fine Day tho with a very strong cold wind, Miss Sheppards here in the Morning, we dined at Mr Reads, meeting only Mr Jeat & his Niece disappointed in not meeting the Ovens family. play'd at whist. rec'd Letters from Mrs. Rollinson & my Dear Francis.

Tuesday Ap: 5th.

A cold stormy day with strong signs of rain but kept dry, left home between 11 & 12 for Bath to hire a Servant in Prissicks place & several other bussinesses, dined at Petty france & got to the White Lyon at 5 in the afternoon walk'd a little, conversed much with my new Servant elect Horsington. my Brother Travell sat an hour here. rec'd a Letter from Mrs. Buxton

Wensday Ap: 6th.

An intire Day of steady rain from Morning to night, better suited to the benefit of the fruits of the earth, than to my moving about on many bussinesses wch I was obliged to accomplish as well as I could in the Carriage, my Brot Travell breakfasted with us, we dined & spent the whole evening alone at the Inn. rec'd a Letter from Mrs. Naper, asnwer'd it & wrote to Mrs. Buxton.

Thursday Ap: 7th.

A charming reverse of weather being fine, mild, & constant sunshine, Mrs. C: Western breakfasted with us, walk'd about much, dined very agreably at Mr Wiltshires, meeting Mr Jeffries & Mrs. C: Western. play'd at Whist, & staid to a very merry supper.

Friday Ap: 8th.

Nearly as fine a day, but more cloudy tho very growing & spring like, much enjoyed all the early part of the Morning with a variety of tradespeople, left bath at 12 o'clock dined

78. *St. Michaels, the Abbey and South Parade.*

again at Petty France, & home in a most delightfull evening just as it was dark finding Boys quite well. rec'd a Letter from Mrs. Hyett.

Saturday Ap: 9th.
A thick wetting mist in the Morning but clear'd off to be a beautifull fine Day, Mr. J. Wathen call'd here early, & Mrs. Savage her Bro^{r.} & Sister Anne the two Miss Sheppards & Mr. Schutz call'd here late Mr. Witts rode to the Hill House &c. to see the Snows who arrived there the night before. we walk'd in our own premises in the afternoon.

Sunday Ap: 10th.
Fine but close in the Morning, but was very wet all the afternoon, went to Stroud Church in the Morning, after which to Sr. George Pauls to see the three Miss Snows sat an hour; in spite of the rain spent an hour in the hot Houses & Green house in the afternoon. busy at accompts in the evening & wrote to Miss Gorges.

Monday Ap: 11th.
A wetting fog till 12 o'clock when it became fine & pleasant, & allow'd me to walk a little & Mr. Witts rode, to Dinner came Sr. George Paul & his three Ladies, M^{r.} & Mrs. Hyett & Miss Hunt the two Mr. Wathens & Cap^{tn.} Forster, a Whist & Cribb: Table, & very lively & chearfull were the whole party, the Hill House set went away before Supper.

Tuesday Ap: 12th.
Quite a warm beautifull Day from Morn: to night, our Painswick Friends did not leave us till mid-day walking much about the place, we Dined at Mr. Wathens a party of 10, no Ladies but Mrs. Wathen & an old Maid a Lady of the name of Goffe, play'd at Ving'tun & staid supper, bringing home Cap^{tn.} Forster to Stroud. rec'd Letters from Mrs. Naper, Mrs. Buxton, & my Dear Francis.

Wensday Ap: 13th.
A strong fog in the Morning, which at Noon turn'd to violent hard rain, which continued all Day & night, Mr. Witts set out early on horseback for Oxon. Miss Snows spent the Morning with me & I return'd with them to the Hill House, to Dine & spend the whole evening, much agreable & friendly conversation the Baronet particularly chearfull & easy.

Thursday Ap: 14th.
A very charming warm growing Day after the rain, I walk'd a little, but was too busy in writting & other bussiness to go to any distance the Boys dined with me & I went to drink Tea at Mrs. Sheppards at Hampton, Miss Beale & Mr. Schutz there besides their own family play'd at Whist with success rec'd a Letter from my Sis^{r.} Catherine, & wrote to Mrs. Naper, Mrs. Buxton & my Dear Francis.

Friday Ap: 15th.
A most uncommon fine warm Day ever known at the time of Year, quite like summer very much engaged all the Morning with dismissing Prissick who made her departure after she had dressed me for Dinner; Miss Clutterbuck here for an hour or two in the Morning, I went

to Dine at the Hill House where besides their own Party were, M.ʳ & M.ʳˢ Hyett, M.ʳ & M.ʳˢ Hawkins, M.ʳ Kingscote, & M.ʳ Peter Hawker, a very agreable Day, walk'd after Dinner two Tables at whist where I was very successfull not at home till a late hour.

Saturday Ap: 16ᵗʰ

Very nearly if not quite as fine a Day I went in the Morning to Tetbury, not so fortunate as to meet with M.ʳˢ Savage at home, but meeting her on my road home had some agreable chat dined again at Sʳ George Pauls meeting M.ʳ & M.ʳˢ Pettat only besides their own party; M.ʳ Witts on his arrival at Bownham sent for me home & I found him at supper with much joy, happy to see him well & hear an account of his adventures in Oxfordshire. M.ʳ Josiah Wathen call'd in the Morning when I was out Sarah Horsington enter'd my service as my own Maid

Sunday Ap: 17ᵗʰ

A much colder air & more Stormy but little or no rain fell, went to Rodbro' Church in the Morn: where we met the three Miss Snows & brought them home with us to Survey our Garden M.ʳ Brice from Bristol & a Son with him came unexpectedly to Dinner & staid all night, walk'd out in the evening. wrote to M.ʳˢ Rollinson & heard from Francis

Monday Ap: 18ᵗʰ

A very damp air, with some small rain early in the Day, but soon cleard off, M.ʳ Witts rode to call on M.ʳˢ Clutterbuck &c., walk'd in the evening with the Boys in our own fields & garden afterwards very busy in accompts.

Tuesday Ap: 19ᵗʰ

Rather, a windy cloudy Day, but growing & not unpleasant in the Vale Land. Went on horseback in the Morning trying a new double Horse which carried me famously, first to the Hill House to call on the Ladies, then to M.ʳ Tyndales at Woodchester & afterwards on some errands to Stroud. Miss Snows dined with us quite én fámile & very happily to all parties play'd at Whist & they staid till 11.

Wensday Ap: 20ᵗʰ

A strong cold wind with three or four heavy showers of rain in the Morning, but a very bright afternoon, imediately after breakfast I set out for Elmore Court to fetch my Dear Boy for the holidays for a week taking Miss Anne Snow with me, who was much pleased with the expedition & we brought him home looking charmingly & as happy as possible. walk'd in the afternoon. M.ʳ Witts walking with Miss Snow about Sʳ Georges premises in the Morn: when M.ʳ & M.ʳˢ Hawkins here.

Thursday Ap: 21ˢᵗ

A very bright fine Morning cloudy noon & afternoon, & very wet Night, walk'd after breakfast with M.ʳ Witts & Francis as far as Littleworth, dined at M.ʳ Jeffries at Hampton meeting there besides M.ʳ & M.ʳˢ Douglass his Brother & Sister M.ʳ & M.ʳˢ Hawkins of Bisley, & Miss Clutterbuck a handsome Dinner & a pleasant visit, 2 Tables at Whist staid Supper home in the rain before twelve rec'd a Letter from Miss Gorges. wrote to M.ʳˢ Granville

Friday Ap: 22ᵈ·

Hard showers & very lowering in the Morning but dry & fine in the afternoon, went to Church at Stroud, a long but excellent sermon from Mʳ Ellis another Clergyman reading Prayers, returnd home by the Hill House the Ladies not at home, but the Bart: sent after us to invite us to Dinner, where we went & Franˢ· with us, took a walk before Tea & home before it was late. rec'd a Letter from my Sisʳ Travell & Mʳˢ· Hyett answer'd the latter.

Saturday Ap: 23ᵈ·

High wind & dark clouds tho with some sunshine, & rain in the afternoon so as to prevent our walking, busy all Day with various employs & not in very high spirits or quite well rec'd a Letter from Mʳˢ· Naper.

Sunday Ap: 24ᵗʰ·

After a hard night of rain, a moist falling morning but held up to let us go dry to Stroud Church where we were kept several hours, by the various duties of the Day, Franˢ· visited Capᵗⁿ· Forster while we were at the Sacrament, tho the afternoon proved very stormy & lowering, for the sake of indulging the Boys took a very long walk, at the back of Sʳ G: O: Pauls premises & round by the Fort. wrote to my Sisʳ Catherine.

Monday Ap: 25ᵗʰ·

Quite a beautifull fine Day throughout walk'd to Littleworth after breakfast with the three Boys, Mʳ Douglass here in the Morning, went to Mʳ Hyetts at Painswick to Dinner, Franˢ· with us & staid all night, meeting the Hill House party all but Miss Anne, a handsome Dinner, play'd at Whist, but not a very lively brilliant visit all together.

Tuesday Ap: 26ᵗʰ·

Dry till Night but very stormy, the parties seperated soon after Breakfast; we came home time enough to Dress to Dine at Mʳˢ· Clutterbucks meeting Miss Sheppards & Mʳ Schutz a chearfull visit, play'd at Whist & Cribbage, sup't & came home in extreme dark & hard rain rec'd a letter from Miss Sabine

Wensday Ap: 27ᵗʰ·

Not a pleasant Day, but a thick air apparently something of a blight from Morn: to night went early to Gloucester transacted many little matters & survey'd the Gaol with much accuracy, & was well amused by it, dined very moderately at the Bell finish'd our bussiness, & drop'd poor Francis on Quedgley Green, where a Servant met him to take him to Elmore Court; not at home till dark.

Thursday Ap: 28ᵗʰ·

Another thick Morning, very fine clear noon, & wet afternoon, Mʳ Witts went very early to Bibury on bussiness, returning to Dinner the Boys & I walk'd to the Hill House in the Morning for an hour or two, very busy the whole of the Day afterwards. rec'd a Letter from Mʳˢ· Hyett & answer'd it.

79. Bisley.

Friday Ap: 29th.

After having been an extreme wet night, it was an intire wet Day with very small intervals, just sufficient to suffer Miss Snows to come up from the Hill House to stay, Miss Jane & Miss Pettat attended them for a quar^{t.} of an hour much conversation & a rubber at Whist finished the Day pleasantly.

Saturday Ap: 30th.

Dry till the afternoon when it became very wet again, but was very stormy & quite cold & uncomfortable, yet I ventured to mount my Pillion & Mr Witts with me to visit M^r & Mrs. Hawkins at Bisley,[13] found the roads better & the place worse than I expected came back well blown but not tired. evening as before. Miss Hawkins here in the Morn.

Sunday May 1st.

Very unlike what this Day should be in point of weather or warmth, being damp & foggy till Noon & perfectly wet afterwards, Mr Witts Miss Anne Snow & I went to Church at Stroud & on our return the Ladies went to visit Mrs. Sheppard at Hampton. Sir G: O: Paul & his Niece dined here the former uncommonly agreable & conversible all the evening. rec'd a sweet Letter from my Francis.

---

13. Edward Hawkins was vicar of Bisley (1782–1806). He was also rector of Kelston in Somerset from 1798. He was the son of Sir Caesar Hawkins (1711–1786), Serjeant Surgeon to kings George II and George III and surgeon at St George's Hospital.

Monday May 2ᵈ·

No change for the better in the weather, being almost perpetual rain the whole Day, Mʳ Peter Hawker in the Morning, & Mʳ & Mʳˢ· Hawkins, Mʳ & Mʳˢ· Douglass, & Capᵗᵐ· Forster dined here, & the former staid all night, a very pleasant agreable Day, a party at whist & Cribbage in the evening, & all well pleased & merry.

Tuesday May 3ᵈ·

No rain any part of the Day but a thick air & very cold & unpleasant, yet we were all so glad to get out that we walk'd from breakfast time till the Hawkins's went away, soon after which my Broʳ Travell very unexpectedly arrived from Cheltenham, & Mʳ & Mʳˢ· Pettat, Miss Jane Snow, Miss Sheppards, Mʳ Schutz & Mʳ Wathen dined here, a full party but not near so agreable as the Day before, a Whist & Commerce Table. rec'd a Letter fᵐ· My Sisʳ Travell & wrote to Francis.

Wensday May 4ᵗʰ·

Very much such another Day, soon after breakfast we all walk'd to the Hill House to shew the glories of it to my Broʳ tho in the absence of its owner, when we returnd home my Broʳ set off for Bath, we were not sorry once again to dine our own snug party of 4 play'd at Whist as usual. rec'd Letters from Mʳˢ· Buxton & Mʳˢ· Naper.

Thursday May 5ᵗʰ·

A much better Day being clear bright sun, but still a cold wind & blighting, walk'd for an hour or two after breakfast with our friends; Miss Sheppards & Mʳ Schutz call'd here in the Morning, dined at Mʳ Peter Hawkers at Woodchester,[14] meeting Sʳ G: O Paul & his Niece wᶜʰ with their own family made the party 13 a most excellent, but <u>wonderfully</u> handsome Dinner a comic visit alltogether. a Table at Whist & unlimitted Loo at which I play'd not at home till late. rec'd a Letter from Lady Dyke requiring the character of Prissick.

Friday May 6ᵗʰ·

Not so good a Day, being less sun & colder wind, the Hill House Bart. Brought up his Niece after breakfast to join her Aunts who were to take her with them to Town, they all left us at mid-day always sorry to say adieu to them; walk'd again in the afternoon but starved almost to death with cold: wrote to Lady Dyke & my Sisʳ Travell.

Saturday May 7ᵗʰ·

Much the same weather, dry but rather cold & stormy, walk'd a little both Morning & evening but much engaged in packing up & preparing for our proposed Journey into Worcestershire work & some writting & accompts in the evening.

Sunday May 8ᵗʰ·

A universal bright clear Day with hot Sun & cold North wind, went to Church at Hampton

---

14. Peter Hawker was rector of Woodchester from 1756 to 1808, when he was succeeded by his son, also named Peter Hawker.

where Mr Dallaway perform'd the service,[15] made a long visit at Mrs Sheppards afterwards, surveying her Park & Garden. wrote to Mrs Naper, Miss Gorges & Miss Sabine.

Monday May 9th

Quite a lowering Morning, but clear'd up by degrees & was a bright afternoon, left home between 8 & 9, drank Coffee at the Bell at Glocester visited Mrs Raikes, & Mrs Comerline,[16] dined moderately at the White Lyon at Upton on Severn, & got to the Hop Pole at Worcester to Tea, thro a beautifull rich country; walk'd about the Town a little & when dark wrote to Mrs Buxton.

Tuesday May 10th

Had been a Night of hard rain but clear'd early, & was very little if any the rest of the day tho lowering & very growing; left Worcester at 11 & got to Hagley at ½ past two a very pleasant drive of 21 miles thro Bromsgrove & a very rich delightfull country; met with a very pleasing reception from M^r B: Dewes with whom we found besides his Daughter & her Governess Miss Cardan,[17] M^r & Mrs Granville, & Miss Delabere arrived at night, very lively & conversible & a smart party at Whist rec'd a Letter from my beloved Francis.

Wensday May 11th

A very fine Day tho without much sun but hard rain in the evening, our whole party walk'd a great deal in Hagley Park surveying it is many beauties, a M^r M^rs & Miss Lyell dined here, as well as supt nothing very lively or clever, 2 Tables at Whist. rec'd a Letter from Miss Anne Snow.

Thursday May 12th

Cloudy with some trifling showers till afternoon when it was very fine, some company here in the Morning, Mrs Granville & I attended by Mr Dewes strolled only about the home premises, the rest went farther, all walk'd together in the afternoon, in part of the Domain of the Hall, evening spent as before wrote to Miss Anne Snow.

Friday May 13th

A most beautifull Day quite summer Miss Delabere, & the Gentlemen rode tho different ways Mr Dewes, Mrs Granville & I again stroled chiefly in the Gardens of the Hall House. M^r & Mrs Phillpot & their Son dined here 2 Tables again at Whist. rec'd Letters from Miss Anne Snow & my Sister.

---

15. The Revd James Dallaway (1763–1834), curate of Rodborough (1787–1793). During the early part of his residence in the area he lived at Rodborough Fort, and afterwards moved to Gloucester. He was the only son of James Dallaway, banker at Stroud. He took an early interest in antiquities and was elected a member of the Society of Antiquaries in 1798. From about 1785 to 1796 he was employed as editor of Bigland's *Gloucestershire Collections*. He later left the area, but enjoyed a distinguished career as an antiquary, funded by several livings in the Church.

16. Although Agnes has written 'Comerline', the name was 'Commeline.' The Commelines of Gloucester were a family of bankers, lawyers and clerics. Thomas Commeline was Mayor of Gloucester in 1816.

17. Bernard Dewes (D'Ewes; 1743–1822) of Wellesbourne and Hagley. Bernard was the brother of John Granville, who had been born Dewes but changed his name to Granville on inheriting Calwich Abbey. Bernard Dewes was a magistrate and at the end of his career was the chairman of the quarter sessions and one of the oldest magistrates in the county.

80. The Leasowes.

Saturday May 14th.

A very bright fine Morning but became very lowering at Noon with some trifling showers, but not of any consequence. the three Ladies in the Chaise & the Gents on Horseback went in the Morning to survey & walk over the Leasowes, much entertain'd by it; found Mr Waddington on our return, walk'd in the Garden a little in the evening & play'd at Cribbage wrote to my sweet Francis.

Sunday May 15th.

A prodigeous fine warm Day quite summer, tho towards evening it became cold & lowering went to Morning Church at Hagley, a pretty Church standing in the Park & still prettier Chancel. The service very indifferently perform'd by Mr Durant the Rector. after Church all walk'd to Pedmore to call on M^r & Mrs. Phillpot, a pretty walk but found it disagreably hot, which so tired me that I did not venture to attend the party in their evening walk rec'd a Letter from Mrs. Naper & wrote Lady Edward Bentinck

Monday May 16th.

Not so fine a Day but dry & very pleasant, Harriet Mr Dewes & I walk'd in part of the Park, the rest rode, M^r & Mrs. Walsh Paster, Mr Amphlet & Captain Pitcock dined here, the former people of the world & very amusing, she very pretty, two Tables at Whist. rec'd a Letter from my Dear Francis, & one from Molly with a good account of the Boys wrote to George.

Tuesday May 17th.

Quite a stormy disagreable Day with strong appearance of rain, but none of any consequence fell, Mr Granville & Mr Witts rode to Stourport, & the Ladies & Mr Dewes walk'd to Pedmore, I confined myself to the Garden. the two Mr Phillpots dined here two Tables of Whist as usual.

Wensday May 18th.

Weather very little mended, quite as stormy but a little sunshine tho very cold, no walking in the Morning, we all both Dined & supt at Mr Lyells at Clent, meeting Mr & Mrs. Porter, handsome entertainment, & a chearfull visit with much Whist. rec'd a Letter from Miss Snow & wrote to Mrs. Naper.

Thursday May ye. 19th.

Again a very boisterous & disagreable Day, but with very little rain, Mrs. Gran. Miss Beresford & I in the Chaise & the Gentlemen on Horseback went to Stourbridge to survey the Glass works much amused by it. the two Mr Phillpots dined here & Mr Cosier supt. rec'd Letters from Mrs. Tyrwhitt & Mrs. Buxton.

Friday May 20th.

Very much the same weather, quite as disagreable, Mrs. Granville, Miss Beresford, & I in the Chaise & Mr Dewes on Horseback, went to Brook Hall to call on Mrs. Porter but did not find her at home, call'd afterwards on Mrs. Amphlet at Clent with equal success. Mr Warner of Warwick both dined & supt here a most singular character the Gentlemen amused themselves with Archery till it was dark & then Whist.

Witts Family Papers F180

1791

Saturday May 21st.

No change for the better in the weather still very cold & stormy, & great expectations of rain tho none of any consequence fell, but the fear of it confined the whole party, to home rides & walks Mr & Mrs. Phillpot & their Son Humphrey dined & play'd at whist with usual spirit. wrote to my Sister Travell.

Sunday May 22d.

Still cold & very windy but having some sunshine made it more pleasant, Miss Delabere went away imediately after breakfast, we all went to Church, after which survey'd the Hall House, & then walk'd to Pedmore to pay a visit very busy all the afternoon in selecting & packg. off Plants.

Monday May 23d.

A very blustering Morning & very heavy showers from 9 till 12 when it cleard up & was a bright afternoon tho very cold. our agreable party broke up after breakfast our good Landlord attending his other Friends to Calwich & we proceeded to Worcester where we dined, & made some trivial purchases, & purposed sleeping at Tewkesbury but on the road changed our scheme & got into the Upton & Malvern road, where at the Well House we took up our abode for the night found little or no company; & it was too late & cold to venture up the Hill. wrote to Miss Snow.

Tuesday May 24th.

A most happy change, in the weather being a mild calm Day with perpetual sun & consequently very warm after an early breakfast took courage to mount the Hills & without being much fatigued & well rewarded by the clearest Day of views I ever saw left Malvern between 10 & 11, & without stopping more than for Hay & water at the Inn on Corse Lawn got to Glocester near three, much delighted with the richness of the drive, dined at the Bell and after walking about a little, set out for home where we arrived as it was dark finding the Boys quite well rec'd a Letter from my Sisr Travell & wrote to Francis

Wensday May 25th.

Quite as beautifull a Day if not superior, much engaged both in House & Garden the whole of it by settling & arranging various matters Mr Reade here in the Morning & Mr John Witts arrived late in the evening as we were returning from a walk with the Boys, rec'd a Letter fm. Frans.

81. The winding valley, Malvern.

Thursday May 26th.

Another fine Day, & the evening still more warm & fine than any of the proceeding ones did not walk to any distance in the Morning but much out with my Green House Plants wch. were setting out. drank Coffee early & set out at 6 o'clock to Take a ride to shew my Brother the country, going to Selsley Hill & thro' Lord Ducie's roads not at home till 9 o'clock wonderfully pleasant. rec'd a Letter from Mrs. Naper & wrote to Mrs. Buxton & Miss Gorges.

Friday May 27th.

Equally fine & pleasant through the whole Day, tho colder & more wind in the evening walk'd a little in the Morning & a very long walk in the evening Boys & all, by St G: Pauls Little London &c.[18] rec'd Letters from Miss Louisa Lee, Miss Snow & my Dear Francis & wrote to Mrs. Granville

Saturday May 28th.

A very fine Day tho with a strong wind which sunk in the evening, Mr & Mrs. Scott of Kings Stanley & their Neice Miss Scott here in the Morning, in the evening we took a most charming ride to Horsley, survey'd the Bridewell there & return'd home thro' Woodchester being out 3 hours & a ½ & were much entertain'd

18.   An area of Rodborough by Kingscourt.

Sunday May 29th.

A most glorious Day, went to Church at Stroud in the Morning, & to Hampton in the afternoon; a dull sermon from Mr Ellis on the Restoration, & a charming one from Mr Douglass on a more usefull subject, dined after both churches, & walk'd in the evening to the Fort on Rodbro' common, Mr Wathen Join'd us on our return. rec'd Letters from Miss Nettleship & Francis answer'd the former & wrote to Miss Louisa Lee

Monday May 30th.

A still warmer Day than any of the former, Mr Witts took his Bror John after an early Breakfast to Elmore Court to see Francis who they found well & most happy to see them & return'd to Dinner, I mounted my Pillion & went to Hampton, visited first at Mrs. Sheppards, & then sat an hour with Mrs. Douglass very agreably Mr Jeffries rode part of the way home with me after Tea walk'd to Sir G: Pauls, & nearly round his walks well tired on my return. wrote to Mrs. Naper & rec'd a Letter from Miss Gorges.

Tuesday May 31st.

Another Day equally warm & fine nearly almost oppressively so, Mr John Witts went away imediately after Breakfast, Mr & Mrs. Douglass spent an hour here chiefly in surveying the Plants we dined at Mr Scotts at Kings Stanley, meeting Mr Reades family, Mrs. & Miss Holbrow, & Mrs. Purnell a very amusing visit alltogether, staid supper not at home till one in the Morn: a Table at Whist & another at Commerce & Ving'tun at which I play'd wrote to Mrs. Savage.

82. Kings Stanley.

Wensday June 1st

No change in the weather but to be hotter, I scarce stirr'd the whole Morn, not being very well, Mr Witts rode to Hampton &'c, the three Miss Sheppards & Mr Schutz drank Tea here, & after walk'd in the Garden & woods & not gone till near 10.

Thursday June 2d

A most dreadfull oppressive hot Day nearly equal to the 22nd of this month last Year, not able to keep myself even tolerably cool the whole Day tho with sitting perfectly still till after sun set, made really quite ill by it. dawdled about the Garden till quite dark. no comfort in anything or body.

Friday June 3d

Very nearly if not quite as hot as yesterday but grew somewhat cooler towards night Mr Hyett drank Tea with us, & Mrs Hawkins calld 5 minutes after we were set out on our ride, & over took us before we got to Sir George's & sat on our Horses & talk'd for sometime; stopp'd at Mr P. Hawkers at Woodchester to leave a message, from there went to Mr Reades at Ebley, where we staid near an hour walking over their Gardens not at home till 10 o'clock when it was quite pleasant

Saturday June 4th

Still most oppressive weather, tho some trifling showers fell in the Morning, & scarce any Sun the whole Day, at Dinner time several loud claps of thunder, & sharp rain for an hour or two, but the evening was cooler & much more pleasant, & after Tea rode to Mrs Clutterbucks at Hyde where we made a short visit meeting Mr Phill: Sheppard. rec'd a Letter from Mrs Savage.

Sunday June 5th

A most charming Day, hot sun but fine air, & the evening delightfull & not very hot went to Church at Stroud, from thence to see Miss Wathen who was just return'd home, & with her Mrs Hunt, came home the Brimscomb road; after Tea, Mr W. George & I went in the Chaise a drive to Uley, much pleased with the road & country about, call'd at Mr Edwd Sheppards who we did not find at home.[19] rec'd a Letter from my Sisr Travell & my sweet Francis

Monday June 6th

Much such another Day only rather hotter, Mr & Mrs Reade & Miss Reade & Captn Forster dined here & the latter staid all night from the oddity of the former Gentleman rather a trick visit. walk'd about after Tea rec'd a Letter from Mrs Naper.

---

19. Edward Sheppard was connected to the Sheppards of Minchinhampton and would have been a cousin in some degree to Edward Sheppard of Gatcombe. This branch of the Sheppards appears to have moved to Uley House in about 1745. By 1789 Edward Sheppard and Henry Hicks took a ten-year lease on what became known as Sheppard's Mill and about £50,000 were spent on a Boulton & Watt steam engine and other machinery. This was the first steam engine used in the clothing industry in Gloucestershire. More than 1,000 people were employed at the mill and when a collapse came in 1837 it was one of the most spectacular bankruptcies in the county. As a village, Uley stagnated for the remainder of the nineteenth century.

Tuesday June 7ᵗʰ·

Another beautifull fine Day being a clear charming air, Mᵣ Forster & Mᵣ Witts walkd & I kept quite quiet to receive a large Party at Dinner Mᵣ & Mʳˢ· Savage, Sir George Paul, Mᵣ & Mʳˢ· P: Hawker & 2 eldest Daughters, a very chearfull agreable Day, walk'd about after Tea for an hour & some of the party staid late playing at Ving'tun.

Wednesday June 8ᵗʰ·

In the Morning, a thick air with flying mists not to be call'd rain tho strong appearance of it & very fine & clear in the evening, Capᵗⁿ· Forster went away after breakfast, & Mᵣ Witts & I rode to Rye Ford to drink Tea with Mᵣ & Mʳˢ· Pettat finding them both very indifferent. wrote to Miss Anne Snow.

Thursday June 9ᵗʰ·

A remarkable pleasant fine Day & tho the sun was uninterrupted none too hot, the two Mᵣ Wathens, Miss Wathen, & Mʳˢ· Hunt with them, Mᵣ James Clutterbuck, Miss Clutterbuck & Mᵣ Sheppard from Uley dined here lively enough & we all walk'd out after Tea. wrote to my Sisᵣ Travell

Friday June 10ᵗʰ·

Strong appearance of rain in the Morning indeed some flying showers fell, but soon clear'd & the evening was beautiful, Mᵣ Witts walk'd to Hampton & call'd on Mᵣ Jeffries, Miss S. Sheppard here for an hour or two in the Morning, in the evening we rode to survey Stanley Park, rather disappointed in it, return'd home by Ebley, to enquire after a Poney wrote to my Dear Francis.

Saturday June 11ᵗʰ·

Cloudy & very much the same weather, rain much expected but none fell, Mʳˢ· John Pettat made me a very long Morning visit with much interesting conversation, in the evening we walk'd with the Boys to Brimscombe & home by Mᵣ Wathens Mill where we met with the Ladies who walk'd some way with us. wrote to Mʳˢ· Naper

Sunday June 12ᵗʰ·

A smart shower in the Morning & another at Dinner time, or else the Day was fine tho very unnaturaly cold & in the night a sharp frost, went to Stroud Church & staid the Sacrement drank Tea at Mʳˢ· Sheppards nothing very lively rec'd a Letter from Francis & Miss Anne Snow & answer'd the latter.

Monday June 13ᵗʰ·

Stormy in the Morning, & after Breakfast a sharp shower of hail, but dry & fine the remainder of the Day tho strong signs of rain, went early to Dine with Mᵣ Sheppard at Uley to meet Mᵣ & Miss Wathen & Mʳˢ· Hunt, but not finding the party assembled, we drove 2 miles farther to survey Dursley, on our return walk'd round Uley Berry before Dinner, much pleased both by the extensive & near views, a good Dinner & polite reception, not at home till ½ past 10 by the light of a beautifull Moon.

Tuesday June 14th.

Very much the same kind of Day dry but cold & uncomfortable, M^rs. Pettat of the Rye Ford, made me a long visit in the Morning in consequence of which Mr Witts & I rode to M^r J: Pettats at Stonehouse in the afternoon, much disagreable altercation between the Bro^rs. & very little gain'd by the meeting, came home almost starved to Death with cold between 10 & 11.

Wensday June 15th.

No change of weather but still dry & cold, after an early breakfast Mr Witts & I went in the Chaise taking George with us, to Petty France to meet a Man Servant recommended from Bath who disappointing us, made it a hopeless & tiresome Morning excursion, work'd while there, & much amused by reading Numa Pompelius[20] on the road to & fro. too cold, & unpleasant to walk out of our own premises in the evening.

Thursday June 16th.

Almost an intire Day of rain attended with cold & strong wind which render'd it less beneficial. never once sitrr'd out of the house, but very busy with work & other employments. rec'd a Letter from M^rs. Rollinson & wrote to Miss A: Snow

Friday June 17th.

A very stormy cold disagreable Day early in the Morning a severe storm. towards even^g. much finer. hard at work all Morning, after Tea walk'd to the Canal side taking the Boys, much fatigued by Jogging up the Hill home rec'd a Letter from Miss Sabine.[21]

Saturday June 18th.

Frequent gentle showers till Noon when it became dry but not pleasant being cold & without sun. Mr Witts rode early on several little calls, in his absence S^r G: O Paul sat an hour with me, & brought me the sad news from Dr Cheston, of Mr Napers having had another Paralytic stroke much hurt by it I went alone in the Chaise intending to drink Tea with M^rs. Clutterbuck but found no one at home returnd to Tea & afterwards air'd to Hampton & on the common, rec'd Letters from M^rs. Buxton & Miss Anne Snow & answer'd them both.

Sunday June 19th.

Fine tho clear & cold, but towards evening dark & stormy, went to Stroud Church in the Morn: the service ill perform'd by Mr Lloyd far better by Mr Jeffries at Hampton in the afternoon to which we went before our Dinner too cold & uncomfortable to walk in the evening rec'd a Letter from M^rs. Savage & wrote to Lord Edwd. Bentinck & M^rs. Eliza Tracy.

Monday June 20th.

Another cold uncomfortable Day tho rather milder towards the evening, Mr Witts spent much of the Morning at Hampton Fair unsuccessfully looking after a Poney for Francis,

---

20.   Numa Pompilius: this probably refers to a novel, *Honoria Somerville*, by Elizabeth and Jane Purbeck, published in 1789.
21.   Although the distance was very short, the rise from the canal to Bownham House was about 400 feet on gradients exceeding one in three.

Mᵣ & Mʳˢ· John Pettat spent two hours with me talking over the old Story,²² we rode in the evening to Woodchester & home by Nailsworth Hill. rec'd a Letter from Franˢ·

Tuesday June 21ˢᵗ·

A milder Day tho cloudy & with little sun, tho very fine in the evening, after an early breakfast George & I went in the Chaise to fetch Dear Francis home from Elmore our errand made the drive there & home delightfull mounted him in the evening on a Poney, & walk'd while he rode on the common. rec'd a Letter from Mʳˢ· Granville & Miss Anne Snow, & several packages.

Wensday June 22ᵈ·

A very fine Day thro'out tho rather cold, Francis rode in the Mornᵍ· attended by John & with us in the evening without the least notion of fear, to Woodchester & Stroud rec'd a Letter from Mʳˢ· Buxton with not quite so bad an account of Mᵣ Naper, & one from Miss Louisa Lee which I answerd & wrote to Miss Anne Snow. & Mʳˢ· Granville

Thursday June 23ᵈ·

Very much the same kind of Day only not quite so much sun, Mᵣ Witts & I went to Dine at Mᵣ Hawkins's at Bisley, found the roads much better than we expected, a very agreable visit finding there Miss Hawkins, Mᵣ Jeffries, Capᵗⁿ· Forster & a Mᵣ Richards not at home till 10 o'clock.

Friday June 24ᵗʰ·

A fine Day with constant sun, tho a strong wind, Miss S: Sheppard here in the Morning & in the afternoon Mᵣ Witts, Francis, & I rode to Drink Tea at Mʳˢ· Clutterbucks at Hyde, where we found Mᵣ Lysons & his two Daughters,²³ a charming ride home near dark.

Saturday June 25ᵗʰ·

As fine a Day, & very warm we began mowing our field, Mᵣ Witts took a long coasting ride, & the 2 Miss Lees came to Dinner from Cheltenham, walk'd a little after Tea, & play'd at Cribbage before supper. rec'd a Letter from Lord Edward Bentinck.

Sunday June 26ᵗʰ·

Quite a hot Day tho with much wind, the three Ladies in the Chaise & the Father & Son on horseback went to Stroud Church, heard a sermon from Dᵣ Surgrove the Master of Pem: Coll: made a visit at Mᵣ Reades at Ebley a compliment to Mʳˢ· Jennings who was there, a wonderfull large circle. drank Tea at Sᵣ G: O: Pauls where was the whole family of the Hawkers to the number of 8, all walk'd to the Towers & back again, & I realy was but little fatigued not at home till dark.

---

22. This is sadly enigmatic. There is the possibility that it involved the financial difficulties of Edward Witts and John Pettat's brother, Richard. Edward had many financial dealings in the area and Richard, although seemingly retired from trade, seems to have had connections with the woollen cloth industry.
23. Samuel Lysons (1730–1804), rector of Rodmarton, antiquary and artist. The fine aquatint illustration of Woodchester in the colour section of this book is his work. One of his daughters was Mary Lysons (1765–1848). The other is unknown.

Monday June 27th.

Another as fine a Day, the three Boys began being drill'd by Cap.tn. Forsters Sergeant M.r Witts & Miss L. Lee took a long ride in the Morning, My Bro.r & Sis.r Witts arrived to Dinner & M.r Jeffries & Cap.tn. Forster dined here also, whist in the evening. rec'd Letters from M.rs. Savage & M.rs. Buxton with a dreadfull acco.t of poor M.r Naper.

Tuesday June 28th.

No sort of change in the weather too warm for riding or indeed any exercise in the Morning, which was agreably spent in work & conversation, in the evening, Miss Lee, M.r Witts, my Husband, Francis, & myself took a ride to Survey Dunkirk &'c & home early,[24] when we found M.r N. Wathen with the Ladies.

Wensday June 29th.

A very hot Day much more so than any of the former ones, I very civilly left M.rs. Witts to take care of herself the whole Day,[25] & accompanied Miss Lees on their road to Bristol, the two Brothers on horseback, & Francis with their Maid we went thro L.d. Ducies Park to Uley, & Dursley & so on to Berkeley Castle which we survey'd, & dined & drank Tea at Newport, when the Ladies proceeded on their route & we return'd home at 10, finding my Brother Travell had arrived to Dinner.

83. Berkeley Castle.

---

24.   The area between Woodchester and Nailsworth on the Nailsworth Stream, housing John Cooper's mills.
25.   Agnes does not seem to have liked her sister-in-law.

Thursday June 30ᵗʰ·

Some small showers in the Morning & indeed in a trifling manner the greater part of the Day, we had 14 to Dinner, viz, Mʳ & Mʳˢ· & Miss Pettat from Stonehouse & a Miss Saunders with them, Mʳ & Mʳˢ· & Miss Scott, & a Mʳˢ· Keller, & a Miss Renell with them, rather too many for pleasure but the Day went off well enough rec'd a Letter from Mʳˢ· Buxton with a better accoᵗ· of Mʳ Naper

July 1ˢᵗ·

Fine & dry, tho cloudy & lowering at times but not very hot. Mʳ & Miss Holbrow in the Morn: here, & we all Dined at Mʳ Reades, a very large party their own family being so numerous, but not very lively, & alarm'd coming home by the kicking of of the Chaise Horses. rec'd Letters from Mʳˢ· Eliza Tracy & my Sister Travell

Saturday July 2ᵈ·

Cloudy & strong appearance of rain, but very little fell of any consequence my Broᵗ Travell went away after breakfast we walk'd in our own premises after Tea received a Letter from Miss Anne Snow & answer'd it & wrote to Mʳˢ· Buxton.

Sunday July 3ᵈ·

Very much the same kind of Day after noon perpetual little trifling showers w.ʰ a strong east wind, all went to Stroud Church in the Morning, where a Stranger did the whole Duty, Mʳˢ· Witts, Francis, & I went to evening service at Hampton, & home to Dinner. Mʳ Wathen drank Tea here, too misty in the evening to walk out. rec'd a Letter from my Sisʳ Travell & answer'd it.

Monday July 4ᵗʰ·

A prodigeous high wind with very frequent Showers, some very violent, we dined at Mʳ Savages at Tetbury taking Francis with us, none but their own family wᶜʰ· was numerous their Girls being at home from School. on our return home found Mʳˢ· & Miss Witts arrived from Bristol the latter a very great invalid indeed.[26]

Tuesday July 5ᵗʰ·

Very fine till afternoon when there was some trifling showers, Mʳˢ· Wathen, & a Lady & her Daughter with her here in the Morning, the three Mʳˢ· Witts's in the Chaise & the Gents walking went to survey the beauties of the Hill House in the evening & walk'd in the walks. rec'd a Letter from Mʳˢ· Naper.

Wensday July 6ᵗʰ·

A very fine Day tho rather windy but a particular pleasant evening, we all walk'd our different ways in the Morning, & in the evening I carried Mʳˢ· Witts my Sister staying with Miss Witts in

26. There were three children of the marriage that survived into adulthood: Anne (1775–1839), John (1777–1857), who became a captain in the Royal Marines, and Apphia (1781–1859), named after her aunt, Apphia, Lady Lyttelton. It appears that this sickly schoolchild was a fourth, and she died in September (*see* diary entry below, 18 September 1791).

the Chaise over Rodbro Hill, up Woodchester Valley to Selsley Hill & home thro Woodchester Park & Woods, my Husband & Son attending us part of the way on Horseback.

Thursday July 7th.

Damp & Showery all the Day & towards evening very cold & unpleasant, M$^{rs.}$ & Miss Witts went away after breakfast, glad to see the poor invalid rather better than when she came disappointed & much vex'd at not seeing Miss Anne Nettleship & my Sis^t Travell to Dinner as was proposed, & more to receive an account that the former was going to L. Slaughter.[27] much hurt & vex'd. rec'd Letters from my Sister & Miss Anne, & answer'd the latter[28]

Friday July 8th.

Quite a fine Day tho still the air very cold, my Brother & Sister Witts left us, Mr Witts went to Tetbury, & on his return dined with a party of Gents at Mr Thornburys at Avening, not at home till late the Boys dined with me, & Francis I took a ride to Mr Tyndales &'c &'c, & a walk after we came home. rec'd a long entertaining Letter from Miss Snow.

Saturday July 9th.

Fine tho cloudy in the Morning, but dark & showery in the afternoon, M$^{rs.}$ Savage & her Daughter Elizabeth came here to Breakfast, the two youngest Miss Sheppards here at Noon, & M$^{rs.}$ Reade & Miss Reade, M$^{rs.}$ Jennings & Miss Willoughby, & Mr Wathen dined here, evening being wet play'd a lively game at Vingt"un

Sunday July 10th.

Perpetual soaking rain from 10 o'clock in the Morning, the whole Day, Miss Hawker came here from breakfast, I carried her with myself & Francis to Church at Stroud in the Chaise, after which set her down at her Brothers at Light Pill drank Tea chearfully enough at M$^{rs.}$ Sheppards at Hampton meeting a M$^{rs.}$ Wesley & her Niece wrote to M$^{rs.}$ Tyrwhitt, & Miss Sabine.

Monday July 11th.

No rain of any consequence, but very cloudy, cold & stormy, & the wind violent, quite unlike July, walk'd & work'd in the Morning & the same in the afternoon, Francis began riding his pretty new Poney with much success

Tuesday July 12th.

Cloudy in the Morning, but fine at noon & very fine in the evening tho cold & not much like summer. Tho$^s.$ Adams a new Man Servant arrived; Mr Witts, Francis & I rode in the afternoon to survey Mr Sevills Garden & on our return call'd for ½ an hour on M$^{rs.}$ Clutterbuck at Hyde. rec'd Letters from M$^{rs.}$ Tyrwhitt, M$^{rs.}$ Naper, M$^{rs.}$ Witts, & M$^{rs.}$ Commeline answer'd M$^{rs.}$ Napers.

---

27. It is difficult not to sense the feeling of pique displayed here to find her sister was going straight to Slaughter, but as Mr Naper was on his death-bed, perhaps the pique was misplaced.

28. Anne Nettleship was to marry a very worthy 'catch' in 1797 when she wed Dodington Hunt, widower, of Charlton Kings.

Wensday July 13ᵗʰ·

A mild fine Day, tho with little Sun & strong wind & clouds. after breakfast, taking Francis in the chaise with me went to call on Mʳˢ· Pettat &'c at the Hill House, then to Stanley to return Mʳˢ· Holbrows visit pleasant & agreable enough, in the evening wᶜʰ· was very fine & pleasant walk'd with the Boys in our own fields & premises. wrote to Miss Snow.

Thursday July 14ᵗʰ·

A very fine Day from Morn: to night sun quite hot, in a great bustle in the Morning getting ready to go to Mʳ Savages for the time of Tetbury Races, went to Dine at the Ordinary where was 30 Ladies,²⁹ but nothing could be more formal & stupid, took Miss Wiltshire with me to the Race where was moderate sport, a great shew of company, & very pretty scenery: home in haste to dress, but the Ball did not commence till past 10; which was very select & good tho not very numerous, a chearfull lively party at Supper not at home till three o'clock in the Morning.

Friday July 15ᵗʰ·

A truly hot summer Day quite delightfull, all the Ladies kept quite quiet all the Morn: while the Gentlemen follow'd their various inventions, Miss Wiltshire went with me to dine at the Ordinary where was only 18 Ladies, but not quite so stupid as the former Day, went with Mʳˢ· Savage to the Course, where was pretty good sport, but so long about we returnd before it was over, a very excellent Ball, much fuller than the night before a fine scramble at Supper but very amusing, not in bed till near 4 in the Morning.

Saturday July 16ᵗʰ·

Still hotter but very fine & true summer did not rise very early, & after a comfortable breakfast at home went to the Jug end of the public breakfast, to make our curteseys to the higher powers, returnd home to Dinner, finding the Dear Boys all we could wish & well pleased with our passt amusements, walk'd out in the evening about home rec'd Letters from Miss Snow & Miss Louisa Lee.

Sunday July 17ᵗʰ·

A wonderfull hot Day very oppressive tho clear & bright, all went to church at Stroud, Papa & Boy riding; after church attempted to make Mʳˢ· Forster a visit at Capᵗⁿ· Forsters Lodgings, but she was dressing & did not appear, but there was a large circle of Gentlemen the three Miss Sheppards drank Tea with us & staid late rec'd a Letter from Mʳˢ· Witts fʳᵐ· Witney & wrote to Mʳˢ· Commeline

Monday July 18ᵗʰ·

A hot cloudy Morning, & at 9 began raining very hard, & the showers were very frequent the whole of the Day, & a most tremendous one attend'd by thunder & Lightening in the afternoon; but in spite of these inauspicious appearances, Mʳ Witts Francis & I set forth on our Welsh Tour which had been long pland, our first

---

29. An Ordinary was a meal at a public house set to a fixed menu at a fixed price, or when at a function, a body of people sat down to such a set meal.

stage thro a rich pretty country by
Frampton &'c, was to Newnham but
before we could reach that place were
obliged to cross the Severn in a boat
in which Carriage, Horses, & all were
stationed not a very easy or pleasant
bussiness, & very tedious as it was
near an hour & half about, but luckily
was dry the whole of the passage,[30]
very glad to find ourselves safely
landed at the Bear Inn at Newnham
a neat comfortable house where we
got a good Dinner,[31] & set out as

84. *Newnham Ferry.*

soon as the storm ceased for Chepstow, the road very hilly & in general full of holes
& rough, the country rich & beautifull, the forest of Dean on the right & the Severn
& distant hills on the left, about half way between Newnham & Chepstow is Lidney
M[r] Bathursts an old Dull place too near the road but the Park behind pretty ground,
& well planted, the descent to the town of Chepstow is beautifull & the view of the
Castle fine the wooden Bridge curious & the River Wye which runs thro' it rapid &
the tide was coming in, the Town has nothing much to recommend it but the Beaufort
Arms a pretty good Inn: Bownham to Newnham 15 miles, to Chepstow 16 miles.

85. *Chepstow Castle and Bridge.*

---

30. Arlingham Passage. A ferry service ran here from Roman times up to the end of the Second World War. In times of
    antiquity it was a major salt route.
31. The Bear Inn was the main coaching inn for those using the ferry service.

86. *Chepstow Castle.*

Tuesday July 19ᵗʰ·

A very fine shewey Morning, but grew cloudy at Noon, & some very trifling showers fell in the afternoon but not enough to spoil our intended schemes. at 8 o'clock in the Morning we got into a clever Boat row'd by 4 men, with the Master at the Rudder for wᶜʰ· we paid a guinea, & half a Crown to the rowers, to take us to Tintern Abbey, which is 3 leagues or rather more distant, up the Wye & 5 miles by land over a dreadfull road; the River winds most beautifully between stupendous Rocks finely wooded on one side Gloucestershire & the other Monmouth on which side extends for near half the way, Mᵣ Smiths beautifull place of Piercefield,³² the first view of Tintern Abbey from the River is most striking & still more

---

32. George Smith, a Durham banker, bought Piercefield in 1785 for £26,200. Smith commissioned John Soane to design a new mansion in the neo-classical style. Work began in 1792, and the new three-storey stone building had reached roof level when Smith found himself in financial difficulties. He sold Piercefield in 1794 to Colonel Mark Wood, who continued and modified the work, incorporating a Doric portico and wings, and commissioning the long stone wall which runs along the edge of the estate. Agnes was looking at the old house which had been built in the early seventeenth century and added to about 1700. It had been bought in 1740 by Colonel Valentine Morris (1678?–1743), the son of a sugar planter from Antigua. The estate was inherited by his son, also Valentine Morris (1727–1789), who began living at Piercefield with his family in 1753. Morris soon added to the magnificent splendour of the estate and its setting by landscaping the parkland in the fashionable style of Capability Brown. Piercefield was developed into a park of national reputation, as one of the earliest examples of Picturesque landscaping. In the 1770s Morris' gambling, business and political dealings bankrupted him, and he was forced to leave his beloved Piercefield and set sail for the West Indies. Agnes' son Francis commented on the house in his entry for 21 September 1803, when he spent three hours wandering around the grounds. He referred to Smith again in his entry for Monday 8 September 1817 when on tour in the Lake District: '*Behind the village of Coniston, down the barren sides of the loftiest mountain, a cataract is precipitated, issuing from its inner recesses. On the bosom of the lake a skiff with sails was gliding along, forming an interesting addition to the view. Besides the pleasing groupes of white cottages among the fields on the opposite side of the lake, two very charming villas attracted our notice on the Eastern side. The first of these, the property of M. North, and on sale, is, however, not so enviable a spot, as the second, belonging to Col. Smith, whose lot it has been to reside in places remarkable for picturesque beauty, as Piercefield on the banks of the Wye was once his abode.*'

*87. Piercefield,
Monmouthshire.*

so on entering it, it was built by Roger Strongbow Earl of Pembroke in the Year 1115 is 77 yards in Length & 53 in depth, & most justly esteem'd the most perfect ruin of its kind in the kingdom, being very light & the Windows elegant & beautifull to a great degree, after contemplating with admiration this wonderfull Pile we return'd to our Vessels, which carried us back in an hour & half, not so much in going. walk'd on the Quay on our return, & into the Church w$^{ch.}$ is ancient & built in the Saxon stile of architecture; here we were fortunate enough to find the Organist who is a Woman, entertaining a party by singing extremely well some of the favourite airs in the Messiah. Dresst ourselves got a very comfortable Dinner & between 4 & 5 drove to Piecefield having previously obtain leave tho not the show Day to walk over it & rec'd an invitation from M^r & M$^{rs.}$ Smith whom we once were acquainted with to drink Tea with them w$^{ch.}$ we did very agreably & rec'd a most polite reception, & very high entertainment as nothing can exceed the beauty of the scenery nor nice keeping of the walks, on the whole we walk'd better than three miles, & to conclude drove to Wine Cliff, a high wooded Promontory from whence is the most glorious view possible of the Bristol Channel, the junction of the Severn & the Wye, & the view extending from Stinchcombe Hill on the left down the Coast to Swansea.

Wensday July 20$^{th.}$

A mild fine Day in general, strong clouds at times with appearance of showers but none of any consequence fell & towards afternoon fine gleams of sunshine, which show'd off the beautifull country thro' which we pass'd to great advantage. Left Chepstow at 9 o'clock, & proceeded 13 miles to Ragland over a very hilly country & the roads rough & bad, but the scenes so beautifully diversified that we were highly amused, tho were three hours going the stage, Ragland is a miserable villiage, with a moderate ale house, Inn, the Beaufort Arms, a quar^t of a mile distant are the ruins of Ragland Castle in the possession of the Duke

88. Tintern Abbey.

of Beaufort demolish'd by Oliver Cromwell, a fine venerable Pile of building on a rising situation, but in sad preservation, 9 miles to Abbergaveny, a much better road & thro an inchanting Country, where Mountains succeed each other without end or number, with the finest rich valleys beneath that the eye can imagine a happy mixture of Corn & Woodland, about half way is a place call'd Cleyton belonging to a Mr Jones who here built on the opposite Hill an ornamented Castle within a mile of the Town is Colebrook a Seat of Mr Hanbury Williams's, fine ground & well planted. Abergaveny is surrounded by Mountains among the most considerable of which, is Boorange, the Sugar Loaf, the Holy Mountain &'c &'c. we were much disappointed in the Town which is old, dull, & dirty, the Angel rather a showey Inn but nothing comfortable about it, & we got a sad dinner, & having nothing to see, set off soon after for Crick Howel, 6 miles, about half way enter'd Brenockshire when the country grows rather less cultivated, & the Mountains more barren, it is rather a desolate place tho has a Market once a week, the Bear Inn little better than an alehouse.

Thursday July 21st.

A most charming day for travelling being constant sunshine without being hot, the air being clear, which was most propitious for the views left Crick Howel at 9 o clock 14 miles to Brechinoch of rather a rough road but only one principal Hill call'd Buelch, the country charming, & tho Mountanous rich & fertile, & full of fine cultivation both of Hay & corn Brechinoch is a very old Town, stands pleasantly at the foot of some of the highest Mountains in Wales call'd Beacons, the Priory Walks all pleasant, & the old Church of St John the Evangelist near it well worth seeing from its antiquity; the Golden Lyon an excellent Inn in point of accomodation, but a very old house in a very narrow Street, we got a very good Dinner & proceeded on 10 miles to Trecastle of so hilly & bad a road that we were 2 hours & ½ going it, about half way is a very pleasant seat belonging to a Mr Williams at Pen Pont. we drank Tea at Trecastle, & then had 9 miles of a charming new road made within

89. Raglan Castle

these two years to Llandovery, thro the most Romantic Wooded Valleys possible, thro' which the River Bruine winds in a rapid fine stile, the Town of Llandovery is large & straggling but rather desolate & truly Welch in its appearance, indeed some of the Cottages or rather hutts both in it & its Neighbourhood are more like Pig sties than dwellings for human Creatures. the Castle is a very tolerable Inn & wonderfully civil people, & so are the Welch people in general, which probably arises more from Nature than commerce with the rest of the world. wrote to M$^{rs.}$ Witts at Clifton

Friday July 22$^{d.}$

Had been a little rain in the night, was a cloudy lowering Morning but kept dry till mid-day was small flying rain all the afternoon, & very hard rain all the evening & night. left Landovery at 9, going 12 miles to Landilo, over the most moderate country we had seen, roads rough & stony, frequent hills & the land neither so good or well cultivated, some mountains at a distance, or else no object worthy note till within 2 miles of the Town, when Bewton Park with Denevor Castle in it, & Golden Grove Mr Vaughans opposite to it on the other side of the river Towey presented themselves in a fine stile Landilo is a most miserable Welsh Town, full of little but beggars, & the Bear as bad an Inn as possible, & our Dinner proved the worst meal we had as yet made, while it was preparing drove to Newton Park which is fine bold ground & much wooded tho the timber is not fine, the House stands low & commands very little view & its environs appear to want many alterations & repairs, the old Denevor Castle about ½ a mile from it, stands on a noble eminence & well worthy of observation, was once the residence of the Princes of Wales, the round Tower the only part that remains at all intire, commands as fine a view of the adjacent country as it can afford but much inferior to most we had seen, the chief object is Golden Grove 3 miles distant, w$^{ch.}$ did not appear to me attractive enough to go so far out of our way; to Carmarthen is 15 miles of a better road, not very hilly, & a much richer country, tho the wretched huts still continued, & every sign of poverty in

90. Brecon Priory.

their inhabitants, at the end of a Village call'd Aberywilly 2 miles from the Town is the Palace of the Bishop of St. Davids Carmarthen is a miserable Town for a County one its Suburbs are more wretched than can be imagined, & what we saw of the Town driving thro' little better, but raining so hard were confined wholly to the Inn, the Ivy Buck; a dark old House with middling accomodation wrote to Mrs. Elizabeth Tracy.

Saturday July 23^{d.}

Wet early in the Morning, & during the course of the Day frequent small showers, but in the afternoon & evening rain'd as hard as the last night rather unpropitious for our wish of seeing the Country left Carmarthen at the usual hour, went 9 miles to Kidwelly a Small Market Town, the road bad & hilly & the country somewhat desolate & uncultivated, but the road made chearfull by the great numbers of people going to Carmarthen Market among which the fair sex strongly prevail'd; some way from the Town we had a first view of the boundless Ocean which floats up to the Town of Kidwelly, where is a fine old ruininated Castle, here we only stopped for hay & water & went on 8 miles farther to Llanely, over a continuation of hilly country, with charming Sea views, the land ones nothing very striking it is a very singular Town the Church has both a Tower & Spire belonging to it, it is very long & dark, in the church yard we saw almost universally on every grave the custom of the country herbs & flowers planted, a pleasing rememberance of departed friends: the Falcon tho a wretched looking Inn, proved very comfortable for Dining at; our first stage in the afternoon was to Pontardilais 7 miles where we did not stop but went on 9 more to Swansea, the evening proved so very wet & misty I could judge little of the country, but that it still continued hilly, the first enterance to Swansea was not very favorable, we again met great numbers returning from that market quite amusing, the Mackworth Arms a great shewey Inn, full of noise & bustle & no comfort, scarce possible to get accomodated at any rate. Mr. Sheldon call'd on us for a quarter of an hour. rec'd a Letter from Mrs. Naper & wrote to Miss Snow.

Sunday July 24th.

Fine in the Morning early, but a small shower after breakfast, after which bright & dry till quite evening, when it became violent wet again went to Church in the Morning sat in Mr Sheldons pew a large handsome church, ceil'd & supported by Pillars, a tolerable well toned Organ, & very pleasing singing, & a good sermon, on our return found M^r & Mrs. Sheldon had call'd on us to ask us to Dinner which we accepted going on the sands towards their House wch. is call'd Sketty Hall being more than two miles distant,[33] the house is good, being greatest part new built, & commands a fine Sea View of the Mumbles, its Town & Castle, but around it is sadly unfinish'd & uncomfortable, they gave us a pleasing friendly reception & we spent an agreable Day as they are grown very domestic & fond of their Children, heard some musick in the evening & did not return to Swansea till quite late by the Turnpike road which not knowing exactly brought us into some distresses. upon the whole I was disappointed in Swansea, it is a large Town, & apparently of much trade, not only as lying on the Sea Shore but having several Copper & lead Works close to the Town; it is often full of company for the purpose of Sea bathing but is thin this Year on the Sands is a house erected call'd the Bathing house, which accomodates company to the number of 30 to lodge & board. wrote to Mrs. Naper.

Monday July 25th.

A very miserable Day for travellers being frequently most violent showers, but not being continued rain, we bustled thro' it & endeavor'd not to mind it tho it was a cruel interruption to our promised pleasure of the Day during which we had much to see & do; left Swansea at 10 to go to Neath 8 miles the first 4 of which is thro a dreadfull bad country intersected with numbers of coal Pits, copper & lead works, the working of which proved an entertainment to look at as we pass'd by before we reach Neath have a fine view of Sir Herbert Mackworths House & plantations on the other side of the Town, which is call'd Noll,[34] its a Castle building, with 12 Cannon planted, at a small distance below, but the place is much infused by the smoke of his own Copper Works below, wch. must be very disagreeable; at Neath is the Ruin of an old Abbey which is of very large extent, but capable of being inhabited by poor people at the Turnpike before we enterd the Town, we turn'd off into another road to go 2 miles to a Villiage call'd Aberdyllis to see a noble Waterfall over some rocks were highly gratified tho caught in a violent hard shower while surveying it but by the help of Umbrellas were not materialy wet, return'd by the same road to Neath again thro' which we went 3 miles to Britton Ferry, where we stopp'd to bait the Horses & dine at little better than, an ale House but got a tolerable Dinner, while it was getting walkd over some part of Ld. Vernons domain just by which is an old place much out of repair but here some fine Sea views & craggy Rocks within itself, were very hospitably taken into the House for ½ an hour during a storm by Miss Fauquier Lady Vernons Sister,[35] to Pyle is 9 miles, a

33. The Sheldon family had lived at Weston, Long Compton, Warwickshire, since 1532. Ralph Sheldon (1741? –1822) was a colonel of the Oxford Loyal Volunteers and later became M.P. for Wilton (1804–1822). During the 1790s Ralph Sheldon lived at Sketty Hall, near Swansea. Edward and Agnes would have known the family from their time in Oxfordshire.
34. Herbert Mackworth of Gnoll, Neath (1737–1791), 1st Baronet (1776–1791); M.P. for Cardiff (1766–1790). *See* Mackworth-Praed below, F182.
35. George Venables Vernon, 2nd Lord Vernon (1735–1813). Vernon was related to the Dolphin family and had been a patron or benefactor to John Dolphin, curate of Lower Slaughter. Vernon married Jane Georgiana, daughter of William Fauquier of Hanover, Germany.

91. *Briton
Ferry.*

pretty good road but rather a dull desolate country, at 6 miles we stoppd to see the famous Orangerie at Margam belonging to Mᵣ Talbot, which I found <u>nearly</u> as fine as reported, tho they seem to propogate rather for numbers than the large size they used to have, there is a fine new Green house just finish'd, highly ornamented on the outside is 327 feet long, 30 wide, & 20 high, at one end a Library, & the other a statuary neither fitted up as yet; the Orange Trees were all standing on a kind of bowling Green, well shelterd by high Trees the House which appears to have been a very large one is almost wholly pulled down, very near to it is a fine ruin of an ancient Chapter House, wᶜʰ· is likewise suffer'd to tumble down peace meal a great pity, but everything about the place seems the face of misery arising from being deserted. The Inn at Pyle is just built by Mᵣ Talbot is a very large one & upon a very good plan is scarcely finish'd, but furnish'd quite elegantly the people that keep it very civil.

Tuesday July 26ᵗʰ·

Very wet early in the Morning but was dry & pretty fine from Breakfast till the afternoon when it was again wet & showery, set out at the usual hour, but diverged from the great road to go to see the Bathing House at Newton & the Wonderfull Well close to the Sea which rises to a great height as the tide goes out & falls as it comes in; the Bathing House will accomodate 18 to board & Lodge but I should be sorry to make one, as it is a very dull coast, & the sand deep & disagreable, from hence we found our way as well as we could across the country to Sᵗ· Donatts Castle which we were anxious to see being Mᵣ Tyrwhitts property, it is a very fine old ruin standing on a great rocky eminence above the Sea of which it commands a noble view, & of the opposite Somerset & Devonshire coast it is a very large Pile of building, & now in its ruin'd state is the residence of three families the Curate of the Parish, & 2 farmers Tenants, the latter, refresh'd our Horses, & the former ourselves & Serᵗˢ. in the best manner he could, tho not as his hospitality led him to wish, & he shew'd us the

92. Cardiff Castle

Castle & all the domain in a good stile, both he & his Wife were great invalids, but very well behaved poor people, & happen'd to know several people we knew; which made our visit give them pleasure, from thence we went to Cowbridge across the country, which was much mended since the Morning, & towards the Town rich & fine, the Landlord of the Inn told us we had made it 24 miles from Pyle & had 12 to go to Cardiff, which we ventured to go tho rather late but as the road was good got there just as it was dark, passing by several good places & overlooking a very fine vale with difficulty got admitted at the Cardiff Arms a very good Inn close to the Castle.

Wensday July 27th.

After a night of violent rain, it was an intire, dry, nay fine beautifull Day, which well suited the various things we had to see, but were prevented leaving Cardiff from one which wanting repairs till 12 o'clock, in the meantime walk'd, round the Castle walls & walks & were much pleased, look'd into 2 or 3 of the new repair'd rooms in the Castle to see some family Pictures; Lord Mountstewart keeps up the place in an excellent manner that does him credit;[36] from Cardiff to Ponty: Prid Bridge is 13 miles of a rough road, but intirely thro' a fine Valley between wooded Rocks by the side of the River Taaf, which is a very noble wide one, & at times both rocky & rapid, for the first two miles from Cardiff you have a pleasing view of the Town & Cathedral of Landaff at about 2 miles distance which tho Picturesque, gives one little idea of being a Bishops See; on the Banks of the river in two or three places are Iron forges which carry on great bussiness, but are no injury to the beauty of the scenery, which is quite charming & very fertile in corn & meadow lands; the Bridge is over a wide part of the Taaf, & surrounded by most Romantic Rocks & woods, in one intire Circle which is

---

36.   John (Stuart), Earl of Bute (1744–1792).

93. Cardiff Castle

144 feet wide from Base to Base, 59 feet in depth from the Centre of the arch to the surface of the water, & is reckond the largest arch in the kingdom, very the surrounding people say in Europe, it certainly is very well worth seeing. being aware of the necessity of stopping here both to refresh ourselves & Horses, & knowing our accomodations would be had, we carried some little provisions from Cardiff & managed to get a very tolerable scrambling Dinner, which we assisted to cook ourselves. while we were there came in a large party on the same errand who had not been so provident, but they added much to our amusement after staying 2 hours & a half, we went 8 miles to Caerphilly, the last 3 miles of which were horrid road up a most dreadfull stoney Hill, so narrow the Chaise could but just pass, a mile from the Town the Castle presents itself in a noble stile, it is an imense Pile of building, many Towers, is reputed to have coverd 10 acres of ground, one principal Tower from a supposed failure of the ground under it is considerably out of the level & lays in a wonderfull manner the account given of the Castle is rather beyond belief that it was built 400 years before the birth of Christ by one Beli Gawr who then govern'd all Brittan, & was totaly demolish'd in the reign of Edward the Second in a war with his Barons; it stands close to the Town wch. is a straggling little Market Town & the adjacent Country nothing remarkable, the Boars Head so miserable an ale house that we thought it impossible to sleep there with any comfort & too late to proceed on to Newport, therefore got Beds from the hospitality of a Mercer who had a good new built house in the Town whither we went after Supper. I omitted to mention that in the Villiage of S^t. Donnats the Day before, we saw an old Man of the name of John Hany, whose age was known to be 106, able to move, blind only with one eye, & not quite deaf, his name is registered in the Parish of Wick two miles distant.

Thursday July 28th.
A mixture of clouds & sunshine, but no rain, & mild, & upon the whole a favorable Day both for travelling & views, left our miserable habitation at Caerphilly as soon as we could & went

12 miles to Newport, thro' a very picturesque fine country of hill & dale, wood & corn land & thro several Viliages, the view of the Castle from a distance most noble, the roads very bad & tedious, three miles from Newport pass Mr Morgans seat at Tredegar, indeed the road goes thro part of the domain, it is a large old place finely timber'd, but the House unfortunately stands in the lowest worst part of the ground on a Hill rising from Tredegar, we got a very fine view of the Channel, the flat & steep Holmes, & the river Usk which is navigable to Newport which is a moderate Town on the banks & a large heavy ruin of a Castle standing near the foot of the Bridge w$^{ch.}$ is wooden as are most in this part of the Country, here we staid to bait the horses & eat cold meat, & proceeded on 12 miles more to Usk over a very striking country, thro the Market Town of Caerlion to Usk is a tremendous steep hill indeed the whole stage there were not half a mile without hills, at Usk we only stopp'd for Hay & water, it is a miserable Town on the River of its name, & here a small ruin of a Castle nearly overgrown with Ivy, from Usk we went 5 miles to Ragland, thro w$^{ch.}$ Town is the only part of the road we went over twice on the whole Tour, here we got some excellent Tea & Coffee &'c which made up for the want of Dinner, & leaving our own Horses to walk quietly after us, took a pair of Post Horses to carry us 8 miles to Monmouth, on a most charming road with very little hill, but the views around quite delightfull, recognised with much pleasure the sweet Mountains around Abergaveny, Monmouth appear'd a very good Town, & the Beaufort Arms an excellent Inn, Just before it was dark walk'd in the Church yard which is planted in walks with Lime Trees, the body of the Church is large & newly built, the Spire old & beautifull, we got a good supper & slept well in a most excellent bed & room.

94. Newport Castle.

95. Newport Castle and Bridge.

Friday July 29th.

A sad wet Morning, with a violent strong wind, we waited till 12 o'clock hoping it might clear up, which it did & suffer'd us to go to Ross 10 miles tolerably dry, but was again wet, & rain'd in the severest manner the whole afternoon; from Monmouth to Ross is a very pretty road extremely romantic, rich, & varied, with perpetual fine views of the river Wye wch. is often both wide & rapid, the entrance into Ross each way is horrid, & the Town very old & miserable, it rain'd so soon, we had not time to walk into the Church yard, where is a good view but were wholly confined to the Inn, where tho we were at the second best house, we got a very good Dinner & were perfectly well satisfied with the mistaking the Kings Head for the Kings Arms it

96. Monmouth Bridge.

97. Monnow Bridge, Monmouth.

is 16 miles to Glocester, of a hilly moderate road what the Country is I know not as the violence of the rain prevented any possiblity of seeing a yard from the Carriage & a very disagreable drive we had & Servants quite wet thro' 2 miles or a little more from Glocester is Highnam the Seat of Sir John Guise, a large handsome House but a very unpleasant looking place close to the Turnpike road; we found ourselves very uncomfortably accomodated at the Kings Head, literally going in a manner Supperless to Bed. wrote to M^rs. Savage & Miss Louisa Lee.

98. Highnam Court.

Bownham to Newham- 14
Newnham to Chepstow-16
Chepstow to Piercefield &'c- 8
Chepstow to Ragland-13
Ragland to Abergaveny- 9
Abergaveny to Crick: Howel- 6
Crick: Howel to Brechinoch-14
Brechinoch to Trecastle-10
Trecastle to Llandovery- 9
Llandovery to Llandilo-12
Llandilo to Carmarthan-15
Carmarthan to Kidwelly- 9
Kidwelly to Llannely- 8
Llannely to Pontardilais- 7
Pontardilais to Swansea- 9
Swansea to Shietty Hall & back- 5
Swansea to Neath- 8
Neath to Aberdgliss & back- 5
Neath to Britton Ferry- 3
Britton Ferry to Dyle- 9
Dyle to St. Donnats-17
St. Donnats to Cowbridge- 7
Cowbridge to Cardiff-<u>12</u>
 225

Cardiff to Ponty: Pridd-13
Ponty: Pridd to Caerphilly- 8
Caerphilly to Newport-12
Newport to Usk-12
Usk to Monmouth-13
Monmouth to Ross-10
Ross to Glocester-16
Glocester to Bownham-<u>13</u>
 322

Saturday July 30th.
A very windy disagreable Day but without absolute rain, & grew tolerably fine in the evening, Breakfasted by invitation with M^r & Mrs. Commeline, afterwards call'd on Dr Cheston, the Dean & Mrs. Tucker, & Mrs. Jennings, & refused every one of them to take Dinner with them, proposing to return home, but meeting Mr Hyett, he tempted us to go home the Painswick road & dine with them to meet Mr Sabine & his Daughter from Bath which we did & like the change of plan very much having a very pleasant drive in the evening getting home just before dark, finding the little dears quite well. rec'd Letters from Mr Hunt, Miss Sabine & my Sister Travell.

Sunday July 31st.

Quite an intire wet Day excepting an hour or two in the middle of the Day, did not attempt going to Church in the Morning for various reasons dined at one o'clock to set out in time for Hampton evening service, which was perform'd by Mr Moore from Bisley, sat in Mrs. Sheppards Seat & return'd with them to Tea & spend the afternoon finding there a Mr Castleman. rec'd Letters from my Sis^r Travell & Mrs. Master, answer'd the latter & wrote to Mr Hunt.

Monday Aug^{st.} 1st.

Very hard rain till noon when it clear'd off & was fine the remainder of the Day, much engaged in various employs, but unwell & very much out of spirits with the thought of my Dear Francis's speedy departure, he rode out in the evening & we all walk'd afterwards. wrote to Mrs. Tyrwhitt.

Tuesday Aug: 2^{d.}

A pleasant dry day, tho strong clouds & sometimes sunshine, Mr Wathen call'd here in the Morning after which we rode out to please Francis, going down Nailsworth Hill to Woodchester &'c Mrs. Savage came early in the afternoon to bring her Son John for me to take to Elmore Court, she staid to drink Tea & returnd with a heavy heart, we walk'd afterwards rec'd a Letter from Mrs. Buxton & wrote to Mrs. Rollinson

Wensday Aug^{st.} 3^{d.}

Quite a beautiful summer Day, without being oppressively hot. Mr Witts went after Breakfast to survey North Nibley for his Bro^r taking Mr Sheppard of Uley with him, with whom he

99. *Nailsworth from Watledge Hill.*

afterwards dined; I went with John Savage & my Dear Francis to Elmore getting there an hour before Dinner where I found M^r. & M^rs. Cresswell & Miss Cresswell who had brought their Sons also. felt more than I ought at quitting my beloved Child, or else my drive home would have been most pleasant rec'd a Letter from Miss Anne Snow.

Thursday Aug^st. 4th.

A very fine Day with a mixture of clouds & sunshine much engaged with Mantua Maker & Taylor & a good deal perplex'd with the continued illness of poor Thos. the footman who had not been out of his Bed since Sunday to speak on rode in the evening to Stroud to send M^r. Thornton to him again from thence went to call on M^rs. A: Pettat at Ganycocks, where we found a circle of 12 drinking Tea staid an hour & was amused wrote to my Sister Travell.

Friday Aug^st. 5th.

Still warmer weather & in the afternoon so close & cloudy it was much like Thunder; very busy all the Morning, walk'd in our own premises after Tea with the Boys, & were visited on horseback by Miss Sheppards & a young Lady with them. write to Miss Anne Snow.

Saturday Aug^st. 6th.

Still charming summer weather, tho too hot to move much in the Morning, when Col: Durouse made a long visit & was agreable; walk'd after Tea as usual with the Boys in our own fields, rec'd a Letter from M^rs. Granville.

Sunday Aug^st. 7th.

Rather a hotter day tho sun being quite broiling but delightfull in the evening, obliged to ride to Stroud Church, the Chaise being under going repairs; M^r. Ellis gave a very good Sermon, call'd afterwards on M^rs. Burgh after her lying in, walk'd late on Rodbro common extremely pleasant the Boys much happy & playfull rec'd a Letter from my Dear Fran^s

Monday Aug^st. 8th.

A remarkable pleasant Day, perfectly clear & fine & not so intensely hot, Col: & M^rs. Durouse & Miss Wynne made a very long Morning visit here walking about to survey everything, rode in the afternoon to Hampton, went into the Church to look for a Seat to rent, return'd home by M^r. James Clutterbucks House at Holcombe, Walking evening. rec'd a Letter from M^rs. Naper.

Tuesday Aug^st. 9th.

Another very fine Day, M^r. Witts rode to Hampton & about, we walk'd in the evening calling on poor sick people &'c. wrote to M^rs. Naper, & M^rs. Master

Wensday Aug^st. 10th.

Still dry & fine but windy, very busy all Morning in the Garden &'c, in the afternoon rode to call on M^rs. Pettat at Ryeford not at home till late but it was very warm & pleasant. rec'd a long Letter from Miss Snow & one from M^rs. Master, wrote to Fran^s.

Thursday Aug^(st.) 11^(th.)

Hot & close with strong appearance of rain
but none came, much engaged all Morning
with packing & preparation for going the next
Day to Cheltenham, M^(r) J: Delabere came very
unexpectedly to Dinner, walk'd with him in the
evening & had much conversation on various
subjects with him.

Friday Aug^(st.) 12^(th.)

Violent hard rain from 9 in the Morning till 12
at noon when it cleard off, & was very fine tho
extreme hot & close & much like thunder, left
home as soon as it was dry, M^(r) Witts & M^(r) J:
Delabere on Horseback, George, Horsington &
myself in the Chaise reach'd Cheltenham just
at Dinner time where my Sisters had arrived
the Day before, M^(r) J: Delabere drank Tea &
walk'd out afterwards with us, concluding with

*100. The Old Well Walk, Cheltenham, from the
Sherborne entrance.*

looking at the company at the Ball room Door. rec'd a Letter from M^(rs.) Hyett.

Saturday Aug^(st.) 13^(th.)

Extremely hot in the Morning with much scorching sunshine, cloudy in the afternoon &
a little thick misty rain in the evening, went to the Well & began drinking the water, a
wonderfull numerous succession of Morning visitors, went out late to make more, M^(r) J:
Delabere dined here & Miss Hughes drank Tea, the former went with us to a crowded Play
House where were very poorly entertain'd, by the Chapter of Accidents & Bon Ton.[37]

Sunday Aug^(st.) 14^(th.)

A wonderfull hot Day, hardly possible to bear moving about, such a hot wind, went to
Church both Morning & evening, a good sermon from D^(r) Small in the Morning, much
visiting till Dinner time, sat an hour with M^(rs.) Markham after even^(g.) church, M^(r) & M^(rs.)
Round & their Son drank Tea here, walk'd till dark & then went to the Rooms for an hour
full & lively. rec'd a Letter from Francis

Monday Aug^(st.) y^(e.) 15^(th.)

More & more oppressively hot at Dinner time a most violent storm of Thunder Lightening, &
rain which continued more or less the whole evening & night & was quite tremendous, went
to the Pump with M^(rs.) Round in her Chaise, a little visiting after Breakfast, M^(rs.) Tracys from

37. Sophia Lee (1750–1824), novelist and dramatist. She was the daughter of John Lee (d. 1781), actor and theatrical
manager, and was born in London. Her first piece, *The Chapter of Accidents*, a three-act opera based on Denis
Diderot's *Père de famille*, was produced by George Colman the Elder at the Haymarket Theatre on 5 August 1780
and was an immediate success. David Garrick (1717–1779), *Bon Ton, or High Life above Stairs* (Drury Lane,
March 1775), acted at Tunbridge in September 1787.

Sandywell & Miss Hughes dined here, & M^rs. Cox drank Tea dull & stupid the whole Day Miss Hughes went with me to the Ball which was a very indifferent one. wrote to M^rs. Hyett

Tuesday Aug^st. 16th.

Very disagreably hot & close, quite a thick air, & in the evening very hard rain, went alone to the Pump in M^rs. Rounds chaise, Mr Witts went into Oxfordshire after breakfast, we visited & dawdled as usual & went to see the little Polish Count a very curious wonder in nature,[38] drank Tea at Mr Delaberes, & went with Mr John & his Sister to see the Distresst Mother very well perform'd in general; Halman certainly a very good Actor.[39]

Wensday Aug^st. 17th.

A much pleasanter Day being not near so hot, but clear with much sunshine Morning pass'd much as usual, Mr Chapeau, Mr B. Dewes, & his Daughter & M^r J: Delabere dined here M^rs. Jennings, Miss Willoughby, & Miss Reade drank Tea, very brilliant rooms, many Card Tables, among the rest a Pharoah one; play'd at Whist with M^rs. Fraines party with bad success. wrote to Miss Snow.

Thursday Aug^st. 18th.

The same glorious weather without being oppressively hot, again to the Well for the last time with M^rs. Round, walk'd to the Cottage &'c in the Morning, Miss Nevilles drank Tea here, my Sis^r Cath: George & I went to the Play, the Wonder & the Critic both very well perform'd to a full house.[40]

Friday Aug^st. 19th.

No change in the weather, was taken to the Well by M^rs. Cox, breakfasted a second time late at the Lower Rooms for the benifit of the Polish Count, who exhibited, playing on the Guittar to a large & genteel company, went afterwards to see the tall Woman & the representation of the Woollen Manufactory, M^rs. Jennings dined here alone drank Tea at Mr Hughes's meeting old M^r & M^rs. Fuller, went to a full & brilliant Ball play'd at whist in a mix'd party wrote to Miss Andrew to condole on her Grandmothers Death.

Saturday Aug^st. 20th.

Quite as fine a Day towards evening still hotter, did not go to the Well, the Morning spent as usual, Mr Witts returned at Noon happy to see him He & I dined at Mr Delaberes to meet Mr Swinfin & Mr Reppington besides their own large family party,

38. Joseph Boruwlaski (1739–1837). Boruwlaski, 'the Little' Count, grew to only thirty-nine inches in height during his long lifetime. A Polish musician, he lived for much of his time in Durham, where he is buried. His best friend was the actor John Kemble. Boruwlaski's clothes are on permanent display at Durham Town Hall.
39. Ambrose Philips (1674–1749), *The Distressed Mother*, first acted at Drury Lane, 17 March 1712.
40. Susannah Centlivre (1667–1723), *The Wonder! A Woman Keeps a Secret*. A comedy first performed at Drury Lane in 1724 and frequently revived. Richard Brinsley Sheridan (1751–1816). In June 1776 Sheridan purchased Garrick's share of the Drury Lane Theatre and became its manager. In October 1779 he produced the last play of his own authorship, *The Critic*, in which he deftly mocked the follies of everyone, from playwright to spectator, connected with the theatre.

went to the Rooms which were better than common on a Play night play'd at Whist in a pleasant party. wrote to Francis

Sunday Aug$^{st.}$ 21$^{st.}$

Much the same weather not quite so much sun & more wind, went to Church in the Morning only, Dr Walters preach'd, visited afterwards Miss Delabere drank Tea, after walking in the street went with her to the Rooms, which were very full but agreable enough to stay there 2 hours rec'd a Letter from my sweet Francis.

Monday Aug$^{st.}$ 22$^{d.}$

Cloudy Morning, & a sharp shower at Noon which did not last long, nor prevent our usual Morning stroles, Sr Willm. Altham, M^r B: Dewes M^r J: Delabere, M^r B: Hughes dined here, & Miss Hughes drank Tea & all went to the Ball together full but not very lively or agreable play'd at whist in the same set as on Saturday

Tuesday Aug$^{st.}$ 23$^{d.}$

One of the hottest Days that had been constant sunshine & very close hot air, walk'd & dawdled a little about, M$^{rs.}$ & Miss Markham, & Mr Tyndale dined here, Major & M$^{rs.}$ Hatrell & M$^{rs.}$ Cox drank Tea, & went to the Rooms, thin but pleasant play'd at Whist with success. rec'd a Letter from Miss Anne Snow. Mr Witts at Sandywell in the Morn$^g.$

Wensday Aug$^{st.}$ 24$^{th.}$

Had been a very wet night, & tho dry all Day, was very dabbling walking in the Morning to the Well; at noon walk'd with my Sis^r Travell & Mr John Delabere to Sandford to see M$^{rs.}$ Ram, where we met a large party of Morning callers; M$^{rs.}$ Jennings & her Neice & the 2 youngest Miss Reades dined here. My Sis^r Catherine went to the Concert & all the rest of us to very full & agreable rooms play'd at Whist in the same party.

Thursday Aug$^{st.}$ 25$^{th.}$

Frequent showers in the course of the Morning but dry in the afternoon, much visiting as usual Miss Hughes dined here, we all drank Tea late at Mr Adairs, & went to the Rooms which were moderately full & very agreable play'd at whist in the old set.

Friday Aug$^{st.}$ 26$^{th.}$

Quite a pleasant Day, neither hot nor cold, a pleasant morning circle at home, & visiting afterwards, dined at Mr Hughes's in a very agreable party of 13, 8 Gentlemen & 5 Ladies, & Dr Napleton added to Tea who was just arrived, all went to the Ball w$^{ch.}$ was a tolerable good one, play'd 2 rubbers at whist with a different set, excepting Mr Bernard Dewes.

Saturday Aug$^{st.}$ 27$^{th.}$

Much the same sort of weather till the evening when it was wet & disagreable, walk'd a little in the Morning with Miss Delabere, picked up on the way by M$^{rs.}$ Cookes & her Daughter in their Coach & taken on dull airing on the Dowdeswell road, Mr Witts rode to Sr John

Guises. Dr Napleton dined here & M^r & M^rs. Chamberlayne drank Tea, went to the rooms & play'd at Whist agreably.

Sunday Aug^st. 28th.

Rather cold & stormy, but not wet went to church in the Morning, heard a good sermon from Mr Neane, visited Miss Delabere & M^rs. Burslem afterwards, dined at Mr Cox's at the Cottage meeting St Willm. Altham & Admiral Wolseley very agreable & an excellent Dinner look'd in at the Rooms for an hour, Dr Napleton & Miss Delabere supt here much spirited conversation. rec'd a Letter from my beloved Francis.

Monday Aug^st. 29th.

Quite a cold Autumn Day, but dry & pleasant for exercise, Dr Napleton breakfasted here Mr Witts, my Sis^r Travell, George & I walk'd to see M^rs. Ram, M^r & M^rs. Hyett &'c here afterwards, M^rs. Evans, M^rs. Phipps, Miss Hibbert & Cap^tn. Forster dined here & most of us went to a large handsome looking Ball I play'd at Whist in an odd party. wrote to M^rs. Buxton

Tuesday Aug^st. 30th.

Very much the same kind of weather but quite cold & windy, walk'd in the fields with my Sisters as well as visited in the Morning, Miss Vernon & Sir Willm. Altham dined here, & Lady Cullen & her little Niece drank Tea, & went with us to the Play, where we took George, for the sake of seeing Harlequin, the next Door Neighbours & the Critic,[41] all very tolerably well perform'd. rec'd a Letter from M^rs. Naper.

Wensday Aug^st. 31st.

A Day of perpetual hard rain except for 2 hours at Noon when Mr Witts ventured to take his purposed ride to Lower Slaughter; St Willm. Altham & M^r J: Delabere made long Morning visits here, Miss Delabere dined & drank Tea as did M^rs. Ledwell & M^rs. Leonard with the latter I went to full & agreable Rooms & play'd at Whist with success in the old set wrote to Miss Anne Snow.

Thursday Sepr 1st.

A beautifull clear fine Day, visited & walk'd in Prestbury field with Miss Delabere & her Bro^r Mr Witts return'd to Dinner, to meet M^r & M^rs. Burslem[42] & Miss Amphlet & Dr Napleton, Miss Nevilles & Miss Hughes drank Tea & as usual all went to the Rooms. rec'd a Letter from Miss Snow.

---

41. Elizabeth Inchbald, *née* Simpson (1753–1821), novelist, actress and dramatist. *Next Door Neighbours* (1791). No specific reference has been found to *Harlequin*. John Rich (1681–1761) developed the role of Harlequin, and thereafter it was a popular theme of a pantomime nature with many plays and set-piece entertainments based on it.

42. William Burslem (1747–1820). Burslem was ordained in 1770 and became rector of Lightpill, Shropshire (1774–1820) and of Hanbury, Worcestershire (1780–1820), residing at the latter place. He married Miss Harvey, of Hoon-hay, Derbyshire, in 1785, and they had at least one child, Henry Burslem (1790–1866), who followed him into the Church and was a successful cricketer, playing for England. Burslem was a very old friend of Edward and Agnes Witts and there are frequent references to him through the years. Later on, Burslem was recruited in the effort to find (or develop) a career for Francis, Edward and Agnes' eldest son. Burslem was the clergyman who married Francis Witts to his future wife, Margaret, in 1808.

Friday Sep.ʳ 2.ᵈ

Cold & stormy, & in the evening, a little rain but very trifling, very little out of the house in the Morning; Major & Mʳˢ· Hatsell, Dʳ Napleton & Miss Morris dined here, & Mʳˢ· & Miss Andre's drank Tea, & the young Ladies went with us to the Ball as did Miss Mill. went late & not a full Ball.

Saturday Sep.ʳ 3.ᵈ

Dry tho cloudy till noon when it became showery, & in the afternoon perpetual hard rain, visited till late kept by the rain Mʳ Hughes, his Daughter & 2 Sons dined here & Mʳ Llewellyn took Miss Hughes with me to the Play, where Miss Mill joind us, well entertain'd by the Battle of Hexham & Inhele & Yarico;⁴³ rec'd a charming Letter from sweet Francis.

Sunday Sep.ʳ 4ᵗʰ·

Frequent hard showers during the whole Day, Mʳ Witts defied them & went home after breakfast, went to Church both times, Mʳˢ· Ram drank Tea here & was very agreable, went with her to a miserable thin Tea drinking at the rooms tho our own party was pleasant.

Monday Sep.ʳ 5ᵗʰ·

A universal bright fine Day, tho a little rain fell in the evening Mʳ B: Hughes & his Sister dined here, Lady Guise & Miss Guise, & Miss Amphlet also drank Tea here we all went to the Ball where I also took Miss Tippets, Mʳ Witts return'd to Dinner. rec'd a Letter from Mʳˢ· Charles Western & wrote to Mʳˢ· Naper.

Tuesday Sep.ʳ 6ᵗʰ·

Rain tho very close & damp to allow me to go to the Well, but wet & very wet the remainder of the Day, Mʳ Burslem conversing here for three hours in the Morning most agreably, Mʳ John Delabere dined here, & we drank Tea with Miss Delabere to meet the Andre family & Miss Hughes, play'd at Cribbage there & did not go to the Rooms. wrote to Mʳˢ· C. Western.

Wensday Sep.ʳ 7ᵗʰ·

Quite a reverse in weather being a most beautifull fine Day after a damp foggy Morning, several callers here in the Morning & a little walking, Miss Vernon dined here & went with us to Mʳˢ· Rams at Sandford to a large Party at Tea & Cards, who all adjourned late to the Rooms, where I play'd at Whist with success with 5 Gentlemen wrote to Francis.

Thursday Sep.ʳ 8ᵗʰ·

An uncommon hot close Day, & with very little sun, walk'd & visited as usual, Mʳ Burslem dined here & was as ever most agreable, & went with us to the Play the Child of Nature

---

43. George Colman the Younger (1762–1836), English dramatist and miscellaneous writer, was the son of George Colman the Elder. In 1782 he produced, at his father's playhouse in the Haymarket, his first play, *The Female Dramatist*, for which Smollett's *Roderick Random* supplied the materials. It was unanimously condemned, but *Two to One* (1784) was very successful. It was followed by *Turk and no Turk* (1785), a musical comedy, and *Inkle and Yarico* (1787). *The Battle of Hexham, or Days of Old* was first performed on 11 August 1789 at the Haymarket.

& many &c's &c's sat in the front row of the Centre Box with Lady Guise & her family & upon the whole was very well amused. rec'd a Letter from M^rs. Buxton.[44]

Friday Sepr. 9th.

Another Day quite as hot, tho with much sunshine & strong wind, Mr W. Palmer came from Upper Slaughter to Breakfast & was very agreable, so many callers succeeded him that we scarce went out at all; Mr Nettleship dined here we went to drink Tea at Mr Burslems & from thence to the Ball which was lively tho not full play'd at Whist in M^rs. Fraines party.

Saturday Sepr. 10th.

A most uncommon hot Day even at any time of the Year, being a strong hot wind, tho so oppressive as to make all moving dreadfull, Miss Benfield breakfasted here, & M^rs. Burslem sat a quiet hour before we set out for Sandywell, where we all three went to Dinner & to stay three nights, & met with a pleasing reception from the three Ladies.

Sunday Sepr. 11th.

Nearly as hot a Day, almost overcome at Church with the sun shining into the Seat rather a long Day having nothing to do, air'd in the Coach after Tea on the Glocester road, & talk'd till every subject was nearly exhausted. Mr Thomas dined & went away early. —

---

44. *The Child of Nature* (1788) by Elizabeth Inchbald.

Witts Family Papers F181

1791

Monday Sepr 12th.

Not quite so oppresively hot, but still too much so to walk or move off ones chair with any comfort, work'd & talk'd a great deal & Mrs. Tracy & Mr Witts walk'd in the evening. rec'd a sweet Letter from my Dear Francis.

Tuesday Sepr 13th.

A very strong fog in the Morning but clear'd off & was a very beautifull Day, & not quite so hot as the former ones, return'd to Chelten. at noon; call'd on Lady Guise & eat some good fruit, Mr H. Hughes & Mr Bignal dined here, went to the Play, the Grecian Daughter & the Irish Widow both moderately perform'd & a very thin house rec'd a Letter from Lady Mill.[1]

Wensday Sepr 14th.

Fog still stronger than the Morning before quite wetting, but when it clear'd off was most prodigeously hot the remainder of the Day, much fatigued both by that, making many take leave visits & some packing, Lady Frances Bulkeley & General Rowley dined & we drank Tea with L^{dy.} Guise, going afterwards to the Rooms which were good for the time of year 6 Card Tables play'd at whist with success.

Thursday Sepr 15th.

A clear Morning, & very bright fine Day, tho the sun oppresively hot, bid a final adiew to Cheltenham at mid Day, going to Glocester to dine at Mr Commelines, who we found too much indisposed to appear but she was as pleasant as possible, & to crown the fact, Mr Parsons from Elmore Court was invited to bring our Dear Francis to all our mutual joy, carried him to see the Polish Count &'c, & on our return home in the evening, I went with Mr Parsons in his Gig & Francis rode his Poney with his Papa till our roads seperated, had a charming drive by the light of the Moon & found Edward quite well. wrote to L^{dy.} Mill

---

1. Arthur Murphy (1727–1805), Irish actor and dramatist. From 1738 to 1744, under the name of Arthur French, he was a student at the English college at St Omer. By the autumn of 1752 he was publishing the *Gray's Inn Journal*, a periodical in the style of the *Spectator*. Two years later he became an actor, and appeared in the title roles of *Richard III* and *Othello*. His first farce, *The Apprentice*, premiered at Drury Lane on 2 January 1756. It was followed by numerous other plays and *The Grecian Daughter* was first performed in 1772. His plays were almost all adaptations from the French, and were very successful, securing for their author both fame and wealth. Oliver Goldsmith (1730?–1774) was an Anglo-Irish writer, poet and physician known for his novel *The Vicar of Wakefield* (1766), his pastoral poem *The Deserted Village* (1770) and his plays *The Good-natur'd Man* (1768) and *She Stoops to Conquer* (1771, first performed in 1773). *The Irish Widow* was written in 1772.

Friday Sepr 16th.

Still bright & fine weather, tho not so intensely hot at least we were not so sensible of it at Bownham, full of bussiness all Morn: in setting all matters to rights, walk'd with the Boys about home before Tea, rec'd Letters from Mrs Naper & Miss Anne Snow, & wrote to my Sister Travell

Saturday Sepr 17th.

Very much the same Day as yesterday rather more cloudy, still busy all Morning, M.^r W rode to Hampton, walk'd in the evening with the Boys a new circuit, rec'd a Letter from my Sis.^t Travell & wrote to Mrs Savage & Miss Anne Snow

Sunday Sepr 18th.

A cloudy Morning, a hard shower of rain at Noon, but a fine afternoon, went to Stroud Church in the Morning, a very good sermon from Mr Ellis, went to Hampton Church before Dinner rec'd a Letter from Mrs Witts with the account of Miss Witts's death,[2] answer'd it & wrote to Mrs Granville

Monday Sepr 19th.

Had been a frost in the night & was a clear, very cold air, all Day, tho with constant sunshine, Mrs Sheppard of Hampton & her two youngest Daughters here in the Morning. I only walk'd in the home premises in the afternoon. rec'd a Letter from Mrs Savage.

Tuesday Sepr 20th.

A mild pleasant Day without either much sun or wind, very favourable for riding, in which we spent most of the Morning, making first a visit at Mr Peter Hawkers, then shopping at Mr Tyndales at Woodchester, from there to Nailsworth, & so by the new road to Hampton,[3] where we call'd on Mr Jeffries & his Sister & so home, walk'd a little in the evening rec'd a Letter from Miss Anne Snow & wrote to Mrs Buxton. Mrs Savage call'd in the Morn: in my absence

Wensday Sepr 21st.

A thick damp Day, with frequent but very trifling flying showers not sufficient to keep one in the house, very busy in the flower garden &'c drank Tea at Mrs Sheppards at Hampton meeting only Mrs Lee's, play'd 3 rubbers at whist with ill success. rec'd a Letter from Mrs Charles Western.

Thursday Sepr 22^{d.}

A most brilliant fine Day, quite warm & pleasant in the Morn.^g but dark & lowering in the afternoon, Mr Witts rode to several places in the Morning on various bussinesses, & we took a long walk after Dinner with the Boys towards the Fort &'c.

---

2.   This is presumably Mrs John Witts. There is no record of any other death in the family for 1791 and the assumption must be that there were four children of the marriage.

3.   The New Road, still called 'New Road,' was a turnpike built under the auspices of Sir George Onesiphorus Paul, who was chairman of the local turnpike trust. It ran from Nailsworth along Pensile Road to West End in Minchinhampton. There was also a small spur leading from the new Nailsworth–Avening turnpike at the Weighbridge Inn which met it at the Pensile Road / New Road junction.

Friday Sep.ᵣ 23.ᵈ

A mild fine Day tho rather cloudy, till towards afternoon when there was fine gleams of sunshine, M.ʳˢ Tracy & M.ʳˢ Eliza Tracy came here from Sandywell by one clock & before I was ready to receive them but they were much pleased & happy, play'd at Whist in the evening & all things went off well & comfortable

Saturday Sep.ᵣ 24.ᵗʰ

In the Morning thick & Misty, clearer at noon, & very fine in the afternoon, went in the two Chaises after breakfast first to survey the whole of the G: O: Pauls House & premises but he not at home, then thro the Woodchester vale, up Nailsworth Hill to Hampton & home by the Blue Boys.⁴ M.ʳ & M.ʳˢ Peter Hawker & a Son & daughter, M.ʳ Josiah Wathen, & a M.ʳ Clayfield with him dined here, disappointed in seeing M.ʳ & M.ʳˢ Jeffries by his having the Gout, a Table at Whist & Ving'tun. rec'd a Letter from M.ʳˢ Savage.

Sunday Sep.ᵣ 25.ᵗʰ

One of the most beautifull Days ever known at the time of Year, quite warm & perpetual sunshine, & the clearest air possible, went in the Chaises taking the Boys to Stroud Church, service miserably perform'd by M.ʳ Lloyd, afterwards took an airing upon Selsley Hill & home thro Woodchester Park, the Ladies highly delighted with the views rather a long idle evening.

Monday Sep.ᵣ 26.ᵗʰ

Not quite so fine a Day being rather cloudy & more stormy & cold, set out early again on on our ramble, going by the Bath road & Kingscote to Stinchcombe Hill,⁵ charmed beyond

*101. Leonard
Stanley*

4.   The Blue Boys coaching inn formerly stood at Blue Boys Corner in Minchinhampton. It is said to have derived its name from the young boys who worked there and coated themselves with more blue woad dye than the sheep they were marking.

measure by the views, on the Hill we were join'd by the Wathen party & had some confab, they went to Berkeley & we to Froster to Dinner where we were well entertaind & got home soon after dark,[6] thro the Stanleys Ebley &'c well pleased with our Days excursion & regaled ourselves with Tea & whist & the best of all to me rec'd a Letter from my Dear Francis. M^rs· & Miss Holbrow had been here in the Morning in my absence

Tuesday Sep^r· 27th·

Very much the same Day as the former but quite fine & pleasant walk'd about & shew'd the Ladies our own premises, M^r & M^rs· Ellis, the two Mr Wathens, M^rs· Jenkins & with her Miss Clayfield, & a Miss Sheppard dined here, & Mr Commeline from Gloster came in to Tea & staid all night a Table at Whist & a merry one at Ving'tun. rec'd a Letter from Miss A: Snow.

Wensday Sep^r· 28th·

A most charming Day again tho rather a strong east wind, went with our Aunts in the two Chaises to Sapperton, a little way from the Cirencester road at the 6 miles stone, an old desolate Villiage in a pretty situation, hanging over the new Canal, & just by the mouth of the Tunnel, went into the Church w^ch· was made interesting to us from being the burial place formerly of the Atkyns family returnd home to Dinner & Whist in the evening.[7] rec'd a Letter from M^rs· Tyrwhitt, & wrote to M^rs· Rollinson.

102. *The Thames and Severn Canal at the Tunnel House (eastern portal).*

5.   Stinchcombe Hill, above the parishes of Dursley and Cam, is a promontory of the Cotswolds above the Severn Vale with very extensive views north, west and south. To the north the Malvern and Lickey Hills can be seen south of Birmingham, to the west are the Black Mountains, with the Sugar Loaf being prominent, and to the south can be seen the Bristol Channel.
6.   The George Inn at Frocester. This was a coaching inn built to accommodate the needs of travellers on the new turnpike road from Gloucester to Bath. This road spurred off the old Bristol / Gloucester road, passing Eastington and going through the village of Frocester, up onto the Cotswolds via Frocester Hill, passing Nympsfield and eventually joining the Dursley / Tetbury road at Kingscote.
7.   Sir Robert Atkyns of Sapperton, Gloucestershire, the author of the first major county history, *The Ancient and Present State of Glostershire* (1712). Sir Robert was buried at Sapperton and he was Agnes' great-grandfather.

Thursday Sep. 29*th.*

No change in the weather only to be rather colder & more high wind, walk'd in the Morn^g. in the Wood &'c with the Ladies, M^rs. John Pettat & her Son, & M^r & M^rs. Richard Pettat dined here, & M^rs. Sheppard & her two youngest Daughters were added to our Tea & Card party, at Table at Whist & one at Ving'tun at which I was very unsuccessfull wrote to M^rs. Naper.

Friday Sep. 30*th.*

Weather still as fine & pleasant walk'd again in the Morning in the Woods & Garden & Dined at Mr Peter Hawkers 12 in number but no one but their own family, an excellent Dinner & chearfull reception; Whist & Ving'tun at which I was again a great loser. wrote to my Dear Francis

Saturday Oct. 1*st.*

A South Wind & therefore warmer but tho constant sunshine it was neither so clear or pleasant as the former Days, M^rs. Tracys waiting in anxious expectation for their Carriage horses made the Morning long & tiresome, & at length they arrived too late for them to reach Sandywell to Dinner, so we dined early, to give them an opportunity of getting home by dark, sorry to part with them & much pleased that our endeavours to amuse & please them had so well succeeded. Irving sent the Poney to fetch Francis home for a week, he arrived at noon one of the happiest of human beings, took a long walk with the three Boys after our friends left us wrote to M^rs. Hyett & rec'd a Letter f^m. Francis.

Sunday Oct. 2*d.*

A lowering Day with frequent signs of rain but none fell to speak on, went to Stroud Church in the Morning & staid the Sacrament, & again to Hampton Church before Dinner where Mr Dallaway did the duty for Mr Jeffries dined too late to walk in the evening rec'd Letters from M^rs. Naper & M^rs. Rollinson, answerd the latter & wrote to M^rs. Charles Western & my Sister Travell.

Monday Oct. 3*d.*

Quite a thick wetting fog, but clearing off at noon became a mild fine Day, Francis went with us a ride to call at Mr Reades & at Mr Pettats at the Rye Ford, walk'd a little in the evening most pleasant & play'd at Goose with the Boys. rec'd a Letter from M^rs. Hyett & wrote to M^rs. Tyrwhitt.

Tuesday Oct. 4*th.*

An almost intire Day of steady warm rain, more beneficial than pleasant, went to dine at M^rs. Clutterbucks at Hyde taking Francis with us & meeting M^r & M^rs. Reade & Miss Reade a chearful pleasant visit play'd at whist & home safely tho with little light but the stars. wrote to M^rs. Savage

Wensday Oct. 5*th.*

A direct contrast to the former Day; being clear bright sunshine from Morn: till night & warm like July without any wind, took a ride Fran^s. of the party to call on M^r & M^rs. Ellis at Stroud much pleased by our visit in all respects & highly amused by hearing him play on the musical glasses & surveying his drawings, call'd afterwards on M^r & Mrs Burgh not at home much before Dinner time, prowled about in the evening till quite dark it was so warm & play'd at Snake with the Boys. wrote to Miss Snow. Mrs Wathen & Miss Clayfield here in the Morn: in my absense.

Thursday Octr 6th

Thick fog & small rain in showers till noon, when it clear'd off & was fine, Mr Witts & Frans. took a ride, & pick'd up on their road hither Mr Hughes his Daughter & 2 Sons, coming from Bath as we were engaged to Dine at Mr Wathens took Mr Bridges & his Sis^t with us, leaving the Boys to entertain the other Gents; sat down 13 to Dinner tho none but their own family party excepting Mr Burgh & Mr Blackwell a Table at Whist & Ving'tun at both of which I play'd, staid supper & not at home till past 12. rec'd a Letter fr^m Mrs Elizabeth Tracy & Mrs Savage.

Friday Octr 7th

Very bright & fine early in the Morn: but soon grew lowering, cold, & stormy tho without rain, the three Mr Hughes's, Mr Witts & his three Sons, 5 of them in & about their Chaise & Mr W. & Francis on horseback went to survey prospects, Miss Hughes & I in our Chaise went just to call on M^rs & Miss Holbrow, who we did not find at home, & then on Mrs Pettat at Stonehouse where we found a large Morning circle, my Bro^r Broome Witts came very unexpectedly to Dinner, we play'd whist in the evening, but talk'd more.

Saturday Octr 8th

A continued bright fine Day tho rather cold & promising future rain, my Brother went away early, not so the Hughes, who did not get away till near noon, M^r & Mrs Savage, Mr Jeffries, Mr Thornbury, & Miss J: Sheppard dined here, the three of Tetbury country went away early leaving us to beat the Hampton pair 3 rubbers at Whist. rec'd Letters from Mrs Granville & my Sis^t Travell & answer'd the latter.

Sunday Octr 9th

Such an uninterrupted Day of violent hard rain there was no attempting to go to Church either Morning or evening, scarce could stir out as far as the Garden, much delight in my Dear Francis's tho chequer'd by the idea that he must return to school tomorrow.

Monday Octr 10th

A bright fine Day excepting one short shower at Noon, my sweet Boy after breakfast set out for Elmore, always a heart breaking to part with him, a variety of employment help'd to dissipate my chagrin, rec'd a Letter from my Sis^t Travell & wrote to Mrs Naper & Mrs Eliza Tracy.

Tuesday Octr 11th

Another bright fine Autumn Day now & then interrupted by strong clouds wch form'd fine light & shade, walk'd a good deal about in the Morning, dined at Mr Ellis's at Stroud, a plain entertainment, tho a hearty & pleasant welcome Mrs Wathen & a Miss Milton there, a variety of pleasing amusements fill'd up the evening without cards.

Wensday Octr 12th.

Quite as fine a Day with rather a milder air, walk'd out & about a great deal in the Morning being very busy in the Garden, M^r & M^rs. Burgh, M^rs. Jenkins, Miss Clayfield, Miss Sheppard & Mr Wathen dined here, very lively & pleasant, play'd a great deal at Ving'tun the party going away quite late.

Thursday Octr 13th.

A sharp frost in the night, but a bright fine Day till afternoon when it became cold & stormy & at night very hard rain, Miss Clutterbuck made a long Morning visit here as did Mr Schutz & Miss Sheppards, hardly allowing me time to Dress to dine at Mr Jeffries' where we met besides his Bro^r & Sister Mr Peter Hawkers family & a Mr Jackson, a pleasant visit two tables at Whist, staid Supper, & as it rain'd so hard brought Miss Mary Hawker home to sleep. rec'd Letters from M^rs. Naper & Miss Snow

Friday Octr 14th.

Continued hard rain till noon, when it lessen'd & became more showery, & dry & fine in the evening, Miss M. Hawker walk'd home as soon as the weather would permit her, full of bussiness all Day preparing for our Slaughter Jaunt!

Saturday Octr 15th.

Windy & cold, but no rain tho often stormy left home after breakfast, baited ourselves & Horses at the Ram at Cirencester & eat a very early Dinner of Beef steaks, & reach'd L. Slaughter between 5 & 6 realy quite cold with going over the bleak horrid country, found poor Mr Naper in the same miserable state, Jane looking, & being well to a great degree of admiration, & her little Boy all that could be wish'd poor old Isaacs no great improvement to our party.

Sunday Octr 16th.

A thick wetting fog till noon when it clear'd off & was fine, went to Church in the Morn: a good sermon but a very strange reader a dull unemploy'd Day, saving talking

103. Cirencester.

whenever M^rs· Naper was out of Mr Napers room & writting 3 Letters to M^rs· Tyrwhitt, M^rs· Burslem, & Miss Snow.

Monday Octr 17th·

Had been a sharp hoar frost in the night but was a beautifull bright warm Day, Mr Witts went into Oxfordshire after breakfast, M^rs· Naper & I air'd to Bourton & back, M^rs· Leigh from Addlestrop made a Morning visit here & was both pretty, & agreable, & served to vary the sameness & soberness of the scene.

Tuesday Octr 18th·

Very hard rain in the Morning, & quite stormy all Day, we air'd to the bottom of Stow Hill, talkd much Mr Witts return'd after it was dark & entertain'd us much by a variety of anecdotes he had heard, & adventures he had met with on his Travels, he brought me a Letter from M^rs· Tyrwhitt with a pretty good account of her Children under inoculation

Wensday Octr 19th·

After having been a night of extreme hard rain, it was a very fine mild Day with constant sun, we air'd to Upper Slaughter, & survey'd my Brothers flower house & visited Molly Blandford, on my return walk'd in the Garden & Shrubbery. in the evening took in Mr Isaac to make a fourth at Cribbage wrote to M^rs· Rollinson on the death of her Sister, & recd Letters from Miss Snow & my Dear Francis.

Thursday Octr 20th·

Had been again a severe night of rain, M^rs· N. & I just air'd to Bourton, & then to Upper Slaughter, where I staid ½ an hour in the flower house & the Chaise came for me again. Cribbage again in the evening.

Friday Octr 21st·

A Day of violent storms both of wind & rain, which Mr Witts was obliged to brave & go through to Chip: Norton too bad for us to air in the Morning but dined earlier & went in the afternoon to Stow to a Shop. Mr Witts return'd to Tea. Cribbage again. wrote to M^rs· Buxton.

Saturday Octr 22^d·

Upon the whole a dry fine Day, tho cold & stormy, left our poor suffering friends after Breakfast, stopp'd an hour & ½ at Cirencester, & from the badness of the roads & a tired Horse did not get home till near 5 in the afternoon, well sick of the drive; glad to find our Dear Boys & everything well & in order to welcome us home.

Sunday Octr 23^d·

Had been a frost in the night, & tho cold & sometimes cloudy, was a beautifull Day went to Church at Stroud detain'd a long time, by the slowness of the Clocke there,[8]

---

8.   This entry is enigmatic but informative. In the eighteenth century local time varied and it was not standardised until forty
      years later with the advent of travel by rail. Was it simply local time, or was the church clock literally running late?

THE LADY OF RODBOROUGH

spent much time in the Garden on our return. rec'd a Letter from M^rs· Burslem & wrote to M^rs· Hyett & M^rs· Granville & my Sis^r· Travell.

Monday Oct^r· 24th·

Another Frost, but as fine & bright a Day as possible, M^r· Witts rode to Stroud, Hampton &c I as busy as possible all Morning, but found time to be much in the Green, & Hot houses. rec'd a Letter from M^rs· Hyett & my Dear Boy & answerd the latter.

Tuesday Oct^r· 25th·

Bright & fine in the Morning, but changed before noon, to wind & constant steady rain, being before engaged went thro it to drink Tea & play at whist at M^rs· Sheppards at Hampton where the 4 Ladies were so glad to see us it could not be unpleasant

Wensday Oct^r· 26th·

A very thick fog in the Morning but clear'd at noon & was bright & pleasant, M^rs· Pettat walk'd up from the Hill house & staid two hours rather a hindrance to much bussiness I was engaged in.[9]

Thursday Oct^r· 27th·

Again a sharp frost, but very fine & weather glass rising, w^ch· appear'd propitious for our approaching journey the preparations for which fully occupied me the whole day. rec'd Letters from M^rs· Rollinson & M^rs· Naper so kind a one as to give me much pleasure.

Friday Oct^r· 28th·

Another frost, cold & rather foggy in the Morning, but soon became bright & fine, was in the Chaise at 8 o'clock, stopp'd to bait the horses & have a second breakfast at Glocester, dined at Upton, & reach'd Worcester soon after dark, very little pleased with our reception at the Hop Pole. George proved a most excellent little traveller on his braket.[10] wrote to M^rs· Naper.

Saturday Oct^r· 29th·

Much the same kind of weather only more stormy at times but no rain, walk'd about Worcester after breakfast & visited M^rs· Penyston & M^rs· Chapeau, & at noon set out for M^r· Burslems at Hanbury 3 miles from Droitwich on the left hand going thro the Park & by the Hall house. met with a very pleasing reception from our agreable friend, whose good new built Parsonage does not stand in a very disirable situation; play'd at whist & conversed much.

Sunday Oct^r· 30th·

Very cold & stormy but dry. went to Church twice, highly pleased both with M^r· Burslems reading & preaching; the Church stands on a very high hill above the Rectors house, the

---

9.   This was Jane Pettat, *née* Paul (1739–1810). Jane was the daughter of Sir George Onesiphorous Paul and wife of Thomas Pettat (1737–1804), brother of John and Richard.

10. The word here is indistinct, but appears to be 'braket'. If Agnes meant 'bracket,' it could be a vertical support to strap to, in other words, a form of child seat / child restraint.

walk up to which is up a flight of 175 steps, something very singular & rather trying to the breath, a fine extensive view from the church yard did not find the Day long, with much entertaining converse & looking over Prints &'c

Monday Oct.ᵣ 31ˢᵗ·

No frost, but a very cold high wind, tho almost constant sunshine Mᵣ Burslem ourselves & Boys walk'd to survey the House & premises at the Hall, wᶜʰ· was interesting from the idea of the late inhabitants on our return the Gents. rode out; play'd in the evening at new Cribbage[11]

Tuesday Nov.ᵣ 1ˢᵗ·

More cold & stormy, with at times trifling showers of rain, the Gentlemen rode to Bromsgrove &'c, on their return I walk'd with them to Survey the remains of Mᵣ Cecils whimsical Garden for fruit Trees. play'd at whist with bad success.

Wensday Nov.ᵣ 2ᵈ·

A very lowering Morning which soon turn'd to hard rain the whole Day with very small intervals; left our aimable friends with regret after an early breakfast & found it a most tedious stage of 19 miles to Birmingham thro' Bromsgrove, did some little bussiness & hoped to get to Litchfield at night but by a drunken driver who took us out of our road we were compel'd to sit near two hours in a turnpike house, till we could get a pair of horses from another Inn in the Town, wᶜʰ· brought us in safety but almost all the way in the dark to Sutton Colfield not quite half way a very tolerable Inn

Thursday Nov.ᵣ 3ᵈ·

Very stormy throughout the whole Day & frequent small showers, but nothing in comparison of the former Day, left Sutton Colfield after an early Breakfast, & reached Calwich a little after three never getting out of the Carriage, changing Horses at Litchfield & Uttoxorter; found our reception as ever most kind from our aimable friends with whom we found Miss Snows & Mᵣ J: Delabere; play'd at Whist with great success & a Table at Tradrille[12] rec'd Letters from Mʳˢ· Elizabeth Tracy & my Dear Francis.

---

11.   Cribbage was invented in the early 1600s by Sir John Suckling, an English courtier, poet, gamester and gambler. It derives from the earlier game of Noddy. Originally the five-card game was played where only one card was discarded to the crib by each player. Now the six-card game is more popular with two cards each being discarded to the crib. Precisely what 'new cribbage' meant is unclear, but it may have referred to the additional card.

12.   Thomas William, writing from India in 1810, said the following: 'Those who are partial to cards, as an amusement, may find abundance of parties during the evenings, where, for the most part, tradrille and whist (the favourite games) are played at such low stakes as not to be productive of regret, or inconvenience. Quadrille is barely known in India, nor are what we term 'round-games' much in use: cribbage is played in some families, and, occasionally, loo.' In the eighteenth century the name quadrille was given to a card game that was played by four players (in pairs), with a deck of forty cards (the eights, nines and tens being removed). By the end to the nineteenth century the game was totally out of fashion. Jane Austen's *Pride and Prejudice* includes four references to quadrille being played by an upper-class character (Lady Catherine de Bourgh) and her guests. Tradrille was clearly a variation of this game, and from other references it is clear that it was the most popular card game in colonial India.

104. Calwich Abbey.

Friday Nov.ʳ 4ᵗʰ·

A beautifull clear Day & the sun quite warm, Miss Snows went away after Breakfast to Mᵣ Harts for a week,[13] we took a charming walk dined at Mᵣ Newdigates at Wooton Hall no one but their own family, play'd both at Commerce & Vingt'un at each of which I was successfull wrote to Mʳˢ· Tyrwhitt.

Saturday Nov.ʳ 5ᵗʰ·

A sharp hoar frost but a clear fine Day with constant sun, walk'd in the meadows & were out & about for 2 hours or more, a very conversable pleasant Day & a merry game at Quadrille in the evening. rec'd Letters from Mʳˢ· Naper & my Sister Travell.

Sunday Nov.ʳ 6ᵗʰ·

Much such another Day, went to Church in the Coach to Elaston, service perform'd in a dull manner by Mᵣ Manwaring, at whose house we made a short visit after Church, on our return home, Mʳˢ· Unwin & Mᵣ & Mʳˢ· Barwell visited here, after which we walk'd for an hour wrote to Mʳˢ· Naper & Mʳˢ· Burslem.

Monday Nov.ʳ 7ᵗʰ·

A still sharper frost & very cold Mʳˢ· & Miss Hayne making so long a Morning visit here prevented our walking till it was time to dress to dine at Mʳˢ· Mills's at Snelson, no one but their own family, a good dinner but a dull bussiness all together, play'd at whist, much laughing coming home thro' the rough roads.

Tuesday Nov.ʳ 8ᵗʰ·

Very wet early in the Day, but cleared to be very fine for the remainder of the Day in time for me to go to Ashborn, Mᵣ J: Delabere with the Ladies in the chaise & Mᵣ Witts on horseback, first to make a visit to Mʳˢ· Beresfords, & then to survey Sir Brooke Boothbys House,[14] place,

---

13. The Snow family were related to the Pauls of Hill House. It is noteworthy that clans of friends, usually linked by family associations, arranged their social circuits purposely to coincide. Elaborate planning was required and accidental coincidence was the exception rather than the rule.

14. Ashbourne Hall, the property of Sir Brooke Boothby (1744–1824).

& plants at Ashborn Green, the house is fitted up in an elegant, fanciful shewy stile, & the collection of plants charming both in hot house & green house brought away a few not at home till quite Dinner time, play'd at Quadrille. rec'd Letters from Francis & from Molly w.ᵗʰ a good account of Edward.

Wensday Novʳ 9ᵗʰ·

A very serious wet Day almost from Morn to night, ill suited to a long drive to dine at Mᵉ Clives at Ilam; but it were a very pleasant visit, & light & fine to come home but at a late hour. besides Mᵉ & Mʳˢ· Clive were 3 Lady Percivals sisters to Lord Egmont & Miss Clive a Table at whist & commerce.

Thursday Novʳ 10ᵗʰ·

Something of a frost & very bright & fine till noon when it clouded & was wet again in the evening, Mᵉ & Mʳˢ· Newdigate, Mᵉ & Mʳˢ· Barwell, Mᵉ & Mʳˢ· Unwin drank Tea here previous to all going together to the Ashborn Assembly which was esteem'd a full & good one, but I thought very dull. I play'd at Whist, not at home till between one & two.

Friday Novʳ 11ᵗʰ·

A mild quiet Day without sun or rain & very pleasant walking, were very agreable & quiet all Day without any company, Mᵉ J: Delabere read Shakespear's As you like it, in the Morning & we play'd at Quadrille in the evening.

Saturday Novʳ 12ᵗʰ·

Very much the same weather, a trifling shower at noon, we dined at Mᵉ Gilberts at Cotton 19 in number meeting the Ilam family, Mʳˢ· Mill's family &'c, a very handsome entertainment & a chearfull pleasant visit. a Table at Commerce & whist. rec'd a Letter from Mʳˢ· Buxton.

Sunday Novʳ 13ᵗʰ·

Almost a universal wet Day went to Church in the Coach, where Mᵉ J: Delabere did the whole of the duty; Miss Snows return'd to dinner from Mᵉ Harts, evening spent variously in chatting writting, looking over prints &'c. wrote to Miss Chaplin & my Dear Francis.

Monday Novʳ 14ᵗʰ·

A day of universal rain from Morn: to night without a possibility of stirring out therefore a fine Morning for employment, Mᵉ & Mʳˢ· Newdigate, & Miss Harriet Beresford dined here, & in the evening almost unexpectedly arrived Mᵉ Bernard Dewes, his Daughter & Miss Cardin, & a Mᵉ Chambers with them which extended our party to a very large one. Whist, Cribbage, & Ving'tun I was very successful at the two last.

Tuesday Novʳ 15ᵗʰ·

Something of a frost & was bright & fine till mid-day when it was again wet all the evening. our party went various ways, following their different pursuits, Mʳˢ· Granville, the three Children & I took a long dirty walk. Mᵉ & Mʳˢ· Clive & their four young Ladies dined here & were very lively & pleasant. Whist & Commerce at the latter of which I won everything. rec'd a Letter from M^rs. Naper with a wretched account of Mr Naper & one from my sweet Francis.

Wensday Novr 16th.

Very much the same kind of weather but sooner in the Day became wet & stormy so that I never went out M^r & M^rs. Barwell & Mr Unwin call'd here; we were very merry & joyous all Day, play'd at Quadrille & whist at the former of which I was very successful, wrote to M^rs. Naper & M^rs. Buxton.

Thursday Novr 17th.

Frosty in the Morning but wet again at noon, the Gentlemen as usual out a Shooting of the rest some walk'd & some staid at home of which latter number I was one Mr Delabere finish'd reading the Orphan & concluded with the Romp. Mr Bingham of Norbury dined & supt here, very merry parties both at Whist & Quadrille. wrote to my Sis^r Travell & recd a Letter from Miss Sabine & heard a very good account of little Edward.

Friday Novr 18th.

Had been a night of severe rain, but tho rather stormy was a fine Day, & very fine late in the Day when all the Ladies attended by M^r J: Delabere walk'd for two hours evening spent as usual with a large mixture of Cards & converse.

Saturday Novr 19th.

A day of uninterrupted rain from Morn: to night, which obliged Miss Anne Snow & I to indulge the Gentlemen with playing a large Pool of Quadrille with some of them. much laughing & talking. rec'd a melancholly Letter from poor M^rs. Naper, & wrote to M^rs. Elizabeth Tracy.

Sunday Novr 20th.

A very misty cold disagreable Day thoroughly cold & miserable at Church, where Mr Chambers preach'd for Mr Manwaring,[15] I did not feel inclined to leave the fireside the remainder of the Day evening spent in hearing some sacred music on the Organ & looking over drawings.

Monday Novr 21st.

Rather a better Day tho at times some trifling showers but not enough to prevent our all going to follow our different pursuits. Mr Witts went in a Coach from Ashborn, to Leicester on business; M^rs. Granville & Miss Snow went to Ashborn to make visits, Miss Anne rode & M^r J: Delabere & I walk'd. the other Gentlemen shooting. Mr Manwaring dined & supt here. play'd at Whist at Quadrille.

Tuesday Novr 22^d.

A very moderate Day damp & rather misty & disagreable; to please the Gentlemen we some of us play'd at Quadrille after breakfast, & at noon the four Ladies sallied forth in the Coach to call on M^rs. Newdigate at Wooton, a very funny visit. evening pass'd as usual

---

15. James Eyton Mainwaring (1751–1809), vicar of Ellaston, Staffordshire (1783–1808).

Wensday Nov. 23*.*

Small rain at intervals the whole of the Day which made walking impossible, M.ʳ Witts return'd from Leicester at mid:day. M.ʳ J: Delabere read to us in the Morning the moving Tragedy of Isabela.[16] Cards as ever in the evening. rec'd a Letter from my Dear Francis & one from Molly with a very good account of Edward. My birth Day.[17]

Thursday Nov. 24*th.*

A fine bright mild Day, which carried the whole of the party many different ways, M.ʳˢ Granville & I in the Chaise to Wooton Lodge M.ʳˢ Unwins where we only saw M.ʳˢ Barwell, M.ʳ Bingham dined & supt here. wrote to little Edward.

Friday Nov. 25*th.*

Wet early in the Day, but grew very fine after breakfast. M.ʳ J: Delabere read the Tragedy of Zara to our great entertainment,[18] after which we walk'd for 2 hours. rec'd a Letter from my Sis.ᵗ Travell with an increased bad account of poor M.ʳ Naper.

Saturday Nov. 26*th.*

Cloudy & misty early in the Day but turn'd out a most beautifull Day for the time of Year, our whole party excepting the shooting Gentlemen walk'd thro' the meadows to the Ware in the hope of seeing some Salmon leap but in vain return'd home as dirty as possible; did not dine till past 5 the sporting Gentlemen coming home so late. play'd a Pool at Quadrille while waiting for Dinner. M.ʳ Bingham dined & supt here. write to M.ʳˢ Naper.

Sunday Nov. 27*th.*

A cold raw disagreable Day with strong wind & at times small showers of rain all went to Church at Ellason, where M.ʳ John Delabere preach'd a very good sermon, the Day fill'd up with the usual employments. but rather long & tedious. wrote to M.ʳˢ Rollinson.

Monday Nov. 28*th.*

A most tremendous Day of uninterrupted rain & wind so as to keep every one within Doors that were not obliged to go out Miss Snows went away after breakfast, much conversation all the Morning so as to preclude reading. I suffer'd much from the rhumatism in my head & face; a table at Quadrille, & Picquet.

Tuesday Nov. 29*th.*

Still wet & very stormy, tho not so bad as the former Day; M.ʳ Delabere read to us the Play of Cymbyline,[19] M.ʳ & M.ʳˢ Clive & Miss Clive made a late Morning visit here, in a Curricle & on horseback, modes of moving little suited to the day or season; Cards the same as the former evening. rec'd a charming Letter from my Dear Fran.ˢ & heard that Edward was very well.

---

16. This was presumably Shakespeare's *Measure for Measure*.
17. This was an unusual reference. Agnes' normal style was simply to underline the date for family birthdays.
18. Aaron Hill (1685–1750). Hill was a poet, dramatist and essayist whose adaptations of Voltaire's play *Zaïre* (*The Tragedy of Zara*, 1736) enjoyed considerable success.
19. William Shakespeare, *The Tragedy of Cymbeline, King of Britain*.

Wensday Nov.ʳ 30ᵗʰ·

Dark & very stormy, & towards noon most violent rain which continued the whole Day & night. all the Gentlemen except Mʳ J: Delabere dined with a party at Mʳ Manwarings & did not return till supper. we play'd at Quadrille with a dumb fourth. rec'd a Letter from my Sister Travell with a wretched account of Mʳ Naper

Thursday Dec.ʳ 1ˢᵗ·

Still cold & stormy with frequent rain we breakfasted very early, that Mʳˢ· Granville & I might accompany Mʳ Delabere in the Chaise as far as Uttoxeter, where he went into a Coach on our return made a visit at Crakemarsh to Mʳˢ· Hodgson. Mʳ Manwaring & 2 Gentlemen with him dined & supt here wᶜʰ· made two tables at Whist.

Friday Dec.ʳ 2ᵈ·

Had been a slight frost in the night which made the day clear & fine tho at times rather stormy; Mʳˢ· Granville & I in the Chaise & Mʳ Witts on horseback went to Ashborn for the joint purpose of shopping & visiting: calling both on Mʳˢ· Hayne & Mʳˢ· Beresford. Whist in the evening. rec'd a Letter from Mʳˢ· Tyrwhitt & wrote to Francis.

Saturday Dec.ʳ 3ᵈ·

Something of a frost again, with a disagreable thick air, & very cold & like snow I was the only one who thought it too unpleasant to stir out. much amused by reading in Boswells Life of Johnson. Whist in the evening again.

Sunday Dec.ʳ 4ᵗʰ·

A pretty deep snow, & continued falling till noon when it clear'd up to be a severe frost. impossible for any of us to go to Church so the Gentlemen among them perform'd the service in the Dining Parlour. read a good deal in the course of the Day. & in the evening wrote to my Sisᵗ Travell

Monday Dec.ʳ 5ᵗʰ·

A very sharp frost, but being bright sun, it was not unpleasant walking on the Gravel where the snow was swept; Cards & much conversation in the evening as usual. rec'd a Letter from my Broᵗ Ferdinand with the melancholly news of the death of poor Mʳ Naper. & answer'd it.[20]

Tuesday Dec.ʳ 6ᵗʰ·

Continued Frost, & had been a little more snow & was very bitterly cold; but being engaged to dine at Mʳˢ· Unwins at Wooton Lodge, we ventured thro' it all 6 in the Coach, but not without small alarms tho got there & back very safely; rather a cold visit & not very lively 2 Tables at Whist.

---

20.   William Naper (1749–1791). Naper was the younger brother of James Dutton, 1st Baron Sherborne. His health had been in decline for more than a year and yet during a respite he had the strength to father a son. He was married to Jane Tracy Travell, the daughter of Ferdinando Tracy Travell, rector of Upper Slaughter and elder brother to Agnes.

Wensday Dec.[r] 7[th.]

Weather very changeable the whole of the Day
one hour freezing the next thawing & rain yet
we had courage to venture thro' it to dine at M[r]
Clives at Ilam, & found the roads better than
could be expected & return'd home very safely
tho late, had a very chearful pleasant visit. a
Table at Whist & commerce. rec'd a Letter from
my Sis[t] Travell with a melancholly detail of
painful events at L. Slaughter

Thursday Dec.[r] 8[th.]

Worse weather than ever, being constant
showers of snow & hail the whole of the
Day with strong wind & extremely cold &
miserable, hardly warm over the fire; M[r]
Witts read to me in the Morning in Boswells
Johnson. M[r] Port came in the evening as did
John Granville from school. rec'd Letters from
M[rs.] Burslem, my Dear Fran[s.] & Molly.

105. *Master John Granville of Calwich Abbey.*

Friday Dec.[r] 9[th.]

No change for the better in point of weather, frost & snow often falling, little moving out
of the house for any one that could stay within. M[r] Port still here, so the Card parties were
strong. wrote to my Sister Travell.

Saturday Dec.[r] 10[th.]

Had been a very considerable fall of Snow in the night which made all idea of moving
difficult & dangerous, yet M[r] Port went away but M[r] & M[rs.] Clive were prevented dining
here from the Ilam roads being fill'd up; which we were all sorry for, much liking them rec'd
a very entertaining Letter from Miss Snow

Sunday Dec.[r] 11[th.]

No abatement in the snow, the frost being still hard & very cold tho some sunshine, only M[r]
Granville ventured to Church, the Morning service performd in the Parlour as the
Sunday before by M[r] Chambers & M[r] Witts, writting, reading & talking fill'd up the Day
wrote to Miss Snow at Lord Middletons.[21]

Monday Dec.[r] 12[th.]

A most tremendous yet changeable Day, beginning with hard snow, & ending with violent
rain tho at night again inclineable to freeze, M[r] Witts read in the Morning, & we play'd at

---

21. Henry Willoughby, Baron Middleton (1726–1800). The Middleton family lived in Yorkshire and the connection is
not known.

Battledore & Billiards to keep ourselves warm & whist as usual at night. obliged to give up the idea of beginning our Journey till the roads were more beaten

Tuesday Dec.ʳ 13.ᵗʰ

Had been a sharp frost in the night & was a bright clear Day, & during the warmth of the sun a ground thaw our Coachman & Horses coming at Noon we prepared for our Journey next Day with the best hopes we could; very busy in collecting some plants from the hothouse to carry away with us Whist & Billiards in the evening.

Wensday Dec.ʳ 14.ᵗʰ

A clear pleasant winter Day tho with little or no sun, the middle of the Day there was again a ground thaw which made the roads not so good after an early breakfast bid adieu to our hospitable friends with much regret after a very agreable visit of six weeks, with the help of their horses added to our own, we got with tolerable ease to Uttoxeter tho in places the snow was very deep, to Lichfield the first 10 milles we took P: Horses & then went on w.ᵗʰ our own to the Swan where we dined excellently, & with the assistance of a pair of Horses reach'd Sutton Colfield soon after dark where we halted for the night, having went over some very indifferent roads from the snow indeed the common road impassable.

Thursday Dec.ʳ 15.ᵗʰ

A very severe Day, but being strong sunshine from rising to Setting at Night, it was a very bright pleasant day & not cold in the carriage left Sutton between 8 & 9, & by the help of P: horses got safely the 8 miles to Birmingham, tho the road was very wretched from the snow being partialy broke in holes, stopp'd there an hour & proceeded on again to Bromsgrove with 4 horses, some part of the way still very disagreable from the Snow & the Lickey very slippery

106. View of Worcester.

where it was steep. got a moderate Dinner at the Golden Cross at Bromsgrove from whence 13 miles to Worcester the roads were so good we ventured with our own horses only, getting their between 5 & 6, but being a remarkable light clear evening, it was not unpleasant, went to the Star & Garter Inn to make trial if we did not prefer it to the Hop pole; & found it comfortable, tho in a very singular stile. wrote to M.rs Burslem & my Sis.r Travell.

Friday Dec.r 16.th

Very much such another Day, only rather a sharper frost, left Worcester as the sun rose, which was a peculiar fine object being so very clear went with our own horses to Tewkesbury 15 miles, where we baited for an hour, & then on in the same way 11 miles to Glocester, roads good & very little snow tho some Ice, stopp'd an hour & ½ at Glocester to dine at the Kings head & go to some shops, & got home between 6 & 7 with the help of a pair of horses, with great comfort, & very glad our long & much apprehended journey was so well concluded. Found Edward almost better than well rec'd Letters from M.rs Buxton & my Sister Travell & wrote to my Dear Francis.

Saturday Dec.r 17.th

Probably a harder frost than any of the past Days, but bright & fine, but we found it very cold indeed, in an house that had been so long without inhabitants, very busy all Morning unpacking &'c but went into the Garden &'c. rec'd a Letter from my Sister Travell answer'd it, & wrote to M.rs Granville & Miss Dewes.

Sunday Dec.r 18.th

A dark & rather cloudy looking morning & not near so sharp a frost, & at noon it became a gentle thaw & so continued the rest of the Day went to Hampton Church in the Morning where the service was perform'd by M.r Cocking who is again Curate there, after Church call'd at M.rs Sheppards, & from thence went to Hyde to make a visit of condolence to Miss Clutterbuck on the death of her poor Aunt. wrote to M.rs Savage.

Monday Dec.r 19.th

Quite a confirm'd thaw being a thick wetting fog till it was night when it again took to freezing very sharp, hard at work all Day & in the evening M.r Witts & the Boys read to me a little rec'd two Letters from Fran.s one returned from Calwich

Tuesday Dec.r 20.th

Cold sharp frost with rather a strong wind, ventured no farther out than to the hot house M.r Witts walk'd to call on Sir. G: O: Paul, busy again in compleating my Mourning, to be ready to set out to see M.rs Naper, wrote to M.rs Hyett

Wensday Dec.r 21.st

A damp thawing Morning, with something of a Fog, but at noon cleard, was bright sunshine & again at night a very sharp frost, set out soon after breakfast for Glocester, where on our arrival at M.r Commelines our Dear Francis met us for the holidays. staid there an hour very pleasantly, & then went on with Post Horses to Cheltenham taking our Dear Boy w.th us, found the roads horrid, both rough, dirty, & slippery the meeting with Mrs. Naper very trying to my feelings tho found her better than I expected, my Sis^{r} Travell with her, & her Lodgings at Miss Wills's much what she liked, much conversation the whole of the evening on a variety of interesting subjects.

Thursday Decr 22^{d.}

Quite a bitter cold day, being a severe frost, & piercing cold wind, I never stirr'd from the fireside, except to receive several friends who call'd on me; Mr Witts rode to Sandywell Park & Francis walk'd to Charlton to call on his school fellow Phipps, a continuation of the same interesting subjects all day; wrote to Mrs. Commeline.

Friday Decr 23^{d.}

Again a thaw, & at times very hard rain tho chiefly in showers, & the air mild & warm the two Mrs. Tracys, made their first visit to poor Mrs. Naper which proved a trying scene to all parties, after they went, the rest of my Cheltenham friends call'd on me & Mr Witts made 2 visits in the evening Poor Fran^{s.} confined to his chair all Day from bad broken Chilblains

Saturday Decr 24th.

A very severe frost with a cutting cold wind & had been a little snow in the night, our own horses came from home early enough in the morning, to take us to Glocester, after many hearty adieus & wishes to our Dear Niece, & stopp'd at Mr Commelines more than an hour for the horses to bait which was very necessary after the execrable bad roads they had gone thro, & did several useful bussiness while we staid. did not get home to our Dinner till near 5 o'clock both cold & tired, our Dear little Boys both glad to see us & their Brother. in the evening wrote to Mrs. Naper.

Sunday Decr 25th.

As usual an alternate change in the weather being again a thaw, with mist or flying rain & extremely damp & uncomfortable, went to Morning Church at Stroud & staid the Sacrament, where we were kept near three hours, read a great deal with & to the Boys; & wrote to my Brother Travell & Mrs. Buxton, & received a Letter from Miss Dewes.

Monday Decr 26th.

Frost tho slight, but dry & after the sun shone, Mr Witts rode to Hampton &'c I walk'd no farther than to the flower houses, being much engaged all Day with various employs, & my Dear Francis still confined to Slippers & the House all Day. wrote to Lady Lyttelton.

Tuesday Decr 27th.

A very nasty thick wetting fog, almost the whole Day accompanied by high wind & flying storms of small snow & sleet, & perfectly uncomfortable yet I having bussiness ventur'd in the Chaise & Francis with me by way of exercise for his Chilblains, to Mr Tyndales at Woodchester to order a variety of articles call'd at Mr Peter Hawkers & found some of the family at home. rec'd a Letter from Mrs. Hyett & Mrs. Witts of Friday Street, & play'd with the Boys at Snake.

Wensday Dec^r *28*^{th.}

Something of a frost but nothing mature yet day with such a bitter cold wind that I judged it best not to stir out of the house, Miss Sheppards & their two Nieces Miss Boughtons made a long Morning visit here, M^r N: Wathen dined here, & before Tea came Dr Napleton who we had expected the night before always happy to see him, play'd 2 Rubbers at Whist.

Thursday Dec^r *29*^{th.}

A pretty sharp hoare frost but calm, rather mild, & pleasant, with constant sunshine, very favorable for moving, Dr Napleton & Mr Witts walk'd a great deal to St George Pauls &'c, & I a little in the home domain the Boys all with me.

Friday Dec^r *30*^{th.}

Quite a nasty day, being an uninterrupted wetting fog from Morn to night, tho with a strong damp wind very adverse to my feelings & I was miserably low all Day. Dr Napleton left us after breakfast for Bath, truly sorry to lose his brilliant & pleasing conversation; play'd at Commerce at night with the Boys.

Saturday Dec^r *31*^{st.}

A tolerable clear fine Morning, tho had been much rain in the night, & at noon turn'd to hard rain in sharp showers, which lasted at least till it was dark. I just got into the hot houses before it began very busy all Morning rec'd a Letter from my Sister Travell.

rec'd 212 Letters
wrote 179 Letters

1792

Sunday Jan: 1st.

The new Year did not open with very brilliant weather being an uninterrupted thick wetting fog from Morn: to night. the 2 eldest Boys went with me to Church at Hampton, a good useful sermon from Mr Cocking; I made a visit afterwards at Mrs. Sheppards meeting Miss Beale & one of her Nephews rec'd Letters from Mrs. Granville, Miss Anne Snow & a short one from my Sis^t Travell, & wrote to Mrs. Tyrwhitt

Monday Jan: 2^{d.}

A pleasant Morning mild with light gleams but at noon grew more stormy, with flying showers; began having Morning Prayers in the family before breakfast. Francis & I went in the Chaise to Cirencester, for me to wait on Mrs. Master I drop'd him with his schoolfellow Lawrence felt much on seeing Mrs. Master who was very civil & obliging;[22] Mr Witts took a ride in my absence, & rec'd a visit from Mr Josiah Wathen in the evening wrote to Mrs. Witts Friday Street & to Miss Sabine.

---

22. Mary Master, *née* Dutton (d. 1819), the younger sister of William Naper.

Tuesday Jan: 3ᵈ·

Something of a fog in the Morning in the Morn: damp, close & disagreable, but towards noon clearer & more pleasant, I was backwards & forwards a great deal overlooking some alterations in the hot house Mʳ Witts & Francis rode out. we play'd at Commerce with the Boys. wrote to my Sisʳ Travell.

Wensday Jan: 4ᵗʰ·

Had been something of a frost, & was rather dry, tho an unpleasant thick foggy air wᶜʰ· never went off the whole Day, tho with a very high weather glass; after breakfast I set forth & Fransˢ· with me to make a string of Morning visits first to Mʳ Pettats at Rye ford, then to Mʳˢ· Holbrows which was very pleasant, & concluding at Mʳ Reades at Ebley not so much so. Not at home till late.

Thursday Jan: 5ᵗʰ·

The same very unpleasant weather being a constant thick air; & at night became quite a wetting fog, dined at Mʳ Wathens, meeting besides their own family, Mʳˢ· J: Wathen from Stroud, Mʳ Thornbury, & Mʳ Edward Sheppard, sociable & pleasant enough, play'd at Ving'tun at which I was very successfull, staid supper & at home between 11 & 12.

Friday Jan: 6ᵗʰ·

Not so much fog, but still a very damp disagreable air, much hurt by my Dear Francis having got a most dreadful cough wᶜʰ· confined him to the house; went to dine & Sup at Mʳ J: Pettats at Stonehouse, meeting Mʳˢ· & Miss Holbrow, Mʳ & Mʳˢ· R: Pettat, & a Mʳ H: Wise the friend of Tom Pettat & a very handsome young Man, a good lively visit, play'd with spirit at Lottery Tickets at wᶜʰ· both Mʳ Witts & I were lucky & not at home till after 12:

Saturday Jan: 7ᵗʰ·

Tolerably fine early in the Morning but soon changed to Mist or small rain, & at night violent gusts of wind which made our chimnies smoke sadly my poor Boys cough still very bad; play'd at Goose in the hope of amusing wrote to Miss Anne Snow.

Sunday Jan: 8ᵗʰ·

An uncommon hard hoar frost for one night, perfectly dry & cold tho constant sunshine, felt it much so at Stroud Church, where Edwᵈ· only went with his Broʳ colds being too bad to venture, & he in cloth Cloaths for the first time, return'd home from Church thro' Cains Cross & Woodchester, calling at Mʳ Peter Hawkers Door. rec'd Letters from Miss Chaplin, Miss Gorges & my Sister Travell, & wrote to Mʳˢ· Granville & Mʳˢ· Commeline.

Monday Jan: 9ᵗʰ·

Frost gone, for an hour or two in the morning flying Snow in showers, with great appearance of more, but it turn'd to small rain & was a thorough uncomfortable Day. Mʳˢ· & Miss Holbrow, Miss Hawker & Mʳ N: Wathen dined here disappointed in 2 or 3 Gents more that were to have dined here; play'd both at 5 Card Loo & Ving'tun unfortunate at both & so was Mʳ W.

Tuesday Jan: 10th.

Pretty fine early in the Day but before noon, severe showers of Snow, which determind us to give up drinking Tea at Mrs. Sheppards as we were engaged to do, I having got a bad cold, not sorry for the excuse, spent the evening much happier with the Boys, & beginning to make a pair of fancy Skreens. rec'd a Letter from Miss Snow.

Wensday Jan: 11th.

Another very sharp frost with very cold wind, I never ventur'd out nor Mr Witts very little he having symptoms of a cold, Fran^{s.} rode with John on some messages. The two youngest Miss Sheppards here in the Morning; we finish'd the Skreens but not till the evening. rec'd a Letter from Mrs. Buxton from Cheltenham with a good account of Mrs. Naper.[23]

Thursday Jan 12th.

Frost again, with clear sun, I only ventured out so far as the garden fearful of enerving my cold which was got better, expected Miss M: Hawker, to dine &'c but she did not come, play'd at Cards with the Boys & wrote to my Sis^r Travell, & rec'd a Letter f.^m Miss Sabine

Friday Jan: 13th.

A still harder frost, bitterly cold tho a constant sunshine, Miss M: Hawker came soon after breakfast, to dress ready to attend us to the Archers Ball at Wotten under edge, for which purpose we dined very early, & set out near three getting there in two hours, taking possession of the sorry rooms provided for us at our ale house Inn till the commencement of the Ball which was full & agreable, the members of the Club all in their archers uniform, & the Ladies tho much varied all in dresses composed of Green & white; the Room tho a pretty good one extremely full, but so cold was the night there was no possibility of keeping warm I play'd both at Whist & Ving'tun, a very handsome ornamented Supper between 2 & 3, much singing afterwards from the Gentlemen, & we did not break up till near 5 in the Morning, went to Bed but got little or no Sleep.

Saturday Jan: 14th.

A dismal miserable cold day with a very thick air & strong appearance of snow & towards evening a cruel cold piercing wind, after a late Breakfast Mr Peter Hawker breakfasting with us, we set forth to survey my Bro^r Witts's new taken House & place at Nibley,[24] where to our great surprize we found him just arrived there before us to shew off the premises, which upon the whole I was rather disappointed in, & almost starved to death with walking about it; brought my Brother home with us, & set Miss M: Hawker down at her Fathers; had a very late Dinner, & went to bed a little after nine dead with sleep.

---

23. Martha Buxton was the sister of Jane Naper; both were daughters of Ferdinando Tracy Travell.
24. Nibley House, North Nibley. Broome Witts had taken a tenancy at Nibley House on cheap terms from the Smythe family, but after a while there he grew to dislike it and by 1802 had managed to extricate himself from the tenancy and bought a property at Cookham Dean in Berkshire.

*107. Nibley House,
North Nibley.*

Sunday Jan: 15ᵗʰ·

Tho a very damp unpleasant Day, yet a very happy change in the weather being a confirmed thaw, & at various times in the day hard rain went to Church at Hampton, an excellent Sermon from Mᵣ Cocking, visited at Mʳˢ· Sheppards afterwards; rec'd a Letter from Miss Anne Snow & wrote to Miss Gorges.

Monday Jan: 16ᵗʰ·

Still a damp air with fogg & now & then small rain, my Dear Francis had been so ill the night before in his Stomach that I sent to Mᵣ Thornton & nursed him all Day, the two Broʳˢ· took a long ride to Salperton &'c, much conversation the whole of the Day chiefly on my Broʳˢ· proposed schemes at Nibley & all play'd at Commerce in the evening to please the Boys.

Tuesday Jan: 17ᵗʰ·

An uncommon thick fog in the Morning, & when it rather clear'd off at noon, became very wet & so continued the whole of the evening, very unsuitable to our long drive to dine at Mᵣ Savages at Tetbury, Franˢ· going with us my Broᵣ Witts being returnd to Bristol. No one there but young Mᵣ Paul of the Town & Mᵣ John Wiltshire; but our numbers large their whole family being at home for the holidays play'd at Commerce before Supper.

Wensday Jan: 18ᵗʰ·

Had been a little of a frost & the weather glass considerably risen, but a thick air, without sunshine, & very cold indeed; staid at Tetbury till one o'clock, returning home a little before Dinner time. play'd at Cards with the Boys in the evening. rec'd a Letter from my Sister Travell & wrote to Mʳˢ· Buxton

Thursday Jan: 19ᵗʰ·

A very miserable Day, severe frost, with constant flying storms of small snow, coming with strong N. East Wind not possible to keep oneself warm in any room: busy in the evenᵍ· repairing a fancy work Basket.

Friday Jan: 20ᵗʰ·

No change or amendment in the weather but that no snow fell, but the wind was higher & if possible still more cold than ever, totally confined again fortunately a Box of Books from Hookhams arrived & began reading Celestina.[25] very far from well all Day & much out of spirits. wrote to Miss Snow.

Saturday Jan: 21ˢᵗ·

Very much the same kind of confining weather & in the afternoon a tremendous thick fog, very busy all Day & happy with the Boys play'd at Commerce with them; & in the evening Mʳ Witts read in Boswells Johnson.[26] rec'd a Letter from Mʳˢ· Hyett & answerd it & wrote to Mʳˢ· Savage.

Sunday Jan: 22ᵈ·

Some snow had fallen in the night, but was a very thick wetting fog which soon melted it & made it too damp to think of venturing to Church a long Day of reading, writting, & conversation rec'd a Letter from Mʳˢ· Savage.

Monday Jan: 23ᵈ·

Another trifling fall of snow, still a thaw but being without fog, I determined to walk out, being quite ill with so long a confinement to the house, & the Boys with me, Mʳ Witts rode to Hampton &'c, & we drank Tea at Mʳˢ· Sheppards more agreable than usual, a party at Whist & one at Commerce for the young people. rec'd a Letter from Mʳˢ· Master.

Tuesday Jan: 24ᵗʰ·

One of the most uncomfortable of the many bad days, being a thick fog a very damp air, & in the afternoon rain, & towards night violent rain & wind we dined at Mʳ Pettats at Gannicocks, meeting Mʳ & Mʳˢ· Hill of Stonehouse & a Miss Turner with them, Miss Scott of Bowel Hill & Mʳ John Pettat & his Son, a laughable but not disagreable visit, a Table at Whist & Ving't'un at the latter of which I play'd; dismal dark & wet to come home at 11 o'clock; wrote to Mʳˢ· Master & rec'd a Letter from Miss Gorges & answer it.

---

25. Hookhams of 15 Old Bond Street, London, was one of the leading circulating libraries of the time. They also undertook some publishing, but not in a large way. The *Celestina*, or more fully *Tragicomedia de Calisto y Melibea or Libro de Calisto y Melibea y de la puta vieja Celestina* is a novel published anonymously by Fernando de Rojas in 1499. It is considered to be one of the greatest in Spanish literature, and traditionally marks the end of mediaeval literature and the beginning of the literary renaissance in Spain. The book is written against the machinations of servants of the low nobility and the story tells of Calisto, a bourgeois who falls in love with Melibea, the daughter of a nobleman; they become engaged following the machinations of Celestina, but their love has a tragic end after an accident in which Calisto falls off a ladder. On seeing this, Melibea subsequently decides to jump from a tower to her death.

26. James Boswell (1740–1795), Scottish lawyer and essayist, best known for his two-volume biography *The Life of Samuel Johnson* (1791), published seven years after the death of its subject.

Wensday Jan: 25th.

Very much the same kind of weather rather mended at Noon, but as bad again in the afternoon & night, I walk'd a little with the Boys before dressing to dine at Sir George Pauls, where we met M^{r.} & Mrs. Hyett & Miss Adams D^{r.} & Mrs. Egre, very agreable people, M^{r.} & Mrs. Sandiford, Mr. Mee, & M^{r.} Jo: Chestern all from Glocester & M^{rs.} & Miss Holbrow; handsome Dinner & Supper, 2 Tables at Whist and one at Loo at both of which I playd not at home till between 12 & one. rec'd a Letter f.^m Mrs. Buxton

Thursday Jan: 26th.

A most dreadful Morning of thick small rain & high wind & dreadfully damp, M^{r.} & Mrs. Hyett & Miss Adams came up here from the Hill House at Noon, & dresst before Dinner, where they were joind by Sir George Paul, M^{r.} & Mrs. Savage & their two Daughters, & Mr. Jeffries, a very pleasant party & all went off extremely well, 2 Tables at Whist, all staid supper, & all slept except the first & last Gent. rec'd Letters from Mrs. Rollinson & Mrs. Drake with the happy news of Mrs. Tyrwhitts being brought to Bed of a Daughter which I answerd.

Friday Jan: 27th.

A most happy change in the weather being bright & fine, yet mild & very pleasant & rather drying air, quite fortunate for all our party to walk about & enjoy the place & garden, at Noon they all took their leaves, I was very far from well all Day finding the want of sleep. wrote to my Sister Travell.

Saturday Jan: 28th.

A sad reverse of weather being a most miserable wet, damp Day from Morn: to night, a day fit only for in doors employments of which I had many; my sweet Francis read to me in the evening in Boswells Johnson & we play'd at Commerce. wrote to Mrs. Rollinson.

Sunday Jan: 29th.

Cloudy & damp in the Morning, but clear & fine before Noon, with frequent temporary gleams of sunshine, I went to Stroud Church, taking the two eldest Boys Mr. Witts prevented by writting Letters for the Post & receiving John Salmons. I walk'd w.th them after I came back. rec'd Letters from Mrs. Granville & Miss Forrest.

Monday Jan: 30th.

Rather foggy, but dry till afternoon when it became wet & stormy, Mr. Witts & Francis rode out, & the Boys walk'd I contented myself with pursuing many useful employments. heard Johnson again in the evening, play'd at Commerce & wrote to Miss Forrest a Letter shamefully long owe'd.

Tuesday Jan: 31st.

Rather a tolerable fine Day; tho extremely windy, but some sunshine, tho at night very wet again Mr. Witts & Francis took a long ride I walk'd with the Boys, but was very far from well all Day & dreadfully nervous. rec'd a Letter from my Sis^{t.} Travell, Mrs. Naper not yet brought to Bed.

Wensday Feb: 1ˢᵗ

A most wonderful high wind but no rain of any consequence, but very damp, not enough tempting to walk out; we dined & Francis with us at Mʳˢ Sheppards at Hampton meeting Mʳ & Mʳˢ Savage Charlotte & John, chearful & pleasant enough, a Table at Whist & Cribbage at which I play'd & won a little not at home till between 10 & 11.

Thursday Feb: 2ᵈ

One of the worst of all bad Days being violent high wind, & perpetual rain & damp to a great degree, fit for nothing but staying at home to be employ'd. John Savage came to Dinner to be ready to go with poor Francis to School the next day play'd at Commerce with them.

Friday Feb: 3ᵈ

A fine shewy Day with much Sun & wind, but changed at Noon, to hard rain in showers I set off after an early breakfast with my two Boys for Elmore, roads dirty but not particularly bad, staid two hours, & parted from my sweet Boy with unfeign'd regret. Mʳ Witts had been to Cirencester to see Mʳ Master &'c. rec'd a Letter from Mʳˢ Rollinson

Saturday Feb: 4ᵗʰ

Had been a trifling frost in the night, but was a beautifull fine warm Day with constant sunshine; Mʳˢ Master & Miss Master came here early & staid 2 or 3 hours, pleasant as ever, Miss Clutterbuck here also in the Morning & Miss Gorges came to Dinner. very lively & pleasant play'd a little while at Loo.

Sunday Feb: 5ᵗʰ

Very much the same kind of weather but not quite so fine, we went to Church at Stroud & return'd home thro Woodchester Vale, & walk'd a little in the garden afterwards, Mʳ Wathen dined here & was lively & pleasant. rec'd an account of old Mʳ Edwᵈ Hunts death which will oblige us to go into Mourning.[27] rec'd a Letter from Mʳˢ Buxton & I answer'd it & wrote to Mʳ Edward Hunt.[28]

Monday Feb: 6ᵗʰ

Not so good a Day, being damp & inclined to wetting fog Mʳˢ Read & her three Daughters made a tiresome Morning visit we dined at Mʳˢ Holbrows[29] Mʳ Witts riding, where we met Mʳˢ Purnel,[30] Mʳ Mʳˢ & Miss Austin, Miss Guise, Sʳ George Paul, Mʳ

---

27. It is unclear why such a distant connection would oblige Edward and Agnes to go into mourning. Furthermore, it is unclear who this particular Edward Hunt was. Edward Witts' aunt Sarah Witts (1715–1766) had married Thomas Hunt of Boreatton in Shropshire (1704–1777). There is no reference in the Hunt pedigree of an Edward Hunt having died in 1792.
28. Edward Hunt (1759–1822), son of Thomas Hunt and Sarah Hunt, *née* Witts.
29. John Holbrow came from Uley and had owned the mill now taken over by Edward Sheppard. By 1789 the Holbrow family had moved to Kings Stanley, where Holbrow had other interests, being the tenant of Stanley Mill. He had married Elizabath, the daughter of Samuel and Elizabeth Phillimore of Hocker Hill, Cam.
30. Mrs Purnell was Ann, the widow of John Small, who had married Thomas P. Purnell of Kingshill House, Dursley. She was also a daughter of Samuel and Elizabeth Phillimore, and therefore sister to Mrs Holbrow.

Kingscote[31] & M[r] Phillimore,[32] to the number of 14; a chearful odd visit playd both at Ving'tun, & Lottery Tickets, staid Supper not at home till past one in the Morning.

Tuesday Feb: 7th
Wet in the Morning, dry at Noon & wet again in the afternoon, M[r] Witts went early in the Morning on bussiness to Fairford & staid the whole Day the Ladies & I talked & worked without ceasing & in the evening we play'd at Loo. rec'd Letters from Miss Snow, M[rs] Master & M[rs] Buxton with the joyfull news of M[rs] Napers being brought to Bed of a Daughter[33] wrote to Miss Anne Snow & M[r] Edward Witts

Wensday Feb: 8th
A tolerably fine Day, tho very stormy I only walk'd in the Garden, being very busy with the young Ladies drawing a work'd Petticoat, very merry all Day much conversation & a little reading aloud & Loo again at night. rec'd a Letter from M[rs] Buxton, wrote to her & M[rs] Master

Thursday Feb: 9th
A mild pleasant Day with gleams of sunshine, we all walk'd for an hour at Noon much work, more conversation, a great deal of laughing, & a great deal of Loo in the evening.

Friday Feb: 10th
Very much the same kind of weather but not quite so fine, we dined at M[r] Reades, where we met M[r] & M[rs] John Pettat & a M[r] Webb, a splendid setting out of Dinner but a miserable dull visit all together, play'd both at Commerce & Ving'tun heartily glad to come home at 10 o'clock. rec'd Letters from M[rs] Commeline & my Sis[t] Travell & wrote to my Dear Francis

Saturday Feb: 11th
A mild pleasant day tho without sun, the greater part of the Morning spent in the Cape House, new arranging the Plants which caused much laughing & amusement to all parties. Loo & conversation in the evening

Sunday Feb: 12th
A very fine Morning, & a most charming Day throughout, but constant sunshine & very mild warm air, Miss Gorges myself & Boys all went to Hampton Church, & walk'd a good deal on our return but talk'd more, we three Ladies went to drink Tea with the 4 Ladies at M[rs] Sheppards at Hampton a very dull performance, & return'd home in time to reading & prayers. rec'd Letters from M[rs] Buxton & my sweet Francis & wrote to M[rs] Eliza Tracy.

---

31. Colonel Robert Kingscote (d. 1840). The Kingscote family had lived at Kingscote, between Dursley and Tetbury, for 500 years. Colonel Kingscote was a bachelor. His younger brother Thomas L. P. Kingscote married, in 1794, Harriet, daughter of Sir Henry Dashwood Peyton of Doddington, Ely, and the estate devolved to this side of the family.
32. John Phillimore (1753–1825) lived at Symondshall (between Wotton-under-Edge and Kingscote) and at Uley Lodge. He was the elder brother of Mrs Holbrow and Mrs Purnell.
33. Jane Naper (1792–1853). She married Sir George Cornewall of Moccas Court, (1774–1835).

Monday Feb: 13th.

As fine, if not a still finer Day, tho had been a trifling frost in the night, quite hot when we all walk'd on the common towards Littleworth, Mrs. Rollinson & Miss Biscoe with her came from Chadlington before it was dark, a good deal agitated with seeing my old friend look so very far from well, play'd all at Loo very merry & pleasant.

Tuesday Feb: 14th.

Quite as fine a Day, if not more brilliant, after a working party we all walk'd out in a slow solemn manner, Miss I: Sheppard made visit here on her horse, we all went to Dine at S^t G: Pauls where we met M^{rs.} & Miss Holbrow, Mr Peter Hawker & Mr Kingscote, a very handsome Dinner & Supper & a very pleasant meeting a table at Cribbage & another at Lottery Tickets at which I was very successful home about 12 o'clock.

Wensday Feb: 15th.

Weather somewhat similar but not quite so fine, Miss Gorges return'd to Leighterton afer breakfast, the other 2 Ladies & I went an airing in the Woodchester Vale & home up Nailsworth Hall in the evening talk'd much & play'd at Cribbage. wrote to Mrs. Peter Hawker a Letter of reconciliation[34] rec'd her answer & a Letter from Miss Anne Snow

Thursday Feb: 16th.

A most wonderfull & cruel change in the weather, to extreme bitter cold with a strong North east wind, & from the thickness of the air a great propensity to snow, no temptation to stir from the fireside, besides being far from well, & <u>much</u> out of spirits. Mr Palmer from Chip: coming here on bussiness staid Dinner. Cribbage again in the evening rec'd a Letter from my Sis^r Travell & answer'd it.

Friday Feb: 17th.

Quite as cold a Day with perpetual flights of small snow tho with very little to lye, Mrs. Rollinson & Miss Biscoe left us after breakfast to go to Cheltenham in their way back into Oxfordshire, I spent some time in the Morning in the hot house all I was able to do being still very unwell, wrote to Mrs. Tyrwhitt & Mrs. Granville.

Saturday Feb: 18th.

Had been a sharp fall of snow in the night, & snow'd the greater part of the Day in storms tho bright & strong sun between whiles, & most extremely cold being a piercing wind; We went to Dine & sleep at Leighterton with Miss Gorges meeting Mr Kingscote & Mr Edward Sheppard, an odd but pleasant Day, play'd at Loo with great success in the evening. rec'd a Letter from Mrs. Buxton.

Sunday Feb: 19th.

Rather a worse Day being still colder, & the storms of Snow more constant & with^t any

---

34. It is not made clear what caused the two ladies to fall out, but presumably the evening before, when Peter Hawker was unaccompanied, he may have intimated that a previous comment from Agnes may have caused offence.

chearing sun; went to Leighterton Church the service very moderately perform'd by Mr R. Huntly suffer'd much from the cold there, sat an hour or two with our friends afterwards & came home brisk to Dinner the roads being excellent. wrote to Miss Snow.

Monday Feb: 20^(th.)

A continued hard frost but a bright fine Day, the snow only melting from constant sunshine during which I enjoy'd my visits to the hot house much but in the evening was very ill & had a strong hysteric fit. Rec'd a Letter from my Dearest Francis & wrote to Lady Edward Bentinck, a very <u>interesting Letter</u>.

Tuesday Feb: 21^(st.)

Very much the same sort of weather till towards evening, when it became fast thick snow the two eldest Miss Sheppards & Mr Schutz here for an hour or two in the Morning, walk'd a little in the Morn: two or three times wrote to my Dear Francis

Wensday Feb: 22^(d.)

A constant ground thaw the whole day very moderate, with^t fog or any wet to be perceived consequently mild & rather pleasant to be out of doors. I was very far from well all Day Mr Witts read to me a good deal in Boswells Johnson. rec'd Letters from M^(rs.) Savage & my Sister Travell with rather an indifferent account of M^(rs.) Naper.

Thursday Feb: 23^(d.)

Very much the same kind of day only the snow melted still faster from a still milder air, I walk'd a good deal round the house, work'd hard at my Petticoat, my Husband read in Boswells Johnson, & we play'd at Commerce to please George, rec'd an entertaining Letter from Miss Gorges & wrote to M^(rs.) Buxton.

Friday Feb: 24^(th.)

Dry early in the Morning, but very soon after breakfast became, severe rain accompanied with some sleet, & severe wind & cold which altogether made me give up the idea tho quite prepared & even the P: Chaise at the Door to go out & make some Morning calls. in the evening was again very far from well received a Letter from M^(rs.) Eliza: Tracy

Saturday Feb: 25^(th.)

A miserable thick wetting fog in the Morning, but towards Noon & afternoon very hard & perpetual rain, I just went into the hot house or else was hard at work the whole Day & evening & Mr Witts read a good deal to me.

Sunday Feb: 26^(th.)

Very thick fog, attended by frequent rain till quite afternoon when it became clear & fine: quite prevented from thinking of going to Church the day only memorable for being my sweet Francis's Birth Day writting the whole day in the Morning at accompts & at night wrote to M^(rs.) Savage & Miss Gorges, & received Letters from my Sis^r Travell & my sweet School Boy.

Monday Feb: 27ᵗʰ·

Tolerably fine in the Morning, alternate gleams of sunshine with trivial showers, but towards afternoon steady strong rain came on; I went to make a string of Morning calls first to Mʳˢ· Holbrows, then to Mʳˢ· Pettats at the Ryeford, to Mʳ Peter Hawkers, & to Mʳ Tyndales shop. Mʳ Witts having also been out on horseback.

Tuesday Feb: 28ᵗʰ·

Damp & stormy with foggy thick air & a most unpleasant air alltogether, I walk'd a little but soon driven in by flying rain. Mʳ Witts had ridden to Woodchester & Hampton. in the evening read to me in Johnson as usual.

Wensday Feb: 29ᵗʰ·

A thick misty air but not wet in the Morning which tempted us to venture to set out for the sale at Nibley & to meet my Broʳ Witts there, but it turn'd out a sad wet miserable uncomfortable Day, but yet we did not much regard it the roads being excellent all the way tho we went a different route from usual a dull sale of bad things & but little company there. yet some amusement to George not at home till very late. rec'd Letters from Mʳˢ· Granville & my Sisʳ Travell

Witts Family Papers F182

1792

Thursday March 1ˢᵗ·

Still foggy & uncomfortable tho better than the former day I walk'd a little but soon driven in by small flying rain & extremely damp, work'd & read a good deal but in the evening much plagued by domestic plagues wᶜʰ· made me very ill, & extremely so in the night. rec'd a Letter from Lady Lyttelton & wrote to Mʳˢ· Commeline & my Sister Travell.

Friday Mar: 2ᵈ·

Tolerably fine in the Morning which tempted Mʳ Witts to ride as far as Mʳ Hawkins's of Bisley, & Mʳˢ· Pettat of Stonehouse to ride up here, but it became very wet & bad at noon, & obliged Mʳˢ· Pettat to stay here till 4 o'clock when it grew a little better & she venturd home: I was very indifferent all day.

Saturday Mar: 3ᵈ·

Fine & very pleasant in the Morning, but quite the reverse at Noon, when it began raining & so continued the whole Day with violence, Mʳˢ· & Miss Holbrow, & Miss Guise with them, Mʳ & Mʳˢ· Peter Hawker & Miss Mary, & Mʳ Jeffries dined & supt here disappointed in seeing Mʳ Hawkins & his Nephew a table at Loo & whist at which I play'd. received Letters from Mʳˢ· Buxton & Miss Snow

Sunday Mar: 4ᵗʰ·

After a miserable wet night was as miserable a wet Day being perpetual rain & that violent, notwithstanding, went to Church at Stroud, for the purpose chiefly of receiving the Sacrament heard an excellent Sermon from Mʳ Ellis. wrote accompts all the evening.

Monday Mar: 5ᵗʰ·

Wet again early in the Morning but soon blew off to be a very bright, very fine Day much enlivening sunshine, Mʳ Witts went early to meet some one on bussiness at Bibury, wᶜʰ· proved unsuccessful, but he return'd to a late Dinner, Mʳ Hawkins & his Nephew Sir Ceasar here in the Morning.[1] I walk'd a good deal & had the joy of receiving a Letter from my sweet Francis. & wrote to Miss Sabine

---

1. Sir Caesar Hawkins. This is something of a surprise as Edward Hawkins' late father, Sir Caesar Hawkins (1711–1786), and his own son, Sir Caesar Hawkins (1798–1884), were both famous surgeons and were knighted, and neither were alive at this period, yet there seems to be a third Sir Caesar in the person of his nephew.

Tuesday Mar: 6th.

After a night of great rain was bright & fine with a strong wind till afternoon when it became very cold & violent hard rain the whole evening, but I had fortunately taken a good long walk about our own premises first. Mr Wathen call'd here in the Morning. rec'd a long Letter from both the Miss Gorges, & wrote to Miss Snow & Mr Tyndale, & my Dear Francis

Wensday Mar: 7th.

Had been a considerable fall of snow on the preceeding evening & in the night, & after breakfast snow'd again with great violence for 2 or 3 hours to which succeeded wetting fog & small rain which prevented its lying to any great degree on the ground but was a truly miserable Day for the time of Year rec'd Letters from Mrs. Tyrwhitt & my Sister Travell & wrote to Mrs. Granville & Miss Gorges.

Thursday Mar: 8th.

A very severe Frost, with very cold wind tho constant sunshine wch. by degrees lessend the snow on the ground, Mr Witts rode in the Morning to Leighterton to call on Miss Gorges & we dined at Mr Jeffries's very agreably, meeting Mr Hawkin's & his Nephew <u>not</u> Sr Caesar, & M^r & Mrs. Peter Hawker & 2 Daughters an excellent Dinner & Supper 2 Tables at Whist, & home by a bright sharp Moon between 12 & one.

Friday Mar: 9th.

Frost still as hard or more severe wind being higher & more cold, Mr Witts set out very early on horseback for Cheltenham to call on Mrs. Naper &'c & return'd home again before 6 in the evening, having had a very propitious Journey in all respects; I walk'd in & about the Kitchen Garden only I work'd hard all day. in the evening wrote to Miss Sheppard.

Saturday Mar: 10th.

Another frost as sharp, & still colder if possible, from the severity of the wind, the sun being always out, I sallied forth directly after breakfast to make several visits & first go to 2 or 3 shops in Stroud; then call'd at Mr Ellis's at the Green where found only him & M^{rs.} J: Wathen, then to see Mrs. Burgh & concluded with M^{rs.} J: Pettat at Stonehouse not at home till 4 o'clock

Sunday Mar: 11th.

Very much the same kind of weather extremely cold at Church at Hampton where we arrived so much too early we went on a short airing on the Tetbury road first, a very good sermon from Mr Cocking, walk'd in the Garden on our return rec'd a Letter from my Dear Francis & wrote to Mrs. Tyrwhitt & Mrs. Buxton.

Monday Mar. 12th.

Still a frost & bitter cold tho bright & fine, I left Mr Witts & Boys soon after breakfast to take care of themselves, & set off by myself to go to Cheltenham to see Mrs. Naper, went the Painswick road, part of which I found very bad indeed, towards the end of my journey particularly found her tolerable well, her dear Babes quite so, & the little Girl a very fine child. my Sis^{rs.} both with her a very comfortable conversible evening.

Tuesday Mar: 13th.

A black cold morning, with a very bitter high wind that portended hasty change of weather which arrived by noon in the shape of both snow & rain & continued the whole of the evening. before it fell much, I went out in the Town to make some visits & do some bussiness, evening much the same as the former wrote to Mrs. Elizabeth Tracy.

Wensday Mar: 14th.

Frost quite vanish'd having been severe rain, & was bright & stormy by turns till near afternoon when it became again wet to a great degree, having allow'd me first to walk out in the Town with M^r J: Delabere & make more visits.

Thursday Mar: 15th.

Again fine in the Morning part but stormy & lowering at Noon, with some trifling rain but tolerably fine again in the afternoon, I left my Friends at eleven, & went to Glocester where Mr Witts met me at the Coachmakers to give our joint orders for the repairs of our Chaise; made some visits & having a little bussiness to do, did not think of returning home to Dinner, but had a good one at the Kings Head & reach'd home at seven finding the Boys quite well & gay. rec'd Letters from Mrs. Tyrwhitt, Mrs. Witts Friday Street & Miss Gorges, & wrote to Francis.

Friday Mar: 16th.

Quite a bright fine Morning, but grew stormy & dark towards Noon tho scarce any perceptable rain fell. I was full of employs all Day, conversing much with a person that came to offer for a servant & many other bussinesses. rec'd a Letter from Miss Snow & wrote to Mrs. Naper.

Saturday Mar: 17th.

A disagreable Day of wetting fog or rather flying rain, so I only went into the Garden indeed was fully employ'd all Day, with packing up in readiness for our Mondays Journey. rec'd a Letter from Mr Tyndale & wrote to Miss Gorges.

Sunday Mar: 18th.

Rather stormy tho scarce any rain fell, & was very bright & fine after the Morning went to Church at Stroud, from whence Mr Witts rode to call on Mr Hyett at Painswick: much writting & bussiness all the evening rec'd a Letter from Miss Gorges & wrote to Mr Tyndale.

Monday Mar: 19th.

A very fine bright Day from rising to setting sun, which shone constantly little wind & mild air. left home at 9 o'clock, George with us, to go to Upper Slaughter, stopp'd at Foss Bridge for an hour & ½ to bait the Horses a miserable place for that or any purpose, got to our Journeys end at 4 o'clock well tired w.th climbing so many barren Hills. found my Bro^r very indifferent Mrs. Buxton & children well play'd at Cribbage. rec'd a Letter from Francis.

Tuesday Mar: 20th.

Pleasant but windy till afternoon when it was wet & stormy, M^r & Mrs. Bourk & the two

Mᵣ Leighs from Addlestrop here in the Morning² Mʳˢ. Buxton & I walk'd a little, & talk'd more. play'd again at Cribbage & wrote to my Sister Travell.

Wensday Mar: 21ˢᵗ.

A still finer Day than most former ones, being warm & without wind walk'd a good deal in the home premises, evening the same spent as the former ones. rec'd Letters from Miss Sheppard & my Sister Travell & wrote to Miss Snow & my Dear Boy

Thursday Mar: 22ᵈ.

A very fine day from Morn to night well suited to our Oxfordshire drive left our friends soon after breakfast, & George under their care, my Brothers Horses carried us to C: Norton, & Mʳˢ. Buxtons chaise the whole of the way, got to Mᵣ Tyrwhitts a little while before Dinner with Post Horses & met with a most friendly reception from our kind friends whom with their charming little family of seven I was delighted to find so well, much friendly converse the whole of the evening.

Friday Mar: 23ᵈ.

Small rain & mist in the Morning which clear'd off & was only showery the remainder of the Day; Mᵣ Tyrwhitt went early a Hunting, & Mᵣ Witts on bussiness to Banbury from whence he did not return till tea time, but I spent a most happy Day with my aimable friends. too much to talk of, to think of cards.

Saturday Mar: 24ᵗʰ.

An almost universal wet Day much work, talk & play with the Dear Children & in the evening play'd at Cribbage, rec'd a Letter from my Sister Travell with an amended account of Mʳˢ. Naper.

Sunday Mar: 25ᵗʰ.

Very wet again early in the Morn: but became fine tho very windy the rest of the Day went in the Coach to church, service moderately perform'd by a young Curate, walk'd on our return for a considerable time in the Garden much talk & play with the Children &c in the evening

Monday Mar: 26ᵗʰ.

A bright but very stormy day, tho without rain excepting a smart shower at Noon Mᵣ Witts & Mᵣ Tyrwhitt rode to see Mᵣ Lyster at Enstone; day & evening spent as before. rec'd a Letter from Mʳˢ. Holford & answer'd it.

Tuesday Mar: 27ᵗʰ.

Very wet early in the Morning, & severe showers during the course of the Day; we bid adieu to our highly favor'd friends after breakfast stopp'd for an hour & ½ at Chipping: Norton to

2. Grace Brabazon, *née* Leigh (1743?–1812), was the daughter of John Leigh of Rosegarland, County Wexford. She married Anthony Brabazon (1721–1790), 8th Earl of Meath, on 20 May 1758. Their daughter was Lady Catherine Bourke. Presumably these were the Irish Leigh connections.

see some old Friends & reach'd Upper Slaughter just at Dinner time, finding my George quite well. thought, everything wore a very sombre face rec'd a Letter from my Dear Francis.

Wensday Mar: 28th.

Bright & fine in the Morning tho cold & stormy & in the afternoon rather wet M^rs. Naper & my Sister Travell with her came up from Lower Slaughter for an hour or two rejoiced to see the former so much recover'd. rec'd Letters from Miss Snow, Miss Gorges, & Molly with a favorable account of Edward.

Thursday Mar: 29th.

Much the same sort of weather rather cold & stormy, & a flying shower in the afternoon. Poor M^rs. Buxton confined to her room the greater part of the Day with a severe head ache wch. did not mend our dull scenery here. my Sis^r Travell here for an hour in the afternoon.

Friday Mar: 30th.

Fine early in the Day, but about noon steady mild rain, M^rs. Naper & my Sister Travell spent the greater part of the Morning here, Mr Witts & George attempted to take a long walk but were caught in the rain. play'd at Cribbage at night.

Saturday Mar: 31st.

Tolerably fine early in the Morning but as usual turn'd to rain at Noon, & was a very dismal wet stormy evening. Mr Witts spent the whole Day at Chipping: Norton, & the evening here alone as we went to drink Tea at Lower Slaughter & not at home till supper time.

Sunday Ap: 1st.

A most dismal uninterrupted wet day from Morn to night, no possibility of either M^rs. Buxtons or my going to Church; a very tiresome long day, Mr Williams & Farmer Cook dined here our Gardiner from Bownham came, & brought a good account of Edward; wrote to M^rs. Tyrwhitt & to Edward.

Monday Ap: 2d.

Fine, but wet & stormy at intervals & wind extremely high, in the Morning M^rs. Buxton & I went to make visits to both the families of Leighs at Adlestrop,[3] extremely pleasant one to M^rs. Leigh & delighted with her little Boy; play'd at Cribbage in the evening. rec'd Letters from Lord Edward Bentinck Miss Forrest & my Dear Francis.

Tuesday Ap: 3d.

Cold & stormy in the Morning & extremely wet in the afternoon & night, Mr Witts went to Chipping Norton in the Morning & was prevented from returning at Night by the rain. M^rs. Buxton & I spent the Morning at Lower Slaughter, having first gone to a shop at Bourton on the water. a dismal long evening. wrote to Miss Gorges, & Miss Snow.

---

3. James Henry Leigh of Adlestrop (1765–1823) married, in 1786, Julia Judith Twisleton (17?? –1843), daughter of Thomas Twisleton, 13th Baron Saye & Sele. The other Leigh family was presumably that of the Revd Thomas Leigh (17??–1813).

Wensday Ap: 4ᵗʰ·

Dry & pleasant till Noon when as usual it became wet & stormy, Mᵉ Witts return'd before Dinner, & Mʳˢ· Ugnall & Miss Buxton came to Tea, play'd at Whist. rec'd a Letter from Mᵉ Tyndale, humble, civil, & properly obliging.

Thursday Ap: 5ᵗʰ·

Prodigeous high wind, & at times trifling showers, my sweet Francis arrived at mid-day having rode from Cheltenham where he had slept, much delighted to see him. Mʳˢ· Naper & my Sisᵗ Travell here all the Morning, & Mᵉ & Mʳˢ· Bourke & Miss Praed dined here, lively agreable people.⁴ play'd at Whist.

Friday Ap: 6ᵗʰ·

Happily a day without any rain & the storms much abated, all went to Church & found Mʳˢ· Naper & my Sisᵗ here on our return; I was very low & far from well. play'd at Pope Joan with the Boys, & whist with the elders.

Saturday Ap: 7ᵗʰ·

Another fine day & wholly without rain, we were all dispersed different ways in the Morning my Broᵉ & Mᵉ Witts going to visit Mᵉ Hastings at Dailsford, the 4 Ladies spent the Morn at L. Slaughter, & Francis rode to see Mᵉ Jones at Naunton; I was again very indifferent. play'd at Commerce & whist. wrote to Mʳˢ· Granville

Sunday Ap: 8ᵗʰ·

A very fine Day tho with less sunshine but a mild air, I was so ill during Church time I was obliged to come home before it was over, the Boys dined at Lower Slaughter & their Papa drank Tea there to walk home with them rather a long tiresome day little done but talking I wrote to my Sister Catherine.

Monday Ap: 9ᵗʰ·

A most beautiful warm Day from Morn: to night, Mʳˢ· Buxton her little Girls & I spent the greater part of the Morning with Mʳˢ· Naper to meet Mᵉ Clarke, Mᵉ Witts & Francis rode to Adlestrop to visit both families of the Leighs, walk'd in the evening & play'd both at Pope Joan & whist.

Tuesday Ap: 10ᵗʰ·

Another as fine a day & still warmer but not quite so pleasant from being a strong blighting wind.

108. Warren Hastings.

---

4.   Arabella Mackworth-Praed (1766–1843) married, in 1792, John Bourke, 4th Earl of Mayo (1766–1849). Miss Praed was obviously on the point of marriage to John Bourke.

Mrs Ugnall air'd with Mrs Naper, Mr Witts went to C: Norton, & Francis rode out with his Uncle, & Mrs Naper & my Sister Travell drank Tea here; & after they were gone we play'd at Whist rec'd Letters from Lady Lyttelton, Mrs Tyrwhitt, Mrs Granville & my Sis^{r} Catherine & wrote to Lady Lyttelton.

Wensday Ap: 11th

A most glorious day warm like summer, in the sun, too hot for comfort; imediately after breakfast Mrs Buxton, Miss Buxton & myself, set out on a string of visits first to Lady Reades, then to Mrs Hippisley, & lastly to Mrs Bourke at Swell, all agreable in their different ways, on my return I went to Dine with Mrs Naper, where Mr Witts & Boys join'd me, & we return'd in her Chaise to Upper Slaughter between 8 & 9 & play'd at Whist.

Thursday Ap: 12th

Still warm & & very pleasant quite uncommon for the time of Year, a working Morning, with little walking; Mrs Naper & my Sis^{r} Travell came in the afternoon, & while we were at Tea came for half an hour M^{r} & Mrs Bourke & Miss Praed. Whist as usual. wrote to Mr Parsons.

Friday Ap: 13th

Fine in the Morning, but very hot & close & toward Noon grew quite cloudy, with frequent distant claps of Thunder, Mrs Thos. Leigh & Mrs Elizabeth Leigh made long Morning visits my Bro^{r} & Mr Witts rode to Mr Bourkes, Mrs Naper & my Sis^{r} here in the afternoon. whist as usual

Saturday Ap: 14th

Very cloudy in the Morning, with something of a fog, but clear'd & was fine & pleasant at Noon & afternoon, left Slaughter soon after Breakfast, not very sorry to quit such a dismal scene, Mr Witts & Francis on horseback, Mrs Buxtons Chaise & Post horses, reach'd Cheltenham at three where we intended visiting my Sis^{r} Catherine for 2 or three Days found her well & comfortable walk'd before Tea, when Miss Hughes & Mr John Delabere join'd us. play'd at Quadrille with success.

Sunday Ap: 15th

A change for the worse in the weather being stormy & cold & very little sun, went to church twice the service very well perform'd by a Mr Cummins. after Morning church went to survey the melancholly ruins of 5 houses that had been burnt down early in the Morning & made several visits. drank Tea at Mr Nettleships there own family party large,[5] & Mr J. & Miss Delabere added to it

Monday Ap: 16th

Rather a fine Day, but still blustering & rather cold, were about the greater part of the Morning, dawdling & visiting, walk'd as far as Sandford to call on Mrs Ram but did not find

---

5. Thomas Nettleship was one of the gentry resident in Cheltenham. His daughter, Anne Nettleship, married Dodington Hunt of Charlton Kings in 1797.

her at home drank Tea at Mr Hughes's, meeting M$^{rs.}$ Ram, play'd a merry game at Quadrille rec'd Letters from Mr Parsons & my Sister Travell.

Tuesday Ap: 17$^{th.}$

Cloudy & cold in the Morning, & turn'd to small steady rain before noon, but was dry again in the evening tho neither fine or pleasant bid my Sis^r Catherine adieu after breakfast, & went thro' Glocester to Elmore Court, Mr Witts & Fran^s on horseback, & George Horsington, & myself, in S^r G: O: Pauls old Chaise for want of our own & a most wretched inconvenient old tumbrell it proved dined early at the School, & left our sweet Boy with the accustom'd regret after Tea, & did not get home till past nine, but not very dark tho no moon. I was very ill, & much out of spirits the whole day. found Edward all alive & merry.

Wensday Ap: 18$^{th.}$

Dry, tho very cold & disagreable in the Morning, but before noon turn'd to a very constant & severe rain the whole Day & night, I put to the Hothouse &'c before it began, & was very busy from Morn: to night, in setting things to rights.

Thursday Ap: 19$^{th.}$

Constant hard rain, accompanied with sleet or hail & at times very high wind till quite evening when it became fine, & the sun shew'd itself before setting much engaged all Day & at night wrote to M$^{rs.}$ Naper & M$^{rs.}$ Savage.

Friday Ap: 20$^{th.}$

Scarce any rain fell the whole day, but it was cold & stormy, & little like the time of Year, yet I walk'd for a considerable time in our own premises Mr Witts read to me in the evening in Dr Johnson I was very indifferent & low. rec'd a Letter f^m Miss Snow

Saturday Ap: 21$^{st.}$

Still much the same kind of weather only wind higher, & more cold & unpleasant as it had been a sharp frost in the night; Mr W. went early on bussiness to Lechlade & did not return till night; I went after breakfast to Leighterton to see the three Miss Gorges who easily prevail'd on me to stay Dinner a very chatty visit & got home just as it was dark.

Sunday Ap: 22$^{d.}$

Weather very little if any mended only rather more pleasant from some gleams of sunshine, but the wind was intolerably high, went to Church at Stroud, the service very ill perform'd by Mr Lloyd; rec'd a Letter from my Dear School Boy & wrote to my Sis^r Catherine

Monday Ap: 23$^{d.}$

Tolerably mild & pleasant in the morning, but wet again at Noon & all the rest of the Day the three Miss Gorges came at noon & Miss Sheppard drank Tea here, all play'd a chearfull game at Loo.

Tuesday Ap: 24ᵗʰ·

Very wet till Noon when it ceased & was very fine in the afternoon, walk'd in the Garden &'c as soon as it grew fine with our 3 Misses the youngest of whom went at Noon in the Coach from the Bear to Glocester, the others return'd home to Leighterton after Tea. wrote to my Dear Francis. & rec'd a Letter from my Sisᵗ Travell.

Wensday Ap: 25ᵗʰ·

Quite a pleasant Day after the rain warm sun, mild air & no wind, was out a good deal at various times in the Day, Mᵉ Witts rode to Hampton &'c in the evening busy at accompts & wrote to Mʳˢ· Buxton.

Thursday Ap: 26ᵗʰ·

Not near so agreable a Day, tho dry & much sunshine, but a cold high wind dined at Mᵉ Peter Hawkers meeting only Mᵉ Hunt & his Son from Charlton,[6] a great entertainment others being expected, 2 Tables at Whist in the evening staid supper & home in the dark between 12 & one not a very enjoyable visit.

Friday Ap 27ᵗʰ·

Still wind, & stormy clouds tho dry & now & then some sun, went in the Morning in the Chaise with the new hired Horse, to spend an hour with Mʳˢ· Sheppard at Hampton, then went to buy some Grocery at Mᵉ Tyndales at Woodchester walk'd in the Garden &'c after Dinner.

Saturday Ap: 28ᵗʰ·

Had been some useful mild rain in the night, & was a moist & very growing Morning Mᵉ Wathen call'd here, & I was much engaged in preparation for our purposed Bath Jaunt, but walk'd in the afternoon when it became very fine. wrote to Miss Anne Snow. & rec'd one fᵐ· Mʳˢ· Savage

Sunday Ap: 29ᵗʰ·

A close & rather foggy Morning but grew clear & fine at mid day & delightfully warm & pleasant, went to Church at Stroud a very full congregation & an excellent <u>long</u> sermon from Mᵉ Ellis. took a very long walk between Dinner & Tea not at home till 8 o'clock on Sir George Pauls walks. rec'd a Letter from my Sisᵗ Catherine & wrote to Mʳˢ· Tyrwhitt.

Monday Ap: 30ᵗʰ·

Very uncommonly hot for the season till afternoon, being hot sun & no wind, & at 3 o'clock very loud claps of thunder, which soon turn'd the air too cold with a very stormy wind & rain at night left home after breakfast for Bath going to the X hands with our own horses, & from thence past landed at the White Lyon, dined with Mᵉ & Mʳˢ· Witts[7] No 1 Duke Street North Parade where finding a very pleasant parlour apartment vacant we engaged it for a week, dined & supt with our Friends, with whom was Miss Cope, & Mᵉ Spry likewise dined, a Miss Byrek drank Tea & Mʳˢ· Savage & Miss Wiltshire call'd on me rec'd a Letter from my Dear Francis.

---

6. Probably Dodington Hunt from Charlton Kings.
7. Probably Broome and Amelia Witts.

Tuesday May 1ˢᵗ·

Cold & stormy but bright & fine till afternoon when there was some trifling showers & 2 very remarkable rainbows: walk'd about a great deal visiting & shopping, dined at home comfortably & were at a route of Miss Copes upstairs consisting of 16, 2 Tables at whist I play'd 4 rubbers without winning or losing a farthing.

Wensday May 2ᵈ·

Dry & fine, but cold & strong north wind but very suitable to much walking about visiting & shopping, dined at home, & went with Mʳˢ· Savage & Miss Wiltshire to a benifit concert at the Town Hall, pretty well entertain'd; rec'd a Letter from Miss Anne Snow.

Thursday May 3ᵈ·

Very much the same kind of weather, out & about all Morning as usual dined in a pleasant party at Mʳ Wiltshires of 14 & went with some of them to the new Play of the road to ruin,[8] a very good thing & admirably well perform'd. walk'd home afterwards

Friday May 4ᵗʰ·

Small rain early in the Morning & at intervals for the greater part of the Day, wᶜʰ· made it miserable walking about, but I little regarded it. dined at Mʳ Westerns meeting Mʳ & Mʳˢ· Savage & Miss Eliza Wiltshire, Mʳˢ· Western of the Vineyards & others of the family there in the evening, play'd at Cribbage & Cassino & staid supper. rec'd a Letter from my Sisʳ Travell

Saturday May 5ᵗʰ·

Little or no rain, but miserably cold & stormy, walk'd about a great deal, much with Mʳˢ· & Miss Buxton who arrived the night before, dined at Mʳˢ· Birds, meeting Mʳ & Mʳˢ· Charles Western & Miss Charlotte & Miss Willes, a Small party in the evening 2 Tables I play'd Cribbage.

Sunday May 6ᵗʰ·

A miserable windy Day, quite unpleasant tho bright & dry, went to Sᵗ· James's Church much gratified by hearing the service so admirably well perform'd, walk'd afterwards making many visits, & went to dine at Mʳ John Wiltshires at Bath ford with Mʳ & Mʳˢ· Western in a hired Coach, meeting several of the family a very pleasant visit, finish'd the evening with Mʳˢ· Buxton.

Monday May 7ᵗʰ·

If possible still more windy & cold & so dusty it was miserable walking about Miss Sabine & my Broʳ Travell breakfasted which he had frequently done before, trotted about as usual, much with Mʳˢ· Buxton, dined at Mʳ Wiltshires with an agreable large party, more company in the evening 2 Card Tables, went to the Ball for 2 hours with Miss Wiltshires & Miss Buxton not very lively or full. rec'd Letters from Francis & Molly with an account of the Boys.

---

8.   Thomas Holcroft (1745–1809), dramatist and miscellaneous writer. *The Road to Ruin*, Holcroft's most successful play, was first produced in 1792, so the theatre in Bath was pretty well up-to-date.

Tuesday May 8th.

No change for the better in the weather, but not quite so cold much engaged in putting the finishing stroke to all bussiness, Mr W went to Bristol on bussiness & return'd to Dinner dined at home; went in the evening to Tea at Mrs. Hunts to see Mrs. Jenkins, & afterwards at a party of three Tables at Mrs. Muntons at next Door play'd with great success at Lottery Tickets.

Wensday May 9th.

A bright shewey Morning, but very soon became cloudy & looking like rain, but was mild & pleasant thro the whole of the day & very pleasant for travelling as we left Bath after breakfast, sitting half an hour before we set out with Mrs. Buxton; taking away with us a new Man Servant William Brown by name; leaving both Thomas & Horsington behind; went the upper road to Bristol wch. was new to me, drove thro' the Town, getting out of the Carriage to walk the greater part of it, & proceeded on to Kings Weston Lord de Cliffords 4 miles from Bristol, dined at the Inn, & then went into the Gardens merely to Survey the houses & conservatory, having seen the house & place before, not <u>very</u> highly gratified by the plants, except by bringing away some we did not possess a very civil Scotch Gardiner. returnd to Bristol Wells just before it was dark, went to Ferrys Hotel, a very good house & civil people supp'd both agreably & comfortably with Mr & Mrs. Schutz in Hope Square Miss Mary Sheppard with them.

Thursday May 10th.

More warm & fine than several former days but grew cloudy & cold in the afternoon, & slight symptoms of rain but none to signifi, breakfasted, with the Schutz's, & they walk'd with us a little about the place before we set out to return home, again obliged to drive thro' the odious Town of Bristol, went thro Sodbury to Petty France a dull road tho new, of 20 miles, which we performd in a little more than 3 hours, dined very comfortably & staid two hours to rest the Horses, & got home before it was dark finding the Boys well, all but Georges Cough hanging on him; rec'd a Letter from Mrs. Naper & wrote to Francis.

109. Kings Weston.

Friday May 11ᵗʰ·

Rather cold & unpleasant no rain & much cold wind, walk'd a little about home but was too much engaged with resettling, unpacking & various domestic bussiness to do more, my new Maid Martha Lodge came in the evening as did the Post Chaise from Glocester having been painted & repair'd

Saturday May 12ᵗʰ·

More mild & pleasant, tho only sunshine in short gleams, my Sisters came to Dinner from Cheltenham, such great strangers it was quite a wonder to see them, walk'd a little in the garden after Dinner & play'd at Cassino in the evening. rec'd Letters from Mʳˢ· Witts & my Sister Travell.

Sunday May 13ᵗʰ·

Quite a beautiful day from Morn: to night mild air & perpetual sunshine, went to Church at Stroud where Mʳ Dalaway did the duty, from there took my Sisʳˢ· an airing to Selsley Hill &'c, & before Tea walk'd for 2 hours to little London & round the Hill home by Sir G: Pauls. rec'd Letters from Miss Anne Snow & my Dear Francis, & wrote to Mʳˢ· Witts & Mʳˢ· Charles Western.

Monday May 14ᵗʰ·

Incessant mild rain the whole of the Day prodigeously growing & seasonable, & very propitious to in doors employments, my Sisters read to me in Anna Stᵗ Ives[9] not very interesting in the evening a good set to at Cassino. wrote to Mʳˢ· Holford.

Tuesday May 15ᵗʰ·

Much the same kind of weather till the afternoon when it was dry but not fine all went to drink Tea at Mʳˢ· Sheppards a chatty visit & one rubber at whist, play'd at Cassino after Supper wrote to Miss Anne Snow. rec'd a Letter from Mʳˢ· Savage & answer'd it.

Wensday May 16ᵗʰ·

Still wet but more in hard showers & very growing, very fine in the afternoon bright sun which tempted us to walk a little chiefly in the Garden, a great deal of working reading & talking & Cassino after supper. wrote to Mʳˢ· Naper.

Thursday May 17ᵗʰ·

The same moist growing weather little temptation to go out, Mʳ Witts confined by a very bad cough & cold lying in Bed till mid-day a great deal of Cassino in the evening. a good deal agitated by hearing there was a Scarlet Fever among the Boys at Elmore School determined to go the next day to see about it. rec'd a Letter from Mʳˢ· Buxton.

---

9.   *Anna St Ives* by Thomas Holcroft (as above) was the first revolutionary novel to appear in England, fuelling the political debate of the time. Holcroft was an atheist and a key figure in the radical movement of the 1790s.

Friday May 18th.

Very fine in the Morning, & little or no rain the whole of the day, but very stormy & cloudy in the afternoon; M\ Witts & I set out for Elmore after an early breakfast, found our Dear Boy quite well, but 2 others being confined judged it best to bring him away & John Savage also, play'd at commerce with the Boys & also at Cassino.

Saturday May 19th.

A beautiful fine day with hot strong sun till afternoon when it was dark & quite overcast & late in the evening some flying rain. M\ John Wiltshire & his two youngest Sisters rode here from Tedbury[10] to escort John Savage home & staid here two hours, taking M\ Witts & Francis back with them as we all were to dine at M\ Savages, where we met besides their own family M\rs. & Miss Sheppard; not at home till quite dark. M\ & M\rs. Hawkins rode over in the Morning from Bisley, w\ch. made the hurries of the Morning very great.

Sunday May 20th.

Quite a mild pleasant day without any wind, yet no sunshine till within 2 hours of its setting when it was very bright. went to Church at Stroud, dined rather earlier than usual, to take an airing in the afternoon Papa & Son attending us on horseback went to Lord Ducies at Woodchester Park getting out of the chaise to walk up a dreadful steep to see the large ruinous kitchen garden with little or nothing in that or the hot houses, return'd back the same way thro the Park & home thro & up Nailsworth Hill & home to a very late Tea drinking.

Monday May 21st.

A mixture of Clouds, sunshine & rain throughout the whole day, which permitted us to walk but little, M\ Witts & Francis were wetted in returning from making 2 visits at Kings Stanley & doing some bussiness at Stroud. I was very far from well all Day. play'd at Cassino.

110. *Spring Park, Woodchester.*

10.   Agnes was not usually concerned with accurate spelling.

Tuesday May 22ᵈ·

More sunshine & less rain tho there was now & then some small showers. I was very busy at accompts, interrupted at them by the arrival of Mʳˢ· & Miss Savage & Miss E. Wiltshire sent them home loaded with plants & cuttings. rec'd a Letter from Miss Gorges.

Wensday May 23ᵈ·

A still finer day then many past ones, much sun & little if any rain, & the afternoon beautiful, when my Sisᵗ Travell Francis & I went to see & drink Tea with Mʳˢ· Wathen in her new house near Stroud, pleased with the situation, did some little bussiness as we pass'd thro Stroud, Mʳ Witts, my Sisᵗ Catherine & George walk'd in Sᵗ George Pauls walks. play'd at Cassino on our return. wrote to Mʳˢ· Buxton.

Thursday May 24ᵗʰ·

Cold & rather stormy but dry & very bright in the afternoon when we took my Sisʳˢ· accompanied by the Boys a walk down the Hill to Brimscombe & home by the side of the canal; up Mʳ Wathens hill home, where we found Miss Sheppard waiting to drink Tea with us. rec'd a Letter from Mʳˢ· Holford.

Friday May 25ᵗʰ·

Very dark & cloudy all Morn: with strong appearance of rain but none fell till Dinner time, & lasted more or less all the even. which prevented Mʳˢ· Sheppard from fullfilling her engagement to drink Tea here but we were stuck out uncomfortably in the drawing room; read much all Day in Anna Sᵗ Ives at last hearing it. rec'd a melancholly Letter from Mʳˢ· Naper, & one from Mʳˢ· Schutz

*111.
Brimscombe
Port, men
towing trow.*

Saturday May 26th.

Wet early in the Morning, & very stormy the remainder of the Day tho little rain fell but we were deter'd by it from venturing to dine at Mr Hawkins's at Bisley, which was fortunate as Mr John Delabere dined with us & spent some social hours in his way home from Lady Shrewsburys walk'd a little after he was gone in the evening but it was bitterly cold. wrote to Miss Gorges

Sunday May 27th.

Not much like Whit Sunday in point of weather being cloudy & cold in the Morning & very wet all the afternoon, but luckily it permitted us to come home dry from Stroud Church where my Sister Travell & myself staid to receive the Sacrament an excellent sermon suitable to the day from Mr Ellis. busy at accompts all the afternoon.

Monday May 28th.

Very severe storms both of wind & rain thro the whole of the Day, & for 3 or 4 hours at mid-day continued violent rain, which made it quite a stay within day much reading, working, talking & playing at Cassino.

Tuesday May 29th.

A very stormy disagreable Morning, & at noon a very severe storm attended both with hail & Thunder, which kept my Sisters & myself, much longer on a Morning visit at Mrs. Sheppards at Hampton, from whence when it became clear & fine we went down the new road to Nailsworth & Woodchester & to Mr Tyndales shop. the earth too wet to walk in the evening. rec'd a Letter from Miss Snow a very long entertaining one.

Wensday May 30th.

A much better day, tho still little like the season of the year, Mr Witts & Francis rode to several places in the Morning, & we all seven walk'd before Tea to the Post going round the Hill to it.[11] Cassino as usual at night wrote to Mrs. Granville.

Thursday May 31st.

More like a summer day than any we had had, a mild air, & soft clouds with frequent gleams of sunshine but it became very cold again in the evening. my Sis^r Catherine & I went a string of visits in the vale, first to the Ryeford but did not meet Mrs. Pettat at home, at Mrs. Holbrows we found them surrounded by a large party of friends in the house, Mrs. Scott we found alone & very obliging on our return call'd also at Mr Reades at Ebley. walk'd but little in the even^{g.}

Friday June 1st.

Small trifling rain the greater part of the day which made it very damp & uncomfortable, & quite prevented going out, much work & reading, finished Anna St Ives better pleased

---

11. Presumably Tom Long's Post on Minchinhampton Common.

with the last volume. never failing Cassino after supper rec'd a Letter from M^rs· Rollinson a great wonder.

Saturday June 2^d·

Weather very little improved for tho it was not absolute rain, yet it was such a thick disagreable air it was little better & very cold Mr Witts & Francis rode in the Morning & we all tried to walk in the evening but with little pleasure Mr Witts came to Tea from Nibley having been long expected.

Sunday June 3^d·

Much the same thick air in the Morning, but changed at Noon to a boisterous high Wind, with strong sun, but yet it was so cold it was miserable walking in the evening even under the Shelter of our own wood. went to Morning Church at Stroud, & to evening service at Hampton before Dinner to which came my Bro^r Travell from Bath unexpectedly. wrote to M^rs· Naper.

Monday June 4th·

A fine Day tho still with a very cold wind, I was far from well all day, not the better for sending my sweet Francis to school again or from a great variety of morning company, such as M^rs· & Miss Sheppard, Mr Scott & M^r & M^rs· Hyett & Miss Hunt, in the evening before Tea we all 8 walk'd to St George Pauls, play'd at Whist before Supper.

Tuesday June 5th·

Not a very pleasant day being a thick blighting air & still very cold, both my Brothers went away, Mr Witts very early, Mr Travell nearly at mid-day; Mr Cooper & Mr Wathen both dined here we walk'd a little after Tea, & afterwards taught them Cassino till a late hour.

Wensday June 6th·

A better day being rather milder & some gleams of sunshine, & in the evening very clear & fine; after an early Breakfast we all 4 set off for my Bro^r Witts's at Nibley, going over Uley Bury, round which my Sis^rs· walk'd & I followd in the Chaise, & thro Dursley afterwards, walk'd much about the Garden & Feilds, got a tolerable scrambling Dinner, & after Tea returnd home by Wooten Underedge & Simmondil Down.[12]

Thursday June 7th·

Warm & close in the Morning without any sun or wind, but rain again in the afternoon tho very small & gentle, we went to Dine at Mr Hawkins's at Bisley, walking up the Hill to save the Horses, met there only M^rs· Mills & Miss Willis, but the visit was pleasant & we return'd home safe & quick before it was quite dark; having no complaint to make of the roads.

Friday June 8th·

Very showery & cold the whole of the Day, yet we continued to go to dine at Mr Hyetts at Painswick without much annoyance from it tho Mr Witts was as usual on horseback met

---

12. Wotton-under-Edge and Symondhall Down. From Symondhall the road took them through Horsley and Nailsworth to home.

there only Dr Cheston[13] & Mr Raikes[14] besides their own trio, an excellent Dinner & very lively & agreable it was, not at home till near ten but still very good driving light. rec'd a Letter from Mrs Granville.

Saturday June 9th

Much a finer Morning than usual but grew cold again as usual towards evening, tho still dry with great signs of rain. Mr Wapshott came unexpectedly on a Journey to call on us to Breakfast,[15] Miss Sheppard spent two hours here in the Morning, we walk'd for a short time in the evening, My Bro^r Witts came from Nibley just as we sat down to supper, play'd at Cassino afterwards. rec'd a Letter from Miss Anne Snow.

Sunday June 10th

One of the same disagreable days that so many had been, being dark & cloudy tho very little rain of any consequence fell, went to church at Stroud in the Morning, & to Hampton in the evening too cold & stormy to make it desirable to walk out in the evening. rec'd Letters from my Dear Francis & Lady Lyttelton & answer'd the latter.

Monday June 11th

Several severe showers in the Morning but at noon clear'd up & was very little more rain the remainder of the day, tho very wet & dirty. my Brother Witts left me after Breakfast & my Sister & myself, went first to visit Mrs Pettat at the Rye ford & then to see Mrs John Pettat at Stonehouse both amusing visits in their way. Cassino in evening.

Tuesday June 12th

Still cold, cloudy, & little or no Sun & less like the approach of midsummer, after an early breakfast, my Sisters bid an adieu to go to Swerford to join my Bro^r Travell, very sorry to part with them, after having had their company for more than a month; Mr Witts & I dined at Mr Scotts at Kings Stanley,[16] meeting M^r M^{rs} & Miss Pettat from Stonehouse, & a M^r & Mrs Crawley that were to stay at Stanley agreable people of the world, a table at Whist & Cassino, & not at home till near 11 o'clock.

Wensday June 13th

The same dark, cold, uncomfortable weather yet no rain fell to speak on, walk'd at two different times in the Morning, & a long walk after Tea with the Boys to Houndscroft &

---

13. Dr Cheston was Richard Brown Cheston of Gloucester, M.D., F.R.S.

14. Robert Raikes (1735–1811). Raikes took over the running of his father's newspaper, the *Gloucester Journal*, on his death in 1757. He held liberal views and used his newspaper to campaign for prison reform and working-class education, and, as such, was know to Sir George Onesiphorus Paul. In July 1780 Raikes and a local curate, Thomas Stock, decided to start a Sunday School at St Mary le Crypt church in Gloucester. Every Sunday the two men gave lessons in reading and writing. Raikes was not the first person to organise a school in a church but by giving it maximum publicity in the *Gloucester Journal*, he was able to spread his ideas to others.

15. Mr Wapshott was a banker in the partnership of Wapshott, Palmer, Matthews & Palmer of Chipping Norton and Edward Witts' bank manager.

16. Thomas Scott was the rector of Kings Stanley, a living to which he was presented in 1779.

home by Littleworth; rec'd a Letter from M^rs. Naper wrote in a very melancholly strain, & wrote to my Dear Francis.

Thursday June 14th.

A better day, air milder, & some sun & in the evening had more the appearance of a summers evening than any this year, being bright & clear & a strong dew; Mr Witts went to Tetbury to call on the Savages in the Morning, we walk'd a little at night calling on M^rs. Tanner. rec'd a Letter from Miss Gorges & wrote to Miss Snow.

Friday June 15th.

Quite a fine Day, throughout from Morn to night much like summer, I walk'd & prowled a good deal about in the Morning & after Tea rode out for the first time for many months went to Cains Cross down Rodbro' Hill & so to Mr Rich^d. Pettats at Ganycocks where we call'd & found a large party assembled, the Stonehouse family, M^r & M^rs. Scott & M^r & M^rs. Winchcombe amused by meeting the latter very much there was a table at Whist & we play'd at Cassino, much press'd to stay supper but withstood it, tho not at home till 10 o'clock. rec'd a Letter from M^rs. Tyrwhitt

Saturday June 16th.

Not so pleasant a day tho still very warm, as the air was blighting & disagreable & I was very far from well all Day, Miss Clutterbuck here for 2 hours in the Morning, & we again rode after Tea thro the Woodchester Vale to Nailsworth up the new road to Hampton, where we calld to see if the Sheppard family were return'd home but in vain. rec'd a Letter from my Sister Travell.

Sunday June 17th.

Rather gloomy in the Morning but turn'd out a very fine pleasant Day & beautiful for views, went to church at Stroud, & from thence to Mr Reades at Ebley to invite them to Dinner walk'd a great deal in their Garden took a fine walk with the Boys after Tea to Littleworth & home by Sinelmer[17] & the back of S^r G: Pauls walks, more than three miles. rec'd Letters from Lady Lyttleton & my Dear Francis.

Monday June 18th.

A sad change in the weather being again turn'd to cold & stormy, & dark & dismal M^r & M^rs. & Miss Savage, M^r & M^rs. Reade, & Mr Hawkins dined here, chearful & pleasant enough wrote to Lady Lyttelton.

Tuesday June 19th.

As bad if not a worse day being still colder with trifling showers & as dark as if winter, little pleasure in being out of doors, glad to keep in the Woods for shelter when we took our

---

17.   This word is extremely difficult to read and this is the nearest that can be ascertained in transcription. She probably meant St Loe, as St Loe House, adjacent to the area known as St Chloe, is on the direct route they would have followed from Littleworth to the back of Sir George Onesiphorus Paul's property.

evening walk; M.ʳ Witts read a good deal to me in the Romance of the Forrest an interesting Novel.[18] wrote to my Sis.ʳ Travell.

Wensday June 20.ᵗʰ

Not intirely so bad a day, but still miserably cold & dark & very unlike the time of Year, I was very far from well, went to drink Tea with Miss Clutterbuck at Hyde meeting M.ʳˢ & both the Miss Sheppards play'd at Whist not at home till it was dark wrote to M.ʳˢ Granville.

Thursday June 21.ˢᵗ

Being a much milder air & some few gleams of sunshine, made it realy a pleasant day & encouraged us to begin cutting our Hay which carried me frequently out in the Morning M.ʳ & M.ʳˢ Ellis & M.ʳˢ Wathen with them, & M.ʳ Nathen Wathen dined here, & behaved so well & seem'd so much pleased it was quite agreable walk'd about the Garden & Wood before Tea wrote to Miss Gorges.

Friday June 22.ᵈ

A very lowering day, tho very little rain fell till afternoon & then only in showers, attended by a most Wonderful bright rainbow of long continuance, my Dear Francis came from School at noon, to the great delight of all, on his Poney. I walk'd a little in the Morning, but too wet in the evening for any to go out so play'd at Cassino to amuse the Boys. wrote to M.ʳˢ Naper.

Saturday June 23.ᵈ

Very much the same sort of weather only the storms more violent which made all going out impossible except to the Garden M.ʳˢ Shellard from Cirencester here for an hour or two in the Morn: to enquire the character of a servant & was very agreable, I was very far from well all Day. play'd again at Cassino in the evening, & the Boys read much to me.

Sunday June 24.ᵗʰ

If possible still more violent storms, yet it allow'd me to go dry to Stroud church but rain'd while we were there, & before we could get home, I was still more unwell than, the day before, after Tea went an airing taking Francis w.ᵗʰ us along the Woodchester vale, up the new road to Hampton, where we stoppd for a few minutes at M.ʳˢ Sheppards door to gossip with the Misses rec'd a Letter from Miss Snow.

Monday June 25.ᵗʰ

In the Morning dry & mild, but very damp & without sun, & at three o'clock began raining small rain very steadily & so continued the rest of the evening, putting a stop to our taking a ride for which we were prepared Boys read much & Cassino with them at night.

---

18.   Ann Radcliffe (1764–1823). Ann Radcliffe, *née* Ward, married William Radcliffe, an editor of the *English Chronicle*, at Bath in 1788. The marriage was childless and, to amuse herself, she began to write fiction, which her husband encouraged. Her works were extremely popular among the upper class and the growing middle class, and especially among young women. Her works include *A Sicilian Romance* (1790), *The Romance of the Forest* (1791), *The Mysteries of Udolpho* (1794) and *The Italian* (1796). The success of *The Romance of the Forest* established Radcliffe as the leading exponent of the historical Gothic romance.

Tuesday June 26th.

The same dull damp kind of weather in the Morning & equally if not more wet in the afternoon, Mrs. Sheppard & the two Miss Sheppards, M^r & Mrs. Pettat, Mrs. John Pettat her Son & Daughter & Mr Brown with them dined here & staid late playing both at Whist & Cassino

Wensday June 27th.

A very fine day quite a pleasing variety, tho it was still close & damp, walk'd a little in the Morning, & after Tea rode, & Fran^{s.} with us on some errands to Stroud, & home thro Cains Cross & up Rodbro' Hill wrote to Mrs. Rollinson

Thursday June 28th.

Quite a thick fog in the Morn: but clear'd off in some degree but was never bright & fine the whole of the day being so wonderfully damp, Mrs. Burgh here in the Morning, walk'd in the evening a little on Hampton common but chiefly in our own domain among the Hay &c rec'd Letters from Lady Lyttelton, Miss Gorges & my Sister Travell.

Friday June 29th.

Very disagreable weather in the Morning being quite a thick blue mist, very hot & damp, but clear'd off tolerably, with an intermixture of strong stormy clouds & sunshine but no rain. Francis & I went in the Chaise to call on M^r & Mrs. Hyett & invite them to Dinner on Monday, from thence went to visit Mrs. Durouse at Paradise both pleasant visits but tired with the exertion of toiling up & down the Hills walk'd only in our own premises in the evening; finish'd reading the Novel of Argus[19] with wch. I had been much entertaind rec'd a Letter from Lady Lyttelton informing us that both she & Lady Clive put off coming to us, tho within 20 miles of us & we had expected them on Saturday evening. much ado about nothing.

Saturday June 30th.

Not the same kind of weather, being dry & windy, but with strong clouds & little sunshine Mr Witts & Francis took a ride in the morning, & to our great surprize as soon as we had dined came an express messenger from Lady Lyttelton to say herself & Lady Clive would be here in the evening which accordingly they were about 8 o'clock such changeable arrangements not pleasant. play'd at Cribbage before Supper. rec'd a Letter from Lady Lyttelton & Mrs. Naper.

Sunday July 1st.

Upon the whole a very fine day being a happy mixture of sun, clouds, & temperate air all went to Stroud Church in the Morning in the two carriages, the Ladies much pleased with Mr Ellis's manner of performing the service staid the Sacrament & drove home by Dudbridge & Sir G. O. Pauls Hill. My Brother Witts came to Dinner & staid all night, & the two Mr Wathens were here in the evening, when we all walk'd a little.

---

19. *Argus* is possibly an early novel by Laetitia Matilda Hawkins (1759–1835), an English novelist associated with Twickenham. She was the daughter of Sir John Hawkins, an acquaintance of Samuel Johnson. She wrote at least five novels, including *The Countess and Gertrude* (1811), and she also acted as an amanuensis for her father. Her work was published anonymously until after Sir John's death in 1789.

Monday July 2^{d.}

A very sober quiet kind of day in point of weather, being without rain, sun, or wind but close & warm, stirr'd very little in the Morning Lady Clive being very indifferent, my Bro^r Witts went away early, M^r & Mrs. Hyett & Miss Hunt, Mr Wathen & a Mr Wassey dined here the latter a young Curate residing at Bisley, the two latter staid later & join'd in a pool at Commerce. wrote to Mrs. Naper

Tuesday July 3^{d.}

Very much the same kind of weather, only both morning & evening there was little flying mists; but on the whole not an unpleasant day, which was fortunate, as our whole party the three Boys & all, spent the Day with my Brother Witts at Nibley, going by Uley Bury & returning by Simmonsil down, not at home till late but the two Ladies much pleased with the jaunt

Wensday July 4th.

Wet early in the Day, & at times very damp & showery the whole of it; walk'd much about our own house & premises with Lady L both Lady Clive & myself, far from well, play'd a long bout at Cribbage in the evening.

Thursday July 5th.

Hard rain till after mid-day when it clear'd & was rather a bright fine evening, our two Ladies took there leave of us at Noon, & M^r & Mrs. Richard Pettat, & a M^{rs.} & 2 Miss Rainsfords sister & Nieces of Mrs. Pettat dined here, pleasant & pretty young women which made the visit go off better than expectation, as we were disappointed in Mr Scotts family who were to have dined here play'd at commerce. rec'd a Letter from Mrs. Buxton.

Friday July 6th.

A very moderate kind of day, dark & dull, & at various intervals flying Mists which could hardly be determined rain, & suffer'd our Hay to be carried in the Morning; Mr Witts & Francis rode to Hampton &c; & after Tea they again rode out with me, on the Cirencester road & home by Gatcombe & Hampton wrote to my Sister Travell.

Saturday July 7th.

A very happy change in the weather being bright & warm, & much like summer in every respect quite reviving if it would but last. Mr Witts & his Son rode to call on the Savages at Tetbury, M^{rs.} & Miss Sheppard, bringing with them, M^{rs.} & Miss Castleman made an early & long morning visit here, & we dined a party of 13 at M^r R: Pettats meeting besides their own family of 5, Mrs. John Pettat & her Son & Daughter & with them Mr Wise & Mr Brown, play'd 11 at Commerce which was so lingering we did not get home till ½ past 11 & then without Supper.

Sunday July 8th.

Dark & lowering in the Morning, & for 3 or 4 hours at mid-day, the same flying Mists which might be call'd serious rain, but clear'd off to be a bright fine evening. Myself & three Boys went to Church at Stroud, dined very early to give Mr Witts, Francis & I the power of going to Drink Tea with Miss Gorges at Leighterton, found them well & rejoiced to see us, had a very pleasant drive home just before dark. wrote to M$^{rs.}$ C: Western.

Monday July 9$^{th.}$
As fine a Day as possible, quite hot being constant bright sunshine from Morn to night M$^{rs.}$ Savage & Miss Wiltshire here for 2 hours in the Morning, Mr Witts, Frank, & I rode in the evening, to Mr Tyndales Woodchester vale &c rather fatigued being very far from well.

Tuesday July 10$^{th.}$
A cruel reverse of weather, being constant small rain the whole of the Morning & as constant a thick fog & mist the evening which put a stop to all moving, except to the hot House for a quart. of an hour, much reading & working & a little Cassino & rec'd a Letter from M$^{rs.}$ Naper.

Wensday July 11$^{th.}$
Quite uninterrupted hard rain from Morn: to night, so much so as seldom to see the like, put a total stop to our engagement to drink Tea at M$^{rs.}$ Sheppards, very ill & much oppress'd scarce able to employ myself

Thursday July 12$^{th.}$
Not quite such uninterrupted hard rain, as it held up for 4 or 5 hours in the middle of the Day, but then was miserably damp & uncomfortable & we had a sad evening to come home from Mr Savages at Tetbury, where we had dined, meeting besides their own family party, M^{r} & M$^{rs.}$ Estcourt,[20] Dr Estcourt & a Captain Pigot, a very lively agreable visit. recd a Letter from Miss Anne Snow & wrote to Miss Snow.

Friday July 13$^{th.}$
The weather full as wet & bad as the former Days, till noon when it clear'd off, & was a beautiful bright fine afternoon; rather an interesting & very agitating Day to me, who was ill able to bear any hurry either of mind & Body, as Dr Cheston came in the Morning, to give me his advice, & M$^{rs.}$ Naper & Miss Western with her, soon after to stay a week truly glad to see the former so well. walk'd a little before Dinner, but thought it better to play Cassino in the evening than encounter the damp. rec'd a Letter from M$^{rs.}$ Granville.

Saturday July 14$^{th.}$
A remarkable fine pleasant Day being bright & fine, with strong light & shade & yet not too hot. Mr Witts & Fran$^{s.}$ rode to Bisley, & the 2 Ladies & I drove thro Woodchester Park, to Uley Bury & home down Froster Hill & thro' the Stanleys much pleased.[21] in the evening walk'd to the Fort Boys & all & play'd at Cassino before & after Supper. rec'd a Letter from M$^{rs.}$ Charles Western.

20. Thomas Estcourt (1748–1818), of Estcourt House, between Shipton Moyne and Long Newnton, near Tetbury. His wife was Jane, *née* Grimston, daughter of James Grimston, 2nd Viscount Grimston. Thomas Estcourt was M.P. for Cricklade (1790–1806).
21. Through the villages of Leonard Stanley and Kings Stanley.

Sunday July 15th.

Very much the same kind of day only rather warmer, went to church at Stroud from whence Mr Witts & Francis rode to call at Painswick I brought the Ladies home thro Woodchester Vale calling at Mr Peter Hawkers, we went to evening service at Hampton, being all rather tired we only stroled on the common. wrote to Mrs. Granville & my Sister Travell.

112. Priory, Leonard Stanley.

Monday July 16th.

Quite a hot old fashion'd summers day, which afforded an excellent means of completing our Hay, very busy in the Morning dressing up the large flower stand which answer'd admirably Miss Boughtons here for ½ an hour in the Morning we only walk'd in the evening in Woods & our own premises & again play'd at Cassino with much spirit. rec'd Letters from Lady Lyttelton & 2 from my Sister Travell & wrote to Lady Edwd. Bentinck

Tuesday July 17th.

Fine in the morning & very warm, but showery at Noon & in the afternoon, Mrs. & Miss Holbrow here in the Morning, & Mrs. & Miss Hawker, & Mr Peter Hawker, Sr George Paul & Mr Wathen dined here disappointed in seeing Mr & Mrs. Hawkins who were invited, the visit pass'd off well, a Table at Loo & one at Cassino, & Sr G: O: P. staid supper & chatted away till late. wrote to Miss Byam.

Wensday July 18th.

Wet early in the Morning, but dry the remainder of the day excepting a shower at Noon Mr Witts & Francis rode to Stonehouse &'c & we three Ladies, aird first to survey Mr Sevilles Garden at Chalfort, & return'd thro Hampton & down the new road to Nailsworth & Woodchester, stopping at Mr Tyndales shop for some trifles. Miss Sheppards & Miss Castleman with them, drank Tea here, & we play'd an almost endless Pool at Commerce.

Thursday July 19th.

A very fine Day excepting a very small shower or two at Noon as it were first to keep up the general practice of rain every Day after walking about the Garden & premises, the three Ladies in the Chaise & Father & son on horseback drove round Selsley Hill a beautiful Day for views. Mr Wasey[22] call'd here before we went & Mr & Mrs. Hyett & Miss Hunt while we were gone, & before Tea the three Ladies attended by the three <u>young</u> Gentlemen, went to Sr George Pauls going all over the House, & a short way in the walks; came home to a late Tea & had a long bout of Cassino afterwards. rec'd Letters from Mrs. Granville & Miss Gorges.

22. George Wasey (1773–1838). Wasey was a fellow of All Souls' College, Oxford, from 1795 to 1812, graduating B.A. in 1795, M.A. in 1799 and B.D. in 1809. He was rector of Whittington, near Cheltenham (1802–1811), and then of Ulcomb, Kent, from 1811 to his death. At this point he was presumably curate to Edward Hawkins at Bisley.

Friday July 20th.

Very fine Day, till afternoon, when it gradually became cloudy, & after sunset began raining hard & so continued all night, Mr Witts & I attended Mrs. Naper & Miss Western so far on their Journey home as Cirencester, where we dined with them at Mr Masters, meeting only Mrs. Shellard excepting their own family, very agreable & pleasant, only too wet for comfort on our return. very sorry to part from Mrs. Naper after having been happy with her.

Saturday July 21st.

Uninterrupted violent rain for the whole of the day, I ventured thro it to the garden in the afternoon, quite as busy as there were hours in the day preparing for going to Cheltenham the next day. rec'd Letters from Lady Edward Bentinck & Dr Cheston, the former as interesting as it was pleasing

Sunday July 22^{d.}

For a great wonder a perfect dry day, & very warm & pleasant, after going to Stroud Church in the Morning, Mr Witts on horseback & Francis, Lodge & I in the Chaise went down to Cheltenham to Dinner, much disappointed but not surprized not to find my Sisters return'd home well & comfortably rec'd by their servants. walk'd in the evening to the Well & in the Street, & saw much of the gay world; M^r & Mrs. Granville call'd on us late. rec'd a Letter from my Sister Travell.

Monday July 23^{d.}

Quite a pleasant fine Day throughout, Mr Witts & Francis went to the Well before breakfast, I visited & walk'd about the great part of the Morning, dined at home our Trio, & dress'd afterwards to go to the Master of the Ceremonies Ball, with Mrs. Granville, which was more crowded than ever known, near 300, very hot & not very pleasant got home about 12.

Tuesday July 24th.

Not so pleasant a day, being a very thick close air but no rain to speak on I walk'd the whole of the Morning till I was tired to death making some visits a little out of the Town, dined again at home alone, & was so in the afternoon, till we carried our Dear Boy in the evening to the Puppet Shew where he was much delighted. on our return home expected to find my Sisters arrived, but instead a Letter that they did not know when they should. much vex'd about it & heartily wish'd ourselves at home again. rec'd a Letter from my Sis^r Travell & answer'd it.

Wensday July 25th.

A very disagreable Day wet almost constantly from Morn: to night, M^r & Mrs. Granville breakfasted here, & Lord Elcho & many others call'd in the Morning,[23] & I made two or three

---

23. Francis Charteris, Lord Elcho (1749–1808). Lord Elcho was the husband of Agnes' first cousin, Susan Charteris, *née* Tracy Keck.

near visits, dined at Mᵣ Delaberes very pleasantly the only addition to their own family party was Mᵣ Dewes.²⁴ Mᵣ & Mʳˢ· Mills drank Tea there, & we all adjourned to good rooms where I play'd in a pleasant set at Cassino. rec'd a Letter from Miss Byam & wrote to Mʳˢ· Naper.

Thursday July 26ᵗʰ·

Was a dry & moderately fine Day. after a very wet night, I went to the Well before breakfast well tired with the exertion. Mʳˢ· Ecles's call'd on us, walk'd about a good deal with them Miss Hughes dined with us, & we carried her with us to drink Tea at Mᵣ Delaberes, went with them all to the Play, the Merchant of Venice & so many &'cs that we were not home till 11. wrote to Lady Edward Bentinck & Miss Anne Snow.

Friday July 27ᵗʰ·

Fine in the Morning but showery again in the afternoon as usual, Mᵣ Witts rode out as usual with some Gentlemen, I walk'd in a party to Mʳˢ· Ecles Lodgings in the fields & made some visits afterwards, drank Tea at Mᵣ Delaberes & play'd at Cassino before going to the Ball, which was full & lively, & very smart, at our return home to supper found my Sisʳˢ· had arrived in the evening sat up talking with them till a late hour. rec'd a Letter from my Sisᵣ Travell, & Miss Gorges.

Saturday July 28ᵗʰ·

A very fine day without much heat & scarce any rain to mention, a variety of visits both at home & abroad all Morning, & went with my Sisᵣ Catherine to a Musical performance at the Rooms, by the 3 young Lindleys,²⁵ most capital players & a high 2 hours entertainment Mᵣ Witts went very early in the Morning into Oxon Mᵣ Granville & Mᵣ John Delabere dined, & the Ladies of the family & Mᵣ Dewes join'd us at Tea, the 2 former carried Francis to the Play, & the rest of us went to full handsome Rooms without playing at Cards. wrote 2 Letters characters of servants

Sunday July 29ᵗʰ·

Dark & very cloudy in the Morning with small rain or flying mists, but suffer'd us to go dry to Church, but at the conclusion of it so violent a storm of rain came on that we were kept half an hour in Church after it was done & walk'd home thro' mud & dirt imediately after which myself & dear Boy set out to return home by the way of Glocester found the roads so good that I got home within 3 hours & ½ & found the Boys quite well, walk'd in the Garden before Tea went early to Bed without supper. rec'd a Letter from Miss Anne Snow & wrote to Mᵣ Parsons.

---

24. John Delabere appears to have remained a bachelor, as there is never a Mrs Delabere referred to. The family circle would have been John Delabere, his sister, Harriet Granville, and his brother-in-law, John Granville. Mr Dewes is Bernard Dewes, elder brother to John Granville, mentioned above. John Granville had been born John Dewes, but changed his name to Granville on inheriting Calwich from his uncle, Bernard Granville—a friend of Georg Frideric Handel and Rousseau. Bernard Dewes' wife was Anne, *née* Delabere; therefore, the two brothers had married two sisters.
25. The Linley family were of great repute. The father was Thomas Linley (1733–1795), born at Badminton, Gloucestershire. The Linleys Agnes referred to must have been Ozias Thurston Linley (1765–1831) and William Linley (1731–1835). The third is a mystery, as the other siblings had all died, Elizabeth very recently, on 28 June 1792; Thomas had died in 1778 and Mary Linley in 1787. Therefore, the third 'Linley' was probably just a colleague player and not a member of the actual family.

Monday July 30ᵗʰ·

A very pleasant Day from Morn: to Night, dry & constant sunshine without being at all too warm, extremely busy all Day, Franˢ· took a long ride in the Morning, & Mᵣ Witts arrivd from L. Slaughter an hour after Dinner, walk'd a little in the evening with him, & play'd at Cassino with the Boys. rec'd a Letter from my Husband & wrote to Lady Lyttelton, Mʳˢ· Savage, & Miss A: Snow:

Tuesday July 31ˢᵗ·

Very wet in the Morning & had been so all night, & tho their was little rain after mid-day it was very dark damp & unpleasant & little like summer; very busy all Morning, & drank Tea & staid late, at Mʳˢ· Sheppards at Hampton where were arrived Mᵣ & Mʳˢ· Schutz, play'd at Whist. wrote to Mʳˢ· Charles Western.

Wensday Augˢᵗ· 1ˢᵗ·

Quite a fine day being dry with constant sunshine yet not oppressively hot, Mᵣ Witts & Francis made some visits in their ride. & Miss Holbrow brought Miss Pettat in a little open Carriage to stay an hour here, which time I could ill spare from much business particularly to prepare everything for the departure of all my Dear Boys the next Morn: wrote to my Sisᵗ Travell & Mʳˢ· Parsons.

Thursday Augˢᵗ· 2ᵈ·

A very fine hot Day true old summer weather, being a gloomy Morning, quite so to my feelings, which could very ill stand parting with all my Dear Boys, sweet Francis to Elmore, & the 2 others with Molly to proceed on to my Sisters house at Cheltenham, for the advantage of becoming day scholars at Mᵣ Fowlers School. Mʳˢ· Schutz & Miss Wiltshire rode here & made me a pleasant visit to them succeeded Mᵣ & Mʳˢ· Scott, & Miss Scott & another Lady, who made a still longer visit, I walk'd a little after Tea. rec'd a satisfactory Letter fᵐ· Sisᵗ Travell

Friday Augˢᵗ· 3ᵈ·

Most uncommonly hot, so sultry that it was with difficulty anyone could move about Mᵣ Witts went to pay a Bridal visit to Mᵣ & Mʳˢ· Wathen at New house, in his absence I rec'd a visit from Mᵣ Jeffries, he was succeeded by Mʳˢ· Holbrow & Mʳˢ· Pearce in their little open carriage to learn many particulars of a route into Derbyshire; before they could possibly be return'd home & while we were at Dinner fell a most violent Thunderstorm, which continued more or less the whole evening; & was dreadfully hot & close wᶜʰ· with the fatigue of packing &'c almost over set me. rec'd a Letter from Mʳˢ· Naper.

Saturday Augˢᵗ· 4ᵗʰ·

A very disagreable thick wetting fog, & extremely close & hot, but it went off between 9 & 10 & gave us a most beautiful day for beginning our Journey to Margate; only stopd at Cirencester for Hay & water, dined at Fairford & staid two hours, drank Tea at Farringdon & staid two hours more, & lay at Kingston Inn having gone 38 miles in the day, it is a very small paltry looking place, but were very well accomodated & comfortable. wrote to Miss Gorges.

113. Fairford Church.

Sunday Aug^{st.} 5th.

A most delightful Day for travelling being warm & bright yet a very fine air, went 14 miles to Dorchester, passing thro' Abingdon before ½ past 10, where we baited near three hours, & took the advantage of going to Church, there, which is a large old Cathedral building, but newly fenc'd, & neatly fitted up, very well satisfied with the service altogether a pretty good reader & preacher, & most excellent singing, a very full band both vocal & instrumental quite in the Oratorio stile; eat some cold meat before we set out for Henly which we found a long hot stage there we dined, & went on in the evening with Post Horses to the Sun at Maidenhead in all 37 miles.

Monday Aug^{st.} 6th.

If possible a still more charming day dull & rather foggy in the Morning early, but grew to be rather hotter than either of the former Days & yet with a fine cool air; left Maidenhead at 9, & went 6 miles to Windsor, a kind of private road but very good & chiefly lying across rich corn fields, pleasing both to the eye & imagination from the appearance of great plenty, only stopp'd at Windsor while the Horses had Hay & water, & went on 7 miles more to Staines, leaving Egham on the left hand, & the road mostly going to the side of the Thames which afforded many delightful views & the roads charming & with little or no Hills. at the Buck at Staines we found a great difficulty to have either ourselves or Horses accomodated, the House running over with travellers going to the Camp at Bagshot, but the Garden being large & pretty took the over flowings went on to Hampton Court, over Sunbury Common

114. Staines Church.

& much fine open ground both of Corn & Heathland about 8 miles, & frequent views of the River very beautiful, order'd our Dinner at the Toy & went to see the Palace which answer'd our expectation more than we expected, very fine suites of appartments some good pictures chiefly portraits, & great quantities of old ornamental china chiefly blue & white got a miserable hurrying hot Dinner, & were very glad to go 10 miles farther to Mitcham in Surrey thro' Kingston, & part of it thro' a pretty country & all an excellent road the Kings Head a moderate Inn.

Witts Family Papers F183

1792

Tuesday Aug^(st.) 7^(th.)

In all respects just such weather as the former Days & as fine as possible for travelling not being oppressively hot, left Mitcham at the usual hour, & passing thro Croyden, Bromley &c were very happy to find ourselves passing by M^(rs.) Dolphins Door on Chislehurst Common, who with her Daughters rec'd us most kindly, & gave us an early Dinner to suffer us to proceed on to Farmingham, where we drank Tea, & had an unexpected visit from M^(r) Henry Dimock who had a curacy in the Neighbourhood, & went on to Wrotham, where we arrived just as it was dark but too much so to permit us to see clearly the very fine view from the Hill which you descend to the Town, but the whole road was beautifull & rich. Wrotham is a poor little Town & a very moderate Inn in point of accomodation. wrote to M^(rs.) Naper.

Wensday Aug^(st.) 8^(th.)

A continuance of the same beautiful weather, as well as of the same delightfull rich country to pass through, for the 11 miles to Maidstone were some of the pleasantest we had pass'd, thro abounding with fine Hop yards as well as other cultivation on the right of the 5 mile stone we left Town Malling a neat looking Town; at Maidstone we stopp'd to bait the Horses for an hour & ½ & walk'd about the Town & went into the Church which is large

115. Maidstone Church.

& handsome from thence to Sittingbourne is 16 miles of a very pretty tho chiefly a retired road thro woods, the Rose Inn there is become most sumptuous in point of furniture & of every kind of accomodation of course we had a famous good Dinner, & reach'd Canterbury 16 miles more as it was dark, the whole of which was a very beautiful road. we found the Fountain Inn very commodious, & being well tired I was glad to get early into a good Bed. wrote to my Sister Travell

116. Canterbury Cathedral.

Thursday Aug^st. the 9th.

A much hotter day than any of the former ones the wind being changed to the south: went to Morning Prayers at the Cathedral much gratified by a fine anthem, set out directly afterwards for Margate where we arrived between 2 & 3 having had a very hot dusty ride found M^r & M^rs. Granville ready to receive us with whom we dined very pleasantly & spent the remainder of the Day with them drinking Tea at Surflius Gallery, & walking till quite dark on the Pier &c & home to supper with them after which retired early to our comfortable Lodging within 2 Doors of them namely at N°. 5 S^t. Johns Place.

Friday Aug^st. 10th.

Quite as hot a day, the air being more thick & oppressive & in the evening heavy black clouds portending rain or thunder but none came, went on the Sea for 2 or 3 hours in the Morning, with the Granvilles in a very pleasant boat, but there was so little wind stirring, & against tide we could go but to a very little distance but I enjoy'd it much. dined very comfortably at home, the Gentlemen rode out to Kingsgate, & M^rs. Granville & I drank Tea & sat till a late hour in Surfleus Gallery,[1] & just look'd in at Halls Library on our return home but too hot to bear to stay long. rec'd a very satisfactory Letter from my Sister Travell.

Saturday Aug^st. 11th.

No change in the weather but almost hot enough to wear out our patience as well as ones strength, which I endeavoured to recruit by going into the sea after breakfast,[2] came home

---

1. The spelling changes in the diary from 'Surflius' to 'Surfleus'.
2. Sea-bathing in the 1790s was a quick total submersion in the water and was intended as a medical treatment rather than a pleasant experience. The bather took off all his or her clothes in the bathing machine and was then plunged into the sea by attendants. Margate's enhancement to the bathing machine came in around 1750, when Benjamin Beale invented a canvas hood which could be pulled down to protect the naked sea-bather from prying eyes. The hiring charge for a bathing machine in around 1770 varied from 9d. for two or more gentlemen bathing themselves to 1/6 for a gentleman taking a machine with a guide. Naked bathing continued until the 1860s when a byelaw was passed stating that male and female bathers were to be segregated by not less than sixty feet, and that all owners of bathing machines would provide gowns or dresses to female bathers and drawers or similar to male bathers.

*117. Kingsgate,
near Broadstairs.*

& dresst for the day & took M^rs. Granville in the chaise to visit L^dy. Lifford at Ramsgate,[3] during which I sat at the Library & was fortunate enough to meet wth M^r. Higginson with whom I went to survey the rooms; M^r & M^rs. Granville drank Tea with us & brought S^r. Thos. Tancred & his Bro^r,[4] Johns Schoolfellows, too hot to move more than to Surfleus Gallery, & Halls library sup'd with our Neighbours.

Sunday Aug^st. 12th.

If possible still hotter than ever almost broil'd at Church, tho we sat in the Chancel much the coolest place, but the crowds were very great, made 2 or 3 visits afterwards, but were unwise in moving so much in the heat. The Granvilles dined with us & at 6 o'clock we went to Kingsgate & Broad Stairs the Gentlemen on Horseback, & John with us in the Chaise, the views beautiful tho the air was thick; drank Tea very badly at Broad Stairs not at home till quite dark & went to the Sunday evenings promenade at the Rooms which were full & brilliant supt with the Granvilles, rec'd a Letter from my sweet Francis & answer'd it.

Monday Aug^st. 13th.

Very much the same weather, extremely hot & sultry having bath'd I walk'd very little in the Morn^g. excepting to a shop or two, dined with the Granvilles & went with them to Drink Tea at Surfleus Gallery in order to be in readiness to see the fireworks that were to be exhibited on a Stage erected on the Sea opposite, in honor of the Prince of Wales's Birthday from numbers obliged like many others to take up with the lower Gallery, but got a good view of some were worth seeing, but more the lively scene both on land & water from the number of the spectators not at home till ½ past ten well tired. wrote to Lady Betty Chaplin & Miss Dolphin.

---

3. Ambrosia Hewitt, *née* Bayley (17??–1807), widow of James Hewitt, 1st Viscount Lifford.
4. Sir Thomas Tancred (1780–1844), 6th Baronet. Thomas succeeded to the baronetcy at the age of four. He was a school friend of John Granville, junior.

118. Dandelion, Garlinge, near Margate.

Tuesday Aug^st. 14th.

Quite a pleasant Day being not near so hot which made moving pleasant, attempted to go soon after breakfast in a Boat fishing for whiting but the tide not serving we defer'd it till the afternoon having an early Dinner for that purpose, but could not set out so soon as we intended being fearful of rain, but at last ventured for 2 hours, but it was so calm it was not pleasant nor very successful in point of fishing, drank Tea afterwards, in Surfleus Gallery, stroled about Halls Library for ½ an hour & sup'd with the Granvilles.

Wensday Aug^st. 15th.

Some appearance of rain in the Morning but it soon dispatchd & was a beautiful fine Day I bathd & between 12 & one our whole party went to the public Breakfast at Dandelion,[5] a pretty Garden about a mile & half from the Town, where great numbers of all discriptions were assembled, & a <u>choice</u> set of Dancers upon a raised platform afforded much amusement did not return home till past three, drank Tea with M^r & Miss Rogers's & play'd at Cards there & sat ½ an hour in a great crowd at Halls & supt with the Granvilles

Thursday Aug^st. 16th.

Some change in the weather having been some rain early in the Morn: as well as in the night, & was very stormy till noon when it became fine again Mr Witts went very little out in the Morn: being very indifferent in his Stomach & bowels; M^rs. G: & I took our work & sat in Miss Surfleus gallery M^rs. Higginson & her Sister made me an agreable visit from Ramsgate; dresst after Dinner & went to the Ball the Rogers family being of our party a large good one & many amusing figures. rec'd a Letter from Lady Edward Bentinck.

---

5.   Dandelion is about a mile to the south-west of Margate, the fortified mansion of a family of that name in the time of Edward I—Dent de Lyon.

Friday Aug^{st.} 17th.

Upon the whole a warm fine Day tho a strong mixture of clouds & sunshine; I bath'd, & after breakfast made a visit or two & then mounted my double Horse & rode to Birchington, attended by Mrs. Granville, Mr Greaves, & my Husband very pleasant tho at times much too hot. the Granvilles drank Tea with us, & we went to the Play where we were join'd by the Rogers family, the Play a humorous Comedy Notoriety,[6] & the Farce a very bad one tho the title all in good humor, a very moderate set of performers thinking merit consisting in making a great noise which sent me home with the headache rec'd a Letter from my Sister Travell with a charming account of my Dear Boys.

119. The Theatre, Hawley Square, Margate.

Saturday Aug^{st.} 18th.

One of the most intire soaking wet days ever known, attended by violent high wind & storms no possibility of moving, Mrs. Granville spent the greater part of the Morning working & most comfortable conversation, they all came in the afternoon, to Tea & staid supper & play'd a merry game at Quadrille. rec'd a Letter from Mrs. Naper & wrote to Mrs. Buxton & Miss Byam condolence on the Death of Lord Tracy.[7]

Sunday Aug^{st.} 19th.

Rather wet in the Morning early but more dry & fine the remainder of the day excepting a most violent high cold wind, which made it very unpleasant moving about, & most disagreable boisterous bathing, went to Church with M^{rs.} G: a most surprizing & disagreable ranting Sermon, after Church, she & I & Mr Witts who was far from well went an airing to Kingsgate &'c, on our return went to Surfleus Gallery to see the violence of the waves, dined with our Neighbours & drank Tea at Surfleus, where we were join'd by an agreable party of Gentlemen who attended us the Sunday evenings promenade at the rooms which were very full supt with the Granvilles.

Monday Aug^{st.} 20th.

A very fine pleasant Day tho towards evening strong symptoms of storm & rain after breakfast walk'd about shopping with Mrs. Granville, & on our return went out on horseback with our own two Gentlemen, a very pleasant ride to Ramsgate, where we made visits & walk'd on the Pier admiring the glorious Sea view from there drank Tea at

---

6. Frederick Reynolds (1764–1841). Reynold's first play was performed in Bath in 1785. *Notoriety*, a comedy, appears to have been first performed in 1792.
7. *See* the note in F178 above. Thomas Charles Tracy died on 10 August 1792. Louisa Bathurst, the sister of Thomas Charles Tracy's late wife Harriet, had married George Byam of Apps Court. Miss Byam was presumably a daughter, and therefore niece to Lord Tracy.

Mr Barwells, meeting Granvilles & others & all adjourn'd to the Rooms in expectation of a Ball but none was made up, & very few card Tables. I play'd at Cassino in an agreable set.

Tuesday Aug$^{st.}$ 21$^{st.}$

Quite a disagreable Day, violent hard rain early in the Morning which made it miserable uncomfortable Bathing, & so wet & damp the remainder of the day that it was quite confining, sat at home all the Morning alone very busy writting &c. M^r & M$^{rs.}$ Granville &

120. Margate.

Son, & Mr Rogers & his two Daughters & Son drank Tea here, & we made up a Table at Whist & Commerce quite grand. wrote to Lady Edwd Bentinck & M$^{rs.}$ Tyrwhitt & rec'd a Letter from my Dear Francis.

Wensday Aug$^{st.}$ 22^d.

Something a better day & not much being wet & stormy at various times of the Day & quite damp & cold, M$^{rs.}$ Granville & I attempted taking drive to Broad Stairs in the Morning, but driven back by a violent Shower, & she spent the remainder of the Morning with me, we dined with them meeting Johns two young Friends the Simpsons, & in the afternoon M$^{rs.}$ G. Mr Witts & I drove to Ramsgate, return'd as it was dark to Drink Tea at Miss Surfleus, at Halls Library made a party with M$^{rs.}$ Sober & Mr Swinnerton to play at Cassino at the Rooms very lively & pleasant. wrote a long Letter to M$^{rs.}$ Naper.

Thursday Aug$^{st.}$ 23^d.

Very stormy & disagreable, with short flying showers but nothing of any consequence detain a great while before we could Bathe in the Morning by the great numbers assembled for that purpose; M$^{rs.}$ Granville & I again sallied forth after breakfast in the Chaise for Broad Stairs, did not find the Gores who I went to see at home, but join'd Mr Graves & Mr Swinnerton in walking about the place return'd home a beautiful drive by Kingsgate went to the Ball but without M$^{rs.}$ G: who was unwell a moderate Ball, play'd at Whist in M$^{rs.}$ Barwells party all <u>strange</u> but herself. rec'd a Letter from Miss Snow & answer'd it.

Friday Aug$^{st.}$ 24$^{th.}$

Windy but rather a fine Day upon the whole, sufficiently so to tempt us <u>all</u> to ride to Ramsgate went the near way, & came back by St Peters, the Granvilles visited Lady Lifford & we Mr Wilmot in a beautiful house in Prospect Row commanding a fine Sea view, the Granvilles dined with us, walk'd to the Pier after Dinner drank Tea with the Granvilles meeting the Rogers family a Table at whist & Cassino & went to Halls Library afterwards; dull enough.

Saturday Aug$^{st.}$ 25$^{th.}$

Had been a little rain in the night & was a doubtful looking Morning, but turn'd out dry & fine tho very windy, bath'd early, & went at <u>**mid-day**</u> with M$^{rs.}$ G: in the chaise to the

121. Old Church, Margate.

'Dandelion' Breakfast which by rain had been postponed from Wensday, not very full but a very gay lively scene, went in the evening to the Cottilion Ball,[8] a very good set, play'd at ½ crown Cassino with a smart party. rec'd a Letter from my Sis.ᵗ Travell with a charming account of the Dear Boys & wrote to M.ʳˢ Guydickens.

Sunday Aug.ˢᵗ y.ᵉ 26.ᵗʰ

Fine early in the Morning, but soon became lowering & while we were at Church a very violent Storm which detain'd us there a considerable time in a very great crowd, & there was frequent hard showers in the course of the day, but dry & fine in the evening; an entertaining political Sermon of a great length, M.ʳˢ Granville & I took an airing between Church & Dinner little regarding the Storms, to Pegwell Bay & home thro' Ramsgate & S.ᵗ Peters, all drank Tea in Surfleus Gallery, & concluded with looking in at the Promenade at the Rooms where were 300 assembled a wonderful sight altogether supt with the Granvilles rec'd a Letter from Miss Snow.

Monday Aug.ˢᵗ 27.ᵗʰ

Early in the day bright but very high wind & rather Stormy, yet M.ʳˢ Granville her Son, M.ᵗ Witts & I ventured in a Boat & were out 3 hours coasting towards Reculver, & as the weather improved we very much liked it, tho at times the Sea ran very high, drank Tea at M.ᵗ Barwells & went with their party to a smart Ball, call'd the first dress'd one, a few laughable minuets & all in form I play'd in the same Cassino set.

Tuesday Aug.ˢᵗ 28.ᵗʰ

A very fine day, little wind & constant sunshine which tempted us again on the water M.ᵗ G. being of the party instead of his Son, were out 4 hours, going very near to Ramsgate, the

---

8. A cotillion ball was one at which the dances were in the French eighteenth-century style; a social dance was based on a continual change of partners with elaborate steps.

122. Ramsgate.

views of which, as well as of Kingsgate & Broad Stairs were very gratifying, were completely tired on our return & the whole evening. drank Tea at Mr Rogers's our two families, & meeting two Ladies a whist & Commerce Party at which I was successful look'd in at Halls Library as we came home but glad to come home early & go to Bed. rec'd Letters from M^rs. Guydickens, Miss Byam, & Dear Francis.

Wensday Aug^st. 29th.

Quite an uncommon day for the season of the year being a most violent strong N: East wind from Morn: to night without any cessation scarce able to stand on ones legs, which prevented our intended jaunt to Dover, M^rs. G & I air'd to Broad Stairs & home by Kingsgate to please ourselves with the fine view of the Ocean there in such a storm, walk'd home from the lower Town & call'd in at the Library, staid at home all the evening the Granvilles drinking Tea with me & play'd at Quadrille with much spirit rec'd Letters from Lady Edward Bentinck Miss Dolphin & Mr Edward Hunt. wrote to Lady Edward & my Dear Francis.

Thursday Aug^st. 30th.

A very strong wind early in the Day but turn'd out a tolerable fine one excepting a smart shower of rain at Noon, walk'd to the Pier with the Granvilles after Breakfast, to survey the waves & learn intelligence about the Dutch Vessel that had been lost on the sounds the night before; M^rs. G: Mr Witts & I air'd in the Chaise to Ramsgate & home by Pegwell Bay; in the evening went to a full handsome Ball, play'd at Cassino in a new Party. rec'd Letters from M^rs. Naper & M^rs. Savage & wrote to my Sis^t Travell.

Friday Aug^{st.} 31st.

A very fine mild day being a happy mixture of
shade & sunshine & little or no wind, bathed
very early, to enable us to set out in good time
on our Dover Jaunt, M^{rs.} G: her Son & I in the
Chaise & the two Gentlemen on Horseback,
went thro Sandwich 9 miles distant a large
struggling Town with three Churches, about
a mile from the Sea with which it is connected
by the River Stour which brings Vessels of
considerable size up to the Town besides which
it has a great Salt Trade, carried on a mile from
the Town, the Sea Water being collected in Pans,

123. *Gateway at Kingsgate.*

to be absorbed by the Sun as at Lymington, here we did not stop, but proceeded on to Deal
seven miles further, over a tolerable good but narrow sandy road. Deal is a large Town with
very narrow streets, & nearer to the Water edge than any Town I ever saw, the Tide was
fortunately in, & floated directly close under the windows of the Hoop & Griffin Inn where
we dined, not very well but very merrily before which we walk'd a little about the Town &
into some smuggling I hope without making any purchases to speak on. Mr Witts exchanged
with John Granville & attended us to Dover 9 miles farther, much the same sort of road but
a more dull country, the first view of Dover Castle on a fine eminence overlooking the Town
& Sea, is very noble, & the Hill down to the Town steep & long. Dover is a very large Town,
tho the streets are narrow, ill built & dirty the Principal Inns are situated on the back water
which at low tide makes them very disagreable, & the smell of the mud horrid, we could gain
no admittance at the York Hotel, & the Ship Inn, was the worst I ever was at both in respect

124. *Sandwich.*

354

125. Dover Castle.

to dirt & accomodation of every kind M^rs· G: & Mr Witts & I play'd at Cassino, got a very moderate supper & went ill satisfied to our bad Beds. rec'd a Letter from Miss Gorges.

Saturday Sep^r· 1st·

Very hot & close in the Morning, some signs of rain at mid.day but none came of any consequence, & it was a pleasant afternoon; after eating an execrable breakfast, we got into a Boat conducted by 4 Men to row under Shakespears Cliff, the tide was high which caused the Sea to be very rough, & I to be dreadfully sick the greater part of the hour we were out, & so were all the party in some degree, but the view of the Cliff was very fine, on our

126. Dover.

127. Dover.

return to the Inn were amus'd by a party of our acquaintance calling on us, who were just landed in the Packet from Calais full of French politics M^r & M^rs· Shode & Mr Accourt;[9] the weather made us fearful of mounting up to the Castle, & breaking the Pole of the Chaise kept us longer in Dover than we liked but when we did set out, went an intire different road to Sandwich, part of the London road, as much richer more cultivated country, dined very well at the Bell at Sandwich, & reach'd Margate pretty thoroughly tired between 8 & 9, & after drinking Tea walk'd by Moonlight to refresh ourselves before we went to Bed.

Sunday Sepr 2^d·

Quite a beautiful day throughout not too hot tho constant sunshine, very charming bathing, a very crowded Church, &c. good Sunday preacher, walk'd afterwards to the Pier & Gallery dined at home & drank Tea with M^rs· Granville at Surfleus, & look'd in at the Rooms which were detestably hot & disagreable, said to be 500 persons in the course of the evening. rec'd a very pleasing Letter from Lady Edward Bentinck.

Monday Sepr 3^d·

Dry but extremely windy & towards evening miserably cold, Mr Wilmot sat an hour with us early in the Day after which we rode with M^rs· Granville to Kingsgate & home by S^t· Peters,

---

9. William Pierce Ashe À'Court of Heytesbury, Wiltshire (1747–1817). À'Court was M.P. for Heytesbury. He was extremely well known in Cheltenham due to the notorious murder of his wife Katherine, who was poisoned with arsenic on 23 September 1776 by a manservant, Joseph Armstrong, whom she had detected in the act of stealing her jewellery.

& on our return sat at Halls Library seeing a great collection of fine folks promenade & ride about; in the afternoon walk'd to Surfleus Gallery where quite unexpectedly were assembled a great crowd to survey many sports exhibiting on the sands such as a foot race for a pair of Stays, men running tyed up in Sack Bags & many &'cs drank Tea with the Granvilles, play'd at Quadrille & supt also wrote to M$^{rs.}$ Savage.

Tuesday Sepr 4$^{th.}$

In the Morning rather cloudy & strong appearance of rain but none fell of any consequence & it was a very fine afternoon, after breakfast made some visits came home early to dress to dine at Mr Higginsons at Ramsgate, where we met Major & M$^{rs.}$ Metcalfe, M^r & M$^{rs.}$ Barwell & a Mr Flayer, very agreable, went with them all to the Ball at 9 o'clock which was not very full, play'd 3 rubbers at Whist in a very sober quiet set, & came home between 12 & one by a delightful Moon rec'd Letters from M$^{rs.}$ Tyrwhitt, My Sis^r Travell & my Dear Francis charming accounts of all my Dear Fellows. wrote to Miss Gorges.

Wensday Sepr 5$^{th.}$

A very pleasant Day tho at times cloudy & at 8 in the evening a most violent storm of rain for an hour; went with the Granvilles to the Dandelion Breakfast, which was particularly brilliant & crowded 850 persons many of rank & numbers very genteel, not at home till near 4 o'clock; drank Tea at Surfleus where we were detain'd by the rain & obliged to come home in chairs the Granvilles attended us to play at Quadrille & eat a bit of supper.

Thursday Sepr 6$^{th.}$

Quite a fine Day, at times very hot gleams & strong clouds but no rain, rode to Broad Stairs, got off to hunt about Lodgings for Miss Snows return'd home by Kingsgate, dined at Mr Granvilles return'd home early to dress for the Ball, took M$^{rs.}$ J. Jones with us, a very fine full Ball, I play'd in the old set at Cassino with some more <u>smarts</u> added to it rec'd a Letter from Miss Anne Snow & answer'd it.

128. Fort Rock, Margate.

Friday Sep.r 7th.

A fine Day tho close & cloudy, & very warm & towards evening little flying rain but of no consequence attended M.rs. Granville to make her take leave visits, & afterwards walk'd with her round & about the Fort &'c ending with the Galleries & Library & after Dinner M.rs. G. & I took an airing to Dandelion Birchington &'c, growing dark very soon, & getting into very moderate roads it was far from pleasant drank Tea at Surfleus, look'd into the Rooms where was none but Gentlemen, & sat an hour at Halls rather more lively than usual, M.rs. G: came home with us & play'd at Cassino. wrote to M.rs. Naper.

Saturday Sep.r 8th.

Very much the same sort of weather in the Morning, but at Noon a most violent storm of rain & hail; M.rs. Granville & I went in the Chaise to Ramsgate, made a very pleasant visit to the Higginsons & eat Sandwichs, came home by Broadstairs to see more about the Snows Lodgings, detain'd by the rain for an hour at Halls but not tired there was so many amusing characters to converse with; went to the Ball, attracted by the idea of Cottilions & reels, which answer'd a very genteel Ball. rec'd Letters from M.rs. Buxton & Miss Anne Snow.

Monday Sep.r 10th.

Dark & stormy & much like rain but none of any consequence fell in the course of the day, bid adieu with much regret to our good friends the Granvilles who set off before nine, & we seemd lost without them. I did not bath till after breakfast having got a bad cold, went imediately after, an new airing to the Village of Pegwell at the side of the Bay & home by Ramsgate, on our return walk'd about till Dinner time & did not stir out afterwards but nursed my cold & work'd & read.

Tuesday Sep.r 11th.

A similar Day to yesterday only rather more rain, a violent storm at mid.day attended with loud thunder & extremely cold. My cold very indifferent yet I went in the Chaise to Broad

129. Ramsgate Harbour.

130. Margate.

Stairs, taking Miss Snows William who had arrived in the Morning to investigate more about their Lodgings. ventured to the Play in the evening much wrapp'd up & in a chair going & returning. met M^r. & M^rs. S: Jones there by appointment, a very full house, the Play bespoke by M^rs. Hastings, very tolerably amused; both by the Country Girl & the Spoilt Child M^rs. Davies a pretty good copiest of M^rs. Jordan.[10] rec'd Letters from my Sis^r. Travell & my Dear Francis most pleasing accounts of all my Dear little fellows.

Wensday Sepr. 12th.

A very disagreable Day, being a high cold wind, & at times sharp rain, I was miserably ill all Day with my cold, unable to do anything but read novels & scarce that. M^r. Witts call'd in the evening on Miss Snows who arrived to a late Dinner at Mitchevers Hottel.[11]

Thursday Sepr. 13th.

Still very Stormy disagreable weather & tho a good deal of sunshine was most bitterly cold Miss Snow call'd on me after breakfast & invited us to dine with them, I air'd to Kingsgate & S^t. Peters & at 3 o'clock went to them, & spent a very chearful Dinner & supper playing many rubbers at Cassino came home late in a Chaise well wrappd up for fear of increasing my cold which was still very bad. –

Friday Sepr. 14th.

A very thick Fog, which at Noon turnd to rain, & so continued very frequently for the remainder of the Day, I just got down to Halls Library before it began, where a great variety of persons were met together, I waited there while M^r. Witts went to find out Lady Hereford who came the night before. she came to take me up in her Carriage to go a Lodging hunting. Miss Snows & Miss Turners dined & supt with us, much Cassino & laughing. wrote to my Sis^r. Travell.

---

10.   *The Country Girl* was a play by David Garrick. *The Spoil'd Child* was probably by Isaac Bickerstaffe.
11.   This is very difficult to read and it could be 'Mitcheners'. No reference has been found.

Saturday Sep.r 15th.

Had been a most uncommon violent Storm of wind, attended by a little rain in the night, & the violence of the wind never abated the whole day, I made some visits & did some bussiness going about in the Carriage, & went also to call on Lady Hereford at Chappel Hill, went to the Cottillion Ball, taking Mrs. & Miss Holbrow with me, full & smart I play'd at Cassino with Mrs. Metcalfe, Mr. Churchill & Captn. Floyer. rec'd a Letter from Mrs. Naper.

Sunday Sep.r 16th.

The Storm quite gone & in its place a sharp frost & very cold tho fine & pleasant, went to Morning church, after which Lady Hereford sat an hour with us, we then walk'd to the Pier &'c dined early, in order to take an airing, which we did to Kingsgate, Ramsgate &'c, the evening so clear I never saw the Country look so beautiful drank Tea tête tete at Surfleus & spent an hour at the Rooms full but not very brilliant.

Monday Sep.r 17th.

Something of a Frost, & a very bright fine Morning, but grew cold & cloudy at Noon & wet at night, went imediately after breakfast on horseback to Broad Stairs to call on Miss Snows who we found pretty comfortably settled in their Lodgings; Dined with Lady Hereford at Chappel Hill, meeting Mr. Lloyd, the Clergyman of Margate, an excellent Dinner & very chearful, after Tea went to the Ball, which was thin & cold, I play'd at Cassino with Mrs. Metcalfe & the same two Gentlemen.

Tuesday Sep.r 18th.

Extremely cold & Stormy but scarce any rain fell, went at 11 o'clock to Broad Stairs in the chaise, to Miss Snows, when I got into Miss Annes Phaeton, the other 4 in & about the Chaise & went to Pegwell Bay to see a Boat race the idea of which had collected great numbers of very genteel people to see it, tho in fact there was little or nothing to see a very good cold collation was the best part of the sport, returnd to Broad Stairs to Dinner very merry, 3 rubbers at Cassino after Tea & came home without fear by the light of our Lamps at 10 o'clock rec'd Letters from Mrs. Granville, my Sisr. Travell & my Dear Francis.

Wensday Sep.r 19th.

Very much the same kind of weather rather more Sun than the former Day, but still very windy & cold, Miss Snows call'd on us to go together to Dandelion breakfast, where there was a genteel set of Company but not very numerous, on our return walk'd about till Dinner Time, in the evening went for an hour to Halls Library which was dull & very stupid. wrote to Lady Edward Bentinck Miss Dolphin & my Sweet Francis.

Thursday Sep.r 20th.

Bright tho windy and cold, till mid.day when it became soon cloudy & afterwards most violent rain for several hours, I went out early to make my take leave visits which were fortunate dined with Lady Hereford only our own trio, took Miss Dickens with us to the

131. Tunbridge Wells, from the Frant Road.

Ball which was a very brilliant one crowded & very smartly dress'd owing to the Dutchess of Cumberlands being there,[12] to whom & a select party a Supper was given by some Gentlemen I play'd at Cribbage & sat much with M[rs.] Holbrow &c — wrote to M[rs.] Granville

Friday Sep[r.] 21[st.]

Very much the same cold, stormy & uncomfortable weather, some showers but not so wet as the former Day, much engaged with packing & other preparations for our departure next day, but dedicated an hour or two in the Morning to Miss Snows who call'd on us & wanted to be walk'd about drank Tea at Miss Surfleus, look'd in at Halls Library & home early.

Saturday Sep[r.] 22[d.]

Had been a night of excessive hard rain, was a bright showey Morning, but a most violent & long storm of rain & hail at mid.day, we left Margate without any prodigeous regret at 10 o'clock dined at Canterbury, where we were detain'd till the rain was over, & had a pleasant drive to Sittingbourne where we slept at the Rose, the best appointed Inn in all respects I was ever at. Lady Blackwood who was likewise there sat an hour with us.[13] we play'd a duett at Cassino.

---

12. Anne, Duchess of Cumberland (1743–1808), widow of H.R.H. Frederick, Duke of Cumberland (1745–1790), the son of Frederick, Prince of Wales. Anne had been born Anne Luttrel. She had married Christopher Horton of Catton Hall, Derbyshire, but following his death she married Frederick in 1771. He was referred to as probably the most foolish of Frederick's sons!

13. Dorcas Blackwood, *née* Stevenson (17?? –1807), wife of Sir John Blackwood, 2nd Baronet, of Ballyleidy (17??–1799). After his death Dorcas was created a peeress of Ireland in her own right as Baroness Dufferin & Claneboye.

Sunday Sep.ʳ 23.ᵈ

Quite a bright beautiful Day tho still very cold till
3 o'clock when a violent storm of rain came on,
& tho it did not last long it remain'd dark & cold
the remainder of the Day; reach'd Maidstone in
<u>tolerable</u> time to go to Church, a fine old building
& well fill'd both a good reader & preacher, the
latter in a very peculiar style, but much to the
purpose eat some cold meat & came on 19 miles
to Tunbridge Wells, thro a most beautiful country,
the scenery much improved by the Hop yards being
in a state of perfection, & in full picking; a tedious
5 miles from Tunbridge Town to the Wells both
as to Hills & deep sands, did not reach the Sussex
Tavern till 5 in the afternoon, got a pretty good
Dinner which we had scarcely finish'd, when M.ʳ
Cumberland came & sat an hour with us.[14] rec'd
Letters from M.ʳˢ Dolphin & my Sister Travell.

132. Richard Cumberland.

Monday Sep.ʳ 24.ᵗʰ

A truly miserable Day, being thick driving rain from Morn: to Night, making everything as
damp dirty & disagreable as possible, quite unsuitable to our first entrance to Tunbridge, it
just held up sufficiently to allow us to walk to breakfast at M.ʳ Cumberlands, on Sion Hill,
M.ʳˢ C. too ill to appear the whole Day, after breakfast, visited Lady Dacre,[15] M.ʳˢ Barwell
&'c, dined at M.ʳ Cumberlands where was no one but his youngest Son & a M.ʳ Brace
went with them to the Theatre which was crowded & brilliant, the part of Othello being
perform'd by M.ʳ William Cumberland[16] in a most capital manner & Iago by M.ʳ Badcock,
who tho esteem'd a great Actor did not shine so much as was expected in that most difficult
part but on the whole, it was a high entertainment, I sat by old Cumberland w.ᶜʰ made it still
more pleasant a stupid Farce seem'd wretched afterwards. wrote to M.ʳˢ Naper.

Tuesday Sep.ʳ 25.ᵗʰ

Still most miserably cold & Stormy & at Noon wet again for the greater part of the Day
went to the Well in Morning to drink water finding it agree with me wonderfully, & went
to look after a Lodging being quite tired of the Sussex Tavern fix'd upon apartments in Sion
House determing to stay a week but did not take possession of them till we went to Bed,
paddled about in the wet at Noon to drink water & pay visits & walk on the Pantiles, Dined

---

14.   Richard Cumberland (1732–1811), dramatist. *See* the note in F174 above.

15.   Anna Maria Barrett-Lennard, *née* Pratt (17??–1806). Anna Maria had married, in 1739, Thomas Barrett-Lennard,
       17th Baron Dacre (1717–1784).

16.   Richard Cumberland had four sons: Richard, who married the eldest daughter of the Earl of Buckinghamshire and
       died at Tobago; George, who entered the Royal Navy and died at the siege of Charleston; Charles, in the army; and
       William, here, who was in the navy. These last two sons survived their father. The eldest daughter (out of three),
       Elizabeth, married Lord Edward Bentinck and is detailed above.

133. Tunbridge Wells, the Walk.

at Lady Dacres most agreably, meeting M^rs. Munster, Miss Harding, M^r R: Harding, & Mr John Pelham, play'd both at Cribage & Cassino, went to the Ball with M^r & M^rs. Barwell which was full lively & pleasant, play'd 2 rubbers at Cassino with M^rs. Barwell & some other smarts not at home till past 12. rec'd Letters from Lady Edwd. Bentinck, Miss Gorges, & my Dear Francis & wrote to Miss Snow.

Wensday Sepr 26th.

For a wonder a day without any rain & clear uninterrupted sunshine from Morn: to night but still the air very cold, as usual drinking Water & walking on the Pantiles before Breakfast & at Noon made some visits, one to poor M^rs. Cumberland for 5 minutes only, her health & spirits being in so wretched a state, walk'd up to the Race ground, spent the whole evening at home writting & reading. wrote to my Sister Travell & my Dear Francis.

Thursday Sepr 27th.

Very foggy in the Morning, & tho that went off in great measure, yet it remain'd a dull quiet day without either sun or wind & after dark rain again, after breakfast ventured to mount my double Horse, & had a fine ride of 10 or 12 miles, to Eridge Place Lord Abergavenneys on the Lewes road to Grombridge,[17] over a fine country & fine rich views interspersed with both rocky & forest ground, the bye roads very moderate & all very hilly, walk'd after my

---

17. Eridge was the country seat of Henry Nevill, Earl of Abergavenny (1755–1826). Nevill succeeded to the earldom in 1785 and by 1790 was busily restoring the old family house of Eridge, where in 1573 Queen Elizabeth had been entertained by an ancestor.

return dress'd after Dinner to go with M^r & M$^{rs.}$ Barwell to a Public Tea drinking at the Rooms very pleasant & a smart dance afterwards of 12 or 14 couple I play'd at Cassino. rec'd a Letter from my Sis^r Travell

Friday Sepr 28$^{th.}$

A very disagreable dripping Morning & at Noon extreme rain for 2 or 3 hours; dry in the afternoon, but still very stormy & unpleasant Mr Cumberland sat an hour with us in the Morning & after I had drank my Water we went to call on Lady Dacre, kept there a considerable time by uncommon hard rain, drank Tea with M^r & M$^{rs.}$ Barwell & play'd several rubbers at Cassino with very bad success wrote to M$^{rs.}$ Buxton.

Saturday Sepr 29$^{th.}$

Very showery in the Morning, but clearing up a little after breakfast, we ventured to set out to survey Penshurst at about 6 miles, anciently the Seat of Sir Phillip Sidney, but now much dismantled in every respect is in the possession of a Minor of the name of Shelly, a very old place in a low situation on the Banks of the Medway, the state apartments still wear the face of much grandeur, the furniture being rich & costly, many good old Pictures & some envious pieces of Sculpture, but upon the whole the place is much out of repair,[18] & shews plainly it has been without an inhabitant for many years the roads tho turnpikes very bad the greater part of the of the way renderd much worse by the inundation of rain as it never ceased the whole time we were out nor indeed the remainder of the day.

Sunday Sepr 30$^{th.}$

Had been a very wet night, but was a more tolerable day than many former ones, the showers being not so frequent & very short, & it was much warmer went to Church in the Morning or rather Chappel w$^{ch.}$ is a very singular one, having no pews, the seats being cross benches, a good Organ, but a quarrel having recently happend among the Singers the singing was not so good as usual, Mr Benson the Minister of the Place, both a good reader & preacher, & crowded promenade afterwards on the Pantiles, where we staid but a short time, going an airing for 2 or 3 miles as far as Woodgate, on the road to Hastings, which shew'd us a variety of country, but the roads were most horrid drank Tea at the Rooms on the walks by appointment to meet M^r & M$^{rs.}$ Barwell &'c very lively & pleasant. rec'd a Letter from Miss Snow.

Monday Octr 1$^{st.}$

Quite a beautiful bright warm day from Morn to night such a rarity, it was matter both of wonder and delight to every one, & very fortunate for us who much wish'd to visit Bayham Abbey Mr Pratts about 6 miles distant in Sussex, the road very bad, the greater part of the way but the views very rich & enchanting, & the place itself extremely well worthy observation, the ruin of the Abbey is very much decay'd, & much overgrown with Ivy &c, the House is modern built but in the gothic stile, very correspondent & stands close to the

---

18.   Sir John Shelley-Sidney, 1st Baronet, of Penshurst (1771–1849).

134. Bayham Abbey.

Abbey, the ancient Gateway which is a very beautiful one leading to both, the River Medway was close by, & the shape of the ground in general very charming & the Meadows fertile & fine & the Hills cloth'd with wood thro' & by which there is walks & drives which we had not leisure to survey, return'd to Tunbridge Wells the same way, made a visit or two before Dinner, & went to a Tea drinking by invitation from M$^{rs.}$ Munster & Miss Hardinge at the great Room at the Sussex Tavern to meet Lady Dacre & many of their family & friends to the number of 16 very chearful & pleasant, after w$^{ch.}$ other company coming in there was 3 or 4 Card Tables which made very lively rooms, carried home in Mr Straceys Coach who Lodged in Sion House with us.

Tuesday Octr 2$^{d.}$

A sad & strange reverse of weather being a thick close misty Day, very dark & damp, little or no rain fell, tho it look'd likely to pour perpetualy sadly unfavourable to shew off all the fine country we were to pass thro on our route from Tunbridge which we left between 11 & 12, after breakfasting most agreably at the rooms on the walk in the same party as had drunk Tea together, by invitation from Lady Dacre, whose pleasing manner makes all parties agreable. were obliged to add a pair of Post Horses to our own to take us to Tunbridge Town & recd enough had we to have taken them all the way to Sevenoakes, as the road was hilly & dreadfully deep & dirty, at Riverhead 14 miles from Tunbridge Wells we stopp'd to bait & dine at what appear'd a miserable little Inn but turn'd out better & we were well accomodated & went afterwards 12 miles to Godstone, very good road & the greater part of the way thro' a most beautiful rich & varied country, interspersed with innumerable handsome seats, & Gentlemens houses, did not reach the White Hart at Godstone till after dark but with^t fear as the road was excellent. rec'd Letters from my Sister Travell & my Dear Francis with a charming acco^t of all my Dear little fellows.

Wensday Oct.ʳ 3ᵈ·

The same disagreable sort of thick damp weather, without rain but so hazzy it was very unpropitious to see the new Country thro' which we were to pass, the road was for the greater part of the 14 miles to Dorking very bad indeed not turnpike & in parts very sandy were near three hours & a ½ going it, the views in general fine, but a great sameness in appearance, at Dorking we baited at a miserable ale house Inn, & went 8 miles more to Mᵣ Richard Witts's at Evershed Place,[19] his Horses met us at Ockley 2 miles distant, & well they did, as the roads were so intolerable we should never have dragg'd thro' the mud, the place stands upon a knoll, but appears rather dull being quite surrounded with wood, Mᵣ & Mᵣˢ· Witts gave us a very pleasing reception a Miss Daniel was with them we play'd at Cribbage in the evening. rec'd a Letter from Mᵣˢ· Naper.

Thursday Oct.ʳ 4ᵗʰ·

Bright & fine for an hour or two early in the Morning, but soon grew too thick & damp to make it pleasant to think of stirring from the fireside & in the evening was again small rain, much work, talk & in the evening Cribbage. wrote to Lady Edward Bentinck.

Friday Oct.ʳ 5ᵗʰ·

Had been a night of very hard rain, & so continued many parts of the day at different times wᶜʰ· made it impossible for females to stir out of the House, very cold & rather stupid, conversation not being very brilliant, books none, so work alone kept me from going to sleep, & Cribbage & Cassino at night. rec'd a charming friendly pleasant Letter fʳᵐ· Mᵣˢ· Granville

Saturday Oct.ʳ 6ᵗʰ·

Still thick lowering weather very dark & misty, & at mid.day small rain or fog at times & continued in the evening; being dry after breakfast we all sallied forth in the Coach making a function of our Coach horses to see Mᵣ Locks at Norbury Park three miles from Dorking,[20] the other side of which the country improves greatly, & we pass'd by several very pretty places, particularly Mᵣ Edwᵈ· Bouveries under Box Hill a very romantic pretty spot.[21] Mᵣ Locks stands beautifully at the top of a very high Hill surrounded by fine Park ground & woods, & commanding an extensive & rich hill & vale view, the house is new & elegant, & the Drawing room more admired than I think it merits being fixed up quite in the Italian taste, paintings on the walls of Landscapes & flowers, but it has a gloomy effect & wants constant sunshine to shew it off, stopp'd an hour at the Red Lyon at Dorking to bait ourselves & horses not at home till 5 o'clock, Cribbage as usual.

---

19. Richard Witts was a trustee for his eldest son, Lee Steere Witts, who had inherited a fortune from his maternal grandfather, Lee Steere, Esq. Richard had done well in his marriage, for the Steere pedigree went back to the Norman Conquest, and they had lands and wealth to match. Richard married Martha Steere (1755–1815) in 1774 and later in the same year Lee Steere Witts was born. There were two other children: Richard and an unnamed daughter who became Mrs Daniells. The Lee Steere estate was at Evershed and during Lee Steere Witts' minority Richard managed the affairs, but unfortunately, as will be shown in later diaries, he managed them badly. The Miss Daniells referred to by Agnes must be a sister of Richard's son-in-law.
20. Norbury Park, near Box Hill, was built by William Lock (1732–1810) in 1770.
21. Edward Bouverie (1760–1824), M.P. for Downton (1796–1803). If the home of Edward was under Box Hill it must have been Betchworth House, the home of his elder brother, Charles Henry Bouverie (1752–1836), M.P. for Dorchester (1811–1812) and Downton (1812–1813). Edward Bouverie later moved to Squerries Court, Kent.

135. Boxhill and Burford Bridge.

Sunday Oct[r.] *7*[th.]

So very wet a Morning it was quite impossible to think of going to Church at Ockily 2 or 3 miles distant, but it ceased at mid.day, tho was very damp & miserable all day, & was one of the most dull long & stupid days I ever spent in my life, no books, little real conversation tho much talk; wrote to M[rs.] Granville & Miss Anne Snow but much disappointed at not having any Letters.

136. Norbury Park.

Monday Octr. 8th.

No rain the whole day, tho at times it look'd very likely & was at times very windy & stormy but the sun shew'd itself for a little while at mid.day, I mounted my double horse, but went a very little way the Pillion being so uneasy, & the roads such as to alarm me walk'd a little, but it was so miserably dirty I could only go about the Stables Cribbage as usual in the evening & commerce after Supper. wrote to Francis & Molly Braxton

Tuesday Octr. 9th.

Most discouraging weather still, as it rain'd small rain, more or less the whole of the day & was miserably cold & damp, & our home party not being very lively it was as usual a bitter long day, not even the Gentlemen could be out of the house long much Cribbage at night by way of a concluding Game. rec'd a Letter from L^dy. Edwd. Bentinck & my Dear Francis.

Wensday Octr. 10th.

Sad to tell, weather worse than ever being constant hard rain from Morn: to night & the wet & dirt beyond discription, which we fully experienced in attending M^r & M^rs. Witts & Miss Daniel in their Coach to Leatherhead about 12 miles to an annual Fair held there, & which if it had been dry weather is usually a very gay thing one booth being fill'd with many pretty ingenious things made by some Ladies in the Neighbourhood, & sold for the benefit of the poor, by which I benefited tho I never stirr'd'out of the Inn my Bro^r bringing me a pretty fairing; when our Friends set out to return home we got into our own Chaise & went 4 miles to Epsom to the Spread Eagle a good Inn thro' pouring rain. wrote to M^rs. Witts Friday Street & Miss Louisa Lee.

137.
Leatherhead Church.

138. St. Paul's and Blackfriars Bridge.

Thursday Oct.ʳ 11ᵗʰ·

A charming reverse in the weather, being a bright fine day from Morning to night quite delightful, left Epsom between 11 & 12 first having walk'd to see Dill Place at the end of the Town lately in the Possession of Mʳ Fitzherbert, now of a Mʳ Jedwyn an uncommon pretty place in a very singular stile, & in nice keeping, the drawing room very elegant opening into a very beautiful conservatory hot houses &'c in a capital stile, as likewise the Kitchin Garden farm yard &'c. 15 miles of excellent road to London tho very heavy from the late rains enterd the great Metropolis on Black Friars Bridge & were soon landed with our worthy Cousins in Friday Street who rec'd us most kindly, & we spent a very chearful evening playing at Whist. rec'd a Letter from Miss Anne Snow & Molly Braxton.

Friday Oct.ʳ 12ᵗʰ·

Another dry day till quite evening when it was again wet, but scarce any sunshine, Mʳˢ· Witts kindly lending me her Carriage, we were out near 4 hours in it making some visits & doing some bussiness Mʳ Richard Witts's two sons dined here & we went seven Witts's alltogether to Covent Garden Theatre, to see the Consious Lovers & two Strings to the Bow the performance of either very moderate,[22] but the view of the house from being newly & very superbly fitted up well worth observation return'd to a merry supper. rec'd a Letter from Miss Snow

Saturday Oct.ʳ 13ᵗʰ·

Very wet in the Morning early, tolerably dry in the middle of the Day, but cruelly wet again in the afternoon, I attended Mʳˢ· Witts after breakfast to be Electrified, amused

---

22. Sir Richard Steele (1672–1729), essayist and dramatist. Steele's comedy, *The Conscious Lovers*, was first performed in 1722. Robert Jephson (1736–1803), playwright. Born to an Anglo-Irish family in County Cork, Jephson served in the army and settled in London, associating there with Edmund Burke and others. *The Count of Narbonne* (1781), a successful stage version of his friend Horace Walpole's *Castle of Otranto*, played in London and Dublin. His farce *The Hotel, or the Servant with Two Masters* (1784) first appeared at Smock Alley, while Robert Owenson opened his Irish National Theatre with *The Carmelite* (1784). Among other plays were *Braganza* (1775), a tragedy, and *Two Strings to Your Bow* (1791), a farce.

by the sight of the operation & the Performers scientific observations upon it, M.rs & Miss Witts accompanied me afterwards to several shops, we dined comfortably only our own family party & had much conversation & a little Cards rec'd Letters from both my Sisters with a good account of the Dear Boys.

139. Covent Garden Theatre.

Sunday Oct.r 14.th

More violent rain than ever till ten o'clock & was little more the remainder of the Day, we attended the family to the Dissenting Meeting in Carter Lane, very well pleased with the Service, on our return M.rs Witts had provided a <u>hot</u> collation for us, to enable us to perform our little Journey before a very late Dinner, we left our good friends at one with much regret, being much indebted to them for their kind & friendly hospitality to us, & well pleased with each one of the Quartetto found the roads so very heavy & bad that we did not reach Michelefield Green till near ½ past 5, found neither Lord or Lady Edward Bentinck well, but truly obliging in their reception of us, Lord Clarendon & Miss Hughes with them, much lively & interesting conversation kept us up till one o'clock. rec'd a Letter from M.rs Buxton.

Monday Oct.r 15.th

Extremely wet the whole of the Day, & most of the time violently so, no one not obliged to it would think of stirring out, Miss Hughes went away, Lady Edward was very indifferent, but still chearful & the party so agreable & pleasant it was by no means a long Day, Lord Clarendon a very sensible agreable Man with much droll conversation.[23] a little Cards in the evening but more talk. wrote to M.rs Naper.

Tuesday Oct.r 16.th

Flattering hopes of the weather in the Morning, but it proved too bright to last, & before Noon was as violently wet as ever, but chiefly in hard darking storms, no possibility again of stirring out even into the Garden tho so near; Day spent much as the former, my sweet Friend rather better. wrote & rec'd a Letter from Miss Lee, & a charming one from my Dear Francis.

Wensday Oct.r 17.th

The same bright appearing Morning but soon grew cloudy & stormy tho but little rain fell in the course of the Day & the air was more mild Lord Clarendon left us to go to Lord Salisburys, Lord Edw.d & M.r Witts kept house with bad colds, Lady Edward not quite convalescent, so I alone ventured to walk out for an hour, glad to find the use of my Legs play'd at whist in the evening, much lively chat wrote to my Sister Travell & Francis.

---

23.   Thomas Villiers, Earl of Clarendon (1753–1824).

Thursday Oct.ᵣ 18th.

Quite a bright pleasant day a most happy change, & continued without rain from Morn: to night Lady Edward & I went in our Chaise to see our old Servant Nelly, who was Married & well settled at Rickmansworth, eat cold meat &'c with her on our return found the Duke of Portland making a Morning call;²⁴ Lord Clarendon returnd to us to Dinner a most pleasant evening, much lively & improving conversation & a little Cards. wrote to Miss Snow.

Friday Oct.ᵣ 19th.

Had been a little Frost in the night & was bright & fine till mid.day, when it became cloudy & in the evening again wet, bid adieu with much regret to our agreable old Friends, & new acquaintance at one o'clock, & passing thro' Wolford, & over Bushey Heath about 13 miles in the whole arrived at Dinner time at M.ʳˢ Lee's at Totteridge Park with whom besides her two Daughters we found M.ᵣ Arrowsmith & met with a very obliging reception, & good entertainment, play'd at Cribbage & Cassino.

Saturday Oct.ᵣ 20th.

A miserable wet Day throughout at times very hard rain, quite confining to the house work'd hard, & M.ᵣ Witts read to me in the Morning in Lavaters Phisiognomy not much amused by it,²⁵ M.ᵣ & M.ʳˢ Fiott dined with us as well as supt, 2 Tables at Cards I play'd Whist & Cassino.

Sunday Oct.ᵣ 21st.

Foggy in the Morning, but before 11 o'clock became very hard rain, which continued more or less the whole of the day, particularly so as we were going to Totteridge Church, & the Coach not being able to go up to the Door were considerably wetted, a pretty little new built Church, or rather a Chappel of ease to Hatfield service pretty well perform'd by a M.ᵣ Marsham, too wet to go anywhere, or do anything but just into the Greenhouse &'c, the day did not appear long from a happy mixture of books & conversation.

Monday Oct.ᵣ 22d.

Bright & pretty fine early in the Day but soon became stormy, & many very violent showers fell in the course of it; M.ᵣ Witts went early in the Chaise to a Nursery Garden near London & took M.ᵣ Arrowsmith with him who did not return, the former return'd to Dinner. we Ladies just visited M.ʳˢ Fiott where we found a large circle of Morning company afterwards M.ʳˢ Lee, Miss Lee & myself took an airing in their Chaise to Barnet, Hadley M.ᵣ Bethels &c liked it much in spite of rain w.ᶜʰ sometimes overtook us, a very comfortable chatty evening & a little cards rec'd a Letter from my Sister Travell.

---

24. Lord George Augustus Henry Cavendish, 3rd Duke of Portland (1738–1809). The duke was the Whig leader and prime minister in 1783 and from 1807 to 1809 and the elder brother of Edward. He had more than once rescued Edward from his financial scrapes. Of Edward's marriage to Elizabeth Cumberland, the gossip Mrs Mary Delaney had said the alliance was likely to produce serious consequences to the health of the Duke of Portland.

25. Johann Kaspar Lavater (1741–1801), physiognomist, theologian and writer, born in Zürich. In 1769 he received Protestant orders and made himself known by a volume of poems. He was a close friend of the artist Fuseli. He also invented the science of phrenology, which was based on the reading of significance into the bumps on the heads of a remarkable range of gullible clients. His works on physiognomy were written with the assistance of Goethe. He died of wounds sustained at the capture of Zürich by Masséna and after tending others among the wounded.

Tuesday Oct.ʳ 23.ᵈ

Had been a frost in the night, was a bright shewey Morning, which soon became dull tho did not rain the whole of the day & in the afternoon was again bright & fine, we walk'd between 2 & 3 hours all of us about the Gardens & premises & were entertain'd by seeing a fine course with Greyhounds & poor dress afforded us much sport; went to dine at M.ʳ Fiotts no adititional company, but the party large from their six Children, Whist & Cassino in the evening staid supper & return'd home only to go to Bed. rec'd a Letter from M.ʳˢ Naper & wrote to my Sister Travell.

Wensday Oct.ʳ 24.ᵗʰ

Another dry day, & still more fine than the former one having more sunshine, very fortunate for our intended expedition to Trent Farm Lord Cholmondelys about 6 miles distant,²⁶ on the borders of Endfield chace, & formerly a part of it, a woody pretty scene, & a very pretty, tho Singular House, most elegantly fitted up quite in the french stile much pleased with the sight of it. M.ʳˢ Lee took M.ʳ Witts in her Chaise, I took the Miss Lee's in mine, & M.ʳ & M.ʳˢ Fiott follow'd in their own Chariott, & return'd home to Dinner with us, before which we some of us took a walk in the Garden &'c, a very free chearful evening & a little Cards. sorry it was a concluding evening.

Thursday Oct.ʳ 25.ᵗʰ

Very much the same kind of weather dry tho rather a thick air, tho at intervals lively gleams of sunshine which made it a pleasant day for moving & we found the roads much dried as we proceeded on our Journey, leaving our agreable friends with regret after an early breakfast, & passing thro Watford went to Berkhamstead 20 miles before we stopt good roads & in the general a pleasing country, diversified with many pretty & handsome places, got an excellent Dinner at the King's Arms, which sent us on merrily to M.ʳ Stones at Hartwell 2 miles beyond Aylesbury which was 12, roads very good but country miserable got to our Journeys end before it was dark, found Miss Stone absent from home, her Parents very well & trying all in their power to make their sad house & work accomodations as comfortable as they could.²⁷

Friday Oct.ʳ 26.ᵗʰ

Still dry but cold & gloomy being an east wind but it matter'd little to me, as I never stirr'd from the fireside, the Gentlemen walk'd to Aylesbury &'c S.ʳ William & Lady Elizabeth Lee paid us visits in the Morning at seperate times & were very obliging a long evening of conversation . wrote to M.ʳˢ Tyrwhitt

Saturday Oct.ʳ 27.ᵗʰ

Foggy in the Morning but soon clear'd off, but was again misty at Noon but bright & fine in the afternoon. left Hartwell after an early breakfast & found the 21 miles stage to Oxford

---

26. George James Cholmondeley, Viscount Cholmondeley (1749–1827). Cholmondeley had been envoy to Berlin (June–September 1782) and was Chamberlain to the Prince of Wales (1795–1800) and Lord Steward of the Household (1812–1821).

27. Sarah and Edward Stone, sister and brother-in-law to Edward Witts.

140. Oxford from the meadows.

thro' Thame a dismal long one in every respect, the country being naturaly flat & ugly, & now nearly under water & the roads most horrid which made us 4 hours & ½ going to Oxford, had a very good Dinner at the Star during which Mr Henry Wise & Mr Thos. Pettat sat with us & were very lively & agreable; reach'd Witney 10 miles soon after it was dark; thro a watry world. wrote to Lady Edward Bentinck & Mr Edwd London Witts.

Sunday Octr. 28th.

Quite a mild beautiful Day from Morn: to night, & the light & shade very fine, of the country I had to pass thro had been worthy observation, only stopt at Burford for Hay & water & Mr Witts to get into a Post Chaise to go to Chipping Norton I dined at Northleach very miserably, & reach'd Cheltenham just as it was dark, found both my Bro^r Travell & Miss Susan Charteris with my Sisters which fill'd their house far beyond comfort. my Dear Boys were rejoiced to see me, & look'd as well as possible rather a long stupid evening, & had a very sleepless night. rec'd Letters from M^rs. Granville Miss Gorges & my Dear Francis.

Monday Octr 29th.

A dark cloudy Morning but turn'd out if possible a still finer Day being quite warm, a little walking & much visiting in the Morning, M^rs. Tracy from Sandywell & Miss Coxwell with her here for two hours. Miss Charteris dined out & M^rs. Chollet dined here & was very entertaining, M^rs. Durouse & Miss Wynne Mr Bernard Dewes & his Daughter & M^r J: Delabere drank Tea here a Table at Whist & Commerce rec'd a Letter from my Husband & answerd it, & wrote to Miss Gorges.

*141. Witney
from the
Market Cross.*

Tuesday Octr 30th.

A sad reverse in the weather, being almost constant rain the whole Day, & after mid.day
most violent high wind, fit for nothing but staying at home walk'd much, talk'd more, read
a little, a set or two of Morning callers & a dull rubber or two at Whist in the evening
concluded the Day. rec'd a Letter from my Husband & wrote to my Dear Francis.

Wensday Octr 31st.

Quite a delightful mild fine Day with constant sunshine, made the most of it, by being out
nearly the whole Morning but chiefly walking about the Town & visiting sundry people, M^r
Witts return'd to me to Dinner Miss Hamiltons drank Tea here, & we had a Table at Whist &
another at Cassino very lively & pleasant. rec'd Letters from Miss Snow & Miss Louisa Lee.

Thursday Novr 1st.

Another very miserable Day being wet more or less the whole of the day & at times
extremely windy & stormy, yet we had a succession of Morning callers, & I ventured out
a little in spite of mud & dirt before Dinner. a very quiet sombre evening of talk & whist,
wrote to Miss Louisa Lee.

Friday Novr 2^{d.}

A most beautiful Day, perpetual sunshine from rising to setting, & quite mild & warm
visiting & walking as usual, my sweet Francis arrived from School just as we had dined most
general Joy, he attended us to drink Tea at Mr Hughes's where we met M^r & Mrs. Newell &
Mr Clarke, & all adjourn'd to the Town Ball which was a good one & amusing, my sweet
Boy went down a dance or two for the first time, I play'd 2 rubbers at Whist & was not at
home till past one rec'd a Letter from Mr Edward Hunt & wrote to Mrs. Granville.

142. *Sandywell*

Saturday Nov.ʳ 3ᵈ·

Another Day quite as beautiful & fine was out & about the greater part of the Morning Mʳ Witts & his Son rode to Sandywell, Mʳ John Delabere dined & drank Tea here as did Miss Nettleship, a table at Whist & another at Cassino. had the pleasure of receiving a delightful Letter from Lady Edward Bentinck.

Sunday Nov.ʳ 4ᵗʰ·

Very much the same agreable weather more like Spring than winter, went to Morning Church & staid the Sacrament, afterwards rec'd visits, & went an airing on the London road with Mʳˢ· Chollet, to church again, in the afternoon a strange Sermon from Dʳ Berkeley, Miss Charteris dined out & Mʳ Clark dined here.²⁸ wrote to Mʳˢ· Naper.

Monday Nov.ʳ 5ᵗʰ·

Notwithstanding there had been something of a frost in the night it was a most beautiful warm bright Day, Mʳ Witts went to Mʳˢ· Napers to meet my Broᵗ Ferdinand on bussiness I walk'd & air'd again very agreably with Mʳˢ· Chollet, & Francis took two different rides. Mʳˢ· Chollet & Miss Hamiltons & Miss Hughes drank Tea here, Whist & Cassino again very chearful wrote to Mʳ Edward Hunt.²⁹

Tuesday Nov.ʳ 6ᵗʰ·

Quite as fine weather till mid.day when it became cold & lowering & a wetting fog came on, walk'd about a great deal with Miss Charteris before she set out to return home to Stanway,

---

28.   Miss Charteris was one of the daughters of Lord and Lady Elcho. Susan Charteris, Lady Elcho (1745–1835), was first cousin to Agnes Witts and to Mrs Travell.
29.   Edward Hunt (1759–1822), first cousin to Edward Witts.

143. Charlton Kings, the seat of Dodington Hunt Esq.

& visits afterwards, M[r] Witts return'd home to Dinner, & he & I & Francis went to drink Tea with Miss Delabere meeting M[r] & M[rs.] Newell & Miss Nettleships, Whist & Cassino. rec'd a Letter from M[r] Edw[d]. London Witts

Wensday Nov[r.] 7[th.]

Neither a bad or good day, being dry tho & misty thick air, my sweet Francis went off again to school, a painful pendent necessity to part with him so soon, walk'd with him as far on his road as the Turnpike from whence M[r] John Delabere escorting my Sister & I, we went to survey M[r] Hunts Garden & Hothouses at Charlton & to visit M[rs.] Lane & M[rs.] Phipps, thoroughly tired by the time I came home. M[r] & M[rs.] Newell, & Miss Delabere drank Tea here, the same party at Cards rec'd a Letter from Miss Louisa Lee & wrote to M[rs.] Parsons by Francis.

Thursday Nov[r.] 8[th.]

Very much the same kind of weather dry but thick & hazzy, I walk'd & visited a little, but was too much tired by my former days walk to wish to try again much, drank Tea at M[rs.] Chollets very pleasantly tho a party of 12 in her small room, play'd at Loo with success, another Table at Whist. rec'd Letters from M[rs.] Catherine Thornton & Miss Forrest & wrote to Miss Snow.

Friday Nov[r.] 9[th.]

No kind of change in the weather, left Cheltenham after breakfast, & went with Post horses to Lord Elcho's at Stanway leaving the two Boys to remain with their Aunts, stopp'd at Sandywell Park for an hour by the way, happy to find M[rs.] Eliza: Tracy better than I expected, M[rs.] Coxwell there as well as her Daughter; find the roads very bad tho proved them safe met with a very pleasing reception from Lord & Lady Elcho & their large party, which ourselves made 14, besides their own family, the two Miss Hamiltons, Captain Hamilton &

his Daughter, & M[r] Principal Gordon,[30] very chearful & lively & the old house made quite gay & pleasant. Whist, Cassino & Cribbage.

Saturday Nov[r] 10th

A very fine Day with much bright sunshine, which shew'd the country & views off to very great advantage, our large party were seperated in different ways walking & riding, Lady Elcho & I walk'd a tetetete, M[r] Winniat here for an hour in the afternoon or else the evening was spent much as the former in much agreable chearfulness.

Sunday Nov[r] 11th

Not a fine Day at all being cold & windy with now & then flying mists or fog, went to Church both Morning & evening, the service very moderately perform'd by M[r] Heyden, who dined here the Principal Gordon so ill all Day as to keep his Bed & room, much talking & laughing, much writting some reading & Lord Elcho read a Sermon at Night wrote to Lady Edward Bentinck & Miss Forrest.

Monday Nov[r] 12th

After being something of a frost in the night it was a most beautiful Day constant warm sunshine & a very clear air, we made the best use of it by being out almost all the morning, some on Horseback some walking & I in the Phaeton, all went just to see the poor old Mansion at Toddington, & then to drive in the Park, very chearful all the evening much laughing, Cards & Music. wrote to M[rs] Naper

Tuesday Nov[r] 13th

Hard rain in the Morning, stormy at noon & fine in the afternoon, but still it was quite a stay at home day, some work, much talk, & laughing, a great deal of Cards, rec'd Letters from Miss Anne Snow & my Sister Travell.

Wensday Nov[r] 14th

Fine & shewey in the Morning, but before noon turn'd to violent rain & storms & so continued the rest of the day, & prevented all going out, day passd very pleasantly like all the former ones, but nothing material to relate. wrote to M[rs] Catherine Thornton.

Thursday Nov[r] 15th

A tolerable day being dry, tho the wind was extremely high & cold, yet pretty constant sunshine made a little walking not unpleasant. M[r] Witts rode with some of the young Ladies, evening spent much as usual, excepting Miss Charteris shewing off delightfully in a very fine minuet.

---

30. Principal Gordon is something of a mystery. He was to become a close friend of Agnes Witts during the Edinburgh years (*see* Volume Two: 'Exile') and he was frequently mentioned in her diaries from 1793 onwards, but especially between 1793 and 1798, when the family lived in Edinburgh. Exactly who he was is not known. He could have been the Principal Gordon referred to in respect of the affairs of Sir John Gordon, Baronet (1775), or he could be the Principal Gordon who was the head of the Scots College in Paris in 1792. With unrest in France it would not be surprising if he were the latter, and either escaped or was expelled from France. Circumstantial evidence surrounding his movements and references in the diaries would tend to support the latter supposition. This gathering at Stanway may have been the first time they met.

Friday Novr 16th.

Very bright & shewey in the Morning tho cold & windy & at Noon several hard Storms of rain & hail but clear again in the afternoon we left Stanway at Noon, & were 4 hours performing our little Journey back to Cheltenham, from the increased badness of the roads & a tired Post Horse found my Bro^r Sisters & Boys well, play'd three dull rubbers at Whist in the family stile. rec'd Letters from Mrs. Naper & my Dear Francis.

Saturday Novr 17th.

Had been quite a sharp hoar frost in the night, but was a universal warm fine day walk'd about & visited a great deal, went to Drink Tea at Mrs. Chollets meeting the same party we had met there before I spent a very pleasant evening, playing a merry & successful Game at Loo & staying to eat a cold supper wrote to Mrs. Hyett.

Sunday Novr 18th.

Dry & cold tho without either sun or wind went to Church in the Morning hearing M^r J: Delabere send prayers, & Dr Berkeley preach an unpleasant sermon, walk'd between churches with Mr John & of course talk'd, evening service dismally perform'd by Mr Llewellyn. Miss Hughes & Miss Beves drank Tea here, altogether a very trite party. rec'd a Letter from Mrs. Granville & wrote to Mrs. Naper.

Monday Novr 19th.

A very moderate Day cold & windy & at noon, flying mists of rain but none fell of any consequence we walk'd & shopt a little in the Morning, & in the evening went again to Mrs. Chollets meeting only Mrs. Kenning, a chearful game at Loo, & the same kind of cold supper we had before. wrote a Letter to Miss Anne Snow.

Tuesday Novr 20th.

Not much a better day being still colder tho quite dry, some Morning visitors, after which I walk'd to Sandford with Miss Hughes & her friend, Mr J. Delabere, & my Sis^r Travell, did not find Mrs. Ram at home, but staid to rest ourselves & eat sandwichs sat an hour with Mrs. Chollet on my return, drank Tea with Miss Nettleships rather dull, met Mr John Delabere a table at Whist & Cassino. wrote to my Dear Francis.

Wensday Novr 21st.

A very stormy wet disagreable Day rather better at Noon, but still worse in the afternoon was out for two or three hours at mid.day on necessary bussiness & visits Mr Markham dined wth. us, & Mrs. Ram & Miss Hughes & Miss Beves drank Tea a Table at Whist & Cassino, rec'd a Letter from Miss Gorges.

Thursday Novr 22^d.

Very bright & fine early in the Day but, very stormy cold, & disagreable the remainder with many hard Showers of rain & hail, left Chelt: at Noon & had a very long & wretched drive home, from one of the horses refusing to take the Collar up hill was aware of his tricks & had a post horse rode by to supply his place but still was not at home till near dark, very unwell & much fatigued & nervous with these attempts. found the Boys well & all things in high order. rec'd a melancholly Letter from Miss Snow in regard to her Sis.ᵗ Paul & wrote to M.ʳˢ· Granville.

Friday Nov.ʳ 23.ᵈ·

Tollerably bright & fine in the Morning but was afterwards damp, cloudy, & cold the remainder of the day, fortunately took the best part of the day to be out & about the premises. tired myself to death with standing & fidgetting about to set things in order & at night was quite ill. rec'd a Letter from M.ʳˢ· Naper.

Saturday Nov.ʳ 24.ᵗʰ·

No change in the weather, being much finer in the Morning than it was afterwards, which was no inducement to me to be much out of the house as well as being very much engaged with a variety of employs. Miss Sheppard here for an hour rec'd Letters from Lady Lyttelton & M.ʳˢ· Hyett & wrote some Letters on bussiness..

Sunday Nov.ʳ 25.ᵗʰ·

Not a very pleasant day being dark cold & damp, & at times small flying mists, went to Church at Hampton, visited at M.ʳˢ· Sheppards both before & after church & took them with us & sat in their seat; went into the hot house before Dinner. rec'd a Letter from my sweet Francis & wrote to Miss Snow & M.ᵗ Burslem.

Monday Nov.ʳ 26.ᵗʰ·

Very similar weather which only tempted me to walk a very little, besides I was very low & indifferent, & had much domestic bussiness to transact work'd & read a little & at night wrote a very interesting Letter to M.ʳˢ· Buxton.

Tuesday Nov.ʳ 27.ᵗʰ·

Quite the same sort of weather only the wetting fog lasted more hours, I went after breakfast in the Chaise first thro Stroud, where I did some little bussiness, call'd on old M.ʳˢ· Wathen who was not well enough to receive me, & went on to the New House to make my first visit to young M.ʳˢ· Wathen, who I found at home & alone & was much pleased with her appearance & manner the roads very bad, but the Horse perform'd as well as possible. rec'd a Letter from Miss Anne Snow with a very sad account of M.ʳˢ· Paul, & wrote to Miss Louisa Lee & my Sister Travell.

Wensday Nov.ʳ 28.ᵗʰ·

Very much the same kind of weather and at, & afternoon was a thick wetting fog, walk'd about & was much engaged till at one o'clock M.ᵗ Witts & I set out to spend two nights at M.ᵗ Witts's at Nibley went round by Hampton for the contents of the Post & so up Nailsworth Hill & over Simonshill Down roads excellent & drive quick, found our friends well & pretty well settled in their new habitation, but their House miserably cold & wanting in minor comforts. rather a long evening with nothing to do. rec'd a Letter from my Sis.ᵗ Travell & wrote to M.ʳˢ· Chollet.

Thursday Nov.ʳ 29ᵗʰ·

Rather a better day, being dry tho cold & the air clear, but yet I did not venture from the fireside having a very bad cold, & Mʳ Witts near as bad a one, but he & his Brother were out & about all Morning when Mʳˢ· Witts & I had much conversation. evening as dark & sombre as the former one had been.

Friday Nov.ʳ 30ᵗʰ·

A very fine Winter day, being much sunshine, & the air dry tho somewhat cold & windy, yet we found our drive home from Nibley realy pleasant returning thro' Dursley & Uley, where we just stopp'd for 5 minutes at Mʳ Edward Sheppards Door. My cold very little mended Mʳ Witts's much so. Boys, well

Saturday Dec.ʳ 1ˢᵗ·

Quite a thick gloomy day tho dry, very busy all Morning went to Dine at Mʳˢ· Sheppards at Hampton meeting Mʳ Mʳˢ· & Miss Savage, & Mʳ Schutz just arrived. a very lively pleasant day. staid late playing at Whist & Cassino.

Sunday Dec.ʳ 2ᵈ·

Very much the same weather dry & cold tho thick & gloomy, went to Church at Stroud, service excellently perform'd as usual by Mʳ Ellis, on my way home went to call on Mʳˢ· Pettat at the Hill House but did not find her at home; wrote to Mʳˢ· Naper & Mʳˢ· Witts friday Street, & rec'd a Letter from Miss Snow

Monday Dec.ʳ 3ᵈ·

No change in the weather which tempted me to go but little out. Mʳˢ· S. Wathen, & her Sister Mʳˢ· Sheppard &'c calld here in the Morning but too late for me to see them excepting in the Carriage as I was going to dress to receive Mʳ & Mʳˢ· Savage & Miss Savage to Dinner who staid all night, & Mʳˢ· & two Miss Sheppards & Mʳˢ· Schutz to Dinner very comfortable & friendly & play'd at Whist & Cassino.

Tuesday Dec.ʳ 4ᵗʰ·

Very thick fog all Morning, but when clearing off at Noon it began to be very stormy, & at Night was wet & very tempestuous, our Tetbury friends staid with us till near one; we dined at Mʳ Peter Hawkers meeting besides their own family, Mʳ & Mʳˢ· Pettat from the Hill house, sat down 10 to a most famous good & well dresst Dinner, a merry table at Whist & Cassino return'd home before supper, carrying Mʳˢ· Pettat home to the Hill House. S: Maclausin the new Gardiner came.

Wensday Dec.ʳ 5ᵗʰ·

An intire change in the wind which made it quite mild & damp, with an uncommon high wind & at times flying mists of rain, a very Nervous day with me was much in the Garden &'c with the Gardiner. rec'd a very unpleasing Letter from Mʳˢ· Buxton, one quite the contrary from Lady Edward Bentinck, another from Mʳˢ· Chollet, & one from my beloved Francis, answerd his & wrote to Miss Anne Snow.

Thursday Decr 6th.

Much a worse day than the former, being most wet & damp, & the wind most wonderfully high & unpleasant, but just able to get into the hot.house dined at Mr Wathens at the New house meeting only Mr Wasey, & M.^r N: Wathen, but liked the visit very much it was so easy & pleasant, & every thing smart & in a pretty new stile, play'd at Vingt'un, with very great success both Mr Witts & I, staid there all night with much comfort.

Friday Decr 7th.

Quite a happy change in the weather being very drying, strong wind & sun both left our pleasant Neighbours soon after breakfast & on my return home made a string of Morning visits first to the elder Mrs. Wathen, then Mrs. Ellis, & concluding with Mrs. Burgh, which brought me home but little before Dinner. Edward Herbert my Sis.^{rs.} Servant came to commence being our temporary Servant; after Dinner had the pain of receiving an account from Elmore Court that my beloved Francis was far from well with the Measles or some other eruptive complaint very miserable about him; which deranged me quite rec'd a Letter from Mr Burslem.

Saturday Decr 8th.

Had been a sharp frost in the night more Ice visible than the season before, dress'd by candle light & set out at 9 o'clock for Elmore Court, arrived there in little more than 2 hours tho some of the road was very bad, rejoiced to find my sweet Boy suffering little tho in Bed, & his disorder pronounced a slight degree of a Scarlet fever, yet the worst was past & he grew better every hour, & sat up in the afternoon for a short time. found Mr Jones of Hay Hill & his younger Daughter at Elmore which over fill'd the old Mansion. play'd at Whist with success in the evening & went to Bed in more comfort than I rose.

Sunday Decr 9th.

A very dark gloomy Morning with high wind & strong appearance of rain, which came on at Noon & continued with great violence attended by Hail & tempestuous wind all the day; My Sweet Boy having had a good night was so much better that we could leave him with comfort, therefore return'd to Bownham after breakfast & return'd again after an early Dinner having to settle & finish all matters with David Stewart the old Gardiner before he went away & other bussiness. found Francis charming & Mr Nayler the Apothecary with him for the last time. wrote to my Sis.^r Travell.

Monday Decr 10th.

Again dark & gloomy, with high wind & very damp air but little or no rain. rejoiced to bring our Dear Boy down with us to Breakfast much recovered, tho his spirits sunk at our leaving him which we felt necessary as he was in a manner well, made a visit at Mr Pettats at Stonehouse as we came home. very busy at accompts all the evening. rec'd a Letter from my Sister Travell & wrote to Mrs. Chollet.

Tuesday Decr 11th.

Dry tho stormy in the Morning, but at mid.day was too much rain to be able to walk out & violent high wind all the evening; Mr Witts rode to Hampton, I work'd hard all the

Morning, & wrote hard all the evening. rec'd a Letter from Miss Anne Snow, & wrote to M^rs. Elizabeth Tracy.

Wensday Decr 12th.
A pleasant dry air tho without frost, with small gleams of sunshine upon the whole a fine winter day, tho I made but small use of it, being detain'd in the house when I meant to walk by a long visit from M^r & M^rs. S. Pettat & Miss Pettat. Mr Witts walk'd to Hampton, & visited at M^rs. Sheppards

Thursday Decr 13th.
Quite a disagreable Day being a very thick fog throughout, & after noon almost amounting to rain & as dark as possible, altogether it made me very Nervous & ill able to support Dinner company as M^r & M^rs. Pettat from the Hill House, M^r & M^rs. Wathen & Mr Nathan & a Mr Wasey who staid all night, chearful & lively upon the whole. whist & Cassino. –

Witts Family Papers F184

1792

Friday Decr 14th.

By no means an unpleasant winter day, the air being mild tho dry, & not at all stormy I walk'd a good deal about the premises after Breakfast with Mr Wasey before he went away, & went to drink Tea at Mrs. Sheppards, play'd many rubbers at Whist with very ill success, came home between 10 & 11 & went to Bed directly, having had the satisfaction of receiving a Letter fr.^{m.} Mr Parsons with a most excellent account of my Dear Francis.

Saturday Decr 15th.

A most uncommon fine Day for the season of the Year, being mild & dry without frost little wind & frequent soft gleams of sunshine very fortunate for my first winter excursion on horseback, wch. I set out on soon after Breakfast going to Mr Tyndales at Woodchester on errands return'd home by the New road to Hampton &c. rec'd a Letter from Mrs. Chollet & answer'd it.

Sunday Decr 16th.

An unpleasant day on the whole being a thick damp air, & in the afternoon quite a thick fog, I was far from well & much out of spirits, went to church at Stroud in the Morning busy writting all the afternoon; wrote to Mrs. Tyrwhitt, Mrs. Buxton & Miss Snow, & rec'd a Letter from my sweet Francis with a pretty good account of himself, but still I was not quite easy about him.

Monday Decr 17th.

Much a better day, being a dry air, tho not being clear or warm, having had a very bad night, I mounted on my double Horse, & rode to call at Mr Peter Hawkers at Woodchester, & home by Dudbridge & Rodbro' Hill, Mrs. Chollet came here to a late Dinner from Cheltenham, & Mr Wasey also Dined here & staid all night we had a very lively game at Loo, M.^r & Mrs. R. Pettat here & much conversation

Tuesday Decr 18th.

Quite a miserable Day & a worse night, being a thick wetting Fog with a strong wind & in the evening violent rain, & tempestuous wind we went to dine at Mr Ellis's at Stroud, where we met the three Brothers Mr Wathens, & had a very chearful pleasant day, with much music on the Glasses & lively converse very dark & dismal coming home rec'd Letters from Mrs. Manwaring & My Sister Travell.

Wensday Decr 19th.

Dry & cold, with at times gleams of Sunshine & strong cold wind, walk'd with Mrs. Chollet about our own premises. M^r & Mrs. Hawker & Miss Hawker & Mr Peter Hawker dined here as did M^r J: Wathen who also slept here, a table at Whist & Loo. rec'd a Letter from Mrs. Elizabeth Tracy.

Thursday Decr 20

Quite a miserable Morning, of high wind & flying rain, I got up before it was well light to set out to fetch my Dear Francis from School, prevented having the pleasure of having Mrs. Chollets company by her having so violent a cold that I left her in Bed, took George with me, found the roads very bad but went quick, did not find my sweet Boy so stoutly recover'd as I could wish, wch. made me very anxious & I wrote at night to Mr Nayler to learn his opinion. return'd home to a very late Dinner play'd at Commerce with the Boys &'c.

Friday Decr 21st.

Still very stormy, & a transitory flight of Snow early in the morning wch. lasted only a bit but proved the air to be very cold which it remain all Day, & the night was remarkably clear & bright. We went to Dine at M^r J: Pettats at Stonehouse, where we met besides their own Quartetto M^r & Mrs. Reade, M^r & M^{rs.} R: Pettat, & Mr Brown play'd at Loo & a Table at Whist, staid supper & return'd home about 12. My Dear Francis a good deal mended the whole of the day; rec'd an answer from Mr Nayler about him & wrote to Mrs. Mainwaring.

Saturday Decr 22^{d.}

A very miserable day of mist, rain & terrible high wind & excessive damp, which made us in a scene of smoke the whole Day, Mrs. Chollet left us after breakfast to go to Bath, I work'd & tryd to amuse my sweet Francis & in the evening play'd a rubber at Cassino with him & George. rec'd a Letter from Miss Gorges & answer'd it

Sunday Decr 23^{d.}

Quite a change in the weather being a sharp frost, & tho the sun was constantly out, it was extremely cold from a piercing high wind, went to Church at Hampton taking the two eldest Boys, sat in Mrs. Sheppards seat & visited them afterwards, walk'd a little in the Garden on my return for the sake of my Dear Francis who I thought very indifferent which made me compleatly miserable wrote to Mrs. Hyett & my Sis^t Travell

Monday Decr 24th.

Another very sharp frost but the wind being quite fallen, & the sun strong & constant it was a very fine Day for the time of Year which tempted us to attend our poor invalid Boy out on horseback, to Hampton &'c but sweet fellow he was so very indifferent all Day that we were quite distres'd & low about him Mr Josiah Wathen here in the Morning. play'd at Cassino & wrote to Mr Nayler.

Tuesday Decr 25th.

A little of a frost, but chang'd at Noon to be a thaw, & in the evening was rain & snow together, went to Church at Stroud where Miss Sheppard join'd us, & where the various services of the day kept us so long that we were not at home till near three Francis continuing so very indifferent we had sent for M.̱ Nayler to come to him w.̱ᶜʰ he did after Dinner order'd him some medicines & a blister on his Chest, all this made us very unhappy & I sat up with him the greater part of the night. rec'd Letters from M.̱ʳˢ Granville, Miss Snow, M.̱ʳˢ Savage & M.̱ʳˢ Witts & answer'd the two latter.

Wensday Dec.̱ᵗ 26.̱ᵗʰ

In every sense of the word a dismal day, being constant small rain & violent damp wind, & my feelings too much corresponded, as my Dear Boy was very indifferent, & confined to his Bed, I scarce ever left his room, wrote much in accounts. rec'd an agreable Letter from M.̱ʳˢ Chollet.

Thursday Dec.̱ᵗ 27.̱ᵗʰ

A happy change both in the weather & my Dear Child, as it was a sharp frost & tho very cold was pleasant from constant sunshine Francis certainly better, & able to sit up a great deal M.̱ᵉ Witts went early on business to Tetbury & returning by Hampton, join'd the association on a plan of Royalty,[1] & did not return till 4 o'clock. M.̱ᵉ & M.̱ʳˢ Parsons from Elmore Court came here an hour or two before Dinner, the evening rather dull & painfull, from not being quite satisfied about my sweet Boy, & very unhappy on the receipt of a strange Letter from M.̱ʳˢ Naper. wrote to M.̱ᵉ Nayler & rec'd a satisfactory answer.

Friday Dec.̱ᵗ 28.̱ᵗʰ

Again frosty & very pleasant & warm but in the evening was a thaw & late hard rain M.̱ᵉ Witts went again to Tetbury, M.̱ᵉ & M.̱ʳˢ Parsons & I walk'd my spirits much mended by Francis's being greatly better, w.̱ᶜʰ sufferd me to go with comfort to Dine at M.̱ʳˢ Holbrows, where we met the Stonehouse family & M.̱ᵉ Henry Wise with them it was a very chearful lively Day, a Table at Loo & Cassino at w.̱ᶜʰ I play'd with success; staid supper not at home till one o'clock. rec'd a letter from M.̱ʳˢ Tyrwhitt.

Saturday Dec.̱ᵗ 29.̱ᵗʰ

Another change in the weather, being mild & damp with frequent small showers, or rather flying mists, I only went into the Garden the Gents took a long ride, & my sweet Francis was so well I ventured to let him move into the Dressing room M.̱ᵉ Wasey dined here & staid all night, & Miss Sheppard & Miss Boughton drank Tea. play'd both at Whist & Loo.

Sunday Dec.̱ᵗ 30.̱ᵗʰ

After a great deal of rain in the night, it was a mild yet dry very fine day being little wind & constant bright sun quite pleasant took M.̱ᵉ & M.̱ʳˢ Parsons with me in the Chaise to Stroud Church, M.̱ᵉ Witts on horseback, where M.̱ᵉ Wasey read Prayers & M.̱ᵉ Parsons preach'd very excellently to an attentive congregation, brought them home thro' Woodchester Vale, on our return found M.̱ᵉ Nayler, & my Dearest Boy again very ill suffering much from a

---

1.   The Association on a Plan of Royalty may have something to do with what was going on in France, where, a few months earlier, royalty had been abolished.

violent pain in his head & Bilious complaint in his stomach most miserable about him & much occupied in trying various means to relieve him, which happily succeeded by night. Mr Nayler obliged to leave us.

Monday Decr 31st.

A sharp frost but a beautiful clear fine day, my sweet Boy so much better it was quite charming, for prudence I kept him in Bed till after Dark when he sat up two or three hours & play'd at Cassino. M^r & Mrs. Parsons left us after breakfast, truly sorry to part with them being much pleased with their manner & behaviour wrote to Mr Nayler by them.

rec'd 219 Letters:
wrote 195

1793

Tuesday Jan: 1st.

A dismal day in point of weather for the opening of the new year, being constant storms of wind & rain & flying snow or Sleet & & extremely dark, damp, & cold, my sweet Invalid much the same, still necessary to keep in the room for fear of catching cold. Whole Day, & evening spent with him as usual. rec'd a Letter from Mr Nayler & wrote to Mrs. Chollet.

Wensday Jan: 2^{d.}

Alternate Frost, & turn'd out a beautiful fine day much sun, no wind quite mild. my Dear Boy confined later to his Bed by taking an Emetic early in the Morning which appeard to be of much service to him, & he was better than usual & very lively all the evening. I walkd out for sometime in the Morning & found it quite pleasant. wrote to Lady Edward Bentinck Mr Nayler & Miss Snow.

Thursday Jan: 3^{d.}

A sharp hoar frost clear & fine till noon when suddenly came on a tremendous thick wetting fog & so continued all the evening my Dear Boy being pure well I ventured to take a ride, having left him in my Bed chamber by way of change of air for the air for the day.[2] went first to call on Mr Pettal at the Hill House, from whence Mr Pettal attended us to call at Mrs. Sheppards at Hampton, came home starved by being wet thro' by the Fog. play'd a merry game at Cassino with the Boys. rec'd a Letter from my Sister Travell & answerd it.

Friday Jan: 4th.

Quite a disagreable Morning, being perpetual Storms of snow & wind & some had lain on the ground so very cold I was fearful of letting my Dear invalid stir out of his room all Day, being engaged to go to Dine & sleep at Mr Wathens we braved it, being well wrapp'd up in Great Coat &'c, met there Mr Wise 2 Mr Sheppards Mrs. Wathens Brothers, Mr Josiah & M^r

---

2.   This makes little sense, but she may have been writing in haste and without due care.

Nathan Wathen, & Mr Moore from Bisley, a very lively pleasant meeting, a Table at Whist, & a very merry one at Bragge at which I play'd, & we all play'd after supper to a very late hour indeed. wrote to M^rs. Parsons.

Saturday Jan: 5th.

A thorough change in the weather being warm mild rain accompanied by some wind, & at times showery throughout the whole day; breakfasted very late, which of course did not bring us home early tho I was impatient, to see my poor Boy, who I found pure well, & soon removed him into my Bed room where we play'd at Cards as usual in the evening & went to Bed very early after our great raking. rec'd a Letter from M^rs. Hyett.

Sunday Jan: 6th.

A very pleasant fine day, a little of a frost but warm from constant sunshine & no wind, went to Church at Stroud taking George with us, happy in having my Dear Francis so much better that I ventured him down into the Parlour to Dinner & spend the evening. rec'd a Letter from Mr Nayler & answer'd it.

Monday Jan: 7th.

Quite continuing weather, being miserably damp & cold, & a thick wetting fog all Day, Mr Witts obliged to take a long ride in the Morning, many employments filld up mine, my Dear Boy again spent the better part of the day in the Parlour & we play'd at Cassino. wrote a very interesting Letter to M^rs. Naper.

Tuesday Jan: 8th.

As usual an alternate change in the weather being an uncommon clear fine day tho very little frost & constant sunshine. quite warm & mild wch. tempted me to let my Dear Invalid go out in the Chaise to air accompanied by myself & George went to Nailsworth & home by the new road to Hampton. expected a good deal of company to Dinner but disappointed in all but the 2 Mr Wathens, Mr Henry Wise, & Mr Thornbury, Miss Sheppards came to Tea & staid Supper, each persons playing at Bragge, did not go to Bed till 2 in the Morning. rec'd a melancholly Letter from Miss A: Snow

Wensday Jan: 9th.

Much contrast in the weather, being a mixture of fog & frost, both very cold & damp afraid to let Francis stir out of the House, tho he certainly he mends gradualy every day. Miss Clutterbuck made a visit of two or three hours in the Morning, & by receiving her quite in a free way in my Boys bedchamber it realy was not as pleasant as usual play'd at Cassino after the Boys went to Bed, Mr Witts read to me, in Adam Smiths Theory of Moral Sentiments,[3] both improving & entertaining, rec'd Letters, from L^dy. Elcho, Lady E^d. Bentinck & my Sis^r Travell. All most pleasing & satisfactory in their different ways.

---

3.   Adam Smith (1723–1790). *The Theory of Moral Sentiments* was first published in 1759, and it was this book, and not *The Wealth of Nations*, which laid the foundation of his career. This was Smith's first book, written while he was a professor of moral philosophy at the University of Glasgow. It is here that Smith first introduced the

Thursday Jan: 10th.

A very thick fog early in the day which afterwards turn'd to hard rain, but chiefly in showers with gleams of sunshine between, but so transient it was not pendent to go out as usual constantly with my Dear Francis schooling & a great variety of employs going forwards. rec'd Letters from Mrs. Witts from Nibley House & Mr Nayler & wrote to Mrs. Granville & my Sister Travell

Friday Jan: 11th.

Dark & lowering in the Morning, rather better at Noon, & much worse in the afternoon being violent showers of rain, hail & wind & so extremely dark it was hardly possible to see, happily we had taken an airing of an hour & ½ to the Post & on the Cirencester road before it began, evening spent much as usual Francis purely. wrote to Miss A: Snow

Saturday Jan: 12th.

A moderate day rather stormy, tho dry, at times gleams of sunshine, Mr Witts went to Tetbury on bussiness, I walk'd a little with Francis in the Garden, the first time of his going alone, evening spent much as usual not very gay rec'd a Letter from Mrs. Savage.

Sunday Jan. 13th.

Foggy in the Morning, rather wet at Noon, but fine towards afternoon, went to Church at Stroud taking George, after I came back, exchanged Francis for his Papa in the Post Chaise & took him an airing on the Tetbury road to the top of Avening Hill. wrote to Mrs. Eliza Tracy & Mr Nayler.

Monday Jan: 14th.

A thorough unpleasant day, very high wind & cold, with now & then hard storms of rain & hail, no chance either of my own or Fran^{s.s.} stirring from the fireside, a tedious long Day, Mr Witts spending many hours at the meeting of the Stroud dispensary not at home till 9 o'clock wrote to Mr John Delabere on the death of his poor Father.

Tuesday Jan: 15th.

Weather none the better, some hope in the Morning, but truly overclouded at Noon with storms of Snow or rather sleet which quite put a stop to our intention of taking an airing Mr Witts set out after breakfast to go into Oxfordshire, a dismal bussiness. Mr Pettat here for a long Morning visit, Cassino in the evening wth. Francis & George. rec'd Letters from Mrs. Mainwaring & Miss Gorges. & wrote to Lady Edward Bentinck & Mrs. Chollet.

Wensday Jan: 16th.

A sharp frost, with a high cold North Wind & no sun with strong inclination to falling sleet yet I ventured to take Francis out an airing thinking else we should go on to our

increase the welfare of society as a whole. Smith shows that the desire for improvement of one's condition, which he says is essential for any human progress, also includes improvement of the condition of others. Among the topics he discusses are prosperity and adversity, justice and beneficence, rewards and punishments, and the nature of benevolence. Smith shows why free markets, with all of their unequal outcomes and income disparities, still do a better job of providing assistance to the truly needy than do government-mandated income redistribution schemes.

chairs, call'd at Mr Tyndales for some trifles home by
Nailsworth Hill new road to Hampton for Letters.
rec'd one from my Sister Travell & my Dear Husband
answer'd his & wrote to Lady Lyttelton.

Thursday Jan: 17th.

No frost or else very much the same kind of cold
stormy weather, frequently falling no safety therefore
in stirring out of the House, & indeed I was miserably
low & ill the whole Day; the two Miss Sheppards &
their Niece Anne Boughton staid two hours with me
in the Morning & I kept the latter all Day & all night,
& devoted myself the whole afternoon to entertain all
my young people rec'd Letters from Miss Snow & M^{rs.}
Witts & wrote to Lady Elcho.

144. *Tom Paine.*

Friday Jan: 18th.

Quite a severe frost but it turn'd out quite a beautiful Winter Day being warm sun & no
wind, I set out soon after breakfast accompanied by Anne Boughton & Francis to make a
Morning visit at Mrs. Savages at Tetbury the roads so excellent the drive was realy pleasant
staid there more than two hours, a great bustle in the Town from the silly exhibition of
burning Tom Payne[4] I stopp'd at Hampton on my return to dine at Mrs. Sheppards sending
Francis home for fear of the night air made a very friendly visit, play'd at whist partner
with the old Lady with great success & got home only in time to go to Bed. Rec'd a very
satisfactory Letter from my Dear Husband. Mrs. Pettat here in my absence

---

4.   Thomas Paine (1737–1809). Paine was a pamphleteer, revolutionary, radical, liberal and intellectual. Born in England,
     he lived in America during the Revolution and was the author of the powerful and widely read pamphlet *Common
     Sense* (1776), advocating independence for the American colonies. Later, Paine was a great influence on the French
     Revolution. He wrote *The Rights of Man* (1791) as a guide to the ideas of the Enlightenment. Despite an inability to
     speak French, he was elected to the French National Assembly in 1792. Paine was arrested in Paris and imprisoned in
     December 1793; he was released in 1794. He became notorious with his book *The Age of Reason* (1793–1794), which
     advocated deism and took issue with Christian doctrines. Paine remained in France during the early Napoleonic era,
     but condemned Napoleon's moves towards dictatorship. He stayed in France until 1802, when he returned to America
     at the invitation of Thomas Jefferson, who had been elected president. Meanwhile, returning to January 1793, his
     work was not without criticism in England and many pamphlets were being written and circulated, whipping up
     opinion, including: *An Address to the Inhabitants of Great Britain and Ireland Rights of Man* (1793); *An Answer to
     the Second Part of the Rights of Man* (1792); Brooke Boothby, *Observations on the Appeal from the New to the Old
     Whigs, and on Mr Paine's Rights of Man* (1792); John Bowles, *A Protest Against Thomas Paine's 'Rights of Man'*
     (1792); *Constitutional Letters, in Answer to Mr Paine's Rights of Man* (1792); *A Fourth Letter to Thomas Paine,
     in Answer to the Second Part of the Rights of Man* (1792); Charles Hawtrey, *Various Opinions of the Philosophical
     Reformers Considered; Particularly Paine's Rights of Man* (1792); *A Letter to Mr Paine on His Late Publication*
     (1792); *Paine and Burke Contrasted* (1792); Alexander Peter, *Strictures on the Character and Principles of Thomas
     Paine* (1792); *A Rod in Brine, or a Tickler for Tom Paine* (1792); *A Whipper for Levelling Tommy; in Which the
     Modern Doctrines of the Rights of Man are Properly Stated* (1793); John Riland, *The Rights of God, Occasioned by
     Mr Paine's 'Rights of Man'* (2nd edn, 1792); and Thomas Hearn, *A Short View of the Rise and Progress of Freedom in
     Modern Europe* (1792). Agnes Witts blithely let the events of the world go past her and only mentioned in passing the
     problems in France, but here in Tetbury, she could not avoid witnessing intense political and patriotic fervour.

Saturday Jan: 19th.

A still harder frost, but such an intire fog till Dinner time there could be no going out for any of us poor Francis waiting with great hopes, but much patience to take his first ride, I just went into the hot house before Dinner, Mr Wathen here for 5 minutes in the Morning. Cassino as usual with the Boys in the evening. rec'd another Letter from my Dear best friend & wrote to my Sister Travell

Sunday Jan: 20th.

Again very hard frost, but a charming fine Day the sun so much getting the better of the fog that it was quite warm & pleasant, much pleasure in taking my dear Francis to church for the first time at Stroud George of the party, walk'd in the Garden after we came home rec'd a Letter from Mrs. Chollet & answer'd it, & wrote to Miss Snow.

Monday Jan: 21st.

Frost in the Night & early in the Morning, but the air grew damp & mild, tho the earth was dry, which tempted me to let my Dear Boy go out on horseback for the first time since his illness & he was all the better for it. Mr Witts return'd home to Dinner to our general Joy, last from Sandywell Park chearful & well. rec'd a Letter from Lady Lyttelton & Mr Delabere.

Tuesday Jan: 22^{d.}

Little or no frost, tho the air still remain'd dry & cold, Francis rode to Stroud & back on a message He went with me to Mr Savages at Tetbury to dine & shop where we met the Miss Sheppards, Miss Boughton & M^r J: Wiltshire, pleasant & lively, a Table at Bragge for the old ones & Commerce for the young. rec'd a Letter too long delay'd from Mr Witts.

Wensday Jan: 23^{d.}

Very much the same kind of Day only rather more foggy, particularly so towards the afternoon left Tetbury at Noon, & dropping Mr Witts at Hampton My Boy & I went to make an unsuccessful visit to Miss Clutterbuck at Hyde not finding her at home return'd home an hour or two before Dinner play'd at Cassino in the evening. Fran^{s.} got so well it was delightful.

Thursday Jan: 24th.

A wretched Day being an extreme thick fog, & nearly incessant, constant, & soaking rain which prevented Mr Witts from joining his many Loyal Neighbours at Stroud on a declaration,[5] Lady Lyttelton, & M^r & Mrs. Witts came from Nibley to Dinner, being no Card players the evening was long & very sombre the conversation being by no means brilliant enough to supply the want. rec'd a Letter from Lady Elcho.

Friday Jan: 25th.

Weather very similar only the rain was not quite so hard or constant, but it was very damp

---

5. Louis XVI had been guillotined in Paris on 21 January 1793. There was real concern among the landed classes that revolution might take hold in England. The Loyal Declaration was part of a campaign to maintain the status quo and instill loyalty and patriotism among the mass of the population.

& miserably uncomfortable, Miss Sheppards here in the Morning to invite us all to Tea & Cards in the evening which we accepted finding M^r & M^rs. Schutz there, a Table at Whist & Cassino at which I play'd with success.

Saturday Jan: 26th.

Not much better prospects of weather early in the day, but clear'd & mended at noon when our Friends went away, & Mr Witts & Francis took a ride; domestic Cassino early in the evening, & accompts when the Boys were gone to Bed. rec'd a very pleasant Lett^r from M^rs. Chollet. wrote to M^rs. Granville

Sunday Jan: 27th.

Fine, clear, & mild in the Morning & at Noon when the sun made its appearance pleasant like Spring, went to church at Stroud taking Francis with us, on my way home went to the Hill House, to call on M^rs. Pettat, but did not find her at home, but saw Sir G: O: Paul getting on his Horse at his own Door. walk'd in Garden &c till near Dinner time it was so mild & pleasant. rec'd Letters from Miss Snow & my Sister Travell & wrote to Miss Gorges.

Monday Jan: 28th.

Such a very fine Day as is seldom known at this Season of the Year, mild, constant sun & no wind, went out on horseback soon after breakfast with my Husband & Francis, & most pleasant it was, going first to Stroud on several little errands then to make an unsuccessful visit at Gannicocks from thence to Mr Reades at Ebley, & home thro' the Woodchester Vale well tired, Cassino as usual. & afterwards complicated accompts.

Tuesday Jan: 29th.

A sad reverse in point of weather being a wetting fog, & some small rain & on the whole miserably damp & uncomfortable, hard at work all Morning, after Tea went to our first Stroud Ball & assembly of which Mr Wathen was Steward, a better meeting than was expected, 21 Ladies & full 40 Gents. a proper cold Supper, several Card Tables, I play'd at Vingt'un with a great variety of Gentlemen the worst part of the whole affair, was its being extended so late an hour, as we were not at home till near four in the Morning.

Wensday Jan: 30th.

Clear, dry & bright, but still very cold being a North wind, I never ventured out for fear of taking cold being much fatigued with the evenings exertion, Mr Witts & Francis rode out, & Mr Schutz & Miss Sheppard sat an hour with me in a very friendly manner. wrote to M^rs. Chollet & my Sis^r Travell.

Thursday Jan: 31st.

A mild dry day, with rather a thick air & no sunshine, I walk'd out longer than usual thro' both the woods, hoping to gain benefit from it of which I stood much in need being far from well both in health & spirits. Francis rode out evening spent as usual rec'd a Letter from M^rs. Granville & wrote to M^rs. Hyett & Miss Snow.

Friday Feb: 1st.

A most cruel day of constant flying rain or mist, with violent high wind & very damp quite impossible to do anything but stay in the house & bear smoking chimneys with all the patience we could; had a pleasing cordial in receiving a sweet Letter from Lady Edward Bentinck.

Saturday Feb: 2d.

Still rather stormy but dry till noon when it was a little wet, & very wet in the evening tempted to go out on horseback, for the sake of taking a last ride with my Dear Boy, call'd on Mrs. Pettat at the Hill House, on Mr & Mrs. Hawker at Woodchester and at Mr Tyndales on some business came home in small rain. so very ill & low all the evening I was scarce able to play at Cassino.

Sunday Feb: 3d.

Very stormy the whole of the day, tho pretty constant sunshine between the storms which were often of hail, being unwell myself & Francis shewing symptoms of a cold, we did not go to church, tenacious of every moment of his Dear company, having fixd of his going to school the next Day, had him much with me tho busy in many trivial & useful matters. wrote to Lady Elcho.

Monday Feb: 4th.

A fine shewy day upon the whole tho rather stormy & two or three times some showers fell, but a very tristeful day to me taking my beloved Francis back to Elmore Court, his Papa went also, the common road being esteem'd almost dangerously bad we went by Whitminster wch. took us thro a much more beautiful country. The Dear fellows cough & cold being bad made the parting more griving on both sides, & I never came home in worse spirits in my life. sorry to learn the death of poor Lord Tracy in the Glocester Paper[6] James Bidmead enter'd our service as Footman. wrote to Francis wth. the key of his trunk wch. had been forgotten

Tuesday Feb: 5th.

Very thick fog in the Morning, but clear'd off soon & became quite a fine winter day, I could avail myself very little of it, being too much engaged in preparations for our Bath Journey to walk out more than to the Hothouse, & much writting & accompts in the evening. rec'd a Letter from Miss Anne Snow with a sad account of the health of all their family party, & one from Mrs. Parsons with a very satisfactory account of my sweet Boys cold & spirits.

Wensday Feb: 6th.

A very fine Morning with mild air & sun but grew foggy towards afternoon, left home at 10 o'clock for Bath, the drive quite pleasant the roads were so excellent stopp'd to bait more than an hour at Petty France & reach'd Mrs. Chollets No. 3 North Parade before 4 met with a most friendly reception, found her very far from well, My Brot Travell dined here, but going away early we only play'd at Piquet & went to Bed in good time. rec'd a long Letter from Miss Snow.

---

6.   This was John Tracy (1722–1793); he had succeeded his brother Thomas as 7th Baron and Viscount Tracy of Rathcoole only six months earlier.

145. Bath from the Avon.

Thursday Feb: 7ᵗʰ·

Quite a thick fog in the Morning, bright & very fine at noon, but colder & more cloudy towards afternoon, some visiting & shopping, a little driving, a great deal of lounging & seeing the world, & some walking fill'd up the Morning, dined at 5 pleasantly our own trio, & went to the fancy Ball at the Upper rooms which was full & agreable by meeting great numbers of my acquaintance.

Friday Feb: 8ᵗʰ·

A miserable day, quite hard rain till after mid.day, & afterwards very stormy & dirty to a dreadful degree, which only permited me to go out & call on Mʳˢ· Badcock on the South Parade, Mʳ Witts set off for London at 5 in the afternoon in the Mail Coach having eaten a Mutton Chop at the White Hart, much concernd to part with him; Mʳˢ· Chollet & I went to Dine at Major Callanders, a party of 5 Ladies & 8 Gentlemen none very smart, & all very ill bred getting shamefully drunk & never appearing to Cards till 11 o'clock, we staid supper not at home till between one & two heartily tired with losing my money in a very stupid way at Whist, & with the noisy ill breeding of the Gentlemen rec'd a most satisfactory account of my beloved Boy from Mʳˢ· Parsons & wrote to Miss Anne Snow.

Saturday Feb: 9ᵗʰ·

Rather foggy in the Morning, but was a tolerable day tho without sunshine, Morning pass'd as usual, part in the Carriage & part on foot, dined chearfully our own tete tete & went to the Play together disappointed of a large party, very well amused with the West Indian & Hartford Bridge,[7] a thin dull Hour yet tedious getting away. rec'd a Letter from my Sister Travell.

---

7. *The West Indian* was by Richard Cumberland, first performed at Drury Lane in 1771. *Hartford-bridge: or, The Skirts of the Camp an Operatic Farce* by William Pearce was first performed in London in 1793.

146. The Comforts of Bath — Supper.

Sunday Feby. 10th.

Tolerably fine tho very cold in the morning, at noon & afternoon, frequent showers of hail
& sleet & the wind most high & disagreable went to Church at the abbey, miserably cold,
but our attention much caught, & our feelings much tried with a very fine Sermon, wherein
the wretched sufferings of the French King were minutely detail'd went to the Pump Room
made many visits & in vain attempted to walk on the Crescent; went to afternoon Church
at S^t. James's which kept us from our Dinner till ½ past five. evening spent comfortably tho
I was very low at being disappointed in not hearing of my Dear Husbands safe arrival in
Town. wrote to him & Lady Edward Bentinck.

Monday Feb: 11th.

Had been something of a frost, was cold & without sun but good walking in the Morning,
but wet again in the evening, much visiting both at home & abroad in the Morning. great
hair dressing distresses which prevented M^rs. Chollet from going to the Ball at all, I went
with M^rs. Callander & M^rs. Badcock a most excellent one very full & agreable rec'd a Letter
from Miss Gorges.

Tuesday Feb: 12th.

A very cold windy disagreable Day & as usual wet again in the afternoon. I walk'd so much
in the Morning I quite tired myself down & was very very low & indifferent all Day several
agitating circumstances taking place, went to the fancy Ball at the lower Rooms much

against my will, stupid to a degree should have gone to sleep had I staid not being a creature there I was acquainted with, when the company went to Tea we went to spend the evening at Major Callanders a very small party, I play'd at Whist with some Success rec'd a Letter from my Dear Husband & ^fm. George & answerd it.

Wensday Feb: 13th.

By no means a pleasant day, a strong mist the whole day tho it was tolerable walking about & again wet & very windy in the afternoon. Morning pass'd as usual, I drank Tea at M^rs. Westerns meeting a very small party, & play'd at Cassino, afterwards join'd M^rs. Chollett at Major Calanders where I play'd 3 rubbers at Whist, scarce any but their own family party, staid supper after which Mr Anstruther sang delightfully. rec'd Letters from Lady Lyttelton, & 2 from my Husband one that was long delay'd & one from my Francis with a good account of himself.

Thursday Feb: 14th.

Fog in the Morning which produced a beautiful fine warm Day, but as ever was wet again at night rather, a busy Morning first going to see poor Lady Tracy,[8] a very melancholly visit, & some other calls, & then walking with M^rs. Chollet & a merry party, went to the Ball at the lower rooms with M^rs. Chollet & M^rs. Badcock, not so gay as at the Upper Rooms, but meeting many pleasant people I liked it well enough. rec'd a Letter from Mr Witts answer'd it & wrote to Francis.

Friday Feb: 15th.

A most beautiful warm fine Day for the time of year, rather hot for walking, being upon my Legs for four hours I was quite tired down & very glad to sit quiet at home all the evening our own tete tete play'd many games at Picquet & wrote a long Letter to my Sis^r Travell

Saturday Feb: 16th.

Something of a frost but was fine & pleasant the whole of the day, soon after breakfast I went in M^rs. Chollets Chaise taking M^rs. Western with me to Bathford to see M^r & M^rs. Charles Western spent an hour or two very pleasantly liking their little place much, went to the Play with M^rs. Calander & her party, & brought them, Mr Anstruther & Miss Rutherford to an oyster Supper to which were added Mr Blackshaw, Mr Butler & Dr Holman, a great deal of singing & too much noise till past two in the Morning. rec'd a Letter from Miss Snow & Mr Witts

Sunday Feb: 17th.

Quite a warm, beautiful day, mild air & constant sunshine, disappointed in getting a Seat at the Octagon Chappel, obliged to return to the Abbey, a very disagreable crowd in the Pump room, walk'd & drove with M^rs. Callander & M^rs. Anstruther in her Coach on the Crescent very full & gay, spent the evening at Major Callanders no one there but Mr Butler, Whist & Vingt'un staid supper & home very late. rec'd a Letter from Mr Witts & my dear Francis, wrote to Miss Snow & Mr Witts.

---

8. Selina Tracy, *née* Shirley (17??–1795). Selina was the daughter of Robert Shirley, 1st Earl Ferrers. She married Thomas Charles Tracy in 1755. Selina, Lady Tracy, lived in Pulteney Street and there were no recorded children of the marriage.

Monday Feb: 18ᵗʰ·

Had been considerable rain in the night, but cleard off & was fine, excepting being more miserably dirty walking than ever I saw it, but impossible at Bath to stay within. Much plagued by the unpunctuality of Hair dresser which kept me from going to Dine at Mᴿ Wiltshires till near an hour after the time a party of 12 there very pleasant, play'd at Whist before we went to the Ball, where I went in their party, a very full one, very gay & pleasant but for the extreme crowding which almost tore ones cloaths off ones back

Tuesday Feb: 19ᵗʰ·

Had been a hoar frost, but was bright & very fine all Day, a long & very interesting conversation with Dᴿ Baker after breakfast indeed had had the same the Morning before visited & walk'd much, went to Drink Tea at Major Callanders to make up a Card party for her who was ill. play'd at Loo with great success return'd home to supper. rec'd a Letter from Lady Edward Bentinck & my Husband & answer'd it. at night rec'd one from George.

Wensday Feb: yᵉ· 20ᵗʰ·

Had been rain in the night but was a charming fine Day quite warm & constant sun poor little Edward Sabine came & spent the early part of the Morning with me & I took him to see the representation of the gold, & silver mines joining a large party,⁹ afterwards I trotted about as much as time would permit before dressing to go to Dine at Mʳˢ· Holfords, where a party of 10 Ladies sat down to Dinner not at all dull, a large party for the House in the evening I play'd many rubbers at Cassino, afterwards went to a most elegant tho very crowded rout at Mʳˢ· Prover's. wrote to George

Thursday Feb: 21ˢᵗ·

A colder day & rather more stormy but still dry & pleasant morning, set out soon after breakfast Lodging hunting, & found one in Bond Street very suitable both to Mʳˢ· Chollet & myself which we agreed to enter on, on Monday next walk'd a great deal on the Crescent & about very much tired, & heartily glad to sit all the evening at home & play at Picquet, rec'd rather a dismal Letter from my Dear Husband, answerd it & wrote to Francis.

Friday Feb: 22ᵈ·

A day without either fog, sun or wind, but rather mild & pleasant, not ill suited for moving,

---

9. Edward Sabine (1788–1883) was just four years old at this time. His mother, Sarah, had died a month after his birth in October 1788. Edward, in adulthood, became an officer in the Royal Artillery, but the Duke of Wellington granted him general leave of absence on the understanding 'that he was usefully employed in scientific pursuits.' On 9 May 1813 the packet *Manchester* sailed out of Falmouth bound for Canada. The surgeon aboard was a 'Mr Sabine,' as was his cousin, Edward, in his official capacity of astronomer. Eight days out from Falmouth the *Manchester* was attacked by an American privateer, the *Yorktown*, and in the ensuing running battle, which lasted twenty hours, Edward Sabine and his young soldier attendant handled a gun 'to good effect.' The *Manchester* was, however, 'compelled to strike her colours.' Two months later she was recaptured by a British frigate, and, after a short spell of service at Quebec, Edward returned to England. Two expeditions followed: in 1818 under Commander Ross in the *Isabella* and in May of the following year under Sir Edward Parry. Edward was an authority on Arctic bird-life. Elected a fellow of the Royal Society in 1818, he was treasurer from 1850 until 1861 and president for the next ten years. He was president of the British Association for the Advancement of Science and was created a K.C.B. in 1860. He died in 1883 at the ripe age of ninety-five.

147. The Comforts of Bath — Dancing.

I left Bath between 11 & 12 stopp'd to bait at Petty France where I dined on Veal cutlets very dull & lonesome all the way home with only Lodge by my side, & a stupid novel in my hand, made worse on my arrival at home just before it was dark not to find any Letter from Mʳ Witts. found the Boys quite well & gay wrote to my Sisʳ Travell.

Saturday Feb: 23ᵈ·

A truly sad comfortable day in every respect the weather being damp & misty & my spirits sunk even to dejection by getting no Letter from my Husband; in vain did variety of employments keep me up at night I quite sank. wrote to Mʳ Witts.

Sunday Feb: 24ᵗʰ·

A very fine Day particularly in the early part when the air was clear yet mild & some sunshine, but towards night a falling mist came on. after a very early Breakfast George & I set out for Elmore Court to see my Dear Francis who came running down the hill with a chearful face to meet us, rejoiced to see him much himself again both in health & spirits, went to Chapell both Morning & evening had an excellent & very comfortable Dinner much gratified with the manner in the which the whole Day had been spent return'd home in 2 hours & ½ the Whitminster road. rec'd Letters from Miss Anne Snow, my Sisʳ Travell & my Dear Husband wrote to the latter.

Monday Feb: 25ᵗʰ·

Dark & cloudy in the Morning at noon grew very stormy with small rain very disagreable for my drive down to Bath, baited at the X hands for more than an hour got to my new

Lodging N⁰· 12 Bond Street between 3 & 4 dined at Mᵣ Wiltshires, only a family party, staid to play 2 rubbers at Whist with the old Gentleman before I return'd home to my lonesome supper my gay little friend being gone to the Ball. rec'd a Letter from my Dear Francis. had a very bad headache

Tuesday Feb: 26ᵗʰ·

A dry fine day, tho cold & windy walk'd about on various pursuits the greater part of the Morning till quite tired down, & very glad it was my fate to sit quietly at home our own tetetete all the evening & go to Bed very early. rec'd a Letter from Mᵣ Witts which did not mend my spirits wᶜʰ· were very low indeed.

Wensday Feb: 27ᵗʰ·

Quite a cold comfortless day, thick air tho high wind, My Brother Travell breakfasted with us, after which accompanied by Dᵣ Baker as a Chaperon & introductor I went to make a very anxious visit to my Broᵣ Ferdinand & both his Daughters, which pass'd off well, tho with strong feelings on each side, home early to dress to dine at Mᵣ Wiltshires, a very pleasant party of 13, ran away imediately after, all of us to a Concert at the Upper rooms for the benifit of the Pauper charity, the chief of the performers being Gentlemen & Ladies, Miss Glasse a most wonderful fine singer, the crowd prodigious the room so full it was dreadful, & yet hundreds could never enter it tho had tickets, heat excessive & yet the amusement was great, went home with Major & Mʳˢ· Callander to their house to sup at a late hour. wrote to Mᵣ Witts.

148. The Comforts of Bath — The Concert.

Thursday Feb: 28th.

Wet early in the Morning but was fine at breakfast time, & thro the whole of the Day tho very dirty moving about, I had an infinity of callers in the course of the Morning, & walk'd out for a little time, dined by invitation at my Brother Ferdinands to meet Dr Baker, rather a trying visit but the affectionate manner of both my Nieces was a great alleviation; Mrs. Callander call'd on me in her Coach to take me in her party & joining Mrs. Chollet to the Play of Love in a Village & the Irishman in Town being Huttleys benifit,[10] the performance but moderate & the house not so full as was expected. rec'd a disappointing Letter from my Husband, his return being still farther postponed. answerd it.

Friday Mar: 1st.

An intire wet day till quite afternoon when it remaind very stormy, of course quite a stay at home Morning, much talk, a little work some writting, & a lively visit from Mr Blackshaw fill'd up the Morning, I went to Drink Tea at Mrs. Westerns to meet my Brother & his Daughters play'd two rubbers at whist & then went to Mrs. Hunts in Portland place taking Mrs. C. with me a party assembled of 25 people chiefly Ladies to hear Madame Grandjean play on the Harp; a Table at Whist very agreable. rec'd a Letter from Mr Witts & answer'd it & wrote to Miss Anne Snow.

Saturday Mar: 2d.

Not a very pleasant day being a thick foggy air & yet a very disagreable high wind, after having rec'd many visitors we went to the Pump room, Crescent &'c & made some visits, I went to Drink Tea at Mrs. Foleys to meet my Brothers family & a small party of two Tables, & afterwards join'd Mrs. Chollet at the Cottilion Ball at the Upper rooms, rather thin but genteel & agreable; rec'd a Letter from my Husband & wrote to Mrs. Granville.

149. Royal and Lansdown Crescents.

---

10. *Love in a Village* by Isaac Bickerstaffe, first performed 1762; *The Irishman in Town* was by probably by John O'Keefe.

Sunday Mar: 3ᵈ·

Dry having been a sharp frost, but violent Hail storms in the evening, & the wind most miserably high & cold no moving about with any comfort, but in the Carriage, walk'd a little in the Crescent, went to Drink Tea with Mʳˢ· Redwood, meeting Mʳ Blackshaw, Dʳ Holman Col: Blundel & Mʳ Mee, play'd both at Whist & Loo, but I could find no enjoyment, my spirits being so damp'd by receiving a very melancholly Letter from Mʳ Witts which I answer'd.[11]

Monday Mar: 4ᵗʰ·

Fine in the Morning, very showery at Noon but fine again in the afternoon, walk'd a little, caught in the rain, & went in the Carriage went to a large smart party at Miss Wiltshires play'd at Cassino, went with some of their family to the Ball, where I join'd Mʳˢ· Chollet & her party, a good smart Ball but I was dull & therefore hard to be amused. rec'd a Letter from my Sister Travell.

Tuesday Mar: 5ᵗʰ·

An intire Day of hard rain from Morn: to night, dismal to a great degree, tho but too consonant to my own feelings as I was low & miserable, & in the afternoon so ill with Hysterics that I was obliged to send to an apothecary, spent an hour or two in the Morning with Mʳˢ· Naper & was to have taken Mʳˢ· Chollet with me to a party at Mʳˢ· Holfords but I was too ill to attempt it & we pass'd a painful evening. rec'd a Letter from Mʳ Witts & answer'd it, & one from George.

Wensday Mar: 6ᵗʰ·

Dry but very cold being a sharp severe North east wind & no sun; I was so indifferent I never stirr'd out the whole Morning, but by staying at home rec'd a large circle of visitors, once perswaded by Miss Wiltshire to go with them in a Coach to dine at their Brothers at Bath Ford, meeting Mʳ Western, Mʳ & Mʳˢ· Walter & Miss Horlock, a very pleasant day, came away soon after Tea to our several parties I to one at Mʳˢ· Strodes, where I play'd pleasantly at Whist & with success. Rec'd a Letter from Mʳ Witts & wrote to Fransˢ·

Thursday Mar: 7ᵗʰ·

Very much the same kind of weather only rather better from the sun now & then making its appearance for a short time, my Dear Husband arrived after breakfast in the Mail Coach from Town much fatigued & harrass'd, & the joy of our meeting greatly damp'd by cruel perplexities, persuaded him to go to Bed for two or three hours to make up for sitting up all night, & enable him to go with me to Dine at Mʳ Wiltshires at Bath ford whither we went with Miss Wiltshires & Miss Western in a Coach meeting both my Brothers, Mʳˢ· Buxton & Mʳˢ· Naper & Mʳ J: Wiltshire, not very brilliant, by being detaind at Cards, did not get back to Bath till ½ past nine, when Mʳ Witts & I went to the Ball at the lower rooms to join Mʳˢ· Chollet by appointment as well as Balls usually are at those rooms but I was truly low & uncomfortable. rec'd a Letter from Miss Anne Snow.

---

11.   It was probably this letter which indicated to Agnes that their financial problems could not be resolved.

Friday Mar: 8th.

A very severe cold day for the time of year being
violent high N: east wind, & tho the sun was
constantly shining it was very difficult to keep ones
self warm while moving ever so fast; the Day past very
manfully by the recapitulation of many dismal events
from Mr Witts's detail of his London bussinesses
which terminated far worse than I expected & gave me
little powers of supporting myself, walk'd miserably
about with him in the Morning, & was very ill all the
evening with Hysterics.

Saturday Mar: 9th.

Still very cold but not quite so severe the wind
being more moderate, & I was better in health &
from recollection not quite so wretched tho much
interesting conversation took place with my Bro^r &
his Daughters, visited L^{dy.} Tracy &'c in the Morning,
dined at Mrs. Birds meeting only Mr Bowdler & my
eldest Brother, but it was a pleasant conversible visit
after Tea went to join a party of two Card Tables at
my Brother Ferdinands being all particular friends it
was pleasant enough play'd many rubbers at Cassino.

150. *Hysterics and fainting.*

Sunday Mar: 10th.

Another very severe day of wind & cold, perfectly dry & much sunshine, Mr Witts & I
starved ourselves to Death with going to church at the Abbey, after which visited the Pump
room then took Mrs. Naper an airing on the Landsdown road & on our return walk'd a little
on the Crescent dined with my Bro^r Ferdinand & his Daughters most painful conversations
afterwards, went home to drink Tea with Mrs. Chollet, & I was so ill as to be under the
necessity of sending for an apothecary relieved happily before I went to Bed rec'd a Letter
from Dear Francis & wrote to my Sister Travell

Monday Mar: 11th.

Quite as cold as ever being little or no sun, & a great tendency to snow & sleet falling,
much conversation, a great deal of finishing up bussiness, some visiting, & of course a little
walking fill'd up a long Morning, dining late at home, Mr Witts & I went to drink Tea with
Mrs. Buxton & Mrs. Naper their father being gone to Salisbury, went to the Ball with M^{rs.}
Naper & Mrs. Chollet, not very full, but very pleasant, & being determined for the time to
cast all anxiety realy enjoy'd it. wrote to Lady Elcho.

Tuesday Mar: 12th.

A better day till quite evening, when it began raining & was very stormy; My Brother
Travell breakfasted with us by way of taking leave so much business of various kinds that

we were kept from leaving Bath till one o'clock dined at Petty france & reach'd home as it was dark, in very poor spirits & much agitation, found the Boys quite well

Wensday Mar: 13th

Had been a trifling fall of Snow in the night which very soon melted away, the air being warm & mild I was very busy all Morning unpacking &'c, & all the evening writting rec'd a Letter from Miss Louisa Lee & wrote to Miss Anne Snow, Miss Gorges & Francis.

Thursday Mar: 14th

Rather stormy in the Morning but clear'd off & was a beautiful fine Day, with much sun & clear air very favourable for our intended Jaunt to Lord Elcho's at Stanway whether we were going for the purpose of taking their mutual advice on a new material plan of life we were about to adopt,[12] went the Whitminster road to Glocester where we only stopt for Hay & water dined at Tewkesbury & tho the roads were rough & very bad from thence to Stanway reach'd it long ere dark meeting with a most pleasing reception from the whole party which excepting their own family were Cap^n. Hamilton & his Daughter & Mon^se Mont Farron; play'd at Whist rec'd a Letter from my Sis^r Travell

Friday Mar: 15th

Fine tho rather stormy in the Morning but turn'd to confirm'd rain hard & settled at Noon which soon sent home even the Hunters & confined every one else & proved a most tempestuous night, Lady Elcho so indifferent she was little out of her Bed & room but as well as my Lord full of useful & kind communication. Mr Talbot added to our party, private conversation took place of Cards in great measure in the evening.

Saturday Mar: 16th

A miserable Stormy Morning but before Noon became settled violent hard rain & so continued till quite night, very uncomfortable for our Journey home, which did not commence till past 11 yet we got home safely between 8 & 9 much obliged for the help of the Moon transposed the matter of baiting, by Dining at Glocester. rec'd Letters from Miss Gorges & my Dear Francis & wrote to my Sis^r Travell on our return home dispatched our good for nothing Servant James Bidmead before we went to Bed.

Sunday Mar: 17th

Rather a more shewey Morn: being some sunshine but still very stormy & in the course of the day & night violent showers of rain & snow alternately & very cold, having much of the Rhumatism I did not venture to church rec'd a very interesting Letter from Miss Anne Snow & wrote to my Sis^r Travell, Lady Edwd. Bentinck & M^rs. Buxton both long & very interesting Letters.

---

12. Agnes probably intended to write 'whither' rather than 'whether,' but obviously she was under great stress. The advice they were seeking was whether or not Edinburgh might prove a much cheaper place to educate the boys now that financial collapse was looming.

Monday Mar: 18th.

Weather worse rather than better being violent wind accompanied by Snow & sleet which made me break my appointment to drink Tea at Mrs. Sheppards for fear of increasing my Rhumatism, very low & unhappy all day, which writting very interesting Letters did not improve. rec'd a Letter from Mrs. Granville, & wrote to Mrs. Tracy, Mrs. Naper, & Mrs. Chollet.

Tuesday Mar: 19th.

A very fine day throughout, warm & mild I walk'd out a good while, Mrs. & Miss Sheppard made a long Morning visit here, & before they went arrived my Br Witts from Nibley, much interesting & distressing conversation the whole day, & in the evening much more so from Mr Bignels clerk being here. never more low in my life.

Wensday Mar: 20th.

Not a good day wind being high & flying mists or small rain frequently, My Brother went away at Noon, various employs all Morng. and at night much writting. Mr Joshiah Wathen here in the Morning. rec'd Letters from Miss Snow & My Sisr Travell, & wrote to Miss Snow & Mrs. Granville.

Thursday Mar: 21st.

Another very mild & pleasant day, walk'd out a considerable time, meeting wth. Mr Sheppards Hounds & several Gentlemen with them, Mr Wathen sat an hour here in the Morning, & my Sisters came from Cheltenham to Dinner an affecting meeting, & much painful conversation at several times of the day, enliven'd by a little Cassino at night.

Friday Mar: 22d.

Had been a very wet night, & was but a moderate day, very damp & frequent showers which prevented all going out, much injoyment & comfort in my Sisters, evening spent as the former.

151.Gatcombe.

Saturday Mar: 23ᵈ·

A bitter cold, & stormy day, & at times flights of snow or hail, yet we all walk'd out for sometime by way of bracing. very needful to my strength & spirits. rec'd Letters Jointly one from my Broᵗ Ferdinand & Mʳˢ· Buxton, & another from Lady Edward Bentinck most sweetly soothing & consolatary

Sunday Mar: 24ᵗʰ·

Quite as cold & windy but dry till afternoon, when it became miserably wet & quite tempestuous, My Sister Travell & I only went to church at Stroud, on our return Mʳ J: Witts here visited here from Tetbury, little else done all day but constant conversation had the Joy of receiving a Letter from my Franˢ·

Monday Mar: 25ᵗʰ·

A very miserable & constant violent wet day accompanied by wind, did much work in the Morning, too ill & Hysterical in the evening to do anything but complain, & lament very bad & improper employment tho but too natural in my situation

Tuesday Mar: 26ᵗʰ·

Tho not absolutely wet, yet it was quite a confining Day, being extremely cold, & violent high wind; most agreably surprized at Noon by the arrival of Mʳ Delabere from Cheltenham, much interesting conversation with him the whole of the Day, & as ever much pleased with his friendly kindness. rec'd Letters from Mʳˢ· Tracy & Mʳˢ· Naper.

Wensday Mar: 27ᵗʰ·

Very much the same kind of weather no warmer or better; poor Mʳ Delabere left us after breakfast, the parting scene a great trial to all parties, such feeling sympathy & affection I never saw express'd, & tried me to the utmost which was continued on the whole day by speaking to all the Servants of our intended removal rec'd a very affectionate Letter from Miss Anne Snow & wrote to Mʳˢ· Parsons & my Dear Francis

Thursday Mar: 28ᵗʰ·

Rather a better day being something warmer & the wind not quite to high, which tempted us to walk a little in our own premises, Mʳ Wasey & his Brother here in the Morning, & my sweet Francis arrived from School before Dinner rejoiced to see him so well, but the meeting was peculiarly tender & affecting. play'd at Cassino in the evening. wrote to Lady Lyttelton Mʳˢ· Buxton & Robert Braxton about his Daughter.

Friday Mar: 29ᵗʰ·

Quite a sharp white Frost, & tho almost constant sunshine was a bitter cold Day we all went to Morning Church at Stroud, Papa & Francis riding, a very long Sermon from Mʳ Ellis a little Cards in the evening, but a very gloomy melancholly day throughout at least my feelings made it so.

Saturday Mar: 30ᵗʰ·

Again a frost, but it was not near so cold being no wind & constant sunshine, we all walk'd on the common as soon as we had breakfasted, on the supposition of meeting the Staffordshire Militia on their March but was disappointed they having gone early in the Morn: Francis read to us in the evening. rec'd Letters from Mʳˢ· Granville & Mʳˢ· Chollet.

Sunday Mar: 31ˢᵗ·

Much such another Morning but grew more cold & stormy at Noon, all went to Church at Stroud, where Mʳ Colbourne assisted Mʳ Ellis in performing all the service we staid the Sacrament being Easter Day, very low & unhappy in the evening rec'd a Letter from Lady Lyttelton & wrote to Mʳˢ· Parsons about Catherine Newman

Monday Ap: 1ˢᵗ·

A dismal day for the time of Year being a good deal of snow & rain at various parts of the day, but with such a damp wind that it did not lye at all on the ground & towards evening was dry & clear, a day full of a variety of bussiness as usual & in the evening play'd at Commerce to amuse the Boys. rec'd a very pleasing Letter from Mʳˢ· Parsons.

Tuesday Ap: 2ᵈ·

Had been a very severe fall of Snow in the night, accompanied by such a high wind that it was drifted very deep in many places, but melted a great deal in the course of the day, tho sometimes it snow'd on. very busy again. wrote to Lady Lyttelton, Mʳˢ· C. Western & Mʳ Delabere.

Wensday Ap: 3ᵈ·

Something of a frost in the Morning but not sharp enough to keep the Snow from melting away very fast the air being damp & mild, extremely busy all the Morning, looking over household Linnen &c ready for packing & doing many other things. rec'd a Letter from Mʳ Delabere & Miss Snow, & wrote to Miss A: Snow & Mʳˢ· Naper.

Thursday Ap: 4ᵗʰ·

Still a frost but very mild air & constant sun which made the snow nearly depart I was much too busy to think of stirring out pack'd up two very large Boxes. my mind much agitated by Molly Braxtons Parents writting a Letter of refusal to her going with me into the North, greatly relieved by Catherine Newmans not objecting to attend one, most thoroughly overcome with fatigue little able to do anything at night. rec'd a Letter from Mʳˢ· Savage & answer'd it.

Friday Ap: 5ᵗʰ·

Very much the same weather, clear & frosty, but tolerably fine being constant sunshine I made time to walk out for an hour, every hour & minute in the day fully fill'd up with various employs; quite knock'd up by fatigue. wrote to Lady Elcho.

Saturday Ap: 6ᵗʰ·

A very brilliant fine Day tho still frosty, Mʳ Witts, Franˢ· myself, & Cath: Newman in & about the Chaise, went to Upper Slaughter by the way of Painswick stopping for an hour at Kilkenny to bait the horses, arrived there at ¼ past 4, finding my Bro^r. & M^rs. Buxton very well. M^r. Bignell & M^r. Cornish came to Tea, wch. from much painfull intelligence & conversation made the evening pass dismally.

Sunday Ap: 7th.

Very much such another day, rather a cold east wind, I was dreadfully ill & most unhappy all Day, having had a sleepless night, the Morning wholly spent in lamentable consultation with M^r. Bignell, & many interesting points decided on; M^rs. Naper came to Tea, the whole evening past in converse on her affairs. wrote to my Sis^r. Travell.

Monday Ap: 8th.

Still a frost, but being no wind & most constant sunshine, it was quite warm & pleasant I left Slaughter after breakfast to return home Francis my only companion, My Dear Husband staying behind for proper reasons, which also carried me to Bownham. eat a hasty Dinner at the Ram at Cirencester when we baited an hour ½ & got to my own Door at 5 to the great surprize of my Sis^rs. & Sons, roads excellent the journey was not unpleasant.

Tuesday Ap: 9th.

Not near so fine a day tho still constant sunshine, frost being sharper, & wind quite high & severe, but I had little time to regard it, being much engaged in a great variety of bussiness mostly accompts. wrote to M^rs. Granville.

Wensday Ap: 10th.

A most extreme cold day strong & high North east wind, which we very sensibly felt passing over the bleak country to Upper Slaughter where my Sisters attended me, in a hired chaise, meeting M^rs. Napers chaise at Foss bridge where we baited an hour & ½ & got to my Bro^rs. in very good time, finding my Dear Husband well in health but ill in spirits; play'd at Cassino at night rec'd a Letter from M^r. Delabere.

Thursday Ap: 11th.

Still cold, frosty, & miserable, but everything wore a dismal aspect to my eye sight, as my mind was miserable & I was almost broken hearted & at night very hysterical, much sad but very interesting conversation but a great want of consolation; M^rs. Naper & Miss Boddington here for two or three hours in the Morning.

Friday Ap: 12th.

As cold as ever with now & then trifling showers of hail & rain, yet still we all walk'd at several times My Sis^r. Travell went to Lower Slaughter to keep Miss Boddington company in M^rs. Napers absence, My Dear Fran^s. so ill all Day with a complaint in his Stomach that much affected his head with a strong degree of fever, which obliged him to keep up stairs all Day & to take James Powder at night which had a strong effect, all this made me wretched. wrote to Lady Edwd. Bentinck & Miss Snow.

Saturday Ap: 13ᵗʰ·

Rather a milder air & being much less windy & constant sunshine it was realy pleasant being out, my spirits somewhat exhilerated by seeing my Dear Boy made better, my Sisᵗ Travell return'd from L. Slaughter, & my Broᵉ dined there. Mᵉ & Mʳˢ· Dolphin & Mᵉ J: Dolphin made a Morning visit, thought her very pleasant. Cassino & much talk in the evening.

Sunday Ap: 14ᵗʰ·

Still extremely cold & severe tho with sun & little wind, went to Church in the Morning service sadly perform'd by Mᵉ Williams, Mʳˢ· Dolphin visited for a quarter of an hour after Church, went to Lower Slaughter to Dinner, & to remain with Mʳˢ· Naper, sorry to leave Mʳˢ· Buxton with a most dreadful headache, evening pass'd chearfully lik'd Miss Boddington much rec'd a Letter from Lady Lyttelton & wrote to Mʳˢ· Tracy.

Monday Ap: 15ᵗʰ·

As usual very comfortless weather miserably cold & stormy, & at noon & afternoon hard rain which obliged my Sisᵗ Catherine who spent the Morning here go home in the Carriage much pleasant converse, some writting & Cassino in the evening. wrote to Mᵉ Delabere.

Tuesday Ap: 16ᵗʰ·

No change for the better in the season had been a very sharp frost, & perpetual showers of hail & snow interspersed with sunshine I was sadly low & miserable & both Mʳˢ· Naper & my Francis suffering from bad rashes. My Sisᵗ Travell & my Broᵉ here from Upper Slaughter, at different parts of the Morning, evening pass'd as the former. rec'd interesting Letters from Lady Edward Bentinck, Miss Snow, & Mʳˢ· C: Western.

Wensday Ap: 17ᵗʰ·

Weather still worse than ever, being constant sharp snow all the Morning & very hard rain all the afternoon very cold & a truly miserable day, the family from Upper Slaughter dined here, a Table at Whist & Cassino. wrote to Mʳˢ· Chollet & Mʳˢ· Charles Western

Thursday Ap: 18ᵗʰ·

Some little change for the better in the weather, the air being milder & the storms shorter & less frequent, which allow'd us all to walk a little in the Garden & Grove, some very unpleasant events occur'd in regard to our melancholly affairs which made me very miserable & wretched, Mᵉ Fretwell dined here; we play'd much at Cassino wrote to Mʳˢ· Tyrwhitt & Mʳˢ· Savage.

Friday Ap: 19ᵗʰ·

Very sad weather till noon, being violent & frequent storms of hail & snow, & most bitterly cold, which we felt at Church attending the service & duty of the day being a public Fast appointed, a very excellent well adapted sermon from Mᵉ Nicholls the Curate, Mʳˢ· Naper & I went in the chaise to Upper Slaughter, rather a doleful visit being the last time I was to see my Broᵉ Ferdinand perhaps for ever, a day of much bussiness & conversation being the last of our stay at Lower Slaughter.

Saturday Ap: 20th.

Had been a frost in the night, but was a bright fine Day without for a wonder any falling weather, left M^rs. Naper soon after breakfast, my Sis^t Travell coming from Upper Slaughter to attend us home, very sorry to bid adieu to Miss Boddington, Mr Witts on horseback & Francis attending on us in the Chaise, got a bad hasty Dinner at Cirencester, & reach'd home by ten o'clock, finding the Boys well, surprized not to find Mr Bignells Man of bussiness.

Sunday Ap: 21st.

Not so pleasant a day the wind being high & very cold, but dry with sun, not one of the family went to church, a variety of employs, very useful fill'd up the day, Mr Young the Messenger arrived & appear'd a much less terrible object than I expected from his propriety of behaviour. rec'd Letters from Lady Hereford M^rs. Savage & M^rs. Holford, & wrote to Miss Louisa Lee.

Monday Ap: 22d.

Very much the same dry cold weather but it little signified to me as I was too busy to stir out, many things of consequence being transacted & arranged, my mind & body thoroughly fatigued by the exertion; a little Game at Cassino in the evening. rec'd a Letter from M^rs. Granville.

Tuesday Ap: 23d.

Still dry but rather lowering, with signs of rain a continuation of much active bussiness, packing up Books & many other things, recd Letters from M^rs. Halford & Miss Boddington & wrote to M^rs. Naper.

Wensday Ap: 24th.

Rain of a very mild kind the greater part of the day, doubtless very useful at his season but not pleasant being damp & cold, much fatigued by a great deal of packing & rummaging which tired me almost to death. wrote to M^rs. Witts of Nibley

Thursday Ap: 25th.

No rain but a thick foggy air, which made it far from pleasant, the same continuation of unwiarred packing, which left no time but to play a little at Cassino. rec'd a short Letter from Miss M. Sheppard & answerd it.

Friday Ap: 26th.

Rather a soft growing day, damp air & some little sun, & only one shower of any consequence the Boys spent an hour or two in the Morning at M^rs. Sheppards at Hampton as a take leave visit, still more busy than ever in packing & got through a great deal of bussiness. Cassino at night by way of recreation.

Saturday Ap: 27th.

A stormy unpleasant day, with very damp air & frequent short small showers, but weather was of little consequence to such a busy occupied mind as mine tired almost to death before night.

Sunday Ap: 28th.

Upon the whole a fine Day, clear air & much sun, I walk'd a little, but had so much bussiness remaining to do, I was obliged to work hard at packing &'c, & wrote hard in the evening; rec'd Letters from Miss M. Sheppard, & Miss Forrest, & wrote to Lady Lyttelton & Miss Snow.

Monday Ap: 29th.

Gloomy in the Morning & soon became very wet for many hours, bright & dry in the evening. such various claims both on my heart, head, & hands to finish up all our melancholly bussiness of removing that I was incessantly occupied the whole day, yet bore it better than could be supposed. wrote to L^{dy.} Edwd. B.

Tuesday Ap: 30th.

A very bright shewey Morning, which proved as is too common, a wet noon, & very wet afternoon & night, left poor Bownham House <u>for ever</u> after breakfast, with stronger feelings than can <u>be expressed</u> yet I was happily enabled to support it better than I expected, My Sis^r Travell & Francis with me, Kitty Molly Braxton who I took as far as Slaughter on her way into Oxon, with George & Edward in a hired Chaise, met Mrs. Buxtons Carriage at Foss Bridge in which my Sis^r & I & George went on directly Mr Witts & Francis being on horseback; the Maids & Edward, from the restiveness of the Horses, did not arrive at Slaughter till dark, which alarm'd me sadly, but they came safe. Mrs. Naper came to Tea some many anxious schemes & plans for her & her children in view that assisted to wear my Spirits very considerably. rec'd Letters from Mrs. Tracy, Mrs. Tyrwhitt, Mrs. Witts, & Miss Anne Snow most kind.

Wensday May 1st.

Dry in the Morning but at different parts of the day such violent hard Showers of rain that all moving out of the house was impossible the two Mrs. Rices from Bourton on the Water here in the Morning & Mrs. Naper both dined & supt here, & playd at Cassino, much pleasant converse from freedom & ease.

Thursday May 2^{d.}

Still a continuance of Showers but not so frequent or violent & dry in the afternoon yet too damp to walk out, Mrs. Naper again dined here, but did not stay to join in the Cassino party, felt much at dismissing poor John the Coachman for ever, his concern was truly affecting wrote to Mrs. Granville

Friday May 3^{d.}

Weather much better being quite dry the whole day, & warm gleams of sunshine, which made it very pleasant stroling about, the wind having dried it very much, Mr Witts & Francis rode out to Stow &'c in the evening play'd at Pope Joan with the 4 Children rec'd a Letter from Miss Louisa Lee & wrote to Miss Gorges.

Saturday May 4th.

A gloomy unpleasant Day with strong appearance of rain but none of any consequence felt miserably cold & comfortless for the season of the Year Mr Witts & Francis rode out in the

Morning, we all 6 dined with M^rs. Naper the chaise going & returning twice, made the last party late at night after having play'd at Cassino.

Sunday May 5th.
Still cold & winterly, high wind & some sun, realy uncomfortably cold at Church whither we went both Morning & evening, M^rs. Naper came to from church & staid till after Tea, M^r. Fretwell also dined here; I was much hurt by parting with poor Molly Braxton who went home to her Friends rec'd a Letter from M^rs. Hyett.

Monday May 6th.
The same gloomy moderate weather dark & like rain but none fell, Francis took an early ride to Moreton in Marsh with Thos. Blandford, M^rs. Naper spent the greater part of the day here, her children likewise call'd in their walks. rec'd a Letter f^m. Miss Gorges

Tuesday May 7th.
Dry, dark, & cold in the Morning, very Showery at Noon, & hard rain in the afternoon, My Sis^rs. went in the Chaise to Moreton on bussiness, I went with them to Lower Slaughter, & spent the Morning they calling for me on their return; a long bout at Cassino Boys & all.

Wensday May 8th.
Dry, mild & fine in the Morning, with frequent gleams of warm sun, but a hard & long shower in the afternoon, & a very wet night, the <u>Gents</u> rode out My Sis^rs. myself & Boys walk'd to see M^rs. Burrows & M^rs. Buxton accompanied by M^rs. Naper went to see M^rs. Rice at Bourton in the Morning, & brought M^rs. N. to Dinner. rec'd Letters from Lady Elcho & Miss Snow.

Thursday May 9th.
Rather cold & damp after so much rain, with frequent very black clouds & some little rain fell, walk'd but little, Papa & Son rode, M^rs. Naper came to Dinner, & M^rs. Dolphin to a late Tea very pleasant & agreable we play'd as usual at Cassino. wrote to M^rs. Hyett & Miss Anne Snow.

Friday May 10th.
Mild & very pleasant in the Morning but grew cold at noon, & rather showery in the afternoon, I walk'd to L. Slaughter in the Morn^g. & spent the greater part of it with M^rs. Naper, my three Boys & Patty Buxton dined there & M^r. Witts went to drink Tea & bring them home. Cassino as usual.

Saturday May 11th.
Quite a damp, gloomy, oppressive day & for 2 or 3 hours at mid.day hard rain, we were quite a house of invalids My Sis^rs. both with rashes & M^r. Witts with a little fever & sore throat, & myself with giddy headache & miserably low & dejected M^rs. Naper dined here & play'd at Cassino. wrote to Miss Forrest.

Sunday May 12th.
Foggy in the Morning but turn'd out a beautiful fine clear day, rather too warm for exercise,

Mrs. Naper came to Morning church, & staid all Day, she & I only went to church the rest being still too great invalids, & walk'd afterwards to see Mrs. Burrows. rec'd a Letter from Lord Edward Bentinck & wrote to Miss Louisa Lee.

Monday May 13th.
An intire fine, clear, warm day, quite delightful, very busy in the Morning early & at Noon went with Mrs. Naper in my Bro^{rs.} Chaise to call on Mrs. Dolphin at Eyford, an agreable visit, both the Mrs. Dolphins join'd us & we walk'd a little among their improvements, Mrs. Naper returnd home to Dinner. she came again after Tea, the evening turn'd out cold. wrote to Lady Elcho & Mrs. Granville.

Tuesday May 14th.
A pleasant day upon the whole, the rain had been expected, but none came, but much sunshine, Mr Witts went very early in the Morning to Banbury, to the first meeeting, on the unfortunate bussiness, he return'd at night; Mrs. Naper came early in the day, we all took a walk, towards Eyford at Noon, & I nearly walk'd home with Mrs. Naper at night. play'd much at Cassino before and after Tea

Wensday May 15th.
Still delightful weather, my Sisters were again obliged to go to Moreton on law bussiness. I went with them as far as L. Slaughter where I staid 2 hours, principaly to take leave of the Dear children which was very interesting, as in a day or two they were likely to suffer with the small Pox being inoculated on the 11th. Mrs. Naper walk'd back with me to Dinner & staid late in the evening when several of us walkd part of the way home with her. the three Boys drank Tea with Mrs. Dolphin at Eyford.

Thursday May 16th.
Very much the same pleasant weather, Mrs. Naper came early in the Day & as usual staid till quite late in the evening, I was deeply engaged all Morning in packing, our spirits all so much depress'd by our approaching seperation that we could have very little enjoyment in each other Mrs. Buxton made quite ill by it. most terrible parting scenes on all sides at night; requiring all my fortitude to support. rec'd a Letter from Mr Delabere.

Friday May 17th.
Very bright & fine early in the Morn: but was at many times, dark, cloudy & cold, & two or three trifling showers alarm'd us on the road, left <u>poor</u> Slaughter soon after seven, my Sis^r Travell & the little Girls alone able to preside at our breakfast, many tears shed both by high & low, young & old, Mrs. Witts myself & Fran^{s.} in our own Chaise & my Bro^{rs.} Horses, & the two other Boys & Catherine in a hire'd one proceeded in the best spirits we could to Stratford on Avon 23 miles thro' Moreton in Marsh, from thence proceeded to Hockley 12 miles,[13] where we made a very bad Dinner, & afterwards 10 miles more to Birmingham, where we only

13.   Hockley Heath.

stopt to get fresh horses to our own Chaise, & left Catherine to fight her way on to Uttoxeter in a Coach, finding we could go on very well, all 5 in the chaise, 8 miles brought us to Sutton Colfield about 8 o'clock where Tea &'c satisfied us & we went well tired to Bed.

Saturday May 18th.

A very bright shewey Morning, but tho it was dry the whole day excepting small flying mists it was dark & gloomy & very cold; left Sutton Colfield after breakfast, roads excellent, yet we found it a long tedious stage from Litchfield to Uttoxeter of 17 miles at the last place Mr Granvilles Horses met us & convey'd us with comfort to Calwich a little before Dinner, where our kind Friends gave us the welcome such hearts ever bestow, with them we found Mrs. Port & her three Daughters & Miss Delabere in very poor health; a lively game of Quadrille in the evening after having taken a very pleasant little walk.

Sunday May 19th.

Very much the same weather, dry, dark & cold till afternoon, when the sun enliven'd, I was so indifferent having had a bad night that I did not go to Church walk'd afterwards a long walk with Mr & Mrs. Granville Mr Witts & all the young people, they all again walk'd after Tea when I had a pleasant tete tete with Miss Delabere. rec'd a Letter from Miss Anne Snow

Monday May 20th.

Had been something of a frost in the night, but was a beautiful clear fine Day & in the sun quite hot, soon after breakfast Miss Delabere set off for Buxton, & Mrs. Granville accompanied her to see her well settled in her new situation, Mrs. Port & I walk'd, work'd, & read, Miss Berrisford & her Cousin made a short visit, Quadrille in the evening. wrote to Mrs. Buxton.

Tuesday May 21st.

Still most pleasant weather, mild air, & towards the afternoon constant sunshine Morn: I spent much as the last, entertain'd by Murphys Life of Johnson[14], a pleasant walk sitting down at intervals Mrs. Port talking much, our Dear Mrs. Granville return'd to us just as we began Dinner, much joy to have her with us again & to find she left her Sister so tolerable: walking & Cards in the evening. wrote to Mrs. Naper & Mrs. Chollet.

Wensday May 22d.

A most delightful day constant sunshine making all the surrounding beautiful objects appear to peculiar advantage, we four Ladies took a long walk in the meadow by the Dove side, while the Gentlemen follow'd their own inventions, a Clergyman from Ashborn Mr Pickford Dined here little or no walking in the evening but great battling at Quadrille as usual. wrote to Mrs. Pettat.

Thursday May 23d.

A thick foggy air in the Morning, but Soon became bright & hot, soon after breakfast we sallied forth our whole party excepting Mrs. Port to walk to Ellason Church where service

14. Arthur Murphy (1727–1805), *An Essay on the Life and Genius of Samuel Johnson, LL.D.*

was to be perform'd by Mr Pickford being the annual meeting of a Brotherly Club held in that Parish, upon which account all the members present walk in procession to the Church, with Mr Granville & other Gentlemen attending, flag flying & music playing & a great crowd of Spectators, a Sermon preach'd applicable to the subject & on the whole a pleasant sight, from the idea of its benevolent intention, a very hot walk home again, a Mrs Fletcher return'd with us to spend the Day & Mrs Granville brought several Gentlemen home to Tea after having dined with the Society. Had a great treat in receiving a most kind & feeling Letter from Mrs Naper with an excellent account of her Dear Children.

Friday May 24th

Most lovely weather still, bright & fine but none too hot tho the sun was perpetual, M^r & Mrs Granville rode to Ashborn, I only prowled a little about determining to take a long evening walk, which we all eleven did to the Hutts, & tho near 3 miles on the whole I perform'd it to admiration, & a sweet walk it proved. wrote to Miss Snow.

Saturday May 25th

Close & foggy in the Morning, but it was only a sign of a more beautiful bright day which it continued till quite evening, when it became cloudy but dry; we walk'd a good deal before Dinner overlooking the removal of some Trees that interrupted the views. for a wonder so early in the year drank Tea just out of Doors, while the Cows were milking close by, took a long walk afterwards wch knock'd me up almost. rec'd a Letter f^m Miss Snow.